University Casebook Series

December, 1980

ACCOUNTING AND THE LAW, Fourth Edition (1978), with Problems Pamphlet (Successor to Dohr, Phillips, Thompson & Warren)

George C. Thompson, Professor, Columbia University Graduate School of Business.
Robert Whitman, Professor of Law, University of Connecticut.
Ellis L. Phillips, Jr., Member of the New York Bar.
William C. Warren, Professor of Law Emeritus, Columbia University.

ACCOUNTING FOR LAWYERS, MATERIALS ON (1980)

David R. Herwitz, Professor of Law, Harvard University.

ADMINISTRATIVE LAW, Seventh Edition (1979), with 1979 Problems Supplement (Supplement edited in association with Paul R. Verkuil, Dean and Professor of Law, Tulane University)

Walter Gellhorn, University Professor Emeritus, Columbia University.
Clark Byse, Professor of Law, Harvard University.
Peter L. Strauss, Professor of Law, Columbia University.

ADMIRALTY, Second Edition (1978), with Statute and Rule Supplement

Jo Desha Lucas, Professor of Law, University of Chicago.

ADVOCACY, see also Lawyering Process

ADVOCACY, INTRODUCTION TO, Third Edition (1981)

Board of Student Advisers, Harvard Law School.

AGENCY, see also Enterprise Organization

AGENCY–ASSOCIATIONS–EMPLOYMENT–PARTNERSHIPS, Second Edition (1977)

Abridgement from Conard, Knauss & Siegel's Enterprise Organization.

ANTITRUST AND REGULATORY ALTERNATIVES (1977), Fifth Edition

Louis B. Schwartz, Professor of Law, University of Pennsylvania.
John J. Flynn, Professor of Law, University of Utah.

ANTITRUST SUPPLEMENT—SELECTED STATUTES AND RELATED MATERIALS (1977)

John J. Flynn, Professor of Law, University of Utah.

BIOGRAPHY OF A LEGAL DISPUTE, THE: An Introduction to American Civil Procedure (1968)

Marc A. Franklin, Professor of Law, Stanford University.

BUSINESS ORGANIZATION, see also Enterprise Organization

BUSINESS PLANNING (1966), with 1980 Supplement

David R. Herwitz, Professor of Law, Harvard University.

BUSINESS TORTS (1972)

Milton Handler, Professor of Law Emeritus, Columbia University.

CIVIL PROCEDURE, see Procedure

CLINIC, see also Lawyering Process

COMMERCIAL AND CONSUMER TRANSACTIONS, Second Edition (1978)

William D. Warren, Dean of the School of Law, University of California, Los Angeles.
William E. Hogan, Professor of Law, Cornell University.
Robert L. Jordan, Professor of Law, University of California, Los Angeles.

COMMERCIAL LAW, CASES & MATERIALS ON, Third Edition (1976)

E. Allan Farnsworth, Professor of Law, Cornell University.
John Honnold, Professor of Law, University of Pennsylvania.

COMMERCIAL PAPER, Second Edition (1976)

E. Allan Farnsworth, Professor of Law, Columbia University.

COMMERCIAL PAPER AND BANK DEPOSITS AND COLLECTIONS (1967), with Statutory Supplement.

William D. Hawkland, Professor of Law, University of Illinois.

COMMERCIAL TRANSACTIONS—Text, Cases and Problems, Fourth Edition (1968)

Robert Braucher, Professor of Law Emeritus, Harvard University, and
The late Arthur E. Sutherland, Jr., Professor of Law, Harvard University.

COMPARATIVE LAW, Fourth Edition (1980)

Rudolf B. Schlesinger, Professor of Law, Hastings College of the Law.

COMPETITIVE PROCESS, LEGAL REGULATION OF THE, Second Edition (1979), with Statutory Supplement

Edmund W. Kitch, Professor of Law, University of Chicago.
Harvey S. Perlman, Professor of Law, University of Virginia.

CONFLICT OF LAWS, Seventh Edition (1978), with 1980 Supplement

Willis L. M. Reese, Professor of Law, Columbia University, and
Maurice Rosenberg, Professor of Law, Columbia University.

CONSTITUTIONAL LAW, Fifth Edition (1977), with 1980 Supplement

Edward L. Barrett, Jr., Professor of Law, University of California, Davis.

CONSTITUTIONAL LAW, Tenth Edition (1980)

Gerald Gunther, Professor of Law, Stanford University.

CONSTITUTIONAL LAW, INDIVIDUAL RIGHTS IN, Third Edition (1981)

Gerald Gunther, Professor of Law, Stanford University.

CONTRACT LAW AND ITS APPLICATION, Second Edition (1977)

Addison Mueller, Professor of Law Emeritus, University of California, Los Angeles.
Arthur I. Rosett, Professor of Law, University of California, Los Angeles.

CONTRACT LAW, STUDIES IN, Second Edition (1977)

Edward J. Murphy, Professor of Law, University of Notre Dame.
Richard E. Speidel, Professor of Law, University of Virginia.

CONTRACTS, Third Edition (1977)

John P. Dawson, Professor of Law Emeritus, Harvard University, and
William Burnett Harvey, Professor of Law and Political Science, Boston University.

CONTRACTS, Third Edition (1980), with Statutory Supplement

E. Allan Farnsworth, Professor of Law, Columbia University.
William F. Young, Professor of Law, Columbia University.

CONTRACTS, Second Edition (1978), with Statutory and Administrative Law Supplement (1978)

Ian R. Macneil, Professor of Law, Cornell University.

COPYRIGHT, Unfair Competition, and Other Topics Bearing on the Protection of Literary, Musical, and Artistic Works, Third Edition (1978)

Benjamin Kaplan, Professor of Law Emeritus, Harvard University, and
Ralph S. Brown, Jr., Professor of Law, Yale University.

CORPORATE FINANCE, Second Edition (1979), with 1980 New Developments Supplement

Victor Brudney, Professor of Law, Harvard University.
Marvin A. Chirelstein, Professor of Law, Yale University.

CORPORATE READJUSTMENTS AND REORGANIZATIONS (1976)

Walter J. Blum, Professor of Law, University of Chicago.
Stanley A. Kaplan, Professor of Law, University of Chicago.

CORPORATION LAW, BASIC, Second Edition (1979), with Documentary Supplement

Detlev F. Vagts, Professor of Law, Harvard University.

CORPORATIONS, see also Enterprise Organization

CORPORATIONS, Fifth Edition—Unabridged (1980)

William L. Cary, Professor of Law, Columbia University.
Melvin Aron Eisenberg, Professor of Law, University of California, Berkeley.

CORPORATIONS, Fifth Edition—Abridged (1980)

William L. Cary, Professor of Law, Columbia University.
Melvin Aron Eisenberg, Professor of Law, University of California, Berkeley.

CORPORATIONS, THE LAW OF: WHAT CORPORATE LAWYERS DO (1976)

Jan G. Deutsch, Professor of Law, Yale University.
Joseph J. Bianco, Professor of Law, Yeshiva University.

CORPORATIONS COURSE GAME PLAN (1975)

David R. Herwitz, Professor of Law, Harvard University.

CREDIT TRANSACTIONS AND CONSUMER PROTECTION (1976)

John Honnold, Professor of Law, University of Pennsylvania.

CREDITORS' RIGHTS, see also Debtor-Creditor Law

UNIVERSITY CASEBOOK SERIES—Continued

CRIMINAL JUSTICE, THE ADMINISTRATION OF, Second Edition (1969)

Francis C. Sullivan, Professor of Law, Louisiana State University.
Paul Hardin III, Professor of Law, Duke University.
John Huston, Professor of Law, University of Washington.
Frank R. Lacy, Professor of Law, University of Oregon.
Daniel E. Murray, Professor of Law, University of Miami.
George W. Pugh, Professor of Law, Louisiana State University.

CRIMINAL JUSTICE ADMINISTRATION AND RELATED PROCESSES, Successor Edition (1976), with 1980 Supplement

Frank W. Miller, Professor of Law, Washington University.
Robert O. Dawson, Professor of Law, University of Texas.
George E. Dix, Professor of Law, University of Texas.
Raymond I. Parnas, Professor of Law, University of California, Davis.

CRIMINAL JUSTICE, LEADING CONSTITUTIONAL CASES ON (1980)

Lloyd L. Weinreb, Professor of Law, Harvard University.

CRIMINAL LAW, Second Edition (1979)

Fred E. Inbau, Professor of Law Emeritus, Northwestern University.
James R. Thompson, Professor of Law Emeritus, Northwestern University.
Andre A. Moenssens, Professor of Law, University of Richmond.

CRIMINAL LAW, Third Edition (1980)

Lloyd L. Weinreb, Professor of Law, Harvard University.

CRIMINAL LAW AND ITS ADMINISTRATION (1940), with 1956 Supplement

Jerome Michael, late Professor of Law, Columbia University, and
Herbert Wechsler, Professor of Law, Columbia University.

CRIMINAL LAW AND PROCEDURE, Fifth Edition (1977)

Rollin M. Perkins, Professor of Law Emeritus, University of California, Hastings College of the Law.
Ronald N. Boyce, Professor of Law, University of Utah.

CRIMINAL PROCEDURE, Second Edition (1980)

Fred E. Inbau, Professor of Law Emeritus, Northwestern University.
James R. Thompson, Professor of Law Emeritus, Northwestern University.
James B. Haddad, Professor of Law, Northwestern University.
James B. Zagel, Chief, Criminal Justice Division, Office of Attorney General of Illinois.
Gary L. Starkman, Assistant U. S. Attorney, Northern District of Illinois.

CRIMINAL PROCEDURE, CONSTITUTIONAL (1977), with 1980 Supplement

James E. Scarboro, Professor of Law, University of Colorado.
James B. White, Professor of Law, University of Chicago.

CRIMINAL PROCESS, Third Edition (1978), with 1979 Supplement

Lloyd L. Weinreb, Professor of Law, Harvard University.

DAMAGES, Second Edition (1952)

Charles T. McCormick, late Professor of Law, University of Texas, and
William F. Fritz, late Professor of Law, University of Texas.

DEBTOR–CREDITOR LAW (1974), with 1978 Case-Statutory Supplement

William D. Warren, Dean of the School of Law, University of California, Los Angeles.
William E. Hogan, Professor of Law, Cornell University.

DECEDENTS' ESTATES (1971)

Max Rheinstein, late Professor of Law Emeritus, University of Chicago.
Mary Ann Glendon, Professor of Law, Boston College.

DECEDENTS' ESTATES AND TRUSTS, Fifth Edition (1977)

John Ritchie, Professor of Law Emeritus, University of Virginia.
Neill H. Alford, Jr., Professor of Law, University of Virginia.
Richard W. Effland, Professor of Law, Arizona State University.

DECEDENTS' ESTATES AND TRUSTS (1968)

Howard R. Williams, Professor of Law, Stanford University.

DOMESTIC RELATIONS, see also Family Law

DOMESTIC RELATIONS, Third Edition (1978) with 1980 Supplement

Walter Wadlington, Professor of Law, University of Virginia.
Monrad G. Paulsen, Dean of the Law School, Yeshiva University.

DYNAMICS OF AMERICAN LAW, THE: Courts, the Legal Process and Freedom of Expression (1968)

Marc A. Franklin, Professor of Law, Stanford University.

ELECTRONIC MASS MEDIA, Second Edition (1979)

William K. Jones, Professor of Law, Columbia University.

ENTERPRISE ORGANIZATION, Second Edition (1977), with 1979 Statutory and Formulary Supplement

Alfred F. Conard, Professor of Law, University of Michigan.
Robert L. Knauss, Dean of the School of Law, Vanderbilt University.
Stanley Siegel, Professor of Law, University of California, Los Angeles.

EQUITY AND EQUITABLE REMEDIES (1975)

Edward D. Re, Adjunct Professor of Law, St. John's University.

EQUITY, RESTITUTION AND DAMAGES, Second Edition (1974)

Robert Childres, late Professor of Law, Northwestern University.
William F. Johnson, Jr., Professor of Law, New York University.

ESTATE PLANNING PROBLEMS (1973), with 1977 Supplement

David Westfall, Professor of Law, Harvard University.

ETHICS, see Legal Profession, and Professional Responsibility

EVIDENCE, Fourth Edition (1981)

David W. Louisell, late Professor of Law, University of California, Berkeley.
John Kaplan, Professor of Law, Stanford University.
Jon R. Waltz, Professor of Law, Northwestern University.

EVIDENCE, Sixth Edition (1973), with 1980 Supplement

John M. Maguire, late Professor of Law Emeritus, Harvard University.
Jack B. Weinstein, Professor of Law, Columbia University.
James H. Chadbourn, Professor of Law, Harvard University.
John H. Mansfield, Professor of Law, Harvard University.

INSTITUTIONAL INVESTORS, 1978

David L. Ratner, Professor of Law, Cornell University.

INSURANCE (1971)

William F. Young, Professor of Law, Columbia University.

INTERNATIONAL LAW, see also Transnational Legal Problems and United Nations Law

INTERNATIONAL LEGAL SYSTEM (1973), with Documentary Supplement

Noyes E. Leech, Professor of Law, University of Pennsylvania.
Covey T. Oliver, Professor of Law, University of Pennsylvania.
Joseph Modeste Sweeney, Professor of Law, Tulane University.

INTERNATIONAL TRADE AND INVESTMENT, REGULATION OF (1970)

Carl H. Fulda, late Professor of Law, University of Texas.
Warren F. Schwartz, Professor of Law, University of Virginia.

INTERNATIONAL TRANSACTIONS AND RELATIONS (1960)

Milton Katz, Professor of Law, Harvard University, and
Kingman Brewster, Jr., Professor of Law, Harvard University.

INTRODUCTION TO LAW, see also Legal Method, On Law in Courts, and Dynamics of American Law

INTRODUCTION TO THE STUDY OF LAW (1970)

E. Wayne Thode, late Professor of Law, University of Utah.
Leon Lebowitz, Professor of Law, University of Texas.
Lester J. Mazor, Professor of Law, University of Utah.

JUDICIAL CODE and Rules of Procedure in the Federal Courts with Excerpts from the Criminal Code, 1981 Edition

Henry M. Hart, Jr., late Professor of Law, Harvard University.
Herbert Wechsler, Professor of Law, Columbia University.

JURISPRUDENCE (Temporary Edition Hardbound) (1949)

Lon L. Fuller, Professor of Law Emeritus, Harvard University.

JUVENILE COURTS (1967)

Hon. Orman W. Ketcham, Juvenile Court of the District of Columbia.
Monrad G. Paulsen, Dean of the Law School, Yeshiva University.

JUVENILE JUSTICE PROCESS, Second Edition (1976), with 1980 Supplement

Frank W. Miller, Professor of Law, Washington University.
Robert O. Dawson, Professor of Law, University of Texas.
George E. Dix, Professor of Law, University of Texas.
Raymond I. Parnas, Professor of Law, University of California, Davis.

LABOR LAW, Eighth Edition (1977), with Statutory Supplement, and 1979 Case Supplement

Archibald Cox, Professor of Law, Harvard University, and
Derek C. Bok, President, Harvard University.
Robert A. Gorman, Professor of Law, University of Pennsylvania.

LABOR LAW (1968), with Statutory Supplement and 1974 Case Supplement

Clyde W. Summers, Professor of Law, University of Pennsylvania.
Harry H. Wellington, Dean of the Law School, Yale University.

LAND FINANCING, Second Edition (1977)

Norman Penney, Professor of Law, Cornell University.
Richard F. Broude, of the California Bar.

LAW AND MEDICINE (1980)

Walter Wadlington, Professor of Law and Professor of Legal Medicine, University of Virginia.
Jon R. Waltz, Professor of Law, Northwestern University.
Roger B. Dworkin, Professor of Law, Indiana University, and Professor of Biomedical History, University of Washington.

LAW, LANGUAGE AND ETHICS (1972)

William R. Bishin, Professor of Law, University of Southern California.
Christopher D. Stone, Professor of Law, University of Southern California.

LAWYERING PROCESS (1978), with Civil Problem Supplement and Criminal Problem Supplement

Gary Bellow, Professor of Law, Harvard University.
Bea Moulton, Professor of Law, Arizona State University.

LEGAL METHOD

Harry W. Jones, Professor of Law Emeritus, Columbia University.
John M. Kernochan, Professor of Law, Columbia University.
Arthur W. Murphy, Professor of Law, Columbia University.

LEGAL METHODS (1969)

Robert N. Covington, Professor of Law, Vanderbilt University.
E. Blythe Stason, late Professor of Law, Vanderbilt University.
John W. Wade, Professor of Law, Vanderbilt University.
Elliott E. Cheatham, late Professor of Law, Vanderbilt University.
Theodore A. Smedley, Professor of Law, Vanderbilt University.

LEGAL PROFESSION (1970)

Samuel D. Thurman, Dean of the College of Law, University of Utah.
Ellis L. Phillips, Jr., Professor of Law, Columbia University.
Elliott E. Cheatham, late Professor of Law, Vanderbilt University.

LEGISLATION, Third Edition (1973)

Horace E. Read, late Vice President, Dalhousie University.
John W. MacDonald, Professor of Law Emeritus, Cornell Law School.
Jefferson B. Fordham, Professor of Law, University of Utah, and
William J. Pierce, Professor of Law, University of Michigan.

LEGISLATIVE AND ADMINISTRATIVE PROCESSES (1976)

Hans A. Linde, Professor of Law, University of Oregon.
George Bunn, Professor of Law, University of Wisconsin.

LOCAL GOVERNMENT LAW, Revised Edition (1975)

Jefferson B. Fordham, Professor of Law, University of Utah.

MASS MEDIA LAW (1976), with 1979 Supplement

Marc A. Franklin, Professor of Law, Stanford University.

MENTAL HEALTH PROCESS, Second Edition (1976)

Frank W. Miller, Professor of Law, Washington University.
Robert O. Dawson, Professor of Law, University of Texas.
George E. Dix, Professor of Law, University of Texas.
Raymond I. Parnas, Professor of Law, University of California, Davis.

UNIVERSITY CASEBOOK SERIES—Continued

MUNICIPAL CORPORATIONS, see Local Government Law

NEGOTIABLE INSTRUMENTS, see Commercial Paper

NEW YORK PRACTICE, Fourth Edition (1978)

Herbert Peterfreund, Professor of Law, New York University.
Joseph M. McLaughlin, Dean of the Law School, Fordham University.

OIL AND GAS, Fourth Edition (1979)

Howard R. Williams, Professor of Law, Stanford University
Richard C. Maxwell, Professor of Law, University of California, Los Angeles.
Charles J. Meyers, Dean of the Law School, Stanford University.

ON LAW IN COURTS (1965)

Paul J. Mishkin, Professor of Law, University of California, Berkeley.
Clarence Morris, Professor of Law Emeritus, University of Pennsylvania.

OWNERSHIP AND DEVELOPMENT OF LAND (1965)

Jan Krasnowiecki, Professor of Law, University of Pennsylvania.

PARTNERSHIP PLANNING (1970) (Pamphlet)

William L. Cary, Professor of Law, Columbia University.

PERSPECTIVES ON THE LAWYER AS PLANNER (Reprint of Chapters One through Five of Planning by Lawyers) (1978)

Louis M. Brown, Professor of Law, University of Southern California.
Edward A. Dauer, Professor of Law, Yale University.

PLANNING BY LAWYERS, MATERIALS ON A NONADVERSARIAL LEGAL PROCESS (1978)

Louis M. Brown, Professor of Law, University of Southern California.
Edward A. Dauer, Professor of Law, Yale University.

PLEADING AND PROCEDURE, see Procedure, Civil

POLICE FUNCTION (1976) (Pamphlet)

Chapters 1–11 of Miller, Dawson, Dix & Parnas' Criminal Justice Administration, Second Edition.

PREVENTIVE LAW, see also Planning by Lawyers

PROCEDURE—Biography of a Legal Dispute (1968)

Marc A. Franklin, Professor of Law, Stanford University.

PROCEDURE—CIVIL PROCEDURE, Second Edition (1974), with 1979 Supplement

James H. Chadbourn, Professor of Law, Harvard University.
A. Leo Levin, Professor of Law, University of Pennsylvania.
Philip Shuchman, Professor of Law, University of Connecticut.

PROCEDURE—CIVIL PROCEDURE, Fourth Edition (1978), with 1980 Supplement

Richard H. Field, late Professor of Law, Harvard University.
Benjamin Kaplan, Professor of Law Emeritus, Harvard University.
Kevin M. Clermont, Professor of Law, Cornell University.

PROCEDURE—CIVIL PROCEDURE, Third Edition (1976), with 1978 Supplement

Maurice Rosenberg, Professor of Law, Columbia University.
Jack B. Weinstein, Professor, of Law, Columbia University.
Hans Smit, Professor of Law, Columbia University.
Harold L. Korn, Professor of Law, Columbia University.

PROCEDURE—PLEADING AND PROCEDURE: State and Federal, Fourth Edition (1979)

David W. Louisell, late Professor of Law, University of California, Berkeley.
Geoffrey C. Hazard, Jr., Professor of Law, Yale University.

PROCEDURE—FEDERAL RULES OF CIVIL PROCEDURE, 1980 Edition

PROCEDURE PORTFOLIO (1962)

James H. Chadbourn, Professor of Law, Harvard University, and
A. Leo Levin, Professor of Law, University of Pennsylvania.

PRODUCTS LIABILITY (1980)

Marshall S. Shapo, Professor of Law, Northwestern University.

PRODUCTS LIABILITY AND SAFETY (1980), with Statutory Supplement

W. Page Keeton, Professor of Law, University of Texas.
David G. Owen, Professor of Law, University of South Carolina.
John E. Montgomery, Professor of Law, University of South Carolina.

PROFESSIONAL RESPONSIBILITY (1976), with 1979 Problems, Cases and Readings, Supplement, 1980 Statutory (National) Supplement, and 1980 Statutory (California) Supplement

Thomas D. Morgan, Professor of Law, University of Illinois.
Ronald D. Rotunda, Professor of Law, University of Illinois.

PROPERTY, Fourth Edition (1978)

John E. Cribbet, Dean of the Law School, University of Illinois.
Corwin W. Johnson, Professor of Law, University of Texas.

PROPERTY—PERSONAL (1953)

S. Kenneth Skolfield, late Professor of Law Emeritus, Boston University.

PROPERTY—PERSONAL, Third Edition (1954)

Everett Fraser, late Dean of the Law School Emeritus, University of Minnesota.
Third Edition by Charles W. Taintor, late Professor of Law, University of Pittsburgh.

PROPERTY—INTRODUCTION, TO REAL PROPERTY, Third Edition (1954)

Everett Fraser, late Dean of the Law School Emeritus, University of Minnesota.

PROPERTY—REAL PROPERTY AND CONVEYANCING (1954)

Edward E. Bade, late Professor of Law, University of Minnesota.

PROPERTY—FUNDAMENTALS OF MODERN REAL PROPERTY (1974), with 1980 Supplement

Edward H. Rabin, Professor of Law, University of California, Davis.

PROPERTY—PROBLEMS IN REAL PROPERTY (Pamphlet) (1969)

Edward H. Rabin, Professor of Law, University of California, Davis.

PROSECUTION AND ADJUDICATION (1976) (Pamphlet)

Chapters 12–16 of Miller, Dawson, Dix & Parnas' Criminal Justice Administration, Successor Edition.

PUBLIC REGULATION OF DANGEROUS PRODUCTS (paperback) (1980)

Marshall S. Shapo, Professor of Law, Northwestern University.

PUBLIC UTILITY LAW, see Free Enterprise, also Regulated Industries

REAL ESTATE PLANNING (1980), with 1980 Problems, Statutes and New Materials Supplement

Norton L. Steuben, Professor of Law, University of Colorado.

RECEIVERSHIP AND CORPORATE REORGANIZATION, see Creditors' Rights

REGULATED INDUSTRIES, Second Edition, 1976

William K. Jones, Professor of Law, Columbia University.

RESTITUTION, Second Edition (1966)

John W. Wade, Professor of Law, Vanderbilt University.

SALES (1980)

Marion W. Benfield, Jr., Professor of Law, University of Illinois.
William D. Hawkland, Chancellor, Louisiana State University Law Center.

SALES AND SALES FINANCING, Fourth Edition (1976)

John Honnold, Professor of Law, University of Pennsylvania.

SECURITY, Third Edition (1959)

John Hanna, late Professor of Law Emeritus, Columbia University.

SECURITIES REGULATION, Fourth Edition (1977), with 1980 Selected Statutes Supplement and 1980 Cases and Releases Supplement

Richard W. Jennings, Professor of Law, University of California, Berkeley.
Harold Marsh, Jr., Member of the California Bar.

SENTENCING AND THE CORRECTIONAL PROCESS, Second Edition (1976)

Frank W. Miller, Professor of Law, Washington University.
Robert O. Dawson, Professor of Law, University of Texas.
George E. Dix, Professor of Law, University of Texas.
Raymond I. Parnas, Professor of Law, University of California, Davis.

SOCIAL WELFARE AND THE INDIVIDUAL (1971)

Robert J. Levy, Professor of Law, University of Minnesota.
Thomas P. Lewis, Dean of the College of Law, University of Kentucky.
Peter W. Martin, Professor of Law, Cornell University.

TAX, POLICY ANALYSIS OF THE FEDERAL INCOME (1976)

William A. Klein, Professor of Law, University of California, Los Angeles.

TAXATION, FEDERAL INCOME (1976), with 1980 Supplement

Erwin N. Griswold, Dean Emeritus, Harvard Law School.
Michael J. Graetz, Professor of Law, University of Virginia.

TAXATION, FEDERAL INCOME, Second Edition (1977), with 1979 Supplement

James J. Freeland, Professor of Law, University of Florida.
Stephen A. Lind, Professor of Law, University of Florida.
Richard B. Stephens, Professor of Law Emeritus, University of Florida.

TAXATION, FEDERAL INCOME, Volume I, Personal Income Taxation (1972), with 1979 Supplement; Volume II, Taxation of Partnerships and Corporations, Second Edition (1980)

Stanley S. Surrey, Professor of Law, Harvard University.
William C. Warren, Professor of Law Emeritus, Columbia University.
Paul R. McDaniel, Professor of Law, Boston College Law School.
Hugh J. Ault, Professor of Law, Boston College Law School.

TAXATION, FEDERAL WEALTH TRANSFER (1977)

Stanley S. Surrey, Professor of Law, Harvard University.
William C. Warren, Professor of Law Emeritus, Columbia University, and
Paul R. McDaniel, Professor of Law, Boston College Law School.
Harry L. Gutman, Instructor, Harvard Law School and Boston College Law School.

TAXATION OF INDIVIDUALS, PARTNERSHIPS AND CORPORATIONS, PROBLEMS in the (1978)

Norton L. Steuben, Professor of Law, University of Colorado.
William J. Turnier, Professor of Law, University of North Carolina.

TAXES AND FINANCE—STATE AND LOCAL (1974)

Oliver Oldman, Professor of Law, Harvard University.
Ferdinand P. Schoettle, Professor of Law, University of Minnesota.

TORT LAW AND ALTERNATIVES: INJURIES AND REMEDIES, Second Edition (1979)

Marc A. Franklin, Professor of Law, Stanford University.

TORTS, Sixth Edition (1976)

William L. Prosser, late Professor of Law, University of California, Hastings College.
John W. Wade, Professor of Law, Vanderbilt University.
Victor E. Schwartz, Professor of Law, American University.

TORTS, Third Edition (1976)

Harry Shulman, late Dean of the Law School, Yale University.
Fleming James, Jr., Professor of Law Emeritus, Yale University.
Oscar S. Gray, Professor of Law, University of Maryland.

TRADE REGULATION (1975), with 1979 Supplement

Milton Handler, Professor of Law Emeritus, Columbia University.
Harlan M. Blake, Professor of Law, Columbia University.
Robert Pitofsky, Professor of Law, Georgetown University.
Harvey J. Goldschmid, Professor of Law, Columbia University.

TRADE REGULATION, see Antitrust

TRANSNATIONAL LEGAL PROBLEMS, Second Edition (1976), with Documentary Supplement

Henry J. Steiner, Professor of Law, Harvard University.
Detlev F. Vagts, Professor of Law, Harvard University.

TRIAL, see also Lawyering Process

TRIAL ADVOCACY (1968)

A. Leo Levin, Professor of Law, University of Pennsylvania.
Harold Cramer, of the Pennsylvania Bar.
Maurice Rosenberg, Professor of Law, Columbia University, Consultant.

TRUSTS, Fifth Edition (1978)

George G. Bogert, late Professor of Law Emeritus, University of Chicago.
Dallin H. Oaks, President, Brigham Young University.

TRUSTS AND SUCCESSION (Palmer's), Third Edition (1978)

Richard V. Wellman, Professor of Law, University of Georgia.
Lawrence W. Waggoner, Professor of Law, University of Michigan.
Olin L. Browder, Jr., Professor of Law, University of Michigan.

University Casebook Series

EDITORIAL BOARD

THE LAWYERING PROCESS:

PREPARING AND PRESENTING THE CASE

By

GARY BELLOW

Professor of Law, Harvard University

and

BEA MOULTON

Legal Services Corporation

Mineola, New York

THE FOUNDATION PRESS, INC.

1981

COPYRIGHT © 1981 By THE FOUNDATION PRESS, INC.

All rights reserved

Printed in the United States of America

Library of Congress Catalog Card Number: 81-67655

ISBN   0-88277-040-3

B. & M. Prepar. & Present Case Pamph. UCB

INTRODUCTION

The following material is drawn from a larger work on lawyering skills and roles.[1] It is reorganized here to be used in a separate course on trial and appellate advocacy or as a supplement to materials now used in existing trial practice courses and programs.

Our primary focus is on helping you reflect on and make sense of the skills a lawyer uses in litigation. Chapter One addresses problems arising out of planning and investigating the case. Chapters Two and Three are concerned with witness examination and argument.

Each of these chapters is organized along familiar lines. First, we begin with excerpts from a variety of sources designed to encourage you to think about what is involved when a lawyer engages in preparing or presenting testimony and argument at trial. For example, readings on classical rhetoric and acting are offered as useful analogues in understanding the lawyer's tasks. The readings from these sorts of materials are less likely to tell you how to do the task than to provide a framework for analyzing and reflecting on it. Our belief is that, although such questions are elusive, these materials offer a way of approaching them. We would suggest that in each subject area at least one class be devoted to such a general inquiry.

The introductory material is then followed by a more detailed analysis of the components of the task. It is best assigned piecemeal, in conjunction with a simulated performance and/or actual clinical experience. There are a number of collections of problem materials available, including two problem supplements to the longer work from which these readings are drawn, which contain a large number of exercises and several criminal and civil files.[2] Such exercises will help you develop a "feel" for the dynamics of the task involved and provide a structure for thinking about how the particular problems might be solved. The connection between reflection and action explored in such a context is central to your ability to improve and enlarge your own skill and understanding in the future.

Finally, we turn to the ethical dimension of each of these tasks. Strategic choices inevitably have moral consequences and doing well may or may not involve doing good. It's our hope that you will look

---

1. Bellow & Moulton, *The Lawyering Process: Materials for Clinical Instruction in Advocacy* © 1978, The Foundation Press.

2. *Id., Civil Problem Supplement* and *Criminal Problem Supplement,* © 1978, The Foundation Press.

hard at the transcripts we've provided [3] in light of the Code of Professional Responsibility, your own experience with the task involved, and your own values and aspirations. It is well worth remembering how much of what we are becomes defined by how and what we do.

GARY BELLOW
BEA MOULTON

July, 1981

3. Videotapes of the transcripts are available from the American Bar Association's Consortium for Professional Education.

ACKNOWLEDGEMENTS

The problem with trying to list those who have helped us is the risk of omission. This work has been through many drafts and is, in a number of ways, the work of many hands. Its development parallels much of the debate, discussion, and experimentation that has accompanied the most recent efforts to introduce clinical education into the law school curriculum. It is impossible to distinguish between our involvement in that process and what we hope will be a contribution to it.

We owe a debt to scholars in a number of fields and many of our own colleagues, but first we would like to thank the people without whose help this book literally could never have been published: Donna Colletta of the Arizona State University College of Law, who typed and prepared many drafts and most of the final manuscript, and Cheryl Burg of the Harvard Law School, who also typed countless drafts. They have met our often unreasonable demands with grace, good humor and efficiency, and we would have been lost without them. They received substantial assistance from a number of others at both schools, including Carolyn Barone, Jeri Fitzgerald, Alice Fuhr, Mary O'Leary and Eileen Walker. In addition, Linda Beyer, Patricia Keairns, Fran Kendall, Iris Nissen, Virginia Stewart, Ellen Stone, and Dorothy Swanton helped out whenever they were asked, as did a number of other administrative and clerical personnel. We really are unable to name all those who assisted.

We also want particularly to thank Jeanne Kettleson, who made substantial contributions to a number of chapters, and had the temerity to teach with earlier drafts. She has consistently been a tough critic and a good friend.

As we have mentioned, we borrowed heavily from authors in a variety of fields. The list on the following pages only partially represents the debt we owe to a good many writers. Some of those whose writing we drew on gave us a considerable amount of personal help as well, including David Binder, Jeffrey Browne, John Cosier, Monroe Freedman, Charles Fried, Kenney Hegland, John Scanlan, George Shadoan, Tom Shaffer, William Simon and Andrew Watson. We also owe a debt to a number of people who actually worked on drafts or helped us work through some of the conceptual and pedagogical problems with which we struggled: Chris Argyris, Lee Bolman, Robert Condlin, John Cratsley, David Kaye, Bob Keeton, Jack Himmelstein, Michael Meltsner and Phil Schrag. Our failure to resolve these problems, of course, is our responsibility alone.

ACKNOWLEDGEMENTS

During the several years in which this work has been in progress, many teachers and lawyers—particularly those in the teaching fellow program at Harvard Law School—have taught or worked with students using these materials. Their comments and criticism have been most helpful. We want particularly to thank Mike Altman, Arthur John Anderson, David Barnhizer, Bob Bohn, Dorian Bowman, John Bowman, Clarissa Bronson, Barbara Buell, Barbara Burkett, Paul Collier, Nathan Crystal, Steve Fagan, Gene Fleming, Marty Gideonse, Dwight Golann, Jesse Goldner, Ann Greenberg, Rick Gross, Joe Harbaugh, Walter Heiser, Michelle Hermann, Rick Ireland, Rod Jones, Bill Joyner, Jeffrey Kobrick, Kenneth Kreiling, Nick Littlefield, Gary Lowenthal, Ken MacIver, Margorie McDiarmid, Kathy Mitchell, Fred Moss, Steve Morse, Steve Pepe, Mike Reiss, Dean Rivkin, David Rosenberg, Frank Samford, and Valerie Vanaman.

A number of other colleagues and friends have contributed in other ways, including Mike Brennan, Lou Brown, Hal Bruff, Edgar Cahn, Jean Cahn, Dick Carter, David Cavers, Phil Heymann, Earl Johnson, Rosabeth Kantor, Duncan Kennedy, Susan Kupfer, Marty Levine, Dorothy Nelson, Charles Nesson, Bill Pincus, Steve Rosenfeld, Frank Sander, Alan Stone, Sam Sutton, Roberto Unger and Lloyd Weinreb. In addition, throughout the years we have drawn on the experience of numerous others in legal aid and public defender practice, as well as on the insights of many other clinical teachers and students. The people in this category to whom we owe a real debt of gratitude are simply too numerous to name.

We also wish to thank Deans Willard Pedrick, Ernest Gellhorn and Alan Matheson of Arizona State and Dean Albert Sacks of Harvard; their cooperation and willingness to devote substantial resources to this project have in large part made it possible. Their support enabled us to employ a number of research assistants over the years, from whose efforts we have greatly benefitted: Frank Fanning, Mark Greenberg, Louraine Gutterman, Kathy Hillman, Virginia Richter, Nelson Rose, Layna Taylor, Glenda Ulfers, Karen Walker and especially Peter Puciloski, who kept working long after the money ran out.

Finally, we would like to thank the many authors and publishers who have given us permission to reprint copyrighted material. In addition to acknowledgements noted by special request on the first page of specific excerpts, we wish to thank the authors and publishers of the following materials:

ABA Consortium for Professional Education, Dilemmas in Legal Ethics, Parts One Through Five. © 1977 by the American Bar Association. Reprinted with permission.

ABA Project on Standards for Criminal Justice, Standards Relating to the Prosecution Function and the Defense Function. © 1971 by the American Bar Association. Reprinted with permission.

ACKNOWLEDGEMENTS

ABA Code of Professional Responsibility and Opinions of the Committee on Ethics and Professional Responsibility. Excerpts reprinted by permission of the American Bar Association.

Appleman (ed.), Successful Jury Trials, A Symposium, 127, 268-73, 275. © 1952 by Bobbs-Merrill Co., Inc. Reprinted with permission.

Bailey and Rothblatt, Successful Techniques for Criminal Trials, 92-98, 488-97. © 1974 by the Lawyers Co-Operative Publishing Company. Reprinted with permission.

Barthold, Attorney's Guide to Effective Discovery Techniques, 64, 67-69, 70. © 1975 by Prentice Hall, Inc., Englewood Cliffs, New Jersey. Reprinted with permission.

Bellow and Shadoan, Criminal Practice Institute Trial Manual, 2-1, 2-4 to 2-7, 2-10 to 2-11, 3-9 to 3-12. © 1964 by Lerner Law Book Co., Inc.

Bernstein and Woodward, All the President's Men, 63-69. © 1974 by Carl Bernstein and Bob Woodward. Reprinted by permission of Simon & Schuster, a Division of Gulf & Western Corporation.

Blumberg, Criminal Justice, 124-30, 137-42. © 1967 by Abraham S. Blumberg. Reprinted by permission of Franklin Watts, Inc.

Bodin, "Marshalling the Evidence," Civil Litigation and Trial Techniques, 18, 27, (Bodin, ed.). © 1976 by Practising Law Institute. Reprinted by permission.

Brock, Chesebro, Cragan & Klump, Public Policy Decision-Making: Systems Analysis and Comparative Advantages Debate, 27-29, 50-52, 56-59, 61-68. © 1973 by Harper & Row Publishers, Inc. Reprinted by permission.

Brooks and Warren, Understanding Fiction, 2d edition, 170-73, 272-77. © 1959 by Prentice-Hall, Inc., Englewood Cliffs, New Jersey. Reprinted with permission.

Capaldi, The Art of Deception, 76-80, 84, 87, 100-101. © 1975 by Prometheus Brooks, Buffalo, New York. Reprinted with permission.

Clark, Rhetoric in Greco-Roman Education, 71-92, 100-102, 118-124. © 1957 by Columbia University Press. Reprinted by permission of Columbia University Press.

Colman, Cross-Examination. A Practical Handbook, 39-40, 61, 64, 66, 89-90, 136-142, 144-150. Published by Juta and Company, Limited, 1970.

Davis, J., "The Argument of an Appeal," 26 ABAJ 895, 896-98. © 1940. Reprinted with permission of the American Bar Association Journal.

ACKNOWLEDGEMENTS

Erikson, "The Nature of Clinical Evidence," Evidence and Inference (Lerner, ed.), 74–77. © 1959 by the Free Press, a Corporation. Reprinted with permission of Macmillan Publishing Co., Inc.

Fitzpatrick, "Closing Argument for the Plaintiff," in Successful Jury Trials (Appleman, ed.) 411–31. © 1952 by the Bobbs-Merrill Company, Inc. Reprinted with permission.

Freedman, Lawyer's Ethics in an Adversary System, 43–49, 67–69, 71–75. © 1975 by the Bobbs-Merrill Co., Inc. Reprinted with permission. All rights reserved.

Gelatt, H. B., "Decision Making: A Conceptual Frame of Reference for Counseling," 9 J. of Couns. Psychology 240, 241–44. © 1962 by the American Psychological Association. Reprinted by permission of the American Psychological Association and the author.

Goldstein, "The Cardinal Principles of Cross-Examination," 3 Trial Lawyer's Guide 331, 354–58, 380–83. © 1960. Reprinted with permission from Trial Lawyer's Guide, 1959 Annual, published by Callaghan & Company, 3201 Old Glenview Road, Wilmette, Illinois 60091.

Gordon, "Non-Jury Summations," 6 Am.Jur. Trials (1967) p. 792. © 1967. Reprinted with permission of Bancroft-Whitney Company.

Hegland, Trial and Practice Skills in a Nutshell. © 1978 by West Publishing Company. Excerpts from the unpublished manuscript. Reprinted by permission of the author.

Hermann, "Winning Your Lawsuit by Deposition," 448 Ins.L.J. 297–300. © 1960 by Commerce Clearing House, Inc., Chicago, Ill. Reprinted by permission of Commerce Clearing House, Inc. and the author.

Huber, Influencing Through Argument. © 1969 by Longman Inc. Previously published by David McKay Company, Inc. Reprinted by permission of Longman Inc.

Hughes and Duhamel, Rhetoric: Principles and Usage, pp. 15–23. © 1967. Reprinted by permission of Prentice-Hall, Inc., Englewood Cliffs, New Jersey.

Jackson, "Direct Examination of Defendant", 6 American Jury Trials, 270–72, 282–83. © 1967. Reprinted with permission of Lawyers Co-Operative Publishing Company.

Jeans, Trial Advocacy, 372–74, 377–79. © 1975. Reprinted with permission of West Publishing Company.

Kaplan & Waltz, The Trial of Jack Ruby, 325–81. © 1965 by John Kaplan and Jon R. Waltz. Reprinted with permission of Macmillan Publishing Co., Inc.

ACKNOWLEDGEMENTS

Keeton, Trial Tactics and Methods, 2–3, 4, 42–44, 79–80, 303–05, 307–09, 311–17, 326–27. © 1973. Reprinted with permission of Little, Brown & Company and the author.

Kemelman, "The Nine Mile Walk." © 1947 by the American Mercury, Inc. Copyright renewed 1970 by Harry Kemelman. Reprinted by permission of the author and the author's literary agents, Scott Meredith Literary Agency, Inc., 845 Third Avenue, New York, N.Y. 10022.

Knapp, "The Civil and the Criminal Appeal" Compared in Counsel on Appeal (Arthur A. Charpentier, ed.) 66–69. © 1968. Reprinted with permission of McGraw-Hill Book Company and Shepard's Citations.

Lake, How to Cross-Examine Witnesses Successfully, 14, 16–18, 43, 92, 102, 185–88, 195–98, 328–29. © 1957 by Prentice-Hall, Inc. Reprinted by permission of Prentice-Hall, Inc., Englewood Cliffs, New Jersey.

Lindblom, "The Science of Muddling Through," The Public Administration Review, 79, 80–87. © 1959. Reprinted with permission.

Lindsay, New Techniques for Management Decision-Making, 48–53. © 1958 by McGraw-Hill, Inc. Reprinted with permission of McGraw-Hill Book Company.

Low, How to Prepare and Try a Negligence Case, 58, 70–74. © 1957 by Prentice-Hall, Inc., Englewood Cliffs, New Jersey. Reprinted with permission.

Lustgarten, Defender's Triumph, 56–63. © 1951 by Edgar Lustgarten. Reprinted with the permission of Charles Scribner's Sons.

McBurney & Mills, Argumentation and Debate, Techniques of a Free Society, 156–163. © 1964 by Macmillan Publishing Co., Inc. Reprinted with permission.

Maier, "Reasoning in Humans . . ." 12 J.Comp.Psych. 181, 182–83, 189–91. © 1931 by the American Psychological Association. Reprinted by permission.

Marshall, Law and Psychology in Conflict 13, 15–17, 19, 22–24, 25–26, 36–37. © 1966 by the Bobbs-Merrill Co., Inc. Reprinted by permission. All rights reserved.

Musmanno, Verdict!, 248–52. © 1958 by Doubleday & Company, Inc., copyright assigned to the author. Reprinted by permission of the author's estate.

O'Neill and McBurney, The Working Principles of Argument, 285–87, 293, 298–302. © 1932 by McMillan Publishing Co., Inc.

Parker, "Applied Psychology in Trial Practice," 7 Defense Law Journal 33–36, 38–45. © 1960. Reprinted with permission of The Allen Smith Co., Publishers.

Pierson, The Defense Attorney and Basic Defense Tactics, 228, 233–34, 247–48, 251–52. © 1956 by the Bobbs-Merrill Company, Inc. Reprinted by permission of the Michie Company.

Prettyman, Jr., Death and the Supreme Court, 65–70, 75–77, 87–89. © 1961 by Barrett Prettyman, Jr. Reprinted by permission of Harcourt Brace Jovanovich, Inc.

Probert, "Courtroom Semantics," 5 Am.Jur. Trials, 723–725, 735–738, 743–751, 754–755, 762–763. © 1966. Reprinted with permission of Bancroft-Whitney Company.

Redmount, "Handling Perception and Distortion in Testimony," 5 Am.Jur. Trials, 812, 816–17, 896–99, 902. © 1966. Reprinted with permission of the Lawyers Co-Operative Publishing Company.

Report of the Joint Conference of Professional Responsibility, 44 A.B.A.J. 1159, 1160–61. © 1958. Fuller and Randall, Co-Chairmen. Reprinted with permission of American Bar Association Journal.

Schwartz, Proof, Persuasion, and Cross-Examination, 104–107, 203–204, 207–208, 1605–06, 1703, 1803, 1910, 2103, 2205. © 1973. Reprinted with permission of Executive Reports Corporation, Englewood Cliffs, New Jersey.

Schweitzer, Cyclopedia of Trial Practice, Vol. I, 614–15. © 1970. Reprinted with permission of Lawyers Co-Operative Publishing Company.

Schweitzer, Trial Guide, Vol. 3, 1275, 1277–81, 1298–1305. © 1945 by Baker, Voorhis & Company.

Shadoan, Law and Tactics in Federal Criminal Cases, 1–21. © 1964.

Silver, Guilty Plea Negotiations: Criminal Defense Techniques, (Vol. 1A), 13–06 through 13–07. © 1977. Reprinted with permission of Matthew Bender & Company, Inc.

Simmons, Winning Before Trial: How to Prepare Cases for the Best Settlement or Trial Result, 205–06, 208–09, 223–25, 227–29, 231–32, 234–36, 305–13, 410–12. © 1974. Reprinted with permission of Executive Reports Corporation, Englewood Cliffs, New Jersey.

Simon, The Jury and the Defense of Insanity, 106, 107, 108, 118, 119. © 1967. Reprinted with permission of Little, Brown and Company.

Sink, Political Criminal Trials, How to Defend Them, 418–21, 651–52. © 1974. Reprinted with permission of Clark Boardman Company, Ltd. and the author.

Spellman, Direct Examination of Witnesses, 61–63, 66–69, 72, 85, 87–88, 90, 92. © 1968. Reprinted with permission of Prentice-Hall, Inc., Englewood Cliffs, New Jersey.

Stein, Closing Argument, 122-27. © 1969. Reprinted with permission from Closing Argument (The Art and the Law) published by Callaghan & Company, 3201 Old Glenview Road, Wilmette, Illinois.

Tessmer, Criminal Trial Strategy, 76-78, 80-81. © 1968 by John R. Mara Law Books.

Vetter, Successful Civil Litigation, 21, 27, 30-33. © 1977. Reprinted with permission of Prentice-Hall, Inc., Englewood Cliffs, New Jersey.

Whiting, An Introduction to the Theatre, 198, 200-211 (3rd ed.). © 1954 by Harper & Row Publishers, Inc. © 1961, 1969 by Frank M. Whiting. Reprinted with permission. A fourth edition of this work was published in 1978.

Wiener, Briefing & Arguing Federal Appeals, 287-89, 320-22, 328-29. © 1967. Reprinted with permission of The Bureau of National Affairs, Inc.

Wiener, "Oral Advocacy," 62 Harv.L.Rev. 56, 60-63, 69-75. © 1948. Reprinted by permission of the author.

Wigmore, Science of Judicial Proof, 9-11, 18-21, 24-28, 29-31, 34-37, 43-46. © 1937 by Little, Brown and Company.

Winterowd, Rhetoric: A Synthesis, 14-16. © 1968 by Holt, Rinehart & Winston, Inc. Reprinted with permission.

Zimbardo, "The Tactics and Ethics of Persuasion," Attitudes, Conflict and Social Change (E. McGinnies & B. King, eds.), 81, 84-92. © 1972 by Academic Press, Inc. Reprinted with permission.

*

SUMMARY OF CONTENTS

*

TABLE OF CONTENTS

CHAPTER TWO. WITNESS EXAMINATION: THE CASE RECONSTRUCTED

CHAPTER THREE. ARGUMENT: THE CASE PRESENTED

TABLE OF CONTENTS

THE LAWYERING PROCESS:

PREPARING AND PRESENTING THE CASE

*

Chapter One

CONSTRUCTING THE CASE: PREPARATION AND INVESTIGATION

SECTION ONE. PRELIMINARY PERSPECTIVES

A. IMAGES AND FRAGMENTS

KEMELMAN, 'THE NINE MILE WALK'

(1947).

I had made an ass of myself in a speech I had given at the Good Government Association dinner, and Nicky Welt had cornered me at breakfast at the Blue Moon, where we both ate occasionally, for the pleasure of rubbing it in. I had made the mistake of departing from my prepared speech to criticize a statement my predecessor in the office of County Attorney had made to the press. I had drawn a number of inferences from his statement and had thus left myself open to a rebuttal which he had promptly made and which had the effect of making me appear intellectually dishonest. I was new to this political game, having but a few months before left the Law School faculty to become the Reform Party candidate for County Attorney. I said as much in extenuation, but Nicholas Welt, who could never drop his pedagogical manner (he was Snowdon Professor of English Language and Literature), replied in much the same tone that he would dismiss a request from a sophomore for an extension on a term paper, "That's no excuse."

Although he is only two or three years older than I, in his late forties, he always treats me like a schoolmaster hectoring a stupid pupil. And I, perhaps because he looks so much older with his white hair and lined, gnomelike face, suffer it.

"They were perfectly logical inferences," I pleaded.

"My dear boy," he purred, "although human intercourse is well-nigh impossible without inference, most inferences are usually wrong. The percentage of error is particularly high in the legal profession where the intention is not to discover what the speaker wishes to convey, but rather what he wishes to conceal."

I picked up my check and eased out from behind the table.

1

"I suppose you are referring to cross-examination of witnesses in court. Well, there's always an opposing counsel who will object if the inference is illogical."

"Who said anything about logic?" he retorted. "An inference can be logical and still not be true."

He followed me down the aisle to the cashier's booth. I paid my check and waited impatiently while he searched in an old-fashioned change purse, fishing out coins one by one and placing them on the counter beside his check, only to discover that the total was insufficient. He slid them back into his purse and with a tiny sigh extracted a bill from another compartment of the purse and handed it to the cashier.

"Give me any sentence of ten or twelve words," he said, "and I'll build you a logical chain of inferences that you never dreamed of when you framed the sentence."

Other customers were coming in, and since the space in front of the cashier's booth was small, I decided to wait outside until Nicky completed his transaction with the cashier. I remember being mildly amused at the idea that he probably thought I was still at his elbow and was going right ahead with his discourse.

When he joined me on the sidewalk I said, "A nine mile walk is no joke, especially in the rain."

"No, I shouldn't think it would be," he agreed absently. Then he stopped in his stride and looked at me sharply. "What the devil are you talking about?"

"It's a sentence and it has eleven words," I insisted. And I repeated the sentence, ticking off the words on my fingers.

"What about it?"

"You said that given a sentence of ten or twelve words—"

"Oh, yes." He looked at me suspiciously. "Where did you get it?"

"It just popped into my head. Come on now, build your inferences."

"You're serious about this?" he asked, his little blue eyes glittering with amusement. "You really want me to?"

It was just like him to issue a challenge and then to appear amused when I accepted it. And it made me angry.

"Put up or shut up," I said.

"All right," he said mildly. "No need to be huffy. I'll play. Hm-m, let me see, how did the sentence go? 'A nine mile walk is no joke, especially in the rain.' Not much to go on there."

"It's more than ten words," I rejoined.

"Very well." His voice became crisp as he mentally squared off to the problem. "First inference: the speaker is aggrieved."

"I'll grant that," I said, "although it hardly seems to be an inference. It's really implicit in the statement."

He nodded impatiently. "Next inference: the rain was unforeseen, otherwise he would have said, 'A nine mile walk in the rain is no joke,' instead of using the 'especially' phrase as an afterthought."

"I'll allow that," I said, "although it's pretty obvious."

"First inferences should be obvious," said Nicky tartly.

I let it go at that. He seemed to be floundering and I didn't want to rub it in.

"Next inference: the speaker is not an athlete or an outdoors man."

"You'll have to explain that one," I said.

"It's the 'especially' phrase again," he said. "The speaker does not say that a nine mile walk in the rain is no joke, but merely the walk—just the distance, mind you—is no joke. Now, nine miles is not such a terribly long distance. You walk more than half that in eighteen holes of golf—and golf is an old man's game," he added slyly. *I* play golf.

"Well, that would be all right under ordinary circumstances," I said, "but there are other possibilities. The speaker might be a soldier in the jungle, in which case nine miles would be a pretty good hike, rain or no rain."

"Yes," and Nicky was sarcastic, "and the speaker might be one-legged. For that matter, the speaker might be a graduate student writting a Ph.D. thesis on humor and starting by listing all the things that are not funny. See here, I'll have to make a couple of assumptions before I continue."

"How do you mean?" I asked, suspiciously.

"Remember, I'm taking this sentence *in vacuo*, as it were. I don't know who said it or what the occasion was. Normally a sentence belongs in the framework of a situation."

"I see. What assumptions do you want to make?"

"For one thing, I want to assume that the intention was not frivolous, that the speaker is referring to a walk that was actually taken, and that the purpose of the walk was not to win a bet or something of that sort."

"That seems reasonable enough," I said.

"And I also want to assume that the locale of the walk is here."

"You mean here in Fairfield?"

"Not necessarily. I mean in this general section of the country."

"Fair enough."

"Then, if you grant those assumptions, you'll have to accept my last inference that the speaker is no athlete or outdoors man."

"Well, all right, go on."

"Then my next inference is that the walk was taken very late at night or very early in the morning—say, between midnight and five or six in the morning."

"How do you figure that one?" I asked.

"Consider the distance, nine miles. We're in a fairly well-populated section. Take any road and you'll find a community of some sort in less than nine miles. Hadley is five miles away, Hadley Falls is seven and a half, Goreton is eleven, but East Goreton is only eight and you strike East Goreton before you come to Goreton. There is local train service along the Goreton road and bus service along the others. All the highways are pretty well traveled. Would anyone have to walk nine miles in a rain unless it were late at night when no buses or trains were running and when the few automobiles that were out would hesitate to pick up a stranger on the highway?"

"He might not have wanted to be seen," I suggested.

Nicky smiled pityingly. "You think he would be less noticeable trudging along the highway than he would be riding in a public conveyance where everyone is usually absorbed in his newspaper?"

"Well, I won't press the point," I said brusquely.

"Then try this one: he was walking toward a town rather than away from one."

I nodded. "It is more likely, I suppose. If he were in a town, he could probably arrange for some sort of transportation. Is that the basis for your inference?"

"Partly that," said Nicky, "but there is also an inference to be drawn from the distance. Remember, it's a *nine* mile walk and nine is one of the exact numbers."

"I'm afraid I don't understand."

That exasperated schoolteacher-look appeared on Nicky's face again. "Suppose you say, 'I took a ten mile walk' or 'a hundred mile drive'; I would assume that you actually walked anywhere from eight to a dozen miles, or that you rode between ninety and a hundred and ten miles. In other words, *ten* and *hundred* are round numbers. You might have walked *exactly* ten miles or just as likely you might have walked *approximately* ten miles. But when you speak of walking *nine* miles, I have a right to assume that you have named an exact figure. Now, we are far more likely to know the distance of the city from a given point than we are to know the distance of a given point from the city. That is, ask anyone in the city how far out Farmer Brown lives, and if he knows him, he will say, 'Three or four miles.' But ask Farmer Brown how far he lives from the city and he will tell you, 'Three and six-tenths miles—measured it on my speedometer many a time.'"

"It's weak, Nicky," I said.

"But in conjunction with your own suggestion that he could have arranged transportation if he had been in a city—"

"Yes, that would do it," I said. "I'll pass it. Any more?"

"I've just begun to hit my stride," he boasted. "My next inference is that he was going to a definite destination and that he had to be there at a particular time. It was not a case of going off to get help because his car broke down or his wife was going to have a baby or somebody was trying to break into his house."

"Oh, come now," I said, "the car breaking down is really the most likely situation. He could have known the exact distance from having checked the mileage just as he was leaving the town."

Nicky shook his head. "Rather than walk nine miles in the rain, he would have curled up on the back seat and gone to sleep, or at least stayed by his car and tried to flag another motorist. Remember, it's nine miles. What would be the least it would take him to hike it?"

"Four hours," I offered.

He nodded. "Certainly no less, considering the rain. We've agreed that it happened very late at night or very early in the morning. Suppose he had his breakdown at one o'clock in the morning. It would be five o'clock before he would arrive. That's daybreak. You begin to see a lot of cars on the road. The buses start just a little later. In fact, the first buses hit Fairfield around five-thirty. Besides, if he were going for help, he would not have to go all the way to town—only as far as the nearest telephone. No, he had a definite appointment, and it was in a town, and it was for some time before five-thirty."

"Then why couldn't he have got there earlier and waited?" I asked. "He could have taken the last bus, arrived around one o'clock, and waited until his appointment. He walks nine miles in the rain instead, and you said he was no athlete."

We had arrived at the Municipal Building where my office is. Normally, any arguments begun at the Blue Moon ended at the entrance to the Municipal Building. But I was interested in Nicky's demonstration and I suggested that he come up for a few minutes.

When we were seated I said, "How about it, Nicky, why couldn't he have arrived early and waited?"

"He could have," Nicky retorted. "But since he did not, we must assume that he was either detained until after the last bus left, or that he had to wait where he was for a signal of some sort, perhaps a telephone call."

"Then according to you, he had an appointment some time between midnight and five-thirty—"

"We can draw it much finer than that. Remember, it takes him four hours to walk the distance. The last bus stops at twelve-thirty A.M. If he doesn't take that, but starts at the same time, he won't arrive at his destination until four-thirty. On the other hand, if he takes the first bus in the morning, he will arrive around five-thirty. That would mean that his appointment was for some time between four-thirty and five-thirty."

"You mean that if his appointment was earlier than four-thirty, he would have taken the last night bus, and if it was later than five-thirty, he would have taken the first morning bus?"

"Precisely. And another thing: if he was waiting for a signal or a phone call, it must have come not much later than one o'clock."

"Yes, I see that," I said. "If his appointment is around five o'clock and it takes him four hours to walk the distance, he'd have to start around one."

He nodded, silent and thoughtful. For some queer reason I could not explain, I did not feel like interrupting his thoughts. On the wall was a large map of the county and I walked over to it and began to study it.

"You're right, Nicky," I remarked over my shoulder, "there's no place as far as nine miles away from Fairfield that doesn't hit another town first, Fairchild is right in the middle of a bunch of smaller towns."

He joined me at the map. "It doesn't have to be Fairfield, you know," he said quietly. "It was probably one of the outlying towns he had to reach. Try Hadley."

"Why Hadley? What would anyone want in Hadley at five o'clock in the morning?"

"The Washington Flyer stops there to take on water about that time," he said quietly.

"That's right, too," I said. "I've heard that train many a night when I couldn't sleep. I'd hear it pulling in and then a minute or two later I'd hear the clock on the Methodist Church banging out five." I went back to my desk for a timetable. "The Flyer leaves Washington at twelve forty-seven A.M. and gets into Boston at eight A.M."

Nicky was still at the map measuring distances with a pencil.

"Exactly nine miles from Hadley is the Old Sumter Inn," he announced.

"Old Sumter Inn," I echoed. "But that upsets the whole theory. You can arrange for transportation there as easily as you can in a town."

He shook his head. "The cars are kept in an enclosure and you have to get an attendant to check you through the gate. The attendant would remember anyone taking out his car at a strange hour. It's a pretty conservative place. He could have waited in his room until he got a call from Washington about someone on the Flyer—maybe the number of the car and the berth. Then he could just slip out of the hotel and walk to Hadley."

I stared at him, hypnotized.

"It wouldn't be difficult to slip aboard while the train was taking on water, and then if he knew the car number and the berth—"

"Nicky," I said portentously, "as the Reform District Attorney who campaigned on an economy program, I am going to waste the taxpayers' money and call Boston long distance. It's ridiculous, it's insane—but I'm going to do it!"

His little blue eyes glittered and he moistened his lips with the tip of his tongue.

"Go ahead," he said hoarsely.

I replaced the telephone in its cradle.

"Nicky," I said, "this is probably the most remarkable coincidence in the history of criminal investigation: *a man was found murdered in his berth on last night's twelve-forty-seven from Washington!* He'd been dead about three hours, which would make it exactly right for Hadley."

"I thought it was something like that," said Nicky. "But you're wrong about its being a coincidence. It can't be. Where did you get that sentence?"

"It was just a sentence. It simply popped into my head."

"It couldn't have! It's not the sort of sentence that pops into one's head. If you had taught composition as long as I have, you'd know that when you ask someone for a sentence of ten words or so, you get an ordinary statement such as 'I like milk'—with the other words made up by a modifying clause like, 'because it is good for my health.' The sentence you offered related to a *particular situation*."

"But I tell you I talked to no one this morning. And I was alone with you at the Blue Moon."

"You weren't with me all the time I paid my check," he said sharply. "Did you meet anyone while you were waiting on the sidewalk for me to come out of the Blue Moon?"

I shook my head. "I was outside for less than a minute before you joined me. You see, a couple of men came in while you were digging out your change and one of them bumped me, so I thought I'd wait—"

"Did you ever see them before?"

"Who?"

"The two men who came in," he said, the note of exasperation creeping into his voice again.

"Why, no—they weren't anyone I knew."

"Were they talking?"

"I guess so. Yes, they were. Quite absorbed in their conversation, as a matter of fact—otherwise, they would have noticed me and I would not have been bumped."

"Not many strangers come into the Blue Moon," he remarked.

"Do you think it was they?" I asked eagerly. "I think I'd know them again if I saw them."

Nicky's eyes narrowed. "It's possible. There had to be two—one to trail the victim in Washington and ascertain his berth number, the other to wait here and do the job. The Washington man would be likely to come down here afterwards. If there was theft as well as murder, it would be to divide the spoils. If it was just murder, he would probably have to come down to pay off his confederate."

I reached for the telephone.

"We've been gone less than half an hour," Nicky went on. "They were just coming in and service is slow at the Blue Moon. The one who walked all the way to Hadley must certainly be hungry and the other probably drove all night from Washington."

"Call me immediately if you make an arrest," I said into the phone and hung up.

Neither of us spoke a word while we waited. We paced the floor, avoiding each other almost as though we had done something we were ashamed of.

The telephone rang at last. I picked it up and listened. Then I said, "O. K." and turned to Nicky.

"One of them tried to escape through the kitchen but Winn had someone stationed at the back and they got him."

"That would seem to prove it," said Nicky with a frosty little smile.

I nodded agreement.

He glanced at his watch. "Gracious," he exclaimed, "I wanted to make an early start on my work this morning, and here I've already wasted all this time talking with you."

I let him get to the door. "Oh, Nicky," I called, "what was it you set out to prove?"

"That a chain of inferences could be logical and still not be true," he said.

"Oh."

"What are you laughing at?" he asked snappishly. And then he laughed too.

BERNSTEIN AND WOODWARD, ALL THE PRESIDENT'S MEN *

63–69 (1975).

On the evening of September 14, Bernstein knocked at the front door of a small tract house in the Washington suburbs. Ever since he had lunched with the woman from CRP, he had had a feeling that the owner of this house was the person who had gone back to the prosecutors. He had asked around. "She knows a lot," he was told. The woman worked for Maurice Stans.

A woman opened the door and let Bernstein in. "You don't want me, you want my sister," she said. Her sister came into the room. He had expected a woman in her fifties, probably gray; it was his image of a bookkeeper, which is what she was. But she was much younger.

"Oh, my God," the Bookkeeper said, "you're from the *Washington Post*. You'll have to go, I'm sorry."

Bernstein started figuring ways to hold his ground. The sister was smoking and he noticed a pack of cigarettes on the dinette table; he asked for one. "I'll get it," he said as the sister moved to get the pack, "don't bother." That got him 10 feet into the house. He bluffed, telling the Bookkeeper that he understood her being afraid; there were a lot of people like her at the committee who wanted to tell the truth, but some people didn't want to listen. He knew that certain people had gone back to the FBI and the prosecutors to give more information. . . . He hesitated.

"Where do you reporters get your information anyhow?" she asked. "That's what nobody at the committee can figure out."

Bernstein asked if he could sit down and finish his cigarette.

"Yes, but then you'll have to go, I really have nothing to say." She was drinking coffee, and her sister asked if Bernstein would like some. The Bookkeeper winced, but it was too late. Bernstein started sipping, slowly.

She was curious. "Somebody is certainly giving you good information if you knew I went back to the prosecutors." Then she rattled off a few names that Bernstein tried to keep in his head; if she was mentioning them as possible sources, they must be people who either had some information or were unhappy with the way things were going down at the committee.

He went into a monologue about all the fine people he and Woodward had met who wanted to help but didn't have hard information, only what they had picked up third and fourth hand.

"You guys keep digging," she said. "You've really struck close to home."

How did she know?

"I ran the totals for the people. I have an adding machine and a deft hand." The way she said it was almost mocking, as if she knew she had been watching *Naked City* too much. She shook her head and laughed at herself. "Sometimes I don't know whether to laugh or cry. I'm an accountant. I'm apolitical. I didn't do anything wrong. But in some way, something is rotten in Denmark and I'm part of it." Then she started guessing sources again and Bernstein tried to keep the names straight in his head. She was glancing at his coffee cup. He tried not to look tense, and played with her dog. She seemed to want to talk about what she knew. But to the *Washington Post*, the enemy? Bernstein had the feeling he was either going out the door any minute or staying till she had told the whole story.

"My only loyalties are to Maurice Stans, the President's re-election and the truth," she said.

Bernstein had heard that Stans' wife was sick and in the hospital. He asked how Mrs. Stans was, and then inquired if the Secretary was going to end up a fall guy for John Mitchell.

"If you could get John Mitchell, it would be beautiful. But I just don't have any real evidence that would stand up in court that he knew. Maybe his guys got carried away, the men close to him."

What guys?

Her hands were shaking. She looked at her sister, who shrugged her shoulders noncommittally. Bernstein thought he had an ally there. The sister got up to get another cup of coffee. He took a gulp and handed his cup to her. She refilled it. Bernstein decided to take a chance. He removed a notebook and pencil from his inner breast pocket. The Bookkeeper stared at him. She was not going to say anything that they probably didn't know already, Bernstein told her, and absolutely nothing would go into the paper that couldn't be verified elsewhere.

"There are a lot of things that are wrong and a lot of things that are bad at the committee," the Bookkeeper said. "I was called by the grand jury very early, but nobody knew what questions to ask. People had already lied to them."

Sally Harmony?

"She and I have not discussed it. . . . But Sally—and others —lied." The Bookkeeper had worked for Hugh Sloan, and after he quit, she was promoted to work for Stans. "There were a few of us they were worried about who got promotions.

"Sloan is the sacrificial lamb. His wife was going to leave him if he didn't stand up and do what was right. He left because he saw it and didn't want any part of it. We didn't know before June 17, but we put two and two together on June 19 and figured it out."

She changed the subject. A few days earlier, the *Post* had reported that there was another participant in the bugging whose identity had not been disclosed; and that he had been granted immunity from prosecution and was talking.

The Bookkeeper started to speculate out loud: "Baldwin? He wasn't even on the payroll."

She tried two other names.

Bernstein shook his head. (He had no idea who it was.)

"It has to be one of those three," she said. "I'm pretty sure it's Baldwin."

Bernstein asked if she knew who had received transcripts of wire-tapped conversations.

"I don't know anything about how the operational end of the espionage worked," she said. "I just know who got the money and who approved the allocations. And from what I can see, you've got all the names. Track a little upstairs and out of the finance committee," she advised. "It was the political people. . . . It won't make any difference. You've got to get the law on your side if anything is going to be done. The indictments are going to get the seven and that's it. The power of the politicians is too strong."

How many people were paid?

"Thirteen or fourteen from the fund, but only six or seven are involved. The grand jury didn't even ask if there were any payments that were extra-legal."

Did Stans know who received such payments?

"He knew less than I knew. My loyalty is to Hugh and Mr. Stans," she stressed. "For some reason, Mr. Stans feels we have to take the heat for a while." She had talked to Sloan that morning and he had mentioned a story in the *New York Daily News* that gave the impression that Sloan knew of the bugging operation. "I told him he should sue, but all he said was 'I want out.' The grand jury didn't ask him the right questions either, I guess."

Who knew all the answers to the right questions?

"Liddy and Sally Harmony. She has more information than I have. But she has never talked to me about what she knows. I urged her time and time again to do what's right. Sally got promoted, too." She was now working for Robert Odle.

Was Odle involved?

"Certainly not in knowing anything about the bugging. He's a glorified office boy, Magruder's runner. Jeb's definitely involved, of course. It was all done on the political side, that's common knowledge. All the people involved are with the political committee, not finance." But she wouldn't say who, beyond Magruder. Magruder was CRP's second-in-command. Bernstein started guessing, picking

names that he remembered from the GAO list. Lang Washburn?
He had forgotten that Washburn was in finance, not on the political
side.

"Are you kidding? Lang's so dumb that the Monday after the
bugging he called everybody in finance together to say that we had
nothing to do with it. And then he asked Gordon to say a few words
to the kids. At which point Gordon Liddy got up and made a speech
about how this one bad apple, McCord, shouldn't be allowed to spoil
the whole barrel."

Bernstein asked the sister for another cup of coffee and tried
another name.

"Never. The White House got him out because he didn't like
to do all the crazy things they wanted."

Who?

"Right under Mitchell," the Bookkeeper suggested.

Bernstein tried LaRue and Porter. She didn't respond. He tried
again.

Silence.

What evidence did she have that Mitchell's assistants were involved?

"I had the evidence, but all the records were destroyed. . . .
I don't know who destroyed them, but I'm sure Gordon did some
shredding."

Was it hard evidence?

"It wouldn't positively say they planned the bugging; it wouldn't
necessarily implicate them with this, but it would come pretty close."

How could she tell it linked them to the bugging?

"There was a special account before April 7. Back then, they
were just expenditures as far as I was concerned; I didn't have any
idea then what it was all about. But after June 17 you didn't have
to be any genius to figure it out. I'd seen the figures and I'd seen
all the people. And there were no receipts." Liddy was among those
who received the money, she said. "Gordon's a case of loyalty to the
President. He'll never crack. He'll take the whole rap."

The Bookkeeper was looking at Bernstein's coffee cup again,
having second thoughts. "There are too many people watching me,"
she said. "They know I'm privy and they watch me like a hawk."
She was convinced her phones were tapped.

How much money was paid out?

"A lot."

More than half a million?

"You've had it in print."

Finally it clicked. Sometimes he could be incredibly slow, Bernstein thought to himself. It was the slush fund of cash kept in Stans' safe.

"I never knew it was a 'security fund' or whatever they called it," she said, "until after June 17. I just thought it was an all-purpose political fund that you didn't talk about—like to take fat cats to dinner, but all strictly legal."

$350,000 in dinners? How was it paid out?

"Not in one chunk. I know what happened to it, I added up the figures." There had been a single sheet of paper on which the account was kept; it had been destroyed, the only record. "It was a lined sheet with names on about half the sheet, about fifteen names with the amount distributed to each person next to the name. I saw it more than once. The amounts kept getting bigger." She had updated the sheet each time a disbursement was made. Sloan knew the whole story too. He had handed out the money.

Bernstein asked about the names again. He was confused because there were about 15 names on the sheet, yet she thought only six were involved. Which six?

"Go down the GAO report; I think they've all been before the grand jury. They're easy to isolate; a couple have been named in the press but not necessarily in connection with this."

How were the funds allocated?

Telephone calls had something to do with how the money was doled out. Only three of the six had actually received money. "The involvement of the others includes answering some telephone calls," she stated.

Who were the six? he asked again.

"Mitchell's principal assistants . . . the top echelon. Magruder is one."

He started throwing out more names. No use. He tried initials: if she told him their initials, she could truthfully say that she had never given Bernstein the names, and he would at least be able to narrow down the candidates. Early in the conversation, she had not answered when he had asked if LaRue and Porter were involved. He tried L.

"L and M and P, and that's all I'm going to give you," the Bookkeeper said.

Bernstein finished his coffee. He wanted to be able to come back, and he had already pushed too hard. Thanking her at the door, he asked who at the committee might know something and be willing to talk about it. She mentioned the name of the woman who had been followed to lunch with Bernstein.

Heading for the Beltway, Bernstein stopped at a phone booth and called Woodward at home. Between the coffee jag, the euphoria of the moment and the information he was trying to keep straight in his head, Bernstein sounded overexcited. He also didn't want to say too much on the phone—the paranoia was catching. He said he'd be right over.

Woodward typed as Bernstein dictated his notes and filled in the gaps. The implications seemed clear. The money in Stans' safe was related to the bugging operation; Liddy had received some of it; but, most important, Mitchell's assistants—including Magruder— had also gotten some of the money and were aware of the espionage operation.

PRETTYMAN, JR., DEATH AND THE SUPREME COURT

65–70, 75–77 (1961).

The jury was out for two hours and a half.

Its verdict was announced by the foreman:

"We, the jury, find the defendant Everett D. Green guilty of arson on count one.

"We find the defendant guilty of second degree murder on the second count."

Green had escaped the death penalty. Judge McLaughlin sentenced him to two prison terms—from one to three years on count one, and from five to twenty years on count two, the two sentences to run concurrently.

Green himself wrote a letter to the Court of Appeals, which the court interpreted as an appeal of the conviction. In such cases, when defendants cannot afford to hire counsel, the Court of Appeals appoints attorneys to represent them. These attorneys serve without compensation. And so here, the Court of Appeals appointed as Green's counsel a young attorney less than one year out of the University of Virginia Law School. George Blow was tall and thin, with a shock of slightly curly hair above a high forehead. He was not handsome, but a wide grin surrounded prominent white teeth, and the effect was good. He delayed his laugh; it came a fraction after it was expected. But its arrival was punctuated by loud staccato sounds that amply compensated for the delay. His job with Washington's largest law firm had not, to date, included any trial work or any criminal work.

Blow obtained a copy of the transcript of the trial and studied it in great detail. Carefully he went over, time and again, every aspect of the proceedings. He spent hours reviewing the opinions in criminal cases in the District of Columbia. On several occasions, he interviewed Green at the jail.

Finally, he returned to Green with very sober news. There was, he felt, an error in the record, but presenting that error to the Court of Appeals would place Green's life in danger.

Judge McLaughlin had allowed the jury to consider both first and second degree murder. The only evidence at the trial as to the cause of Bettie Brown's death was rendered by Dr. Rosenberg, and he had concluded that she died as the result of the fire. The jury had decided, by its finding of arson under count one, that Green had set the fire. Therefore, explained Blow, if Green had caused the death, he necessarily did it in the course of committing arson, a felony.

The District of Columbia has a "felony murder" statute. This law provides that if anyone causes the death of another while committing a felony, he shall be guilty of first degree murder, even if he did not intend to kill. Thus, reasoned Blow, if Green had caused Bettie Brown's death while committing the felony of arson, he *must* be guilty of first degree murder; there was no evidence whatever to support a verdict of second degree murder, and Judge McLaughlin had been in error in even instructing the jury on second degree murder.

With great care and precision, Blow explained to Green the possible consequences of an appeal on this point. If the Court of Appeals reversed the second degree murder conviction, it would return the case for a new trial, and at a second trial the jury would be instructed only on first degree murder. If the verdict was guilty. Green would have to be sentenced to death, because the death penalty is mandatory for first degree murder in the District of Columbia.

It is true, said Blow, that he had devised a theory by which he hoped to avoid a second trial. But he had no guarantee whatever of its validity, or of its ultimate success.

Green was given time to think over his desperate situation. Shouldn't he, after all, be content with a jail sentence? Isn't confined life far better than the risk of no life at all? How could this mild, almost timid, man gamble with stakes that were so high and with odds so poor? And for *any* man, was the chance of freedom worth the agony of another trial, of standing once more while a nameless foreman stated the short, pungent, expressionless words which told you whether you would walk out free or walk to your death?

But it was not a searing decision for Green. He said he fully understood the consequences, but he would rather go to the chair than spend the rest of his life in jail. In fact, he added, he would rather die than spend another day in jail. He adamantly instructed Blow to file the appeal.

And so George Blow wrote a lengthy brief setting forth his contentions, and he argued the case orally before a three-judge panel of the Court of Appeals.

Two months after the argument, the court rendered its decision. By a vote of two to one, the court agreed with Blow and reversed the conviction. After quoting at length from Dr. Rosenberg's testimony, the court concluded that "all the testimony as to what occurred in the burning house pointed to murder in the first degree and nothing else. . . . In seeking a new trial at which—if the evidence is substantially as before—the jury will have no choice except to find him guilty of first degree murder or to acquit him, Green is manifestly taking a desperate chance. He may suffer the death penalty. At oral argument we inquired of his counsel [Blow] whether Green clearly understood the possible consequences of success on this appeal, and were told the appellant, who is 64 years of age, says he prefers death to spending the rest of his life in prison. He is entitled to a new trial."

* * *

And so, four months later, Green prepared for his second trial in Federal District Court. Since he had not appealed from his conviction of arson, that issue was no longer involved. And the Court of Appeals had now held that no instruction could be given on second degree murder. The sole issue was whether Green was guilty of first degree murder. If so, the judge was required by statute to condemn him to death.

The United States Attorney's Office was not enthusiastic about this turn of events. As Flannery had said, this was a pathetic case rather than a brutal one, and the thought of asking a jury to send Green to his death was not pleasing. After a number of consultations within the United States Attorney's Office, word was sent to George Blow that a plea of guilty to manslaughter would be acceptable to the prosecution.

Once again, Blow returned to the jail. Once again he explained patiently and with great care the alternatives open to Green. A plea to manslaughter would involve a relatively short jail sentence. A new trial, on the other hand, would mean the chance of an adverse verdict, and of death in the electric chair. Blow urged his client, with all the persuasive force he could marshal, to accept the prosecution's offer.

Green said no. He said he would not plead guilty to anything because he was not guilty of anything. He had faith in the future and in his own destiny, and he would take his chances with a new trial. George Blow, feeling solemn and old beyond his years, left the jail and turned his thoughts to the preparation of his first trial.

* * *

Prior to trial, Green's attorneys presented a motion to dismiss the indictment. This was the move which Blow had outlined to Green, a desperate effort to kill the first degree murder charge.

Their argument was this. The jury in the first trial not only had found Green guilty of second degree murder but had, in effect, found him *not* guilty of first degree murder. Or, to put it another way, Green had once been in jeopardy of a first degree murder conviction, and the jury had failed to convict. Therefore, argued Green's attorneys, he no longer could be tried for first degree murder; to do so would put him twice in jeopardy for the same offense in violation of the Fifth Amendment to the Constitution.

Judge Letts rejected their argument and proceeded to trial. It lasted one day longer than the first trial and included twenty-five witnesses compared with the nineteen who had appeared previously.

* * *

[The jurors] deliberated for six hours and twenty minutes. At 10:30 P.M., they notified the marshal that they were ready. The courthouse was completely dark except for the one room into which they filed. They formed a long line, facing Green. The clerk asked the foreman, "What say you as to the defendant Everett D. Green on Count 2?"

The reply came firmly: "Guilty as charged."

* * *

Judge Letts . . . proceeded on to what surely must be the most distasteful duty that rests on a judge. "Everett D. Green, you have been found guilty . . . and . . . you are hereby sentenced to the punishment of death by electrocution. . . ."

* * *

Back to the Court of Appeals went his attorneys. As they had argued to Judge Letts, they now argued to the appellate court that this conviction was void because in violation of the Constitution. Green had been twice tried for the same offense.

[When the Court of Appeals rejected their claims, they turned to the Supreme Court of the United States.]

* * *

[The argument turned on whether Green's earlier appeal waived his protection from being retried for first degree murder.] Under the Fifth Amendment when a jury finds a defendant not guilty, the government cannot appeal the verdict, regardless of how many errors were made during the trial. And "a defendant is placed in jeopardy once he is put to trial before a jury so that if the jury is discharged without his consent he cannot be tried again." However, if a jury cannot agree on *any* verdict, a new trial can be ordered. Finally, if a defendant appeals and wins a reversal, he can be tried again for the *same* offense with which he was originally charged, by appealing, he "waives" his right to claim double jeopardy.

But what about Green's situation? He had appealed and won a reversal of his conviction for second degree murder, but the government had not prosecuted him again for second degree murder. It had prosecuted him the second time for *first* degree murder. Green's attorneys claimed that Green, by appealing the *second* degree murder conviction, did not waive his rights in regard to the *first* degree acquittal.

On Monday morning, December 16, 1967 . . . the first decision announced by the Court was Green v. United States. The opinion ran thirteen and a half printed pages and was joined by Warren, Brennan, . . . Whittaker, Black and Douglas. These five justices reversed the conviction . . . Green . . . was free.

———

NOTES

Somewhere during, after, or even before your interview with your client, your attention will shift to "what to do next." The nature of this aspect of thinking and acting like a lawyer is the focus of this chapter.

Identifying the legal rules relevant to a particular statement of facts is probably familiar to you (at least your first year teachers hope so). But how will you construct the complete statement of "what happened" from the fragments of what a client has offered? How close is the logic of this process to the way Nicky Welt worked with the statement, "A nine mile walk is no joke, especially in the rain?" If you needed to fill in gaps in the narrative, and they could be supplied by a witness reluctant to talk to you, how would you proceed? Would you insinuate yourself into the witness' home as Bernstein did?

Perhaps more difficult is the problem of looking forward. Imagine yourself representing Everett Green in his grim situation. Would you have been able to plan the arguments to be made in the case, and to foresee their impact? To what extent are judgments about what arguments to make to an appellate court similar to those a lawyer makes about the believability of factual claims? Even if we limit our inquiry to litigated situations (where there is, at least, a focused dispute rather than an effort to anticipate all possible consequences), planning and investigation are complex processes.

Whatever their difficulty, however, most skillful lawyers see these tasks as central to the lawyer's job. Because legal rules and roles are relatively fluid, they can be "taken advantage of" to make things happen according to a particular plan. Good lawyering is, whatever else, a purposive, practical activity. Whenever you interview a witness, answer interrogatories, appear on a preliminary motion, or work with an expert to organize a mass of technical data, what you do and say will almost certainly—even if incidentally—influence the way others (witnesses, clients, officials) view you and the case, and may even change the case itself. Such influences, in turn, can determine how a dispute is ultimately resolved across a bargaining table or in court. Good cases—and, to a large extent, good facts—are often made, not found.

In contrast to client interviewing, then, case preparation is a very instrumental aspect of the lawyer's job. What will the process of "putting a case together" mean to you? What knowledge and skills does it require? What doubts does it create? As you begin to sort out answers to these questions, you may be surprised to find that the facts do not speak for themselves. You and your client—as well as witnesses, opponents and their counsel—will select and order them not only so that they make sense, but also so that, as much as possible, they work toward your goals. That is, what is "learned" from an investigation is never an end in itself; it is always the starting point for new inquiries and choices. A fact is inevitably, as Pirandello remarked, "like a sack"—it won't stand up unless you put something into it.

Second, you will continually find yourself making predictions—imagining the consequences of particular actions or "moves" you and others might make. Consider, for example, Prettyman's comments on the role of particular Supreme Court Justices in the Green case:

> From hindsight, the interesting man in the case was Justice Whittaker. The votes of Black and Douglas were in line with their often-expressed desire for a broad application of the Fifth Amendment, and the votes of Warren and Brennan now seem in keeping with their later approach to these problems. But Whittaker has developed along different lines.
>
> * * *
>
> On the Supreme Court, he has tended to side with Frankfurter and Harlan on questions involving the criminal law, and to keep strictly to proper lines of criminal procedure. It must be recalled that the Green case was one of the first on which Whittaker sat when he came to the Court, and the awful specter of death hung over the result. Who can gauge the psychological impact of arriving at Olympus and being asked to decide, as one of his first acts, whether an elderly man should be electrocuted? It is probably safe to assume that it was Whittaker, as much as any other Justice, who wanted reargument in the case so as to help him resolve his many doubts.
>
> Green's timing was undesignedly perfect. If he had arrived at the Supreme Court a few months earlier, he would have been faced with Reed and Minton rather than Brennan and Whittaker, and his reception no doubt would have been less cordial than it was. On the other hand, if he had arrived a few months later, after Whittaker had more fully adjusted to the demands and rigors of the Court, perhaps he would have lost Whittaker's crucial vote.[1]

In this situation, George Blow might not have been able to foresee that Whittaker would be more likely to vote with him during the Justice's early months on the Court, but there are ways of controlling the timing of appeal and argument to take advantage of such possi-

1. B. Prettyman, Jr., DEATH AND THE SUPREME COURT 87–89 (1961).

bilities. How would you go about identifying the elements in such circumstances which can be predicted and controlled, and how will you learn to manage them?

Finally, you will continually be faced, not with a single coherent view of what happened, but with multiple narrations of the same story—*e. g.*, your client's, your opponent's, the version that is legally relevant, or the story you would like to tell at trial, across a bargaining table or to a hostile witness. All these narratives must be kept in mind as you investigate your case and build it in ways that are most favorable to your client's position.

The interpersonal skills needed to make your plans a reality have a similar instrumental quality. Carl Bernstein's interview with the CRP bookkeeper indicates some of the ways in which the conventions and patterns of everyday life can be "used" to accomplish one's goals. Notice how he relied on the common tendency to respond to direct requests (here for a cigarette) to get in the door, and the common understanding of what is polite (once offered a cup of coffee, one will normally be allowed to finish it or to have a second cup) as a way of staying in the house. He also encouraged her to talk by letting her know that many others whom she knew had spoken to him, and by expressing sympathy for Maurice Stans' ill wife. Effectively preparing a case seems to involve constantly searching for such "opportunities."

Such demands pose troubling questions. Some of you may find such a calculating mode of thinking and acting unnatural or morally questionable. The ethical boundaries here are very hard to draw. You might want to ask yourself whether it is possible or desirable for any practitioner to be so partisan in dealing with adversaries, officials and witnesses, and yet uncontrolling when dealing with clients. Or whether it really can be said that lawyers are strategic and manipulative only within very limited circumstances. You might also want to think about the ways in which you will change when so much of your life is invested in efforts of this kind. There are many such unasked questions in the profession's often stated catechism that a good lawyer is "tough, tactical, tenacious, and prepared."

B. AN ORIENTING MODEL: CASE PREPARATION AS PLANNING

———

A general model of what is involved when a lawyer initially plans and investigates a case turns out to be surprisingly elusive. No simple analogy is available which captures the reasoning and actions required by this task *and* the peculiar way it looks both to the past and the future. For example, the lawyer constructing a case is in some sense like an historian, particularly if one recognizes the selective nature of historical inquiry. But historiography is still too past-looking and too accountable to norms of objectivity and detachment to be an apt analogy for the sort of strategic preparation and investigation in which lawyers engage.

As we think about the way lawyers prepare, what finally comes most readily to mind is the work of the planner in any field. Whether he or she seeks to design a building or implement a complex government program, the planner must marshal the relevant materials to achieve a set of concrete purposes. As part of the process, problems must be defined and redefined, alternatives generated, and the relevant facts identified, selected, and evaluated or explained. The following excerpt outlines the framework that this perspective provides.

GELATT, DECISION–MAKING: A CONCEPTUAL FRAME OF REFERENCE . . .

9 J.COUNSELING PSYCH. 240–45 (1962).[2]

. . . Our society continually confronts people with situations where they must choose between alternate courses of action. Tyler suggests that "a person to some extent shapes the pattern of his life by the choices and decisions he makes at successive stages".

*   *   *

Decisions about the immediate future are partly determined by the more vague decisions about the intermediate and distant future, whereas . . . decisions about the . . . distant future are continually being modified by the results of the more immediate decisions. All of these decisions are, of course, altered as [one] learns more about [self] and environment. . . .

Decision Theory

Much of the work on decision and game theory to date has been in the field of economics and mathematics. However, [many] . . . contributors to decision theory . . . indicate that the applicability of decision theory ". . . ranges from almost all inductive sciences to many situations that people face in everyday life when it is not perfectly obvious what they should do."

A decision-making frame of reference will require that we define our objectives clearly, collect data and analyze its relevancy, study the possible alternatives, and evaluate the possible consequences.

---

2. This article was written as application of decision theory to counseling decisions. We have eliminated the references to this concern in order to highlight the general applicability of the model Gelatt sets out.

Proposed Decision-Making Framework

All decisions   .   .   .   have essentially the same characteristics.
.   .   .   [I]n the first place,   .   .   .   a decision is required.   There
are two or more possible courses of action to be taken and the decision
is to be made on the basis of information.   Cronback and Gleser use
this sequence for their model and suggest that a decision may be terminal (final) or investigatory (calling for additional information).
The investigatory decision becomes a cycle, involving information
gathering and decision making, until a terminal decision is made.   The
terminal decision may also suggest a cycle, since the outcome of such
a decision may yield additional information which would serve to
modify the result of the terminal decision.

Bross designs a "decision maker" requiring information as "fuel"
and resulting in a recommended course of action.   The process of deciding requires a "predictive system" (assessing the possible alternative actions, the possible outcomes, and the probabilities) a "value
system" (weighing the desirability associated with outcomes), and a
"decision criterion" (to integrate and select an appropriate action).

The model in Figure 1 incorporates the above processes and suggests the cyclical nature of decisions.   Thus, the strategy requires
knowing the alternatives and outcomes, applying a value scale, and
evaluation.   The "decision" may lead to collecting more data or to
outcomes which alter the situation and require the application of a
new strategy, or the outcome may alter the objectives, or achieve the
purpose.   A decision can be final only in the sense that an immediate
goal is reached.   But the achievement of this goal may itself influence or modify other related choices.   .   .   .   As Cronback and Gleser point out "   .   .   .   it is necessary to distill from a limited quantity of information the most intelligent possible decision.   The problem is to find the procedure which, in the time available, offers the
greatest yield of important, relevant, and interpretable information".

.   .   .   The objective would be [defined].   .   .   .   Information
related to the objective would be organized and considered.   Test results,   .   .   .   interests, and the relation of this decision to future
choices are examples of data to be used.   In order to discuss the possible outcomes of alternative choices and their probabilities it is essential to know something about the degree of relevancy these data have
for each alternative.   What is the empirical basis for the relevance of
a particular datum for a specific decision?   Can success be predicted?
Would other data be more suggestive?   These and other questions are
part of the strategy.   Then the possible outcomes are evaluated in
terms of some scale of desirability and the actual selection of a decision is made utilizing a criterion based on the purpose.

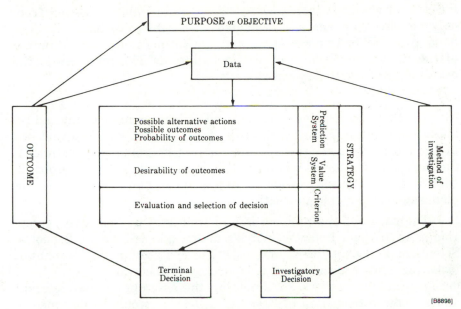

Fig. 1. The Sequential Decision-Making Process

Bross suggests that this notion of decision-making presupposes a way of looking at the real world. That is, in judging any system or a decision the test is: does it work? The court of final appeal is the result in the real world. This pragmatic principle, in turn, presupposes that the individual has a value scale and requires the individual to compare one group of situations with another group. The use of the pragmatic principle assumes that what has been successful in the past will continue to be successful in the future and that experience (direct and indirect) will be used in assessing alternatives.

Although the problem of individual value scales is extremely complex and will not be discussed in detail, one comment from the field of philosophy is offered. Thomas shows us that valuing can be conceived as an active transaction between desires and certain conditions leading to anticipated consequences. Our decision-maker must be careful not to commit . . . the "positivistic fallacy"—equating the desired with the desirable. "Something is considered valuable and desirable (not merely desired) when it is wanted in the light of perceived relationships to other things of interest". Thus, when the possible outcomes are evaluated in terms of chances of success, the same odds have different meanings for different individuals or for the same individual under varying circumstances.

The use of a decision-making framework is actually the application of the scientific method. . . . [It does not] tell us what the content of an individual's choice should be; rather it indicates a process of choosing. [In using this method, the decision maker's] freedom of choice is increased. . . . Rather than choosing from only perceived alternatives evaluated with subjective bias, . . . he is aware of more alternatives and has an increased understanding of the factors involved in choice, including his determination of the desirability of the consequences.

* * *

[In this process] the collection and utilization of relevant and reliable information is essential. [I]t seems generally agreed that one of the most frequent problems encountered by guidance personnel is the inability of students and parents to assess accurately the probabilities of given alternatives and/or the lack of knowledge of the complete range of possible alternatives.

The cause of the problem is also well known—selective perception. As Michael Demiashkevitch's motto, adopted by the School of Scientific Police in Paris, tells us, "The eye sees in things what it looks for, and it looks for what is already in the mind". A . . . decision-making framework, accepting the assumption that relevant and reliable information is essential, . . . would be designed to teach students Dewey's reflective thinking and to encourage them to be tentative in their conclusions. . . . An appeal to empirical data is essential to establish any generalization.

NOTES

Gelatt's model is drawn from an extensive literature concerned with planning and decision-making in human experience. Some of this research seeks to identify influences on decision or to describe the actual thought processes involved.[3] Much of it, like the forgoing reading, presents the model as a standard against which the process a decision-maker chooses to follow might be judged. In the background is an ongoing debate over whether it is possible, desirable, or necessary to develop decisional models at all.[4]

3. *See, e. g.*, J. Bruner, S. Goodnow & G. Austin, A STUDY OF THINKING (1956); F. George, MODELS OF THINKING (1970); J. March & H. Simon, ORGANIZATIONS (1958); H. Simon, THE NEW SCIENCE OF MANAGEMENT DECISION (1960); Feldman & Kanter, *Organizational Decision-Making*, HANDBOOK OF ORGANIZATIONS (J. March, ed., 1965); Wilson & Alexsis, *Basic Framework for Decisions*, 5 J.ACAD.MANAGEMENT SCI. 151 (1962). For a summary of the work trying to adapt such an analysis to computer technology, *see* G. Miller, E. Galanter & M. Pribram, PLANS AND THE STRUCTURE OF BEHAVIOR (1960).

4. *See generally* K. Boulding, THE IMAGE (1956); D. Braybrooke & C. Lindblom, A STRATEGY OF DECISION: POLICY EVALUATION AS A SOCIAL PROCESS (1963); I. Bross, DESIGN FOR DECISION: AN INTRODUCTION TO STATISTICAL DECISION-MAKING (1953); J. Dewey, HOW WE THINK (1933); R. Ebert & T. Mitchell, ORGANIZATIONAL DECISION PROCESSES: CONCEPTS AND ANALYSIS (1975); A. Faludi, PLANNING THEORY

Look carefully at the model Gelatt offers and think about whether it describes a process you do or would want to follow in practice. Under this model, each decision requires (i) gauging an existing situation in terms of what is known (data) and what is desired; (ii) generating alternatives; (iii) projecting the probability of the possible outcomes of each alternative (prediction system); (iv) judging and choosing among these consequences (value system and criteria); (v) acting on the decisions that are made; (vi) evaluating the process again as new information is obtained. Is it possible to make these steps concrete? How does one give content to the risks and value judgments that the model requires? Can one be assured that important steps have not been left out?

Despite many, many difficulties, we have found the decision theorists' efforts to answer these questions surprisingly helpful in clinical work. Perhaps the following best expresses our own reactions to struggling with structured approaches to decision making:

> Knowledge of the complexity of the decision making process may lead to increased tolerance for ambiguity and to increased ability to accept the consequences of an occasional poorly made decision.

> Second, a need exists to become aware of the decision making process so that persons will develop an understanding of the use of data in making a decision. Seldom will one have readily available all the data necessary. The individual . . . need[s] to know when to search for additional data and when the cost of the search in terms of time, money, and energy probably is not worthwhile.

> Third, a study of decision making enables one to see the relationship between goals, action, and decision. Goal attainment can be facilitated or deterred by the quality of decisions made. . . .

> * * *

> Fourth, decision making should be studied so that persons can learn to ascertain the quality of the decision. To differentiate between the merits of possible consequences of choices is a necessary learning. In the rush of accomplishing daily tasks, persons often fail to consider long term consequences of present actions, to see relationships among decisions, or to develop a framework for priorities. . . .

> Fifth, [the study of] decision making . . . helps the person realize that he himself does not enter into the decision of another except as the other person chooses to let others enter into the decision. In the last analysis each person selects those individuals, facts, or situa-

(1973); A. Kaplan, THE CONDUCT OF INQUIRY: METHODOLOGY FOR BEHAVIORAL SCIENCE (1964); R. Luce & H. Raiffa, GAMES AND DECISIONS (1957); H. Raiffa, DECISION ANALYSIS: INTRODUCTORY LECTURES ON CHOICES UNDER UNCERTAINTY (1968); H. Raiffa & R. Schlaifer, APPLIED STATISTICAL DECISION THEORY (1961); I. Robinson, DECISION-MAKING IN URBAN PLANNING (1972); E. Banfield, *Ends and Means in Planning*, 11 AM.SOC.SCI.J. 361 (1959). Many of the debates are summarized in A READER IN PLANNING THEORY (A. Faludi. ed., 1973).

tions which he is going to allow to influence his decision making. The person sees "he does not *cause* pleasure or pain. . . . He knows now that 'you hurt me' means 'I choose to hurt myself about you,' and 'you make me love you' means 'I choose to care about you.' "

Sixth, persons need to understand decision making since it is so critical to other human processes and functions such as showing gratitude, aspiring, and caring.

Decision making is affected by how one perceives, the values one holds, the knowledge one prizes, the persons one admires, the modes of communication one utilizes. The process does not stand alone.[5]

Moreover, the particular decision model Gelatt articulates offers a useful heuristic for systematically approaching the way lawyers plan and handle cases. It is a model on which we rely, either explicitly or implicitly, in a number of the following chapters. At least part of its value for us lies in the fact that it requires us to focus on the following aspects of decision.

Maximizing Information—The emphasis on fully identifying and exploring alternatives makes lawyers more sensitive to information. Since command of the data, events, and circumstances relevant to a case is crucial to a lawyer's confidence and performance, any set of "steps" which encourages such inquiries can perform useful functions.

Minimizing Risks—Explicitly attending to prediction and probability judgments keeps risks and risk avoidance in the foreground of lawyer decisions. Inexperienced lawyers often seem willing to run unnecessary procedural risks—*e. g.*, acting on the most "reasonable" rather than the most conservative view of when a statute of limitations tolls. Discussing choices systematically highlights decision criteria and "reversibility"—the value of alternatives that offer some chance of benefit and no loss if the hoped-for gains do not materialize. At the same time, an explicit analysis of costs and benefits can be an antidote to risk-aversion or overcaution in situations where adverse effects are only one factor to be weighed in the balance.

Exerting Control—The planner's orientation also directs attention and energy to the importance of actively influencing and controlling the development of a case. That is, it fosters a view (which we share) that the facts and relative strategic position of the parties are as much a result of what lawyers do as of the situations in which they find themselves.

Perhaps carefully studying the following dialogue will give you some further insight into what such an orientation involves. Assume an experienced lawyer is helping a young associate decide how to proceed against a retailer who has been defrauding consumers. The seller has threatened to sue several clients on the original sales con-

5. L. Berman, NEW PRIORITIES IN
THE CURRICULUM 102–04 (1968).

tracts, and counsel is considering an affirmative action against the retailer.

Look carefully at the way each lawyer deals with informational needs and concerns, analyzes potential risks and benefits, and conceives opportunities for controlling or managing the variables in the situation. Also notice how explicitly goal-oriented the experienced lawyer is. She essentially develops a strategy by working backwards from what she wants to achieve to what she might do; by contrast the inexperienced lawyer seems to move forward, trying to evaluate the possibilities without having a clear idea of where he is going.

COUNSEL: (Coun) You've said that our next step is to draft a pleading. Frankly I don't see why that's our problem right now; we're not even sure whether the company will accept some settlement.

SENIOR
COUNSEL: (Sr) I know. But I usually try to make some of the decisions which would be made if the case went forward, even before I negotiate. It gives me a much better feel for my tactical position and bargaining options when settlement is discussed.

COUN: I don't quite understand that. Does that mean we will or will not contact the company before we file the pleading? I'm having a lot of trouble drafting it. I don't really know where to begin.

SR: I'm not sure what we'll do about negotiation. We'll play it by ear. Right now the job is getting the pleading done. You have the facts, and we've uncovered several theories that will support recovery.

COUN: But we've only talked to the clients and looked at the contracts. We have no idea what our opponent's story is. Don't we need to do some investigating before we do anything else?

SR: Probably yes, but again, I've found that drafting a pleading or even sketching a tentative closing argument helps me identify the holes and develop lines of inquiry. It also gives me a better sense of what to be careful of in early contacts with opponents or witnesses.

COUN: Okay, that makes sense, but I'm still unsure how to begin.

SR: Why don't you start by listing the objectives you want to accomplish with your pleading?

COUN: Like establishing a basis for formal discovery or avoiding a motion to dismiss?

SR: Well, those are two important goals. For example, you'd have to be sure you properly allege all the elements of the claim. But there are many more. Ask yourself what would occur if you took one approach or another—or, alternatively, what you'd want to occur.

COUN: I'm stumped again. I just don't have enough experience to know what could happen in this case, or even what I want— except to be in the best position possible, of course.

SR: You know more than you think. We have a superior court and a municipal court in this jurisdiction. What would you rather be in, if you had the option?

COUN: Well, the discovery rules are more liberal in superior court, and I'd get a jury trial. On the other hand, there would be considerably more delay.

SR: That's right, under the statutes in this jurisdiction, we'd waive our right to a jury trial if we filed directly in municipal court. But the calender is much less crowded.

Now, assume that you've balanced those considerations and you've decided that you want to get into superior court. Under the jurisdictional rules in this state you can do that in a number of ways: by framing the complaint as one for declaratory or equitable relief, by joining a claim solely cognizable in the superior court, or by pleading above the jurisdictional amount. On the basis of the facts you've described to me, we would be well within our rights to plead punitive as well as actual damages and thereby to bring the amount in controversy above the jurisdictional limit.

COUN: But there are risks in that. If we lost, I understand that we could be assessed higher costs in the superior court.

SR: And that's one of the factors you'd then weigh in deciding whether you really wanted to get into superior court after all. You could always plead less than the jurisdictional amount and file in municipal court. You'd use the same analysis in considering objectives and alternatives with respect to whom you would join as parties, when you wanted to have the case tried, what substantive theories you'd rely on, and what remedies you'd seek.

COUN: Can you give me one more example?

SR: Sure. You told me earlier that the wrong here is essentially the tort of fraud or negligent misrepresentation. But if we wanted to take advantage of the rule that suits in contract may be brought where the plaintiff resides, or that contract actions get preference on the superior court trial calendar, or if our immediate problem was to avoid the shorter statute of limitations governing tort, we could characterize our claim in terms of breach of contract. In fact, as I read the cases, the contract theory would be successful even if this jurisdiction doesn't accept negligent misrepresentation as a basis of recovery, or would allow contributory negligence as a defense to a tort claim. On the other hand, pleading in contract would mean a different measure of damages, and probably less discovery if we wanted to inquire into whether there was a pattern or practice of this sort of conduct.

COUN: So what you suggest is that I try to project the position I what to be in after the pleading is filed, and then analyze all the advantages and disadvantages of the different ways of getting to that position?

SR: Essentially, that's correct. If you don't want a jury trial or you want to get temporary equitable relief, for example, you'd frame your contract theory or request for damages as an action for rescission.

COUN: Can that be done?

SR: Of course. You control the remedy you are asking for. You'd have to be ready to return the property, though, if you took that approach.

COUN: It's just too complicated. I would never have thought of any of those considerations on the basis of what I know about the requirements of equity pleading, or contract law, for that matter. Even if I did, I would have no idea how to weigh all the advantages or disadvantages you've mentioned. It seems to me that there's only a "psuedo-system" here. Every one of those decisions involves, at best, *guesses* about how a court would interpret the requirements you mention, and how our client would want the risks and possibilities balanced. And we haven't even discussed how our adversaries might react or respond to each of these approaches. Are you saying that all lawyering decisions involve this sort of judgment?

SR: Yes.

There are a number of respects in which the thinking and analysis of the experienced lawyer illustrates the planning process at work:

(a) Immediate choices (first negotiate, then file pleading; first file pleading, then negotiate; file pleading only after they have sued) are deferred to permit an analysis of each one separately. Drafting a pleading (or thinking through drafting a pleading) is seen as a source of insights and "feedback" on the more general decisions counsel must make.

(b) The problem of maximizing the clients' interests (general goal) is broken down and analyzed as a series of subproblems, only one of which is where to file the action. Others include (i) who should be sued; (ii) what the content, form, sequence, tone of the pleading should be; (iii) what theories the pleading should embody; (iv) how a potential statute of limitations defense should be handled; (v) what scope of discovery the pleading would support; and (vi) what remedies should be sought. Some of these subproblems are considered critical and some not. Some are seen as interdependent (remedy, venue).

(c) Alternatives are discussed in terms of projections of future consequences (both negative—avoiding a motion to dismiss; and positive—access to discovery, jury trial) and the desirability, likelihood and significance of these outcomes. That is, counsel is directed by senior counsel to imagine (i) how the pleading would look; (ii) how it would probably be interpreted in the face of a challenge (including how the court might respond to arguments made by counsel at a hearing on a motion to dismiss); (iii) what events/opportunities would follow from its being filed in a particular court or written in a particular way.

This step might be presented on a matrix as follows:

Alternatives

Desired Consequences	File in superior court	File in municipal court
Resolution of problem within a few months	unlikely	likely
Responsive judge	likely	50/50
Liberal attitude by judges toward complaint on motion to dismiss	likely	likely
Jury trial available	certain	no chance
Extensive Discovery available	50/50	unlikely
Low costs of filing, service, etc.	no chance	certain

[B8902]

Counsel has simply estimated that each alternative is certain to produce one of the desired consequences, likely to produce two of them, unlikely to produce another and so forth. Some of the consequences, however, are valued or desired *more* than others; these different "weights" can be depicted in the above matrix by listing the consequences in order of their importance to the decision maker. It thus becomes possible not only to identify the consequences attached to each alternative, but also to gain some notion of the relative desirability of those consequences and the likelihood that they will occur.

(d) Finally, the lawyers make a judgment about the net advantages and disadvantages of each of the anticipated outcomes (discounted by their probability) in ways that allow the two choices to be compared.[6]

6. This is a very complex subject in itself. *See generally* K. Arrow, SO-CIAL CHOICE AND INDIVIDUAL VALUES (2d ed. 1970); J. Marschak,

(e) If this were done with the client (as it ought to be) they would have to sort out whether the accessibility and lower costs associated with the municipal court action were "worth" the lower chance (50–50) of a favorable reaction from the judge.

A similar framework can be used to analyze every investigative decision in a case—*e. g.*, what witnesses to see, whether to proceed formally or informally, the timing of depositions and the use of other discovery, how much information to reveal.

In each instance, the gap between what a "rational, maximizing" decision-maker would have done and your own judgments and actions provides a useful *benchmark* (not a standard) for evaluating your work. Whether you can articulate goals, strategies and predicted consequences in dealing with a problem or case is usually a good check on the extent to which you have the problem under control.

What is left out of all of this, of course, is the role of intuition, creativity and imagination in the decision process itself. Despite some excellent efforts, the models of how such thought processes actually work are still very undeveloped.[7] The visual and the verbal enter into decisions in ways that are vaguely understood. Nevertheless, disciplined experience seems to be the source of a "logic of experience" that can be developed over time. The following, written about skills in chess reasoning, captures something of this elusive quality:

> It is . . . the treasury of read 'experience' which puts the master that much ahead of the others. His . . . knowledge and experience enables him, first, to recognize immediately a chess position as one belonging to an unwritten category of . . . means to be applied, and second, to 'see' immediately and in a highly adequate way its specific, individual features against the background of the category.
>
> It is no accident that the word 'seeing,' as used here stands both for perception and abstraction. The two processes tend to fuse together; they are difficult to distinguish. But if a master and a weaker player are compared, often the former literally 'sees' possibilities that are deeply hidden for the latter, possibilities that the latter must first try to discover, calculate, think out, or deduce in order in his turn to be able to 'see' them. In other words, the difference in achievement be-

Scaling of Utilities and Probability, GAME THEORY AND RELATED APPROACHES TO SOCIAL BEHAVIOR 95 (1964). We deal with some aspects of the "combination" problem, as well as the task of making predictions, in Chapter Eight of THE LAW YERING PROCESS (1978). On the latter problem *see generally* W. Feller, AN INTRODUCTION TO PROBABILITY THEORY AND ITS APPLICATIONS (1950); E. Parzen, MOD-ERN PROBABILITY THEORY AND ITS APPLICATIONS (1960). Some of you might want to test your present knowledge against J. Dixon, A PROGRAMMED INTRODUCTION TO PROBABILITY (1964).

7. For a very provocative and beautifully written work on this subject see A. Koestler, THE ACT OF CREATION (1964); *see also* H. Sachs, THE CREATIVE UNCONSCIOUS (1942).

tween master and non-master rests primarily on the fact that the master, basing himself on an enormous experience, can start his operational thinking at a much more advanced stage and can consequently function much more specifically and efficiently in his problem-solving field.

[The expert has what might be called] a perceptual advantage—an ability . . . [to reproduce in his mind] completion of the perceived situation . . . In fact, the more 'experience' a person has collected in any field, the more difficult it becomes for him to understand the behavior of the have-nots. Thus every teacher knows the following frequent brand of over-estimating his students: opining that from the given problem situation his students can 'immediately' derive (see) some property or means that he himself finds quite obvious—whereas in reality, in order to 'see' it, much perceptive and abstractive experience is required. The teacher has had this experience for so long that he is no longer aware of it. An experienced problem solver in any field is particularly apt to forget about his primary and fundamental problem transformations even before he starts his own consciously operational thinking. This is especially true when these problem transformations have shifted, over the long run, from the field of thought to the perceptual field. . . .[8]

* * *

An effective lawyer may "know" in similar ways how to react to resistance in a deposition or how to organize the initial plan for investigating a case. But this knowledge, like that of his or her chess counterpart, seems to be gained by going back over past decisions again and again. At some point experienced players begin to "see the future" of possible strategies. One day we may be able to learn from them (and from our own experience) how this reservoir of images is used.

SECTION TWO. THE SKILL DIMENSION

___

A. ASSESSMENT: DECIDING WHAT YOU NEED TO KNOW

1. Developing a Preliminary Approach to the Case

___

Once you have some initial facts to work with, you must begin the problem solving process we have just described—defining the problem, analyzing the "givens" and the opportunities in the particu-

8. A. DeGroot, THOUGHT AND CHOICE IN CHESS (1965), *cited in* THINKING AND REASONING 145–46 (P. Wason & P. Johnson-Laird, eds., 1968). DeGroot's work is representative of a continuing interest among psychologists with the chess master. There are many sides to this particu- lar metaphor. *See* R. Fine, THE PSYCHOLOGY OF THE CHESS PLAYER (1956); B. Karpman, *The Psychology of Chess*, 24 PSYCH.REV. 54 (1937); E. Jones, *The Problem of Paul Morphy: A Contribution to the Psychology of Chess*, ESSAYS IN APPLIED PSYCHOANALYSIS (1951).

lar situation, generating possible solutions, and choosing the courses of action which will allow these working hypotheses to be tested and refined. Basic to these judgments is a theory of the case—a view of how fact, law and circumstance can be put together to produce the outcome you and your client seek. Although such a framework cannot be exclusive or static, here, as elsewhere, inquiry needs tentative hypotheses.

These hypotheses must be more than a general notion of the conclusions you want the fact-finder to reach. At some point, early in planning and investigation, you must develop a detailed, coherent, accurate story of what occurred, which can be asserted in negotiation and at trial. It must account for the bad facts as well as the favorable ones, and must focus explicitly on the inferences you wish the fact-finder to draw from specific evidence. Since your opponent will be shaping a competing version of what happened and what it means, your working model must also take these competing explanations into account, anticipating what your opponent will try to prove and finding ways to counter it. Analyzing a case in such detail is no simple task, particularly since it is attempted at a stage when the factual picture is far from complete. But it is only in light of such a comprehensive, particularized conception of what must be proved that specific lines of inquiry can be selected and pursued in the course of case preparation.

There are no simple formulas for developing such guiding concepts, but we have found it helpful to think of the facts we hope to prove in terms of a hypothetical closing argument: what arguments do we hope to be able to make at the close of trial, and what evidence would we like to be able to point to? It then becomes possible to work backward from this set of propositions to assemble the testimony and other evidence that will be needed to prove them at trial.

The following very different readings—one from a practitioner and the other from a scholar on evidence—may be helpful to you in sorting through what is involved in this critical step in the planning process.

VETTER, SUCCESSFUL CIVIL LITIGATION *

21, 27, 30–33 (1977).

A hit-or-miss approach to a case is an invitation to disaster. You might miss or glide over strong points. You might expose or emphasize weak points. Worst of all you probably will not try the case with an eye focused on persuading the jury. To make sure that you do try the case that way, you must try the case with a theory of the case.

In the broad sense, the theory of the case is how you hope to win the case. It is your plan of action. It is the perspective you want the jury to view the case from. It is your formula for persuading the

* © 1977 by Prentice-Hall, Inc. Published by Prentice-Hall, Englewood Cliffs, New Jersey.

jury to find in your favor. It is the persuasive theme you integrate the case with . . . . [It is the perspective] through which you want [the jury] to view the facts and assess what the case is all about.

Defense counsel have a stock theme in medical malpractice actions—the Healer. Some cases lend themselves to a variation on this theme—the Ungrateful Patient. Combined as a theme and variation, they can be lethal—the dedicated physician who has done all he could for the patient who in disappointment at a less than perfect result lashes out at the person who tried to help him.

Successful theories regardless of type share certain features. Six of these features have become bench marks for working up a winning theory for a particular case.

First, the theory must have a firm foundation in strong facts and the fair inferences to be drawn from the facts.

Second, if possible, the theory should be built around the so-called "high cards" of litigation, incontestable or virtually incontestable facts, such as self-certifying documents, patently undoctored pictures, admissions against interest, the testimony of independent witnesses, clear scientific facts, and so on.

The principle behind this rule should be mentioned. The jury reconstructs what happened from the evidence. Often the evidence is in sharp conflict. Naturally, then, the jury will seize upon the facts that seem fixed and certain and true. These facts then serve three functions. They, themselves, become part of the foundation for the jury's reconstruction. They become the means by which the jury tests other facts and inferences. And they become the basis for inferences.

Third, and as a corollary of the second bench mark, the theory should not be inconsistent with, or fly in the face of, incontestable facts.

Fourth, the theory should explain away in a plausible manner as many unfavorable facts as it can.

Fifth, the theory should be down-to-earth and have a common-sense appeal. It must be readily acceptable by a jury. A theory gets an "A" if it persuades a jury to say, "Yes, that's the way it is."

Sixth, the theory cannot be based on wishful thinking about any phase of the case.

* * *

There is no magic formula on how to develop a theory of the case, but there are guidelines.

To start with be sure you understand the theory behind the concept of a theory of the case. At the risk of repetition, you must appreciate that first, last, and always a trial is an exercise in persuasion.

Next, get a feel for the different types of theories. Start looking at cases in terms of theories. After awhile you will find yourself instinctively fitting cases into the various categories.

The formulation of a theory for a particular case usually happens in one of two ways. Sometimes a theory becomes obvious as the contours of the case emerge. In those instances, your main job is to test and re-test the theory against the bench marks.

If a theory does not spring to mind, you must construct one step by step.

First, isolate the legal and factual issues in the case. Be sure about the nodes on which the case will turn. In cases where the legal principles are broad, much of the analysis will be factual. In cases where the legal principles are narrower, the analysis will be a mix of law and fact.

Next, take an objective look at the proof pro and con on these issues.

Third, pin-point the critical areas. This means assessing and weighing the results of the analysis on the first two points in terms of the presentation at trial. At this stage, you must begin to think about how to exploit your strong points and your opponent's weak points, and how to shore up your weak points and attack your opponent's strong points.

Fourth, come up with a tentative theory and check it against the five bench marks. If it falls way below the marks, scrap it. If it partially passes muster, set about strengthening it. This usually means searching out further facts or getting expert tesimony.

Fifth, as you strengthen and develop the theory, keep checking it against the bench marks.

Finally, from the time you begin to develop a theory try it out on a colleague. It is too easy to miss the forest for the trees deep in the preparation of a case.

WIGMORE, THE SCIENCE OF JUDICIAL PROOF

9–11, 18–21, 24–28, 29–31, 34–37, 43–46 (1937).

Evidence is always a relative term. It signifies a relation between two facts, the factum probandum, or proposition to be proved, and the factum probans, or material evidencing the proposition. The former is necessarily hypothetical; the latter is brought forward as a reality for the purpose of convincing the tribunal that the former is also a reality. No correct and sure comprehension of the nature of any evidential question can ever be had unless this double or relative aspect of it is distinctly pictured in each instance. On each occasion the questions must be asked, What is the Proposition (Probandum) desired to be proved? What is the Evidentiary Fact (Probans) offered to prove it?

Part of the confusion often found arises from the circumstance that each Evidentiary Fact may in turn become a Proposition to be proved, until finally some ultimate Evidentiary Fact is reached. For example, to prove the Proposition that a murder was committed by John Doe, the Evidentiary Fact may be offered that John Doe left the victim's house shortly after the murder; this in turn becoming a Proposition, the Evidentiary Fact may be offered that John Doe's shoes fit the track left near the house by the murderer; and this, again becoming a Proposition, may be evidenced by the statement of a witness on the sand who has placed the shoe in the tracks. Here each Evidentiary Fact in its turn becomes a Proposition requiring the marshaling of new Evidentiary Facts, more or fewer according to its complexity. Any specific matter may be Proposition or Evidentiary Fact, according to the point of view of the moment.

* * *

Inference is the persuasive operation of *each separate* evidentiary fact, as to an Interim Probandum. Proof is the persuasive operation of the *total mass* of evidentiary facts, as to a Probandum.

* * *

Note then the term "inference" signifies merely the *process* of thinking about a piece of evidence, not the *result*. The inference may be weak, medium or strong; *e. g.*, if A approaches us on the street without a hat, the inference is the process of thinking whether he lost his hat by the wind or whether he started from the house without it. This process may or may not result in our belief that he lost it or that he never put it on; but in either case our *belief* as to one or the other proposition is distinct from our *inference*. The advocate asks the tribunal to infer; and the tribunal proceeds to infer, *i. e.* to think probatively, but this inference may or may not result in belief. The term "inference" has been sometimes used ambiguously to include either or both the process and the result; in the present work it is applied to the process.

* * *

The process of passing upon judicial evidence is and must be based ultimately on the canons of ordinary reasoning, whether explicitly or implicitly employed. It is therefore necessary to review the distinction which Logic makes between the two great types of Argument or Inference,—the Deductive and the Inductive forms.

1. The Deductive form is this (known as a "syllogism"): "Persons related by blood to a party are biased in their testimony" (major premise); "This witness is related by blood to a party" (minor premise); "Therefore, this witness is biased in his testimony" (conclusion). The Inductive form is this: "This witness is related by blood to a party" (thesis); "Therefore, he is biased in his testimony" (conclusion).

Modern Logic looks at this distinction without prejudice. Its tendency is to accept both types as capable of reduction to a single one.

Nevertheless the distinction is a practical and substantial one, particularly in litigious proof.

* * *

2.   A brief examination will show that in the offering of evidence in court the form of inference is usually *inductive*.

Suppose, to prove a charge of murder, evidence is offered of the defendant's fixed design to kill the deceased.   The form of the inference is: "A planned to kill B; therefore, A probably did kill B."   It is clear that we have here no semblance of a syllogism.   The form of inference is exactly the same when we argue: "Yesterday, Dec. 31, A slipped on the sidewalk and fell; therefore, the sidewalk was probably coated with ice"; or, "Today A, who was bitten by a dog yesterday, died in convulsions; therefore, the dog probably had hydrophobia."   So with all other legal evidentiary facts, whether circumstantial or testimonial, we may argue: "Last week the witness A had a quarrel with the defendant B; therefore, A is probably biased against B"; "A was found with a bloody knife in B's house; therefore, A is probably the murderer of B"; "After B's injury at A's machinery, A repaired the machinery; therefore, A probably acknowledged that the machinery was negligently defective"; "A, an adult of sound mind and senses, and apparently impartial, was present at an affray between B and C, and testifies that B struck first; therefore, it is probably true that B did strike first."   In all these cases, we take a single or isolated fact, and upon it base immediately an inference as to the proposition in question.   This is the Inductive, or Empiric, process.

* * *

The peculiar danger   .   .   .   of Inductive Inference is that there may be *other explanations, i. e.* possible inferences, than the alleged Probandum one, from the fact taken as the basis of proof.

Let us now examine this principle from the point of view of the opposing parties in a legal trial.   Since our system of procedure is based on the method of leaving the production of evidence to the parties themselves, the proceeding is an antiphonal one.   Proponent and opponent in turn offer evidence.   Both counsel and jury therefore need to examine each piece of evidence, first, from the proponent's point of view, next, from the opponent's point of view, and finally, from the jury's point of view.

* * *

If the potential defect of Inductive Evidence is that the fact offered as the basis of the conclusion may be open to one or more other explanations or inferences, the failure to exclude a single other rational inference would be, from the standpoint of *Proof,* a fatal defect; and yet, if only that single other inference were open, there might still be an extremely high degree of probability for the *Inference* desired. When Robinson Crusoe saw the human footprint on the sand, he could not argue inductively that the presence of another human being was absolutely proved; there was at least (for example) the possible inference of his own somnambulism. Nevertheless, the fact of the footprint was, as a basis of *Inference,* evidence of an extraordinary degree of probability. The provisional test, then, from the point of view of valuing the Inference, would be something like this: *Does the evidentiary fact point to the desired conclusion* (not as the only rational inference, but) *as the inference* (or explanation) *most plausible or most natural out of the various ones that are conceivable?* Or (to state the requirement more weakly), is the desired conclusion (not, the most natural, but) *a* natural or plausible one among the various conceivable ones? After all the other evidential facts have been introduced and considered, the net conclusion can be attempted. But in dealing with each separate fact, the only inquiry is a provisional one: How probable is the Probandum as the explanation of this Probans?

This test for the probative value of a proposed inference may be illustrated from various sorts of evidentiary facts:

(1) The fact that A left the city soon after a crime was committed will raise a slight probability that he left because of his consciousness of guilt, but a greater one if his knowledge that he was suspected be first shown. Here the evident notion is that the mere fact of departure by one unaware of the charge is open to too many innocent explanations; but the addition of the fact that A knew of the charge tends to put these other inferences into the background, and makes the desired explanation or conclusion—*i. e.*, a guilty consciousness—stand out prominently as a more probable and plausible one. Even then there are other possible inferences—such as a summons from a dying relative or the fear of a yellow-fever epidemic in the city; but these are not the immediately natural ones, and the greater naturalness of the desired explanation makes it highly probable.

(2) The fact that A before a robbery had no money, but after it had a large sum, is offered to indicate that he by robbery became possessed of the large sum of money. There are several other possible explanations,—the receipt of a legacy, the receipt of a debt, the winning of a gambling game, and the like. Nevertheless, the desired explanation rises, among other explanations, to a fair degree of plausibility.

(3) The fact that A, charged with stealing a suit of clothes, was a poor man is offered to show him to be the thief. Now the conclusion of theft from the mere fact of poverty is, among the various possible conclusions, one of the least probable; for the conclusions that he would preferably work or beg or borrow are all equally or more probable, and the inference of stealing, being also a dangerous one to adopt as the habitual construction to be put on poor men's conduct, has the double defect of being less probable and more hard upon the innocent. Such evidence, then, is of slight value to show that conclusion.

* * *

(5) The fact that A makes his statement on the witness stand in response to a leading question of his counsel is not of great value to show the fact asserted by him, because in experience the chances are so great that his answer is based on the counsel's suggestion and not on his own knowledge. On the other hand, where the leading question deals merely with the preliminary matters of his name, age, and residence, the answer is fairly probative, because, there being so little motive for falsification on those subjects, the conclusion that he answered truly is far the most probable one.

* * *

Thus, throughout the whole realm of evidence, circumstantial and testimonial, the theory of the inductive inference, as practically applied, is that the evidentiary fact has probative value only so far as the desired conclusion based upon it is a more probable or natural inference, and as the other inferences or explanations of the fact, if any, are less probable or natural.

* * *

The pure scientist works alone in his laboratory; there is no one at hand to dispute his every step of inference. But in judicial trials, there are always two parties; the partisan proponent offers his evidence, without pointing out its weakness; then the partisan opponent points out the weaknesses, *i. e.*, the possible explanations. Therefore it is important to notice the double treatment of which every offer of evidence may admit.

Where the scientist is dealing with the subject of Proof in Logic, the single stage of the inquiry is whether the argument offered as involving Proof does really fulfill the logical requirements. But wherever, in the applications of logical principles to specific practical purposes, two parties are found contending, the proponent and the opponent—as in a formal debate, and, preëminently, a trial at law— the treatment of the Inference falls into two stages. Whenever, on the evidential fact offered by the proponent, a single other inference remains open, complete Proof fails; the desired conclusion is merely the more probable, or a probable Inference; the other possible inferences, less probable or equally probable, remain open. It is thus apparent that, by the very nature of this process, a specific course is suggested for the opponent. *He may now properly show, by adducing other facts*, that one or another of these inferences, thus left open, is not merely possible and speculative, but is more probable and natural as the true explanation of the originally offered evidentiary fact. That fact has been admitted in evidence, but its force may now be diminished or annulled by showing that some explanation of it other than the proponent's is the true one.

Thus every sort of evidentiary fact may call for treatment in a second aspect, by the opponent, viz.: *What are the other possible inferences which are available for the opponent as explaining away* the force of the fact already admitted? To illustrate:

(1) In showing the defendant's connection with a murder, the fact is admitted of the finding of a knife, bearing his name, near the body of the deceased; the defendant, to refute the claimed conclusion that he was present with the knife at the murder, may show that he lost the knife a month before; thus giving greater color of probability to the inference that some one else was present with the knife.

(2) To show the defendant's animosity against the deceased, the fact of a serious quarrel ten years before is offered; the claimed conclusion, namely, that the animosity existed at the time of the killing, is an inference of low relative probability; for the opponent may show, by the fact of a reconciliation in the interim, that the fact of the quarrel does not lead to the conclusion claimed.

* * *

Thus far, in considering the process of Inference from a particular evidentiary fact, we have noticed that its weaknesses give rise to the Opponent's process of Explanation.

But are there no other processes used by the Opponent, in opposing this proposed Inference?

There are, indeed, two other processes, and only two. He has three processes in all. He may, (1) as already seen, seek to *explain* away the proposed inference. Or, (2) he may *deny* the existence of the evidentiary fact itself. Or, (3) he may offer some *new and rival* evidentiary fact, tending independently to disprove the Probandum.

But in neither of the latter two cases is he using any new logical principle. In (2) he is not contesting the logical value of the proponent's inference, but is denying that its basis, the evidentiary fact, is a fact; and thus for that purpose he becomes a proponent of new data, and offers inferences from new evidentiary facts tending to disprove the proponent's original evidentiary fact. In (3) he neither explains away the force of the proponent's inference, nor disputes the fact on which it rests; he offers a new fact, with an inference pointing directly at the Probandum, but negatively; he thus becomes a Proponent, in turn, as to that new rival evidentiary fact; and the same logical principle applies, in valuing his new proposed inference, that applied to the proponent's original inference.

To illustrate:

To charge A with murder, the prosecution shows a specific threat, an old quarrel, and traces of blood on his clothes. The defendant may answer: (1) *Explaining* away the old quarrel by showing an intervening reconciliation; explaining away the blood traces by showing the recent killing of a chicken; this is the complementary process of Explanation suggested by the evidentiary facts of quarrel and blood, and is directed to diminishing their force; this complementary process depends for its conditions and possibilities upon those original facts;

(2) *Denying* the specific threat; this in itself does not affect the logical probative value of the threat as circumstantial evidence; it introduces a new issue of evidence, raising a doubt as to the very existence of the circumstantial fact;

(3) *Advancing the rival facts* of an alibi and of good character for peaceableness; here the defendant is simply a proponent of new evidentiary facts, just as the prosecution was for its own evidence; this new question of relevancy depends on precisely the same tests as the prosecution's original evidence.

All an opponent's modes are reducible to these three. In the first, he is an opponent by logical nature of his argument. In the second, he is an opponent from the contradictory point of view, but this may require him to become a proponent of either a new circumstance or a new witness. In the third, he becomes himself the proponent of a new argument, which the original proponent may now attack as an opponent. The first is inherent in the probative use of the proponent's original fact; the other two are not inherent, and may or may not be resorted to.

*   *   *

Symbols. In further discussion, the symbol C will, for brevity, be used for a piece of circumstantial evidence; the symbol T for a piece of testimonial evidence; the symbol P for the probandum; the symbol ⟫→ denotes the proposed inference. . . .

*   *   *

From the foregoing exposition of the kinds of evidence and processes of probative reasoning, it will be seen that the essential thing, in preparing to estimate the effect of evidence, is to *analyze accurately the inference proposed* in each instance. Every evidential fact is offered as tending to prove a Probandum. We know that in most instances it may not completely prove. Therefore it is necessary to place it in the light and dissect it to see what are its shortcomings. For practical purposes this analysis has four steps.

(a) The *first step* is to *state to ourselves, in words, precisely what the offered evidence is*, and then *precisely what is its supposed Probandum*. Until this is done, it is useless to go further. For example, a policeman tells his story about capturing the accused after an affray. Out of that story let us select two or three supposed facts; *e. g.* (1) that the accused had no hat, and (2) that his hand was cut.

This (1) first supposed fact we may then analyze into the inferences as alleged or implied by the proponent; *e. g.*

C—The fact of having no hat   →P—it was lost by running;

C—The fact that he lost it by running   →P—he was running away;

C—The fact that he was running away   →P—his consciousness of guilt;

C—His consciousness of guilt   →P—his actual guilt of the assault charged.

[B8912]

Now at any one of these four steps a lack of certainty in the inference may become important; whether and just where the doubt will become important will depend upon the opponent's attitude in the case in hand.

The (2) second supposed fact we may analyze thus:

C—The fact of having a cut hand   →P—the recent contact with a sharp weapon;

C—Recent contact with a sharp weapon

C—Contact with the weapon used in the affray   →P—contact with the weapon used in the affray;

     →P—taking part in the affray.

[B8841]

Here, too, there is an opening for dispute as to the successive inferences. The analysis enables us to estimate the strength of the final inference, and to prepare for the various possibilities of dispute at any possible point.

(*b*) The *second step* is to *set down, in words, precisely what the logical possibilities are for the opponent to explain away the inference* at any one of the successive stages, and to estimate the probabilities of any one of them being more correct, in the case in hand, than the inference towards our own probandum. Thus, in the first instance above taken:

C—The fact of having no hat, may be explained by four possible other inferences:

     > Hat was blown off by a gust of wind;

     or> Hat was already off when the accused came out of his store to learn the cause of the commotion;

     or> Hat was off because the day was hot;

     or> Hat was off because he never wore one.

[B8840]

One or more of these explanations may be absurd; but the necessary process is first to set them down in black and white.

Again, in the next step of inference, assuming that the proponent's inference is sound, nevertheless—

C—The fact of losing the hat by running, may be explained thus:
> He was running to board a street car;
or> He was running to give an alarm of fire;
or> He was running to evade a third person.

[B8839]

Any one of these may be improbable; but the needful thing is to determine explictly how many and what they are.

(*c*) The *third step* is to *investigate the evidential probabilities* for the opponent in dealing with the above evidential facts. Thus, in (*a*) 1 above, C, the fact that the accused when arrested had no hat, may be (OE) explained away, (OD) denied, or (OR) rivalled. For which of these is there any actual prospect of use by the opponent?

Let us examine them, in the above order:

OE. In (*b*) above, we say that there are at least four other possible Explanations. But these are hypothetical only, or imaginary, as yet. It now remains to find out whether there is any evidence-basis for inferring any one of them to be facts.—The first one was that "the hat was blown off by a gust of wind"; so, investigate to learn whether at that time and place there *was* a gusty wind.—The second one was that "the hat was already off before the affray"; so, investigate to learn the time *when* the hat came off.—The third one was that "the hat was off because the day was hot"; so investigate to learn what the temperature *was* at that time and place.—The fourth one was that "the hat was off because he never wore one," so, investigate to learn the man's *personal habits*.

And so on for each of the hypothetical explanations noted (under *b* above) as applicable to each of the other successive inferences that lie between the proponent's evidentiary fact and the probandum.

OD. This Denial might hypothetically be effected by
T=another witness, who contradicts the policeman's assertion that the accused had no hat; or by
C=the circumstance that the accused still had on his hat a few minutes later; which C would in turn need a witness T.

[B8903]

So, investigate to learn whether such witnesses are available.

OR. This Rival Fact may be any one of many, *e. g.* that the accused had no motive for making an assault. But these possible rival facts have no direct bearing on the original evidential fact, and depend upon the case at large.

Whether the opponent will explain, or deny, or adduce rival facts, cannot always be told beforehand; but the directions which his refutation may take must be thought out beforehand and prepared for.

(*d*) The *final step* consists in the analysis of the effect of a mass of evidential facts. This is something larger than the analysis of each separate fact, though it involves no new canons of reasoning.

*   *   *

Does Corroborative Evidence involve any new or additional logical process other than those already analyzed?

It does not. Whereabouts, then, does it belong, in the scheme above expounded?

Let us first eliminate an ambiguity in the term as currently used. "Corroboration" means literally "strengthening." But there may be several mental processes equally included under this loose idea:

(1) A frequent use of the term "corroboration" applies it to the production of an *additional witness* or two, duplicating the assertion of some prior witness. But this is not a new logical process. It is simply the addition of another T $\ggg\!\!\rightarrow$ P.

*   *   *

(2) But the term "corroboration" is also used to signify the auxiliary evidential facts offered by a proponent to *negative the explanations* by which the opponent seeks to weaken the inference from some original evidentiary fact of the proponent; and in this aspect "corroboration" involves (not a new logical process, but) a *new stage in the presentation* of evidence.

For example, in the case put *ante*, § 17, where the policeman testifies that the accused when arrested had no hat, and the proposed inference is that he lost it when running away to escape capture, we saw that this inference might be annulled or weakened by at least four explanations, hypothetically suggested by the opponent. If now the proponent can negative one or more of these explanations, he strengthens ("corroborates") the inference to that extent. Thus, in the above cited example, if the proponent offers the evidentiary fact that there was no gust of wind (indicating that the hat was not thus lost), and that the hat was on when the accused came out of the store (indicating that he had not taken it off in the store), and that the day was a cold one (indicating that he had not removed the hat because of the heat), and that the accused habitually wore his hat (indicating that his habit could not account for his hatless condition),—thus, one by one, he blocks up the possible explanations, and to that extent strengthens ("corroborates") the original proposed inference.

*   *   *

As applied to testimonial evidence, Corroboration consists in offering data which refute possible discrediting circumstances. . . .

. . . the rule of practice which forbids most sorts of so-called corroboration until after an attempted impeachment is a rule of orderly convenience only, and its distinction has no correspondence to any logical feature of Corroboration.

Every fact, then, which closes up an exit of *possible* distrust of the testimony, *i. e.* which prevents or refutes a possible discrediting hypothesis, is a corroborative fact. Hence the varieties of corroboration are as numerous as the varieties of impeachment.

However, since the presentation of Corroborative Evidence may not come until after the opponent has presented his explanations and denials, Corroboration may be regarded as a fifth possible stage or probative process, in addition to the four already analyzed.

* * *

Hence, the five probative processes applicable to any piece of evidence are as follows:

PA = proponent's assertion of a fact to evidence a probandum;

OE = opponent's explanation of other facts taking away the value of this inference PA;

OD = opponent's denial of the evidentiary fact on which the inference PA is based;

OR = opponent's rival fact, adduced against the probandum, without any reference to the inference PA;

PC = proponent's corroborative facts, negating the explanations OE.

NOTES

1. *Case Planning: General Perspectives*

Despite the importance of selection and organization in preparation, the trial literature is surprisingly sparse in articulating a framework for dealing with this aspect of the process. The typical discussion of investigating cases for trial—which will usually be a chapter or a few pages in a manual dealing with trial practice in its entirety—tends to assume that the investigator knows what he or she is after, and is primarily concerned with where and how to obtain it. Similarly, the legal literature on formal discovery proceedings seems almost universally to be addressed to the lawyer who knows what he or she wants. Starting with the assumption that the lawyer knows that a specific piece of information is relevant and significant, discussions of rules, cases and treatises on discovery address the question of whether it can be obtained and whether it will be admissible at trial.

Given traditional modes of legal analysis, it may be that questions of content—of *what* to look for rather than how or where to seek it—deserve less attention than do questions of method. Certainly the study of legal rules involves considerable discussion of the relevance of particular facts and the inferences that can be drawn from them. It has been our experience, however, that many lawyers give insufficient consideration to questions like "what do I need to know?" and "when do I stop looking?" To use Vetter's perspective, they do not formulate "theories" of what happened or what they want to prove. As a result, they may fail to probe for details in their clients' descriptions of the facts, or overlook lines of investigation that would open up new avenues of defense or recovery. Whatever the sources of failings in this area, they suggest that before you develop such habits, you need to consider how a lawyer analyzes a sketchy or tentative version of the facts, and develops it into a complete, reliable and understandable body of information that will provide a basis for the subsequent handling of the case.[9]

One aspect of this task simply involves developing a working sense of "what happened." Obviously these ideas should start with the "strong facts" and the fair inferences that can be drawn from them. But such images are also constructed, tested against the "proof," and refined and modified as the investigation progresses. Bodin goes into this process in a little more detail:

> From the evidence available you should be able to formulate a tentative working hypothesis as to the course of events. A few examples will serve to illustrate the meaning of such hypothesis and the importance of analyzing a case in that manner.

> Let us take first one of the simplest types of cases in which the formulation of such a hypothesis would be of great help in keeping before you the essential elements of the case and pointing the direction in which the evidence should be concentrated.

> A plaintiff has been injured by an automobile which struck him while he was crossing a street. A number of elements must be considered in arriving at a conclusion as to how the accident happened. Was the road dry or wet? If it was wet, were there any indications that the car skidded? Were the brakes defective? Was the car being operated at an excessive speed? Was the driver intoxicated? Were there any lights controlling the traffic? Were there other cars in the vicinity of the defendant's car which had any effect on the operation of the defendant's car? These elements and others that may be rele-

9. Those of you who are interested in the general subject of "theory building" might want to see R. Reynolds, A PRIMER ON THEORY CONSTRUCTION (1971); R. Rudner, PHILOSOPHY OF SOCIAL SCIENCE (1966); A. Stinchcombe, CONSTRUCTING SOCIAL THEORIES (1968). The relationship of theory to action has bedeviled scholars for centuries. Modern ideas about this relationship are well worth your consideration as you struggle with the way you use theory in lawyer work. For an excellent treatment of this subject, see R. Bernstein, THE RESTRUCTURING OF SOCIAL AND POLITICAL THEORY (1976).

vant in a particular case must be considered in formulating a hypothesis as to how the accident happened, and the facts which are gathered by the lawyer must be scrutinized from the point of view of the hypothesis adopted, in order to determine whether all of the facts point in the direction of that hypothesis. If they do not, it may be necessary to revise the hypothesis before formulating a factual theory as to how the accident happened.

* * *

Whatever hypothesis is adopted, it must be checked against all ascertainable facts. If some of the facts do not fit the hypothesis, it may be necessary to change the factual theory of the action or of the defense. It is important to make this type of analysis of the case before interviewing all of the witnesses, because it is helpful to know the direction in which you are going. Some witnesses should not be bothered too often. If you go off on the wrong theory you may not be able to obtain the cooperation of those witnesses when you seek to interview them again.[10]

Nor should such theories be limited to the reconstruction of a narrative; they should also address the question of *why* the client should prevail.[11] This obviously includes an understanding of how rule and fact combine to require (or at least make more probable) a particular judge or jury decision. But it also means developing a rationale for why this result is desirable or just. Vetter's reference to characterizing medical malpractice cases as "the Healer attacked by the Ungrateful Patient" is an example of such a "theory." Most lawyers have such heuristics which they use in working up a case. If counsel for the doctor limited his or her investigation to theories of what happened—*e. g.*, "the doctor was not negligent in this case because she followed approved procedures"—evidence relating to the patient's motivation might be missed.

Finally, an initial approach to the case should reflect recognition of the gap that inevitably exists between an authoritative decision and what the client might want. Enforcement of a favorable judgment, or even an agreed-upon settlement, rarely follows a straightforward progression.

10. Bodin, *Marshalling the Evidence*, in CIVIL LITIGATION AND TRIAL TECHNIQUES 18, 27 (H. Bodin, ed. 1976).

11. This is the same problem confronted by the historian, who must work with theories not only of what happened in the past, but what meanings should be attached to it. Those who would like to pursue this analogy should find the following works of interest: M. Cohen, THE MEANING OF HUMAN HISTORY (1947); R. Collingwood, THE IDEA OF HISTO-

RY (1946); A. Danto, ANALYTICAL PHILOSOPHY OF HISTORY (1965); GENERALIZATION IN THE WRITING OF HISTORY AND THEORY (L. Gottschalk, ed. 1965); L. Gottschalk, UNDERSTANDING HISTORY: A PRIMER OF HISTORICAL METHOD (1950); PHILOSOPHY OF HISTORY IN OUR TIME (H. Meyerhoff, ed. 1959); M. Postan, FACT & RELEVANCE: ESSAYS ON HISTORICAL METHOD (1971); M. White, THE FOUNDATIONS OF HISTORICAL KNOWLEDGE (1965).

One way to look at these concerns is to adapt a simple picture of law in operation, suggested by Jerome Frank. Achievement of client goals is a function of:

$$F \text{ (facts)} \times L \text{ (law)} \times D \text{ (decision)} \times I \text{ (implementation)}$$

Any litigation plan must take account of how each of these elements will/can be influenced.[12]

---

12. *See* J. Frank, *What Courts Do In Fact*, 26 ILL.L.REV. 645, 761 (1932); COURTS ON TRIAL 14–24 (1950). This is, of course, merely a heuristic; there are countless complexities. Brown and Dauer, for example, offer the following elaboration of this simple model:

[In] the simplest of transactions or plans . . . there are but four identifiable stages. An example of such an elementary form would be: Purpose—to effectuate an estate plan with a minimum threat of erosive litigation; Result—to deter potential contestants by penalizing them if they litigate against the will; Law—a person loses a bequest if he or she contests a will in which there is a no-contest/forfeiture clause; Fact—draft such a clause into an enforceable will. Even in this elementary example, however, the concepts are not unchanging. Had we begun with "Purpose—to create a charitable foundation to be funded with $X after the client's death," the next step back could be "have a valid testamentary transfer with a minimum threat of erosive litigation." Then, the Fact would be, "to deter potential contestants . . . etc." Alternatively, we might consider the ". . . valid testamentary transfer . . . ." as a sub-Purpose. The point is, that the categories are never fixed in practice, *nor need they be.* Graphically, the process might be viewed as:

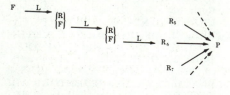

—where the result of each stage becomes the fact of the next. The

Process, then, might be of a "decision-tree" form:

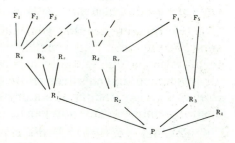

—and the process is that of reasoning from one stage (P, e. g.) back to the next (its constituents, related to it by some causal route such as a rule of law) and so on until we have reached the stage of discrete physical events. Quaere: would it be possible for, say, F_3 to be the same as non-R_3? For F_5 to be impossible? For F_2 to eventuate, by the operation of some *other* rule of law, in some Result that will lead to non-P? . . . (Suppose, to take an extreme example, that the penalty for usury is forfeiture of some portion of the principal sum . . . ?) Again, the fact that the contents of the Result category not only are changeable and relative but also, in many cases, arbitrary, is not of crucial significance. What is important is the process of continual subdivision which these variables suggest. Each stage is the result of the preceding stage; each stage suggests the elements which must be accomplished in the preceding. L. Brown & E. Dauer, PLANNING BY LAWYERS: MATERIALS ON A NONADVERSARIAL LEGAL PROCESS 275–276 (1978).

2. *Case Planning: Identifying Specific Lines of Inquiry*

Looking carefully at Dean Wigmore's analysis of what must be proven at trial begins to give this planning process more specificity. What Wigmore identifies as the process of proof essentially involves reasoning from fact to conclusion—from the Probans, or fact-offered-as-evidence, to the Probandum, or proposition to be proved. The more probable it is that the proposed inference is *the* explanation of the evidentiary fact, the greater the probative value of the evidence. In developing lines of inquiry in the investigatory stages of a case, one reverses this process, reasoning from desired conclusion to possible or probable fact, and pursuing lines of inquiry accordingly. There are a number of ways of going about this; the following represents one formulation of analytic steps that you might find helpful:

(1) **Imagine arguing your client's story to a judge or jury.** Assume, at the start, that your client's perceptions, recollections and interpretation are essentially accurate. Then develop (or write out) an argument that resolves inconsistencies and fills in gaps in your client's favor. Rework the story until it is consistent with the most desirable outcome the rules permit.

(2) **Ask yourself, "If my client's story as I just argued it were true, what else would be true?"** The purpose here is to move from your conclusions and inferences to the "data" that would support them. For example, suppose you represent a client who claims she was defrauded in the door-to-door sale of a food freezer plan. She understood the salesman to say that she was leasing the freezer and could cancel at any time. She tried to cancel, but the company now insists that no such option was offered and is suing her for the balance. If the client's story were true, what else would be true? The following possibilities come immediately to mind: (i) the freezer, not the food plan, would be the money-maker for the company; (ii) the salesman might have been "working" the area and made similar representations to other purchasers; (iii) there may be company training manuals or written instructions to salesmen on the sales "pitch"; (iv) complaints about similar practices may be on file with better business or consumer protection agencies; (v) the salesman may have been under some particular pressure to make sales at the time he visited your client. Each of these suggests possible lines of inquiry and could lead to facts that corroborate your client's story.

(3) **Imagine you are counsel for your opponent and argue his or her "best" case to a jury.** As Wigmore points out, partisan investigation requires that you plan for and adjust your story to rebut or avoid counter-explanations. In order to do this, you need to put yourself in the place of opposing counsel and construct an argument as you did for your client. This act of imagination, aided by some preliminary inquiries, will begin to give you a sense of the case you have to undermine or explain away.

(4) **Ask yourself, "If my opponent's story were true, what else would be true?"** This is the same thought process that you used in analyzing your client's story. The lines of inquiry developed here point you to facts you hope are *not* there. If you do find them, you will have to revise your client's story to explain them or find ways to discredit or undermine them. Generally it is preferable to incorporate what seem to be unfavorable facts into your story or explain them rather than attempt the risky, inherently uncertain task of trying to contradict them. This means, for example, that your primary goal in interviewing most hostile witnesses is to establish as much congruence as possible between their recollections and what you can prove to be true. Eliciting material for impeachment becomes the main focus only when all else has failed.

(5) **List sources of information for all the lines of inquiry that seem worth pursuing.** Sometimes there won't appear to be any good ways of pursuing a line of inquiry. At other times, the possibilities will be so numerous you will find it difficult to choose among them. Part of this problem is resolved as you get more deeply into the case, or as circumstances change, but even at the planning stage there are many ways to be more creative about investigative possibilities. For example, some of the following suggestions may be helpful:

—Brainstorm, *i. e.*, in a group of two or three people let your imagination run free. Don't criticize any suggestions until you have a full list and don't stop to explore the details of any particular possibility. Use each idea as a jumping off place for another.[13]

—Visualize each piece of evidence you would like to have and where it might be located. Identify the obstacles you would encounter if you went directly to each source and focus on how you could avoid these barriers.

—Ask a friend or stranger who is "outside" your problem or frame of reference. Sometimes a fresh, more distanced view is the most creative one.

—Use libraries and research guides, and ask research people (journalists, reference librarians, research firms, claims adjusters, police investigators) how they develop leads in analogous areas.

—Forget the problem for awhile—go to a movie, think about something else—and come back to it later. A rest period often permits you to begin again in new ways.

13. There is an extensive literature cataloging suggestions and procedures of this nature. *See, e. g.,* W. Gordon, SYNECTICS (1961); C. Clark, BRAINSTORMING (1958); A. Simberg, CREATIVITY AT WORK (1964); G. Davis & J. Scott, TRAINING CREATIVE THINKING (1971). For work in education devoted to training the imagination, *see* S. Parnes, CREATIVE BEHAVIOR GUIDEBOOK (1967); A SOURCE BOOK FOR CREATIVE THINKING (S. Parnes & A. Harding, eds., 1962).

(6) **Select the lines of inquiry you will pursue and the order in which you will pursue them.** Identifying a line of inquiry doesn't necessarily mean you will pursue it. Sometimes costs will be prohibitive, time will be a problem, or other considerations will be more important. You will often need to decide which lines of inquiry to pursue, and when. Comparing and choosing among alternatives is difficult and inevitably dependent on the particular case and context. For example, in many cases you will do a great deal of investigation and preparation before a deposition, in order to maximize the likelihood of obtaining the statements or admissions you want. At other times, it is best to depose or interview a witness quickly, before many facts are known, and before he or she can be "prepared" by the other side.

The most we can offer here are some general criteria for choosing among or sequencing lines of inquiry: (i) How much information (that you would not otherwise choose to divulge) will you have to disclose in order to get what you want? Generally you disclose least when you investigate physical evidence—documents, photographs, objects, scenes, etc.—and more when you seek testimony. (ii) Who has the advantage of delay or avoidance? (iii) Is your choice reversible? That is, if the inquiry is not successful, have you committed yourself to propositions you can't back up or have you closed off options that would otherwise be available? (iv) Have you expanded possibilities for further inquiry? (*E. g.*, collecting documentary evidence and obtaining a few admissions from an opponent may improve your chances of getting assistance from an expert.) (v) Is the information likely to become available without expensive and time-consuming investigation? The rule of thumb, not surprisingly, is to select and sequence your inquiries so as to maximize the information you get and minimize costs and risks.

(7) **Inquire—Assess—Revise story—Develop new lines of inquiry—Inquire—Assess—Revise** . . . In this spiral fashion you will build your case—that is, you will refine and adapt your original story, enlarge the base of solid facts, and progressively eliminate alternative, unfavorable explanations.

Through some such means you will learn to analyze your case, develop lines of inquiry, and devise some method of deciding whether and when to pursue them. Each time you thoroughly investigate a case you will expand your knowledge of what to look for the next time, because in this area, as in others, experience accumulates and informs your subsequent choices and actions. You will also become more adept at seeking and shaping the facts you need to meet your clients' purposes, going down fewer "blind alleys" and reducing the amount of irrelevant information you collect. That is, you will de-

velop a sense of what fits and what does not in a given set of circumstances—a sort of Holmesian sense of the logic of things:

> [Inspector Gregory:] "Is there any point to which you would wish
> to draw my attention?
>
> [Holmes:] "To the curious incident of the dog in the night-time."
>
> "The dog did nothing in the night-time."
>
> "That was the curious incident," remarked Sherlock Holmes.[14]

For a detective, he wouldn't have made a bad lawyer at all.

---

2. Understanding the Larger Context

Developing a theory of the case, of course, involves more than
evolving a story which will tie together uncontroverted facts. One
cannot understand what was said or done by the parties to a particular dispute without some sense of its larger context. Indeed, understanding the larger context is sometimes the only way to determine
how it should be handled—*e. g.*, should the client file suit only against
a local contractor or should a federal regulatory agency be involved?
Is what happened to the client unusual or is it standard practice in a
given industry? Who else might be interested in the outcome? As
these questions indicate, planning in a particular case may frequently
require an understanding of the *system* of which it is a part. The
following reading may be of some help in making clear what thinking
about systems might entail.

BROCK, CHESEBRO, CRAGAN AND KLUMPP, PUBLIC POLICY DECISION MAKING [AND] SYSTEMS ANALYSIS . . .

27–29, 50–52, 56–59, 61–68, 74 (1973).

[All decision making depends on having a picture of the decisional context—a sense of the terrain which defines the actor's options
and limits. Each such conception can be thought of as a "system"—
that is] . . . an assembly of objects all of which are related to
one another by some form of regular interaction or interdependence
so that the assembly can be viewed as an organic or organized whole.
According to this definition the solar system, a telegraph system, and
a network of television stations are clearly systems.

We wish to highlight four characteristics of a system which are
essential elements in a general systems theory. First, there is an *interdependence of objects* within a system. . . .

* * *

14. A. Doyle, *Silver Blaze*, in THE
MEMOIRS OF SHERLOCK HOLMES
(1894).

The solar system . . . is a system because the planets and the sun are dependent upon each other and mutually define the nature of each other. If the sun should undergo a major change, then the entire system would undergo a change in which all of the planets would be affected.

* * *

Second, a system contains an *ordered sequence of events*. The words "ordered sequence" draw our attention to the fact that there are temporal relationships between the objects which constitute the system. . . . In order to identify or describe any system, one must be able to detect or observe a series of acts over time. . . .

Third, the objects within a system are *connected and controlled* by each other. The objects within a system mutually influence each other; a change in one object necessarily requires a change in the other objects within a system and thus the objects can be said to control each other.

* * *

Fourth, it ought to be noted that a system possesses both *a structure and a set of processes*. A set of processes may be the foundation for defining what a structure is, or the structure may be the basis for defining a set of processes within a system. One can best identify a set of processes by viewing them as major paths of interactions (actions between objects that persistently repeat themselves). These paths of interaction can be the basis for a description of the structure of a system. From a student's perspective, the structure of the educational system is defined by the three major paths of interaction between the instructor and himself: (1) listening to lectures, (2) writing examinations, and (3) receiving grades. In this case, the processes of a system determine the nature of the structure of the system.

* * *

Four terms appear to capture the major features of any system. These four terms are identified and defined in [the figure below.] This

Function	Terms	Definitions
Description	Components	The discrete, unique, or constituent parts that compose a system.
	Relationships	The identity that exists between two or more components; the action of a system, that is, the nature or characteristics of the activity that exists between two or more things taken together.

Function	Terms	Definitions
Evaluation	Goals	The stated or operational objectives, designs, aims, or intentions of the men interacting with their environment; the critical decisionmaking process is designed to maximize or achieve these goals.
	Effects	The assessment, fulfillment, accomplishment, impression, or outcome of a system as a result of certain components interacting in relationships toward certain goals; an evaluation of the elements of the system as measured against the goals of the system.

systemic model allows a critic to make two kinds of assessments. First, the critic is able to make a *descriptive analysis* of a system. The components and relationships generally provide the foundation for the descriptive statements regarding the function or operation of a system. A critic would examine a system to identify the components within the system, which ought to lead him to the discovery of relationships within a system. However, the critic might well reverse the process and look for commonly recognized relationships in order to detect the major components . . . .

Second, the model allows the critic to make an *evaluative assessment* of a system. Goals and effects are generally the basis for an evaluation of a system. The concept of an effect is essentially a derived concept. Effects are interpretative assessments based upon a comparison of the relationships within a system and the stated goals or operational goals of a system. From this perspective, a critic is asking if the quantitative or qualitative interaction of certain components (relationships) are achieving desired goals or to what extent the relationships are consistent with desired goals. For example, a 5 percent unemployment rate would be viewed as an effect of a system if the relationships within a system produce a 5 percent level of unemployment (a descriptive claim) and that rate of unemployment is explicitly or implicitly compared to a stated goal of 3 percent unemployment or full employment (a standard for an assessment). The wise critic would be aware of both the descriptive characteristics of a relationship and the evaluative function of a stated goal if a relationship is examined in terms of a goal. The systemic model, then, provides the basis for both descriptive and evaluative judgments of a system.

As with any model for analysis, the insights and meaning which can be derived from its use depend upon the creativity of the critic. We have viewed a system made up of components, relationships, goals, and effects. It is our belief that human interactions can be described and evaluated fairly completely by using these four terms. However, the critic's creativity is the decisive factor. If a critic begins an analysis by looking for things called components, relationships, goals or effects, his analysis will undoubtedly be mundane. If, on the other hand, the critic perceives the four terms as points of view that he might employ in creative ways, then novel, often insightful, analyses will emerge. . . .

*   *   *

The Area of Concern

As the public policy, [or any other,] decision-maker begins his investigation, he faces the tremendous mass of data created by the information explosion. In addition, he confronts an extremely complex society, the complexity of which is intensified by the recognition that multiple causes and multiple effects tie many branches together in complex social relationships. To hope to deal with the information and complexity by treating society as a whole probably would be folly. To make his study manageable, he must first limit the scope of his analysis.

To begin his study, then, the decision-maker will specify an "area of concern"—a complex of correlated goals and mechanisms. . . . By focusing research and isolating components, relationships, and subsystems of the area of concern, the policy analyst may organize the tremendous complexity of society into social systems.

*   *   *

Once he has drawn boundaries around the area of concern, the researcher must begin making some statements about its actions, processes, and more stable characteristics. . . . The researcher will describe the activity or the identity between two elements in specifying and explaining relationships, he will summarize the more stable characteristics of the system's elements in describing components, and he will group closely tied relationships in organizing the subsystems. Through this process he will organize the area of concern into social systems.

In the specification and organization of the elements of the system he makes many choices. For example, frequently he must choose between treating an element as a component or treating it as a relationship. When describing individual exchanges between buyer and seller in the economic system, price is the expression of a relationship. Yet, when describing the macroeconomic system, price is a component, as in the relationship between price and money supply. The investigator must choose which interpretation of price is more useful.

*   *   *

[Tools to Find Relationships]

[We have defined a relationship as the action of a system or the identity that exists among two or more elements.]

.   .   .   Looking for relationships is simply a matter of looking for any repetitive activity, path of interaction, or procedural rule in the system.   However, the tools [the investigator] develops, such as the ones suggested below, will help him find less obvious relationships and understand the relationships that he does find.

(1) *Look for Relationships Between Components Already Isolated.*   The decision-maker analyzing the American court system immediately notes the difference between the trial court and the appellate court.   "What is the relationship between the trial court and the appellate court?" he asks and begins to look at the activity between the two.   To say that relationships are the activities among components and that components are the elements in the activity is a useful circular definition of the two terms.   It helps illustrate that once the analyst isolates components he should look for the relationships involved.

(2) *Look at Organizational Charts.*   An organizational chart of the executive branch of the federal government recognizes that the President has a foreign affairs adviser and a domestic affairs adviser on his staff reporting directly to him.   Important activities might be expected to occur within the context of these relationships.   Frequently organizational charts will give clues to where activities occur.

The researcher will find, however, that an organizational chart may become a blinder rather than an illuminator.   There are always informal activities that are important but not shown on the chart.
.   .   .

The same observation may be made about the rules of the system. Often dictated rules that regulate interaction are clues to relationships.   However, the specified rules frequently are not observed.   For example, laws regulating access to the ballot box for blacks were circumvented for years.   To avoid this pitfall, the analyst ought to differentiate between stated and operational rules of the system.   He can use the organizational chart and the rules as clues to relationships if he realizes the limitations and dangers of the tool.

(3) *Use Functional Analysis.*   Functional analysis assumes that certain activities necessarily occur in any system.   By searching for the activity that fulfills the system's functional needs, the analyst isolates relationships within the system.

The public policy decision-maker using this tool might look for eight basic functions.   (a) The *production* function is the task accomplishment function.   Once he determines the system's desired product, he isolates the activities involved in the system's producing it.   (b) The *input* function is designed to attract the necessary raw materials and energy of money and people so that the system may perform its tasks. (c) The *output* function distributes the products of the task accomplishment. When the system's task is a service, the production and output functions are identical. (d) The *monitoring* function continually assesses the system's performance to determine which procedures are appropriate for present conditions and how successful the procedures are in achieving their goal. (e) Closely related is the *adaptive* function which also asks how well the system is performing, but determines where new procedures need to be developed rather than which procedures should be used. (f) The *maintenance* function standardizes procedures and brings stability to the system by teaching new members the proper procedures. (g) The *public relations* function regulates the system's relationship with other systems. The public relations function's responsibility is to ensure that the system has a proper image beyond its boundaries. (h) The *management* function is designed to orchestrate the system, ensuring that the system operates properly and deciding on changes in the system and its main tasks.

Each function may be performed by more than one component of a system or a component may perform more than one function. The important thing for the researcher to remember is that a health system will include activities designed to perform these functions, so he can find activity by looking for them.

(4) *Look at the Social System's Needs.* Taking a broader perspective, the decision-maker may borrow from the sociologists who list basic needs of a society: (a) mastery of nature, the need to develop activities to maintain life, such as providing food, clothing, shelter, and so on, (b) socialization, the need to develop methods of teaching the new members the pattern of activities, and (c) social control, the need to insure that no one deviates significantly from the norms for these activities. He may look for activities designed to fulfill each of these needs. He will probably find this framework most useful in looking at society's overall structure.

(5) *Develop Questions to Help Understand Relationships.* Once the decision-maker has isolated relationships, the kinds of things he wants to know about them are relatively constant, so he may decide to develop a list of standard questions to ask about a relationship. One set of these that he may find useful is: What is done? By whom? In what way? To whom or what? With what effect? At what time? In response to what? With what purpose? He will undoubtedly discover other questions relevant in some cases and other questions that he could ask in all cases, but having a list of questions will help him thoroughly explore the nature of the relationships.

(6) *Use Causal Mapping.* We have argued elsewhere that the changing view of the world has changed the concept of causal links. Because of this change, the old methods of mapping causes and effects

seem less appropriate. But the investigator may want a way of mapping the relationships so he can understand the activities within the system. [The figure below] is an example of a technique of causal mapping that preserves the idea of multiple causes and multiple effects. Note that any one component may be related to many others.

There are two ways to view the relationships on the map. It may serve to illustrate that a relationship exists, for example, changes in bank loans affect business investment. Such a relationship is represented on the map by a line connecting the components. The map may give more specific information, for example, an increase in prices increases business profits, but usually leads to Federal Reserve action to decrease the money supply. A quantitative relationship between the components is represented on the map by a (+) to indicate a positive relationship or a (−) to indicate a negative relationship.

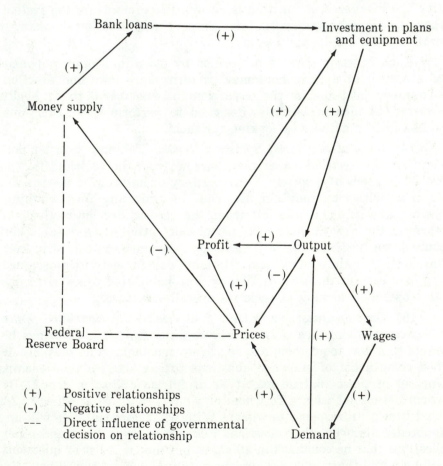

(+)   Positive relationships
(-)   Negative relationships
---   Direct influence of governmental
      decision on relationship

A View of the Quantitative Relationships in the Economy

[B8899]

Of course, maps are more useful for pointing to relationships than for explaining their characteristics, and no map can illustrate all the relationships in a system. The mapping is simply a way of seeing the links between components. Relationships are of differing importance and most maps will illustrate the most important relationships while ignoring the more insignificant ones.

Regardless of the methods used to find or understand the relationships, when he has described them properly, the researcher should have an account of the activities important to the operation of the system. His inquiry should focus attention on the characteristics of these interactions, since judgments about the system's ability to achieve its goals return the policy-maker to the characteristics of the system's activities. Because the system's perspective defines the system in terms of the activity within it, the study of relationships is the cornerstone of inquiry through systems analysis.

[Tools to Find] Components

. . . [Earlier, we] defined components as the discrete, unique, or constituent parts that compose a system. Components are of two types: (1) the individuals, groups, subsystems, institutions, classes, or agencies that participate in the interaction and (2) the material involved in the interaction. The latter category includes items that characteristically are inputs, throughputs, or outputs of the system, such as money or information exchanged or raw materials converted to finished products. While relationships describe the activity within the system, the components describe the participants and materials in the interaction.

. . . [I]n this section we are interested in examples of tools that help the policy-maker find and understand the important components in a system.

(1) *Look for Information and Matter Involved in Exchange.* An analyst looking at the economic system sees money changing hands and expects to find a good or service being exchanged in conjunction with the same process. The exchange of the money indicates to him that an activity is occurring. Similarly, he may find reports or other communication being transferred from one agency of government to another. The report suggests that the agencies are related, one dependent on the other for information. In another case he may be able to isolate a raw material or a product passing through various stages of development and discover activities connected with the processing. Because systems analysis talks about relationships between components in terms of energy and information exchange, isolating these exchanged components will lead to the discovery of important relationships.

(2) *Look for Inputs and Outputs.* When looking at the foreign policy decision-making system, the student of public policy will see

that decisions are important components. When he looks at the health care system, he will examine carefully the quality of the health care provided by the system. The various items brought into the system (inputs) or sent from it (outputs) may be key components because of their importance in evaluating the system. Inputs and outputs are especially important when evaluation requires quantification of the system's costs and benefits.

(3) *Look for Relationships That May Profitably Be Treated as Components*. Earlier this chapter stated that although from one perspective price is a relationship between buyer and seller, in explaining the macroeconomic system the analyst may want to treat price as a component and money supply as another component and look at the relationship between them. Especially when tracing the effects of a change through a system, instead of talking in terms of relationships between relationships, it is useful to treat the relationships as components and determine the relationships between them. This is a common procedure when quantifying the relationship.

The selection of components is an important step in describing the system. If the decision-maker can find the discrete individuals, groups, or objects that compose the system, he will be less likely to overlook important relationships and the characteristics of the components that influence the nature of the system's activity. A thorough understanding of the system requires an understanding of the nature of the components participating in the interaction.

[Tools for Finding Subsystems]

After isolating the important relationships and components, an analyst will organize them into a description of the processes that define the structure of the system. Usually some relationships and components are more closely associated than others. These form processes within the general process—subsystems within the system.

* * *

Just as he develops certain methods of finding and understanding relationships and components, the decision-maker will find certain methods for designating subsystems repeatedly useful. In this section we want to develop some examples of tools for organizing subsystems.

(1) *Functional Subsystems*. When considering relationships we discussed functional analysis. Isolation of one of the eight functions listed there may facilitate understanding the relationships and components involved in the performance of the function. For example, the student of the welfare system will find it useful to isolate and describe the distribution (output) function as a system.

(2) *Geographic Subsystems*. A decision-maker investigating the transportation system may find it wise to differentiate between transportation in coastal areas and inland areas, or between trans-

portation in urban areas and rural areas. The boundaries of a system mark the locus of the weaker relationships. In some systems, physical distance or different physical characteristics may be important barriers to closer relationships, and so regional subsystems may be useful.

(3) *Relationships Groups.* An analyst may want to describe foreign affairs by isolating the political, military, economic, and cultural subsystems and examining them separately. A decision-making system may be viewed within the framework of information gathering, evaluation and decision, and execution subsystems. Sometimes, special groupings of relationships may be useful in analysis. The policy-maker simply groups those relationships that form consistent patterns within the system and treats them as subsystems.

Analysis of subsystems helps the policy-maker understand the processes within the subsystem in more detail. His interest in the subsystem, however, is within the framework of the broader system. After the microanalysis he must still relate the subsystem to other subsystems and components of the broader system. Thus, the specification of subsystems, like the specification of relationships and components, contributes to general understanding of the area of concern.

*   *   *

The Final Description of the Area of Concern

After he has isolated the components and relationships and organized them into subsystems and into a system, the decision-maker has the information for his description of the present system within the area of concern. . . . [We] delineated [above] the characteristics of a final description of the area of concern. It describes an ordered sequence of events and emphasizes the system's purposive operation. It emphasizes the interdependence among components and illustrates the influence of one component on the state of the others.

The system will highlight the characteristics of the components and relationships that determine the final structure and processes of the system. The decision-maker will describe the different processes that operate within the system's structure. In short, he has before him a montage of people, institutions, materials, and laws interacting with each other systematically to achieve the purposes defined by the area of concern. He describes the activity that he recognizes in the montage.

*   *   *

NOTES

1. *The Strategic Importance of Complete Description*

A case starts with a client and a problem, and begins to take shape as preliminary inquiries are made. At some point the relationship and events which the case touches will also come into view. "Mapping this terrain," to use the language of the reading, is an important part of preparation.

Mapping involves making the context of a problem explicit. Take as an example the case of a distraught client, Ms. A, who appears in your office with an eviction summons in hand, fearful that she and her family will be physically removed from their apartment in a matter of days. In the "foreground" of the problem are the client and her family, the building in which her apartment is located, a court and its processes, a landlord and perhaps a sheriff or opposing counsel. Information about these immediate features of the case must be obtained before the lawyer can do more than simply react to the landlord's initiatives.

In the background of the case, however, are (i) the economic circumstances of the landlord; (ii) the procedures and practices of public agencies and officials with authority to intervene in Ms. A's housing situation; (iii) the banking and financial institutions that influence the market of which her housing unit is a part. In short, Ms. A's housing problem is enmeshed in a broad network of relationships and processes. The way lawyers understand this broader context will often determine the way they define the alternatives available to them.

Mapping skills, then, are of fundamental strategic importance. As the reading suggests, by thinking in terms of maps or systems we impose order on otherwise unrelated facts. At the same time such perceptions, being human creations, are capable of distorting as well as elucidating the realities of particular situations. As one author puts it:

> A person's conception of *"things as they are"* includes his conceptual map of his society. Any inaccuracies or distortions of that map will be reflected in his behavior. For example, the best navigator in the world will get into trouble if his maps are false. Actually, when the maps are false the more conscientious navigator may get into worse trouble than the slap-dash navigator who goes less by his maps and more by hunch and by the little he can see." [15]

The descriptions you rely on, then—whether explicit or implicit, accurate or distorted—will influence the way you "see" and therefore plan, build, and investigate your cases. In addition, our own experience has been that attending to such maps has the following benefits:

—It provides a framework for handling what would otherwise be overwhelming quantities of information. For example,

_____

15. This excerpt was offered by one of our students. We have been unable to locate its source.

think about how limited and pressured you would feel if you were Ms. A's counsel and knew nothing about the people and practices involved in the summary eviction subsystem, or the larger housing and legal systems. On the other hand, imagine that in addition to your general familiarity with the summary process and housing systems, you learned that Ms. A's landlord had a large number of financially unstable, poor quality residential properties. It is worth reflecting for a moment on the very different ways in which you would handle the same case under these separate circumstances.

—It abstracts and orders key features of the situation by linking smaller subparts into larger wholes. It thus permits a focus on parts without losing the connections between them.

—It assists in predicting and explaining the responses of others. For example, if you knew the financial situation or business plans of Ms. A's landlord, you would be better able to assess his response to litigation delays.

—It suggests ideas for further investigation. Turning again to Ms. A's case, if you wanted to explore the vulnerabilities of Ms. A's landlord, you might (i) check the court dockets for the volume of evictions he files; (ii) find out whether he has other holdings or operates in any other business forms; (iii) look for other holdings in the neighborhood (Do they fit a plan for further development? Are they well managed and maintained? Are tenants satisfied?); (iv) find out about his other property in the city (Is it commercial or residential? What sort of tenants live in residential properties? How many government programs and oversight agencies are involved? Are the developments profitable, well-maintained, attractive, well-managed?); (v) find out if he has proposals, requests, appeals pending before any public agency (What sort of development is planned? What changes will result in the neighborhood? Who stands to benefit? What opportunities are there for integration?). Much of this information is available from public records, and a broad inquiry of this sort in one case becomes the starting point for a map of the housing system which is used in many others.

For all these reasons, we would encourage you to try to analyze and understand the various systems that provide the context of the typical cases in your practice. In clinical work involving indigents, for example, you would need a map of the housing system (factors that determine housing opportunities and conditions in the public and regulated private sector), the consumer system (regulated, retail markets for goods and services), the public welfare system (government supported income maintenance and human services programs), the work system (factors that influence work opportunities and conditions, including the nexus between school, "training" institutions, and subsequent work patterns). There might be many others depending on the sorts of client problems on which an office focuses. Whatever the field of practice, we are convinced that you will benefit from being systematic about it rather than working from partial, untested assumptions about the way things are. The good lawyers, in our experience, always have a grasp of this larger picture. It is one reason why they are able to break away from routinized patterns in their work.

----

2. *The Mapping Process*

As the foregoing excerpt suggests, the first step in describing any situation is to identify the area with which you are concerned and to set some tentative limits on what you want to analyze. You might begin, for example, with a case you are presently handling. Work out the network of relationships the parties are involved in, perhaps by simply listing the people and organizations connected to a client and his or her opponent. Then group these "actors" into subsystems, stopping where the information or relationship begins to seem tangential.

A logical place to begin is with formal or legal relationships in the situation, since this is familiar ground. You would also want to pay special attention to formal lines of communication and authority, and to the people that you consider most important. Then begin to chart informal procedures and practices. Where are formal lines short-cut or ignored? What new lines are established? Often the gaps between the formal and informal system can be sources of leverage or benefit for your clients.

As Ms. A's lawyer, for example, you might proceed to map the housing system as follows:

(1) *Setting Boundaries*—The need here is to identify the formal organizations, relationships and lines of communication and authority that make up this system. There will be no hard, formal limits; you will have to set them. Our own approach to any new area is to start with a broader, more inclusive definition and narrow the focus later. In the housing system, for example, you might begin by pursuing the following sources of general information: (i) publications of lobbies and interest groups, (*e. g.*, National Association of Home Builders, National Tenants' Organization, the National Association of Housing and Renewal Officials); (ii) market analyses, trade association reports, census data, government statistics; (iii) texts on planning and housing problems; (iv) design, planning, and urban studies libraries; and (v) financial and real estate pages of local, metropolitan and national newspapers and magazines. All of these

would be potential sources of information about the larger housing system.

(2) *Focusing on Subsystems*—As the reading suggests, government and its organizations and processes enter into many of the systems in which lawyers and their clients are involved. Therefore, an initial division into public and private subsystems makes sense and permits analysis of the interdependence between the two.

Public subsystems in the housing field would include housing and building code enforcement agencies, redevelopment and housing authorities, tax assessors' offices, zoning boards, rent control agencies, and state and federal regulatory departments (*e. g.*, the Department of Housing and Urban Development). For each agency, you would want to know the organization's formal structure; its statutory or regulatory powers; its budget, staff size, and policymaking or enforcement responsibilities and procedures; the formal lines of communication and authority within the organization. Over time, you might begin to identify job structures and career lines (entry routes, salary levels, civil service coverage, promotion policies and practices), be able to chart informal lines of authority and communication, and describe the patterns and practices by which the agency "really" conducts its everyday business.

Sources of such information include official reports, documents, and statistical summaries; systematic observation and recording of data and impressions, interviews (lunch or a friendly cup of coffee) with those who know the organization; internal organization and policy manuals; books and magazine articles; academics and professionals who have expertise in the areas the agency deals with.

Private subsystems such as trade associations, banks, unions, good government groups, tenant organizations, neighborhood improvement associations, business entities (partnerships, trusts, corporations) would be similarly mapped, though in the private sphere economic circumstances would be more pertinent. This information is less likely to be available in the private sphere, but possible sources would include: public relations material such as newsletters and annual reports; statistical data that is required to be kept or filed; reports to regulatory agencies or commissions; formal discovery in law suits; registries of deeds and tax assessors' lists. Personal contact and interviews with those who know the market are apt to be more important here than with public subsystems.

(3) *Charting Relationships and Processes*—The problem here is to link the components and subsystems you have identified in ways which capture how the system actually works. This

involves identifying—in much the same way as is described in the main reading—lines of interaction and interchange with respect to particular problems.[16]

All of this may leave you somewhat overwhelmed. What we seem to be suggesting is that to practice law well you need the knowledge and skills of an accountant, statistician, economist, social psychologist, management consultant, investigative reporter and research librarian. If you modify the statement to read "some" of those skills you would be correct. A successful lawyer tends to work on every case with a large reservoir of case-relevant information.

The question is how to go about obtaining and ordering such encyclopedic knowledge. A common solution in law practice, as in other areas of human endeavor, is specialization. To some extent, this is necessary and useful, but there are limits on both the possibility and desirability of intense specialization. The problems that clients bring to lawyers don't always fit into neat slots, and aspects of almost any problem may be missed by a lawyer who has extremely narrow, though detailed, knowledge. Moreover, the nature of law practice makes it difficult for highly specialized lawyers to exchange information, even when they realize that they lack expertise in an area which may be peripheral to their own experience but related to their client's problem.

A second approach is to make the collection and organization of information a collaborative task. Clinical programs (or the offices in which they function), for example, could (i) keep files or notebooks on individual landlords, social workers, retailers, and employers in order to pick up patterns and practices as well as major offenders; (ii) assign individual attorneys to monitor agencies with recurrent involvement in particular problems (*e. g.*, agencies charged with housing code enforcement or rent control) and report back to the group; (iii) encourage individual lawyers to get to know clerks, secretaries and line people who have regular access to system information; (iv) assign individuals as "readers and reporters" to periodicals and other information sources; (v) begin plotting on area maps sections with a high incidence of school suspensions, housing code violations, etc. As information is collected, more complicated arrangements can be tried out. But the most practical strategy is to gather systemic information incrementally.

---

16. Some lawyers actually set out this sort of information in written form. All of this information could be presented in a narrative report. In addition, charts, graphs and diagrams are used to show relationships and processes. For example, one could indicate the incidence of serious housing code or lead paint violations in a community on an ordinary map of the city. This could be compared to another map that showed geographic areas from which complaints are most likely to originate, and a third that charted the areas where code enforcement efforts were concentrated. The gaps disclosed by such comparisons could become windows on patterns and practices in the larger housing system.

Even if the office in which you eventually find yourself has both specialists and a good information system, you may still rightly feel that you have a tremendous amount to learn before you can represent your clients adequately. It will be necessary, for a while (and perhaps throughout your career), to approach each case not only in terms of what is required to handle it, but with an eye to what you can learn from it. It is no disservice to your clients (though the problem should at least be raised with them) to recognize that your knowledge and skill must be built, and extra time may be required for research and planning in the early stages of your career. If you take advantage of the opportunities that present themselves—*e. g.*, if you browse in the library, ask those with experience, keep notebooks, seek out cases in new areas, review your own work, catalogue memos and letters— you will be surprised at how fast this knowledge and experience accumulates.

B. INQUIRY: BUILDING THE CASE

We turn now to the more specific tasks involved in carrying out an overall investigative plan: convincing a hostile witness to talk with you; looking for authority to support your interpretation of a rule; determining how to get quick access to a document; taking a deposition.

In these discrete tasks, just as in your overall discovery plan, your choices and actions will be guided by: (i) the client's situation and purposes; (ii) the uncontroverted facts of the case; and (iii) the rules and institutional practices which will circumscribe what you can and cannot do. At some point each of these become "givens"—unalterable elements of the case that must be incorporated into any plan you evolve.

This chapter addresses only indirectly the problems and skills involved in understanding and identifying your client's situation, needs and goals. We will deal here with the constraints within which the case is built. The first section discusses establishing the relatively unchangeable factual and legal material relevant to the case. This essentially involves locating, obtaining, and interpreting a variety of pieces of evidence. The second section discusses shaping the somewhat more malleable testimonial aspects of the case—a process that requires difficult issues not only of how but within what limits a lawyer can or should take advantage of the lapses, vulnerabilities, or idiosyncracies of others.

1. Getting All the Pieces: The Hard Data

KEETON, TRIAL TACTICS AND METHODS

303–05, 307–09, 311–17 (2d ed. 1973).

Preparation for trial is never finished until the trial is over. Even then preparation for the prospect of a new trial may be indicated. The time in the courtroom is only a part of the time that, as a careful and thorough lawyer, you must devote to a case during the days it is on trial; you must give attention to such matters of preparation as conferring with witnesses and considering the legal and factual aspects of developments that vary from those you anticipated in your advance preparation. During the period before trial, adequate preparation will require your periodic attention to a case despite your most thorough investigation of facts and law immediately after the case reaches you. Circumstances bearing on the case are changing as the date of trial approaches. In many cases damages will depend partly upon developments during this period. Issues of liability may be directly affected by changing circumstances—for example, by developments supporting waiver or estoppel. Still more important in the average case is the indirect effect that developments during pendency of the case may have upon the availability and the attitudes of witnesses.

* * *

Investigation of Law

The primary and most obvious aim of your investigation of law is to ascertain the substantive rules that will govern your case, or the competing rules that might be asserted by each party if there is doubt about the rule applicable to some phase of the case. Your study of the rules and the authorities available to support your adversary's interests is as important to your preparation as your study of those supporting the interests of your own client. This is true not only because of the necessity of advising your client concerning the question whether he should compromise or litigate the case but also with respect to advocacy during the trial. Urging wholly untenable propositions interfers with your advocacy of those more tenable; your more tenable propositions lose emphasis in the mass, and the judge who has found you wrong in one contention may be inclined against you on another when there is doubt. You therefore need to test each of your legal theories by constructing the best arguments you can against it, and comparing them with the arguments that you would use to support it. If, in doing so, you find that the theory that you were considering is plainly insupportable, abandon it for the sake of improving your chances of success on those with a better basis. As to those theories that you retain for use, your anticipation of the response of your adversary and your planning for meeting that response will obviously improve the effectiveness of your advocacy during the trial.

Your study of the substantive rules applicable to your case should culminate in an outline of the facts required for establishing each legal theory upon which either you or your adversary may rely. This outline is a guide for developing the evidence, and it should note any law that you must prove or of which you must ask the court to take judicial notice, typical examples being foreign law and municipal ordinances. Your outline will be useful to you throughout the litigation— in preparing your pleadings, your statements or arguments to the jury, your plan of evidence, your requests and objections to the charge, your motions during trial and after verdict, and your briefs and arguments in the higher court if either party appeals. With extensive experience in a particular type of litigation, this outline may become so well known to you that you no longer need to put it in written form for each new case. Even the experienced lawyer uses at least a mental check list, however, to avoid oversights.

* * *

Priorities in Early Preparations

Should you give priority to fact investigation or to law investigation in your early preparations?

Unless you have had much experience with other cases of the same type, and often even then, your initial interview with your client about the facts of his case will raise in your mind some questions of law to which you do not know the answers. Frequently the answers to those questions will determine the scope and nature of the fact investigation needed. If you proceed with the fact investigation first, you may find that in part your efforts have been in vain, because the matters investigated prove to be immaterial when the answers to the questions of law are known. This factor indicates that solution of the questions of law before undertaking detailed fact investigation is preferable.

On the other hand, as you proceed with the fact investigation new fact disclosures may make some of your thoroughly investigated legal theories immaterial and may suggest new legal theories that might be asserted either by you or your adversary. These new possibilities in legal theories may also require further study of the law and may suggest new subjects for both legal and factual investigation.

Your two investigations—on the law and on the facts—should proceed simultaneously, the scope of each being influenced by the results of the other. Should either receive priority?

If it were possible to anticipate all of the avenues of fact inquiry needed to support any legal theory you might later assert, or to meet any legal theory that your adversary might later assert, then clearly you should give priority to the fact investigation because of the advantages of completing this investigation while facts are fresh in the minds of witnesses, before the influences of time and discussion have affected their views of the facts, and before your adversary has interviewed them. Truth may be eternal, and facts may not change, but facts do not prove themselves, and factfindings must be made by people with human failings. Furthermore, unlike judges who are expected to investigate the law independently and may reach quite proper conclusions without the aid and even despite the obstructions of counsel, jurors are forbidden to make independent investigation of the facts; it is almost certain that they will fail in their job of making findings that conform to actual facts if those facts have not been discovered and proved by one of the lawyers. In most cases, facts are more easily discovered when they are fresh. This is true not only because witnesses remember more but also because their memory is less confused by reflection. The ideas of the most conscientious witness will undergo some modification as he thinks about and discusses the facts of the case with others. The observations and attitudes of others influence his. He is more than human if his own desire or conviction that one party should prevail in the controversy fails to influence his views as to the facts of the case, and to greater and greater extent as time dims his memory of those facts. Your problem of discovering the facts is less difficult if you see the witnesses early. Furthermore, if your adversary has interviewed them first, you face the added difficulty of the influence of that interview and the priority in time of any statements taken from the witnesses in the earlier interviews. The period of early investigation is a crucial point in the tactical development of litigation.

There are disadvantages to giving priority to fact investigation. It is impossible to anticipate all the legal points that may affect the scope and importance of investigating certain aspects of the facts. You must also take account of limitations of time. Trial practice, though it requires some of the greatest skills, is not the most lucrative law practice. One reason this is true is that it is so time-consuming. Perhaps you will wish to believe that every case you handle demands your best in time and energy; you may be advised that you should not take a case unless you can give it your best. Unless we say that "your best" is qualified by an implied condition—"the best that you can reasonably do under the circumstances"—the advice is visionary. Rarely is a trial lawyer able to devote enough time to preparation of a case that he will feel that there is nothing more that he would do if he had the time. Furthermore, thorough investigation often involves the use of services of others, and incurring expenses that must be borne eventually by the client; the feasibility of incurring expenses will depend on the amount involved in the case and the materiality and probable success of the investigative efforts. In view of these considerations, it becomes important to avoid wasteful investigation of facts that will not possibly be relevant under the theories of law applicable to the case.

* * *

Methods and Leads for Fact Investigation

.   .   .   In your interviews with your client and with each other witness, you should be as much concerned with obtaining information regarding leads to other sources of admissible evidence as with obtaining information on the admissible evidence that the persons you are interviewing can furnish. You will see some persons with the sole aim of finding leads to admissible evidence. Experienced investigators have developed a number of standard methods of locating witnesses, because experience has indicated that they are most likely to be productive. You should treat the methods referred to below as merely suggestive, however. In any individual case, you should seek other sources of information as well; use your imagination to reconstruct the circumstances of any incident that bears on your case, and use your knowledge of people and their habits to guess what persons were there to observe and how they can be found, or who might possess some documentary or real evidence that would be material. This imaginative approach has been responsible for development of many of the standard methods in the list that follows.

(1) Encourage everyone you interview to tell you all he has heard about the case or about any incident or circumstance material to the case. Hearsay is a most productive source of leads, though a hearsay statement may itself be quite inaccurate. Not infrequently you will find that a witness with only hearsay information is more willing to volunteer it than the person who has personal knowledge and fears that he will be called to testify.

(2) Leave your card with each person whom you interview and ask him to call you if he thinks of anything else about the circumstances that he omitted mentioning, or if he hears something new.

(3) Search for and develop demonstrative and documentary evidence.

(4) When you are representing a claimant, give special attention to identifying all potential defendants, so that your choice as to which one or more you shall sue will be the best. If a vehicle is involved, you should check public records as to registration and ownership of the vehicle, with a view toward discovering any relationship of the driver to another legally responsible party. Also, consider the possibility that the driver was engaged in employment as a servant of another, even though using his own car. Known presence in the vehicle of tools used in his emplyment may lead to such disclosures. If a business entity is involved, give careful attention to correct identification of that entity. Sometimes closely associated business enterprises may be operating under the same or related management but under

arrangements such that suit against the wrong one would be fatally defective. Information on corporations is available from the office of a state official; you should ascertain whether the corporation is a local or foreign one, and if foreign, whether licensed to do business in the state. Information on the identity of service agents designated by foreign corporations is also available from the office of a state official. Most jurisdictions provide for some statutory form of registration of assumed names, at least in the case of noncorporate enterprises not registered with the public official keeping records of all corporate licenses to do business in the state. Other sources of information are public utility records and telephone and city directories; information obtained from these sources may be incomplete or inaccurate from the point of view of correct identification of the legal entity involved, and you should always check it against other sources of information. Both for this reason and also as an additional source of information, you should consider using discovery processes either before or after instituting suit; this is usually the surest way of ascertaining whether your original information from other sources is complete and accurate. Some particularly dangerous pitfalls to be avoided are the possibility that there are two separate entities of the same name or very similar names, that a change of entities by incorporation or dissolution may have occurred after the date of an incident on which suit is based, or that a vehicle or other machinery involved in an accident may have been owned by one but leased to another either with or without a "loaned servant."

(5) Consider the financial responsibility of the potential defendants. A perfect case of liability may be practically worthless because of your inability to collect a judgment from the defendant. This is especially true in states with liberal exemption statutes as to property subject to levy of execution. In most states financial responsibility laws afford both protection and a source of information regarding insurance coverage or other financial responsibility of defendants in suits based upon operation of motor vehicles. Other sources of relevant information in any case are public records regarding ownership of realty, personal property subject to *ad valorem* taxation, and motor vehicles, and concerning interests in corporate and other enterprises subject to public control. Often credit reports can be obtained from various credit agencies, disclosing relevant information on financial responsibility. Such a report is frequently not exhaustive, however, and you should use it as an aid to determining financial responsibility rather than as a final determination.

(6) Consider official files that may provide information relating to some phase of your case. State, federal and local governments maintain a variety of official files that may prove to be sources of useful information not only in the typical negligence case based on an automobile collision but also in many other types of cases.

(7) Personally observe as many as possible of the physical objects and scenes that are material to the case. In an accident case, for example, go to the scene of the accident yourself and study it thoroughly. This study not only increases your own understanding of the facts of the case but also may provide you with new ideas and leads for investigation.

(8) If your client or his adversary has employed other persons who may have had some association with circumstances relevant to the case, consider in particular former employees of both parties, since they may be inclined to speak more freely and more critically of the former employer than others would.

(9) If you are defending a personal injury claim, consider using the records of claim index bureaus that will usually be accessible to you and may help you acquire information about previous claims and previous medical history. Since most personal injury claims that reach litigation involve liability insurance, information from index bureaus will be available through the insurance company and usually will have been obtained in the course of investigation before the matter is turned over to you. To a more limited extent, information about previous claims and medical history can be obtained from official files of bodies administering workmen's compensation and from court records, military service and Veteran's Administration files, hospital records, and records of drug prescriptions. Some of these sources are accessible only with the claimant's consent.

(10) Consider court records as a source of information concerning a party or witness to the suit. Convictions of a party or witness may be admissible for impeachment. Records of previous civil litigation may also disclose useful information.

(11) Consider potential sources of scientific evidence material to issues in your case. Following are illustrations of types of issues as to which scientific evidence has sometimes figured prominently: nature, extent, and cause of personal injuries (medical); location of properties (surveying); authenticity of photographs and freedom from distortion and touching; identification or association of a defendant with incidents on which suit is based (laboratory examination of paint marks, clothing fragments, etc., in a hit-and-run driver case, gunpowder tests, fingerprints, blood tests); veracity ("lie detector" tests); intoxication (breath and blood tests); presence of poisons in foods (chemical analysis); existence of defects in machinery or other products (defective metals causing critical failure of automobile part, defective glass causing "exploding" beverage bottle); means of contact with sources of electricity (laws of physics as to "arcing" of current without contact); manufacturing methods (effectiveness of non-human "inspection" devices). This list is merely suggestive. As scientific advances are made, additional opportunities for effective use of scientific evidence will arise. Obviously, you cannot become

familiar with all the scientific fields potentially involved in cases that you may handle, though your preparations are simplified as your knowledge of the sciences increases. Since you will be an amateur in a foreign field, however, you will need the guidance of an expert within the field. You may find it helpful to make use of a good public library as a starting point to get ideas as to sources of available evidence when you recognize the possibility of using scientific evidence in a case, but you cannot rely on that method as an accurate way of determining whether scientific evidence can be useful in the case. The better method is to seek out the experts for consultation and advice, as well as for potential witnesses. If you are uncertain about the stage of development of a science that might be relevant to some issue in your case, frequently the most expeditious approach to the problem is through consultation with scientists in educational institutions.

The following additional suggestions relate particularly to cases based upon an accident:

(12) Check for wrecker drivers, ambulance drivers, and news reporters who may have been at the scene.

(13) Check police records.

(14) Examine all photographs taken at the scene of an accident for the purpose of identifying persons who appear in them so that you may interview them if you have not already done so.

(15) Canvass the neighborhood of the scene of an accident to find persons who may have seen it, and those who went to the scene afterwards and may provide useful information on physical circumstances and on conversations by the parties (perhaps including some admissible declarations), and also information on identity of persons who saw the accident.

(16) Go to the scene of the accident on some succeeding day, at the same hour that the accident occurred and observe passing traffic with the purpose of discovering the identity of persons who customarily pass at that hour of the day and may have observed the accident or may have come upon the scene immediately afterwards. This method is sometimes useful also in identifying the driver and passengers in a vehicle referred to by other witnesses but not identified by them.

Types of Demonstrative Evidence

The available types of demonstrative evidence vary greatly with the type of case as well as the peculiar facts of the individual case. The following is a suggestive list, intended as a point of beginning in considering kinds of evidence to look for and develop. You should also consider the admissibility of the contemplated evidence in the jurisdiction of trial; some of the types of evidence listed below are held inadmissible in particular instances because of concern that their use may distract the minds of jurors from fair consideration of the issues before them.

This list includes not only matters described by the term "real evidence," but also such things as documents and photographs, since they may be offered as exhibits and have the characteristic of independence from some of the human errors affecting testimony. This is one of the characteristics making demonstrative evidence particularly persuasive.

(1) Documents—letters, statements, contracts, telegrams, former pleadings in this or other lawsuits, transcripts of evidence in previous proceedings, accounts, sales slips, orders, and other business records. You should consider the possible sources of evidence of this character carefully, both from the point of view of finding evidence useful to your own case (for example, in the form of admissions of the adversary) and also from the point of view of ascertaining what evidence of this character may be available to strengthen your adversary's case or weaken that of your client. If your case involves correspondence between the parties, examine all of the correspondence for items that you may use and for items that your adversary may use against you. In searching for documents possibly useful in cross-examination of a witness or party, consider not only documents signed by him but also those that he has adopted by reference or approved orally or by separate writing. Your preparations for use of documentary evidence should include attention to the means of authenticating the evidence when you use it (by pretrial stipulation, or admissions concerning authenticating facts, or developing evidence necessary to establish them).

(2) Physical evidence of identity of an actor or a weapon used in a relevant event—fingerprints, footprints, blood tests, powder burns, photographs, bloodstains, false teeth, personal effects, jewelry, laboratory tests of clothing, hair, blood, etc.

(3) Evidence of physical surroundings of the scene of an event—photographs (including aerial photographs, color photographs), maps, charts, models, diagrams. You may increase the effectiveness of models and maps by asking the witness to use some special devices in explaining his testimony—*e. g.*, colored pins to indicate the positions of the witness, other persons, and objects not on the map, and scale model objects such as cars involved in a collision, to clarify and illustrate the witness' testimony.

(4) Evidence of physical condition and personal injuries—X-rays, photographs, moving pictures, exhibition of an injured member, manipulation of an injured member, series photographs (showing changes of condition over a course of time, and perhaps taken in color in the case of burns or other skin conditions more accurately shown by color films), laboratory tests of the medical practice (blood, urine, stomach contents, stools, electrocardiograms, electroencephalograms,

myelograms, spinal fluid tests, etc.). Witnesses may use models effectively to explain their testimony; a medical witness might use a skeleton, for example, in a case involving bone injury or a plastic model of the heart, brain, kidney, or other organs, when injury to one of them is involved.

(5) Evidence of the manner in which an accident occurred—small objects involved in the accident (a carpet on which plaintiff alleges he slipped; a waxing machine and the wax used on a floor; a handcar that struck the plaintiff; a piece of metal that was driven into his body; a shoe that was worn as the plaintiff was dragged for a distance with the shoe scraping); diagrams drawn by the witness as he tells his story (either drawn on a blackboard, which will not be introduced in evidence as an exhibit, or on a paper, which may be introduced in evidence and carried to the jury room).

(6) Other possibilities—The possibilities for demonstrative evidence are almost unlimited. In many instances, it will be possible to conduct an actual experiment in the courtroom. Bottling companies frequently present an experiment, for example, in cases involving a claim of explosion of the bottle from excessive internal pressure. Bottles are taken from the production line of the defendant bottler and subjected, in the courtroom, with specially designed equipment, to tests of internal pressure and breaking pressure of the bottles, with the purpose of demonstrating a large safety margin. Another type of experiment that is occasionally used is the "lie detector." In an appropriate case, a bold lawyer with absolute faith in his client and in the expert tester might challenge the opponent to submission to lie detector tests, with notice that he will undertake to prove the request and refusal if the adversary declines.

SHADOAN (ed.), LAW AND TACTICS IN FEDERAL CRIMINAL CASES

1–9, 16–18, 21 (1964).

STANDARD STEPS IN INVESTIGATING ANY CRIMINAL CASE

There are certain standard steps and principles of investigation appropriate to every criminal case regardless of court or jurisdiction. It would be beneficial to provide to attorneys in every federal district the particulars of how and where they can most effectively gather the facts of their case. However, as it is impossible to present this detailed information for every district, and rather than confine this section to simply stating a few broad general principles, the section presents in considerable detail a recommended procedure for investigating a case in the District of Columbia. While titles and numbers may vary from district to district, similar sources of information are available in every district. The step-by-step procedure outlined provides a guide for the inexperienced attorney and a useful check-list for the experienced attorney.

A. Inspect the File of the Case

Inspect the file of the case (criminal jacket) in the criminal clerk's office in the United States Courthouse. The file is obtainable by giving the clerk the defendant's name and case number. In the criminal jacket the following documents may be found: the indictment, a felony complaint or United States Commissioner's notes and the pauper's affidavit. Often there are other papers relating to the case. If the defendant was taken before a Court of General Sessions judge for a preliminary hearing, a felony complaint should be in the jacket. On the other hand, if the defendant was taken before a United States Commissioner for a preliminary hearing, the commissioner's notes should be in the criminal jacket. Either of these documents will disclose the names and addresses of some prosecution witnesses. Also the documents will give the names of the arresting officers and usually the attorney who represented the defendant at the preliminary hearing. The alleged offense will be described with more particularity than in the indictment. For instance, in an unauthorized use of a vehicle case, the complaint or notes will describe the make and model of the car and from what location in Washington the car was taken.

B. Inspect the Search Warrant

Inspect the search warrant (if any), the affidavit in support thereof, and the marshal's return and inventory. In most cases this information can be found in the defendant's criminal jacket provided the search warrant was issued by the District Court or the United States Commissioner. . . .

C. Inspect the Arrest Warrant

Inspect the arrest warrant (if any), the affidavit in support thereof, and the United States Marshal's or police officer's return. If the warrant was issued by the United States Commissioner, these papers may be found both in the defendant's criminal jacket and in the commissioner's Record of Proceedings.

*   *   *

Inspection of the warrant will reveal the name of the complainant, date of the offense, nature of the offense, and date of issuance of the warrant. Inspection of the affidavit will add the date when application was made for the issuance of the warrant.

This "Application for Warrant" contains a much more detailed description of the offense, as told by the complainant and sworn to before an Assistant United States Attorney. . . .

D. Inspect the Criminal Conviction Record of Government Witnesses

Inspect the criminal conviction record of the government witnesses whose names have been obtained from the criminal jacket.
. . . A certified copy of these convictions can be obtained free of charge and are admissible into evidence.

E. Obtain Copy of the Defendant's Criminal Conviction Record

Obtain a copy of the defendant's criminal record in Room 4080 (Criminal Records) of the Municipal Building. A short form must be filled out to obtain a photostatic copy of the arrest record. There is no charge for the arrest record of a defendant represented by a court-appointed attorney.

F. Inspect Various Police Forms

Inspect the various police forms which have been made out by the arresting officers. . . . These forms may include the following: . . .

. . . a complaint form used for reporting and recording all complaints received by the Metropolitan Police. A copy of this form is also filed at the precinct where the complaint is registered. . . . an offense report. This form is used for reporting crimes and offenses, and it contains complete information about the alleged crime.

. . . a statement of alleged facts which is given to the prosecutor by the reporting officer. Stated on the form is the requirement that the statement of facts "will include any statement made by defendant." Hence, any oral admissions to the police should be included in this form.

G. Interview the Arresting Officers

Interview the arresting officers, the names of whom have been obtained from the criminal jacket. If the officers are members of a specialized squad such as Robbery, Narcotics, Homicide, Sex, etc., they may be located in the squad's office in the Municipal Building. If they are precinct officers they must be located at their respective precinct; the number of which is obtained from the criminal jacket. Precinct officers are most easily contacted when the shift changes at 7:30 A.M., 3:30 P.M. and 11:30 P.M.

H. Interview the Lawyer Who Represented Defendant at Preliminary Hearing

Interview the lawyer who represented the defendant at the preliminary hearing, the name of whom is obtained from the criminal jacket. . . . Some pertinent information may be found in the notes or memory of counsel. Inquiry should be made as to whether a court reporter was present at the hearing.

I. Interview the Assistant United States Attorney Assigned to the Case

Interview the Assistant United States Attorney assigned to prosecute the case. His name will also be found in the criminal jacket or can be obtained by calling the United States Attorney's Office. Such an interview can be mutually advantageous if the prosecutor discloses sufficient information to enable defense counsel to accurately evaluate the desirability of a disposition of the case in advance of trial.

J. Interview the Defendant

After completely covering the preceding nine steps, it is now time for the initial interview with the defendant. Careful investigation before this interview will enable counsel to secure a more complete and accurate story from the defendant.

* * *

The following is a checklist of standard questions to ask a defendant on an initial interview:

(1) *Story.* Name and address; date of birth; place of birth; innocent or guilty; complete narrative of events on the date of the alleged crime; prospective witnesses, and their names, addresses, phones, places they might frequent; employers, relatives, and friends.

(2) *Arrest and Search.* Time; place; people present; activity of defendant at time of arrest; warrant for arrest; resistance (did defendant give police any trouble); sobriety of defendant; property seized from defendant's person; place taken after arrested, which precinct, where booked; conversation (if any) between police officers and defendant or anyone else present at time of arrest; police brutality; name of informer (if any).

(3) *Statement To The Police.* Time arrested; where taken; time of preliminary hearing; who talked to defendant; police coercion; lies, promises, threats made by police to defendant; what defendant told the police and when; whether statement written or oral.

(4) *Insanity.* Prior mental history of defendant or close relatives; auditory or visual hallucinations; drug addiction, average dosage per day, length of time on narcotics, type of narcotics used, *e. g.*, heroin, marijuana, barbiturates; vague recollection of events or no recollection at all; irresistible impulse to commit crime; subnormal mentality—unable to communicate, name three presidents, or do simple mathematics; bizarre type of crime; out of contact with reality; unusual distrust of everyone; inappropriate emotional reaction; type of military discharge, if any; schools attended.

K. Conduct Street Investigation

The eleventh and final step consists of street investigation, which is the most tedious and time-consuming of all the steps in investigation. By now the lawyer should have the names of various witnesses, both government and defense. Both types of witnesses should be extensively interviewed. Quite often, however, real difficulty is encountered in locating key witnesses. Often all one has to go on is a nickname such as "Jabbo" or "Malachi Jet." The following is a checklist on the information needed in tracing a witness:

(1) full name, alias, nickname; (2) address (last known) and phone; (3) physical description; (4) associates—past and present, including girl and boy friends; (5) places he is known to frequent; (6) employers; (7) fraternal lodge; and (8) union.

The witness' whereabouts might be found by checking the Veteran's Administration, phone company, electric company, Department of Public Welfare, city directory, probation officer, voting registers or tax assessment lists. The post office might be checked for changes of address.

Many witnesses interviewed by defense counsel will be from the lower economic group, many of whom instinctively distrust any stranger. Consequently, it is extremely important for counsel attempting to locate a defense witness to properly identify himself as the lawyer for Mr. X and state that he is not a police officer or a bill collector. Also it is important to have someone with counsel for protection.

When interviewing government witnesses, follow the same procedure of identification—but in addition have someone present who will be able to testify in the event of later inconsistent statements, statements indicating bias against the defendant, etc. A personal interview with a witness is preferable to a phone conversation because counsel can assess the demeanor of the witness. However, if counsel telephones a government witness, it is advisable to have someone listening on an extension to protect against subsequent accusations of bribery or threats. Counsel may indicate that Mr. X is working on the case and is listening to the conversation.

After talking to a witness in person for some time, tell him that some notes will be necessary. Then a written statement should be obtained. Counsel may either write questions and fill in answers to each question—or he may write a short narrative. If the witness says he knows nothing, make out a statement to that effect. Then have the witness read the statement and make any corrections. Counsel should make a few deliberate errors so that the witness will make corrections in his own handwriting. Also have him initial each correction and mark "O.K." on each page of the statement. Have him sign the statement or at least initial it.

To obtain additional witnesses and information, it is necessary to canvass the scene of the alleged crime. Interview drugstore clerks, grocery store clerks and managers and other shop keepers and neighbors. . . .

*   *   *

CHECKLIST FOR INVESTIGATING VARIOUS DEFENSES

A. Alibi and Mistaken Identification

The defense of alibi carries with it the corollary defense of mistaken identification. According to careful studies made in the field, the most frequent cause for the conviction of innocent people is mistaken identification. Consequently, the defense attorney should be extremely cautious about eyewitness testimony.

(1) *Prior Acquaintance of Witness and Defendants.*

(2) *Opportunity to Observe.* Length of time, lighting conditions, place, obstructions to vision, distance from defendant.

(3) *Event Anticipated or Unexpected.*

(4) *Condition of Witness at Time of Event.* Intoxicated, drugged, tired, headache, fever, ill, frightened, preoccupied with other thoughts.

(5) *Vision and Hearing of Witness.* Wear glasses or hearing aid; glasses or hearing aid knocked off during crime.

(6) *Conversation between Witness and Police Pre-Identification.* The witness may have been intentionally or inadvertently coached.

(7) *Conversation between Witness and Other Eyewitnesses Pre-Identification.*

(8) *Place of Identification.* In a police line-up with other men of similar build and color; on the street or in an office with no other suspect but the defendant.

(9) *Number of line-ups.* Immediate identification, hesitation, identified another man before identifying defendant.

(10) *Police Photos.* Witness shown pictures of various suspects in area, number of pictures, similarity to defendant, lack of coaching.

(11) *Description of Clothing Worn by Criminal at Time of Crime.*

(12) *Distinctive Physical Characteristics of Criminal.*

(13) *Mental Stability of Witness.* Past or present mental patient, tendency to have hallucinations or to fictionalize incidents.

(14) *Official Time, Date, and Place of Crime.*

(15) *Location of Alibi in Relation to Place of Crime.* Travel time, walking, or driving.

(16) *Point of Time Reference.* How do the alibi witnesses know that they were with the defendant at a particular time and place? A particular television program may have been playing at the time when the alibi witness and defendant were watching. The day in question may have been a holiday or someone's birthday.

(17) *Independent Facts Corroborating the Alibi.* Television guide, train or airplane schedules, and newspapers may corroborate facts in the alibi.

The police keep records of line-ups at each precinct, and sometimes make photographs. These records may yield the time, participants, and identification or lack thereof. These records would have to be subpoenaed.

B. Self Defense

(1) *Type of Weapon Used.* Defendant, complaining witness, or deceased.

(2) *Relative Size, Age, and Physical Condition of Parties.*

(3) *Injuries and Treatment of Parties.* The defendant may have been taken by ambulance to D.C. General Hospital. In that case counsel will want to look at the ambulance log and interview the ambulance drivers. To accomplish this one must obtain special permission from the Fire Marshall's Office in the Old District Building by filing an official request form. The written request must be cleared by the Corporation Counsel's Office.

Counsel will also want to look at the defendant's hospital records at D.C. General Hospital. He will expedite matters by obtaining an authorization from the defendant at the initial interview to examine such records. If the hospital will not allow examination of the records, it is necessary to obtain a court order directing the hospital authorities to allow examination of the defendant's records.

If the defendant was not injured seriously he may have been treated in the D.C. Jail dispensary. Records are kept of the treatment given to each inmate. The jail officials are reluctant to disclose the name of the physician or dentist who treated the defendant; but they may do so if confronted with the possibility of a subpoena for the records. Counsel should contact the D.C. Jail classification office about these matters.

Sometimes the police take pictures of the man booked to protect themselves against charges of police brutality. However, these pictures must be subpoenaed. Obviously, they may show that the defendant was badly injured when arrested.

(4) *Opportunity to Retreat.*

(5) *Position of Parties at Time Witness Was Struck.*

(6) *Excessive Force.*

(7) *Determination of Primary Aggressor.*

(8) *Reputation of Complaining Witness for Violence.*

* * *

GENERAL SOURCES OF INFORMATION

A. Accident Reports

One may obtain a copy of the accident report made by the investigating officers from the Accident Investigation Unit . . . of the Municipal Building. This report will contain the following information: a sketch of the accident scene with the position of the cars at the moment of impact, the driver of each car, his address, and a general description of the accident. It would be well to consult the investigating officer for details.

B. Maps

It is often useful to produce a map of the scene of the crime. The Surveyor's Office in the Old District Building will supply maps of city blocks for a very nominal sum. This office also has area maps covering a wider territory of the city.

C. Weather Reports

The Weather Bureau at the Washington National Airport will supply certified copy of the report of weather readings of any particular day. These reports contain the temperature, the precipitation, the wind velocity, and the cloud formations at almost every hour of the day and night.

NOTES

1. *On the Importance of "Getting the Givens"*

Both of the foregoing selections can be seen as an application of the ways of developing lines of inquiry we outlined in the last section. But such catalogues can also be understood as a specification of those aspects of a case that both sides *must* account for in their theory of the case. They are common ground between opposing parties.

The most obvious of this type of material is the documentary and physical evidence which Keeton and Shadoan describe. Both parties will have to incorporate such evidence into their positions or find a basis for arguing that it is irrelevant or inconsequential. An investigation that misses such material will significantly alter subsequent aspects of the case.[16] Moreover, because these elements are relatively unalterable—*i. e.*, given—they are also the centerpieces of most negotiating and trial strategy. It is obviously easier to show that a

---

16. In the cross-examination that exposed Oscar Wilde's homosexual relationships (and led to his imprisonment at the height of his literary career), Wilde was confronted with letter after letter which he could not effectively explain away. One wonders what the trial would have looked like (or whether it would have taken place) if his representatives had obtained this material before trial.

contract on its face violates the state truth-in-lending law than to prove that your client's version of a conversation is more credible than the salesman's.[17]

Indeed, the presence or absence of this sort of data affects every aspect of the way a case is handled. The questions you ask a prospective witness or the posture you adopt across a bargaining table depend on an operative version of what happened. This version must be tentatively crystallized before you actually interact with witnesses and adversaries. Imagine representing a client who is suing for medical malpractice, who does not recall signing the required consent form and believes she did not consent. You can plead alternatively (on information and belief) that no consent was obtained or that it was not intelligently given. But it is difficult to bargain, prepare, or investigate with such a basic question unresolved. Witnesses will only give you limited amounts of time, and experts feel more comfortable when they are not dealing with alternative versions of underlying circumstances. In addition, your own witnesses and your client tend to fill in details on the basis of assumptions about things that they can't entirely know or remember. If their assumptions are in error, their credibility and confidence are consequently undermined.

Perhaps this is an overly elaborate way of emphasizing that such evidence as documents, the main outline of events, and the existence of witnesses must be ascertained very early in an investigation. But recognizing this imperative is critical to any adequate investigative plan. A negotiating or investigatory posture is almost always more effective if it relies on what can't be controverted and can take into account opposing views of what the case involves.

———

2. *On the Importance of "Knowing the Rules"*

The same reasoning is applicable to the necessity for preliminary legal research. As Robert Keeton points out, a case should not be presented in court, negotiated, or even investigated to any great extent until the lawyer has a clear idea of the applicable legal standards. The open texture of legal rules notwithstanding, most advocacy is conducted within a rule framework which sets clear limits on the theories and strategies counsel can pursue.

17. The same analysis would require developing a list of all the people who observed or might have been involved in aspects of the case. For example, in a case involving unfair and deceptive practices by a used car dealer, it is certain that employees, customers, or business associates will have knowledge of or experience with the sales practices and could say *something* about them. Whether these individuals will talk to a lawyer investigating a customer's claim of fraud, and what they will say if they do, is always unclear. However, if they represent possible sources of favorable or unfavorable testimony, it is important to discover at least who such witnesses are and how they might be located.

Our hunch is that many of you do not yet proceed in this fashion. Despite the amount of law training devoted to finding, reconciling, distinguishing and "Shepardizing" cases, very few students are comfortable with the sort of legal research and analysis that is essential to these preliminary efforts. This observation may not apply to you, but it is worthwhile to reflect on some of the possible causes of these patterns.

First, students are often trained in only one kind of legal research —the complete, painstaking analysis that is necessary in briefing an issue for an appellate court. This means that when a case comes in they either do very little research (because "there's not enough time"), or they retire to the library shortly after the client interview for days or weeks (we know of cases where research at this early stage went on for months), and return with comprehensive memos on issues that may never be pressed because the client has had to cope in other ways with his or her problem.

What are almost always needed in the early stages of a case are a series of frequent, short (20–60 minutes) visits to the library. Early in the case, for example, you should read carefully any immediately relevant statutory or regulatory material. If court-made law controls, a case not in a local law review or annual survey will tell you where your jurisdiction stands on the issue. You might even quickly read the leading or most recent cases. If your jurisdiction is unfavorable to the claim, checking the ALR or a digest will give you a sense both of how strong and how prevalent the contrary authority is.[18]

As you proceed to draft pleadings and investigate the case, a great many other issues will arise that need researching—*e. g.*, who may be sued and in what capacity; what remedies are available; what discovery rules apply to an opponent's expert witness. Several weeks or months into a case, further issues will emerge. Research thus becomes an incremental process from the initial client interview to that stage in the case at which it is most central—the appeal. Preparing for this stage occurs neither at the outset (too soon) nor at the point at which appeal is taken (too late), but in a cumulative fashion.

Second, many students do not handle statutes or regulations well, even though such material is directly relevant and often controlling in many types of law practice. Because statutes and regulations control broad classes of transactions, guide administrative choices and practice, and are more apt to be deferred to by a judge than court-made law, they must be under control at a relatively early stage.

---

18. Although most law students have had some training in legal research, it is helpful to review, from time to time, some of the practical guides that detail research methods and sources. *See, e. g.*, J. Jacobstein & R. Mersky, FUNDAMENTALS OF LEGAL RESEARCH (1977); M. Price & H. Bitner, EFFECTIVE LEGAL RESEARCH (3d ed. 1969); W. Statsky, INTRODUCTION TO PARALEGALISM (1974).

Interpreting a statute involves much more than determining whether it applies, as the following diagram indicates:

[Suppose the original statute reads as follows:]

(1t) *If* the court shall deem it necessary *or* the defendant shall so demand, the jury of twelve freeholders shall be summoned *and whenever* a jury is required such jury shall determine the sanity or insanity of the defendant.

The same set of ideas expressed in this original text can be written in the following *normalized form:*

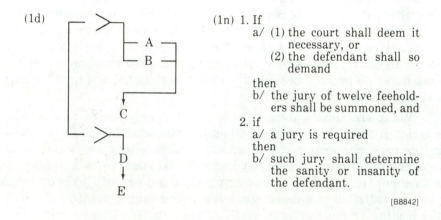

(1d)

(1n) 1. If
     a/ (1) the court shall deem it necessary, or
        (2) the defendant shall so demand
     then
     b/ the jury of twelve feeholders shall be summoned, and

2. if
     a/ a jury is required
     then
     b/ such jury shall determine the sanity or insanity of the defendant.

[B8842]

     In this version, "If," "or," "and" and "whenever" (*the syntax words of the original text*) are replaced by "If-then," "or," and "if-then" (*the syntax words of the normalized version*) and each sentence is itemized. Thus the syntactic relationships among phrases in the original text are expressed visibly and unambiguously in the normalized version (1n) and in its accompanying diagram (1d).[19]

If you are unable to parse a statute in this way—to break it down into its elements or pieces much as you would diagram a sentence—you lack an extremely important practice skill.

     Third, many students have trouble organizing large bodies of law in their heads. In practice, the law will be most usable in black letter or outline form. Written guides, desk references, and annual surveys or updates can provide useful organizational schemes that you can change or elaborate as you learn the law in each case you handle, and as you follow advance sheets and reporting services. Such habits of organization and learning will serve you well in making judgments at any stage of a given case about "what the law is."

     Fourth, students have considerable difficulty deciding when to stop researching. As a consequence, they don't develop usable re-

---

19. Allen & Ohta, *Better Organization of Legal Knowledge,* 1969 U.TOL.L. REV. 491, 492 (1969).

search skills.   In the long run, this makes them less willing and able to do relatively simple research jobs.   You might test your own skills in this area by "tracking" two or more pieces of research you have done, setting out (i) the steps you took; (ii) the references you used; and (iii) the amount of time you spent on each aspect of the process. Compare the conclusions you reached or the memos you wrote with other student's work and—if you can arrange it—with the way an experienced practitioner did the same task.   The comparison may show you strengths and weaknesses in your own approach to research, and give you a better sense of the research habits you are already beginning to form.

---

3.   *Being Creative About Information*

Both Keeton and Shadoan offer a variety of useful suggestions for developing information in a case.   Following such checklists is obviously a sensible way to expand the number and type of approaches to investigation that you consider.   What they do not discuss, however, is the importance of developing ways to obtain information about a case when the usual sources dry up.   Witnesses sometimes refuse to talk, documents may be lost, and even with the availability of sanctions formal discovery may be unproductive.   Consider the possibilities explored in the following dialogue.

> Co-counsel in a manslaughter case are faced with an early trial date and no information concerning the testimony against their client. (Formal and informal discovery efforts have already been attempted.) The first lawyer (A) suggests that they seek a continuance and then interview the arresting officer to get the names of the witnesses against their client and any leads on what the witnesses might say.   He concludes:
>
> We can follow through from there with further interviews. I'm sure the court will grant the continuance because we've only had ten days since our appointment to prepare.
>
> Beyond that, we should probably research the law on the line-up at the police station after his arrest and on his being arrested without a warrant.   On the basis of what he tells us, though, they seem to have handled the line-up properly, and we just don't have anything to go on at all on the basis for the arrest.   Not unless we get the police to talk to us in the interviews.
>
> We'll just have to wait and make any motions on these issues at trial.   If anything develops later we can always raise objections then.   And you needn't worry about losing the opportunity.   On the basis of my research, it's clear that since we didn't have sufficient information before trial to make the motions, the issues would not be considered waived.   There's a case directly on point. As I see it, that's about the best we can do at this stage.

Assume that the second lawyer (B) agrees with her partner's interpretation of the applicable law. However, she adds:

Well, as I see it, the problem is not protecting our options at trial: it's compelling disclosure of what the testimony will be against us *before* trial. I think we should get a continuance and then move to suppress the identification evidence (both the trial identifications and the police station identifications) before the new trial date on Fourth Amendment grounds. We have a colorable basis for a search and seizure motion (we know he was arrested without a warrant and he claims there was no basis to arrest him). We could subpoena all the ID material, line-up records, and police statements at that hearing as part of our claim that they are the "fruits" of the illegal seizure. This would give us a good deal of information about who said what to the police which could help us prepare for trial.

If we wanted to, we could even couple the motion with a direct challenge to the ID on Sixth Amendment and Due Process grounds to strengthen the relevance of this testimony. The client remembers the police talking to the complainant before the line-up and only four people being included in it. Even if we lost the motions (which is likely), we'd have much more impeaching material with which to confront the identification evidence at trial.

Even better, as I think about it, would be a pre-trial opportunity to cross examine the witnesses themselves. The problem is that we don't even know their names. But we could get around that as well. If we make the pre-trial motion to suppress, as I've suggested, and the names of witnesses to the killing or to the identification come out at the hearing, we could, in the course of the hearing, subpoena them to testify. Particularly if our motion is on Fourth, Fifth and Sixth Amendment grounds, the opportunities for observation at the scene and everything about what the police testify was said to them are at issue. If we're not too worried about bringing out damaging material at this stage (the case will be tried before a different judge anyway) we can virtually have pre-trial depositions of all the witnesses.

At this point, lawyer A points out that subpoenas have to be issued before their return date and, if pursued in forma pauperis, would require a showing of the materiality of the testimony being sought. He suggests that his partner's notions are unrealistic. Lawyer B responds:

Of course, that's correct. We can't be *sure* we'd get witnesses' names or any kind of discovery at a pre-trial hearing, and there is only the *possibility* the judge would allow subpoenas. Perhaps, in light of what you say, we should handle our motion for a continuance a little differently. Why not set it to be heard the day of trial? They're usually granted in these circumstances, and we can at least see who comes down to court to testify for the prosecution. I've sometimes been able to interview prosecution witnesses in this way who would never talk to me in their homes. Then we'd subpoena these witnesses to our motion to suppress. You look skeptical. What do you think?

Both lawyers see the problem as getting the information needed to prepare for trial. Both recognize that a motion to suppress the evidence of the line-up is available (the line-up was the "fruit" of an illegal seizure or the line-up was unconstitutionally conducted). However, Lawyer A feels he does not have sufficient facts to make a judgment about how strong these claims are. He suggests that they ask for more time, interview potential witnesses (starting with the arresting officer), and then go to trial. He is aware of the danger of waiver in not making the motion to suppress before trial but has determined that the circumstances fit within the rule allowing such motions to be made at trial for "good cause." His judgment is based on a belief that the "real" problem is getting time to interview—hence the motion for a continuance and his concern with the possible negative consequences of not making it sooner than trial.

Lawyer B, on the other hand, sees the information problem as a function not only of time, but of the difficulties of *compelling* such information in advance of trial. That is, she sees at least two discrete subproblems: (i) the possibility that the witnesses, if interviewed, will not talk, and (ii) the problem of preparing for trial under circumstances where the witnesses have not previously been pinned down to their story under oath—hence her unwillingness to concentrate exclusively on winning the motion and her interest in using the subpoena power and the testimony at the hearing to compel broad disclosure of the circumstances leading to the arrest and the line-up. She also wants to deal with the additional problem of not knowing the witnesses' names (and not being able to subpoena them to a hearing), suggesting that they gamble on setting the request for a continuance on the date of trial, when the witnesses will probably be at the court.

Ask yourself if you have begun to think like either of the two lawyers. Is either one "better" than the other? To what can you attribute the differences between them?

In our view, there is a good deal to be learned from Lawyer B here. Her approach can be applied to any number of "information" problems. Stated simply, it involves explicitly asking yourself, at each stage of the proceeding, how you might maximize the discovery potential available to you. For example, a number of lawyers handling civil cases use (i) the motion for summary judgment; (ii) the motion for a preliminary injunction; (iii) proceedings to attach property; (iv) the subpoena power; and (v) early pretrial conferences to enlarge their discovery. In criminal cases, where formal discovery is more limited, even a larger number of indirect discovery devices have evolved. Some criminal defense lawyers routinely (i) call adverse witnesses at the preliminary hearing; (ii) ask for full factual hearings on pretrial motions to suppress evidence or to sever (*e. g.*, for potential conflict between co-defendants); (iii) file civil actions where the issue of civil liability (*e. g.*, trespass) overlaps the issue in the criminal case (*e. g.*, the lawfulness of a police entry and seizure) —thus making civil discovery devices available. Can you imagine how each of these approaches would actually work? Assuming that none of these strategies is undertaken solely for discovery (which would be improper), what advantages does seeking information through such mechanisms have over formal discovery requests? Did you "see" these possibilities when you studied the rules providing for such procedures?

Interestingly, there is a good deal of psychological literature on the difficulty many people have recognizing ("seeing") alternative (or unfamiliar) uses of familiar objects. A classic demonstration is provided by Maier:

> [An] experiment was carried on in a large room which contained many objects such as poles, ringstands, clamps, pliers, extension cords, tables and chairs. Two cords were hung from the ceiling, and were of such length that they reached the floor. One hung near a wall, the other from the center of the room. The subject was told, "your problem is to tie the ends of those two strings together." He soon learned that if he held either cord in his hand he could not reach the other. He was then told that he could use or do anything he wished. . . .

[B8892]

> When one solution was found the subject was told, "Now do it a different way." If he then attempted a modification of his first solution he was told that it really was no different. Thus he soon learned that a solution involving a different principle was desired. When solution 4 was found the experiment ended. . . .
>
> * * *
>
> [The problem could be solved in the following ways:]
>
> Solution 1. One cord was anchored with a large object (such as a chair) placed part way between the cords, while the other was brought over to it.
>
> Solution 2. One of the cords was lengthened (with the extension cord, for example) and the other reached with the hand.
>
> Solution 3. While holding one cord the other was pulled in with a pole.

Solution 4. A weight was tied to the cord hanging from the center of the room and then put in motion, thus making it a pendulum. The other cord was then brought near the center and the swinging cord caught it as it approached the middle point between the two cords.

.   .   .

.   .   . The manner in which one tried to solve the problem .   .   . was dependent on what one saw the difficulty to be. [That is, the subject might see the problem in any one of the following ways:]

1. How to make one cord stay in the center while the other cord is reached. Solution 1 overcomes this difficulty.

2. What to do to make the cords long enough to bridge the gap. Solution 2 answers the purpose in this case.

3. What can be done to extend the reach. In this case solution 3 applies.

4. As the one cord cannot be reached while holding the other, one cord must in some way be made to move toward the other. In this case solution 4 is the possibility.

In the first three solutions activity on the part of the subject is necessary—he must use some sort of tool, but in the fourth, something must be put in operation—a principle of a machine must be used. Making the cord do something is unusual, [and therefore the most difficult solution to arrive at].

[In addition] the cord must be transformed into something else. It must be seen as a pendulum rather than as a cord hanging from the ceiling. This change in meaning is a decided source of difficulty.

.   .   . [Even] presenting the subject with pliers is of no benefit so long as the pliers are seen as pliers. They become useful, however, when they are seen as a weight.   .   .   .[20]

Most of the participants in this study failed to find Solution 4 because the pair of pliers remained a pair of pliers and was not conceived of as part of a pendulum. In your own approach to the familiar uses of procedural devices you may develop similar blocks. You might counteract this tendency to some extent by:

—Continually posing to yourself the possibility that you are missing options;

—Developing categories of typical problems (and solutions) that might be missed in particular situations;

20. Maier, *Reasoning in Humans II: The Solution of a Problem and Its Appearance in Consciousness*, 12 J. COMP.PSYCH. 18 (1931) (since the situation described in this study is somewhat difficult to visualize, we have taken the liberty of adding a sketch). For other reading on problem solving, *see* M. Wertheimer, PRODUCTIVE THINKING (1959); Birch, *The Relation of Previous Experience to Insightful Problem-Solving*, 38 J. COMP.PSYCHOL. 367 (1945); Duncker, *On Problem Solving*, PSYCHOL. MONOGRAPHS, No. 270 (1945); Luchins & Luchins, *New Experimental Attempts at Preventing Mechanization in Problem Solving*, 42 J.GEN.PSYCHOL. 279 (1950); Sangstad & Rasheim, *Problem Solving, Past Experience and Availability of Functions*, 51 BRITISH J.PSYCHOL., part 2, 97 (1960).

—Working with someone who is willing to engage in a dialogue about options and possibilities;

—Thinking up other "uses" of court rules and practices;

—Doing some of the things listed on pages 321–23, *supra*;

—Brainstorming and mentally "playing" with the problem and its possibilities.

All of these have been suggested as ways of avoiding what has come to be called "functional fixedness" (the tendency to see only routine, stereotyped ways of solving problems). The problem, of course, is that the nature of the difficulty prevents you from knowing what you are missing ("you can't hit what you can't see," as the man said).

2. Obtaining Witness Statements: The Constructed Aspects of Investigation

When investigation moves beyond the basic events, documents and rules in a case, the open-ended character and influenceability of the information increases enormously. Because perceptions and memory are inevitably partial and filtered, a margin of error exists in the accounts of all witnesses. It is within this margin that lawyers often "persuade" witnesses to recount the facts in a way that is most consistent with the outcome they desire.

The first reading below is an analysis of attempts by students to persuade others to take new or different political positions on a broad range of issues. The persuasive character of their efforts and the strategic communication skills involved are remarkably similar to what much of the trial literature suggests about interviewing witnesses. The second reading, by an experienced trial lawyer, offers— far less explicitly—what seems to us to be essentially the same approach.

ZIMBARDO, THE TACTICS AND ETHICS OF PERSUASION

From Attitudes, Conflict and Social Change 81, 84–92
(E. McGinnies & B. King, eds. 1972).

If one . . . has a layman's knowledge of practical psychology, and uses the salesman's approach, he can be successful in reaching into a man's brain and pulling out the facts he wants.

The road to the top is steep and treacherous. To move up, you have to give 100 per cent of your energies and abilities at all times. . . . Whether you sell to industry, to wholesalers, to the retail trade, or to the individual consumer, you are dealing with people. Human beings are generally regarded as unpredictable and unfathomable but over the years the knowledge of human nature has been increased and clarified. Psychology has taught us much about getting along with and motivating people. The *Manual* will show you how to deal successfully with people and motivate them to make decisions in your favor (*Professional Salesman's Desk Manual.* Bureau of Business Practices, 1969, Introduction).

* * *

Just how far should you go to make the "sale," to get the commitment? The answer to such a question depends ultimately on a complex interplay of ethical, ideological, and pragmatic issues. Each individual must establish his own set of weighting coefficients to determine how much pressure he is willing to exert. Assuming that your approach will achieve your purpose, is it "right," "proper," "decent," "humane," "moral" for you to deceive someone, to hit him below his unconscious, to arouse strong negative feelings of guilt, anxiety, shame, or even positive feelings of false pride? Behaving unethically for whatever reason pollutes the psychological environment by replacing trust, understanding, and mutual respect with deceit, lies and cynicism.

Police interrogation manuals state: "When you break a man by torture, he will always hate you. If you break him by your intelligence he will always fear and respect you". This generalization may hold only when he does not realize that you, in fact, have broken him by intention. When deception techniques are employed by a sophisticated, trained practitioner, the "victim"—be he a criminal suspect, collegiate experimental subject, or "mark" in a pool hall hustle—does not realize he has been conned. But *you* always know what your intention was and that you "broke a man" thus. What effect does such knowledge have upon you? Do you respect yourself more because of it? Do you begin to depersonalize other human beings as they become notches on your gun handle, "hits/misses," "easy cases/tough customers"? Thus, you must reflect upon the psychological effects of behaving unethically, both upon the target person and upon yourself. If you are so ideologically committed to your cause or goal that any ends justify the means, then ethical issues will get a zero weighting coefficient. But that alone should give you pause.

(a) Will it be possible to restore ethical precepts after your ends have [been attained]?

(b) If you have been converted to such an extreme view, can others be similarly moved without recourse to deception?

(c) Have you not been duped into the extreme position you now hold?

(d) Are you being honest with yourself in recognizing that you are about to be dishonest with others, and are not covering up the fact with rationalizations about "the other side did it first" (if that's true then the poor victim gets it from both ends).

* * *

Finally, if you cast ethics to the wind, yet proceed firmly convinced that Goodness, Justice, and Truth are what you stand for, then ask one more practical question: "Is it likely to work?" How much effort, training, staging, and time will it take to carry off the caper? Are you the type of person who can be effective at this game? What happens if the person discovers the gimmick? Will each "miss" turn into a "boomerang" or a backlash that will actively work against your cause? Will you then get only the immediate, small behavioral compliance, but blow the hoped-for bigger subsequent commitment and attitude change? Have you "ruined" the person for further persuasion attempts (or experiments) by your colleagues?

Having posed and answered such questions to your own satisfaction, and if you still want to go for broke, then the time has come to go Machiavellian. Once such a decision has been made, your only concern is to find the weak points of the target person, and learn what conditions to manipulate and how best to exploit the unsuspecting victim.

*   *   *

Preparing for the Initial Contact

A. *Be informed.* Get as much accurate, up-to-date, reliable evidence as you can. Commit important facts, arguments, statistics, and quotations to memory so they are "natural" when you need them. You should see yourself as more expert on the particular issue of concern than the people you will try to persuade. Your perceived competence is a very important source trait. However, *do not use information as a put-down.* Do not overkill. Hold your storehouse in reserve and select only the facts you need.

B. *Learn as much as you can about those you will engage.* Be familiar with their neighborhood, local issues, basic values, language style (use of diction, cliches, homilies), source of local pride and discontent, the nature of usual influence media, attitudes on the issue in question, and the like. You can obtain this information from local businessmen (barbers, cab drivers, grocery store employees, bartenders, and others), salesmen, letters to the newspaper, and distinguishing characteristics of the neighborhood or the individual home. You can also encourage people to state their opinions on preliminary telephone surveys. When you are in this learning phase, do not try to exert influence.

C. *Actively role-play with a friend the anticipated situation.* Imagine and then work through as realistically as possible the persuasion situation in which you will operate. If available, tape-record or videotape such dress rehearsals and then critically analyze your performance. Switch roles and try to be the target person in the situation where he is experiencing the pressure to comply to a request for some commitment.

D. *Do a critical self-appraisal.* Analyze your own personal strengths and weaknesses, your appearance, and discuss any source of fear, anxiety, anticipated embarrassment, and so forth with one or more persons with whom you feel comfortable before you actually start out.

E. *Be confident.* Expect that you will be effective more often than not. You must expect some setbacks, but you must be dedicated to winning, to making the "sale." If you do not handle the situation carefully, you may produce the undesirable effect of increasing the person's resistance to any further influence attempts by others, or you may generate a backlash effect yourself. If you blow it once or twice, or if you get doors slammed in your face before you even start talking (this will surely happen in some neighborhoods), keep trying. If you lose your confidence, however, or you get negative results in a variety of neighborhoods with a variety of techniques, then perhaps you are not suited for face-to-face confrontations and your talents could be put to better use elsewhere.

F. *Be sensitive to the varied reasons underlying the attitude(s) in question.* Attitudes are formed and maintained because of needs for information, for social acceptance by other people, or for ego protection from unacceptable impulses and ideas. Deeply held attitudes probably have all three of these motivational bases. Information *per se* is probably the least effective way of *changing* attitudes and behavior. Its effectiveness is maximum at the attitude-formation stage when the person has not yet taken a stand and put his ego on the dotted line. Your general approach must acknowledge that the individual is more than a rational, information processor—sometimes he is irrational, inconsistent, responsive to social rewards, or primarily concerned about how he appears to himself and to others.

G. *Even as a stranger you can exert considerable influence.* You can be an effective agent for change by serving as a model for some behavior by publicly engaging in it, selectively reinforcing some opinions rather than others, and providing a new source of social contact, recognition, and reward for many people.

Gaining Access to and Establishing the Contact

A. Before you can persuade, you must get the person to acknowledge your presence, to attend to you and to follow your presentation. People are wary of an assault on their privacy and "life space" by an unknown person on their doorstep. You might want to consider an initial phone call or letter to contacts to be made at home.

B. If you are making a home contact, be aware of the particular situation you have encountered. Be sure that the person is willing to give you the required time. You might be interrupting dinner, a phone call, a family quarrel, a visit with guests, or some bad news. You do not want the dominant motivation of the homeowner to be to get rid of you as soon as possible.

C.   Although strangers can influence everyday behavior, persuasion is enhanced when the target perceives some basic similarity with the source.   This "strategy of identification" (practiced by all good entertainers and politicians) involves finding something in common between you.   Physical similarity is the most obvious: age, sex, race, ethnic features, dress (distribution of hair).   In addition, similarity is inferred from voice dialect, regionalisms, and appropriate slang, jargon, or group-membership-identifying phrases (for example, "such a lot of *chutzpah* he's got, that Vice President," or "People like us who work for a living have callouses on their hands, a politician like X who talks about working for the people, probably has them only on his mouth.")   Canvassing should be arranged to optimize this perceived similarity by selecting neighborhoods and locations which are approximately matched to the available canvassers.   The canvasser should try to uncover as many points of similarity as possible because similarity breeds familiarity, which breeds liking and enhances credibility and greater acceptance of the message.

D.   Students are not seen as credible sources on most issues that concern them directly, and to be effective, it is important that they increase their source credibility.   This may be accomplished in a number of ways:

1.   Impress the audience with your expertise, concern, and dedication, being forceful but not overbearing.

2.   Make some points which are against your own best interest: indicate the sacrifices you have made and would be willing to make.

3.   Have a respected person introduce you, make the contact for you.

4.   Begin by agreeing with what the audience wants to hear, or with whatever they say first.

5.   Minimize your manipulative intent until you ask for the commitment.

E.   Avoid group situations where the majority are known or expected to be against you, since they will provide support for each other and their cohesion might make salient the group norm that you appear to be attacking (which they never cherished so much before your attack).

Maintaining, Intensifying, Directing the Interpersonal Relationship
Once you have managed to get the person to receive you, then you must hold this attention, while trying to get your message (and yourself) accepted.

A.   You have the power to reinforce many behaviors of the target person, a power you should use judiciously but with conscious awareness of what and how you are reinforcing.

1. Listen attentively to what the other person has to say about anything of personal interest. This not only "opens up" the person for a dialogue, and helps in establishing what are the primary values, beliefs, and organization of his (or her) thinking, but establishes you as someone open to what others have to say. (The opportunity to tell a college student where to get off is very rewarding for many people.)

2. Maintain eye contact with the person and as close physical proximity as seems acceptable to the person.

3. Individuate the person, by using names (with Mr. or Mrs. or titles where there is an age or status discrepancy). Make the person feel you are reacting to his uniqueness and individuality—*which you should be*—and are not reacting in a pro-grammed way to your stereotyped conception of a housewife, blue collar worker, etc. Similarly, help the other person to individuate you, to break through the categorization and pigeon-holing process which makes you just an anonymous canvasser. At some point, describe something personal or unique about your feelings, background, interests, and so forth (which you expect will be acceptable). However, once accomplished, then do not allow yourself to be the exception to the stereotype—say "most other students are like me in how we feel about X."

4. Reinforce specific behaviors explicitly and immediately, by nodding, saying "good," "that's an interesting point," and the like. Reinforce more general classes of behavior by smil-ing, and by making it obvious you enjoy the interaction and by being impressed with the person's openness, sensitivity, intelligence, or articulateness. As a student with a lot of "book learning" you can still learn a lot from people who have gone to the "school of hard knocks," who have "real-life learning" and "street savvy" to offer you. Let them know that this is how you feel when talking to someone who has not had the benefit of your degree of education.

5. The person must perceive that you personally care about and are enthusiastic about the item(s) under discussion; more-over he/she must perceive that *you* as a person really care about the complaint act—at a personal level and not merely as part of your role.

6. Your reinforcement rate should increase over the course of the interaction, so that ideally, at the end of the time, the person is sorry to see you leave.

B. Be aware of sources of resentment against you for what you represent by your physical appearance, group membership (as a stu-dent), and the like, work first to differentiate those biased and often unfounded feelings and reactions from those reactions you want to elicit by your influence attempt.

Working class people in particular will resent you for having an easy life. They have worked with their hands, strained their backs, calloused their knees, scrubbing, lifting, sweating, struggling, ekeing out a measly subsistence, while you (as they see it) sit on your butt and have every need catered to. You can blunt this resentment in at least two ways: (1) by showing respect, even awe, for how hard they work, acknowledging that you found it really tough that summer you worked as a hod carrier, and so forth; (2) by offhandedly noting what a sweat you had studying for that last calculus exam, that while other students may have a lot of money, *you* don't and you don't know whether you can afford to make it through college, and the like— whatever you can honestly say to undercut the perception that you are privileged and spoiled.

In contrast, middle class office workers are likely to resent you for a different set of reasons: that (according to the stereotype) you do not show respect for your elders, that you are an uncouth, dirty, disruptive, pot-smoking libertine, and so forth. A neat appearance and considerate, respectful manner will do much to combat this stereotype.

C.   Plan the organization of your approach well enough so that it seems natural and unplanned, and be flexible enough to modify it as necessary.

1.   Do not surround your best arguments with tangential side arguments or a lot of details. Arguments that come in the middle of a presentation are remembered least well. Put your strongest arguments first if you want to motivate or interest uninvolved people.

2.   Draw your conclusions explicitly. Implicit conclusion drawing should be left for only very intelligent audiences.

3.   Repeat the main points in your argument, and the major points of agreement between you and the target person.

D.   Tailor your approach to the target person.

1.   Do not put him on the defensive, or even encourage or force a public defence of (and thus commitment to) any position against you. Opposing beliefs are seen as providing the opportunity for open discussion, and as a starting point to find areas of common agreement. If the person is for you, then get a public commitment early, and try to make that commitment more stable and more extreme than it was originally.

2.   If possible, have the person restate your ideas and conclusions for himself, in his own words (encourage active participation).

3. If the person appears to be very authoritarian in manner and thinking, then he will probably be more impressed by status sources, decisiveness, and one-sided generalizations than by informational appeals, expert testimony, unbiased presentation of both sides of the issue, and so forth. Make any approach responsive to the dominant personality and social characteristics of the person to whom you are talking.

4. Work in pairs. Although a more personal relationship can be established in a two-person interaction, there is much to be gained from teamwork. Working in pairs provides each student with social support, lowers apprehension about initiating each new contact, and allows one of you to be "off the firing line" appraising the situation, to come in when help is needed, to refocus the direction, or respond to some specific trait detected in the target person. There are several ways in which teams can be composed to produce interesting effects. There is a general principle covering them all, namely, *the two members of the team should differ in some obvious characteristic, such as temperament, age, or sex.* There are two reasons behind this principle: first, it maximizes the chances that either one or the other member will be similar to the target person and therefore can gain a persuasive advantage at the appropriate moment; second, it promotes the subtle idea that even when people differ in outward characteristics, they can still agree on the important issue of peace—therefore, the target person, who may differ from both persuaders, can be encouraged to agree also. The obverse of this "team difference" principle is also important: *it is very inefficient for similar canvassers to accompany each other.*

Getting the Commitment and Terminating the Contact

Do not insist that the person accept and believe what you have said before he makes a behavioral commitment. Get the behavioral commitment anyway, and attitude change will follow. The ideal conclusion of the contact will also leave the person feeling that the time spent was worthwhile and his self-esteem will be greater than it was before you arrived.

A. Do not overstay your welcome or be forced to stay longer than is worthwhile according to your time schedule. Timing is essential both in knowing when to ask for the commitment and in knowing when to quit with an intractable person. For a person who needs more time to think, encourage him if you get a promise to allow you to come back.

B. Provide several levels of possible behavioral alternatives for the person: pushing the most extreme is likely to get a greater level of compliance even if the extreme is rejected.

C.   Be clear as to what actions are requested or what has been agreed upon or concluded.

D.   Use a "bandwagon" effect, if called for, to indicate prestigious others who have joined in the action.

E.   When you believe the target person is about to make the commitment (or after a verbal agreement is made), stress the fact that the decision is his own; it involves free choice, no pressure. This maximizes the dissonance experienced by the decision made and forces the individual to make his behavior internally consistent by generating his own intrinsic justification for his behavior. Each person is his own best persuader. After the final commitment, honestly and openly thank the person and reinforce his behavior.

F.   Broaden the contact in two ways. First, get the name of one or more neighbors who would agree with that person's position—you will talk to them too and use the person's name if that is O.K. with him. Second, honestly react to something about his person which is irrelevant to the main social/political issue at hand—the house, decor, hair, clothes, and avocation mentioned, or a favor which you can do related to something mentioned.

G.   Extend your influence if you can get the target person also to be an agent of influence. Try to enlist his aid in getting at least one other person to agree to do what he has just done. He should be motivated to proselytize at this time, especially if he is an outgoing person good at persuading others. If he convinces others, that will reduce his own doubts about whether he has done the right thing.

SIMMONS, WINNING BEFORE TRIAL: HOW TO PREPARE CASES FOR THE BEST SETTLEMENT OR TRIAL RESULT *

205–36, 305–13 (1974).

INTERVIEWING THE FRIENDLY WITNESS

Economy of effort and time make knowing your interview objectives vital. Have them all in mind when you see the witness the first time, since there is no time like the first time for achieving them. There may not be a second. Even if you can and do hold a second interview, his memory will not be in the same mint condition as it was before.

1.   *Enlist his active and partisan support for your case.* He comes to you almost as a volunteer for duty. Explain his importance to the case and the client's chance of winning it. Explain the merits of the client's cause, his "right" to victory, and the anticipated opposition; then tell the witness what he must do to help overcome the latter to achieve the former.

2. *Obtain and preserve all favorable facts.* Both from the client's interview and your preliminary investigation, you should have a fairly complete grasp of the facts you must prove to win your case. Establish all you can through friendly witnesses during their interviews, then make certain you can do so again at a later settlement conference or trial.

3. *Obtain and subordinate unfavorable facts.* Knowledge of "bad" facts is as important as knowledge of "good" facts, for in a legal setting knowledge is indeed power—power to convert favorable facts to favorable evidence and so prove your essential issues, and power to anticipate unfavorable facts and either extenuate, dilute, or refute them. But after knowledge comes use. And it is the favorable facts, not the unfavorable, you want your friendly witness to use subsequently . . . in his statements to you and your opponent. You must orient the witness in his partisan role by emphasizing his facts that help your case and by subordinating (not suppressing) those that hurt it. . . .

4. *Obtain leads to other facts, evidence, and witnesses.* Like Galahad's quest for the Holy Grail, the treasure a lawyer seeks (decisive, winning evidence) often can only be found by pursuing leads friends supply. So, a friendly witness may not himself be the eyewitness you need, but with patient probing, he may supply you with clues to that witness's identity and whereabouts.

5. *Obtain sufficient personal data about the witness so you can locate him whenever necessary later.* A good witness who cannot be produced when needed is as much use as a million dollars that cannot be spent. Expectations count for very little at the negotiating table. When interviewing such a witness, believe that he will disappear ten minutes after leaving your office. Then gather enough personal information about him so you can trace him if he does.

* * *

By definition, a friendly witness has a commitment to the client stemming from family, social, employment, or friendship ties. You start with a favorable bias. But both commitment and bias start out as negative qualities—he will not knowingly do anything to hurt the client.

The degree to which this witness will actively help your client depends on answers to three questions: How much will his help benefit the client? How much will it benefit *him*? How much will it cost *him*? The answers you supply to these questions will determine whether you have an indifferent helper who volunteers nothing, or a zealous helper, eager to contribute all he can toward victory.

* * *

Interviewing the Unfriendly Witness

Now you are dealing with a witness owing some allegiance to the adverse party, including the adverse party himself. Someone with an inherent bias favoring the other side because of some relationship between them, either family, employment, social or affection, is likely to be unfriendly to you and your cause.

That that someone is a witness and theoretically spurred by a sense of justice and yen for fair play means nothing. He will say and do whatever he can to help his ally beat you . . . within reason. Within reason? This is the qualification that offers lawyers the chance to deal effectively with these witnesses.

* * *

As with the populace generally, some adverse witnesses are basically dishonest. They are so in the habit of lying that they lie on all subjects great and small. They rarely pose a problem for the opposing lawyer, for, making no effort to be plausible, they are soon found out.

The techniques of this section are designed for the bulk of witnesses who are basically honest and want to appear honest to others.

Action rule: The large majority of adverse witnesses you interview will state the whole truth about any event until they learn which facts favor your client and which favor their friend. If the interview takes place after they have learned the difference, they will conceal the first and exaggerate the second, but only so long as they do not thereby reveal themselves untruthful.

Armed with knowledge of these tendencies, interview an adverse witness with these six objectives in mind:

1. *Interview him before he acquires a factual slant—before he learns which facts hurt and help his ally.* The witness will perceive the value of some facts without being told. He does not need an attorney to tell him that driving on the wrong side of the road and misrepresenting features of a house for sale are facts favoring persons injured by those acts. But he does not know legal principles relating to either event to appreciate the refinement of factual advantage. Was the driver forced over the center line? Was the misrepresentation innocent? You must get to the witness before opposing counsel teaches him the refinements and prepares him against your coming.

2. *Obtain and preserve all favorable facts.* The witness is more likely to disclose facts helpful to your side at this stage of the case than at any other. When he does, you must be prepared to preserve them in some form usable later in settlement discussions. . . .

3. *Obtain and preserve unfavorable facts.* Getting an early recital of all facts the witness knows damaging to your client confers three benefits: 1) You learn your opponent's evidence—and can conduct your investigation and preparation accordingly; 2) Having stated all unfavorable facts he knew, the witness cannot subsequently add to them without the threat of impeachment and discredit; 3) The witness cannot later correct obvious errors in his interview disclosures to harmonize with discovered truth without the threat of impeachment and discredit.

4. *Establish his adverse bias and the factual basis of it.* Of course, if the witness is the adverse party, his identity is enough. Similarly, his spouse and close relatives bespeak relationships that presume bias. But other relationships do not create the same presumption even though bias is evident. That the witness is the adverse party's employer does not mean his word will be disbelieved. But if his income is affected by the party (override on sales commissions) or there is a close social intimacy as well, his value as a witness sharply diminishes. Such detail is vital to your successful disparagement of unfriendly witnesses.

5. *Obtain leads to other facts, evidence, and witnesses.* It is not only his version of the events he witnessed you should seek and can get. The witness will often know of witnesses, documents, or physical objects important to the case you never knew existed. Interview him before he is warned against helping you, probe for such leads, and then be pleased at the number you get.

6. *Obtain and preserve impeaching utterances.* Establishing a bias in the witness favoring the adverse party gives you a weapon. But couple that with a glaring untruth he stated and you hold an explosive sufficient to blow credibility right out of the witness. Always seek to induce at least one such untruth in every interview, then preserve it in statement form for later use.

The balance of this [section] supplies techniques for achieving these witness objectives. They carry no warranty against failure. But they succeed for other lawyers and they will for you . . . if only you employ them.

* * *

Able lawyers know that the manner in which they deal with [adverse] witnesses often dictates the success or failure of their case. This is obvious, since the extent to which adverse witnesses can prove claims of their own party, or disprove claims of yours, determines the case outcome.

Dealing effectively with them requires that you interview them effectively, And to do this you must achieve four plateaus: *Get access to them; get them to talk to you; get utterances from them that help your case,* and *put these utterances into a form that you can use subsequently.*

Here is a checklist of techniques that will help you reach each plateau. Each has been pre-tested by use and accomplishment. Employ them in your practice and see if your results are not better than before.

1. *First, identify by name and address* the adverse party and other unfriendly witnesses whose testimony, according to information on hand, is likely to prove or disprove essential issues in your case. Information from your client, friendly witnesses, police reports, newspaper accounts and other early sources of facts provides the identification.

2. *Interview these witnesses* within a week after the identification is made, in order of their potential importance to the case—the adverse party first. Delay of even one day may see a lawyer hired. Interview the most important witness first because this is the order in which your opponent will visit and prepare them against you.

3. *Conduct the interviews yourself* whenever possible. If this is impossible, then use only an associate or investigator whose interviewing ability has been demonstrated.

4. *Interview the witnesses at their homes* during the evening or weekend. Do not call for an appointment first nor give prior notice of your coming. All witnesses are reluctant to submit to a lawyer interview, and unfriendly witnesses most of all. Call for an appointment and it will be refused. Give them advance notice and they will tell you to stay away, not answer the door or leave before you arrive. Explain that you are "out this evening investigating events that concern them" to take some of the sting from your seeming rudeness. That will get you to the next item of procedure.

5. *Identify yourself truthfully* as the lawyer for "so and so," and never dissemble yourself or mission. Say you are trying to learn all the facts of the case, no matter whom they hurt or help, and that you must investigate fully before you can decide whether, and on what basis to settle it. Be courteous and friendly. Never threaten, bluster, or "throw your weight around." The witnesses will probably talk to you about the events now, if only to justify and promote their perspective.

6. *Obtain sufficient personal information* about the witnesses to establish the relationships between them and the adverse party—and the factual basis of their biases.

7. *Ask the witnesses first to narrate the events they witnessed.*
    Then question them specifically about each such event. A
    narration will occasionally disclose helpful facts that de-
    tailed questioning will overlook . . . and vice versa.
    The dual approach requires repetition and targets dis-
    crepancies caused by poor memory, poor articulation, uncer-
    tain conviction, increasing candor, heightening partisan goal
    awareness, and just plain mistakes. Whatever the cause,
    discrepancies taint witness credibility and are important
    to you.

8. *Tell the witnesses about favorable facts you know* that con-
    tradict or are inconsistent with unfavorable facts he has
    stated and ask if they want to change these portions of their
    stories. Sources of such favorable facts may be police
    reports, official documents, disinterested witness state-
    ments, friendly witnesses, and your client. Obviously, the
    more authoritative and disinterested the source of your facts
    the greater the pressure upon unfriendly witnesses to con-
    form their own.

9. *Take a shorthand reporter along* to the interviews whenever
    the witness potential or client's purse warrants the fee (it
    will vary from about $35 to $100 depending on time, dis-
    tance, locale, and reporter). There are occasions when you
    will not have the time or freedom to write up a statement of
    witness utterances and the reporter is your surety of future
    use. A stenotype reporter is preferable to none at all, but
    less valuable than a shorthand reporter because some wit-
    nesses are intimidated to silence by the unfamiliar machine.

10. *Make your own notes of significant portions* of witness ut-
    terances, especially those that benefit your case. Make them
    briefly and discretely, because the witnesses will surely be
    alarmed by the sight of furious writing.

11. *Whether a reporter accompanies you or not,* always write
    out a concise memorandum of witness utterances in his
    presence. . . . Give the memorandum to him for review
    and correction. Have him sign or otherwise authenticate
    it. . . . Make an original only and do not supply the
    witness with a copy unless he insists.

* * *

Up to now we have emphasized one of two main objectives of an
unfriendly witness interview . . . the eliciting of probative facts
(facts tending to prove either the adverse party's claims or defenses
or your own). Now for the second main objective, when his probative
facts are, as is commonly true, substantially unfavorable to you: the
eliciting of impeaching facts (facts tending to impair the validity of
the probative facts or his credibility in stating them).

* * *

.   .   .   [There are] six forms which verbal impeachment may take. Here are the six, illustrated by a hypothetical complainant in a robbery case.

1. *Inconsistent utterances.* Complainant says he positively recognized defendant as the robber. Later he says that within two hours of the robbery he viewed six men in a police line-up, defendant included, and was unable to make a positive identification.

2. *Contradictory utterances.* Complainant first says the robber was about six feet tall wearing a blue sweater. Later he says he was about medium height wearing a blue jacket.

3. *Implausible utterances.*   Complainant says he positively identified defendant as the robber even though he viewed him from 500 feet away.

4. *Irreconcilable utterances.* Complainant says he had a clear view of defendant's face as he ran towards him following the robbery. Later he says the robber wore a broad billed cap pulled low so it masked his face.

5. *Perceptual defect.* Complainant says he wears prescription lenses for nearsightedness, later admits he was not wearing them at the time of the robbery.

6. *Discrediting facts.* Complainant says he positively identified defendant as the robber at the scene. Later he says that two days later police pointed defendant out to him at the police station, saying he was "the man who did it."

Techniques for Getting and Keeping Impeachment

First of all encourage the witness to tell his story in detail and show interest in all he says. Never be impatient because he draws it out. The more he talks, the greater the likelihood he will impeach himself in some way.

Be as receptive to the unfavorable facts he relates as to the favorable. If you cut him off with an "I didn't ask you about my client's speed. I want to hear about your driver's speed," you offend him, increase his suspicion, cheat yourself of facts you should know and destroy any chance of impeaching him.

*   *   *

Encourage exaggeration. Damaging statements can sometimes be completely discredited by exaggeration to the point of absurdity. For example, defense counsel in a divorce case interviewed plaintiff wife's sister and asked about defendant's habits. "He drinks a lot" .   .   .   "Did you see him drunk?"   .   .   .   "Oh, yes, quite a lot" .   .   .   "Every time you saw him?"   .   .   .   "Yes, I'd say so." Counsel secured a written, signed statement from the witness in which she says, "Tom is always drunk." From "drinks a lot" to "always drunk" is some progression, moving from a reasonable statement of fact to an implausible defamation prompted by witness bias.

Note irreconcilable facts in the witness story without comment, as you would an implausible statement. Never tip him off that a conflict exists in his facts and, most importantly, never ask him to explain it. It is shameful how often lawyers free skewered witnesses from their hooks. If the witness tells you he saw your client's face at the crime scene, then later says client's back was turned the whole time, leave it be. Bury both facts in a written statement and get it signed. Never say, as many lawyers would, "Tell me, Mr. Martin, how could you see my client's face if his back was turned to you all the time," because he will answer "Oh, he turned his face toward me one time and I got a good look."

* * *

You can be sure that an unfriendly witness possesses more than just unfriendly facts. No case is ever so cut-and-dried that something good cannot be said for both sides. And the witness can say something good for you if he wants to.

Of course, he never wants to. He is biased in favor of the other side and will not wittingly say anything damaging to his ally. The key word here is "wittingly". Your objective must be to get him to disclose facts which damage the ally unwittingly (the witness will never say his friend was speeding, but you may get him to say that he was going about 55 m. p. h., which you know is in excess of posted speed limit).

Here are some techniques that will help you induce those unwitting disclosures.

1. *Know your case as thoroughly as possible when you commence the interview*, so you have in mind favorable facts disclosed by others. Read your completed client interview and friendly witness interview forms and statements, police reports, and other pertinent material in your possession beforehand.

2. *Use the cross-examining style of questioning . . . but gently.* There is no judge around to enforce rules of evidence, so phrase your questions in a manner that assumes the answers you want. Do not say, "Was M driving about 55 m. p. h.?" Instead say, "Wasn't M driving about 55 m. p. h.?" a subtle but persuasive change of phrasing, as any experienced trial counsel knows. Neither is a judge around to compel the witness to answer your questions. Your interview is not by right or invitation but by his sufferance, so do not be aggressive in your style. If he refuses to say "Yes" to your speed question, let him have his way. Say, "What speed was he travelling, then?" He is likely to an-

swer, "No more than 50 m. p. h.," which may still be over the speed limit.

3. *Ask for facts and not conclusions.* Do not say, "Didn't M fail to yield the right of way?" or "Didn't J act in self-defense?" Instead say, "Didn't M drive into the intersection without stopping for the stop sign?" or "Didn't P throw a punch at J just before J struck him?"

4. *Refer to facts from authoritative sources that conflict with his facts in an effort to change his mind.* If the witness said your client was drunk and the police report has an "x" opposite the phrase, "No sign of drinking," show him the report, and then ask if his opinion may not be mistaken.

5. *Ask the witness about favorable facts you know, but he has not disclosed.* If you learned from another witness that the robber spoke with a southern accent and you know your client does not, ask the complainant detailed questions about what the robber said and how he said it. Try for an admission— at the very least—that his accent was not native to your area.

6. *Prod him for facts you suspect he knows but has not disclosed that are likely sources of advantage.* A passenger in the adverse party's car can tell you about distractions existing in the car prior to the accident; conversations, car radio, cigarette lighting, etc.; whether windshield wipers were working, the windshield dirty . . . and other such details. A next-door neighbor in a divorce case will know much about the couple's personal habits, public manner with each other, condition and appearance of the children, etc. The complainant in a criminal case will know the lighting conditions when the crime occurred, his own state of mind, times, distances and what was said.

7. *Ask the witness to show you any pertinent documents in his possession.* In a contract case, ask the adverse party to see his copy of the contract and examine it for writing not appearing on your copy. Also ask for his copies of correspondence exchanged between himself and your client, paying special attention to originals from the client of which he may not have made copies.

8. *Ask him to repeat any conversations he may have had with your client, the adverse party and any other witness concerning events at issue.* These will often confirm what your client has told you and/or contradict the adverse party and other unfriendly witnesses, since the interviewee does not know what the others have or will tell you.

9. *Ask each unfriendly witness other than the adverse party whether he spoke with opposing counsel. If so, get full de-*

tails of the conversation, when, where and what was said. Was he interviewed personally? Give a written statement? Did that statement deviate from the facts he has given you? In what particulars? What did your opponent tell him about the case?

There are three purposes for these questions. First, you should always know the facts your opponent has to work with. Second, the witness will sometimes disclose different facts that were told opposing counsel than were told you, then must admit he was mistaken to one or the other of you. The third purpose is to distinguish coaching from honest recollection. If pressed the witness will occasionally admit that your opponent fed him facts . . . . "Well, he just reminded me of a few things I'd forgotten". Find out all about those "things" and include it in your written statement.

10. *Finally, ask the witness if there is anything he would like to add to what he has told you.* It is surprising how often this question strikes a vein of untapped lore. I remember asking it of the complainant in a burglary case. "You didn't ask me about the fingerprints of your client the police found," he said. "They found prints on the window that was jimmied open."

This was the first I had heard about prints being found, so I went to the prosecutor to confirm the identification, fully expecting to arrange for a plea of "guilty" on the best terms obtainable. He admitted finding prints but refused to say whether they matched the defendant's. A court order was quickly secured requiring the police to disclose comparison results. The answer was *they did not match!* A *nolle prosequi* soon followed. A case was won because of an innocuous question to a hostile witness . . . "Do you have anything to add"?

Interviewing the Disinterested Witness

This is a witness who possesses relevant facts about your case events and has no personal bias favoring either party, except that which his facts create. He carries a high credibility with those persons whom you wish to persuade, opposing counsel and party, third party (insurance company, indemnitor), judge and jury, such that, if his facts be controlling, he himself will control the outcome of settlement negotiations or trial.

* * *

Without an axe to grind or nest to feather, devoid of any allegiance to either side, this witness prefers not to become involved in your case to any extent. So he has either given his name as a witness and now regrets it, or has concealed his identity and is content to leave it that way.

Such is the profile of the average disinterested witness a lawyer encounters. It poses identification and location problems not usually experienced with friendly and unfriendly witnesses, whose bias prompts a high visibility.

Putting such problems aside, . . . the present concern is with the witness whose name and address are known to you. How do you go about interviewing him so as to maximize his benefit and minimize his detriment to your case?

You should begin by knowing your objectives precisely in advance. Then you must utilize effective techniques during the interview itself to reach them. First the objectives:

1. *Interview the witness quickly and before your opponent does.* An emphasis was placed on holding speedy interviews with previous classes of witnesses already discussed. With them it was highly advisable. In the case of the disinterested witness, however, it is *absolutely imperative.* The usual reason for getting to him while his memory is vivid fits here, but beyond that is the witness' facility for disappearing—and your opponent's proficiency at confusing or influencing his facts.

2. *Obtain all relevant facts he knows about the events of your case, then determine whether, on balance, he is a benefit or detriment to your side.* The sum of the witness' facts usually fits him into one of four qualitative niches. He is either . . entirely favorable (as where all he saw was the other side drive into the rear of your stopped car) . . . entirely unfavorable (your client drove into the rear of the adverse party's car and that is all he saw) . . . more favorable than unfavorable (he saw adverse party drive into the rear of your car which had no brake lights working) . . . more unfavorable than favorable (reverse last example).

   A decision on the witness' overall effect on your case is a must so you know whether to cope with his resistance to involvement or let it alone; whether to protect yourself against his disappearance or pray for it.

3. *If the witness is likely to benefit you, overcome his resistance to involvement by inducing a personal commitment to the case.* Except for a meager minority who are willing to help because they are busybodies, or egoists, or they revere justice, most witnesses of this type enter an interview with the enthusiasm of a prisoner entering the death house. In their minds, there is no reason for helping you that outweighs the reasons why he should not (inconvenience, loss of income, ner-

vous upset, lawyer "deception", etc.). Your task must be to supply the witness with positive reasons for helping the client that eclipse the negative ones . . . endowing him with an incentive to participate that will last as long as your need of him.

4. *Induce a factual bias benefiting your client and mitigate as much as possible the unfavorable facts.* Instilling a desire to help you in a witness is not the same thing as eliciting facts from him that *will* help you, though the two are linked. Two witnesses rarely see the same event in the same way and never describe it identically. "After hearing sworn witnesses contradict each other concerning events both saw, I worry about history," a lawyer once remarked.

   Having heard so often about sensory fallibility, most witnesses grudgingly concede it in themselves and are amenable to influence up to a point. Your objective must be to find where that point is, i. e., what facts will he alter to conform to reason, logic, and other inconsistent or contradictory facts, and which will he stick to despite everything. Then you must alter what you can, ethically, by reference to the same guidelines of reason, logic, and other facts.

5. *Obtain leads to other facts, evidence, and witnesses you do not possess.* No matter what the value of his own testimony may be, a disinterested witness will sometimes be able to supply you with clues to the identity and whereabouts of that witness all lawyers dream about . . . the conclusive witness. I know a lawyer who, while defending a grocery store robbery/homicide case, interviewed twelve patrons who had been on the scene before finding one who saw the murderer clearly and could exonerate the defendant. Only one of the twelve was identified in a police report. The lawyer learned of the others from successive interviews with each as he became known (the first gave clues leading to the second, the second for the third, etc.).

6. *If the witness' facts generally favor you, obtain sufficient personal data enabling you to locate him whenever necessary later on.* If it is sound advice to anticipate a friendly witness' disappearance during the pendancy of your case and prepare well in advance for it, it is a *commandment* in the case of the disinterested witness. Without any allegiance to your client, he will often sink into oblivion with never a thought for your distress.

A disinterested witness, by definition, has no partisan commitment. You must give him one! Do his recalled facts that favor you strike him as illogical, unreasonable, or contrary to past experience?

You must strengthen them, citing similar facts of others or simply arguing their validity. Do his recalled facts that injure you strike him as logical, reasonable, and consistent? You must weaken them when you can by citing contradictory or inconsistent facts of others, or arguing their invalidity.

Does the witness slough over facts that aid your cause because he thinks them insignificant? Show him their legal significance and emphasize them in his mind and statement. Does he exaggerate the importance of damaging facts? Set them in perspective and minimize them in his mind and statement.

Witness interviewing, then, is fact-gathering raised to an art form. The artists in our profession, lawyers who consistently win better settlements and judgments than average—with average cases— see it as a critical stage in developing a case to win. So must you. Here are several interviewing techniques to use with disinterested witnesses that have proven their worth time and time again.

1. *As soon as the client interview is done,* examine his checklist form and any other readily available source of facts (police report, official records, newspaper story, etc.) for names and addresses of disinterested witnesses who are likely to possess important facts bearing on some issue of your case. List the names in order of potential importance.

2. *After identifying such a disinterested witness*, phone him at his house or employment for an interview appointment as soon as possible. Explain your status and purpose; that you are investigating the case and *must* see and talk with him so that a settlement decision can be made intelligently. Delay the interview one hour longer than necessary and you risk losing the great advantage of priority to your opponent.

3. *If the witness refuses* or is reluctant to see you, tell him the interview is imperative; that you wish to make it as convenient for him as possible, so you will come to his house. Then say if he refuses to cooperate, you will have no choice but to take his testimony under court order *at your office and during the day.* If you do not bluster, but remain courteous throughout, he will surely relent, for the penalty of refusing an interview will seem to him worse than the annoyance from granting it.

4. *Interview the witness at his home* after work or on a weekend (find out during your phone conversation what time he eats, retires or plans some other activity, then schedule the interview to allow at least *two hours* with him). If you are unable to see him at his house within a reasonable period of time, try to persuade him to come to your office. Emphasize how vital he is to the case and the need for haste. A witness

will sometimes be so flattered by your attention that he will deal generously with you.

*   *   *

5. *When interviewing at his home, ask if the two of you can go to a room away from the rest of the family* where you can talk alone. Privacy is essential for two reasons: 1) The physical and vocal presence of [other family members] is distracting; it interferes with the flow of questions and answers and the desired empathy between you; and 2) The effect of an audience on a witness is the same as it is on an actor . . both tend to emote and grandstand. He is conscious of his "image," and is much less ready to admit he may be wrong on some fact or recollection.

6. *Ask the witness to narrate events* he witnessed while you make notes of relevant facts. Underline those facts which have a marked bearing on a case issue. Then question him closely about the underlined material while you test the following: 1) The consistency of his story (i. e., Do details change from one time to the next?); 2) The degree of certainty with which he holds and relates the facts (i. e., Does he hesitate or look evasive, his manner suggesting doubt? Do his words suggest it? . . . "I think it happened this way" . . . "It seems to me that he said . . ."); 3) Whether his facts are general and undiscriminating ("There was a stop sign at the corner but I don't remember much about it.") or detailed and precise ("It was two feet from the curb and a foot from the cross-walk.")

7. *Whenever the witness evinces uncertainty* about favorable facts and you obtained the same facts from another source (client or friendly witness interview, official reports, personal investigation, etc.), identify the source to him and reinforce the facts in his mind. When his uncertainty relates to unfavorable facts and you obtained conflicting facts from another source, identify the source and other facts. Seek an admission from the witness that he may be mistaken.

8. *Write a memorandum statement* of the witness' facts . . . Have him sign or initial each page and give him a copy bearing your name, address, and phone number. *Ask him to read his statement privately before discussing the case with the lawyer or representative of the adverse party.* Explain that he will be less likely to make an inconsistent or contradictory statement if he does.

*   *   *

[9] *If the witness is favorable,* for your case, find out if he has present plans to move and, if so, where, and when. Also ask him about his health. If he is aged or infirm, make

prominent note of it on your file jacket so that his deposition will be taken if settlement negotiations fail and suit is filed.

[10] *If your case involves a spatial event* (traffic accident, crime, trespass, or nuisance) have him diagram whatever he witnessed, then sign or initial the diagram. If a picture is worth a thousand words, a diagram is worth ten thousand because it bears the personal imprint of the diagrammer.

[11] *If the witness denies seeing anything of value* and sticks to the denial under your questioning, take his statement anyway and quote the denial. How often has such a know-nothing witness miraculously discovered a recollection at some later date? The experience of every lawyer is peppered with such surprises. Have his written disclaimer and he is impeached. Fail to have it and you may be duped.

[12] *Interview a witness by phone only when no other interview can be obtained*. It is like reeling in a catfish when you are fishing for pike. Something is better than nothing. That small something could grow much larger if, for example, you ask him on the witness stand, "Didn't you tell me on the phone that you never saw the accident at all?" . . . and he answers, "Yes."

* * *

It is true that lacking the kind of relationship with a party that spurs a friendly or unfriendly witness to a partisan stance, a disinterested witness does not much care who wins or loses and would rather not get involved at all.

Action Rule: At the outset of the interview, seek to create a favorable bias in the witness by personalizing your client and his cause. Build a verbal image so that the witness is forced to think of him as a flesh and blood being who may be helped or hurt by what the witness says or does.

Describe your client and his family in detail, as though answering the question, "Who is he and what is he like?" Speak of him as if he were a friend as well as a client. ("Mr. Jones, I represent Dan Smith who was one of the drivers involved in the accident you know about. Dan's a young man, 26, and big . . . about 6 feet 2 I'd say. He and his wife, Sue, have three children, all boys. They live on the south side of town in a small bungalow they own . . . together with a bank, of course. Dan's a hard-working guy with a good driving record. This was his first accident, I understand, and no arrests.")

Then describe the client's injury and/or damages if he is the claimant or the demands made of him if he is the defendant, and explain the nature of the recovery you seek to obtain for the client (claimant) or the nature of the jeopardy you are defending him from (defendant).

I'm trying to get a settlement from the other driver's insurance company that will put Dan back on his feet again; pay his bills, pay his lost wages, protect him against any future disability and compensate him in a small way for the pain and trouble he's had.

Or . . .

I'm trying to protect Dan and Sue against losing their home and everything they've worked so hard to get. The other driver's demanding much more than their insurance coverage. Then, too, there's Dan's insurance premiums. If he loses this case he'll be paying much higher premiums for years, no matter what the other man gets.

Then ask the witness point blank to help you "in any way he can" so that you can help your client.

It is vital that you convey absolute sincerity and earnestness in your description of the client. That means (unless you are a consummate actor) telling only truth about him. If he is a drunken slob who beats his wife and gets stoned every other day, you need not mention it. But do not portray him as a loving husband of good habits.

The reward of an induced witness bias favorable to your client is an end to indifference and a beginning of a desire to help. The witness is now ready and willing to cooperate with you, to be interviewed at length and respond truthfully; ready to give you a written statement, to be open-minded (amenable to fact persuasion) and to appear for pre-trial discovery and trial testimony if necessary.

*   *   *

With all its charm and value, a good bias is no cure for bad facts. (No silk purse can be made from a sow's ear.) If a witness' facts are entirely adverse to you, he is convinced of their accuracy and cannot be shaken, then no amount of bias building will make an asset of him.

But what about making a pigskin purse? Even the most antagonistic witness can usually be left better than you find him. He may not renounce his damaging facts but he is likely to soften them. "He was racing down the road like a hot rodder" becomes . . . "He was driving a bit fast." "There's no doubt it was him holding the gun" becomes . . . "I think it was him holding the gun." The difference amounts to winning or losing.

NOTES

1. *The Malleability of Witness Testimony*

Before we address these observations directly, it is useful to focus on the sources of malleability that both Zimbardo and Simmons assume—the margin of error in people's perceptions, recollections and understanding of what they know and experience.

James Marshall has discussed the psychology of these gaps in the particular context of witness testimony at trial. His analysis includes the following comments on the sources of inaccuracies in what a witness perceived about the events in question:

> [S]cientific explorations of the most elementary perceptions have been carried from the laboratory test situation to the more sophisticated occurrences of daily life, and applied to *aural* as well as visual perception. Witnesses testify to what they heard as well as to what they saw. What do they hear? Kilpatrick reports that the novel sound of an oncoming tornado was conformed to past experience by many hearers who accepted it as the sound of an oncoming train; thus perceptual similarities are converted by the observer into identities in order to maintain the stability of his environment and thus his harmony with it.
>
> As Thucydides suggested, we do something very similar when we *recall* spoken words. We reconstruct conversations "of course adhering as closely as possible to the general sense of what was really said." None of us hears all the words or other sounds that occur in our presence. Many of us are deaf to certain tones and we miss the words or syllables in that tonal range, or we have some other diminution in hearing. What we do to adjust to such phenomena in normal conversation, or in listening to lecturers or arguments, is to fill in blanks as we believe the speaker might have meant them. We put together what we have heard with what we sense we might have missed in order to make a whole which is acceptable to us, thereby conforming our perceptions to our expectations. Obviously, this provides an opportunity to realize our expectations, to engage in wishful thinking. Thus a witness can in good honor swear to the truth of what he did not hear, to a damaging statement which a party never made or perhaps made in terms that were in reality not damaging to him.
>
>   *   *   *
>
> We sometimes read drama into perception. For example, when two moving dots are shown on a screen, the larger behind the smaller, the larger is perceived as "chasing" the smaller. But when the larger is shown in front, it is generally seen as "leading." The perception reflects some of our earliest childhood experiences. What we define as "good" or "bad" reflects in our perception of such matters as the facial expression of men on a picket line. To the management it appears "threatening," to labor "determined."
>
> An automobile accident is an exceedingly complex and sudden occurrence taking less than ten seconds. No matter how accurately it is observed, it cannot be perceived in an exact manner by any witness. In other words, not only is eyewitness testimony of such an occurrence necessarily inaccurate; it is also in essential points incomplete.
>
> In many tort and criminal cases *duration of events* is an important factor. Witnesses are asked to testify as to the interval between an occurrence and the action of a party or some third person. Experiments have demonstrated that we do not judge the passage of time accurately, and that "visual durations that were the same as auditory durations were judged shorter," by about twenty percent.

Danger and stress also affect the estimate of time and distance. This overestimate tends to increase as danger increases. As laymen we are accustomed to the concept that in emergencies time seems endless, but as lawyers we ignore the reality that with increasing danger "space and time stretch," and so accept the validity of a party's testimony that the car was a hundred yards away when he stepped off the curb, or the statement of a car driver as to when he sounded his horn. Not only the duration, but the *sequence* of events may be difficult to perceive. This too may be an important issue of fact, as when the question in an assault case is who struck first, or in a matrimonial proceeding, who spoke first.

* * *

The importance of judging distance when observing an automobile accident is obvious. Yet if *distance perception* is merely a secondary or derivative perception, as has been shown, then any witness's report of distance must be subject to so many other conditions that it may be unreliable. Another essential of any eyewitness report of an automobile accident is perception of motion, and this too has been demonstrated to be a secondary, or derivative, characteristic, dependent upon size, apparent distance, lighting, angle of vision, and the known attributes of the object perceived in motion.

With respect to relative size, Gardner notes that we tend to overestimate the length of verticals, and to exaggerate the difference if one average-sized person is surrounded by many exceptionally short or tall ones, and find that the one person is the exception and the others are the average.

* * *

Comparative brightness may indicate movement. Since brightness has some of the constant characteristics of size and will dominate those "cues" of lesser constancy, when the strength of a pinpoint of light is varied in a darkened room the observer concludes that the point is moving, toward him when it becomes brighter, away when it becomes dimmer. Brightness may also be taken as a cue to distance. Early astronomers, for example, assumed that the brightest stars were certainly closest to the earth. Since there was no experiential information about the actual size of a star, its brightness was taken as an indication of its distance from the observer.

Motion, in terms of *direction and velocity,* has also been found to be governed largely by cues of size and overlay, overlay being the apparent sequence of objects in space as related to the observer, indicated by what commonly appears to be the obstructed perception of one object by another object seemingly nearer to the observer. . . .

Filling gaps in perception is a betting process. We select what we believe will be harmonious with those elements we have perceived and repress those that will create dissonance for us. *The elements that we choose or repress will depend on what bet, or what selection, we make as the likeliest explanation for what we see; and that bet will, of course, be conditioned by past experience in similar situations.*[21]

21. J. Marshall, LAW & PSYCHOLOGY IN CONFLICT 13, 15–18 (1966). See also Redmount, *Handling Perception and Distortion in Testimony.* 5 AM.JUR.TRIALS 807 (1966).

It is with this "betting process" (by which perceptual gaps are filled) that a lawyer works. Think for example what might cause a witness to err on the side of understating rather than overstating speed, distance, or time. What would cause a witness to develop a stake or see some self-interest in a particular "slant" on the facts? Suppose an eyewitness to a mugging, Mr. A, saw what happened but cannot identify the defendant, and has boasted of the accuracy and detail of his perceptual abilities. Mr. A could probably be led to overstate distances or to "remember" that the lighting and physical layout of the scene would not permit a person with average powers of observation to identify the defendant. Such statements could be used to impeach him by contrasting them with the actual distances or conditions; or they could be used to undermine the testimony of another eyewitness, Ms. B, who claims that conditions for observing were much better, and that this permitted her to make a positive identification of the defendant. You might look again at the main readings and consider the ways in which Zimbardo's and Simmons' suggestions could be used to plan for and conduct an interview of A that would lead him to the sort of overstatements described above.

Marshall also discusses the sources of memory lapses:

> Considerable transformation of a happening and its initial perception occurs in recollection. . . . Witnesses are historians and autobiographers; on the witness stand they are reconstructing past events. Many of them to the best of their ability attempt to do it honestly, but it is not strange to find the grossest imperfection even in the memory of an honest man. Not only may his hearing and his eyesight be defective, but all his recollections often are the product of an association of ideas, commingled and confused with rationalization, and "all his memory may be tinctured by a bias, sometimes subconscious, or colored by suggestion." Not only do people vary in their native or trained capacities to recall what has occurred or what they have learned, but recollection is also affected by the circumstances in which the events have occurred, the learning taken place, or the story retold.

> Observers commonly see more than they can report. It has been found that "at the time of exposure, and for a few tenths of a second thereafter, observers have two to three times as much information available as they can later report. The availability of this information declines rapidly. . . ." The location of stimuli in the field of vision may affect the degree of an observer's recall as may the sequence with which certain items are reported, for memory is somewhat better with respect to the first items reported than those later reported. It would seem probable, however, that some of the "forgotten" material is suppressed, repressed, or subliminal and may be brought back to consciousness by new stimuli, such as direct or cross-examination or the testimony of other witnesses. By the time a witness testifies, the true order or recall has been lost.

* * *

Just as observation may be influenced by what the observer feels would be to his advantage, so a witness who knows that it would be advantageous if he were to remember that the light was red, or that the fire engine was sounding its siren, or the suspect had declared his intention to avenge himself on the victim, may ultimately believe that this was what he saw or heard. . . . If a witness's actual recollection is vague or nonexistent then any dissonance or contradiction can be removed or any void filled by slight but welcome advantage to himself, especially some psychological ego advantage.[22]

Finally, Marshall suggests that a witness' interpretations of events are not fixed at the time of the occurrence; they are constructed and reconstructed over time:

. . . Just as perception is colored by the past, giving rise to the expectation that what has been will be repeated, so interpretation makes use of values that have demonstrated their validity in similar transactions, happenings, or events to give significance to the present. In other words, what we call interpretation is similar to the transactional nature of perception; perhaps it is a phase of it—a more conscious application of the same process by which we read into our perceptions of distance the cue offered by experience with the size of objects in the environment.

* * *

Interpretive judgments are conditioned not only by the observer's experience as *a* human being but as a *particular* human being. They are not only the product of limitations of sense perception that are common to all of us but also of the unique characteristics of the individual. The significances he assigns to things and happenings are the result of his values and of subjective attitudes that may be derived from his age, race, nationality, sex, profession, religion—all his lifetime experience.

* * *

[Again, f]illing gaps in perception is a betting process. We select what we believe will be harmonious with those elements we have perceived and repress those that will create dissonance for us. The elements that we choose or repress will depend on what bet, or what selection, we make as the likeliest explanation for what we see; and that bet will, of course, be conditioned by past experience in similar situations.[23]

What do these observations tell you about witness interviewing? Zimbardo and Simmons would suggest the following:

First, the margin of error in a witness' statement is affected by the witness' own motives, circumstances, and personality. The ability of an investigator to recognize and deal with distortions will be enhanced by knowing as much as possible about these personal factors in advance of the interview.

22. *Id.* at 25–26, 36–37.   23. *Id.* at 22–24.

Second, most witnesses are aware of and feel they must deal with documents, objects, spatial arrangements and physical conditions in their versions of what happened. The ways in which such facts are presented or introduced into an interview can significantly influence a witness' account. In some instances—*e. g.*, with a hostile witness—a lawyer will avoid providing any of the details, permitting any discrepancies between the witness' statement and a physical fact to go uncorrected, for possible later use in impeachment. At other times, counsel will control a hostile witness by mentioning such detail early in the interview.

Third, timing—who gets to a witness first—can be very important. If Marshall is right, a witness' testimony is influenced as much by the story he or she becomes "committed to" as by what he or she perceived, understood, or remembers. Note that this consideration is in conflict with the first two generalizations. That is, a lawyer may get to a witness first but not be properly prepared to conduct the interview.

Fourth, there are always practical limits on how much someone else's perceptions, memory, and ways of understanding can be influenced. A heavy-handed, obvious approach is likely to produce doubt, resistance, and a firming-up of the facts away from your position. Malleability exists only at the margin of the details of what the witness saw and heard.

Do you agree with these generalizations? What others would you add? What weaknesses do you see in this approach? Our own experience would support Marshall's observations and make the advice of Simmons and Zimbardo practical, though at times troubling. A good deal of recent writing in social psychology suggests that attempts to influence recollections and perception in counsel's favor will be unsuccessful, because the witness will realize that he or she is being led. We have seldom found this to be so. The ethical questions here are substantial, and we discuss them explicitly in the next section. But the reality of influenceability exists.

In many interviews, lawyers do no more than suggest and reinforce an account that—from the witness' point of view—is at least as likely to be true as the one the witness would otherwise provide. There is no complete image of what happened in the witness' mind to be retrieved. Moreover, witnesses have needs and interests that cause them—whether consciously or not—to cooperate in producing a particular version of the facts. Without any improper conduct by counsel (who may never know what really happened either), in a surprising number of instances, the witness comes to believe and be personally committed to the account that counsel has helped generate. It is this characteristic more than any other that makes strategic investigation and preparation both possible and, in disconcerting ways, much like a confidence game.

2.   *The Investigative Interview Process*

While investigative interviewing raises many of the central puzzles in lawyering and the lawyer's role, it also involves a good deal of hard, practical, mundane work. It is worth addressing, at least briefly, some of the typical problems which you will face in doing this task. These include: (i) gaining access to a witness; (ii) deciding in what order to interview witnesses; and (iii) preserving a witness' statements.

Access

Access problems take a number of forms. Sometimes the task is simply to locate the witness. This is a particular problem with "disinterested witnesses" who, by definition, may be strangers to both parties in the case, and have only a chance relationship to the place where an incident occurred. If the case involves a crime or a traffic accident, potential witnesses may be identified in a police report. Other witnesses are also an important source of such information, though some interviewing skill may be required to get the lead you need. Consider, for example, the following excerpt from a police training manual:

> Some officers seem never to be able to find witnesses; others have little difficulty. One officer in the former category would shoulder his way through a crowd. "Did anybody see this accident?" he would shout. "How about you?" "How about you?" He would all but push the people about. Naturally, he found very few witnesses. In reporting back to his partner he would say, "There weren't any witnesses. I went through the crowd four times asking everybody, but nobody saw the accident." An adroit officer uses his head rather than his lung power. He goes about the job quietly. Perhaps he spots a talkative woman— at least one such person is to be found at most accidents. "How do you do, madam," he says. "Did I understand you to say that you saw this accident?" "Why, no, officer," she replies, probably feeling flattered that he singled her out, "I didn't see it, but that man in the straw hat over there was telling me all about it. He was right here when it happened." In approaching the man, the officer is very courteous but just a little more brisk and businesslike. He plans his questions carefully. He does not say, "Did you see this accident?" but rather, "Pardon me, sir, would you mind telling me what you saw in connection with this accident?" This officer seldom has difficulty in finding witnesses.

> He listens carefully to their accounts of the accident. Then, if they are willing to write out a statement, he provides them with notebook and pencil and asks them to sign what they write. If they will not write the statement, he writes it, reads it to them aloud, then has them sign it. If they refuse to sign, he does not insist; they are still his witnesses and he wants their good will when they appear on the stand in the trial, if a trial follows.

In brief, the good investigator usually seeks his witnesses indirectly. He finds somebody who knows that somebody else saw the accident.[24]

In many areas of law practice, the problem of finding unidentified witnesses rarely arises. We have focused on it here because it underscores the tenacity and effort involved in good investigative work. Simmons' checklist for finding unknown witnesses provides an example:

Checklist For Finding A Witness Who Is Not Known

1. If the witness was a bystander or you do not know how he got there, always canvass the neighborhood of the scene. If it is a residential neighborhood, question all available occupants of every house on both sides of the street and in both directions from the event site. If a business neighborhood, question all available employees (be sure to get the employer's consent) at each nearby establishment. A good rule of thumb to use for placing geographical limits is to check out every structure within possible sight or hearing of the event.

   —*Time your canvass* to coincide with the hour when the event occurred (also the same day of the week, if possible) to profit from the chance that the witness is usually in the neighborhood then.

   —*Tell each person* you question the importance of your search; that a witness may make the difference and lead to a just case result. Then briefly describe the event and ask him if he knows anything about it. (Do not ask if he "witnessed" it. He will answer "no" and still have witnessed important post-event facts, such as skid marks, vehicle locations, crime scene physical conditions or admissions by the adverse party.)

   —*Always ask* each person you question if anyone discussed the event with him in a way that suggested the other person witnessed it, or personally knew some fact connected with it. If someone did, get his name and address, suspend your canvass and seek to question him immediately.

   —*Ask each person* you question if another person at his home or business place, but not now present, was in the building or neighborhood when the event occurred. If there was, get his name and telephone number and call him later.

2. If an account of the event appeared in a local newspaper, interview the reporter who wrote the story. An experienced investigator himself, he is often more thorough than policemen in beating the bushes for witnesses. If he found one, his notes will yield the witness' identity.

24. Northwestern University Traffic Institute, ACCIDENT INVESTIGATION MANUAL 171–72 (1948).

3. Question people who are known to have been at the scene but whom you have not interviewed (e. g., policemen who assisted the investigating officer, ambulance or tow truck drivers, building or street repairmen, utility repairmen, newspapermen, news or free-lance photographers).

4. Question people who are regularly at or near the scene at the day and hour of the event (e. g., mail man, milk man, rubbish collector, home delivery man, newspaper boy). You can find out who they are from building occupants you question.

5. If the case warrants the expense, place a small ad in the local newspaper several days in succession. Have it spotted on a news page and not with classified ads. (How often do you read the "personal" column?) For a few extra dollars you can surround the ad with a heavy, black border and make it much more distinguishable.

6. If the expense is warranted, buy spot announcements on a local radio station, several days running. Specify 7–9 A.M. and 4–6 P.M. time slots when the audience is largest.

7. If the witness was in a car and its license plate number is known, trace the owner through the police department, local office of the American Automobile Association, or State motor vehicle department. It helps if you belong to AAA, and are friendly with the police or motor vehicles office, but even if you are not, an explanation of your search is usually enough to win fast cooperation.

8. If the event occurred shortly before or after a normal shift change (commonly 7 a. m., 3 p. m. and 11 p. m.) and the witness was in a car, contact all industries in the area. Explain the importance of your search and ask for an announcement over the public address system, a notice on plant bulletin boards or an ad in the plant newspaper (preferably all three).

Of all these search techniques, the neighborhood canvass is usually the most productive. Every veteran lawyer with whom I have discussed fact investigations emphasized its importance, for each had the experience of discovering witnesses by its means who never would have surfaced otherwise. On the negative side, canvassing is time-consuming, plodding, and often discouraging work. You may prefer sending an independent investigator to do it . . . or a young attorney in your office. If you do, be sure to instruct him to be thorough and skip no building within the zone you define.[25]

---

25. R. Simmons, WINNING BEFORE TRIAL: HOW TO PREPARE CASES FOR THE BEST SETTLEMENT OR TRIAL RESULT 410–12 (1974).

Beyond the specifics Simmons suggests, the tediousness of the efforts required here surely comes through in this excerpt. In the end, a good deal of self-discipline and will are necessary, but most good lawyers find ways to protect themselves against the pressure to stop short of thorough, complete work. In many instances you can and should work with co-counsel or involve an assistant in handling routine tasks and keeping details in order. At the very least you should be sensitive to how easy it is to find rationalizations for not doing mundane tasks.

Imagine yourself "on the street" carrying out these tasks. How will you maintain the discipline and concentration that seems to be required?

Access problems also include getting reluctant witnesses, whose identity and location are known, to talk to you. There are many reasons why a witness might be unwilling to be interviewed—*e. g.*, a general reluctance to "get involved"; distrust or dislike of legal proceedings and/or lawyers; unwillingness to "take sides" in a dispute; concerns about exposure or public statement of views; resistance to devoting the time and effort required; and doubts about your credibility, competence, or ability to protect the witness and make him or her look good. Many times a witness can be asked directly why he or she is reluctant to see you. In other cases, you will have no choice but to infer the source of the resistance and act accordingly.

Zimbardo suggests ways of gaining and keeping the attention and involvement of an interviewee and you might reread his piece with this issue in mind. Ask yourself if you would or should follow his advice. In his interview with the CRP bookkeeper at the beginning of this chapter, Carl Bernstein demonstrated one of these strategies: appear at a place where the witness would otherwise be free to talk to you (this obviously depends on the witness), and apply pressure, via the conventions and forms of everyday social interchange, to keep the witness in the room and talking to you. In addition to Bernstein's direct, mildly pressuring approach you might (i) have the client or another friendly witness initially seek out and interview the reluctant witness; (ii) proceed in steps ("I just want to hear your account. I'm not asking you to testify or talk to anyone else")—trial is often a long way off, and once you have made contact and begun to build a relationship, you can ask for more effort and commitment; (iii) indicate, in a low-key way, that you can compel testimony through a subpoena or deposition; (iv) set a deposition or issue a subpoena for a hearing at which the witness' statement can be taken: when faced with a formal proceeding or an informal conversation, witnesses often choose the latter; or (v) set a hearing or motion at which you know the witness will be present and try to interview him or her informally before or after the proceeding.

Finally, access involves making sure that witnesses remain available to you. Get an address or telephone number, and inquire about plans to travel or move. When the delay between investigation and trial is long, you may want to depose certain key witnesses, in order to assure that their testimony is preserved. At a minimum you should periodically call or, in some other way, make contact to let witnesses know where things stand, and that their testimony continues to be needed.

Sequence

Deciding the order in which to conduct various aspects of the investigation is also problematic. Generally, you will proceed from friendly to hostile, peripheral to central, low risk to high risk, willing to reluctant witnesses. Since you will get less time and cooperation from hostile or reluctant witnesses, no matter how important their testimony may be, you will need to be well-prepared in order to get the information you desire. For example, the fact that Carl Bernstein had talked with many other officials at the Committee to Re-elect the President, and had detailed knowledge of the Watergate events, allowed him to take maximum advantage of the opening he had with the bookkeeper.

Sequence choices are also involved in deciding whether to proceed formally or informally. Careful planning and preparation usually requires getting as much "hard" information as possible through informal means and interrogatories or requests to produce, *before* depositions or critical interviews with important witnesses. At other times you will need to commit a witness to his or her story in an informal setting in order to get the admissions you want in a deposition. For example, a public health inspector who would be very careful if approached in a formal deposition, might, over a cup of coffee, exaggerate the efficiency and accomplishments of his staff beyond what the actual data will show. If the same interviewer deposes the health inspector, it will usually be possible to hold him to the informal statements he made.

Preserving Statements

Finally, once a statement or admission has been obtained, it must be preserved in a usable form. Often this means getting the statement in writing. Keeton lists five reasons for obtaining written statements: [26]

> (i) To avoid misunderstanding between lawyer and client.
>
> (ii) To serve as a basis for trial preparations. (This is especially important where some of the interviews are conducted by investigators other than the lawyer in charge of the case.)
>
> (iii) To serve as the basis for settlement appraisal.
>
> (iv) To refresh the memory of the lawyer's own witnesses immediately before trial.
>
> (v) To impeach a hostile or adverse witness.

Even witnesses who are quite willing to be interviewed, however, may be reluctant to sign a written statement. A number of lawyers suggest the following methods of obtaining a signature:

> (i) asking the witness to make out the entire statement (thereby increasing the likelihood that he or she will sign it);

---

26. R. Keeton, TRIAL TACTICS AND METHODS 317–19 (1973).

(ii) asking the witness to make additions to the document prepared by the lawyer;

(iii) intentionally making an error in the document, pointing it out to the witness so that changes will be in the witness' hand;

(iv) asking the witness to initial the statement (on the theory that people are less reluctant to initial than to sign);

(v) sending someone to the witness' house with a typed version of the statement (the theory being that the witness will find it more difficult to refuse to sign in such circumstances).

Ask yourself which of Keeton's purposes these devices are designed to serve, what assumptions they rely on, and whether you would be willing to employ them.

———

3. *The Investigative Interview in a Formal Setting: Depositions*

Many of the techniques suggested by Zimbardo and Simmons are equally applicable to the sort of "interview" which takes place during a deposition. Obviously the setting is more adversarial, the witness often has counsel present, and answers can be compelled. Nevertheless, memory and motive are used to obtain information and admissions in the deposition much as they are in the informal interview.

For example, consider the following comments by Walter Barthold on "making the most of a deposition." He lists five primary goals for this procedure:

1. To gain information, including the identity and location of sources of evidence;

2. To preserve testimony for possible use during the trial;

3. To find out how much the person to be examined knows, both about his own case and about yours;

4. To commit the party or witness to a version of the facts from which he cannot later deviate so as to adapt to a changed complexion of the case;

5. To confront the party to be examined with damaging evidence, or otherwise to show him the weaknesses in this case, thereby inducing him to drop the case or make a settlement favorable to examining counsel.[27]

27. W. Barthold, ATTORNEY'S GUIDE TO EFFECTIVE DISCOVERY TECHNIQUES 64 (1975). For works on this and other aspects of discovery *see* W. Barron & A. Holtzoff, FEDERAL PRACTICE AND PROCEDURE vol. 2A (Wright, ed., 1961); H. Hickam & T. Scanlon, PREPARATION FOR TRIAL (1963); Armstrong, *The Use of Pre-trial and Discovery Rules: Expedition and Economy in Federal Civil Cases*, 43 A. B.A.J. 693 (1957); Glieberman, *Depositions and Divorce Actions*, 12 PRAC.LAWYER 53 (Oct.1966); Savell, *Basic Use of Discovery Procedures—Some Practical Problems* 3 FORUM 197 (1968); Thompson, *How to Use Written Interrogatories Effectively*, 16 PRAC.LAWYER 81 (Feb. 1970).

He goes on to suggest the following approaches to questioning:

Your selection of the goal or goals of your deposition should take you a long way toward deciding the strategy of your examination. If, for example, you decide that your objective in the deposition will be to determine how much a hostile witness really knows about the strengths and weaknesses of your own or your adversary's case, you might think it best to assume the role of a friendly, sympathetic listener. You hope thereby to draw the witness into making admissions or revealing facts that might not come to light were he more on his guard. If, on the other hand, you decided that you wish mainly to commit the witness to the narrowest possible set of facts, you might think it wisest to assume a sterner role, hoping to impress the witness with the seriousness of the case and with the solemnity of his oath. There are, of course, many variations to these two basic techniques and many others as well. What is important is that you make up your mind, in advance if you can, what demeanor or style is going to do the most for you in a particular examination and how you should deal with specific situations likely to arise.

* * *

As a help in formulating this part of your deposition plan, here is a list of questions to ask yourself in preparation for, or if necessary, during, any deposition:

1. Should you appear, by silence and perhaps an occasional nod of the head, to accept the witness's version of the facts, no matter how outrageous you know it to be?

2. Would it, on the other hand, do more for your case to try to undermine the witness's self-confidence by indicating, in one way or another, that you have reason (not necessarily to be disclosed) to doubt his story?

3. If the witness claims to have forgotten a particular event, are you going to try to refresh his recollection or let the record stand so that any revival of his memory at trial will appear suspicious?

4. If the person being examined makes a statement that you can disprove by documentary or photographic evidence, will you reveal his inaccuracy to him or let him remain in ignorance until the trial?

5. How will you deal with overt hostility on the witness's part, particularly if it takes the form of long, gratuitous tirades on the merits of the case?

6. How do you propose to deal with the opposite attitude, i. e., friendliness on the witness's part? Will you respond to it in kind, hoping thereby to win the witness's confidence, or will you display coolness in the hope of impressing the witness with the gravity of the situation?

A contract action illustrates the problem posed by the first two of the above questions:

Plaintiff has charged defendant with breach of contract. His lawyer is taking the deposition of defendant's assistant director of purchases. The witness relates a conversation in which, he says, plaintiff's sales manager waived the alleged breach. Plaintiff's counsel knows that he may be able to "shake" this damaging story by pointing out inconsistencies with the witness's testimony earlier in the day. Having thought the matter out beforehand, he nevertheless resists the temptation to embarrass the witness. He realizes that he can exploit the contradiction more effectively at trial. He gives, therefore, every appearance of taking the testimony at face value.

Counsel in this situation has, of course, taken into account the possibility that the witness or his lawyer may notice and attempt to correct the inconsistency in reading the transcript of the deposition before signing it.

Let us consider an example of the type of problem posed by the fourth of our questions:

An elderly lady has sued a stock-brokerage firm. She alleges that the executive in charge of her account caused her substantial losses by misusing his discretionary authority and "churning" her account to enhance his own and the firm's income. Defense counsel has a handwritten letter from plaintiff, written a few months before the transactions of which she is complaining, at a time when market conditions were more favorable. Plaintiff's letter thanks and praises the account executive for his astute advice in making so many profitable trades and encourages him to "keep up the good work." Defense counsel feels safe in assuming that plaintiff, like most individuals, did not keep a copy of her handwritten letter. He ponders what to do.

We may envy defendant's attorney such a potent piece of evidence, but it does pose problems for him. He knows that if he shows the letter to plaintiff at her deposition for the purpose of authenticating it, he may discourage her and her attorney from continuing the action. This, of course, will save his client great expense. He realizes, on the other hand, that revealing this crucial exhibit at a preliminary stage may provide his adversary with time to explain it away or rebuild the case in some way not inconsistent with the letter. He must, therefore, consider withholding the document until he can confront plaintiff with it at trial.

The latter course of action also presents problems. First, if plaintiff dies or becomes incompetent before trial, defense counsel may fail to get the document into evidence. Secondly, plaintiff, even though she did not keep a copy of the letter, may remember it. She may, for all defense counsel knows, be prepared to explain it by, for example, saying that the account executive solicited it as a favor to help him keep his job in the face of a retrenchment then taking place at the firm. If defense counsel keeps the letter to himself until trial, he may thus receive an unpleasant surprise. Had he brought it out at plaintiff's deposition and heard her explanation, he might have decided not to use the letter or perhaps have conducted further factual research and developed a counter-explanation. The decision of what to do with so favorable a piece of evidence is not necessarily an easy one.[28]

Philip Hermann adds similarly adversarial advice:

How many lawyers prepare witnesses or parties for deposition as well as they do for trial? How many lawyers take the witness, prior to a deposition, to the scene of the accident as they do in preparation for trial? How many lawyers take the deposition process so casually that they do not even bother to prepare their witnesses? How often have you wished that the lawyer who had ordered a deposition had scheduled it for a more convenient time or day? How often has the press of the business of the day encroached upon preparation time? Have you ever met a witness, favorable to your client's cause, in the opposing attorney's law offices about to have his deposition taken without any preparation? *Let's face it—most witnesses and parties to a lawsuit who are presented for deposition are not adequately prepared.* With diamonds of admissions and of material destructive to the opposing side in our own backyard just waiting to be gathered, why content ourselves with using the deposition merely as a discovery process? Of course, any deposition may develop inconsistencies and secure valuable admissions, but why content ourselves with mere rubies when, in a properly planned and handled deposition, we can harvest acres of diamonds toward minimizing or destroying the opposing case?

* * *

Technique

Some lawyers subscribe to the theory that a witness should be treated roughly, in the hope that you can shake some admissions out of him. Actually, depositions taken in such a manner rarely gather many admissions. It is far better to disarm the witness. Win his confidence. You may be surprised at the admissions your smile will encourage. Recently, an injured witness who was suing for substantial injuries confided that the accident was her husband's fault because he had failed to see a stop sign. You can imagine how surprised his attorney was. The witness felt so relaxed that she didn't realize her mistake until too late. Another witness, to his lawyer's amazement, readily admitted to facts which indicated his fault. He topped it off by saying that he knew the accident was his fault, but he asked whether I could help him get some money from the insurance company. When asked by his lawyer why he had made such admissions, he was stunned to discover I was a member of the opposition.

It is suggested that you greet the witness with a friendly smile and take his coat. Be courteous to him at all times. Make him comfortable. Ask permission to use his first name, or nickname, except in the case of persons to whom respect is due. If this sweet approach doesn't get you some diamonds, then, of course, you can always try the more classic approach.

28. *Id.* at 67–70.

A witness who is not telling the truth must not only keep in mind the accident scene and the action that took place, but in addition must reassociate the answers given by him to the scene and the action. Reassociation can rarely be carried out at high speed, as it entails remembering the answers previously given and the necessity of placing in context these answers and the accident situation. If such a witness is asked questions in rapid sequence, it becomes difficult to carry on such reassociation and, hence, a witness who is not dealing with the truth will tend to expose himself. This is an elementary principle of cross-examination, yet everyday lawyers slow their examination to a snail's pace, taking copious notes. It is suggested that one should rely on the court reporter, so that rapid-fire questioning can be employed.

Most witnesses are prepared on the basis of the sequence of the events that occurred. Questioning a witness in such sequence can rarely be highly successful. On the other hand, questions asked in illogical sequence, such as starting the questioning at the point of impact or some other illogical spot and then jumping around from place to place, not only will dull the veneer of preparation, but makes reassociation difficult. Such questioning may look like the product of a disorganized mind, but will frequently be highly productive of diamonds.

When I was a boy on the farm, I was told that the way to get a horse to the drinking trough was to lead him there. Likewise, to get admissions from a witness, *one must lead him to the admissions.* By using leading questions, a witness can frequently be led to all kinds of admissions that are consistent with your theory of how the accident occurred. If you are questioning concerning injuries, admissions of recovery often can be obtained. *Leading questions frequently bring admissions because untruthful witnesses are led to think that the truth is known and to feel that further denial may be useless.*

A few weeks ago during trial of a lawsuit, a witness who was impeached by his own words from a deposition complained that he could not possibly remember all the answers asked him on deposition as he had been questioned over a period exceeding two hours. Interestingly, this deposition when originally taken, appeared to be completely unsuccessful, as it appeared to contain nothing which appeared to be of value at a trial. However, testimony at the trial itself proved to be so different, in a number of respects, that the witness was effectively impeached by his own previous testimony. Though it was a liability case—a "rear-ender"—the plaintiff's attorney, on the third day of trial, realizing that the jury was lost and that it would be foolish to waste money to put on more testimony, dismissed. Questioning of the jury afterwards confirmed that the attorney was right. *A good deposition should be comprehensive, should cover all relevant material.*

Recently, I showed up in an opposing attorney's office to find that the only disinterested witness in the lawsuit, a next-door neighbor of my client, was waiting to be deposed. Though he was considered to be a witness favorable to our cause, I was concerned with what the passage of two years of time would do to a witness *who was not prepared.* He, of course, like many witnesses will do, had shown up without notifying anyone of his summons. He was questioned superficially for about seven or eight minutes; after the examiner had satisfied himself that this witness was favorable to my client, he ended the deposition. Back in my office, questioning of this witness in the way he probably would have been questioned at trial, or as he should have been questioned on deposition, revealed that thorough questioning at the deposition would have completely destroyed his effectiveness. Interestingly, and probably typically, at the trial this witness was questioned for well over half an hour. He was prepared and he made a good witness. Finally, failing to dent the witness, the opposing lawyer sought to destroy the witness' effectiveness by showing that, as a next-door neighbor, he was just being neighborly and friendly in testifying. Imagine the surprise of the examiner when the witness stated that he was no friend of his neighbor's and that they had not talked for two years because of a boundary-line dispute. Need I say that the case was immediately settled at the right price?

The trial lawyer who questioned concerning the likely hunch of friendly neighbors certainly did so at the wrong place. On deposition, and not at the trial, this should have been explored. During a deposition, we frequently have hunches. Certainly, these should be explored. A social worker, daughter of an injured plaintiff, testified that she had quit a job that she loved to care for her mother and to run her mother's business in her absence. However, questioning revealed that she had quit without seeking a leave of absence. It was a hunch that she had quit her job first, before the accident. The hunch was explored by the use of leading questions. You can imagine what wide eyes the witness had when she admitted that she had resigned before the accident. Another hunch, that the supposedly bedridden mother had gone away to visit a very sick daughter in another city, put the finishing touches on a lawsuit in which the demand dropped from $20,000, with about $8,000 in claimed specials, to $200.

Sometimes we know of embarrassing material, such as convictions for crime. Save embarrassing material for use just before crucial questions. An embarrassed witness frequently will make admissions that he would not otherwise have made.

We should also take advantage of the element of fatigue. By leaving the most important phases of the depositions for last, you are most likely to secure needed admissions. Accordingly, in accident cases, questions as to liability are the very last series that should be asked. Waiting until last with these is more productive of result even if the witness is not tired or upset. He sometimes becomes overconfident; this can lead to his destruction, too.[29]

Although depositions are not available in criminal cases, lawyers discussing the discovery potential of examining witnesses at a preliminary hearing or motion to suppress offer similar guidance.[30]

29. P. Hermann, *Winning Your Lawsuit by Deposition,* 448 INS.L.J. 297–300 (1960).

30. *See, e. g.,* Carlson, *Representation at Preliminary Hearing,* CRIMINAL DEFENSE TECHNIQUES VOL. I, ch. 8 (R. Cipes, ed., 1969), LAW AND TACTICS IN FEDERAL CRIMINAL CASES (G. Shadoan, ed., 1964).

Compare this material with the suggestions of Zimbardo and Simmons. Can these also be classified as Machiavellian strategies? Would you use them?

It might be argued that such an approach is unlikely to be effective—that it would inevitably tend to cut off information that counsel would need to know before trial. Do you agree? Can you articulate the dynamics involved in being the witness or deponent in these situations? How would you react to such strategies? How would you feel using them?

————

4. *Some observations on the Investigator's experience*

All of the foregoing needs to be considered not only in terms of skills and techniques, but also with attention to the experience it involves. What is involved here is a strategic relationship with a person who very often has not chosen to be, and may not be aware of being, an adversary. Consider the following example:

* * *

In preparing for a motion to dismiss charges against my client for selling narcotics, it became obvious that I might benefit from interviewing the undercover agent, B, who made the arrest. If it could be shown that he used narcotics when undercover and was therefore unreliable, and that his job depended on successful prosecution of his sales, my case would be strengthened.

Objectives

I guessed that he was still on probation with the police department (although they officially denied it) and that he had been hospitalized for withdrawals after being undercover, as is sometimes the case, but I couldn't prove it because it would have been under an assumed name. My objective was to get him to admit that fact as well as his anxiety about his probationary status. I hoped to use both at trial.

Strategy and Assumptions

I knew that he was new to undercover work, and, because he was black, had not dealt with defense attorneys much, and was probably not being given much support within the D. C. Police Department. They would often hire recently arrived young black males, send them undercover and, for a variety of reasons, would subsequently wash them out of the force. My theory was that if (a) I treated him with some respect and consideration; (b) sympathized with his situation; (c) appeared to know what I only guessed; and (d) distanced myself from my client, there was a chance that he'd say what more experienced officers would not.

I can't recount the entire conversation (which was over an hour and in a neighborhood bar) but the following gives you some idea of what transpired.

TRANSCRIPT

(WHAT WAS SAID)	(WHAT I WAS THINKING)
ME: They're a pain in the ass— never give you a straight story, never make it easy. Ross is funny, though. I think he'd really rather be in jail than on the streets.	This was part of a general discussion in which I was postured myself as experienced, part of the system, and not taken in by the defendants. On the other hand, since this technique is often used to get information, I couldn't sound too indifferent to my client.
B: Yeah, they really need help. It drove me crazy.	A very uncharacteristic response for an officer. My guesses about his inexperience were partially confirmed.
ME: How are you feeling? I heard you were in a Rockville, Maryland hospital in August but I gather you're okay now.	
B: Who said that?	I probably guessed right.
ME: A friend of mine on the force. Hell, don't look so surprised. Anybody who does this work knows that if you don't shoot once in a while out there, you'll get yourself killed.	If I can reassure him that it is talked about, he may feel free to admit it. I think it sounded certain and casual to him. A friend of mine on the force had said that most undercover officers who got addicted did go to that hospital.
B: Yeah, it's rough.	
ME: I hear the doctors up there can give you a worse time than the junkies. I know a guy that got hooked worse after they began than before. Never really got off it.	If I hinted he might have become addicted, he might admit he was in the hospital but not addicted.
B: Well, they were pretty good with me. I was only in for observation.	I felt he was lying but I got what I wanted.
ME: For a week or so, huh?	This would be too long for merely observation, but he might not have realized that.
B: Yeah.	
ME: It's a tough job—no security—if the cases go sour, where are you?	This referred back to an earlier subject. It really was a terrible practice and he reacted honestly to it.

TRANSCRIPT

(WHAT WAS SAID)   (WHAT I WAS THINKING)

B: You're right about that.
It's a lot of shit, this probationary status.

ME: But you're in good shape—   I wanted him to say he was worried
none of us are going to   and thought he might if he were dis-
tear the courthouse down   agreeing with me.
over these kinds of cases.

B: Well, you never know.

ME: I guess it's always a possibility that you could be
out.

B: Yeah.   I'm sure he didn't realize what he
had admitted to or how it could be
used.

    I used both the statement that he had been in a hospital for ob-
servation concerning narcotics and that he felt he could lose his job
during the trial after being given permission by the court to confront
him with our conversation. (I could not refer to it without such permission because if he denied it, I would have had to testify.) It was
also used in argument in the Court of Appeals. It might have cost him
his job—I'm not sure—he was not given a permanent position on the
force.[31]

    How do you suppose the lawyer in this example got the witness
to talk to him, and why do you think he arranged the meeting in a
bar? Look again at the preliminary comments, as well as the transcript itself, and notice how much information counsel had in advance
of the interview, and how he intentionally used this information to
get admissions he wanted. What human tendencies, idiosyncracies,
or vulnerabilities did he play on?

    The interview is a classic example of the way skillful lawyers
are able to take advantage of the "field" in which an interaction occurs in order to build a case. In particular, notice that the lawyer's
plan during the interview was to treat the officer with some respect
and consideration, and that he seemed to be successful in communicating this disposition to the officer. What do you imagine the lawyer
actually felt towards the officer? Were the respect and consideration just tactical—a cover for other feelings and goals? If so, how
must the lawyer have experienced these two levels—this control of
appearance and reality and the "use" he made of it at trial? On the
other hand, if the lawyer genuinely felt some respect and regard for

31. This transcript was used in a semi-
nar on clinical teaching (1976–77).

the officer and his situation, then what was his experience at trial and afterwards when he pushed aside his sympathetic dispositions and acted in ways that may have hurt the witness? Would different feelings be expected if the officer were an unrepresented party in a civil action? Or if counsel had obtained the same admissions in a deposition with another lawyer present? Would the officer's having counsel change the lawyer's experience?

The next section discusses the ethics of these actions. Here we will only pause to observe that, the profession's norms notwithstanding, we have not found it easy to resolve or rationalize this experience by asserting a simply hierarchy of values and loyalties—clients first, then one's own needs and interests, then friendly others, then neutral others, then opponents and so on . . .; or by resorting to role— "I'm just doing a necessary job." The skillful investigator seems inevitably to be treading dubious moral ground. Movement toward one of the possible extremes (client loyalty, role neutrality, concern for others) may simplify but cannot harmonize the different and competing claims involved in a lawyer's relations with clients and the clients' adversaries.

In the case we have been discussing, the lawyer won on appeal and his client went free. In reflecting on the interview long afterwards, the lawyer said:

> It would not be the last time I depended on someone else's ignorance to help my clients. I've always wondered about it, and whether I'd do it again. I'm afraid I might.

Ross, the client in this case, was almost certainly the victim of illegal police activity and had been wrongly accused. For those who aspire to treat non-clients as well as clients with decency and respect, however, it is not at all clear that—in the long run—such a possibility is justification enough.

SECTION THREE. THE ETHICAL DIMENSION

As the preceding materials amply demonstrate, investigation is not a neutral process. The lawyer as investigator is expected to think and plan as an advocate of the client's cause. Indeed, when serving as an advocate, "doubts as to the bounds of law" are to be resolved "in favor of [the] client." [32] We turn here to the ethical limits of this mandate. Plaintiff E. Z. Finance Co., an assignee of a contract of sale between the defendant and Winkleman Auto Sales, has brought an action for non-payment of the contract price of the car. The defendant, represented by William King, claims (and has so advised his lawyer) that (i) the transmission of the car was defective and (ii) he

32. EC 7–3.

was told that the car was a "good buy." Under applicable state law, the defendant's claims, if established, are a complete defense to plaintiff's action.

The following is a transcript of an interview and subsequent cross-examination of Ronnie Jones, a mechanic employed by Winkleman Auto Sales at the time the car was purchased.

E. Z. FINANCE v. EVANS

SCENE: . . . *King, defendant's attorney, is interviewing Jones, witness for the plaintiff, in Jones' home.*

King: Sorry to hear about the accident. I thought you were still at Winkleman's Auto Sales until I called there last week.

Jones: Nope. I'm out ta pasture, at least for a while. Guess you can see that. Can't be a mechanic with a bum arm and leg.

King: What happened?

Jones: Just what I always told them would happen. It was too damn crowded in the stalls. Winkleman kept hiring young guys and they'd hot rod around. I kept saying they're gonna hit one of them cars when somebody's under it. They didn't do nothing about it, so I just gave up and it happened to me. Ha, I could kick myself.

King: That's a damn shame. The pity of it is, it could have been avoided.

Jones: Well, yeah, you're right. Course, what's done is done.

King: How do you manage now?

Jones: I get workmen's comp. Partial, temporary disability is what they call it. Keeps me and the little lady going, but my God, I had to fight for every penny.

King: That's terrible. There should have been no trouble with a claim as straightforward as yours.

Jones: You don't know Winkleman. No one who's working there would come forward about unsafe conditions. I had to fight 'em every inch. Thank God I got what I did cause a guy like me can't find work with a disability. You know what I mean?

King: Well, it sounds as if you've got grounds to complain, maybe even permanent disability.

Jones: You think so? They keep hounding me to come back to work. Aw, I tell 'em it still hurts, but, ah, they don't hear so good. Maybe I should think about asking 'em for some more money?

King: Maybe so. Wouldn't hurt to ask . . .

I was hoping we could talk a bit about the car my client purchased at Winkleman's.

Jones: Sure.

King: They tell me you examined it before he bought it. What kind of condition was it in?

Jones: Yeah, I saw it a long time before then. A guy wanted to trade it in so, ah, the salesman, Harry Winters was his name, he asked me to check it out. The transmission was ground away, anyone could see that. So they didn't pay the guy much for it and then they give it to me to clean it up so they could put it on the lot.

King: Did anyone else work on the car?

Jones: Na, I doubt it. I did all of Winkleman's checkups and then I made up the work sheets for the other guys. I would have known. Heh, Winkleman told me I was responsible for the cars. Salesmen counted on me and what I told them but, . . . Hell, I was afraid the guy was gonna sue me, you know? Just like Winkleman, too, to put the blame on someone else.

King: Do I understand now that at the time my client bought the car, the transmission was still in bad condition?

Jones: Right.

King: Do you know if the salesman knew that?

Jones: Sure, it was the same guy, Harry Winters. I told him myself. It could keep going anywhere from a month to a year, but that's it. That's what I told him. Course, uh, sometimes you could be wrong.

King: Then, ah, distorting the facts is a pretty common practice with the salesmen out there? Isn't that what you're saying?

Jones: Well, I guess you could put it that way . . . But it don't apply to your guy.

King: Why's that?

Jones: Harry told him straight. I was there. And Jerry Wills. Jerry is another mechanic. Jerry was there too. We was working on this car that was sittin' next to where they was talking and Harry says, "The transmission's bad, I'm telling you that."

King: You're sure he said that?

Jones: Sure as can be.

King: Did he say anything else?

Jones: Uh, now that you ask me about it. Yeah, oh yeah, I remember him ending up . . . Well, let me see how it went. "But for the mon . . . but for the price we're asking, this car is a real good buy." Yeah, yeah, that's his very words and, ah, that's when your guy said he'd take it.

King: Is that other mechanic still at Winkleman's?

Jones: Jerry? I can't say for sure. He was only part-time, even then. He'd be there on and off . . . you can try the Riverton phone book.

King: So both you and Jerry Wills heard the salesman tell my client that the car was a good buy?

Jones: Them's the exact words, like I give 'em to you.

King: Well, what did the lawyer from the finance company say when you told him about the "real good buy" part?

Jones: Well, come to think on it . . . It didn't come up then. I didn't say nothing about it since no one asked me but you. I mean I don't talk just to be talking. You've gotta ask me if you wanna jar me loose.

Hey, speaking about the other lawyers, ah, I was wondering, am I supposed to call them and tell them you're here? Am I supposed to do that?

King: No. I don't think that's required here.

Jones: Yeah, I guess I'll be seeing them soon enough anyway, huh?

King: Since you said they, I assume there's more than one?

Jones: More than one? There's three of 'em. And they all come here three times to take my statement, three times! I told them I just as soon stay out of it, especially the court. But, ah, they said there wasn't no choice.

King: That seems like a bit of an imposition.

Jones: Sure, it was. I don't like them much. They're not like you, you know? Sitting around the table, informal like, talking about the problem. No. They sit like this and then they fire questions at you like you was the one on trial. The same questions, over and over again.

King: Well, I feel even more apologetic about having to go over the same ground again. In fact, it was that sort of pushiness that got my client so upset about this case. Once Winkleman turned it over to the finance company, no one would listen to my client's side of the story.

Jones: I don't doubt it. Them finance boys is tough!

King: Well, I assume their lawyers offered you the usual $25 witness fee?

Jones: No. They didn't even offer me that at first.

King: You're kidding?

Jones: No, they didn't say a word about it. But, ah, the wife's been a witness and she told me there was some money.

King: They sound like real bastards.

Jones: That's for sure . . . But I got 'em this time. Ah, can I say something, ah, off the record, so to speak?

King: Sure, why not.

Jones: I turned them down. I got to have more expenses than that, I says. So, ah, they asked me what I need. So I put in for 200 bucks. Oh, and I meant it too. I figure I got it coming to me. That company never done me no favors. I got nothing but hassles from this whole thing.

King: What happened?

Jones: One guy nods at the other. He nods back and that's that, I get my expenses.

King: And a little extra for your inconvenience?

Jones: Yeah, for the inconvenience.

King: Well, Mr. Jones, it's been good talking with you and I'm very grateful for your help, and the coffee too.

Jones: Nice talking to you, Mr. King.

King: See you in court.

* * *

SCENE: *A courtroom. The trial is in progress.*

Judge: You may cross-examine, Mr. King.

King: You prepared a long time for your testimony about the condition of this car, didn't you, Mr. Jones?

Jones: Yeah, that's right. I started talking with the lawyers . . .

King: Please limit your answers to yes or no. You met as many as three times with plaintiff's counsel, did you not?

Jones: Yeah.

King: And you rehearsed your questions and answers then, did you not?

Jones: Well, I wouldn't exactly say that.

King: Just yes or no.

Jones: Yeah.

King: And those are the questions and answers that we're hearing here today?

Jones: Yeah.

King: Isn't it also a fact that you were paid for your testimony?

Jones: Whaddya mean?

King: Isn't it a fact that you were paid $200 to testify here today?

Jones: Yeah, but uh . . .

King: And you were the one who demanded that sum, weren't you? Plaintiff's attorney offered you $25, the statutory witness fee, but you demanded more.

Jones: Well, I, ah, deserve more, ah, for my expenses.

King: You incurred $200 in expenses while rehearsing this testimony?

Jones: That's right.

King: And that's what you told plaintiff's counsel?

Jones: Yeah.

King: You just didn't make it up?

Jones: No.

King: Mr. Jones, isn't it a fact that all of your present earnings come from workmen's compensation?

Jones: Well, uh . . .

King: Mr. Jones?

Jones: Yeah.

King: So you really had no lost earnings because of the time you spent on this case, did you?

Jones: No.

King: And when you claimed $200 as expenses, you were lying, weren't you?

Jones: Well, uh . . .

King: By the way, Mr. Jones, you testified that you heard the conversation between my client and the salesman at Winkleman's Auto Sales, didn't you?

Jones: Yeah.

King: Did you hear the salesman say, "this car is a real good buy?"

Jones: Yeah.

King: No further questions, your honor.

Judge: You may be excused, Mr. Jones. However, you should be advised that the court is concerned about the amount of your witness fee in this case.

Davis [associate counsel] (whispering): Are you still going to call the other mechanic who was there with Jones?

King: No, not now. He'd only hurt us by testifying that the salesman warned our client about the transmission. I'm afraid our client didn't level with us.

Davis: Say, how did you get that information you were using?

King: Oh, I just interviewed him.

NOTES

1. *Relations with Witnesses: the Guidance of the Code*

At the heart of these interchanges is the problem of fairness: what obligations does King owe to Jones in (i) interviewing him; (ii) cross-examining him?

Assume that King believes that Jones is telling the truth about everything he says in the interview. His client, however, denies that he was ever warned that the transmission was defective or that the "good buy" statement was preceded by any qualification concerning the price. Is what King did required, prohibited or permitted by the ethical mandates of the profession? In the areas in which he had discretion did he act in ways that you find justified? Although there are many ambiguities in the profession's norms here, King's actions stay surprisingly (and, for us, troublingly) close to his professional responsibilities.

The Visit To an Unrepresented, Prospective Party

Although Jones (who apparently fixed the car) may himself be subject to a cross-complaint in the case, there seems to be no restriction on King going out to see him. DR 7–104(A)(1) provides that a lawyer shall not communicate with "a *party* he knows to be represented by a lawyer" without the prior consent of that lawyer. However, the rule apparently does not prohibit *contact* with (i) employees of a party; or (ii) prospective and unrepresented parties.[33] You might ask yourself what rationale would support such distinctions.

Only two prohibitions in the Code limit King in interviewing Jones. First, he may not "give advice to a person who is not represented by a lawyer, other than the advice to secure counsel, if the interests of such person are or have a reasonable possibility of being in conflict with the interests of his client."[34] Although there is an argument that advice may be given, despite this prohibition, when it is apparently in the interests of *both* the witness and the lawyer's client, the rule against advice seems to have been rather strictly construed.[35] King's statements about (i) the possibility that Jones could collect for permanent disability and (ii) the absence of any requirement that he contact plaintiff's attorney, certainly come very close to the line.

Second, King's decision to interview Jones *alone* runs the risk that, if Jones denies what he said in the interview at trial, King would have to testify to impeach him. Writing as a U.S. Court of

---

33. ABA Opinions 117 (1934), 14 (1929), 127 (1935), 187 (1938); EC 7–18. If King were prohibited from seeing Jones he could not send an employee or investigator to see him. See DR 1–102(A)(2); ABA Opinion 95 (1933).

34. DR 7–104(A)(2); *see also* ABA Opinion 58 (1931).

35. ABA Opinion 58 (1931) (attorney may not attempt to induce an adverse party in a divorce action to accede to the action); ABA Informal Opinion 1255 (1972) (improper to submit "appearance and responsive pleading" to unrepresented adverse party for signature); *cf.*, ABA Informal Opinion 1269 (1973) (not improper to seek waiver of issuance and service of summons from an unrepresented defendant). *Cf.* ABA Informal Opinion 575 (1962) (permitting counsel for a defendant in a criminal case to advise a prosecution witness of the dangers of incrimination if he testified at trial).

Appeals Judge about this situation, Chief Justice Burger has said the following:

> In the trial of this case trial counsel asked the detective if he re-called a telephone conversation in which the officer told defense counsel that he did not see the defendant with anything in his hand; that he hadn't seen him drop anything; and that what he said he saw was the defendant making some sort of motion which he in-terpreted to be a pitching motion, and that he didn't see him drop anything. The officer categorically denied such a conversation.
>
> No effort was then made by defense counsel to follow this line of questioning with proof of the alleged "facts" or of the assumptions implicit in the questions. To be sure, it might have been awkward for the lawyer to take the stand and testify, but if he was not prepared to do this, even if it meant withdrawing from the case he should not have asked the questions. Counsel asking such questions with no intention of following them up if the answers were negative, would be subject to severe censure. We assume in this case that it was a thoughtless "shot in the dark" attributable perhaps to lack of experience in the highly practical and difficult art of trial advocacy. Utterances similar to this when made by a prosecutor have led us to reverse criminal convictions.[36]

Here, of course, the risk never materializes. Jones never has to be asked about the conversations at trial. Moreover, the prohibitions of the Code and the ABA Opinions on this subject are not so absolute. The disciplinary rules governing acceptance of employment and with-drawal when counsel "ought to be called as a witness for his client" contain a number of exceptions and apply only where the lawyer "knows or it is obvious" that he will be performing conflicting roles.[37] Most lawyers seem to consider it proper for King to assume that Jones will admit to what he said (as he did) when confronted with it at trial.

Ingratiation

Whatever the parameters of the prohibition against advising po-tentially adverse witnesses, the limits relate only to advice. There seems to be no prohibition in the Code against feigning interest in the witness or sympathy for his or her plight, or assuming any other atti-tude which will lead the witness to talk. This apparently includes King's expression of concern about Jones' injury, his support of Jones'

36. Jackson v. United States, 297 F.2d 195, 198 (D.C.Cir. 1961) (concurring opinion). *See also* EC 5–9.

37. *See generally* DR 5–101(B)(1)–(4); DR 5–102(A); ABA Opinions 50 (1931), 185 (1938); Enker, *Rationale of the Rule that Forbids a Lawyer to be an Advocate and a Witness in the Same Case,* 1977 A.B.F.RES.J. 455; Comment, *Rule Prohibiting an Attor-ney from Testifying at a Client's Trial: An Ethical Paradox,* 45 U.Cin. L.REV. 268 (1976). *But see* DR 5–102(B). Note that if King must with-draw, no member of his firm may handle the case. DR 5–105(D).

negative attitudes toward the opposing party, and even his statements about opposing counsel.[38] A lawyer may not make a false statement of law or fact.[39] Few lawyers, however, seem to feel that this prohibition extends to the sort of devices that King uses to "get Jones to talk." Indeed, the trial manuals are full of suggestions that mirror his actions.

The Use of the Information Obtained

There also seems to be no professional duty which requires King to refrain from using the information he obtains. Having learned that Jones has (i) demanded an excessive witness fee; (ii) misrepresented his actual expenses to opposing counsel; (iii) gone over his testimony several times prior to trial, King could quite properly bring these matters to the attention of the fact finder.[40] The ABA Standards on Criminal Justice do contain some limits on discrediting or undermining a witness believed to be telling the truth. For example, the Standards provide that the investigation should be conducted with due regard for the "dignity and legitimate privacy of the witness" and that counsel "should not misuse the power of cross-examination impeachment by employing it to discredit or undermine a witness if he knows the witness is testifying truthfully."[41] The Code of Professional Responsibility, however, contains no such proscription.

It also seems to be permissible to characterize Jones' preparation as "rehearsed" and his claim of two-hundred dollars as "lying." King could also point out to the court or jury that Jones even lied under oath about his two-hundred dollars in expenses, despite the fact that the tone and sequence of King's examination probably encouraged (and was intended to encourage) him to do so. Indeed, many commentators consider King obligated to engage in such a vigorous impeachment of an adverse witness.[42]

Only two competing obligations in the Code seem to suggest any other conclusion. First, Jones' demand for and acceptance of the two-hundred-dollar fee is probably a fraud on the Court which must "promptly" be revealed to the sitting judge.[43]

---

38. *But see* EC 7–37, 7–10.

39. DR 7–102(A)(5).

40. *See* DR 7–106(C)(1), (2), (5), (6); EC 7–10. Note that King was not asserting his personal knowledge of the facts in questioning Jones about what was said to him in the interview. *Cf.* DR 7–106(C)(3).

41. ABA Standards of Criminal Justice, THE DEFENSE FUNCTION, § 7.6 (1971). *See also* N.Y. County Opinion 43 (1914) ("The Committee considers that wanton, unnecessary or unreasonable inquiry or comment respecting the discreditable past history of a witness or party is unethical or improper professional conduct").

42. M. Freedman, LAWYER'S ETHICS IN AN ADVERSARY SYSTEM 43–49 (1975); *See, e. g.,* Burger, *Standards of Conduct for Prosecution and Defense Personnel,* 5 AM.CRIM.L.Q. 11, 14–15 (1966).

43. DR 7–102(B)(2).

Indeed, the Code requires that King also report opposing counsel's apparent collusion in this conduct.[44] E. Z. Finance's lawyers could pay more than the regular witness fee only as compensation for lost time or for reasonable expenses actually incurred in testifying.[45] However, nothing in these reporting requirements seems to preclude King from waiting until trial to make the improprieties known. Indeed, a communication to the court before trial, at least without notifying counsel, itself might well have been improper.[46]

Second, King learned of Jones' demand for the additional fee "off the record." If this statement could fairly support the inference that Jones was talking to King "as his lawyer" then King would be precluded from using his statements against him.[47] King would also have to withdraw from representing his present client, the defendant in the suit by E. Z. Finance. Although King may have made "a false statement of law or fact" in causing Jones to reveal the information he obtained (which would be improper), one would be hard pressed to find an attorney-client relationship in these circumstances.

Suppressing Unfavorable Evidence

Finally, we should look at King's decisions to (i) ask Jones only about part of the "real good buy" statement (the entire statement by the salesman, according to Jones, was "for the price we're asking, this car is a real good buy"); (ii) refrain from bringing out anything about the salesman's statement to the buyer that the transmission was defective; and (iii) neither seek out nor call Jerry Wills, the other mechanic. Again his conduct probably does not violate the profession's existing norms.

It is clear that King could not "secrete" or advise a witness to leave the jurisdiction.[48] Nor could he refuse to reveal or misrepresent what he learned from Jones if the information were sought in the course of discovery proceedings.[49] However, in general he has no obligation to disclose the name or location of an adverse witness on his own initiative and, on cross-examination, is probably entitled to

---

44. *See* DR 1–103(A); *see also* ABA Informal Opinion 1210 (1972).

45. DR 7–109(C)(1), (2); *see also* N.Y. County Opinion 110 (1917) (money cannot be paid, even in a reasonable amount, to encourage the witness to testify). For recent discussions of the rules relating to the payment of experts, see Note, *Contingent Compensation of Expert Witnesses in Civil Litigation,* 52 IND.L.J. 671 (1977); 81 DICK.L.REV. 655 (1977); 55 N.C.L. REV. 709 (1977); 1977 WIS.L.REV. 603.

46. *See* DR 7–110(B).

47. *See* DR 4–101(A), (B)(1), (2), (3). This could be true even if King chose or was required to reveal Jones' actions to the Court as a "continuing crime." See the discussion of this issue in THE LAWYERING PROCESS (1978) at pages 254–60. On determining the existence of the privilege, *see* H. Wigmore, EVIDENCE, Vol. 8 § 2294 (3d ed. 1942); *see also* ABA Opinion 216 (1941).

48. DR 7–109(B); EC 7–27.

49. DR 7–109(A); 7–102(A)(3); EC 7–27.

bring out part rather than all of a prior statement.[50] Counsel for the opposing party, of course, has the option to bring out the damaging aspects of the statement. But the Code seems to permit counsel to take advantage of the failure of opposing counsel to do so.[51]

The Belief Issue

Note that the foregoing analysis is based on the assumption that King's client has continued to assert his version of what transpired. You might usefully review the same rules under the contrary premise —that the client had later divulged facts that would defeat his claim. King could not "knowingly" assert a breach of warranty claim which was "unwarranted."[52] Moreover, if the state had a rule similar to Rule 11 of the Federal Rules of Civil Procedure, he would have to certify that "he has read the pleading; [and] that to the best of his knowledge, information and belief there is good ground to support it . . . ."[53] If King's client insists that Jones is incorrect, however, neither rule probably precludes his going forward.

On the other hand, these rules considerably complicate the issues we have just discussed. For example, consider (i) how certain counsel would have to be to make an assertion of "good grounds," and (ii) how much investigation would have to be done before filing.[54] Note that DR 7–102(A)(2) permits an unwarranted claim to be advanced "if it can be supported by good faith argument for an extension, modification or reversal of existing law." What do terms like "knowingly" and "good faith" mean in this context? Do they set meaningful limits on the filing of nonmeritorious claims? Wayne Thode makes the following comments on the language adopted by the Code:

* * *

DR 7–102(A)(2) sets the boundary for substantive law representation. A claim or defense is obviously "within the bounds of the law" if consistent with existing law, which arguably is the standard now set by Canon 15 of the Canons of Professional Ethics. The claim

---

50. *See, e. g.*, N.Y. County Opinion 309 (1933) (not improper for defendant's attorney to withhold name and whereabouts of an eyewitness despite dismissal by plaintiff [an infant] because no witness could be located). *See also* S. Williston, LIFE AND LAW 271–72 (1940) (Williston describes winning a case on a finding of fact which he knew to be untrue; he withheld a letter establishing the contrary fact from the court and opposing counsel because it had never been explicitly requested). *But see* ABA Informal Opinion 1169 (1970) (counsel has duty to inform the court that client has died); In re Heimsoth, 229 A.D. 194, 243 N.Y.S. 149, affirmed 255 N.Y. 409, 175 N.E. 112 (1931) (plaintiff's

counsel so narrowly questioned his client in a divorce action that the court remained unaware of another pending separation action; court held this was improper).

51. *See* ABA Informal Opinion 1271 (1973).

52. DR 7–102(A)(2); *Cf.*, ABA Informal Opinion 1271 (1973) (plaintiff may bring a divorce action with knowledge that the defense of recrimination was available to the defendant).

53. *See also* DR 7–102(A)(5).

54. *See* ABA Opinion 335 (1974).

or defense, however, is also "within the bounds of the law" "if it can be supported by good faith argument for an extension, modification, or reversal of existing law." This is an important step forward in defining the scope of the lawyer's duty to his client. Although "good faith" is a spongy term, it is well known to the law and sets a standard that the average lawyer can apply with reasonable certainty when faced with the ethical issue of whether to present a given claim or defense. In a significant way, this provision defines the lawyer's relationship to the legal system as well as to his client. Thus, with regard to issues of substantive claims and defenses, the Code sets an acceptable and understandable standard.[55]

Is this helpful? Why should the lawyer—rather than his or her adversary or the court—screen the validity of the claim? On the other hand, why is the screening function so narrow? What would be lost or gained by modifying the Code to require, or at least permit, the lawyer to refuse to assert a position which he or she believes to be unmeritorious? [56]

––––––

2.   *On the Ethics of Adequate Preparation: Some Reflections*

As troubling as King's methods and purposes may be, he at least makes the most of his opportunity to talk to Jones, and takes full advantage of this preparation at trial. What if he had failed to interview this witness beforehand, or had otherwise failed to prepare for trial? Do his obligations under Canon 6 [57] *require* that he obtain witness statements for use at trial, or is the standard one of minimal effort? And what recourse would King's client have had if the lawyer had failed to uncover these favorable aspects of Jones' testimony or to prepare in other ways?

While the obligation to "represent a client competently" was not a part of the Canons of Professional Responsibility prior to the 1969 adoption of the Code, standards have been articulated by courts and bar committees to give content to this mandate. Lee Gaudineer provides a useful summary:

> Competency, as used in Canon 6 ("*A Lawyer Should Represent a Client Competently*"), embraces: (1) being qualified in an area of the law wherein representation has been undertaken; (2) adequate preparation under the circumstances; and (3) reasonable and proper attention to the client's case. What the lawyer needs to show to establish competency, adequate preparation, and due diligence (absence of neglect) remains unsettled at the present time.

* * *

55.   Thode, *Canons 6 and 7: The Lawyer-Client Relationship*, 48 TEX.L. REV. 367, 369–70 (1970).

56.   *Cf.*, DR 7–101(B)(2); DR 2–110(C).

57.   DR 6–101.

1. Incompetence

Competence, in the sense that an individual has attained the requisite degree of legal learning, generally has not been deemed a subject of inquiry in a disciplinary matter. "There is nothing in the State Bar Act conferring authority upon the board of governors to commence discipline for lack of legal learning, as a general charge." The same position would seem to be valid today under the Code of Professional Responsibility. After all, the lawyer does have a law degree from an accredited school and has passed the bar examination. Prior to the adoption of the present Code of Professional Responsibility by the American Bar Association, several other states also held that ignorance of the law was not grounds for discipline. The California Supreme Court once stated:

> Nor does the Board have power to recommend the discipline of an attorney for a deficiency in legal knowledge when such deficiency is the gravamen of the charge of specific misconduct with relation to a client. . . . In other words, he must perform his duties to the best of his individual ability, not the standard of ability required of lawyers generally in the community. Mere ignorance of the law in conducting the affairs of his client in good faith is not a cause for discipline.[a]

Likewise, various state courts have found that a case for disciplinary action was not presented when a lawyer honestly did not know what the applicable law was, mishandled cases because of inexperience, or otherwise exhibited no culpability or moral turpitude.

The adoption of Canon 6 was not meant to now permit inquiry into whether a lawyer still possesses the requisite degree of legal learning needed to continue in the practice by means of a disciplinary action. However, it was meant to change the rule that ignorance of the law was not grounds for disciplinary action. A lawyer is permitted to take a case in an area in which he is not, at that time, qualified. However, if this occurs, the lawyer must undertake the necessary study and research to become qualified. This not only includes the applicable law, but also any technical data and other information relative to the subject matter of the case. In the alternative, with the consent of his client, a lawyer so qualified may become associated with the case. It follows from these requirements that neither good faith ignorance of the law nor youth and inexperience should now excuse a lawyer from disciplinary action.

DR 6–101(A)(1) carries with it more than the requirement to become qualified in a particular area of the law. The knowledge of the case (legal, technical, and factual) must be applied for the benefit of the client in a professional manner. One could be highly qualified within the meaning of EC 6–3, but, unless the knowledge is applied properly, nothing will be gained for the client. Conduct which evidences indifference, irresponsibility, or a failure to do the best possible service for one's client will be a violation of this disciplinary rule.

a. Friday v. State Bar, 23 Cal.2d 501, 504, 144 P.2d 564, 567 (1943).

For example, the following establish incompetence cognizable under DR 6–101(A)(1): failure to file briefs with the supreme court when specifically ordered to do so; lack of basic knowledge of substantive and procedural law which is essential to the appellate process; failure to effectively represent the interest of one's clients; and advice to a client in conscious disregard of the truth or falsity of the facts upon which one's advice is predicated.

2. Adequate Preparation

Closely related to being knowledgeable and properly applying one's knowledge is being prepared. One can be knowledgeable and skillful in applying that knowledge, but, unless the lawyer is prepared in a given case, the client will suffer. Proper preparation or attention to the details of the matter, both to the law and facts, is mandatory. Disciplinary cases under this rule have been few. Proper preparation, as competency in general, ordinarily was not a basis for disciplinary action prior to the adoption of the Code of Professional Responsibility. However, the changing view was well expressed by the Nebraska Supreme Court:

> We have repeatedly recognized the ancient maxim that ignorance of the law is no excuse. . . . Of all classes and professions the lawyer is most sacredly bound to understand and uphold the law. Respondent was guilty of extreme negligence in his failure to familiarize himself with Section 77–1918, R.R.S. 1943, as amended. The fact that he was extremely busy with criminal prosecutions does not absolve him of his responsibility. It would have taken comparatively little time to have read the statute as amended.[b]

> Respondent was not charged, as he should have been, with . . . lack of proper preparation. It would have been more appropriate to have included DR 6–101(A)(2), which reads as follows: "A lawyer shall not: . . . (2) Handle a legal matter without preparation adequate in the circumstances." It is more in line with respondent's irresponsible conduct. Respondent clearly would have been in violation of this provision of the Code. He admits that he did not know the law. He knew the statute had been amended and made no attempt to ascertain its provision. *It is inexcusable for an attorney to attempt a legal procedure without endeavoring to ascertain the law governing that procedure.*[c]

It is clear that lack of preparation will be no longer condoned. It does not matter whether the preparation was needed in order to become qualified as required by DR 6–101(A)(1) or in order for a qualified lawyer to update his knowledge as required by DR 6–101(A)(2).

b. State ex rel. Nebraska State Bar Ass'n v. Holscher, 193 Neb. 729, 736–738, 230 N.W.2d 75, 80 (1975).

c. *Id.* at 80–81 (emphasis added).

3. Neglect

* * *

Neglect, as previously used as a basis for disciplinary action, was: (1) conduct that demonstrated indifference to the client's cause; (2) conduct that was tantamount to abandonment of the client at his hour of need; or (3) a pattern of conduct which established conscious carelessness or habitual dilatoriness in the handling of a client's affairs It is more than a single act of negligence, whether the negligent act is one of commission or one of omission. It should not now have a broader definition under DR 6–101(A)(3). For instance, the Florida Supreme Court observed that:

> Respondent's failure to follow mandatory appellate procedures in the two misdemeanor cases here involved, in and of itself, is not a mortal sin. Many lawyers of average competence and diligence will stub their toes on appellate time strictures at least once in their careers.[d]

> Proper examples of neglect are failure to appear and defend or prosecute at trial; accepting a retainer fee and, after repeated demands, failing to institute the action; accepting a case and, after repeated requests, failing to communicate with the client or take other appropriate action; and inexcusable delay and carelessness in several instances (*e. g.*, being habitually dilatory or consciously careless).[58]

Gaudineer argues that, in each of the areas of conduct, intent should be shown before disciplinary action is imposed, and that the concept of negligence should be reserved for malpractice actions. No line between "failures to act competently" and malpractice, however, is easily drawn or administered. For example, does the adoption of Canon 6 mean that all malpractice cases are automatically disciplinary cases? Should a violation of DR 6–101(A) give rise to a private cause of action, or at least be evidence of malpractice? Does a jury verdict in a civil case for or against a lawyer preclude a redetermination of his conduct in a subsequent disciplinary action?

Malpractice, as it has traditionally been defined, involves a failure to exercise "that degree of care, skill, diligence and knowledge commonly possessed and exercised by a reasonable, prudent and careful lawyer" in a given jurisdiction.[59] In many cases expert testimony will be required to establish the lawyer's deviation from the standard of acceptable conduct, though in some instances the negligence may be clear enough that the court can rule on it as a matter of law or leave

---

d. Florida Bar v. Reed, 299 So.2d 583, 584–85 (Fla.1974) (a one year suspension was imposed because other factors were present over and above the simple failure to comply with the appellate procedures).

58. L. Gaudineer, *Ethics and Malpractice*, 26 DRAKE L.REV. 88, 94, 96–

101 (1976). *See also* Comment, *Professional Negligence*, 121 U.PA.L.REV. 627 (1973); Kaus & Mallen, *The Misguiding Hand of Counsel: Reflections on Criminal Malpractice*, 21 U.C. L.A.L.REV. 1191 (1974).

59. *Id.* at 107.

the necessary inferences to the jury.   Gaudineer also summarizes the
standards that have evolved in malpractice cases:

> Preparation, adequate in the circumstances, encompasses knowledge
> of the current law on the subject, ascertainment of the facts from the
> client, independent investigation, and employment of necessary dis-
> covery proceedings after a suit is started.   A lawyer is expected to
> possess knowledge of those plain and elementary principles of law which
> are commonly known by well-informed attorneys and to discover those
> additional rules of law which, although not commonly known, may read-
> ily be found by standard research techniques.   The lawyer must educate
> himself on the applicable principles of law so that he may exercise in-
> formed judgment and advise the client accordingly in regard to the
> client's rights.   The court will take notice of those research tools avail-
> able to and commonly used by the lawyer.

> The attorney must also make an adequate investigation of the facts,
> both as they are favorable and unfavorable to the client.   However, a
> lawyer may rely upon the facts related by the client.   Investigation as
> to the truth or falsity of the facts related need not be made, but, if
> critical facts are not related, it is the duty of the lawyer to ascertain
> such facts.   The lawyer may also have the duty to investigate and re-
> port to the client.   If the client does not know what facts are material,
> it is the duty of the lawyer to inquire of the client in respect to such
> facts.   If the client assumes the responsibility of ascertaining the facts,
> the lawyer need not.   In all cases the lawyer's conduct is to be appraised
> in light of the surrounding circumstances existing prior to and during
> the course of such litigation and not solely according to the omniscience
> of hindsight gained after the litigation has been completed.

> Reasonable investigation in order to permit the lawyer to properly
> advise or represent his clients in legal matters other than litigation also
> is required.   For example, it has been held that a lawyer has a duty to
> investigate and advise his client concerning recording requirements to
> perfect a lien; to ascertain and enter of record damages the client has
> sustained; to certify title to real estate; to advise on all material facts
> so that the client can make an informed decision; and to question a
> legal description in a title opinion that a lawyer should reasonably know
> was defective even if the same opinion is made subject to anything that
> would be revealed by a survey.[60]

Gaudineer also summarizes the meaning of malpractice in criminal
cases:

> The general incompetency of the defense lawyer (ineffective assist-
> ance of counsel) in the handling of a criminal case is an issue that is
> frequently raised on appeal.   If the record establishes that the repre-
> sentation by the lawyer was so inadequate as to turn the trial into a
> sham or mockery of justice, the defendant's right to due process of law
> was violated and therefore, the decision of the trial court is vacated.
> An unsuccessful defense does not mean that the defense lawyer was in-
> competent or that the defendant was deprived of effective assistance of

----

60. *Id.* at 108–110.

counsel. Effective assistance of counsel means that the defendant is entitled to conscientious meaningful representation wherein he "is advised of his rights and honest, learned and able counsel is given a reasonable opportunity to perform the task assigned to him."

The defendant's right to have competent counsel obligates an attorney to prepare the client's defense. However, the amount of time needed for preparation and research will vary with the counsel's familiarity with the applicable law, relevant facts, issues presented and the availability of material witnesses. The total record must be examined and the totality of the circumstances evaluated. For the defendant to prevail on this issue, an affirmative factual basis demonstrating defense counsel's inadequacy must appear in the record. Moreover, "the decision on what witnesses to call, whether and how to conduct cross-examination, what jurors to accept or strike, what trial motions should be made, and all other strategic and tactical decisions are the exclusive province of the lawyer after consultation with his client." [e]

* * *

[However] ineffective assistance of counsel has . . . been found if the defense lawyer fails to properly investigate published contradictory statements of the prosecuting witness or call witnesses that could "cast doubt" upon the happening of the crime; fails to make a meaningful presentation of an appeal; fails to timely file an appeal in a criminal matter when instructed to do so by the defendant; fails to file obvious motions to suppress illegally seized evidence; or fails to adequately communicate with the defendant prior to trial.[61]

You might give some thought to whether these standards are clear, enforceable, or fair. What does not emerge from Gaudineer's discussion is a sense of how small a proportion of lawyer work is ever subjected to meaningful evaluation at all. Competence—like so many other aspects of lawyering—may well be an ideal by which you will have to measure yourself.

_____

3. The Larger Puzzle: Purpose, Planning, and Regard for Others

Whether or not the Code permits King's conduct it does not, of course, finally define his moral responsibilities. As we have said elsewhere, he (and you) must still answer the question of whether this conduct is right, good, or just.

Jones' situation poses in concrete form one aspect of the dilemmas of moral responsibility in lawyer work we discussed in earlier chapters. He is a bystander—an "outsider" to the controversy between E. Z. Finance and King's client. Yet King's action affects him and the role he ultimately plays in the outcome of the case. What moral responsibilities does a lawyer have to such persons?

e. State v. McCray, 231 N.W.2d 579, 580 (Iowa 1975), *quoting* ABA STANDARDS RELATING TO THE PROSECUTION FUNCTION AND THE DEFENSE FUNCTION § 5.2(b) (Approved Draft 1971).

61. *Id.* at 102–03.

First, Jones was clearly led to believe that what he said to King would be used to support only that version of the facts that he (Jones) thought to be true. Yet the net effect of his testimony is probably to strengthen the competing version of King's client. Does this have anything to do with Jones? Is there any obligation to insure that witnesses are not "used" to produce what they would consider unfair results? Is there at least some duty to protect or warn a witness who does not fully realize he or she is enmeshed in an adversarial situation when dealing with counsel? Robert Keeton makes the following comments with respect to the use of subterfuge in investigation:

> The Code of Professional Responsibility does not deal specifically with the use of subterfuge in investigation. It is generally considered a permissible practice within reasonable limits, and it is often justified on the basis that it is a practical necessity in discovering falsification by the adverse party or his witnesses. It would be a violation of the Code, of course, for you to use subterfuge as a means of directly interviewing an adverse party who is represented by a lawyer. Doubtlessly, the spirit of the Code may be violated by some uses of subterfuge in interviewing other witnesses, but the absence of an absolute prohibition leaves some area, not clearly defined, in which the use of subterfuge to interview persons other than the adverse party is proper. For example, if as defendant's lawyer in a personal injury case you suspect that the plaintiff is engaging in activities inconsistent with his claim, it is generally considered proper for you (or another person acting under your instructions) to interview under subterfuge (such as preparation of a credit report) persons with personal knowledge of those facts. The justification offered is the necessity for using subterfuge if the plaintiff's falsification is to be discovered without tipping him off. If you do not use subterfuge, he will undoubtedly learn of your interview and will then be warned to guard his activities more closely unless he has chosen the more commendable course of revising his claim (a course that is often more practical from the point of view of his realizing the most from the claim).
>
> In addition to the ethical problem involved in using subterfuges in investigation, the danger of tactical disadvantages deserves your attention. If the fact of your using a subterfuge is disclosed during trial, it may cause an unfavorable reaction on the part of the jury. This danger is particularly apparent if your investigation by subterfuge fails to achieve the aim of revealing falsification by the adverse party. Subterfuges are often used for obtaining information that would otherwise be unavailable, even though it may not directly involve falsification by the adverse party or a witness; this danger of unfavorable reaction indicates, however, that you should be very cautious about using a subterfuge for a purpose other than one leading directly to disclosure of falsification. If you do succeed in exposing false testimony, the typical jury is willing to forgive, as justified, methods to which they might otherwise have reacted adversely.[62]

62. R. Keeton, TRIAL TACTICS AND METHODS 326–27 (2d ed. 1973).

Keeton's concern seems to be primarily with the opposing party. Ask yourself if you would adopt the same stance toward deceptive (though not illegal) treatment of a witness. Suppose, for example, that you believed that Jones was mistaken or lying about the conversation between Evans and the salesman. Would the tactics used by King then be justified?

Second, Jones is exposed to embarrassment and, perhaps, serious legal consequences by King's actions. Is it enough to say that it is his own fault—that he should not have demanded an improper fee or lied in response to King's questions? What if there were no fault involved, or the fault was that of opposing counsel, who did not properly prepare or protect the witness? Monroe Freedman offers an example in the following situation:

> The accused is a drifter who sometimes works as a filling station attendant. He is charged with rape, a capital crime. You are his court-appointed defense counsel. The alleged victim is the twenty-two-year-old daughter of a local bank president. She is engaged to a promising young minister in town. The alleged rape occurred in the early morning hours at a service station some distance from town, where the accused was employed as an attendant. That is all you know about the case when you have your first interview with your client.

> At first the accused will not talk at all. You assure him that you cannot help him unless you know the truth and that he can trust you to treat what he says as confidential. He then says that he had intercourse with the young woman, but that she "consented in every way". He says that he had seen her two or three times before when he was working the day shift at the station, and that she had seemed "very friendly" and had talked with him in a "flirting way". He says that on the night in question she came in for gas; they talked; and she invited him into the car. One thing led to another and, finally, to sexual intercourse. They were interrupted by the lights of an approaching vehicle which pulled into the station. The accused relates that he got out of the young woman's car and waited on the customer. The young woman hurriedly drove off.

> The accused tells you he was tried for rape in California four years ago and acquitted. He has no previous convictions.

> At the grand jury proceedings the victim testifies that she was returning to her father's house in town from the church camp, where her fiancé was a counselor, when she noticed that her fuel gauge registered empty. She stopped at the first station along the road that was open. The attendant, who seemed to be in sole charge of the station, forced his way into her car, terrified her with threats, and forcibly had sexual intercourse with her. She says he was compelled to stop when an approaching car turned into the station. The alleged victim's father testified as to her timely complaint. No other testimony is presented. The grand jury returns a true bill.

> You learn that the victim has had affairs with two local men from good families. Smith, one of these young men, admits that the victim

and he went together for some time, but refuses to say whether he had sexual intercourse with her and indicates he has a low opinion of you for asking. The other, Jones, apparently a bitterly disappointed and jealous suitor, readily states that he frequently had intercourse with the victim, and describes her behavior toward strange men as scandalous. He once took her to a fraternity dance, he says, and, having noticed she had been gone for some time, discovered her upstairs with Smith, a fraternity brother, on a bed in a state of semi-undress. He appears eager to testify and he states that the girl got what she'd always been asking for. You believe Jones, but are somewhat repelled by the disappointed suitor's apparent willingness to smear the young woman's reputation.

Suppose the accused, after you press him, admits that he forced himself on the victim and admits that his first story was a lie. He refuses to plead guilty to the charge or any lesser charge. He says that he can get away with his story, because he did once before in California.

Should the defense lawyer use the information supplied by Jones to impeach the young woman and, if necessary, call Jones as a witness?

* * *

He goes on to suggest the following analysis of the dilemma:

The lawyer [here] knows that the client is guilty and that the prosecutrix is truthful. In cross-examining, the lawyer has one purpose, and one purpose only: to make it appear, contrary to fact, that the prosecutrix is lying in testifying that she was raped.

There is only one difference in practical effect between presenting the defendant's perjured alibi—which the Chief Justice considers to be clearly improper—and impeaching the truthful prosecutrix. In both cases, the lawyer participates in an attempt to free a guilty defendant. In both cases, the lawyer participates in misleading the finder of fact. In the case of the perjured witness, however, the attorney asks only nonleading questions, while in the case of impeachment, the lawyer takes an active, aggressive role, using professional training and skills, including leading questions, in a one-on-one attack upon the client's victim. The lawyer thereby personally and directly adds to the suffering of the prosecutrix, her family, and the minister to whom she is engaged. In short, under the euphemism of "testing the truth of the prosecution's case", the lawyer communicates, to the jury and to the community, the most vicious of lies.

That case takes us to the heart of my disagreement with the traditional approach to dealing with difficult questions of professional responsibility. That approach has two characteristics. First, in a rhetorical flourish, the profession is committed in general terms to all that is good and true. Then, specific questions are answered by uncritical reliance upon legalistic norms, regardless of the context in which the lawyer may be acting, and regardless of the motive and the consequences of the act. Perjury is wrong, and therefore no lawyer, in any circumstance, should knowingly present perjury. Cross-examination, however, is good, and therefore any lawyer, under any circumstances and regardless of the consequences, can properly impeach a witness through cross-examination. [I would], on the other hand, . . . attempt to deal with ethical problems in context—that is, as part of a functional sociopolitical system concerned with the administration of justice in a free society—and giving due regard both to motive and to consequences. . . .

The classic exposition of a legalistic, anti-utilitarian ethical system is that of Immanuel Kant. In assessing moral worth, Kant rejects any concern with motive or purpose, but relies exclusively upon fulfillment of duty as expressed in a maxim of conduct. Thus, says Kant, "the moral worth of an action does not lie in the effect expected from it, nor in any principle of action which requires to borrow its motive from this expected effect".

Kant's only test of the validity of a maxim is whether one is prepared to will the maxim to be a universal law. Referring specifically to lying, Kant suggests that it is improper to reason: "I should not lie, because then no one would thereafter believe me." The error in that, Kant says, is that one would then be telling the truth "from apprehension of injurious consequences", rather than from duty to principle. Assume, for example, that one is in a difficult situation which can be avoided only by telling a lie. One might say that everyone may tell a lie in order to escape a difficulty that otherwise cannot be avoided. However: "I presently become aware that while I can will the lie, I can by no means will that lying should be a universal law." From there, Kant reasons that telling the truth is a universal law, and that it cannot be violated under any circumstances. Thus, if a victim is fleeing from a would-be murderer, one must answer the murderer truthfully when asked where the victim is hiding. Lying—violation of principle—cannot be justified by mere expediency.

In response to that proposition, it would seem to be adequate to observe that there is something wrong with a system of morality that places a higher value upon one's moral rectitude with respect to lying, than upon the preservation of an innocent person's life. The legalistic mind, however, does not recognize such conflicts of principle; for example, what if one had already promised the victim to give him protection, and could only be truthful to the murderer by breaking one's word to the victim? That difficulty, of course, precisely parallels the problems faced by the criminal defense lawyer who has entered into an obligation of trust with the client, and who can avoid violating that trust only by presenting the client's perjury. One can agree with Chief Justice Burger that lying is wrong, and still not know the answer to the question of whether it is worse to lie to the client or to lie to the court.

There is an extremely important aspect of Kant's rejection of utilitarianism, however, which is frequently overlooked. That is, in holding that one must obey a maxim without regard to consequences, Kant is speaking at the level of personal morality. When he leaves the level of personal morality, and addresses himself to morality in systemic terms, Kant is entirely pragmatic. Thus, the fundamental question of whether a maxim is valid in the first instance (as distinguished from whether a valid maxim should be obeyed) is determined by the utilitarian concern with whether that maxim can be universalized, that is, with whether that maxim can be embodied into a viable system. For example, Kant determines that lying in order to extricate oneself from a difficulty cannot be universalized, because "with such a law there would be no promises at all, since it would be in vain to allege my intention in regard to my future actions to those who would not believe this allegation, or if they over-hastily did so, would pay me back in my own coin". Hence, he concludes, "my maxim, as soon as it should be made a universal law, would necessarily destroy itself". In short, in judging the morality of a maxim, considerations of disadvantage "to myself or even to others" are irrelevant, but disadvantage to the system— whether the maxim can "enter as a principle in a possible universal legislation"—is vital.

One of the major flaws in the traditional approach to legal ethics is that it seeks to answer the difficult questions in a legalistic fashion at the personal level, but begs completely the critical questions raised at the systemic level. Thus, if you say to a lawyer: "Lawyers are under a moral duty not to participate in the presentation of perjury, and therefore you are required to act in a way contrary to your client's interest if the client insists upon committing perjury", the lawyer is entitled to respond: "Let us consider your maxim. If it is embodied into the system as a universal law to be applied to all lawyers in all circumstances, would the maxim destroy itself and be destructive of the system?"

As we have seen . . . the system requires the attorney to know everything that the client knows that is relevant to the case. In order to enable the lawyer to obtain that information, the system provides for an obligation of confidentiality, designed to protect the client from being prejudiced by disclosures to the attorney. In addition, the attorney is required to impress upon the client the obligation of confidentiality in order to induce the client to confide freely and fully.

* * *

Obviously . . . the rape case is a . . . hard one, because the injury done to the prosecutrix is far more severe than the more limited humiliation of the public-spirited and truthful witness in the case of the street robbery. In addition, in the rape case, the lawyer is acting pursuant to a manifestly irrational rule, that is, one that permits the defense to argue that the prosecutrix is the kind of person who would have sexual intercourse with a stranger because she has had sexual relations with two men whom she knew in wholly different social circumstances. Irrational or not, however, in those jurisdictions in which the defense of unchastity is still the law, the attorney is bound to provide it on the client's behalf. For the lawyer who finds the presentation of that defense, and perhaps others in rape cases, to go beyond what he or she can in good conscience do, there are two courses that should be followed. The first is to be active in efforts to reform the law in that regard; the second is to decline to accept the defense of rape cases, on the grounds of a conflict of interest (a strong personal view) that would interfere with providing the defendant with his constitutional right to effective assistance of counsel.[63]

Ask yourself whether you concur in this reasoning. To what extent is it a defense of the adversary system itself and the necessity of sacrificing some persons or interests to its requirements? Do you share this view, or would you resolve the dilemma differently? In what ways?

Both these issues—the degree of openness and the degree of protection owed a witness—are rooted in the general limits on client loyalty. Think about what sort of system of obligations would adequately protect both clients *and* the legitimate interests of witnesses in not being embarrassed, harassed or misled. Would it make a difference if judges were more protective, or if counsel were appointed for witnesses more regularly? What if full disclosure were made to every witness who gave damaging information?

Very early in your practice you will encounter witnesses who are or seem to you to be (i) truthful as well as dishonest; (ii) mistaken as well as deliberately deceptive; (iii) friendly as well as hostile; (iv) trusting as well as suspicious; (v) naive as well as knowledgeable and (vi) vulnerable in other respects. If you would respect their humanity—that is, if you would avoid "making them means rather than ends"—you may find that the lawyer's role is rarely a comfortable mantle to wear.

63. M. Freedman, *supra* note 42 at 43–49.

Chapter Two

WITNESS EXAMINATION: THE CASE RECONSTRUCTED

SECTION ONE: PRELIMINARY PERSPECTIVES

A. IMAGES AND FRAGMENTS

NIZER, THE IMPLOSION CONSPIRACY

195–98 (1973).

Long before the defendants took the stand, they and their attorneys had to agree upon strategy. There were two questions which were most troubling.

The first was whether Julius Rosenberg should take the stand and risk cross-examination. Bloch had already announced that Ethel would testify. Sympathy for her plight as a mother could be counted on to soften any blow struck at her. Also she was pretty and intelligent. She could be counted on to charm the jury and cope with a cross-examiner.

Julius had none of these protective elements in his favor. Nevertheless, there was no alternative but to have him testify. The incriminating evidence offered, particularly by the Greenglasses, had to be countered. It was too dangerous to rely on his right to be silent even though the law dictated that no adverse inference was to be drawn therefrom. Only his direct denial, or contrary version of some of the incidents, which I have previously set forth to contrast with the prosecution evidence, might save him from conviction. So, the first question was easily answered by the Rosenbergs and their counsel. Julius and Ethel would take the stand and defend themselves.

However, Sobell and his lawyers, Kuntz and Phillips, disagreed violently on this subject. This was later revealed to the court. Phillips thought that Sobell should testify in his defense. He feared that otherwise his flight from the country, his use of aliases, and Elitcher's testimony, all standing uncontradicted, might convict him. Kuntz, an experienced criminal lawyer, differed. He thought that the government's case was too thin to overcome the presumption of innocence. He feared that cross-examination might worsen Sobell's plight. He preferred to depend on summation, to point out the remoteness of the evidence as it applied to Sobell. Phillips bowed to Kuntz's experience. It was agreed that Sobell would not testify and would put in no defense. The decision put a heavy responsibility on counsel in the event something went wrong. It accounted for the passionate tearful plea by his lawyers for a new trial on newly discovered evidence, when it was too late. I shall come to this extraordinary development later.

The Rosenbergs and the Blochs had even greater difficulty with a second question which had to be answered. What position would they take on cross-examination when they would be asked whether they were Communists? If they conceded that they were, they would be belabored with dozens of questions about their activities in the Party. They would have to reveal that they attended meetings almost nightly; that they engaged in intensive propaganda services; that they sold the *Daily Worker*, going from door to door like school children performing a chore; that they were pleased to do other menial tasks as dedicated servants of revolution; that they read Communist literature almost exclusively, most of it prepared in Russia; that they led debates on theories which denounced capitalism and, therefore, the United States; that they had advanced to the point of giving lectures to cell groups; and perhaps, perhaps the suspicious admission that they had ceased some of these overt activities. This would lead to another series of questions whether their interest in "the cause" had really diminished, or whether they had substituted secret activities for them. The implication would be created by the prosecutor that the higher the rank, the more underground the work.

Of course, the Rosenbergs, even if they admitted being active Communists, would vigorously deny any espionage. This they did and with persuasive emphasis. Nevertheless, if they were harried with fierce cross-examination concerning Communist theory and action, would the jury believe the denials? It was as if their admission of communism was a headlong drive toward betrayal, and then at the last moment they came to a screeching halt. Would the brakes hold against the enormous momentum of prejudice against communism?

The word Communist had come into such disrepute that the courts had held it was libelous.

So Emanuel Bloch urged that when the deadly question was asked by the prosecutor that Julius and Ethel should refuse to answer on the ground that it might tend to incriminate them—or, as was the morbid jest of the day, "tend to incinerate them."

Alexander Bloch reached a different conclusion. Being older and more experienced, he examined the practical consequences of "taking the Fifth."

"Don't you think," he reasoned, "that such a plea will be an admission of communism?" Of course, the jury would be told that no such inference may be drawn. But common sense could not be abrogated by constitutional theories. "If you interview an applicant for a job as a teller in a bank, and you ask him whether he was ever convicted for stealing, and he refuses to answer because it might incriminate him, do you hire him? Or do you hire a sitter for your children, who asserts his privilege not to answer when you ask him if he ever molested youngsters?"

Furthermore, the problem was not as abstract as the discussion indicated. There *had* been evidence that the Rosenbergs were Communists. Elitcher and Greenglass had sworn that they had been indoctrinated by Julius. The jury was, therefore, aware of the Rosenbergs' Communist activities. A plea of Fifth Amendment against this background would surely be taken by the jury as confirmation of facts already presented to them.

Therefore, concluded the older Bloch, it would be wiser to admit their Communist beliefs, but argue strenuously that these were political, and not inconsistent with loyalty to the United States. Even if they were pummeled on cross-examination about their Communist activities, an opportunity would be afforded them to insist that at no time did their beliefs cross the line of espionage.

Their candor and forthrightness in admitting the truth of Communist affiliation would lend credence to their denial that they had anything to do with spy activities. Otherwise, their furtive attitude in "hiding behind the Fifth Amendment" might spill over to disbelief on the vital issue on which their lives depended.

Emanuel Bloch remained unconvinced. He reasoned that if they refused to answer, at least the door would be closed to an inquiry about their dedicated service to communism over many years. They would not have to reveal with whom they met. Perhaps among such people might be a traitor, even though they were innocent. Who knows what the government with its vast investigatory powers might have uncovered? If the defense unlocked the door, by waiving the Fifth Amendment, it might let in incriminating material which could not be overcome. The air was heavy with prejudice against Communists. It was the lawyers' duty to block off the inquiry if it could. Fortunately, the Constitution provided a bullet-proof vest against such attacks. Why take it off? It was not merely the single question "Are you a Communist?" which was involved. If admitted, new avenues of inquiry would follow inevitably. The lawyers were in the position of a doctor who is not as much concerned with the condition the patient has as with the sequelae.

The risk, argued the younger Bloch, was far greater from admitting that they were active Communists than from any improper inference drawn from the plea of self-incrimination. Particularly was this so since the judge recognized his duty to warn the jury against such an inference.

So the argument raged between the lawyers. The emotional strain of the trial, the unexpected blows, particularly of the Greenglasses' testimony, the terrible responsibility that wrong strategy might cost their clients' lives made the difference of opinion an angry exchange. At times, it was necessary for father and son to declare to each other that the harsh words and loud presentation were merely manifestations of mutual deep concern and not personal. The older Bloch was proud of his son, and Emanuel was respectful toward his father. But things were not going well and they had become involved in a contest, which was drawing international attention, and in which they felt insecure. This was evident from their uncertainty in dealing with the prosecutor and the judge. They objected hesitantly and withdrew, sometimes with apology. At other times, they stood their ground angrily. They were caught between psychological forces, asserting their rights on the record, to preserve appellate procedures, and deference toward the judge in order not to offend him. It was he who would hand out punishment, if the Rosenbergs were convicted. This concern for their clients even affected their attitude toward Saypol. It was the prosecutor who would recommend sentence, in the event of conviction. He must not be infuriated.

So, on one hand, they had to fight vigorously for the hard-pressed defendants and, on the other hand, not antagonize too much those who might hold out mercy even if the worst happened. This ambivalence was noticeable in the record.

LUSTGARTEN, VICTORIAN TRUMPETS: EDWARD CLARKE DEFENDS ADELAIDE BARTLETT
DEFENDER'S TRIUMPH

56–63 (1951).

[Editor's note: In 1886 Adelaide Bartlett was charged with murdering her husband, Edward Bartlett, by chloroform poisoning. It was proved that a substantial dose of liquid chloroform had been the cause of death, and the testimony that follows dealt with the question of how the poison had been administered. The Crown was represented by the Attorney General, Sir Charles Russell, Q.C.; Mrs. Bartlett was defended by Mr. Edward Clarke, Q.C.].

The cross-examination of scientific experts falls into a peculiar and isolated category. Others are called to testify to *facts*, and opposing counsel is generally concerned to show that they are either untruthful or mistaken. The experts lead the way into the realm of *theory*, of analytical dissertations and deductive reconstruction. Any contest with them may ultimately turn upon niceties of wording or the shape of formulæ.

Some surprise is occasionally expressed because so many acknowledged experts prove unimpressive witnesses; they are moulded like wax by the cunning hands of advocates who do not rival them in specialised erudition. That is because their mastery of the subject under review is not matched by a mastery of the art of giving evidence. They may be profound, but not quick; thorough, but not selective; accurate, but not lucid. They may find it easier to express themselves on paper; they may find the laboratory more congenial than the court. They may be witnesses who are Experts, without being expert Witnesses.

Few have been both in superlative degree; not more than two or three in any generation. But one such, unquestionably, was Dr Thomas Stevenson, and it was he who had performed, at the Home Office's request, the analysis of Edwin Bartlett's remains. Professor of Medical Jurisprudence at Guy's Hospital, one of the leading consulting physicians of the day, a toxicologist of international repute, Dr Stevenson was above all a tough, shrewd witness; honest and fair enough in forming his opinion, but not easily moved to qualify his blunt expression of it. He could not be rattled and he would not be cajoled.

In the Bartlett trial Dr Stevenson appeared amid distinguished colleagues, each of whom contributed a viewpoint of his own. But on all sides he was considered as their leader, and when on the fourth afternoon he stepped into the box everyone present saw in him the instrument of destiny.

Stevenson was not the man to exploit by style or manner the drama inherent in his situation. He gave his evidence with matter-of-fact composure. He told of finding chloroform in the contents of the stomach, and fixed the quantity at $11\frac{1}{4}$ grams. He described an inflamed patch on the stomach itself—'at the usual spot,' he said, 'after swallowing irritant poison.' He declared unhesitatingly that the chloroform discovered had been the cause of death.

'Could he take a fatal dose,' asked Russell, 'and suppose he was taking some innocent thing?'

'No,' replied the witness, 'I don't believe he could.'

'Is it possible to put liquid down the throat of a person who is insensible, in the sense of being unconscious, but still having the sense of feeling?'

'Yes; you can put liquids down the throat of a person who is fairly moderately under the influence of inhaled chloroform.'

'Would it be difficult?'

'Not if the man was lying on his back with his mouth open.'

Thus was filled in Russell's sketch of the Crown theory. There would be 'no great difficulty' in pouring the *liquid* down if *inhaled* chloroform had taken 'moderate' effect.

But could a person untrained in medical technique produce such a condition, or recognise it when it had been produced? This was the main point Clarke was to take in a cross-examination which he himself regarded as the trial's turning point.   .   .   .

When Russell sat down, Clarke got slowly to his feet.

In front of him was a rampart of massive medical books, the paper markers drooping like a sea of flags becalmed. The moment had arrived—the moment when the close research of many days would bear or stint its fruits.

Signs of the strain inseparable from a long capital trial showed momentarily on the defender's face as he put his first questions.

'Dr. Stevenson, you have for many years given your attention to subjects of this class?'

'I have.'

'And you have had a long experience of the administration of chloroform?'

'I have.'

'And you have also given study to the experience of other doctors?'

'Yes.'

'And you have edited *The Principles and Practice of Medical Jurisprudence*, by Dr Alfred Swaine Taylor, who is well known as one of the greatest authorities in that branch of medical science?'

'Yes.'

'And so far as your skill and experience have enabled you, have you taken care that it is complete in the subject with which it deals?'

'Yes; it is fairly complete, I think.'

Deliberately Clarke was reinforcing Stevenson's prestige. Deliberately he was projecting him as the Supreme Authority; the Expert of Experts; the man who, in dealing with chloroform, knew all there was to know. Now he asked the question for which this had dressed the ground.

'Can you refer me to *any* recorded case, *anywhere*, of murder by the administration of liquid chloroform?'

Stevenson answered as Clarke knew he must.

'No,' he said, 'I know of none.'

So if Mrs. Bartlett had killed her husband by giving him liquid chloroform, she had performed a feat that was apparently unique.

'There are no recorded cases of murder in this fashion,' Clarke went on, 'but have there not been deaths from the swallowing of chloroform by accident?'

'Yes,' said Stevenson.

'How many?'

'About twenty have been recorded.'

So, by the test of statistics, accident was a more feasible hypothesis than murder.

'You say that liquid chloroform could be administered while a person is under the influence of chloroform inhaled?'

'Certainly.'

'You know that the brain appeared normal on post-mortem?'

'I have heard so.'

'But when chloroform has been inhaled just a short time before death would you not expect a distinct odour in the ventricles of the brain?'

'Not always,' Stevenson said, adding, 'It has been observed.'

'Come,' Clarke persisted. 'Is it not one of the most prominent symptoms recognised?'

'Not according to my observations.' Clarke's hand reached out among the books. The witness anticipated the coming thrust. 'I am speaking from my own observation,' he reemphasised.

'I do not want to challenge your book by any other,' Clarke remarked politely, 'but you know *Guy and Ferrier*?'

'Yes.'

'Is it a book of substantial authority?'

'Yes.'

Clarke opened the volume at a place already marked. Stevenson waited, outwardly impassive.

'I am at page 550 of *Guy and Ferrier*.' Clarke began to read. ' "The odour of chloroform is perceptible on opening the body. It is especially observable in the cerebral ventricles." '

He paused enquiringly. Dr Stevenson's response was not entirely unevasive, nor did it possess his usual rigid relevance.

'Asphyxia usually arises from giving too much chloroform,' he said. 'There you would expect to find the smell more prominent.'

Clarke seized his advantage.

'I quite agree it may be a question of quantity, but what I am putting to you is—if you are looking for post-mortem indications of chloroform having been inhaled, the odour in the cerebral ventricles would be one of the principal ones?'

'Oh, I should certainly look for it,' Stevenson conceded.

All this, though highly useful, was subordinate. It set the scene; it provided Clarke with a favourable background against which to open the decisive interchange.

'You spoke earlier,' he said, 'of administering chloroform to persons while in sleep?'

'Yes.'

'Did you speak of adults?'

'Yes.'

'As a matter of your own practice?'

'No,' said Stevenson, 'I have not done it myself.'

'You are speaking of recorded cases?'

'I am.'

'In the case of adults, is it the fact that the attempt to administer chloroform by inhalation during sleep almost invariably wakes the man?'

'Not almost invariably,' Stevenson jibbed at the phrase, which was indeed a little strong. 'Not almost invariably. If I may refer to the largest number of experiments that have been carried out by one individual—Dolbeau—he found that three awoke to one that was chloroformed.'

Clarke extracted another volume from the stack.

'Do you know Wynter Blyth's work on poisons?'

'I do.'

'I am reading from page 136. "Dolbeau has made some interesting experiments in order to ascertain whether under any circumstances a sleeping person might be anæsthetised. The main result appears to answer the question in the affirmative, at least with certain persons; but even with these *it can only be done by using the greatest skill and care. This cautious and scientific narcosis is not likely to be used by the criminal classes, or, if used, to be successful.*" '

Clarke stopped. Dr Stevenson nodded slightly, but made no spoken comment. . . .

The afternoon had lengthened into evening, and still this intensive questioning went on. It was conducted entirely on the plane of general principle; no references were made to the case that was being tried. The talk was not of Mrs Bartlett, but of Wynter Blyth and Dolbeau; not of the man who died at the house in Claverton Street, but of patients in Scotland or the United States; not of what the prisoner had or had not done, but of what, in the light of science, it was possible to do. Yet Clarke's purpose was most relevant and consistently maintained. Each question was directed to the self-same urgent end: to show that the operation which, on the Crown theory, Mrs Bartlett had performed would test the powers of a qualified physician and be utterly beyond her capacity and knowledge.

Toe to toe, counsel and doctor fought the matter out. As book after book was produced and scrutinised, as successive authorities were cited and discussed, the Old Bailey seemed transmuted into some scholastic forum where learned professors contended for the truth.

But there was one who sat apart, in her sombre widow's garb, to bear constant reminder of the stake upon the outcome.

At last the advocate pushed the books aside. They had served him, and he had used them well. The witness was not in any way discredited—this would have been the reverse of Clarke's intention—but he was tied, as a result of the long interrogation, to certain important medical premises. On the basis of these Clarke could now venture upon a series of dramatic, and indeed decisive, questions which related all that had transpired to the case before the court, and garnered the harvest he had so astutely sown.

'Let me put it again,' he said to Stevenson, and there was that in his voice that made everyone alert. 'Let me put it again. You say there is a particular point in the process of chloroforming at which the patient would be able to swallow, though he was sufficiently under the influence of chloroform not to suffer from the pain?'

'I do.'

'How would you yourself ascertain that that time had arrived?'

'By the reflex of the eye. I would not like to pour down the throat if the reflex had been abolished.'

'How would you test it?'

'By touching the eye and watching for the closure of the eyelid.'

'Would you mind touching your own eye; just show us how it is done?'

The jury watched the doctor's practised fingers.

'Like this. You separate the eyelids, see? And . . . just touch the conjunctiva.'

Clarke bowed in acknowledgment.

'I am much obliged. That is the test to ascertain if the sensation of pain has gone?'

'Yes.'

It was time for the concluding strokes.

'Suppose you had to deal with a sleeping man and it was your object to get down his throat without his knowing it a liquid which would cause great pain; do you not agree it would be a very difficult and delicate operation?'

The eye; the reflex; the precise stage of anæsthesia. Stevenson had to bear them all in mind. He replied in somewhat guarded terms.

'I think it would be an operation which would often fail, and might often succeed.'

He had gone far enough; Clarke could afford to insist on his own phrase.

'Would you not look on it as a *delicate* operation?'

Stevenson yielded.

'Yes, I should look on it as delicate; I should be afraid of pouring it down the windpipe.'

'If the patient got into such a state of insensibility as not to reject it, it would go down his windpipe and burn that?'

'Some of it might.'

'If it did so, it would leave its traces?'

'I should expect to find traces.'

As the whole world knew, no such traces had been found. The cross-examination appeared to have reached its culminating point. But Clarke was to add a final, unexpected twist.

'If the post-mortem examination had been performed, *as we know from Dr Leach that Mrs Bartlett wished*, on the very day upon which death took place, there would have been a better opportunity of determining cause of death?'

'There would,' said Dr Stevenson.

Clarke sat down amid a buzz of murmurs which leapt into a hubbub as the hearing was adjourned.

[The morning following this cross-examination, at the close of the Crown's re-direct examination of Dr. Stevenson, the jury asked a number of questions which indicated that they had understood and were troubled by the points Clarke had raised. The defense chose to present no evidence, but Clarke's closing argument, which is regarded as a classic of forensic eloquence, took nearly five hours. After two hours of deliberation the jury returned a verdict in these words: "We have well considered the evidence, and although we think grave suspicion is attached to the prisoner, we do not think there is sufficient evidence to show how or by whom the chloroform was administered.

. . . Not Guilty."]

MUSMANNO, VERDICT!

248–52 (1958).

Occasionally the lawyer can simplify the complications of the law. I was in Criminal Court defending Pete Mardik, an unschooled vegetable huckster indicted on a charge of perjury. He was accused of swearing falsely to an affidavit filed in an action for divorce he had brought against his wife, who, among other things, had once attempted to shoot him. When Mrs. Mardik was brought before a judge on the criminal charge which had followed this attempt, she was paroled on condition that she leave town, whereupon she took up residence in Chicago with a brother. Her husband, however, was required to support her, so that each week he paid into the Non-Support Court a sum of money which was forwarded to her through court channels.

A couple of years later Mardik began his divorce action, and at the request of his attorney (not I) he went to the courthouse to obtain his wife's address so that notice of the divorce proceedings might be served on her. In the courthouse Mardik became bewildered as he wandered through the corridors, courts, and offices in that vast building and he reported to his attorney that he had been unable to obtain the desired information. Later he made the affidavit in which he stated he was ignorant of his wife's whereabouts. His wife's brother in Chicago, learning of this affidavit, came on to Pittsburgh, appeared before a committing magistrate, and charged Mardik with attempting to obtain a divorce fraudulently. The charge of perjury followed, and I was retained to defend Mardik.

I realized the difficulties of my case. Since Mardik's wife's address appeared in the records of the Non-Support Court, the Commonwealth would maintain that all Mardik had to do to get it was to ask for it, and particularly would this be true since he was contributing to her support in that very court every week. Still I believed Mardik was innocent of any intentional wrongdoing.

The only reason he had come away without his wife's address was that, like a sheep in the woods, he could not find his way around in the forest of rooms in the courthouse, but how could I prove that fact to the jury? Merely to assert it was not enough.

I outlined in my mind a plan of defense which was really in the nature of an offense. At the opening of the trial I casually asked Hiram Wilson, the trial assistant district attorney, where I could obtain the records in the divorce proceedings between Mr. and Mrs. Mardik. He replied that he did not know. Later on I asked him if he would be so kind as to locate for me the indictment which had charged Mrs. Mardik with an attempt to shoot her husband. Petulantly he replied: "Find it yourself. I don't know where it is."

Mr. Wilson's first witness was the chief clerk of the Disbursement Section of the Non-Support Court, who testified that Mrs. Mardik's address was on file in his office and that if Mr. Mardik had called for it, it would have been given to him. Cross-examining the clerk, I asked: "Do you receive the money which is paid by husbands for their wives?"

"No, I only disperse it."

"Where is the money received?"

"In the Acceptance Section."

"And where does the money then go?"

"To the Bookkeeping Section."

"And from there where does it go?"

"To the Disbursement Section."

"And that is your section?"

"Yes."

"And you send the money to the wife?"

"Yes."

Wilson then put on the witness stand a clerk from the Acceptance Section, who testified that Mr. Mardik came once a week to pay his support money, and he recalled that on one occasion Mardik asked for his wife's address and he was sent to the Disbursement Division.

In my cross-examination I asked:

"Did you give him the number of the room?"

"No."

"Did it not occur to you that he might lose his way in this big building?"

"No, that did not occur to me."

"Did you give him any instructions on how to get to the Disbursement Section?"

"No, I just told him to go to the Disbursement Section."

"Do you think he understood you?"

"I object," Wilson interjected. "How does he know if the defendant understood?"

The judge sustained the objection.

In his opening statement to the jury Wilson had made a vigorous demand for conviction and he had followed it with documentary and record evidence which seemed incontrovertible. He now rested his case.

I called the defendant to the stand and he testified that he truly did not know where his wife lived, that he had applied for that information at the office where he deposited his weekly support money, that there they had referred him to another office, and from that point he went to still another office, and finally he became lost. He tried unsuccessfully on several other occasions to ascertain his wife's address and at last concluded that he was not supposed to know her whereabouts. He feared the authorities might think he wanted to do her some harm, so he ceased trying to locate her. When he signed the affidavit in which he said that he did not know where his wife lived, he was telling the truth.

At this point in the proceedings I picked up a sheet of paper and, scribbling something on it, I turned to the tipstaff and said: "Mr. Tipstaff, please deliver this paper to the Disbursement Section."

"What is the room number, Mr. Musmanno?"

"I don't know, Mr. Tipstaff, but certainly you ought to know. How long have you been an officer of this court?"

"Ten years."

"And you don't know where the Disbursement Section of the Non-Support Court is?"

"No."

Wilson angrily interposed: "If the Court please, I object to Mr. Musmanno interrogating the tipstaff in open court. The tipstaff is neither a witness, nor is he on trial."

"Well, Mr. District Attorney, perhaps you can tell me where the Disbursement Section is."

"It's in the courthouse somewhere," he replied with a sneer, "and your client could have found it if he really wanted to."

"Really? All right, Mr. District Attorney, I'll ask Court to recess for a few minutes while you direct me to the Disbursement Section."

"If the Court please, I refuse to be annoyed in this manner by defense counsel."

"If the Court please, I rest my case."

I advanced to the jury box and asked: "Members of the jury, do any of you know where the Disbursement Section is? The district attorney does not know, the tipstaff does not know, and they have been in this courthouse for many years, and yet they expect this poor, ignorant huckster to know.

"The machinery of the courts is a complicated one, and it is not given to every person who is caught in its crushing gears to know how it operates. Even many who have a hand in the operation of that machinery do not know the location of the various levers and controls. You will recall that I asked the district attorney at the very outset of the trial how I could obtain the records in the Mardik divorce proceedings and he said he did not know. I later asked him to get for me a copy of the indictment against Mrs. Mardik in the felonious shooting case and he indignantly replied: 'Find it yourself. I don't know where it is.'

"And yet they expect this illiterate, dumb potato peddler to find his way through the labyrinthine passages of this enormous edifice seeking a card among tens of thousands of cards, seeking an address among tens of thousands of addresses, seeking what no one wanted to give him because it might mean a little inconvenience to them. Members of the jury, Pete Mardik did not know the location of the Disbursement Section, but he does know the location of justice. It is right here in this box. I ask you to acquit him of this heinous charge which should never have been brought. I ask you to acquit him and to place the costs of the prosecution on the one responsible for it."

And that is what the jury did. They acquitted Mardik and assessed the costs against the itinerant brother-in-law from Chicago.

NOTES

As you read these excerpts, try to imagine yourself as lawyer and then as witness in these situations. How does it feel? What is being asked of you? How can/will you prepare for it?

These images offer some insight into the tasks and judgments that will be involved as you elicit the testimony of witnesses at trial. In the cross-examination of Dr. Stevenson, Edward Clarke was faced with a situation in which every word was crucial, and one which required extensive and detailed preparation. Musmanno, too, had a plan, but his conduct was governed as much by hunch as by careful analysis, and a great deal depended on his ability to manage the informal as well as the formal aspects of the process. Consider as well the very different decisions involved in calling Ethel and Julius Rosenberg to the stand. That judgment may have cost them their lives, yet may not be fairly considered an error. There are many dimensions to a trial decision. All of these situations, or variations of them, will arise in your own trial practice; you will benefit from thinking now about how you will deal with them and what skills and resources they will require.

Each of these lawyers was faced with (i) a complex of past circumstances, statements and acts; (ii) an existing set of relationships in the courtroom, *i. e.,* lawyer and judge, witness and judge, etc.; (iii) a variety of roles, rules and rituals which constrained their behavior; and (iv) a number of possible actions, reactions and contingencies. How did they determine what they wanted the witness to say (objectives), the resistances that could be expected (problems), the alternatives that were available and the best choice among them? How can such judgments be translated into concrete language and action? What are the appropriate limits on such efforts?

Seen functionally, examining a witness involves a kind of argument, challenging the lawyer to find "the best available means of persuasion in the particular circumstances."[1] The lawyer "speaks" through the voice of witnesses and the logic of the argument may not emerge until the summation, but the classical problems of persuasion—capturing the attention, comprehension and acceptance of the audience—remain the same. To this image, however, must be added a number of complicating factors. First, the context is enormously

---

1. W. Winterowd, RHETORIC: A SYNTHESIS 14 (1968).

variable and complex. Achievement of objectives is limited by the continually changing relationships depicted below.

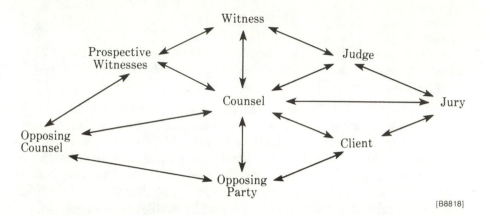

[B8818]

This diagram identifies only some of the affected participants, and the potential interactions which can arise in this setting.

Second, the resources with which counsel works—demeanor, description, interaction—are very hard to control and direct. The "argument" is made more from a stage, with a complete cast of characters, than from a podium. This further complicates the problems of truthfulness and responsibility which are present in any situation involving efforts at persuasion. How will you cope with the strains which such pressures inevitably produce?

In another sense, the pieces of testimony with which a lawyer works have a shifting, almost illusory quality: "time is irreversible, events unique, and any reconstruction of the past at best an approximation." [2] This quality of recalled experience, explored in Chapter One, has further implications for trial. Witness testimony is not only the product of fallible memory and perception, but is also the conscious construction of counsel.

What does this mean for your own efforts as an advocate? What conflicts, opportunities, and obligations does it create? First, it makes clear that the examination of witnesses is a purposeful activity. You will be expected to know what you want a particular witness to say and why. Second, it suggests the importance of the setting in which you work: you will have to seek your objectives not only in situations where evidence is carefully weighed and considered—and where time can be devoted to trial preparation—but also in circumstances where cases are routinely processed rather than tried. Many of you will learn to examine witnesses not in the "hushed courtroom" from which our images are taken, but in the far more constricted

2. J. Maguire, J. Weinstein, J. Chadbourn & J. Mansfield, CASES AND MATERIALS ON EVIDENCE 1 (6th ed. 1973).

setting of lower court practice. If the approach to advocacy we delineate makes sense to you, how will you learn it under these circumstances? What modifications will be necessary? Here, as in other aspects of lawyering, you must become observers as well as participants in the process. When you can describe patterns of examination and cross-examination that you actually see in the courts, you will be better able to define the possibilities which such situations present.

Finally, recognizing the constructed nature of the trial process raises questions about the functions a trial lawyer serves. Even a trial which consumes weeks or months of time is not an "inquiry into truth" or a quest for justice—in any simple sense of those terms. Perhaps it should be. There may be better ways of resolving conflicts, and it may be incumbent on those most closely involved—on judges and lawyers, themselves—to explore them. The following comments by Judge Forer should at least give you pause:

> These questions—Does the litigational process provide just results? Does it promote a belief in law?—we have ignored at our peril.

> At trial, the search for truth and justice must be conducted along very restricted paths. Litigants, witnesses, lawyers and judges are bound by rules developed in other cases, in other generations or centuries, which have little to do with the problems presented to the court today. The trial judge has a very limited scope of discretion. He must apply the rules, though justice be thwarted at every turn.

> In most jurisdictions, if a badly injured plaintiff was ever so slightly negligent and the defendant grossly negligent, the plaintiff cannot recover. If machinery malfunctions, injuring someone, the owner is not liable unless he was negligent in maintaining or inspecting the machinery.

> A person injured in an accident not occurring in the course of his employment who is unable to work is entitled to recover expenses, pain and suffering, and loss of earnings. If the injured party is successful, he or she will recover that sum, perhaps four to eight or more years after the injury. He will not get interest. A factory hand earning $175 a week will recover that amount. An unemployed housewife will not be paid for loss of her time. An executive earning $100,000 a year will recover his loss of earnings. The executive probably has insurance, savings and assets to help him over the period of unemployment due to injury. The factory hand and the housewife may have no resources to help them survive an illness or injury. The law does not grant recovery on the basis of need but only upon provable monetary loss.

> The rules governing the admission of evidence are like the laws of the Medes and the Persians, old and immutable. Hearsay testimony, which is what someone else told the witness, is excluded except in certain well-defined situations. It is excluded because there is no right to cross-examine the first speaker, who is not present at the trial, with respect to the truth of his statement. Often the application of the rule makes no sense. Many arrests are made because an unknown citizen

stopped a police car or phoned the police to report a crime in progress. For example, a policeman is stopped by an excited civilian who says, "Go to the corner of First and Main Streets, a man with a goatee and a green jacket is robbing and beating an old woman." The policeman immediately drives a block to that location, finds a dead woman on the street and a man with a goatee and green jacket running away.

In court the policeman will testify, "I was in my patrol car No. 437, at 8:23 P.M., and driving down Main Street at the corner of Second. I was stopped by an unknown man in a car who said—"

"Objection, Your Honor."

"Sustained. Officer, do not tell us what the man said, but only what you said or did."

"As a result of information received, I proceeded to First and Main Streets where I saw the body of a woman lying on the street and a man in a goatee and green jacket running east. I pursued the man and apprehended him."

It may take an hour or more of testimony to develop what happened. It may be impossible ever to show the connection between the man in the green jacket and the dead woman.

On the other hand, when it is a question of reputation, hearsay is freely admitted and factual evidence is excluded.

"What is the reputation of Mr. Jones, among those who know him, for honesty and peaceful disposition?"

The witness testifies that Jones is known as an honest, law-abiding, peaceable citizen. But unless Jones introduces such evidence, it is not permitted to show that in fact on three previous occasions Jones embezzled money or that before this offense he had committed numerous vicious attacks on other people.

* * *

To assay the difficulties of the litigational process, let us examine a typical case, that of Mrs. Thomas. It was randomly assigned to me by the computer, one of 250 major civil cases, those allegedly involving more than $10,000. More than two-thirds of these cases were over five years old. Many were ten years old. The acts giving rise to the litigation, of course, occurred a number of years before suit was instituted.

In some of my cases in the ten-year age bracket, the defendant was clearly liable. Often the individual defendant pleaded with his insurance company to settle. But the carrier refused to do so. Time and the intervening death of the plaintiff have saved insurance companies and defendants great sums of money which would have been paid if the case had come to trial promptly. Since in a tort suit—accidents of all sorts, defective products and the like—the amount due is in dispute, there is no interest accumulating and no incentive to settle.

Mrs. Thomas' case was one of these where liability was reasonably clear—a rear-end collision. She was driving her car in the afternoon rush-hour traffic and stopped for a traffic light. Arthur Schmidt, who was driving the Robertson Corporation truck on company business, ploughed into the back of her car. Both of them stopped. Schmidt said he was sorry, but the company was insured. She needn't worry. He promptly reported the accident to his employer, who immediately notified the insurance company. Mrs. Thomas went home and called her insurance company. By the next morning she had a splitting headache and a terrible pain in her neck. She could not raise her right arm.

Her insurance company advised her to get a lawyer. Mrs. Thomas went to a reputable doctor, who diagnosed her ailment as a tear of the ligament where the neck and shoulder join. The only remedy was surgery. Since there was but a 50 percent chance of recovery in a woman of her age, he did not recommend it. Mrs. Thomas had to give up her factory job and take occasional light employment. Fortunately she owned a house, which she sold, and with the proceeds and help from her children she managed to stay off relief for *ten* years until her case came to trial. Many others disabled in accidents survive on public assistance for years while awaiting a trial or settlement of the case. The insurance company offered Mrs. Thomas $3,500 just before the trial. She refused the offer.

Fortunately for Mrs. Thomas she had a new jury. Her case was their first one. By the end of the month, after hearing at least six cases of cervical sprain or lumbar strain, a jury will award very little for back injuries. The insurance company had had Mrs. Thomas examined by a doctor of their choice who testified that she had suffered a minor sprain which "should have healed" in three months. He suggested that she was suffering from "compensation neurosis." After all, a menopausal woman could exaggerate her aches and pains. Perhaps she didn't want to work. The judge hears this same doctor testify week in and week out. He never finds that anyone has a real injury. Even amputees had some pre-existing ailment which would have required an amputation irrespective of the accident, the good doctor finds. The jury does not know this. They do not know that there is insurance and they may not be told. Mrs. Thomas was also fortunate that Schmidt was driving the company truck so that she could sue his corporate employer. A jury knows that a company has assets and probably is insured. If the case had been simply Mrs. Thomas against Mr. Schmidt, a nice young man, who knows what the outcome would have been? Would the jury award a large sum against a young man who might have to sell his home to pay for Mrs. Thomas' injuries? The jury awarded Mrs. Thomas $18,000. The defendant (really the insurance company) appealed. Mrs. Thomas' lawyer wisely advised her to take $12,000 now instead of waiting for the outcome of the appeal and possibly a new trial. She cannot wait another three or four years. By then the doctor who treated her may have moved away or died. Where will the witnesses be? And if their testimony at the second trial varies from that given at the first trial, who will believe them?

This case took four days. A courtroom with all the personnel and a jury of twelve citizens plus two alternates were occupied for this entire time. It costs the taxpayers, depending upon the community, from $1,000 to $2,000 a day for a court and jury. Five busy doctors left their patients and came to court to testify. Each of them was paid from $100 to $700 for a courtroom appearance. The jury did not know this. In fact, the jury operates in ignorance of most of the crucial facts. And the system operates in total ignorance of how the jury comes to its decision.[3]

Is it enough to say that such results are necessarily the product of a system which seeks not only truth, but the realization of "independent social policies   .   .   .   ease in prediction and application" and—perhaps most importantly—the "tranquilizing" of conflict?[4] Are there alternative arrangements and views of the lawyer's role which would achieve these purposes with less compromise of truth values? It may be that your efforts to grasp the skills and possibilities in the advocate's role will help you find more satisfactory answers to such questions.

B. AN ORIENTING MODEL: TRIAL PRACTICE AS A PERFORMING ART

---

1.   Structure: The Insights of the Writer

BROOKS AND WARREN, UNDERSTANDING FICTION
23–27, 170–73, 272–76 (1959).*

A piece of fiction is a unity, in so far as the piece of fiction is successful. Its elements are so related that we feel an expressive interpenetration among them, a set of vital relationships.

.   .   .   As a rule, in most pieces of fiction, there is a central character, but there are instances in which this is not true. In such cases, however, the fiction writer is not freed from the obligation to maintain a unity, that is, to build his story so that the characters in action are related to each other and to a dominating idea or theme. .   .   .   [The] decisive matter [in fiction] is .   .   .   structure, that is, the way in which the elements (character, events, meanings) are related to each other. .   .   .   The "truth" which is involved in fiction [refers] to such matters as the following: (1) the consistency and comprehensibility of character; (2) the motivation and credibility of action and (3) the acceptability of the total meaning .   .   . History and biography give us what may be called truth of correspondence. What a true history says "corresponds to the facts." A true biography matches the life of its subject. But fiction is not fact, and its "truth" does not involve a correspondence to something outside life. .   .   .   [I]n fiction, truth of coherence is the primary

---

3. L. Forer, THE DEATH OF THE LAW 143–47 (1975).

4. Weinstein, *Some Difficulties in Devising Rules for Determining Truth in Judicial Trials*, 66 COL.L.REV. 222, 231 (1966).

* © 1959 by Prentice-Hall, Inc., Englewood Cliffs, New Jesey. The first two paragraphs of these excerpts are taken from Hanson Baldwin's *R.M.S. Titanic*, reprinted in UNDERSTANDING FICTION at 11–27.

truth   .   .   .   Successful fiction always involves a coherent relating
of action, character and meaning.   And   .   .   .   failures in fiction
can be stated as failures in coherence.   [This can be seen in every]
domain of fiction.   .   .   .

* * *

From what has been said already, it is plain that the author's
selection of modes of character presentation will depend upon a number of things.   His decision on when to summarize traits or events, on
when to describe directly, and on when to allow the character to express his feelings through dialogue and action, will depend upon the
general end of the story and upon the way in which the action of the
story is to be developed from a beginning, through a complicating middle, to an inevitable end.

* * *

[In critically evaluating each such choice] we are primarily and
unremittingly concerned with truth of coherence—with how the parts
cohere into a total meaningful pattern.

Nowhere are the claims for coherence asserted more plainly than
in the matter of character presentation.   A character must be credible—must make sense, must be able to command our belief.   True,
the character in question may be an eccentric; he may be brutally
criminal; he may even be mad.   But his thoughts and actions must
ultimately be coherent.   If the characters in a story simply don't make
sense, we have to reject the story.   But we must remember that the
kind of sense a character must make is his own kind, not our kind.
For example, a more sensible, less proud woman than Madame Loisel
in "The Necklace"   .   .   .   might have made a clean breast of things
to her friend and been spared the terrible and unnecessary consequences, but it is the coherence of Madame Loisel's character that
Maupassant must convince us of.   If he does not convince us that his
Madame Loisel is really capable of accepting, and persisting through,
the life of hardship that comes with the loss of the necklace, then the
story itself is incredible.   Unless Eudora Welty has convinced us
that Ruby Fisher is capable of entertaining the fantasy which the
chance-read newspaper suggests to her, then her story makes no sense.
An obvious test of fiction then is that the motives and actions of its
characters are rendered coherent.   It is the glory of fiction that the
great artists have been able to render coherent so many strange
.   .   ., often apparently self-contradictory, examples of human
nature.

* * *

[The same claims of coherence relate to the theme, the idea, the
meaning.]   We cannot very long consider the action or the characters
of a story without coming to some concern with theme, for, as we
have already insisted, a story, in so far as it is a good story, is an
organic unity in which all the elements have vital interrelations.
Each element implies the other elements, and implies them in movement toward a significant end.

.   .   .   The theme of a piece of fiction is not to be thought of as merely the topic with which the story may be taken to concern itself—though the word is sometimes loosely used in this sense. For instance, we can say that two stories soon to be encountered, "The Killers," by Ernest Hemingway, and "I Want to Know Why," by Sherwood Anderson, have the same topic—the topic of growing up, the initiation into manhood. But in the two stories the meaning of the initiation is very different. The theme is what is made of the topic. It is the comment on the topic that is implied in the process of the story.

The theme, furthermore, is not to be confused with any ideas or pieces of information, however interesting or important, which we may happen to take away from our reading of a piece of fiction. For instance, Herman Melville's novel *Moby Dick* gives a full and fascinating account of whaling, but that information is not to be confused with either the topic or the theme. The life of whaling is simply the world in which—the background against which—the human experience works itself out meaningfully.

The theme is what a piece of fiction stacks up to. It is the idea, the significance, the interpretation of persons and events, the pervasive and unifying view of life which is embodied in the total narrative. .   .   .

* * *

With fiction, in so far as it is successful, the imagination creates a world, characters and events which exist, as it were, in their own right.   .   .   .

In a successful piece of fiction, out of this sense of an independent world, as the characters act and are acted upon, as one event leads to another, we become more and more aware of the significance of the whole. That is, we gradually sense a developing theme. We *seem* to be caught up in a vital process in which meaning emerges from experience—and that is what, in the end, makes our own lives, in so far as we live above the brute level, interesting to us: the sense of deepening discovery, the satisfaction of learning and achieving, the growth of awareness and appreciation, the fuller understanding of our own experience. Fiction, then, is never the "illustration" of an idea. It is a created image of our very life process by which significance emerges from experience.

* * *

If a story possesses an organic unity, then all the parts are significant and have some bearing on the total significance. All contribute to the total meaning. [In reading fiction]   .   .   .   we try to find what idea, what feeling, what attitude is consistently developing throughout the story.

We can look at what kind of world is presented. We can ask what problems the characters confront, what is at stake for them—

or, if the story is one of developing awareness, what discovery is being made. We can look at the pattern of plot and try to see what significant repetitions appear. We can look at the end and ask, first, if it logically follows from the body of the story; and second, what is the intended significance. We can ask what is the tone of the story? Is it comic, ironical, cold and reportorial, pathetic, or what? We can ask if the author has tried to evoke emotional responses for which there is no justification. We can ask about the speech of the characters and the style of the author—are they in keeping with the rest of the story? All in all, we ask how fully and deeply coherent is the story. As we try to answer these questions, we usually find that we have defined the theme, and have accepted or rejected it.

NOTES

1. *Direct and Cross-Examination as Literature: The Limits and Possibilities of the Metaphor*

The image of the lawyer as "writer of fiction" may, for some of you, appeal to the cynical. We recognize that there are many potential distortions in this analogy. Nevertheless, bear in mind that what is needed here—as elsewhere in your early efforts to learn lawyering—is an orienting image of what the tasks of trial work involve. The elements of any initial metaphor that trouble or puzzle you will help you crystallize your own.

Consider, for example, the extent to which, in presenting a case at trial, the lawyer creates a world of character and theme which exists "in its own right." Of course the writer or director deals with illusion, fiction, a special concept of truth (in different ways and with different degrees of freedom to vary circumstances). But, how different are such questions as: "How do I get the judge or jury to believe that my client didn't know what he or she was signing?" or "How do I establish that my version of events is more likely than theirs?" from those asked by an author wishing to add believability to a plot or credibility to a character? To what degree can a lawyer who wants to persuade avoid paying attention to the coherence of character, events, and themes?

Some insight into these questions might be gained by the following exercise. Assume that you are about to conduct an examination or cross-examination of a witness (you can choose one from a case you are handling or from one of the problem cases in the supplement). Write out the version of the facts you expect to present through testimony as if you were free to tell them in the form of a story, giving due attention to the characters, the sequence of events and anything that explains why your version of the relevant circumstances is more plausible than any other. Now translate your story into questions and anticipated answers from which your statements as to character, theme and plot can be inferred. Annotate or rewrite those questions or anticipated answers which would not be in conformity with the rules of evidence.

Does this exercise add to the detail, scope and unity of your examination? Do the questions and answers convey what you hoped to communicate in your narrative? In performing this exercise you will find that a number of evidentiary rules will have a direct bearing on your attempts to achieve coherence and credibility. Consider, for example, the effect on a direct examination of the rules governing (i) the degree to which background may be brought out by the examiner; (ii) the scope of permissible corroboration (charts, photos, maps, etc.); (iii) the admissibility of prior consistent statements and actions; (iv) the extent to which a witness can testify to his or her mental processes and/or motives, intentions, or justifications for particular conduct; (v) the type of testimony admissible on issues of character. How would you handle these problems? Similar problems are created in cross-examination by the rules governing (i) impeachment through character and prior bad acts; (ii) characterization and conclusory statements by the examiner; and (iii) materiality and relevance. Is it possible and/or desirable to just tell a story with testimony in the same way one does in presenting narrative discourse?

Although they might describe it in different terms, most trial lawyers seem to think of their task as creating coherence. Like the writer of fiction, they are seeking to achieve consistency, acceptability and the kind of unity which will convince the trier of the fact that their client's story is true. And though they must start with "real" evidence—with the testimony of witnesses, documents and other tangible proofs—the process of selection and arrangement, of assembling those building blocks into a coherent whole, is much the same. As Hanson Baldwin points out:

> .   .   .   The fiction writer may choose or create "facts," [but only] in accordance with the pattern of human conduct which he wishes to present   .   .   .   [H]e must convince his reader that the story does not violate the probabilities of human action   .   .   .   .
>
> [One often thinks] of fiction as being opposed to fact. But in one real sense, this is a false opposition. It is simply a matter of what kinds of facts [the writer of] fiction can use and the way in which he can use them.   .   .   .[5]

Obviously, there are differences between a piece of fiction and a body of trial testimony. There are limits beyond consistency and credibility on what can be presented at trial. And there are moral and professional constraints on your ability to build "half-truths" or implications into a believable explanation. Nevertheless, more often than you might imagine, you will find yourself as a trial lawyer arguing inferences which you yourself do not know (or believe) to be true.

5.   In C. Brooks & R. Warren, UNDER-
STANDING FICTION 25–26 (1959).

You may find the insights of the writer a place to begin in making sense of the ethical and practical issues this experience raises.[6]

----

2. *The Logic of Direct and Cross-Examination: The Structure of Coherence*

Another way to understand what Brooks and Warren speak of as the coherence of fiction is to think about the process as explaining something to someone. Following the analogy, a direct or cross-examination would essentially involve a set of statements that say: "It happened this way because . . . and couldn't have happened that way because . . . In so far as X or Y say otherwise they are in error because . . . ."

McBurney and Mills offer a more complete statement of this sort of "logic":

> . . . Explanation is a form of analysis and reasoning in which description, narration, and exposition are used to provide acceptable bases for belief and action by placing a proposition in a context that implies its truth. The method has been described as follows:

> Its plan [that of support by explanation] is simply to portray a situation which gradually, of itself, without compulsion or contention on the part of the speaker, through the compelling power of a developing situation, makes evident to the mind of the hearer the necessity of one certain solution. The method is not in the orthodox and generally accepted sense argumentative, rather it is that of exposition with a goodly dash of narration and description. It does not appear to argue; it merely sets forth—yet slowly definitely, as it proceeds, the lines of descriptive development begin to converge and it becomes compellingly evident to each thinking mind that such a set of conditions implies, necessitates, one thing, the conclusion toward which an approach has been made from the beginning. It is argument in a very true sense, its aim is to convince and persuade, yet it is argument of which exposition, narration, and description are handmaidens.[7]

----

6. For the best collection of law-oriented material drawing on the perspectives of the writer see J. White, THE LEGAL IMAGINATION: STUDIES IN THE NATURE OF LEGAL THOUGHT AND EXPRESSION (1973); *see also* Gilson, *Literary Minds and Judicial Style*, 36 N.Y.U.L.REV. 915 (1961); Probert, *Law and Persuasion: The Language Behavior of Lawyers*, 108 U.PA.L.REV. 35 (1959).

7. The authors define these terms as follows:

> . . . description paints a picture—"exhibits the properties, attributes, and relations of *spacial* objects in their proper order." Narration tells a story—"presents a matter in its *time* relations . . ., exhibits events in their proper order." Exposition exhibits a proposition as "a logical thought whole independent of time or space relations." . . . exposition deals largely with abstract and general conceptions, while pure description and narration are generally occupied with concrete things. Whereas description and narration deal with things seen, heard, depicted (matters of observation), exposition is concerned with things conceived, identified, classified (matters of penetra-

The explanatory approach in argument seeks to involve the proposition in question as a necessary circumstance of the data presented. The key to this is *implication*. The proposition is implied or suggested as naturally to be inferred, often without being expressly stated.

Implication has been defined as "the connection between terms or sets of terms in virtue of a common nature which binds them into parts within a continuous system such that you can tell from one or more parts of it what the other parts of it, or some of them, are and how they are behaving." This is the nature of the inference in argument by explanation. It consists in a juxtaposition of the original data connected with the proposition, and out of the necessities which impose themselves when these data are thus arranged and exhibited arises a datum—a premise which partakes of the nature of a conclusion and is accepted as such.

The Method of Explanation

There are examples of the explanatory approach in argument all around us. In attempting to influence attitudes and beliefs in areas where the relevant data lend themselves to description, narration, or exposition, there does appear to be a "natural" impulse to use this approach. Travel brochures, posters, billboards, radio and television commercials—indeed, the whole field of advertising and selling—attest the confidence that entrepreneurs of all kinds place in the persuasive power of description, narration, and exposition. And most people, in trying to justify their behavior, recommend a course of action, or make a questionable proposition believable, will often resort to explanation. In a quite different area, the reports of scholarly investigations are frequently expositions serving the normal purposes of argument. Scientists, for example, typically support their conclusions by explaining the processes they went through in arriving at these conclusions.

. . . [What is involved is] putting together an *implicative system* that directs an inference to a predetermined conclusion to the exclusion of other possible conclusions.

The implicative system. Such a system may be defined as a logical thought-whole consisting of a set of propositions so related (by implication) that the truth of one is implied by the truth of the others. A proposition may be looked upon as a part of this whole or system. In argument by explanation, the proposition for discussion is always one of the propositions of an implicative system. It is the task of the speaker to present the other related propositions in such a way that the truth

tive and systematic thinking). Description and narration consider traits and acts that distinguish objects as individuals; exposition looks for the traits and acts that unite individuals into classes. Assume, for instance, that you have occasion to explain some controversial religious doctrine or scientific principle. Neither narration nor description would suffice, because such a subject cannot usually be exhibited in relations of time or space. It is an abstract concept which can be adequately explained only by an exposition of its logical relations to other known concepts.
J. McBurney & G. Mills, ARGUMENTATION AND DEBATE 161–62 (1964).

of the proposition under discussion will be implied. The accompanying figure illustrates the point we are making.

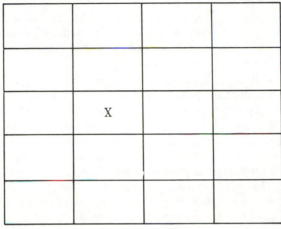

[B8820]

Let us say that the larger square represents an implicative system, and each of the smaller squares a proposition. If we let the square marked by the × indicate the proposition for argument, we suggest that its truth may be implied as we explain the propositions or data represented by the other squares. The more of these related propositions we explain, the more evident will become the proposition under discussion. The whole process is comparable to a picture puzzle which is unintelligible until its various parts are assembled. As the fragments are pieced together, the place of each remaining part becomes increasingly evident from the nature of the picture which is beginning to take form. Propositions, like the pieces of the puzzle, are not intelligible as isolated entities. Their identity as true or false statements, so far as any individual is concerned, is determined by many relationships. It is the task of the speaker to bring these relationships to light. If the proposition under discussion can be identified with a group of other propositions which cannot be logically denied and thus are accepted by the audience, the truth of the proposition is thereby implied. A proposition is thus related to a system as a part is related to the whole. It is the speaker's task to make it clear that the proposition he is defending is a part of a system which the listener cannot safely or logically deny. When that system has been explained, the truth or falsity of the proposition can be implied by it.

The this-or-nothing disjunction. Needless to say, it is a matter of considerable importance that the conclusion drawn by the audience be the conclusion which the speaker intends to be drawn. In other words, the explanation developed should be sufficiently under the control and guidance of the speaker to give reasonable assurance that his purpose will be accomplished. This can best be done by developing the argument so that the only alternative to the acceptance of the suggested proposition is the rejection of all the data presented. . . .

In a tightly drawn argument by explanation, the speaker builds an implicative system that confronts his audience with a this-or-nothing disjunction in which his proposition is the "this" in the disjunction and the rejection of the related propositions implying its truth is the "nothing." This nothing means the absence of all logical grounds— the denial of truth as we know it and commonly accept it.

Topical organization. The outline of explanatory argument is topical rather than enthymematic. In others words, the main points and the subpoints are usually key words or phrases rather than premises. The implicative system may be regarded as a thought whole that is divided into its parts by the main points, and these main points, in turn, divided into their parts by the subpoints. In this organization each coordinate list of points is a descriptive, narrative, or expository breakdown of the point they are intended to explain. The composition (oral or written) developing this outline, then, will be description, narration, exposition, or some combination of these designed to place the suggested proposition in a context that warrants its implication.

* * *

The persuasive values of such an "argument" [are, at least, three-fold]:

It dispels unfamiliarity. Support by explanation has special value as a means of persuading an audience which is inadequately informed on the proposition. What argument could be more persuasive to a person who is indifferent, or opposed to a proposition because he is not informed regarding it, than one which supplies him with this information? Almost invariably, when the opposition has its basis in unfamiliarity, the speaker has only to explain the proposition in order to dispel this opposition and secure the desired action.

The audience is prepared for the conclusion by its own thinking. That you cannot pour conclusions into the heads of people as you would pour water into a receptacle is a matter of common knowledge. Only as the listener is stirred to "purposeful activity" can you expect to influence his thinking or overt conduct. Conclusions arrived at by one's own thinking are thus infinitely stronger than those imposed by others, so far as the individual is concerned. In the explanatory method the persuader does not simply recite his own conclusions before the audience; rather, he sets forth those facts and opinions which led him to conclude as he did in such a way that the hearers will be prodded to go through the same reasoning process.

It avoids the "contrarient idea." This method also avoids what some writers have called the "contrarient idea." When a speaker starts his presentation with certain conclusions, the very announcement of these conclusions invariably sets off inhibitions which might never otherwise occur. Some people seem to resist other people's conclusions and immediately begin a mental argument with the speaker in order to fight him from the first word to the last. In many situations these obstacles can be avoided, or at least minimized by the method of explanation.[8]

The problem for the trial lawyer is developing this form of argument within the confines of presenting evidence through witnesses. Consider the choices involved in preparing to present evidence at trial—the witnesses to call, the order of proof, the questions to be asked, the phrasing and sequence of those questions, the way potential evidentiary objections or difficulties with the witness will be handled. In terms of what objectives should these judgments be made? How does the lawyer communicate through witnesses the propositions he or she desires to establish? Is it appropriate to think of this process as an "implicative system"?

A review of the literature on trial strategy reminds us that direct examination can be employed to perform a number of diverse functions. In particular, it may be used to:

—contribute specific factual elements to the examiner's version of the case;

—corroborate the validity of these elements and other evidentiary matter;

—explain, organize, and clarify the relationship between the factual elements of the case;

—characterize these elements in relation to the appropriate legal standard—*e. g.*, "good cause," negligence, fraud—either explicitly or by inference, depending on the rules of evidence governing the level of abstraction at which a witness can testify;

—characterize the attitudes, dispositions, beliefs, and values of the participants in order to support the examiner's version of the case;

—structure and focus the fact-finder's attention and perception;

—contradict and discredit adverse factual elements and testimony; and

—construct a record for appeal on subsequent proceedings.[9]

Cross-examination, is also used for a number of different purposes, in particular to:

—explain, qualify or supplement the testimony given by the witness on direct examination.

—compel the admission of facts contrary to or inconsistent with the witness' direct testimony.

---

8. *Id.* at 157–62. *See also* S. Toulmin, THE USES OF ARGUMENT (1958).

9. *See generally* R. Keeton, TRIAL TACTICS AND METHODS, 10–11 (2d ed. 1973); S. Schweitzer, TRIAL GUIDE 1273 (1945).

—weaken the effect of the direct examination by attacking the source and extent of the witness' knowledge, by testing his or her memory, and by revealing the witness' inability to consistently and correctly narrate the facts of which he or she pretends to have knowledge.

—show that the witness' testimony is a previously coached and rehearsed story.

—emphasize the improbability of the story testified to on direct examination.

—show the witness' partisanship, bias, prejudice or a willingness to misrepresent or color the facts because of his or her relationship to either of the parties, friendship or hostility for either party, pecuniary interest or other improper motive.

—impeach the witness by showing he or she has made previous statements at variance with the testimony on direct examination.

—show the witness' previous conviction of a crime rendering him or her unworthy of belief, and, to the extent permitted, to show moral delinquencies and misconduct deemed to affect credibility.

—In those jurisdictions following the English rule, to elicit new matter either derogatory to the witness or helpful to the cross-examiner's case.[10]

Although cross-examination introduces fewer new elements and focuses on weakening or discrediting testimony which has already been presented, its goals are similar to the goals of an effective direct examination. The major differences—the likelihood that the witness on cross will assume an adversary stance, and the greater opportunities for control offered by the right to use leading questions—involve distinctions along a continuum rather than two separate processes. Direct and cross-examination are thus essentially variations of the same task.

What is not made explicit in the trial literature, however, is that direct and cross-examination are also both ways of making arguments —or, at least, of offering explanations which will be the basis for arguments. Consider whether this is an important insight and how you might use it. Our own experience is that an appropriate way for attorneys to prepare an examination is to quite literally ask themselves *exactly* what verbal utterances they wish to evoke from a witness and to arrange these propositions in the form of an implicative

---

10. From F. X. Busch, TRIAL PROCE-
DURE MATERIALS 215 (1961) (citations omitted).

system very much like the one suggested by McBurney and Mills. That is, in technical terms, they must juxtapose two (or more) propositions, the second being a probability inference of the first. In direct examination this means that the questions and anticipated answers will be designed to create a chain of such probabilities. In cross-examination the questions and answers would be contrasted to emphasize the improbability of the challenged statement. Thus, if one wanted to establish that a witness was being truthful about making a phone call, the underlying "structure" of the examination might look like this:

Propositions	Anticipated Testimony	Questions
The witness says he made the call	Yes: he answered and we talked—we'd spoken many times over the phone	You called X?
If the call was made, the witness would remember details.	It was about 11:40	What Time?
However, he would only remember the exact time if he had a reason to. He does and it fits with ordinary way people remember things	Well, I'd just come in from a play—and I noted that I had just missed the evening news.	How do you recall?
	Yes—every evening	Which you regularly watch?
People often write down addresses and the like	Yes—I wrote down the address he gave me	Did you make any notation of what was said?
but don't usually save them	No—I threw it away	Do you have those notes?
A phone call to X was the only way he could have known where to go the next morning. Therefore, he made the call.	Yes—He'd just moved	Was that the first time you had X's address?
	At 9:00 the next morning	When did you go to see him?

On cross-examination, the pattern of questions might be something like the following pattern:

Propositions	Anticipated Testimony	Questions
Witness asserts that he obtained address as a result of phone call	Yes	You say that you got the address from X over the phone?
	Yes	That night?
	Yes	You had to see X the next day?
It is not probable that someone needing an address for an urgent 9:00 a. m. appointment would wait until almost midnight to call for it	Well, yes	And you waited until 11:40 that night to get his address?
	Yes	Although it was urgent that you see him immediately?
He could have gotten it elsewhere: the fact that he came next morning doesn't prove he made the phone call. Therefore, he didn't make the call	I could have	You could have gotten the address from Y or Z, couldn't you?
	I suppose so	Or from Information?

Obviously, there are many other lines, details, conclusions these questions could pursue. Further, judgments would have to be made about the number, form and sequence of questions. What we are interested in here is whether this is an appropriate way to think about them. Is this essentially a form of explanation? In what ways is a "story" told in this process?

2.   Method: The Insights of the Actor

WHITING, AN INTRODUCTION TO THE THEATRE *

So far as actual theories of acting are concerned, there are two basic schools of thought: (1) the technical or mechanical school tends toward an approach from the outside, emphasizing the use of body, voice, gesture, inflection, conventions, and techniques; (2) the psychological or creative school tends to approach the problem from the inside, emphasizing such things as understanding, motivation, imagination, purpose, and emotion. Conflict between these two approaches has often been heated. Before we examine them directly, let us consider a closely related controversy that has raged for decades, "Should the actor feel his part?"

*   *   *

. . . Logic tells us that in the final analysis it does not matter whether the actor feels or not, so long as he presents a pattern of voice and action that will make the audience feel. . . . But even though we are thus forced to admit that an actor need not feel in order to make an audience feel, our basic question still remains: is the actor more likely to assume the correct outward pattern—one that will convince and move his audience—when feeling or not feeling?

Logic seems to favor the actor who feels and believes in what he says and does. It may be true that hardened professionals can think or feel one thing while doing another, but for the beginner to attempt this is dangerous. Young actors are likely to convey quite unconsciously and in spite of themselves the way they really think and feel. Thus, many a beginner transmits to his audience not the drives and desires of his character, but the drives and desires that are his own: his personal eagerness to succeed, his struggle to remember the next line, his elation when a comic line gets a laugh, his strained anxiety when it does not, and his growing embarrassment as the love scene draws near. The professional may be able to think such irrelevant thoughts and cover them up with technique, but for the amateur the best way to make an audience understand, feel, and believe is for the actor himself to understand, feel, and believe. It is safer to work with nature than against it.

*   *   *

. . . Assuming that an actor wishes to create a true state of feeling, how is he to do it? . . . Briefly—and we shall consider this in depth later—the answer appears to be: (1) he might begin by trying to understand the play and its author from as many angles as possible; (2) he must humanize the characters in terms of his own life and imagination, tuning in on their drives, desires, hopes, and dreams; (3) he needs to probe again and again with the question,

* Abridged from pages 198–211 of An Introduction to the Theatre by Frank M. Whiting. © 1954 by Harper & Row Publishers, Inc. © 1961, 1969 by Frank M. Whiting. Reprinted by Permission. A fourth edition of this work was published in 1978.

B. & M. Prepar. & Present.Case Pamph. UCB—8

"If I were such a person in such a situation, what would I say and do, how would I deal with the stimulus?"

Out of such depth of understanding and doing can come belief in the character, the situation, the author, and the artistic integrity of what one is required to say and do. Finally, out of such belief is likely to come feeling, not the strained type that confuses and inhibits the actor, but the deeply sincere type that enables him to relax without being dull, to perform with great emotional power and conviction, yet without strain.

* * *

THE CREATIVE APPROACH

Perhaps the most significant element about the Stanislavski method is that it really tries to be creative. . . .

. . . [The] term creative has a somewhat special significance. It implies that the actor himself is fundamentally responsible for creating the patterns of expression that will best express his role.

. . . The actor may use help from any source possible, but it is still his responsibility to play the role, not necessarily according to the textbook, not necessarily according to what the director says, not in imitation of the way Edwin Booth played it, but in the best possible way that he himself can play it. This requires thinking, imagination, and creative effort.

Many of the principles of the creative approach have been mentioned already, but because of the importance of "the method" in modern acting, it seems wise to develop the subject more fully. We shall therefore take a closer look at some of the basic techniques.

Freedom from Unnecessary Muscular Strain

Unnecessary tension can be disastrous to the actor, it not only interferes with the use of voice and body but also blocks the imagination. Freedom from undue strain is a fundamental prerequisite to all creative work, but it is a much greater problem to the performing artist like the actor or singer than to the writer or painter, since the performer must learn to relax unnecessary tension while under the pressure of public performance.

Concentration of Attention

Unnecessary tension and many other ills of acting tend to arise from the actor's failure to concentrate his attention on something within or appropriate to the imaginary situation. The actor needs to be in somewhat the same "inspired" state of mind as the author, the painter, and the composer are when their energies are absorbed by creative work; but whereas other artists usually arrive at this creative state in the quiet of their own rooms and under favorable circumstances, the actor must create at a given time, in a given place, and under very adverse circumstances—glaring lights, offstage dis-

tractions, and the strain of being observed by an audience. The actor's
power to absorb himself in his fundamental task, driving the numerous distractions to the periphery of his consciousness, is thus of tremendous importance.

Object of Concentration: Motives and Dramatic Action

The term dramatic action is closely related to motivation and
purpose—to a sensitive and compelling awareness of the wants, desires, and drives of a character. A desire or objective on stage, as
in life, always calls for some action, something to be done or accomplished. We want to warm ourselves at the fire, to find an article
that has been lost, to convince a friend of our innocence, to win the
lady of our choice. In an effort to achieve such desires we may employ words, inflections, gestures, facial expressions, or whatever type
of activity seems likely to gain the desired end. Under the Stanislavski system the actor pays little direct attention to such things as inflections, gestures, and facial expressions. These, it is assumed, will
take care of themselves if he has a vivid awareness of his objectives.
In other words, the actor does not concentrate on *how* he should say
his lines but on *what he wants* and especially on what can be done to
get what he wants. This, while not the actor's whole task, is his major
task.

Related to all this is another creative method that teachers have
recently begun to emphasize. Essentially it consists of substituting
images for words. Take the great speech by Enobarbus in *Antony
and Cleopatra* in which he describes how the lovers first met. The
great actor not only knows why he is telling the story but in his
"mind's eye" tends to see images of the event, fabricated from his
imagination to be sure, but nevertheless images that are quite as artis-
tically real and vivid as they would have been had he really seen the
meeting of Antony and Cleopatra. Evidence, while sketchy, indicates
that the poor actor tends to see only the images of words from the
printed script or something equally inappropriate.

Memory of Emotion

Probably no other principle is as closely associated with the
Stanislavski method as memory of emotion. This principle has values, although it has often been misapplied and overstressed. Harold
Clurman, one of Stanislavski's most devoted followers, admits that
young actors, upon discovering emotion-memory, tend to "eat it up,"
to wallow in self-induced melancholy until they produce "a kind of
constipation of the soul." All goods things can be overdone. One
cause of difficulty is that the technique of recall is often misunder-
stood. It consists of quietly recalling not emotions, but the details
and images of a past experience that parallels a situation the actor
is required to perform in a play. If the recalling is done carefully

and with enough concentration, some of the emotion that originally accompanied the experience is likely to return. When this happens, it becomes easy to play the scene in the play with sincerity and conviction, for the actor now understands it emotionally as well as intellectually. He can believe it; a similar thing actually happened to him.

In a sense, memory of emotion is nothing but a conscious application of the old principle that we know things only in terms of our own experience. Usually, sensitive artists find that such identification in terms of personal experience functions quite subconsciously and automatically. We read a scene from a play and find it to be deeply moving or exciting without having to probe consciously for the personal experiences that have enabled us to tune in so effectively on its tragedy and excitement. Memory of emotion becomes most valuable when for some reason a scene that should be moving leaves us cold. In such cases, deliberate probing in the storehouse of our own experiences may provide the answer.

Justification and Belief

To act well, most actors find it important to believe in the artistic logic and integrity of what they are doing. If the play is poorly written or the action required by the director is false, the actor finds it difficult to be convincing. On the other hand, the great actor is often a wizard at thinking up reasons that will "justify" even awkward action or bad lines. Charlie Chaplin had an amazing faculty for projecting a naive belief in situations that most actors could only have forced into pure ham. Whether a comedian, a tragedian, or an actor in a fantasy, the actor must seem to believe in the artistic truth of everything he says and does if the audience is to believe in his performance.

The Magic if: Imagination

Closely related to both imagination and belief is a tool that Stanislavski loved to employ, the magic "if." Suppose, for example, that an actor says to himself, "I am Hamlet." His statement is preposterous and his imagination dries up. Instead, let him say, "If I were Hamlet—." Here is an honest, rational assumption, one that is sensible and believable and that sets the imagination and creative faculties to work.

* * *

THE TECHNICAL APPROACH

No responsible person, including Stanislavski, would argue that the creative approach alone is enough. After all, acting is not life. There are obvious differences, and these differences are commonly referred to as the techniques of acting.

Projection

What is said and done on stage must be seen and heard by the audience.   Even in the most intimate scenes "sweet nothings" must be murmured in a voice that projects to the balcony! The simple requirements of audibility and visibility form the basis of numerous stage conventions and techniques: "turn front," "kneel on the downstage knee," "deliver important lines forward," and dozens of others. Obeyed slavishly and without judgment, such rules can make the actor look stilted, conspicuous, and ridiculous. Taken simply as a means of achieving the general ends of being seen and heard, they contain the wisdom of long experience, and the earnest beginner will welcome the help they can give.

The Actor's Body

Related to the problems of audibility and visibility are the instruments of expression themselves, the voice and the body. The value of a free, responsive voice and a rhythmic, expressive body cannot be overemphasized. How to develop such a voice and such a body is another matter.

Actually voice and body are closely interrelated, or more accurately, the production of voice is simply one of the highly specialized functions of the body. Consequently, teachers usually begin the training of either by first considering the body, for it is more general, less complex, and more tangible than voice. Improvement in one is likely to effect improvement in the other, for the root cause of difficulty in both, as far as the beginner is concerned, usually lies in unnecessary muscular strain, which in turn is probably due to such psychological factors as anxiety, fear, stage fright, and insecurity. One approach toward improvement, then, lies in doing something to relieve these unnecessary tensions. . . .

[W]hatever the technique, the objective to strive for is a body that, without strain or affectation, expresses feeling and ideas, not just with the face muscles, not just with the voice, not just with the hands, but with the coordinated power of the entire body. Good acting, while never strained, has vitality.

The Actor's Voice

The training of the human voice is so complicated that we will consider here only [two] general principles.

* * *

[1] Amazing improvements are frequently made in voices simply by working for confidence and better psychological adjustment. Many a voice that rings with assurance and energy in the friendly environment of the playground becomes embarrassingly weak and ineffective in the strained, unfamiliar environment of the stage or platform.   Even the inexperienced teacher can attempt to transfer the confidence and assurance of the one to the other. Anything that re-

lieves fear and strain will almost invariably help the voice—at least it can do no harm.

[2] A general desire to speak with greater audibility and clarity than in ordinary life can also be motivated without particular danger, Most people use a better than ordinary voice when speaking on the telephone, probably because they "instinctively" feel the need for more clarity and care. Students often make remarkable vocal development during the production of a single play simply because they sense the necessity for better than normal voice production.

* * *

Stage Fright

As already indicated, one of the actor's most difficult jobs is to keep his faculties concentrated primarily on the elusive and intangible process of giving convincing theatrical life to his character. This job is hampered by numerous distractions, the worst of all being the actor's consciousness of himself, which usually attacks in the form of stage fright. In the final analysis, this is a personal problem, one that each speaker and actor must conquer for himself. Perhaps the following hints will help.

1. It is reassuring to know that stage fright is natural, and in mild forms even desirable. After all, an appearance before a large audience *is* a social crisis, and nothing can convince the intelligent person otherwise. Nor is the nervousness always an indication that one is self-centered. It may result from fear of letting down the cast, the director, or the school, rather than fear for one's own reputation. To some degree, then, nervousness is a sign of intelligence and sensitivity, and both of these qualities are desirable, if not indispensable.

2. It is comforting to know that the chemical and bodily changes that occur during an attack of stage fright are the same as those that are necessary for the heightened activity of outstanding acting. Athletes, actors, and speakers commonly find that their fear leaves them as soon as they really get into the game, the play, or the speech. Adrenalin poured into the blood under the stress of fear becomes an asset as soon as the individual begins meeting the challenge of his job.

3. Plenty of well-motivated action often helps to relieve stage fright, since it absorbs excess nervous energy and also serves as a distraction technique. One can be reasonably certain that an actor whose first entrance calls for him to "turn on the lights, notice the room, cross to the fireplace, begin making the fire, hear the telephone, and cross to answer it, still dangling a stick of wood in one hand" will not have difficulty with his opening lines.

4. Putting the actor's mind to work may also relieve the tension of stage fright. He should focus his interest on something within the play, and try to make the character's ideas and arguments serve the

same function as his own ideas and arguments would in a real life situation. The psychological significance of this is much greater than most people suppose. It rests on the reasonably well-established theory that when the higher brain centers are active, the emotions, which tend to be localized in the lower brain centers, fall under control. It follows that nothing can be more helpful than a belief in something about the play: its message, its importance, a character's wishes and desires—anything that gives the mind something reasonably tangible to grasp, to work on, to believe in—something outside of and more important than the self. An idea that arouses some emotional conviction is best, partly because it makes concentration easy, and partly because such emotional interest will supplant the emotion of fear, which is the essence of stage fright.

5. One of the best and most practical methods of opposing stage fright is for the young actor to develop gradually. One who begins by working backstage, then progresses to mob scenes, then to bit parts, then to minor roles, next to supporting roles, and at long last to leads is unlikely ever to experience the crippling terrors of acute stage fright.

Condensation and Focus

Perhaps the most important techniques in theatre grow from the fact that art has form and purpose. . . .

. . . Life tends to ramble on endlessly with a complexity largely beyond human comprehension. Its meaningful moments are usually hopelessly cluttered with the ordinary, the uninteresting, and the distracting. Everything in a play, on the other hand, should have significance and interest. Most of the play's problems of condensation and elimination have already been solved by the playwright before the actor enters the picture, and yet much remains to be done. Distracting, meaningless movements, though perfectly natural in life, can ruin a show. Ideas half-formed and fragmentary, as they may be in life, are seldom effective on stage. Mumbled and repeated words, not noticeable in most conversations, can be disastrous to the actor. In mob scenes, unity of effect must sometimes be achieved through the director's insistence that everyone share in the hero's victory, even though from the standpoint of logic some characters would be hostile or indifferent. On stage there is a tendency to "freeze" when the other person speaks. Stage reactions (or surprise especially) tend to be broader than is characteristic of most sophisticated modern adults. In other words, much of the movement and business that a good stage director requires of an actor is primarily for the purpose of composition, picturization, or rhythm, and is not necessarily the most natural thing that the character would do.

Glancing back at the two approaches to acting, the creative approach seems to be fundamental. Generally speaking, the actor can never be too imaginative, too understanding, or too sensitive to the stimulus of the imaginary situation. Stanislavski deserves credit for having evolved a system for developing this indispensable part of the actor's equipment that many had previously considered as fixed and innate. On the other hand, it must never be forgotten that art is not purely a matter of responding to imaginary stimuli. It must be an *effective* response. Such basic things as visibility, audibility, and the demands of composition are indispensable to the actor who would serve his function in the total process of conveying the play to the audience.

NOTES

1. *Trial Practice as Dramatic Technique*

There is an extensive literature on acting and directing which seems clearly applicable to trial work.[11] Indeed, the analogy is a fairly obvious one. Many trial lawyers would readily ascribe to the view stated by Edward Bennett Williams:

> . . . [I]n every action in the trial, a lawyer is producing a great drama, especially vivid because it is circumscribed by the limits of truth. No one who watches a major criminal trial, or even an exciting civil trial, can doubt that trial practice is a creative and powerful form of art.
>
> This sense of the dramatic is in all the great trial lawyers I have met in this country. They all have histrionic flair in staging their productions and, moreover, each of them has a little of the actor in him. In fact, some of the finest actors in America are trial lawyers. They are not actors in any theatrical stage, but in their own legal setting they are almost incomparable in their sense of demonstrating the emotions. Clarence Darrow made some of the most powerful pleas in the history of the American courtroom. He may also have been one of the greatest actors in the history of American drama.[12]

11. *See, e. g.*, J. Dietrich, PLAY DIRECTION (1953); J. Dolman, THE ART OF PLAY PRODUCTION (rev. ed. 1946); S. Moore, THE STANISLAVSKY SYSTEM (1974). For those interested in the original writing of Stanislavsky, *see* AN ACTOR PREPARES (1936); BUILDING A CHARACTER (1949).

12. Cited in J. Scanlan, The Trial As a Communication Process: A Framework for Understanding Direct and Cross-Examination, at note 78 (1975) (unpublished paper on file at the library of the Harvard Law School). Though many lawyers see the parallel, few of them speculate on the long-range effects of playing this kind of role. Haiman makes a perceptive comment:

> . . . A person's character finally takes on the pattern of his acts, not his wishes . . . we become what we do." Just as a good cause can be sullied by the means used to achieve it—"the end pre-exists in the means," said Emerson—so a man can become contaminated by his actions. To manipulate others he must become an actor, and to be an effective actor of this sort requires that he manipulate his own emotions. He must learn to appear sincere when he is not, to be friendly when he is hostile, to seem angry when he feels no anger. Several years of such acting and he no longer knows who he really is or what he really feels. He is nothing but a set of masks, and even he does not know which mask he prefers.

If you have observed even portions of a trial conducted by a skillful trial attorney, you have no doubt developed a sense of what Williams is talking about.

Despite the general recognition that good trial lawyers are also good actors, however, we have encountered a great deal of resistance from colleagues (and, to a lesser extent, students) in discussing trial practice as a problem of acting technique. There is, perhaps, a legitimate fear of distorting or obscuring the real stakes in an actual trial, or inviting distortion of the truth-finding aspects of the process. There is also considerable discomfort with the notion that the trial lawyer may be playing a part rather than participating in the administration of justice. Nevertheless, it seems to us that these objections highlight the very tensions and contradictions in trial practice which we want to emphasize, and that understanding the concepts Whiting describes may help us examine and improve our own performance. Let us follow the comparison a little further.

The trial lawyer engages in a dialogue with others (opposing counsel, witnesses) in front of an audience to whom he or she must convey thought and action which is persuasive and compelling. In doing this, the lawyer must continually deal with the problems that Stanislavski identified for the actor—focus and concentration, adapting emotions and conduct to the situation, communicating coherence in word and action. Consider, for example, the dilemmas of a lawyer who feels that a long jail term for his or her client might well be justified, or who is quite sure that a key witness for the other side is accurate in his or her recollections. Does not counsel have to act "as if" he or she felt otherwise in order to avoid communicating disbelief in the client's position?

In what ways are the elements of scenic action and the modes of responding to them described by Whiting different from the tasks and techniques the trial lawyer must master in presenting evidence to a judge or jury? Would you agree that on direct examination, the witness' testimony must convey "real and vivid" images of the event, told with "power and conviction," but without strain? That on cross-examination, the questioning must be accompanied by a tone and manner which avoids obvious theatricality and expresses a belief in the "integrity" of what one is doing? Does it add or detract from your understanding to speak of these aspects of trial work in such an idiom?

It might be argued that lawyers don't follow lines, that the acting analogy suggests behavior which is too bound by the "script" to apply to lawyering. But lawyers certainly follow relatively prescribed patterns of questions and answers in such trial tasks as intro-

. . . . [He] is a slave of the same game to which he subjects others. Haiman, *Democratic Ethics and the Hidden Persuaders*, 44 Q. J. SPEECH 385 (1958).

ducing a document, or impeaching with a prior inconsistent statement. And few actors feel bound by a script in any mechanical way. Indeed, directors have cautioned against adhering too closely to set patterns.

Similarly, it may be argued that acting takes place upon a stage—that the audience, unlike a judge or jury, has no responsibility in drama and understands this to be the case. Perhaps so. But the belief, imagination, and commitment of the audience is engaged in drama as well as in trial. That a jury is less aware that it is an audience may raise questions concerning the lawyer's responsibilities, but it does not change the nature of the process involved.

On the other hand, it is true that drama is not real: its truth, in the terms we used earlier, is a truth of coherence rather than a truth of correspondence. The art of the stage asks only that the actor "treat things or people *as if* they were what he wants the audience to believe they are." [13] But in what ways is this different from the demands made on the lawyer engaged in witness examination, responding to objections, or making arguments to a jury? Is it not the lawyer's job to persuade the audience that a particular witness is probably lying, or that an objection is unfounded, or that things are what he or she argues they are, regardless of how closely these assertions correspond to some objective truth? What else does the profession mean when it counsels its members that as advocates, they must present each case so as to portray it in the best light possible?

Perhaps even the distinction between the sorts of truth the stage and the trial ideally seek is too simple. The actor's work must also touch, at some level, what we know about human experience. Even fantasy is grounded in plausible views of reality; otherwise, it could not be understood as fantasy. Similarly, the trial may rely far more on consensus as its mode of resolution than we care to recognize. What is the meaning and function of such outcomes as "the defendant is guilty," or the "plaintiff is entitled to recover $5,000"? Are these factual terms? Do they correspond to things done and said at the time of the transaction in question? As we have seen, there are so many variables intervening between event and outcome that it can legitimately be said that the trial is often more the outcome of the investigation process and the relationships it generates than the initial transaction. Is it, nevertheless, an attempt to approximate what happened? Or is it primarily designed to serve other functions, such as resolving the controversy, releasing emotions, or providing a sense of coherence—not necessarily between the event and the outcome, but between the outcome and what happened at the trial itself? Without denying the significance of attempts to screen guilt from innocence, culpability from accident, or cause from coincidence, much of the

13. S. Moore, THE STANISLAVSKI SYSTEM 37 (1974).

legitimacy and acceptability of the trial process is probably rooted in these less truth-oriented functions.[14]

———

2. *The Acting Experience: The Meaning of Having a Method*

Perhaps you might gain further insight into the relevance of the acting analogy to your own work if you "try it on," at least tentatively.

Assume, for a moment, that you are counsel to a defendant in a criminal case, and that you wish to impeach a witness who has testified against your client with that witness' prior criminal record. Your supervisor suggests that you rely on the following "lines" (or some variation of them):

Is your full name John Michael Jones?

And you were born on June 9, 1935?

Are you the same John Michael Jones who was convicted of robbery in the Superior Court of the State of Michigan on January 23, 1957?

And the same John Michael Jones who was convicted of assault with a dangerous weapon on May 5, 1963?

No further questions.

Try role playing these lines (and the affirmative responses) with a friend in front of an audience. You should conduct this exercise at least ten times, discussing your performance periodically with the audience. Feel free to modify the lines—to "improvise"—in any way which feels comfortable without altering their essential meaning.

In what ways did your examination change? What problems of performance did you identify? What modifications of pacing, intonation, emotional tone, emphasis, and physical movement did you make to deal with these problems? Would you expect that you would have similar problems in a courtroom handling an actual case? (Many of our students feel that problems of concentration, coherence in speech and action, responsiveness to both judge (audience) and witness are easier to manage in the courtroom than in role-playing; this has not been supported by our own observation of inexperienced lawyers in court, although our judgments are still very tentative.)

If this sort of exercise intrigues and/or helps you, you might consider exploring the very rich literature on developing acting com-

———

14. *See, e. g.,* C. Curtis, IT'S YOUR LAW 3 (1954): "[It] seems to me that the justification of the adversary proceeding is the satisfaction of the parties . . . not . . . our general conceptions of justice. . . . The best way [to satisfy the parties] is to encourage them to fight it out, and dissolve their differences in dissension."

petency.[15] What this literature offers is a perspective on the way another profession has gone about confronting the problem of training practitioners in a complex communicative art. It draws, as trial practice training must, less on technique than your own resources and life experiences. As Hodgson and Richards have said:

> At every moment throughout our lives, we . . . adjust to whatever happens around us. The more unexpected the happening, the more spontaneous and frank the response is likely to be. Because people are less predictable than things, we are more often called upon to adjust to what is said and done by others in a way which we cannot easily plan. If we are open and receptive, we can make discoveries both about ourselves and others from these moments. If we are less receptive, the tendency will be to reproduce what we consider to be socially accepted responses and these become standardized and stereotyped. Drama improvisation has nothing to do with makeshift or second-best. The aim is to utilize these two elements from everyday life: first the spontaneous response to the unfolding of an unexpected situation: and secondly, employing this in controlled conditions to gain insight into problems presented.
>
> * * *
>
> Acting, then . . . is an interpretation, an impersonation of aspects of the human situation. It may involve playing the role of another person or it may require the imagined response of one's own person to a mood or set of circumstances. In either case, the qualities needed for the best acting are also those qualities required for the fullest living.
>
> Both involve coming to terms with oneself, coming to terms with one's physical environment and learning how to manage relationships with other people. In all aspects of his being the actor needs to be sensitively tuned to be able to respond to whoever or whatever he encounters—and his responses must be within his control.[16]

It may be that you will go through a similar process in learning trial practice. You may also find yourself struggling with similar problems. Whether or not you find helpful the categories that Whiting suggests, it is surely the case that trial practice involves presenting "a pattern of voice and action that will make the audience . . . understand, feel and believe." In this lies not only its challenge, but the source of what is, for many lawyers, its enormous satisfaction.

---

15. Hodgson and Richards, for example, describe exercises for developing concentration, spontaneity, and imagination, many of which can be done alone or in small groups. J. Hodgson and E. Richards, IMPROVISATION: DISCOVERY AND CREATIVITY IN DRAMA, Chapters 5 & 6 (1966). *See also* R. Boleslavsky, ACTING: THE FIRST SIX LESSONS (1933); J. Dolman, Jr., THE ART OF ACTING (1949); C. L. Lees, A PRIMER OF ACTING (1940); V. Spolin, IMPROVISATION FOR THE THEATER (1963).

16. Hodgson & Richards, *supra* note 15 at 3, 11.

SECTION TWO. THE SKILL DIMENSION

A. ASSESSMENT: PREDICTING THE REACTIONS AND RESPONSES OF THE "PLAYERS"

---

1. The Trial Judge

BLUMBERG, CRIMINAL JUSTICE

124–25, 128–30, 127, 128, 137–42 (1967).

By the time he has been elected to the bench, the mean age of a Metropolitan Court judge is fifty-one years. Retirement is mandatory at seventy. In the more than two hundred years of its existence, Metropolitan Court has never had a woman judge.

Of the nine justices who regularly sit in Metropolitan Court, only one is a graduate of a "national" law school; the others are graduates of part-time, proprietary, or "factory" types of schools. Three of the nine justices completed their baccalaureate work before going to law school. In so far as their legal education was concerned, its course content did little to prepare them for their actual functions on the bench. Virtually all courses in most law schools are of the "bread and butter" variety, directed toward the candidate passing the bar examination of the particular state. Only rarely do they concern themselves with the serious issues of law administration, and virtually never do they deal with the social and economic implications of law and legal decision-making. As a result, there is no formal, systematic body of knowledge in legal education which can form the minimum requisite for a judicial career. Metropolitan Court judges—and most criminal court judges—are therefore, for the most part, poorly equipped to deal with the role challenges, dilemmas, and problems which they confront on the bench. A thorough knowledge of the criminal law is only rudimentary knowledge in the context of the onerous demands made by the criminal court bench.

Because he is ill-equipped to be a sophisticated decision-maker in a job that requires decision-making daily and routinely, and at the same time requires him to be an administrator, manager, and overseer, the judge must lean heavily on the services of others. As a consequence, Metropolitan Court justices, when they are initially appointed, are "broken in" by court clerks and other civil service functionaries who socialize them toward the "practical" goals and requirements of the court organization. This socialization is in fact actively sought by the judges in order to make their own work lives easier and to assuage their personal insecurities. As a matter of organizational and personal practicality, regardless of their individual predilections, they learn to accept and internalize the routineering and ritualism of their socializers.

Three of the nine justices in Metropolitan Court had prior judicial experience in courts of inferior criminal jurisdiction. In addition, the only justice who attended a national law school (whom we shall hereinafter refer to as Judge A) had some experience in a lower civil court. All had a history of extensive political activity and close clubhouse ties, four having served briefly as assistant district attorneys in the office of the prosecutor. All had engaged in private law practice for periods ranging from six to twenty years, and they had taken on some "criminal work" as part of their practice. None was employed by a major "Wall Street" type of law firm; instead they were associates or partners in small or medium-sized firms whose major practice was in the lower-level courts.

* * *

Metropolitan Court judges rationalize their more obvious violations of the canons in terms of "community service" and "concern with social problems." They are caught in a bind which, by the nature of their office, compels them to behave with bureaucratic concern for production, efficient administration, and dispassionate enforcement of rules—and at the same time to be instruments of their political benefactors' particularistic designs and concerns.

Another aspect of the anomic character of the judge's conduct is reflected in the reluctance to place an individual on probation if he has been convicted after a jury trial. The justices in Metropolitan Court from time to time publicly affirm the importance of the jury trial as a central element of justice and due process. But privately, in their decision-making process, they will as a rule deny a probation disposition to a jury-convicted offender. In fact, the judges, the district attorney, and the probation report will, upon sentence of such an individual, explicitly note that "the defendant has caused the state to go to the expense of a trial." In 1962 the Metropolitan Court probation division investigated 3,643 out of 4,363 cases processed that year. . . . Of the number investigated, 1,125 were placed on probation; all but three of these had pleaded guilty *before* trial.

Lower-level judges, in their decision-making and administrative conduct, are much more visible than are their appellate colleagues in the middle and upper courts. In a study of thirty appellate judges, three of whom were from federal courts and the others from various state superior courts, the judges were asked to define the least favorable aspects of their work. Two-thirds said isolation was the least favorable aspect of being an appellate judge. "I am segregated from the political, social, and economic arenas of life in which our destinies are shaped," was a comment that tended to summarize other similar comments. Two judges responded simply with one word, "Loneliness." Another judge deplored his "lack of personal contact with the litigants, witnesses, and others who play a part in each case." With judges in Metropolitan Court, the situation is reversed. Here the justices are able to diffuse the anxieties and responsibilities of the decision-making process. As in any other bureaucracy, in the lower-level court the scope of decision-making is limited. Because there is perhaps even greater anxiety generated in the criminal court, the Metropolitan Court judges make an even more active effort than is usual in a bureaucracy to diffuse responsibility and authority. They simply are reluctant to carry the entire burden, and unlike the appellate courts, there are ample intermediaries and groups who can be invoked to share in the responsibilities which are ultimately those of the judge. Reluctant to shoulder the decision-making burden, and ambivalent toward formal rules and criteria which may interfere with his informal relations with political benefactors, lawyers, and other court personnel, the judge tailors each decision to suit his own needs. Thus for different decisions the judge will involve different court personnel, to diffuse responsibility and at the same time alleviate his own formal obligations.

* * *

One of the more significant variables in judicial decision-making is the level of the court. Upper-level judges are more scrupulously concerned with the niceties of legalism, for they do not face the voluminous case pressure and daily administrative tensions of the lower courts. Their distance from the persons involved in the case and the point of origin of the issues allows them to be sage-like, rather than bureaucratic and instrumental.

Similarly, political pressures—visible and invisible—will manifest themselves. Even though there may be no pressures on specific cases, the judge may not wish to offend those who have contributed to his past or may control his future when he comes up for reappointment or renomination. Only federal judges and some higher appellate state justices are appointed for life and are thus presumably above political pressures, but even they may be interested in being promoted. Inasmuch as most judgeships are often political rewards, there is likely to be an assumption of repayment by the judge for the reward. It may be in the form of judicial sympathy for the interests of the sponsors or former associates of the judge when litigation involving such interests comes before him. The judges of Metropolitan Court, being elected for a term of years and not for life, must always maintain a keen sensitivity to the desires, requirements, and interests of their political sponsors. In fact, the "easy" decision is the one that is politically inspired.

Of course, a judge's social biography will affect his decisions. Even the kind of law school he attended, or the nature of his practice before his judicial career, are elements in judicial decision-making. A judge who has come from a corporate or a commercial civil practice may have an entirely different decision pattern than one who has devoted much of his prior practice to criminal law and negligence. And class factors will have been a strong influence in determining the kind of practice the judge had. . . .

* * *

[All these elements come together and are, in turn, affected by a different conception of the judicial role than generally exists] at the appellate level. At the level of Metropolitan Court . . . [there are an] incredibly greater number of decisions that must be made, [a] greater variety of publics that must be served by the judge, and . . . greater anxiety because the legal rules themselves do not furnish adequate guidelines for his behavior. For example, if the Metropolitan Court judges were to permit themselves to be bound by statutory provisions for sentencing procedures, they would meet head on many groups in and out of the court who have vested interests in mitigating sentences and other rules. The judicial ambivalence toward rules is also apparent in connection with institutionalized evasions of the Canons of Judicial Ethics, especially Canon 14 requiring that "a judge should not be swayed by partisan demands," and Canon 28 forbidding his participation in politics except in connection with his own election. He cannot really adhere to these rules because every day he must respond to political commitments. Clubhouse lawyers are part of a constant procession of visitors to the judge's chambers, where there is frequent negotiation over plea and sentence.

Patterns of Judicial Role Performance

As in the case of any other role, there are minimal standards which any judge must meet, and no two judges perform their judicial role obligations in precisely identical fashion. As a source of career and ego satisfaction, the bench furnishes a rich variety of possibilities. Further, organizational requirements appear to harness and exploit the idiosyncracies of individual judges for organizational ends. The distribution of the Metropolitan Court workload is evidence of this feature of organizational life. The judges and their retinue are loath to discuss the distribution of the work load, and the reason for this becomes apparent in Table 8. There were 4,363 cases processed in 1962. Each of the nine judges were rotated among the various "parts" of the court and thus, theoretically at least, had equal access to the court's case load.

No. of cases disposed of	Judge	Per cent of total caseload
1519	A	34.8
112	L	2.6
198	M	4.5
1326	X	30.4
287	J	6.6
132	P	3.0
147	K	3.4
229	D	5.2
413	G	9.5
TOTAL 4363		100.0%

Table 8. *Distribution of Metropolitan Court Judicial Work Load in 1962*

It is readily apparent that two judges, A and X, were responsible for disposing of more than half the court's case load during 1962. Further, the differing participation in the work load reflects the individual performance patterns of the judges. The intellectual and emotional characteristics of each judge are structurally used to advance organization drives, needs, and ends.

In the judges' actual performances, discerned in part from their work load activity, six major judicial role patterns may be perceived.

1. "Intellectual"—Scholar ⎫   "Workhorses" of
2. Routineer—Hack   ⎬   the court
3. Political Adventurer—Careerist
4. Judicial Pensioner
5. "Hatchet Man"
6. "Tyrant"—"Showboat"—"Benevolent Despot"

Actually, the Metropolitan Court during its modern history has always had one or two justices who have carried a substantial portion of the work load. The other justices may secretly chafe under this, but they are remarkably acquiescent about a situation that relieves them of a good deal of burden and responsibility. And as a matter of organizational practicality, in advancing goals of maximum production, it is perhaps more efficient to narrow the circle of individuals whose mission it will be to accomplish these ends.

Judges A and X, who are the workhorses of the court, perform their respective organizational roles in entirely different ways. Judge A, a graduate of an Ivy League law school, is the bench member with intellectual and scholarly leanings but with a great personal need to be continuously involved in the fray of "wheeling and dealing." A not uncommon sight in his courtroom is the tumultuous scene of a trial in progress, interrupted so that Judge A can accept fifteen to twenty lesser pleas of guilty; hear motions on various matters affecting cases before him; sentence several cases previously heard; or consult with lawyers, probation officers, or members of the district attorney's staff. The other justices and members of the court community refer to Judge A's courtroom as a three-ring circus. His fellow judges view with consternation and misgivings the fact that he frequently works on Saturdays, Sundays, holidays, and at odd hours of the night. His passion for work is regarded with suspicion, but all in the court community admit that Judge A "gets results." He is sought after by defense counsel because it is generally known that Judge A is an eminently "practical" man who is more than willing to compromise in return for a plea. He is also very sensitive to political cues, and his office has a veritable procession of individuals seeking his intervention, counsel, and assistance.

Possessed of personal charm, wit, and intelligence, Judge A sees his organizational role as that of maximizing production, even if traditional rules have to be bent. Often he uses his reputation for leniency and "practicality" as a means of disposing of the welter of cases which are for those very reasons funneled to him for disposition.

Judge X is a more traditional political figure on the bench. Like Judge A he has inherited wealth. He is the son of a former important municipal official. Basically, his career aspirations are limited, but he greatly enjoys his work, which he is really incapable of handling in other than a routine fashion. His great production is a result of his easygoing, non-punitive attitude, coupled with his personal desire to make his mark in the organization. Because he is otherwise prosaic and pedestrian, other judges do not consider him as much of a threat as Judge A. The judgeship for him is simply a comfortable slot, a means of maintaining work and other ego needs which would not otherwise be available to him.

Judges G and J are extremely well connected politically, and so their lackluster performance in Metropolitan Court is of no consequence. As "political adventurer-careerist" types their incumbency will be short-lived; the bench is only a steppingstone to other political offices they desire. They have no profound interest in law, or for that matter in the administration of the criminal law. They are more concerned with building their personal and organizational empires elsewhere, and most of their efforts will be directed not toward cases that come before them but toward manipulating the organization for their own ends. At times they will try to develop favorable press publicity about themselves and their judicial careers, as part of their overall career plan. Of course, judges like this sometimes fail and find they have been consigned to a lower court career. The resulting bitterness and querulousness can transform them into "pensioners," "routineers," or "tyrants."

The "judicial pensioner" is a judge who has been rewarded rather late in his political life. He prefers to be left undisturbed, to spend as little of his time as possible in court; he wants an almost anonymous existence. He takes virtually no interest in the administrative activities of the court. It is as though he were already retired. Judges L, M, and P have had long, active political careers at the clubhouse level, and they have been elevated to the bench either to discharge a political obligation or to get them safely out of the way.

The "hatchet man" role is often played by a member of the bench who has previously had a career in the office of the district attorney. He has close ties to that office, the political clubhouse, and other areas of power in municipal government. His role and function in the court are to take care of those cases involving special difficulty because of their "public" nature—in other words, those cases characterized by crimes of delict, malfeasance, or breach of trust committed by public officials and petty civil servants which place the municipal administration on the defensive. Also grist for the "hatchet man's" mill are those accused persons who have refused to cooperate with the prosecuting authorities, or whose cases involve special features of scandal or opprobrium and are being avidly watched by the news media. It is his function to stage manage an impression of swift justice—impassively, clinically, and uniformly administered.

The "tyrant"—"showboat"—"benevolent despot" is usually the same judge on different occasions. He is a deeply hostile, frustrated, ambition-ridden individual who has been defeated in his career aspirations. He is at a dead end and knows it. Possessed of an unbounding contempt and scorn for others, his grandiosity is incredible. He is the terror of his courtroom. Lawyers, accused persons, and probation officers fear him and loathe him. District attorneys simply abide his irascible, acidulous, querulous, surly manner. The social context of the courtroom provides an outlet for the kind of sadistic exhibitionism that is characteristic of this judicial role. Largely rejected by his colleagues, this egocentric individual exploits his judicial post as a vehicle to attract the attention of the press. He glories in the publicity he receives, even if it is negative. His harshness and intemperance are occasionally relieved by acts of charity and forbearance, which he is quick to exploit through publicity in the news media.

The most destructive aspect of his conduct, however, is the way he meets his professional and legal obligations in the courtroom itself. Here he completely dominates the proceedings and manipulates them toward his own ends—or what he perceives to be truth and reality. He has complete control over the court stenographer, virtually furnishing the material the stenographer is to include or exclude from the record in connection with his own comments and statements—which may have been improper. He manipulates juries through smiles, smirks, and unrecorded off-the-cuff comments which may tend to discredit a witness or a defendant's testimony during a trial. He intimidates defendants, privately threatens lawyers. Thus, cloaked in organizational authority and appearing to be performing important activities in furtherance of organizational goals, he is meeting the needs of personal pathology.

In large measure, however, all the judicial types, despite the different character of their performances, contribute to the court organization as a functioning mechanism. The division of labor in the court is not as random and fortuitous as it may appear. Each judicial role type is cultivated, for each contributes in his own way to the total institutional arrangement. Individual needs are capitalized and rationalized in the service of the court organization. As long as individual aberrations do not materially interfere with the achievement of organization objectives, they will be permitted to proceed undisturbed.

NOTES

As a detailed analysis of the operations of a large metropolitan court, *Criminal Justice* provides a useful window on the nature of the pressures that trial court judges generally face. Even these brief excerpts make clear Blumberg's view that lower level courts in many jurisdictions are essentially bureaucracies, concerned more with organizational efficiency than with abstract notions of justice and due process. Needless to say, such concerns radically alter the way a lawyer plans and presents testimony before them.

At the same time, there is considerable difficulty in empirically testing the generalizations that Blumberg offers, for many other factors enter into the complex of attitudes that a lower court judge brings to his or her role.[17] As Blumberg recognizes, there are different judicial "types" even in the central frame of reference he adopts. In our own experience, however, the model he constructs is relatively accurate, at least as applied to courts in metropolitan areas. The question is what effect this will have on your work before such courts. What would it mean if one or the other of Blumberg's "types" seemed likely to be hearing your case? Is there any way to alter the length, sequence, tone or content of your direct and cross-examination to adapt to the reality he describes?

Perhaps the best way to think through these questions is to deal with a problem often encountered by students in clinical programs— extensive interventions by the court. Bailey and Rothblatt identify

---

17. There is a growing literature on these variables and the lower court system. *See, e. g.,* J. Robertson, ROUGH JUSTICE (1974); Cratsley, Materials on Lower Court Justice (unpublished, 1977).

some of the extreme forms such interventions can take, and the way they would cope with them:

The range of possible prejudicial judicial misconduct is a broad one. It may entail outright disregard for your client's rights, remarks which indicate his belief in your client's guilt, sarcastic or vituperative remarks, or it may be his attitude, his facial expressions or the general manner in which he deals with you and the prosecutor.

Prejudicial misconduct can manifest itself at any stage of the proceeding, from arraignment to sentence.

The trial judge's obligation to conduct a fair and impartial trial does not end when the last witness has concluded his testimony. It continues throughout the summations, the charge to the jury and the imposition of sentence.

* * *

Interrupting or Unduly Interfering With Examination of Witnesses

It is improper for the court to interfere with your prerogative to develop the evidence as you see fit. Hence, the judge may not recall the defendant to the stand to interrogate him as to matters not touched upon in his original examination.

A judge's prejudicial attitude may manifest itself with impatience toward the manner in which you examine witnesses. Insist on developing your testimony in a proper order. Do not allow the judge to take over either the direct or cross-examination of your client. If, during your direct and cross-examination of a witness, the judge tells you to "stop wasting time", to "move along onto something else", or if he attempts to take over the questioning himself, state, in a firm but respectful tone, "Your honor, the defendant has the right to develop his proof and conduct his examination in an orderly manner, which he is prepared to do."

If the judge persists in his conduct, you can add, "Your Honor, the defendant respectfully asserts that if he is not permitted to develop his proof (or conduct his cross-examination) in an orderly manner, he will be deprived of his right to effective assistance of counsel as guaranteed by the 6th Amendment of the United States Constitution and of due process of law under the Fourteenth Amendment."

If the judge interrupts your cross-examination of a prosecution witness and tries to rehabilitate him, as often happens, you must gently but firmly insist upon your rights. Say, "Your Honor, I would appreciate it if you would permit me to continue with my examination; I intend to cover the precise points which Your Honor is suggesting." If the judge continues in this vein, you can say, "Your Honor, the defendant excepts to this interruption of the cross-examination. These interruptions break counsel's train of thought and serve to deprive the defendant of his constitutional right to the effective assistance of counsel."

Disparaging the Defendant or His Defense

A trial judge's conduct is prejudicial to your client if it intentionally or inadvertently indicates disbelief in the defense theory or a defense witness, if it tends to embarrass your client or you or if it in-dicates his feeling that your client is guilty. The trial judge must not only be impartial between parties, but must convey the sense of impar-tiality to the jury. The appearance of bias will provide a basis for re-versal even if the trial judge is, in fact, completely impartial and de-tached.

If, during the questioning of your client or of defendant witnesses, the judge intimates, either by the nature of the question or by tone, inflection, or facial expression that he disbelieves the testimony, always interpose an appropriate objection. For example, "Your Honor, the de-fendant respectfully excepts to the tone and inflection in which Your Honor is putting questions to this witness. They suggest to the jury that his testimony is unworthy of belief. He respectfully suggests that the question is improper, as the jury must remain the sole judge of the credibility of witnesses."

It may be wise to ask permission to approach the bench to make such objections in order not to heighten the judge's disbelief in the witness' testimony in the minds of the jurors. In any event, make certain that all such objections are recorded, including those made to the use of gestures and facial expressions.

Your objections on the record will alert them to the possibility that your client was deprived of a fair trial by reason of the judge's prejudicial misconduct. Even if this alone does not result in a reversal, it will cause them to examine other claimed errors with a view toward the possible prejudices suffered by your client and cause them to resolve close questions in his favor.

Witnesses for the defense may not be treated in a manner which conveys the impression that the trial judge does not believe their testimony. Care must be taken in this regard, as such a disbelief can be conveyed indirectly. For example, it is error for the trial judge to question witnesses in an incredulous manner which indicates his doubt as to the veracity of their testimony. If the trial judge indicates his disbelief through the use of gestures or facial expressions, note his conduct for the record and object to it. Most judges will immediately deny any intention to convey a belief to the jurors and will immediately state that fact to them.

The trial judge must act even more scrupulously toward the defend-ant than he does toward defense witnesses. Object immediately if he commits error, either by showing his disbelief in your client's testimony or indicating a belief in his guilt.

* * *

Disparaging Defense Counsel

Any disparagement of defense counsel by the trial judge can have as prejudicial an effect upon the defendant as a direct indication of judicial bias against him. Bias or prejudice directed against you can provide ground for reversal in both jury and nonjury trials. Disparage-ment of defense counsel in the presence of the jurors will almost invari-ably tend to prejudice them against your client.

* * *

Harassment or disparagement of defense counsel can manifest itself in many ways. The trial judge may not embarrass the defense attorney in front of the jury by making disparaging remarks which demean him, nor should he make rulings which prevent defense counsel from making an effective presentation or from obtaining a full and fair consideration of the case by the jury.

Some examples of prejudicial misconduct of this type which have led to reversals are comments in an ironic vein when defense counsel offered to stipulate to a fact, the characterization of a defense motion as "foolish" or "silly," or asking a defense attorney who interposes objections to certain testimony, whether or not he wants to keep the truth from coming out.

* * *

As defense attorney, you are absolutely entitled to be treated by the trial judge in a manner which will not prejudice the rights of your client. You are entitled to this as a matter of right and not of indulgence. Do not allow timidity to prevent you from standing up for your client's rights. Your failure to object to a trial judge's prejudicial misconduct may later be viewed as an intentional waiver of right and may also subject you to later attack for failure to render effective assistance.

Cross-Examination of Defense Witnesses

The cross-examination of defense witnesses is the function of the prosecutor. If the trial judge usurps the questioning, he may be held to have shed his cloak of impartiality. . . . Do not permit the trial judge to follow such a course of conduct.

* * *

Making a Record

Since prejudicial conduct can occur at any stage of the proceeding, you must be constantly on the alert to protect your client's rights. Make certain that the record adequately reflects the events in the courtroom to ensure full appellate review.

* * *

The failure to object to prejudicial misconduct may later be treated as a waiver. It is vital that you never lose your composure at trial. [Also], make certain that all of your objections get into the record.

* * *

. . . If you are told, for example, to sit down and stop objecting, note for the record that you are merely attempting to protect your client's rights. While you should not object unnecessarily for "showboat" purposes, you do have the obligation to ensure that your defendant is given a fair trial. . . . [18]

Bear in mind that Bailey and Rothblatt are dealing in these excerpts with improper conduct. Within the law, however, courts have

---

18. F. L. Bailey & H. Rothblatt, FUNDAMENTALS OF CRIMINAL ADVOCACY 487–98 (1974). You might compare some of these illustrations with the ABA CODE OF JUDICIAL CONDUCT (1972).

considerable latitude to affect the length, clarity and completeness of the evidence, as well as to protect witnesses and the integrity of the process. A court is most likely to do so when counsel appears inexperienced or unfamiliar with the unstated rules of conduct in the court, a particular problem for students in clinical work. How does one limit such interventions, or at least prevent them from reaching the proportions described above?

Most of Bailey and Rothblatt's suggestions involve objecting and making a record for appellate review. Is this always possible? In your clinical work, you may already have found the following to be true: (i) there is still considerable difficulty in obtaining a reporter or a transcript of the proceedings in misdemeanor cases; (ii) in many jurisdictions, there is no appellate review of errors of the trial judge—the defendant is merely afforded a trial de novo; (iii) there is no way an indigent in a civil case can require a reporter at a hearing— or a transcription if a reporter *is* present; (iv) even where appellate review of an accurate lower court record can be obtained, trial judges know that cases—even criminal cases—are rarely reversed on the ground of the prejudicial conduct of the trial judge.

Does this square with your own experience? If resort to the record is futile, what other features of the trial process might be employed to "control" the judge? Bailey and Rothblatt advise counsel to use the phrase "defendant objects" rather than "I object." Others have counseled prefacing objections to interventions by the court with: "Your Honor may not have realized it, but . . . " or "I know it has been inadvertent, Your Honor, but . . . " In light of Blumberg's descriptions of the operative norms and pressures in such courts, how effective would you expect these approaches to be? What assumptions do they make about the nature of trial judging and its orientations?

Obviously, even if one knows which judge will hear the case, it is very hard to prepare for these kinds of interventions. We can make only two observations. First, you should watch for trouble spots—places in the planned testimony where the court might feel something is being done which is improper, excessively time-consuming, or misleading. You might plan to approach the bench (in a jury trial), submit a memorandum of law, or devise some other way of reassuring the court that you know where you are going and how to get there—and that allowing you to get there will advance the judge's performance of his or her role. Needless to say, this is not always possible. A few lawyers actually give the trial judge an outline of the lines of inquiry which are going to be pursued (a copy of which must be given to opposing counsel) in order to offer such assurances.

Second, you should pay attention to building or at least being aware of your own relationship with the court. Although general assessments of the sort Blumberg offers may be helpful, judicial interventions are generally inversely proportional to the amount of confidence the court has in a particular lawyer. In other words, counsel will often be given "room" at trial to the degree to which he or she is perceived as likely to move the proceedings along, to avoid "distorting" the law or evidence in the case, or otherwise to satisfy the norms the judge considers appropriate to lawyer conduct. Indeed, a court with this kind of confidence will often assist counsel in exercising control over the conduct of opposing counsel or witnesses. The problem, of course, is how to gain such trust and acceptance.

If you regularly have coffee with the judge or know him or her socially, of course, this question can be answered very differently. It is a rarely-discussed fact of trial practice that much of what takes place publicly is affected by a network of private social relations between court and counsel. Other than regulating gifts and ex parte communications on particular cases, the bar has had very little to say on this subject.

Even in a single case, however, there are many opportunities to permit the judge to get to know you and the way you define your role. What should be made of these opportunities? To what extent will the court's deference to your conduct of the case depend on your revealing early how well prepared you are? How much depends on the way you act toward clerks and other court personnel, or toward the judge in the informal colloquy in and outside the courtroom? Many lawyers feel that favorable reactions from the court (and non-intervention) can only be generated over time—by "confirming" instances of approved behavior. From this view it is always necessary to weigh the effects of proposed conduct—for example, making a weak (but nonfrivolous) objection, or an exceptionally aggressive argument or attack on a witness—not only on the case itself, but on counsel's overall credibility with a particular judge. Even when a controversial objection or unusual argument is made, it is considered wise to preface such assertions with statements like, "Your Honor, I know this is unusual, but . . . ." or "There are factors here, Your Honor, which make this case different, . . ." A lawyer who argues that every client is the victim of gross injustice—or even that he or she is entitled to consistently favorable evidentiary rulings—will not long be listened to.

There are obvious ethical problems here. Such an approach must be reconciled with obligations to particular clients. The very relationships that will make your assessments of the court accurate and your strategies effective require a much longer time frame than is contemplated by a case-by-case view of legal ethics. No simple generalizations about either judges or court processes afford an adequate substitute.

2. The Jury

FIGG, McCULLOUGH & UNDERWOOD, SELECTION
OF THE JURY

CIVIL TRIAL MANUAL 373, 375–81 (ALI–ABA 1974).

Even the most extraordinary skill in the examination of witnesses
and the presentation of documentary and demonstrative evidence will
not result in a favorable verdict if the trial begins with a jury un-
shakably opposed to the position of counsel's client. The trial lawyer's
primary goal in the selection of a jury is to obtain a jury that will listen to the evidence he presents with a receptive attitude. In jurisdictions in which the attorneys are allowed to participate extensively in
the questioning of potential jurors, the selection process involves more
than merely seeking jurors whose personalities and backgrounds indicate that they will listen attentively to the case. It also affords
counsel his first opportunity to create a favorable impression in the
minds of the jurors for both his client's case and himself.

The focal point of these opportunities is the voir dire. During the
voir dire, questions are put to the potential jurors to determine their
suitability for service. The voir dire is designed to provide information for counsel to use in eliminating jurors from the panel through
either challenges for cause or peremptory challenges. A juror may
be challenged for cause when it can be shown that he probably cannot
render an impartial judgment. Challenges for cause are unlimited in
number. Each party is assigned a set number of peremptory challenges. Unlike the challenge for cause, no reason has to be given for
exercising a peremptory challenge.

* * *

1. Know Pertinent Background Characteristics of the Potential Juror

One should know what kinds of background information may
give him insight into how a juror will perform. Several categories
of background information with this goal in mind may be considered.

a. **Does the Potential Juror Have Any Previous Litigation Experience as a Party or a Juror?** Through a background investigation or through questioning in court, counsel should try to find out
whether or not a panel member had served on juries previously. If
so, what was the outcome of the cases? Is a pattern of favoritism on
behalf of plaintiffs or defendants discernible?

Participation in earlier cases as a party can also be revealing.
For example, a defense attorney in a personal injury case might want
to strike a panel member who was a plaintiff in a similar case, and
lost. Such a juror may have developed a resentment that has spread
toward other defendants in similar cases. . . .

b. **What Is the Jury Candidate's Occupation?** People who pursue a particular occupation for a long time often develop ingrained habits of thought that may affect their conduct as jurors. For example, an accountant may be prone to meticulously check and recheck matters. Such a quality of mind may be helpful when counsel is trying to point out to the jury that the opposition's case is full of holes, which the opposition is trying to disguise by using an emotional appeal.

Caution must be exercised, however, against making sweeping generalizations about a person on the basis of his occupation alone.
. . .

. . . A juror's suitability for service is a mosaic formed from a variety of his experiences and personal characteristics.

A difficult situation to assess occurs when it is learned that a panel member's occupation entitles him to be considered an expert in a field of knowledge on which the case might turn. Counsel's attitude toward that potential juror would depend on his personality, the personalities of other possible jurors, and the nature of the case.

In theory, at least, one of the virtues of the jury, as a decision-making body, is that it is composed of a variety of people, so that its decision will not result from one narrow perspective. If a juror with highly relevant specialized knowledge has a domineering attitude and the other potential jurors are compliant souls, the jury may end up with what is in essence a one-man jury. Whether this is likely to occur should be carefully determined as well as the effect it would have on the case.

A juror who would impose prejudicial views on his fellow jurors should be struck. However, counsel should not place himself in a position that makes the other jurors think he is trying to eliminate the only knowledgeable person in order to deceive the rest of them more easily. After further questioning, the juror's domineering attitude may become more evident to the point that the jury will understand that the juror is being challenged for that reason and not to keep needed knowledge from them.

An entirely different situation may arise if the juror with the specialized knowledge does not have a domineering attitude and the case to be presented is of unusual complexity. Under these circumstances, the juror's specialized knowledge may be helpful to the rest of the jury in accurately evaluating the facts.

Knowledge of a panel member's occupation is also relevant to predict how he will vote on the question of damages. A lawyer who is seeking a large recovery for a plaintiff may find himself defeated on the question of damages, even before he begins to present evidence, if the jury is composed of people with low-salaried positions. Since persons in such an economic position may have trouble keeping ahead of creditors, they may not be able to envision the large sum of money needed to care for a seriously injured person during his lifetime. They are more concerned about the money to pay their own water bill due next week than they are about the plaintiff's payments for a full-time nurse for the next 15 years.

* * *

c.   **What Is the Condition of His Health?**   Selecting a juror with poor sight or hearing should be avoided.   A potential juror's sight is of special importance in cases involving intensive use of demonstrative evidence.   For example, a juror who is not able to correctly gauge the spatial relationship of various objects in a drawing of a geographical area in a borderline dispute case may vote on the basis of completely erroneous impressions.

There are many other health problems that may significantly affect a juror's ability to serve effectively.   He may be unable to concentrate for long periods of time.   He may require frequent medication, and this could result in inopportune interruptions of the court proceedings.

Health information concerning potential jurors should be gathered with great delicacy.   If possible, you should avoid asking embarrassing questions of a juror concerning his health.   He may resent it and vote against you because of that if he ends up on the jury.   In jurisdictions where the composition of the venire is announced prior to the trial date, a discreet background investigation may reveal the needed information.   In some locations, the jury commissioners may be able to supply such information.   If these sources of information are not available, then the panel members should be observed carefully in court—how they walk into the box, how they raise their hands to be sworn, who is wearing thick eyeglasses.

d.   **What Weight, if Any, Should Be Given to the Controversial Factors of Age, Sex, and Ethnic Background?**   The proper criteria to use in the jury selection process is a subject of great controversy among trial lawyers.   The most controversial aspects concern the importance, if any, to attach to the juror's age, sex, and ethnic background.   One lawyer may believe that young people are poor jurors in breach of contract cases from the plaintiff's viewpoint because they have experienced few of the difficulties of life and cannot comprehend the monetary damage that such a breach may cause.   Another equally competent trial lawyer may say that young people today are becoming sophisticated financially, and he, therefore, may reach an opposite conclusion.

One lawyer may say that married women with children are excellent jurors in cases in which damages are sought for injuries to children.   Another lawyer, with equal skill, may entirely disagree.   An attorney representing a beautiful girl may prefer a jury composed of men.   He may assert that women, particularly those of the old-maid variety, may be jealous and therefore vote against her. Another attorney may differ sharply.

Of the controversial factors dealt with in this section, none is more so than ethnic background. Some trial attorneys have developed elaborate schemes, attributing voting characteristics to the various ethnic groups. For example, they may have concluded that a particular nationality is a warm-blooded group and that its members will have more sympathy for a plaintiff. Another lawyer may consider such an idea an inaccurate racial stereotype.

One must make up his own mind on the importance to be given to these controversial factors of age, sex, and ethnic background.

e. **Does the Potential Juror Have a Close Relationship with a Party, a Witness, or an Attorney?** A potential juror might be connected with a party, witness, or attorney in a manner that could affect his vote. A large variety of relationships could endanger the independence of judgment desirable in a juror. Some of the most important of these relationships are [listed] below.

(1) *Is the Potential Juror under the Control of an Opposing Party, His Witness, or His Attorney?*

* * *

(2) *Is the Potential Juror Related by Blood or Marriage to an Opposing Party, His Witness, or His Attorney?*

* * *

(3) *Is the Potential Juror a Friend of an Opposing Party, His Witness, or His Attorney or an Enemy of You, Your Party, or His Witness?*

* * *

f. **Would the Potential Juror Be Personally Affected by the Outcome of the Case?** A juror with a personal stake in the outcome of a case may look after his own interest and not render an impartial judgment. During an inquiry about a potential juror one should be sensitive to the many ways in which he may be financially affected by the case. . . .

* * *

g. **Has the Potential Juror Received Previous Information about the Case?** The effect on a potential juror's qualifications to serve because he has seen newspaper or television accounts reporting factual background of the trial varies widely, depending on the jurisdiction and the nature of the case. However, the view that seems to be gaining currency is that the mere reception of information from the public news media is an insufficient basis for a successful challenge for cause. It would have to be shown that the juror has been so influenced by the media accounts that he is unable to render an impartial verdict.

Few potential jurors will admit such deeply entrenched bias, but questioning their knowledge of news media stories is important for other reasons. The questioning may make it more difficult for the juror who has made up his mind from the news accounts to use his preconceived notions in the jury discussions. He may be put on the spot by his fellow jurors if he shows prejudice in the jury room. At least, some jurors will reevaluate their conclusions when it is pointed out to them during voir dire that they should judge the issues by the evidence produced in court.

Others may start out with preconceived opinions, which they deny stoutly, but which govern their vote anyway. This kind of person is hard to detect and hard to do anything about after detecting him, except to exclude through the use of a peremptory challenge. In all likelihood, insufficient proof would exist to challenge for cause.

h. **Does the Juror Show Signs of Racial, Religious, or Economic Prejudice Against Your Client?** The same points can be made here as were made about prejudice formed from media accounts of the case. Few potential jurors would admit to having such prejudices. Questioning, however, may jar some into keeping a tight control on their feelings. As to others, it will accomplish little.

i. **Is the Juror Opposed to This Type of Legal Action?** Counsel may be representing a client in a cause of action that some jurors feel is unfair. For example, a jury candidate may be opposed to a condemnation suit by an urban renewal district as an unconscionable invasion of private property rights. Counsel may have to try to disarm a potential juror's opposition by asking him whether he will accept the judge's instructions that permitting of such suits is a state policy and that the juror must accept it. If counsel is unable to eliminate from the jury one with an announced attitude against counsel's kind of case, perhaps he can at least dilute the impact of the juror's attitude.

NOTES

1. *Lawyer's Lore on Assessing Juries*

The jury trial affords you a unique opportunity to participate in the selection of the individuals who will hear and evaluate the testimony you present. As a result, most of the writing by lawyers about juries has focused, not on the adaptation of argument or trial strategy to juror attitudes or attributes, but on the criteria which ought to govern challenges and voir dire examination. Indeed it has been pointed out that the voir dire, properly handled, can *create* attitudes as well as inquire into them. The above excerpt is a relatively narrow example of the large amount of sense and nonsense that has been written about the jury as a potential audience.

While the *Manual* emphasizes background factors, a number of writers on the subject have asserted that there is no clear-cut relationship between the background and the voting record of any particular juror, and have recommended that counsel focus on the character of the litigated situation.　For example, in personal injury actions, it has been suggested that the jury will be most heavily influenced by such factors as (i) type of plaintiff (*e. g.*, passenger, minor), (ii) the locality of the trial, (iii) the nature of the defense (*e. g.*, juries don't like brake-failure defenses in rear-end collision cases), (iv) the presence of disinterested witnesses, (v) the quality of the opening statement (as compared to closing), (vi) the demeanor of the judge, (vii) an excessive demand in the prayer (which is seen as dishonest), (viii) the type of defendant (*e. g.*, railroads and local transit companies are given less sympathy than retail shops or individuals), and (ix) the presence of misrepresentation by either party.[19]　Similar factors can be identified in criminal cases, including (i) jury attitudes toward the burden of proof, (ii) perceived sincerity and competence of counsel, (iii) the type of defendant (*e. g.*, status, appearance, personality), (iv) contributory fault of the victim, (v) whether the defendant testifies, (vi) whether the case rests solely on a confession or accomplice testimony, (vii) whether the offense can be considered de minimis, (viii)the type of victim, and (ix) the injuries or losses the defendant may already have suffered.[20]

Although these suggestions seem helpful, the problem is how to "use" such elements in planning testimony or arguments for a jury. How would you determine their possible impact through pretrial investigation or voir dire?　This is a difficult question: it is very hard to estimate the effects of such "case-specific" factors.　Perhaps for this reason, most trial lawyers still rely primarily on background factors, physical appearance and a kind of intuitive sizing up of prospective jurors in their assessments.　The following is a sampling of such judgments:

> (a) Mark their candor, age, humor, intelligence, social stand, occupation, and let your eyes choose the most friendly, liberal and noble faces, young or old but better young than old—better warm than cold faces; better builders than salesmen, better farmers than inventors.

19.　*See, e. g.*, Appleman, *Selection of the Jury*, 1968 TRIAL LAW. GUIDE 33, *Jury Psychology* 1961 PERS.INJ. ANN. 873; Jennings, *What Goes On In the Jury Room*, 30 INS.COUN.J. 279 (1963); Kennelly, *Jury Selection in a Civil Case*, 1965 TRIAL LAW. GUIDE 87, *Proving Damages in a Wrongful Death Case—How to Do It —Part II*, 1975 TRIAL LAW. GUIDE 135, 144–59.

20.　*See, e. g.*, discussion of specific defenses in S. Bernstein & R. Cipes, CRIMINAL DEFENSE TECHNIQUES (1976); I. Goldstein & F. Lane, TRIAL TECHNIQUE, VOL. 1, 9–3 to 9–66 (2nd ed. 1969); C. Tessmer, CRIMINAL TRIAL STRATEGY 51–73 (1968); Blattberg, *Jury Selection by the Prosecution*, 1958 TRIAL LAW. GUIDE 197. *See generally* H. Kalven & H. Zeisel, THE AMERICAN JURY (1966).

Avoid doctors, lawyers, and petti-foggers. There is a little man deformed, narrow, selfish, opinionated; yonder is a captious, caustic, witty man, of stale jokes and street corner argument; and further on is a hard man, grim faced and cold, grey look, white blood and glassy eyes. Rule them all off, if possible. The world has used them ill. They will spread their misery for company's sake.[21]

* * *

(b) As a rule, clergymen, school teachers, lawyers and wives of lawyers do not make desirable jurors. They are too often sought for advice and tend to be opinionated.

Retired businessmen are usually fair but disinclined to render mild verdicts. A reasonably well educated laboring man is not to be despised. Generally, railroad men and their wives are excellent jurors. They are solid, substantial citizens who work hard, are frugal in their personal living, yet have the opportunity to travel and to play more than their fellows.[22]

* * *

(c) Unless the lawyer knows something about prospective jurors, selection of a jury is really a matter of guesswork. Counsel should try not to rely on appearances. The little, twittering, soft-spoken, motherly old lady might easily vote for the death penalty in a homicide case. The burly, shady-looking man whom counsel thinks he would not want to meet in a dark alley may be a kindly husband, father, and grandfather.

I have found the best test to be to size up a juror when he is called into the box, and if I think I could be friendly with such a person, I accept him as one of the jurors.[23]

Ask yourself which of these perspectives makes the most sense to you. What do they suggest about preparing testimony for trial?

---

2. *Social Science and the Assessment of Jury Behavior*

Not surprisingly, there have been a number of more "scientific" attempts to evaluate the kinds of judgments set out above. This methodology has recently been offered to trial lawyers in a number of important trials.[24] In general, the research supports the view that factors specific to the case itself are the most important determinants of outcomes. For example, studies have found important correlations between such features as the type of plaintiff or defendant and the resultant verdict, whatever the attitudes and predisposition of the

21. Donovan, MODERN JURY TRIALS AND ADVOCATES 227 (1887).

22. J. Appleman, SUCCESSFUL JURY TRIALS 127 (1952).

23. L. Friedman, THE ESSENTIALS OF CROSS-EXAMINATION 153 (1968).

24. *See, e. g.*, Cunningham, *The Trial of the Gainesville Eight: The Legal Lessons of a Political Trial*, 10 CRIM. LAW BULL. 215 (1974); Robinson, *How Psychology Helped Free Angela Davis*, EBONY MAGAZINE (May, 1975); Sage, *Psychology and the Angela Davis Jury*, HUMAN BEHAVIOR 58 (Jan.1973); Zeisel & Diamond, *Jury Selection in the Mitchell-Stans Conspiracy Trial*, 1976 ABF RES.J. 151.

jury. Nevertheless, the notion that background factors strongly influence a juror's decisions persists, and considerable research has been done in an attempt to find out whether factors such as race, class, sex and occupation make a difference in jury behavior. Although these studies tend to support some of the beliefs of practicing lawyers, they also reach some surprising results. For example, Simon's work on *The Jury and the Defense of Insanity* reached the following conclusions:

> [Despite the assumption that] persons with more education [would] have greater knowledge and understanding of mental illness, and therefore . . . be more sympathetic to the defense . . . [we found that] jurors with a college education were *less* likely to acquit the defendant on grounds of insanity.
>
> * * *
>
> . . . [What] emerged from our investigation of the effects of social status on verdicts is that the lawyers' lore about the defendant-proneness of lower status jurors generalizes, although in a somewhat weakened form, to jurors' behavior in criminal cases involving a defense of insanity. Specifically, our results were that: Negro jurors are more willing to vote for acquittal on grounds of insanity than jurors of majority ethnic background, and jurors of higher social status, as measured by educational attainment, are more likely to vote for a guilty verdict. Another practical finding, not directly anticipated by the lawyers' lore, is the greater punitiveness of housewives, as opposed to both other women and to men, toward the defendant in the incest case. Finally, a finding that should interest lawyers but about which there is little lore, is that while male jurors who hold important positions in the larger society talk more in the jury room and are more likely to be elected foreman, they do not appear to wield more influence, at least when influence is measured by the ability of the members of a minority faction to persuade the majority to their point of view.[25]

Other studies have examined the influence of factors such as specialized knowledge or experience. Among the most extensive of these is the work of Dale Broeder, who interviewed jurors sitting in a United States district court in the midwest. Although his work has been published in separate articles, some of his conclusions can be summarized as follows:

—Particularized knowledge or experience—*i. e.*, mechanical, engineering, mathematical or medical skill—influences juror perceptions and approaches to related issues in the case. In addition, occupational experience generates bias toward or identification with parties to the litigation.[26]

—The past experience of jurors in prior jury trials, both related and unrelated factually to the case in issue, substantially influences the jurors' handling of cases. The prior cases are discussed in the jury

25. R. Simon, THE JURY AND THE DEFENSE OF INSANITY 106–07, 118–19 (1967).

26. *See* Broeder, *Occupational Expertise and Bias as Affecting Juror Behavior*, 40 N.Y.U.L.REV. 1079 (1965).

room to provide comparative standards, to establish patterns of behavior, to clarify distinctions in the judge's instructions, and to establish expertise among the jurors. At times, the experience generates a certain skepticism or cynicism toward "the legal rules by
which cases are tried." As jurors observe the influence that social
and economic background have on the cases, the perceived necessity for carefully scrutinizing the evidence may decline.[27]

—The out-of-court knowledge of jurors concerning local conditions
(community problems, locations, direction); the parties; the witnesses; the lawyers; and the other jurors likewise can influence juror
perceptions, attitudes and the content of their deliberations concern-
the case.[28]

—Racial bias in jury decision-making, although difficult to isolate,
has some impact on juror decisions in cases involving racial elements
(*e. g.*, witnesses, defendant, etc.).[29]

Such exclusive reliance on the interview is, of course, questionable. A juror's recollection or formulation of what influenced the
jury's deliberations cannot readily be correlated with what actually
took place in the juror's mind or in the jury room.[30] Moreover,
Broeder's examples are taken from a very small cross section of cases.
Nevertheless, trial lawyers have often expressed a need for this type
of information. Again, ask yourself how it might be used in preparing for a trial. How would you obtain and/or adapt such information in a particular case? It is a very long way from ascertaining general attitudes to affecting the discussions of twelve people who must
find common ground for decision.

———

3. *The Ability to Alter Jury Attitudes*

We should not leave this subject without attending briefly to the
fact that assessing jury attitudes may also involve the possibility of
changing them. In those jurisdictions that permit voir dire, counsel
has the opportunity to affect the very attitudes into which he or she
inquires. Consider, for example, the following set of voir dire questions suggested by Bailey and Rothblatt:

Let us take an assault case as an example. While the prosecutor is
questioning, you should note the names of the jurors [and] their occu-
pations . . . . You then approach the first juror, and begin:

1. "Mr. Jones, you live at 200 Central Avenue. Have you ever
served as a juror on a criminal case?"

27. *See* Broeder, *Previous Jury Trial Service Affecting Jury Behavior*, INS. LAW J. 138 (March, 1965).

28. *See* Broeder, *Impact of the Vicinage Requirement*, 45 NEB.L.REV. 101 (1966).

29. *See* D. Broeder, THE NEGRO IN COURT (1966).

30. *See generally* Kalven, *Report on the Jury Project* (Conference on Aims & Methods of Legal Research, 1955).

2.   (If he answers "no"): "Have you ever served as a juror on a civil case?"   (If he answers "yes," then explain the important distinction between criminal and civil cases).

3.   (If he has answered "yes" to Question 1): "Did you ever serve as a juror on a case where the charge was assault?"

4.   "Was the charge felonious assault?"

5.   "How many cases have you served where the charge was assault?"

6.   "Was an agreement as to a verdict reached in each case?"

7.   (If he has served as juror on a case of felonious assault): "Having served as a juror on a case where the charge was felonious assault, do you know what the term felonious assault means?"   (If he answers "no" as to this term, be prepared to explain it. If you are going to urge the plea of self-defense, discuss the elements of self-defense. If your case is based upon no proof of a crime, ask about the meaning of "corpus delecti." If your basis for defense is to be the inadequacy of the circumstantial evidence, discuss the rigid rules applied to circumstantial evidence. In other words, *mold your questions to the defense you will urge.*)

8.   "You know, of course, that the fact that a person was injured must be proved by direct evidence. Do you understand what is meant by the term direct evidence? That is, facts testified to by persons who saw what they are testifying about?"

9.   "You realize, of course, that the indictment in this case is no evidence of any kind? That it is merely a piece of paper used to bring the defendant into court, the same as a complaint in a civil case?"

10.   "Of course, you know a man is presumed innocent until he is proven guilty beyond a reasonable doubt?"

11.   "You also realize, of course, that you must give the defendant the benefit of this presumption of innocence without any mental reservations whatsoever? And that you are to consider this presumption of innocence as actual proof of innocence until it is overcome by proof of guilt beyond a reasonable doubt. Now do I have your promise that you will give the defendant the full benefit of that presumption of innocence?"

12.   "Do you understand that all the elements of the crime charged must be proven beyond a reasonable doubt, and that if one element is not proven, would you then vote not-guilty?"

13.   "If the prosecution fails to prove the guilt of the accused with that degree of moral certainty that amounts to proof beyond a reasonable doubt, would you then vote non-guilty?"

14.   "You understand, do you not, that the burden of proving the defendant guilty beyond a reasonable doubt rests with the prosecution, and that the accused need not introduce any evidence whatsoever?"

15.   "Knowing that, would you require the accused at any time to satisfy you as to his innocence?"

16.   (If you have decided that the accused will not testify): "And knowing that, you realize that the defendant is not bound to explain

his side of the case since the burden of proof does, in fact, rest with the prosecutor. So that you would not consider the accused's failure to testify as an indication of his guilt, would you?"

17. "Knowing the charge against the accused, John X., could you give him the same fair trial that you would give him if he were charged with a lesser crime?"

18. "Do you know anything about the facts of this case other than what you have heard in court today?"

19. "Have you read about this case in the newspapers or heard about it over the radio or television?" (At this point, if the juror answers "yes," you should proceed carefully. Even if the juror admits to an opinion of guilt derived from the newspapers, the court will permit him to remain on the jury, if he declares under oath that he could nonetheless act impartially and fairly. It becomes your job to show the court that he has such an opinion of guilt that it will require evidence to remove it. You must draw out this admission without appearing as if you are out to get the juror, since many prospective jurors will dodge answering in order to stay on the jury.)

20. "What newspapers have you read?"

21. (Nonchalantly): "I suppose you have formed some opinion as to the guilt or innocence of the accused, or about the merits of this case from what you read in the newspapers?"

22. (If he answers "yes," then nonchalantly say): "I suppose it would require evidence to remove or change your opinion?" (If he answers "yes," challenge him for reason.)

23. (If he answered "no" to any of the questions concerning prior opinion gleaned from newspapers): "Knowing what you know about this case and any opinion you have formed about it, would you be satisfied to be tried by a jury having your frame of mind?"

24. "Would you set aside any opinion you may now have and judge this case solely on the evidence introduced during the trial and the instructions of law given to you by the court?"

25. "Do you realize that the court will instruct you as to the law, but that you are the sole and exclusive judge(s) of the facts?"

26. "Would you judge this case solely on the evidence before you, and not allow the fear of later criticism to affect your verdict?"

27. "Would you give the accused the benefit of your individual judgment in arriving at a verdict in this case?"

28. "Now, if you came to the conclusion that the prosecution had not proven the guilt of the accused beyond a reasonable doubt, and you found that a majority of the jurors believed the defendant was guilty, would you change your verdict only because you were in the minority?"

29. "Would the fact that you were in the minority influence your vote at all?"

30. "If the widow of the deceased were to testify, would her appearance so upset or influence you that you could not give the accused a fair trial?"

31. "You understand, of course, that an impartial trial by an unbiased jury is a constitutional guarantee no matter what the charges are against the defendant?"

32. "Do you realize that you are bound to reach a verdict solely on the evidence introduced during the trial?"

33. "If from your experiences you believe or have the feeling that certain facts exist, but these facts have not been proven by satisfactory evidence, would you discard your beliefs or feeling and decide this case only on the evidence or lack of evidence?"

34. "Do you understand that the comments of the prosecutor are not evidence in this case?"

35. "In deciding whether or not you are going to believe a witness, would you consider the witness's conduct on the stand, his opportunity and ability to observe, his bias or prejudice, and the probability or improbability of his story?"

36. (If there will be accomplice testimony against the defendant): "Do you understand what is meant by the term *'accomplice'*?" (Be prepared to explain it if the answer is "no.") . . . .

37. "Do you understand that the testimony of an accomplice is considered to be testimony from a tainted source and must be scrutinized by you with great care and caution?"

38. (In a jurisdiction where corroboration of accomplice testimony is required): "His Honor will instruct you that in order for you to convict the defendant, the testimony of the accomplice must be supported by other evidence that connects the defendant to the crime, and extends to every material fact necessary to establish the crime. His Honor will also instruct that this supporting testimony must come from a believable and unimpeached source. Now, do you promise to follow these instructions?"

39. (If there are child witnesses against the defendant): "In judging the credibility of a child witness, would you take into account his age, intelligence, ability to perceive and observe, realizing that the life or liberty of the accused is at stake? Would you further consider carefully the child's extreme imagination, tendency to mix fact with fiction, and his great susceptibility to suggestions?"

40. (If there may be an identification witness): "In weighing the identification of the defendant, will you consider the witness's capacity for memory, for observation, his familiarity with the defendant and any bias or prejudice he may have toward the accused?"

41. "Will you also consider the amount of time that the witness had to observe the defendant?"

42. "Do you recognize from your daily experiences the frailty of mental observation?"

43. "During the experiences of your personal life, have you ever mistakenly confused a stranger for a person whom you knew well?"

44. "Do you agree that the identity of the defendant as the person who committed the crime must be shown with such certainty as to eliminate any possibility of error?"

45. (If the prosecution's case is based on circumstantial evidence): "Do you know that circumstantial evidence is like a chain which must bind the defendant to the crime, and that that chain is only as strong as its weakest link?"

46. "Do you agree that every element of a circumstantial evidence case must be totally inconsistent with innocence; consistent with and pointing to guilt, and that if the evidence does not point directly to guilt, you must render a verdict of not guilty? Will you faithfully apply that rule of law?"

47. (If the defendant will testify and has a criminal record).

48. "Will you consider and judge the defendant's testimony by the same rules and standards you would use in judging the testimony of any other witness in this case?"

49. (If the defendant is a Negro): "Have you had any dealings or experiences with Negro persons that might make it difficult for you to sit in impartial judgment on this case?"

50. "Will the fact that the defendant is a Negro (or Puerto Rican, etc.) affect in any way your judgment in this case?"

51. "Do you promise to consider only the facts and evidence in this case, and to completely disregard the defendant's race, creed and color?"

52. (If the defendant or any of your witnesses will testify through an interpreter or in poor English): See above matter relating to this situation.

53. (If your defense will be self-defense): "Do you believe that a person is justified in killing another human being if he believes that he is in actual danger of being seriously injured or killed by his attacker?"

54. "Do you have any feeling against a person who uses a knife or a gun to protect himself or his family?"

55. "His Honor will instruct you that a person has a right to use a knife or a gun in self-defense under certain circumstances. Do you promise to heed that information?"

56. "Do you appreciate and understand that the question you will eventually have to decide in this case is whether the defendant acted in proper self-defense?"

57. "Do you further understand that the burden will be upon the prosecution to prove beyond a reasonable doubt that the accused did not act in self-defense?"

58. "You realize, of course, that if a reasonable doubt exists in your mind as to whether or not the defendant was justified in acting in self-defense, then you must resolve that doubt in favor of the defendant, and render a verdict of not-guilty."

59. (If your defense will be intoxication): "Are you a member of any organization which is trying to combat the sale, distribution or use of intoxicating beverages?"

60. "It may develop from the evidence that the defendant was intoxicated at the time he committed the crime charged. His Honor

will instruct you that it is for you to determine the extent of the defendant's intoxication, and whether his intoxication was such as to prevent him from forming the intent necessary to constitute the crime. His Honor will further charge you that should you find the defendant was too intoxicated to form that intent you must render a verdict of not-guilty. Now, do you promise to heed that instruction?"

61. (If your defense will be insanity): "Are you aware that the law does not hold a person responsible for his act, if he was insane at the time he committed the crime?"

62. "Do you agree with that proposition of law?"

63. "His Honor will instruct you that should you find the defendant, when he committed the crime, was acting under such a defect of reason as not to know the nature and quality of his act, he is legally insane and must be acquitted."

64. "Now, do you agree that if the accused was insane, or so insane as not to know the nature and quality of his act or not to know that what he was doing was wrong, he must be acquitted?"

65. "If you find that the defendant was legally insane when he committed the crime, do you promise to follow the court's instruction and render a verdict of not-guilty?" [31]

Give some thought to what these questions would ascertain. What effect would they be likely to have on the jury's predispositions toward these legal and factual questions? Many trial lawyers say that they would give up a good deal of information about a jury's prejudices if doing so would increase the rapport between the jury and their client. Would you agree? If you do, would this alter any of the questions in the preceding list?

3. One's Own Witnesses

SPELLMAN, DIRECT EXAMINATION OF WITNESSES

61–63, 66–69, 72 (1968).*

Where more than one witness is available to prove a point, counsel may be enabled to choose which witness or which several witnesses he will call and, if he determines to call more than one, the order in which they will be brought to the stand.

There is not complete freedom of choice; because there are situations in which the failure to call an available witness may leave a bad impression. For example, if the available witness has been referred to as being present at an important conversation and it is known that that person is friendly to one of the parties, it may be legitimately inferred that the failure of that party to call him as a

---

31. F. L. Bailey & H. Rothblatt, SUC- CESSFUL TECHNIQUES FOR CRIMINAL TRIALS 92–98 (1971).

witness was because he might testify disadvantageously. Some decisions state that the failure to call an available, friendly witness leads to the legal inference that, if called, he would testify adversely to the party failing to call him. Others limit this doctrine and hold that the failure to call an available, friendly witness leads only to the inference that, if called, he would not rebut adverse testimony given by other witnesses. Whichever rule is prevalent in a given jurisdiction, the fact remains that the failure to call an available, friendly witness creates a bad *impression*, no matter what the technical legal result may be.

After counsel's opening statements to the jury (or, in a case tried without a jury, after the presentation of a pre-trial memorandum to the court), the trial of a case assumes many of the aspects of a dramatic theatrical performance. The ultimate aim of counsel (a combination, in this context, of director and actor) is to make favorable points by the production of *proof*. Except for documentary evidence, this proof is established by dialogue between witness and examining counsel. Obviously, as is true in a play or motion picture, the points to be established are strengthened or weakened by the cast of characters (the witnesses) and the construction of the dramatic script (the order in which witnesses are called). The basic question confronting counsel in choosing witnesses and determining the order in which to call them is a simple one. He must ask himself: "What witnesses can I best choose and in what order can I best present them so as to create the ultimate impression that the *story* I am asking the triers of the fact to believe is the truth?" Note the emphasis on the word "story." This is the key to the whole situation. Counsel contends that certain things took place. He unfolds these facts through the mouths of his witnesses. In sum-total they amount to a connected story. He will succeed only if this story is *believed*. It makes no difference, in this context, whether the case is tried to a jury or only before a judge. Although the method of presentation may differ in these two classes of trials, the final aim is the same— that is the procurement of *belief* in a witness-stated *story*.

In determining which of several available witnesses to call, counsel should consider as to each possible witness: (a) his personality; (b) the impression he is likely to make when testifying; and (c) his ability to withstand cross-examination.

* * *

Choosing which witnesses to call is the product of interviews with proposed witnesses. In addition to learning the facts of the case during such interviews, counsel should try to place himself in the position of the trier of the facts, so that he can reach subjective reaction as to the desirability of a given person as a witness. . . . The determination whether to call a given individual should rest in major part on counsel's impression whether that witness would probably be *believed* when testifying.

In the foregoing discussion, we have been considering circumstances in which counsel has a choice whether or not to call a given person as a witness. In situations where a proposed witness is necessary to prove an important fact, the choice disappears.

Instances often arise where counsel cannot interview a witness in advance but must call him to establish a prima facie case or defense. Here, it is desirable to learn as much of the witness' background as possible and to try to gather material to contradict this necessary witness if he proves hostile.

* * *

As all experienced trial counsel know, there is danger in calling *any* witness. The fallibility of human memory combined with the appearance of a witness' unpleasant personality traits conspire to present the problem that even a completely honest witness will either be disbelieved or so disliked that his testimony can be a disadvantage to the party calling him. In addition, there is a subconscious tendency on the part of those hearing the case to identify the witness with a party. As a result, we may be faced with the unstated but existing danger that a verdict may be brought in against one of the parties because the fact-finder disliked a witness so much that he did not want the *witness* to have the satisfaction of "winning" the case.

No matter how grave the danger, the fact remains that we *must* call witnesses in order to prevail on a trial (unless, as attorneys for defendants, we are fortunate enough to obtain a dismissal at the close of the plaintiff's case).

One of the greatest responsibilities of an advocate is his determination as to what witnesses to call where several are available and, conversely, what available witnesses to discard. He must weigh the strong and weak points of each possible witness. If he is fortunate, he can choose the stronger witness. If unfortunate, he is compelled to choose the less weak witness. Indeed, where only several weak witnesses are available, counsel may be compelled to call all of them in the hope that they will, somehow, corroborate one another or that there can be an application of the non-legal axiom that "in numbers there is strength."

The ideal witness is one who gives the appearance that he is simply testifying to his best memory of the facts and that he is not over-eager for "his side" to win. Such a witness is a rare jewel. If he avoids seeming to take sides under the stress of a vigorous cross-examination, he is a jewel without price. A witness who exhibits these potentials should, of course, be called.

Let us now consider the types of persons who should *not* be brought to the witness stand if it is humanly possible to avoid that course.

It should be noted that it is too late after a witness is on the stand to determine that he is a weak witness. This judgment must be made while the witness is being interviewed in preparation for trial. In the course of such preparation, counsel should not only probe the memory of the witness as to the facts, but also should seek to uncover what weaknesses the witness may have *as a person*.

Here are a few (by no means all-encompassing) examples of weak witnesses:

(a) *The exaggerating witness.*—This type of person is very often motivated by a strong desire to "win" the case for the party calling him. However, he may simply be one who has a born tendency for exaggeration. He is liable to testify untruthfully, where his falsity can be demonstrated. He can get himself into a position where he actually *believes* the falsehoods. This often leads to a cumulation of untruths which not only damages the witness' own credibility but may ruin the entire case. This type of witness, on cross-examination, can be led into self-contradictions because, as the old saying goes, "a successful liar must have a good memory."

(b) *The self-centered witness.*—Here, we have the type of egoist who is anxious to demonstrate how sapient he is. Even without his saying so, he gives the impression that he feels that he knows more about the case than the parties, their lawyers, or the other witnesses. He is liable to respond to simple questions on direct examination by tossing in facts which he believes counsel may have forgotten. In so doing, he has the potentiality of destroying the entire strategy planned for trial. His attitude in general and his grimaces in particular can disgust the fact-finder. . . .

(c) *The excessively apprehensive witness.*—Most fact-finders (particularly jurors) are inclined to be somewhat sympathetic to a witness who appears nervous. With rare exceptions, no person likes to be called as a witness. In the strange surroundings of a courtroom and in the unaccustomed position of being the cynosure of all eyes, an average citizen is uncomfortable and will probably exhibit some signs of nervousness. This is not the type of person we are presently discussing. Here, we are considering the *excessively* nervous witness. He is one whose outward manifestations of nervousness are so exaggerated that they can well lead to the impression that he is not telling the truth. Furthermore, a person of this type can be led, through skillful cross-examination, into damaging admissions, which may well be contrary to fact. . . .

Where counsel is confronted by the *necessity* of calling a weak witness, he should try in advance of trial to prevent the weakness of this witness from too greatly damaging his case. This may have to be a laborious process, beginning with the first interview and going on practically to the date of trial. Counsel must make it his business to gain the full confidence of the witness and to appeal to his intelligence to overcome his faults.

In preparing for trial, counsel may be able to reassure a nervous witness. In some instances, in order to alleviate nervousness, trial counsel have deemed it wise to take the proposed witness to court to observe the surroundings and nature of court proceedings in cases with which the witness has no connection. . . .

The exaggerating witness is a harder nut to crack. No matter how much he is warned against exaggeration, it is often impossible to overcome his life-long habits. The important thing is to go over the salient facts of the case, time and time again, and to impress upon the witness the undesirability of testifying to anything other than these salient facts.

The "wise guy" witness is, if possible, to be avoided like the plague. If he *must* be used, counsel should try to frame his questions in such manner as to call for a simple "yes" or "no" answer. However, this is easier said than done. . . .

* * *

Where other witnesses can testify to some of the subjects covered by the weak witness it is wise to present their testimony *directly* before and after the testimony of the weak witness. Although this may have the result of temporarily disturbing chronology, such result is more than over-balanced by the corroborative effect of the testimony of these other witnesses. The strategy, here, is comparable to the calling of witnesses out of the predetermined order after a witness has been damaged on cross-examination.

NOTES

1. *Assessment and Witness Preparation*

The problem of witness assessment in preparing for trial, of course, involves much more than typing. Whatever the function of stereotyping and classification in making initial judgments, work with witnesses inevitably involves interaction as well as perception. The *relationship* between counsel and the witness becomes a central element of what is presented at trial. Some of this discussion, therefore, might be enhanced by a review of some works on client interviewing. Establishing trust, learning from and instructing witnesses are recurrent problems in lawyer work.

With this in mind, consider what can and should be said to a witness before he or she testifies, and how this guidance is likely to affect the impression the witness makes at trial. The following are typical of the sort of instructions which trial lawyers recommend:

It is good practice to make your witnesses familiar with some of the basic rules of testifying. Not all of these rules will apply to each witness, of course, but they are reliable guidelines. You should impress upon your witness the desirability of:

1. Standing upright when taking the oath and saying "I do" in a clear voice.

2. Dressing conservatively and wearing clean clothes.

3. Revisiting the scene of the alleged crime (if applicable to his testimony) to familiarize himself with it prior to trial.

4. Avoiding the memorizing of his testimony.

5. Talking toward the jurors and looking at them most of the time; speaking to them frankly and openly as to a friend or neighbor, in a tone of voice sufficiently clear and loud enough so that the farthest juror can hear the testimony.

6. Listening carefully to all questions. (Impress on your witness the fact that no matter how nice the prosecutor may seem, he is trying to destroy the witness.)

7. Being serious both on and off the stand. Make sure your witness understands that his demeanor can be observed by jurors any place in the courthouse.

8. In the event of answering a question incorrectly, tell your witness he should correct himself immediately.

9. Clarifying at once an answer of his that may be unclear.

10. Explaining his answers if it seems necessary to do so rather than to stick with a simple "yes" or "no". But make sure he understands to answer only the question asked and not to volunteer information.

11. Remaining polite, even under the most intensive cross examination, and at all times avoid appearing to be a cocky witness or a "wise guy."

12. Becoming silent at once if the judge interrupts or if the prosecutor interposes an objection.

13. Avoiding any mannerisms which the jury may interpret as signs of nervousness or falsity. (The mock examination should reveal a witness' offensive mannerisms.)

14. Not looking at defense counsel for answers; and trying not to seem overly partisan.

15. Avoiding the use of technical language. The witness should be instructed that the jury should be able to follow and understand everything he has to say.[32]

32. F. L. Bailey & H. Rothblatt, FUNDAMENTALS OF CRIMINAL ADVOCACY 110–11 (1974). On the general subject of witness preparation, *see* Bodin, FINAL PREPARATION FOR TRIAL (1966); I. Schweitzer, CYCLOPEDIA OF TRIAL PRACTICE, Vol. 4 (1969). A catalogue of witness types similar to Spellman's is found in Figg, McCullough & Underwood, CIVIL

Ask yourself if these sorts of instructions are adequate and/or desirable. What additional information and guidance would you provide? How would you communicate information of this sort?

In addition to going through such a checklist, many lawyers encourage witnesses to (i) attend another trial or to sit through earlier portions of the case in question (assuming they have not been excluded by order of the court)[33]; (ii) visit the scene, handle or reread exhibits and otherwise familiarize themselves again with matters which may come up at trial; (iii) write out or outline their testimony or review counsel's outline; and (iv) participate in a mock examination and cross-examination in counsel's office. Would you consider this sort of preparation desirable? What are the advantages and disadvantages of each of these measures?

Of the preparatory steps listed above, the "rehearsal" seems to be the most controversial among students and the most strongly advised among trial lawyers. Marshall Jox offers the following description of what this entails:

> . . . Since the time element between an occurrence and a trial based thereon is frequently quite lengthy, it is advisable to review the facts, step by step. In fact, some attorneys ask a series of questions just as they would be asked during the trial. By means of such review it may be possible to ascertain when a friendly witness has become hostile, and then to establish the point by some other witness. Statements taken during the initial conference can be used for this purpose. The need for such careful review can be demonstrated by first asking the witness what he recalls of the incident. There will usually be a considerable deviation from the original statement.
>
> It is extremely important that the witness be prepared for a searching cross-examination. This again may be done by asking a series of questions, in as harsh and vicious a manner as possible. The witness can then be informed that in all probability opposing counsel will not engage in such tactics. Among the questions he should be advised to answer truthfully are the following: "Have you discussed the case with anyone?" "Were you subpoenaed to be here or did you come voluntarily?" "Are you being paid for your testimony?" The witness should be informed as to the points the opposition will try to establish on cross-examination.[34]

Others go even further in suggesting ways of ironing out discrepancies and possible vulnerabilities in testimony:

> Bring together at the same time your client and all his witnesses, either at your office or at the home of the client. Explain to them

TRIAL MANUAL 239–40 (ALI–ABA 1974); Redmount, *Handling Perception and Distortion in Testimony*, 5 AM. JUR. TRIALS 807 (1966). On the subject of expert witnesses *see* M. Belli, MODERN TRIALS, Vol. 3 (1954); Gair, *Selecting and Preparing Expert Witnesses*, 2 AM.JUR. TRIALS 585 (1964).

33. *See, e. g.*, Ratner, Instructions for Witnesses, 2 PRAC.LAW 44 (1956).

34. M. Jox, LAWYER'S CONCISE GUIDE TO TRIAL PROCEDURE 11 (1965).

what each is expected to do at the trial, go over the testimony with them collectively, and outline the salient points you hope to establish.

Fasten on the wall a diagram of the scene of the accident drawn to scale (draftsman's tape is excellent for fastening) and have a rehearsal in marking on it the important points, such as where the plaintiff's car was when the defendant's car was first observed, where the defendant's car was at that time, the point of impact, where the cars came to rest, and other pertinent information.

Advantages of the group method. Use of the group method makes for a united front, a dovetailing of testimony, and a uniformity of narration. Each witness sees the case as a whole and the role that he is to play in it. It brings out errors in perception, faulty observations, and improper judgments. It sharpens and refreshes recollections, and thus eliminates the danger of one witness needlessly contradicting another.

* * *

The group method should always be supplemented by the individual preparation of the witness because of the special attention that he may need. This is definitely true of the plaintiff and his key witnesses. For example, with a plaintiff you would spend much time in going over his deposition. With a disinterested eyewitness, you might visit the scene of the accident.

Explain to the witness in simple language the principles of negligence, contributory negligence, and some of the basic rules of evidence. Tell him that negligence means the failure to live up to a standard of ordinary care. Discuss the standard. Have him point out to you how he believes the defendant fell short of such standard. He will then know what to bring out and emphasize in his testimony.

Again, if the witness knows that he can't give hearsay or opinion evidence, his testimony will go in with less interruption and make for a better impression on the jury. Explain to the plaintiff the doctrine of contributory negligence, the fact that no matter how slightly his own negligence may have contributed to the accident he will be denied recovery.

* * *

You cannot anticipate every possible question that the opposing counsel may put to your witness. However, you can fortify your client by giving him an understanding of certain principles to guide him on the perilous journey of cross-examination.

* * *

If you are required to stand in your jurisdiction, stand up when you question the witness; make the witness leave his seat, face the diagram on the wall, and actually use the scale ruler in marking it; use the tone of voice you expect your adversary will use on cross-examination; show the witness no quarter.

In short, have him prepared for the actual ordeal of the courtroom.[35]

Give some thought to both the propriety and potential effectiveness of this sort of preparation. Does it eliminate the risk that the witness will make "mistakes" at trial? What risks does it create? We will come back to some of these questions in our discussion of trial ethics. At this point we are interested in your reflecting on what is involved in preparing and presenting a direct examination. What facts are generated? How do these approaches to preparation alter what is introduced? How might the witness types Spellman identifies react differently to these procedures? Assuming their legitimacy, how would you adjust them?

Note that we have not considered at all the problem of assessing and preparing the expert witness, the defendant in a criminal case, or the adverse witness. Nor have we addressed many of the other problems that must be anticipated and prepared for. For example, the witness may (i) have a criminal record; (ii) have given an earlier inconsistent statement; (iii) exhibit an obvious interest in the case; (iv) be unable to remember much of what occurred; (v) believe that a fact which is clearly refuted by other evidence is true. These and similar problems involve special considerations that warrant much more careful examination.

---

2. *Sources of Distortion in Witness Testimony*

In making the assessments necessary to begin preparing for trial it is essential to bear in mind the degree to which the ordinary process of perception can distort or alter the ways events are seen, understood, and related. Inaccuracies in perception and recall must not only be confronted in the course of witness preparation, but will often be the focus of cross-examination, and the trial lawyer must learn to spot such weaknesses in a witness' testimony. Robert Redmount's summary of the psychological influences on perception serves as a useful reminder of the ways in which inaccuracy can enter into and distort what a witness says:

> Perceiving as a psychological experience has several discrete characteristics, any one of which can result in variations. A variation in perception may fall within the normal range or may be abnormal. These psychological influences may be diagramed as follows:

35. E. Low, HOW TO PREPARE AND TRY A NEGLIGENCE CASE, 70–74 (1957).

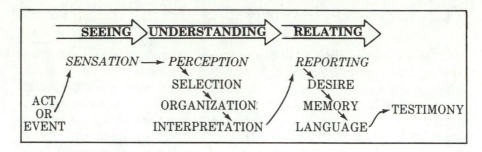

Figure 1. Diagrammatic Representation of Psychological Influences in Perception

[B8821]

As can be seen in Figure 1 perception is a complex psychological process. It is as true of perceptions as it is of machines that the more elements, switches and connections are involved, the more there is to go wrong. Theoretically it is possible for a person who knows the elements well enough to break down or examine any perception to such an extent that he will be able to find components that are ambiguous, reflect oversight, or represent exaggeration. However perception is rarely broken down to that degree, for to do so would be to remove even the approximate meanings and order necessary to life. Nevertheless, for practical trial purposes perception can be examined and tested to some extent for its strength and reliability, and its weakness probed, through knowledge of the perceiver and of the psychological determinants of perception.[36]

In addition to these psychological characteristics that can distort testimony, Redmount identifies the following influences:

—physiological factors (sensory capabilities, nervous system, sensitivity)

—cultural, family and socioeconomic background

—social practices and norms

—age

—sex

—intellectual ability

—mental abnormality or other disorder

—physical disability

—ignorance of the relevance or importance of what is observed

—prior beliefs, knowledge or attitudes

—interest and involvement in the circumstances

—state of mind

36. Redmount, *Handling Perception and Distortion in Testimony*, 5 AM.JUR. TRIALS 810, 816–17 (1966). *See also* the excerpts from J. Marshall, LAW AND PSYCHOLOGY IN CONFLICT (1966), discussed in Chapter One, *supra* at pages 115–120.

—characteristics of who or what is perceived

—time

—the circumstances of testifying

—the attorney's relationship with the witness

As a result of any of these factors, or a combination of them, witnesses can distort consciously, semi-consciously or unconsciously what they in fact observed. This can take a variety of forms.

—contamination (incorporation of additional elements)

—denial (inability or unwillingness to see)

—displacement (attitudes or actions are ascribed to other persons or events)

—embellishment

—uncertainty

—exaggerated certainty

—fragmentation (failure to recognize patterns in a series of events)

—overestimation

—underestimation

—reversal

—uncritical approval

Redmount makes the following suggestions with respect to analyzing a witness' likely performance at trial:

> A witness, in a sense, is being cast in a play. The attorney, as "director" of the court-room drama, must judge how the witness will look and how he will act his part. In the "try out" phase, which usually takes place in the attorney's office, the attorney should examine the witness to determine the latter's testimonial capabilities. He should observe the ability of the witness to (1) associate, analyze and discriminate; (2) organize and interpret; and (3) communicate. Counsel should remember that it is not his own conclusion as to the witness' abilities, but that of the judge and jury, that will determine how effective these abilities are in the courtroom.

> The attorney should discuss casually with the witness any matters of which he himself has knowledge from his own perception and understanding. He may discuss incisively and in depth the matter about which the witness will testify. In the course of such conversation, counsel will be able to make certain observations for himself as to the witness' abilities.

ASSOCIATION, ANALYSIS AND DISCRIMINATION

> In casually discussing some event not relevant to trial of which both the witness and the attorney have personal knowledge, such as a recent parade, the attorney may notice that the witness omits many elements in his associations. For example, the witness may have followed the parade through town but failed to observe or recall the

prize-winning drum and bugle corps or the float bearing the local beauty queen. He may have observed and remember a group in out-landish costumes but he may have been unable to associate the group to anything meaningful or important. In all this, the attorney may observe that the witness has difficulty in developing associations. The witness may not observe important facts, or he may report ob-servation of elements that did not occur. His observations may also indicate some limitation in his ability to discriminate. For example, he may have seen a large group of policemen in the parade but he may not have noticed that there were a number in the group who were not in uniform. Such a limitation may carry over to matters about which the witness is to testify in court.

The attorney should determine whether reminding or encouraging the witness can augment his associations or enable him to be more analytical and discriminating. If the witness reveals impoverished or overelaborated associations, if his analysis of events is too simple or produces error and irrelevancy, the attorney may be forced to use very specific questions of the witness in court. He may ask the witness to testify only on specific, simple matters in which flaws in the witness' perceptual abilities are not likely to occur or to be revealed.

ORGANIZATION AND INTERPRETATION

The attorney's interview with a prospective witness may also reveal whether the witness has the ability to organize and interpret acts and events, and whether any particular pattern of error of the witness is likely to appear in testimony. A prospective witness may overgeneralize in the way he talks about things and construes reality. In talking about something as mundane as the weather, he may as-semble such elements as morning rain, afternoon humidity, total dis-comfort, and the necessity of carrying an umbrella all day long, and overgeneralize his perception by stating that "it rained all day long." In discussing a near riot that he observed in the town square, he may take into account certain elements such as demonstrators throw-ing bottles and the police moving in with clubs. Organizing and construing only these events, he may conclude and report that "the demonstrators started the fight," when the attorney knows that a good deal more occurred that the observer either did not see or report.

Knowing his witness in this way, the attorney can organize his examination so as to avoid questions likely to produce answers vulner-able on cross-examination. He should observe whether the witness can correctly give proper testimony if guided, or whether his abilities to organize and interpret are so limited as to raise serious doubts about his reliability as a witness.

COMMUNICATION

The attorney should observe the witness and assess whether he can communicate clearly and adequately. Does the witness seem to lack sufficient vocabulary to describe an event? Does the witness in his report appear fumbling, halting, slow and unsure? A witness who communicates quickly and volubly, on the other hand, may appear shallow and seem to talk without thinking.

By careful questioning the attorney can sometimes minimize the effects of poor communicative facility. He may ask questions that require brief, simple answers in order that slowness, fumbling and the like may not be so evident. Directing questions to small segments of an observation may provide some means to control or perhaps disguise seeming talkativeness and superficiality in a witness. Slow, deliberate questions may evoke more reasoned, thoughtful answers. If, however, communication disabilities create bad impressions that are likely to be exposed on cross-examination, the attorney should weigh the intrinsic value of the testimony offered against the damaging effects of his limits in communication skill.

Speech patterns and verbal skills may be mostly unconscious and not susceptible to quick improvement. Coaching and suggestion are unlikely to be consistently effective particularly if the witness is put off by some question or approach made to him and loses specific concentration on his speech and verbal skill. It is more realistic for the attorney to accept speech patterns and verbal skills as they exist and adapt his trial strategy accordingly. He may decide to limit the kind and extent of the witness' examination in order to compensate for speech and verbal failings, or, on the other hand, to encourage communication of a witness with verbal skills.

* * *

Handling Witness' Attitudes

Counsel should observe the different attitudes of witnesses and the different consequences flowing from those attitudes, and plan his direct examination accordingly. He may encourage more communication from the confident and self-assured witness and may limit the testimony of an uncertain or confused witness to simple essentials.

If the undesirable consequences of a witness' attitude are likely to be exposed by searching cross-examination, the attorney may need to think in terms of trying to change the witness' attitude in preparing him to testify. A reminder to a witness that his attitude is detrimental because it is overbearing and provocative may make him more careful about his shortcoming. Characteristic attitudes, however, generally do not change greatly nor for long. It may be more realistic simply to weigh the witness' attitude as an asset or liability, and if it is likely to prove harmful, it may be advisable to drop the witness and forgo his testimony.[37]

You might ask yourself if these insights make sense to you. Would a general knowledge of the potential distortions of perception and memory help you deal with these sorts of problems?

------

37. *Id.* at 896–99, 902.

3. *The Other Side of Witness Assessment: The Inevitability of Surprise in Direct Examination*

No matter how well or totally you prepare, there will be unexpected problems at trial. The following are typical:

If, as is usually the case, the defendant has never been in a courtroom before, he may be easily unnerved by the experience of facing, from the witness stand, a critical jury of 12 strangers, a judge, the court attendants, counsel for both sides, and various spectators. Even a defendant who has impressed counsel as being stolid and unemotional may become excited and nervous—sometimes approaching a state of uncontrollable emotion. Although careful pretrial preparation will ease the impact, no office conference can totally prepare the witness for this experience and routine, preliminary questions, such as name, address, age, and occupation, should be asked until the defendant has relaxed sufficiently to proceed into the critical phases of his testimony.

If the defendant does not relax after several preliminary questions have been asked, counsel should proceed to ask questions that he knows will present no problem to the defendant but that will require him to think rather than make automatic answers. This procedure will often relax the defendant by taking his mind off his own feelings. In any event, counsel should not stop the questioning entirely at this point in the hope that it will give the defendant an opportunity to compose himself, for it will be even more disconcerting to the defendant to sit in complete silence, with every eye in the courtroom fixed upon him.

So long as they do not detract from the dignity and the seriousness of the trial, preliminary questions containing light humor, that give the defendant a chance to laugh or smile with the jury, may be appropriate to ease tension.

* * *

Age, sex, personality traits, education level, articulateness or inarticulateness, and the like, all are characteristics affecting the method of examination of the defendant. For example, a timid witness requires firm but gentle handling and encouragement during his examination. An illiterate or slow-witted person frequently becomes timid in the overpowering surroundings of the courtroom, and questions must be put to a defendant of this type slowly and in the most easily understood words. If a defendant so handicapped is still unable to answer, permission of the court to propound leading questions should be requested.

A defendant having an overbearing personality is at the exact opposite end of the personality spectrum from the timid witness. He is absolutely positive of his version of the occurrence, and frequently will resist all efforts of his attorney to reconcile his testimony with known physical facts. Even after extensive pretrial preparation of this type of defendant as a witness, the defense attorney should proceed with the examination cautiously.

The garrulous defendant is probably the most difficult to handle as a witness. Having been asked a question, he will talk until the defense attorney interrupts him and, of course, the more he talks the more suggestions for cross-examination he will furnish the opposing attorney. The greatest hazard with this type of defendant is that he will seldom listen to the question propounded and will usually answer without thinking. Questions addressed to this type of defendant must be in such form as to require a direct and responsive answer. . . .

* * *

On the rare occasion when the defendant has entirely forgotten an important point and no amount of questioning has succeeded in getting it from him, defense counsel should consider asking a leading question. Such question probably will draw an objection but it usually will cause the defendant to recall the desired answer. A question in proper form then should be asked, to give the defendant an opportunity to give the correct answer. This practice should, of course, be followed only when it is of extreme importance to have the answer in the record, since the repeated use of leading questions in this manner casts doubt on the testimony and gives the jury the impression that counsel is putting words in the defendant's mouth.

Other occasions may arise during a trial when the defense attorney will decide to ask obviously objectionable leading questions, even though he knows an objection probably will be made and sustained. A typical instance is that in which the defendant becomes confused, makes a manifest error in his testimony, has a lapse of memory, or otherwise testifies concerning material facts in a manner not consistent with his knowledge. In such circumstances, if the point involved is of substantial importance to the defense, counsel ordinarily should ask the leading questions with the expectation that it will refresh the defendant's memory. The question then can be rephrased and the defendant's testimony continued.

[Similarly,] if an answer given by the defendant has been vague, indefinite, or uncertain, a repetitious question may be asked to clarify the previous answer. This most often occurs in connection with the questioning of the very young or the very old, the former because of embarrassment or confusion and the latter because of defective hearing or mental slowness.

If the defendant, in answering one question, makes a statement concerning a fact that is not a necessary part of the answer to the question asked, it is not improperly repetitious to propound another question directly developing the fact incidentally referred to. Counsel should, in fact, make certain that he does so, lest the fact be overlooked because of its connection with another answer to a different question.

Asking the defendant to repeat his answer may also be proper, under certain circumstances. For example, if the defendant, while answering an important question, lets his voice drop so low that counsel has some doubt of the jury's hearing the answer, it is good practice to have him repeat it and ask him to keep his voice up so that the jury can hear.[38]

* * *

38. D. Jackson, *Direct Examination of the Defendant*, 6 AM.JUR.TRIALS 270–72, 274–75, 282–86 (1966).

The usual response to a witness who leaves out significant testimony, becomes hostile under cross-examination, gives contradictory testimony, or otherwise undermines counsel's careful pretrial planning, is a feeling of helplessness or betrayal. These are obviously of little help in solving such problems at trial, but advice to remain calm enough to quickly and accurately diagnose the cause of the difficulty —and respond to it—is not much more helpful. What is needed is a range of techniques which can be developed in advance to minimize and/or deal with such surprises.

Clearly, it would be desirable to eliminate by preparation the problems described above. Ask yourself, however, whether any of the advice to witnesses would be likely to do so. For example, many lawyers tell the witness (i) what response to make to trap questions; (ii) how to handle prior inconsistent statements (usually involving some form of insistance that his or her present recollection is correct); (iii) to go over any records relevant to the substance of the examination immediately before testifying; and (iv) to write out dates and other matters and refer to the memoranda during testimony. Some discuss the purpose of every question to be put on direct, as well as the dangers that attend any potentially damaging answers and, as we have discussed, many more urge that the witness should be put through an anticipated cross-examination and informed of the consequences of his or her responses to particular questions. Nevertheless, surprise occurs. What are its sources? Do they lie in the nature of perception and recollection itself? In the particular circumstances under which testimony is presented in a courtroom? How much lapse of memory or confusion can be traced to the very methods that are used during preparation? Does it really make sense to give the sort of dogmatic instructions recommended by trial lawyers?

Our own experience is that repetition rather than rehearsal, discussion rather than warnings, and support rather than allusion to dangers help make the witness' performance far more predictable and fluid. Would you agree? Are such efforts also likely to make the witness' testimony more truthful?

A second approach to this problem—in addition to developing a good working relationship with the witness—is for counsel to have available an adaptable, but learned and standardized set of responses to typical surprises. These include the following:

Leading Questions

Faced with something unexpected (and, perhaps, damaging) from a witness, many lawyers resort to leading and suggestive examinations. In some instances, this is obviously counterproductive. In others, it can be very effective.

For example, a witness leaves out an important detail. Counsel may simply ask: "Did anything else happen when you . . . ." or

"Was there any . . . at the time?" Although it would be better if the witness testified to the fact initially, the ability to translate questions into various forms, some of them mildly leading, is a very important trial skill that can be developed with practice.[39]

Recalling the Witness

Some lawyers suggest leaving the problem alone at the time and either recalling the witness or raising the issue on redirect, where counsel is given more leeway in asking leading questions. (This does seem to be the practice, although support for such a distinction under most evidence codes is dubious.) The theory is that this is a far more orderly and less risky way to correct inaccuracies or omissions in testimony. There are, however, many disadvantages in relying on such an approach. For example, if opposing counsel asks no questions, there will be no opportunity for redirect and the court, in its discretion, may not permit the witness to be recalled.

The Use of a Backup Memorandum

Another approach to the possibility of the witness testifying differently than expected is to reduce all anticipated testimony to a writing, which is carefully reviewed prior to the examination. If the witness' testimony at trial differs from the writing, counsel can then use the writing to (i) refresh the witness' recollection if the witness can testify of his or her own knowledge to the matter in question; (ii) impeach the witness with the writing and introduce it as a prior inconsistent statement; or (iii) in some instances, introduce the writing as a past recollection recorded.

You can probably think of other possibilities yourself, as well as ways to enlarge these. If it is any solace, we might remind you that the unexpected in your early trial work becomes the routine of practice in your later years. Indeed, this may someday be the source of a whole new set of problems.

4.   Opposing Witnesses

APPLEMAN, SUCCESSFUL JURY TRIALS

268–73, 275 (1952).

. . . [T]he finest cross-examiners vary their approaches from one witness to another, as an approach which is successful with

---

39. It has been suggested that counsel should arrange ways of signalling to the witness that a question refers to something that has been omitted. For example, whenever a witness hears a phrase—do you recall—he or she is warned that something needs to be added or clarified. Whatever its ethical propriety, this strategy often only increases the anxiety that produced the error or omission in the first place.

one witness may antagonize the jury when employed as to another. Since most people fall into certain personality groups, it is well to consider the reaction of those persons to interrogation and the techniques which are generally the most successful in those instances.

The Timid Witness

Many witnesses fall into this particular category, particularly persons who are not accustomed to speaking before a large audience, who have had little experience in the court room, and who are not too certain of their facts. This is often the situation in a negligence case, where such persons observed only a minimum of the occurrences which are at issue in the lawsuit, but who may be led into committing themselves to a broader position upon direct examination. They are not too sure of their recitals and are somewhat hesitant about the position which they have undertaken. Thus, whether or not they show this uncertainty upon the surface, their thoughts are in somewhat of a turmoil.

It is obvious that it would be dangerous to bully such a witness. Most of the jurors visualize themselves in the witness chair, and the witness who is subpoenaed into court automatically has a certain amount of jury sympathy. The attorney who is rough or blustery tends then to antagonize the juror who visualizes himself in the place of the witness.

This witness must be approached with an air of courteous confidence. The courtesy appeals to the jury; the confidence unnerves the witness. The attorney will ask perhaps two introductory questions to have the witness reiterate a position which he has taken upon direct examination, which will be difficult for him to sustain, and the cross-examiner must then go directly to the weak point of that testimony. . . . There may be a thousand different situations in which such a witness is encountered, but in each instance, if the attorney continues a rapid, confident interrogation, basing each new question upon the preceding answer, he can usually soon excuse that witness with his testimony definitely reduced in value.

* * *

The Liar

There are many ways of destroying this type of a witness, and it is seldom that a perjurer is so skilled that he cannot be destroyed by the cross-examiner. There are two major techniques which the author has found particularly successful in dealing with such persons.

. . . [W]here the circumstances are unusual, and only a person intimately familiar with the circumstances of the case would possess the required knowledge, an out-and-out perjurer can often be tripped up by his lack of knowledge of necessary details. In considering the second method, we must remember that such a person usually comes into the court room prepared to substantiate a certain theory of the case by flat and dogmatic statements. In such event, in order not to disclose his lack of knowledge as to other matters, he will when interrogated thereon take a definite position with regard to them. Thus, a witness of this type can be led along both paths at different portions of the examination to get him committed irretrievably to a flat position as to each. If the two positions then assumed are flagrantly inconsistent, the testimony of the witness is destroyed.

The Bullying Witness

It is not only the attorney who may be accused of bullying techniques. Many witnesses fall in this category. This is generally the man or woman who is quite gracious and positive upon direct examination and then, when cross-examination commences, straightens up in the chair and glares belligerently at the cross-examiner. These witnesses tend to give their answers immediately upon the question being asked and often insert a great deal of irrelevant material in their answers, biting off their words with satisfaction at the discomfort they must be causing the cross-examining lawyer. There are two ways of handling such witnesses. Remember, the jury doesn't like them any better than does the lawyer, so there is not as much risk of antagonizing the jury by a series of questions.

The first technique is by a gentle persistent timidity until the witness has gone further and further out on a limb in the making of the answers. Ability to use this type of interrogation often depends upon the attorney. A very young lawyer or an elderly gentle lawyer could use this technique to perfection. Most of us who have more of a flair for the dramatic find more success in a slightly different method. One can almost always assume that such a witness will give the answer which he believes will cause the most discomfort to the lawyer molesting him. Therefore, a series of machine-gun-like questions couched in an antagonistic manner will most often produce the desired result. Actually the witness is giving the answers you desire, but he thinks he is killing you with his replies. Generally the attorney should be standing, perhaps moving about, facing the witness and firing the questions at him with some scorn in his voice, so as to keep the witness's resentment at fever pitch. If a "yes" answer is desired, the question must be so worded and expressed that the witness is convinced that you want a "no" answer. This is a fairly simple technique when examined and utilized with a little practice. It should almost never be used with any other type of witness.

* * *

The Confused but Honest Witness

When a witness is confused but honest, the jury generally realizes his confusion and will resent it bitterly if the cross-examiner takes advantage of the confusion to belittle or to embarrass the witness. . . .

If the witness is honestly confused, he will welcome the opportunity to correct any mistake which he has made or any erroneous impression which he might have left. A cross-examiner should be very patient with such a witness and help him quietly and politely to straighten out the error. . . .

The Smart Aleck

Again, every cross-examiner is occasionally blessed by having some man or woman upon the witness stand who comes prepared for combat. Often such person possesses a certain crude sense of wit. It is one which may sound very funny for the first remark or two, but thereafter may become extremely boring. The technique of handling such a witness is to permit him or her, as the case may be, to antagonize the jury and not to rise to the bait.

NOTES

1. *Witness Types and the Assessment Problem*

There are a variety of other ways to classify approaches to cross-examination. A number of lawyers prefer to focus on particular types of cases or on the functions performed by particular witnesses. *The Trial Manual for the Defense of Criminal Cases,* for example, organizes cross-examination by the defense around the following: (i) police witnesses; (ii) accomplices turned state's evidence; (iii) complainants in theft cases; (iv) complainants who identify the defendant; (v) rape complainants; (vi) mutual assault complainants; (vii) child complainants or witnesses; (viii) prosecution experts; and (ix) witnesses who have made prior statements.[40]

As we discuss in the next section, such classifications are very useful in cross-examination planning. Here, however, we are interested in focusing your attention on the general features of the case and your predictions about the witnesses who will testify against you. Think back to our discussions in Chapter One. How do you make initial judgments about what witnesses to see, and begin to shape the fragments of their memory and perception into a planned examination? John Sink makes the following observations about this process in *Political Criminal Trials*:

> Preparations do not necessarily mean that there is going to be a cross-examination; they merely assure that when a prosecution witness opens his mouth to testify, the lawyer has made adequate use

40. A. Amsterdam, B. Segal, & M. Miller, eds., TRIAL MANUAL FOR THE DEFENSE OF CRIMINAL

CASES 1–371 to 1–378 (ALI–ABA, 3d ed. 1974).

of all previously available information, so that his mind is free to listen.

* * *

In certain political cases, there will be a school of potential witnesses whose names and (in some cases) statements will have been fished up by the discovery nets. These are not the star witnesses for the prosecution, but persons who nonetheless could be called to the stand at any time.

While the case is in progress, the prosecution may be re-evaluating their testimony and reinterviewing them at night, but without the benefit of fresh, written witness statements. Nothing more will be handed to the defense, to indicate which of them will appear in court. In a large trial, perhaps 10 percent of these people will be called to the stand. Naturally, some minimal state of preparation must be maintained against this entire group at all times. And naturally, the big organizing problems concern materials received from the prosecutor.

Frequently, these will be people who volunteered information to the police that was not central to the subject of the trial. Perhaps someone on the prosecution side thought this information *might* be helpful in proving some element of a crime charged against one of the defendants. As to some of these witnesses, a short statement may have been taken, but it will not always be very indicative of what the witness could contribute. As to the rest, there may be only a brief memorandum from some police officer reflecting a contact on a certain date with a very short reference to what it was about.

Needless to say, the lawyer or his investigator will have made whatever efforts time permitted to contact these people, and so there should be defense investigation notes as to some. But most of those contacts will have been unproductive, either because the person refused to talk to anyone on the defense side, or because he could not be found at all.

The organizational plan here is extremely plain. As to each of these potential witnesses, the pieces of paper relating to that witness should be put together in a little packet with his name on it. All the packets should then be arranged in alphabetical order, or in whatever order the lawyer pleases, and these should be kept within arm's reach throughout the trial.

In a long trial, the lawyer should review these at night from time to time so that he is quite familiar with the modest contents of each packet, and knows, for example, whether his investigator can be expected to come back with more information about this one or that one. The lawyer can add his own notes, annotating and underlining things in whatever bright color pleases the tired eye.

These preparations are childishly simple, but as it happens they are sometimes neglected, apparently on the theory that with so little to go on, there is no point in getting it together. While it may be true that in most cases the little packets make little difference in the sense of adding usable information, not to have organized even this much is to face the witness with a knowledge of things undone, a sense of chaos at the elbow, and guilt. But to have organized even modest materials is to look at the same witness with serenity at the elbow, as much as if the lawyer had spent many hours organizing prolix information. Serenity, of course, if one has not been introduced to him in court, is a great murderer of hostile testimony.[41]

What this involves is maintaining an index on each witness, collecting all prior statements, transcripts, or other evidence relevant to his or her testimony, and organizing this data into an outline of what each witness is expected to testify to and how counsel plans to handle it. The following is an example:

Sample Page From Combined Index
(For Use During Cross-Examination)

Officer Oldbadge (cont'd)
[*Note: portions preceding this section have been omitted*]

II. Observations Before Arrival at Scene

	Grand Jury Transcript	Discovery Motion Transcript
at about 7:30 p. m. was proceeding east on Green Street in the 100 block	3:9–12	9:5–7
saw defendant running along north side of street, going east, in that block; "he observed me and slowed down"	3:14–16	9:7–10
proceeded slowly past defendant, driving up to intersection of Green and Maple Streets, and defendant came abreast of this well-lit corner, and recognized defendant and observed he wore heavy shoes and light colored clothing; can't remember shirt	3:16 to 4:4	
defendant crossed Maple Street at 200 block of East Green Street, and "at about the vicinity of the hotel, I looked in my rear view mirror" and saw defendant talking to victim [marked on grand jury map]	4:8–10	
circled block, returning to make "routine check-out procedure" on parked vehicle; could not see defendant or victim at this time; resumed patrol	5:3–7	
got first radio call at about 8:30 p. m.	5:19–20	10:2–3

contra: crime was committed at 8:10 and reported at 8:20 p. m. see police report [evid. no. 1.01(c)] page 2

* * *

41. J. Sink, POLITICAL CRIMINAL TRIALS: HOW TO DEFEND THEM 418–21 (1974).

Main Objects in Cross-examining This Witness and Reasons:

1. Dislodge time schedule to show the first time he saw defendant was later and compress the time interval between them and when the victim was found. The reason is if defendant takes the stand, the interval of 30–40 minutes would kill him. That would conflict with leaving the store at 8:00 p. m., since the victim could not have been lying there very long. The approach should be: (1) ask him what he did after seeing defendant and before the radio message, minimizing time estimates; (2) shake him up with minor inconsistencies outlined above; (3) emphasize it was dark, that he needed a street light to recognize defendant, and back it up with evidence as to sunset time.

2. Pull the teeth out of that business of defendant running, by asking if there wasn't a traffic light, and if he didn't happen to see the defendant only because he had stopped for it. Obviously running to make the light, not for a guilty motive.

3. Ask him if it was routine to check out parked cars on every block in the city, or just around that park. He will probably say the car was suspicious because it was unfamiliar, but that it was not stolen. This should lead to why anybody would want to watch cars in a certain block so closely as to know when an unfamiliar car was parked there. The answer would be, this damn park is a hotbed of crime; it is the only area in town where two vehicle beats overlap, and that is a good argument point.

N.B. He is winsome with the jury and tends to overdo it with gratuitous explanations. Keep a tight rein, aim for these limited goals, get him off the stand fast, and *don't* get involved in lengthy cross-examination.[42]

Ask yourself whether such preparation is possible in other cases. What tools would be available to you? How would you go about organizing your investigation so that material could be developed in this form?

Bear in mind that often your assessments will have to be much more quickly developed—with far less pre-trial material—than this procedure would suggest. Once in trial, assessment largely depends on your ability to recognize and respond to subtle cues regarding a witness' personality and emotional state. As Louis Nizer has remarked:

> There is a psychological time for venturesomeness with a witness. A question put to him when he is vigorously resistant may be ineffectual. The same question thrown at him when he is stunned and low in morale may induce a confession. Similarly in examination before trial a question asked almost casually after a moment of jest and good will, may be conceded with a gesture of candor. The same question, put when the witness is belligerent, will beget defiance. The converse can be true too. If the mood is hostile, the witness may deny his own name, so to speak, and ultimately pay for his foolish

---

42. *Id.* at 651–52.

anger. The examiner must be sensitive to the moods of the witness and vary his approach in the light of expectations.[43]

No typology of witnesses or approaches is useful unless you have the sensitivity to understand the people whom you examine and your own reactions to them. Here, as elsewhere, the need for both control and empathy makes paradoxical claims on the examiner's craft.

———

2. *The Significance of Preparation in Trial Work*

As we turn from assessment to the related problems of formulating particular lines of examination, we ought not to leave unstated our own assumptions concerning the necessity of preparation in trial work (indeed, in all lawyering). The statements in the practice manuals to this effect are so numerous and their level of generality so unhelpful that we often fail to state what seems obvious: the products of lawyering are shaped by judgments too subtle to be made on the spur of the moment. Whether explicitly stated or not, this has been a dominant theme throughout this book. Our view is shared by countless practitioners, and was perhaps best stated by Emory R. Buckner of the New York Bar:

> If I were a client and knew as much about the trial of cases as I have learned as a lawyer, I would rather have a wholly inconspicuous and utterly unknown man of only mediocre ability who would prepare the case, who would exhaust every possibility of finding out all the facts that are relevant, than to have some very well known and very astute and clever and capable forensic orator, who went in as so many of our specialists and celebrities do, with no particular preparation except to pick up things as they develop.[44]

You will have many opportunities to test this statement and to make it concrete in your own practice. For us, it means that in preparing to cross-examine any witness (and in almost every case) you would have (i) visited any scene involved in the transaction; (ii) thoroughly studied all potential documentary and demonstrative material; (iii) attempted to learn the background of every witness; (iv) carefully analyzed the legal and factual theories applicable to the claims in question; (v) prepared all the possible evidentiary and legal objections you might encounter; and (vi) thought through the case from the perspective of opposing counsel. This, of course, names only a few of the steps that should be taken. What is interesting is why so few lawyers do all or most of these things. In few areas of practice is there a greater discrepancy between the pronouncements of leading practitioners about appropriate conduct and the actual behavior of most of their colleagues in court.

43. L. Nizer, MY LIFE IN COURT 127 (1963).   44. Quoted in A. Cornelius, TRIAL TACTICS (1932).

B. PRESENTATION: CONSTRUCTING AND SUBMITTING THE TESTIMONY

1. Selecting Topics

a. Direct Examination: Building Consistency

SCHWARTZ, PROOF, PERSUASION AND CROSS EXAMINATION

104–07, 203–04, 207–08 (1973)*

The work of the advocate has recently been described by Louis Nizer as the "task of weaving thousands of threads of disconnected testimony into a cloth of persuasive patterns while at the same time dexterously eliminating those strings which would spoil the design." Now, it is true that thousands of threads of testimony must be woven together in the same sense that thousands of notes must be used in a symphony. But, just as there are only seven notes in the diatonic scale which the musician uses in infinite combinations, similarly the thousands of threads of testimony may be classified and reduced to a fundamental or "generic" few.

It is essential that the trial lawyer, too, have a scale—a "testimonial scale," similar to the musician's scale, as the basis for his study and experience. . . .

* * *

Our proposed "testimonial scale" consists of six categories or "notes":

1. The witness' knowledge.
2. The witness' recollection.
3. The witness' perception (sight, hearing, touch, taste, smell).
4. The witness' action (by words or conduct).
5. The witness' state of mind (feelings, emotions, etc.).
6. The witness' operation of mind (opinions, conclusions, etc.).

. . . Irrespective of the nature or subject of the testimony which a witness may give, it must pertain to his knowledge, perceptions, actions, or be a report on the state of his mind or the operation of his mind.

Ordinarily, testimony does not fit exclusively into any one single category. The categories are interrelated and overlapping, but each bit of testimony will predominately concern itself with one category rather than the others. . . . For a complete examination it may

* © 1973 by Louis E. Schwartz. Published by Executive Reports Corporation, Englewood Cliffs, New Jersey.

be necessary to explore all six categories in order to develop the full picture of what the witness is able to convey to the jury.

* * *

There are six *Generic Questions*, each of which is designed to elicit the corresponding "note" of testimony, as follows:

1. Recollection: *Q. What do you recall as to . . . ?*

2. Knowledge: *Q. What, if anything, do you know, of your personal knowledge, as to . . . ?*

3. Perception: *Q. What, if anything, did you perceive (see, hear, touch, taste or smell)?*

4. Action: *Q. What, if anything, did you do (say or write)?*

5. State of Mind: *Q. What are your feelings with respect to . . . ?*

6. Operation of Mind: *Q. What is your opinion as to . . . ?*

All possible questions which may be put to a witness are but variations and combinations of these six. . . . What is important to the advocate is to establish that the witness knows whereof he speaks; his recollection is retentive; his sensory perceptions acute; his state of mind unbiased, to the end that the jury will be persuaded to give credence to his testimony that he indeed had perceived a certain fact, as claimed.

* * *

[Our] thesis . . . is that no matter how varied the subject matter of the trial, no matter how simple or intricate the necessary proof, no matter whether representing the plaintiff or defendant, *all proof can be elicited by means of these six Generic Questions.* Furthermore, that in all questions, no matter how they are worded, *there must be, expressly or implicitly, one or more of these six Generic Questions.*

* * *

. . . [Thus counsel] can guide the witness from one aspect of his testimony to another . . . [When] problems unexpectedly present themselves . . . [he] can choose the appropriate question to put the witness back into the proper channel and evoke the desired testimony. . . . [He] can assure himself that the question is properly framed and that the answer is more likely to be responsive and satisfactory. . . . He can better analyze the compound nature of many question answer sequences.

If a particular bit of testimony is important, the trial lawyer dare not content himself with the bare *Generic Question* and its answer. He must try to develop the theme to a point where it changes from a mere bit of testimony to persuasive proof. The answer of a witness to one *Generic Question* can be strengthened by inferences arising from the answers to other *Generic Questions* put to the same witness. Figuratively speaking, the *Generic Question* is placed in the center of the stage and is illuminated by directing spotlights of inferences from other categories upon it.

The approach is similar to that of a musician. A composer takes a few notes as his motif, he embellishes them with harmony, scale passages, trills, arpeggios; he varies their rhythm and develops them into a movement or sonata. The advocate takes one item of testimony, combines it with other items and creates what may be called a *Thread of Testimony*, which he later combines with other related threads. . . .

The analogy is obvious. One thread of testimony is a weak and flimsy thing. A case made up of many disconnected threads will still be "threadbare." When the proof is loosely knit, it may be ripped apart and torn wide open with one snip by the cross-examiner. *When, however, the threads of testimony are braided together and intertwined with many other such threads, they can form a web to enmesh, a straight-jacket to imprison, or a cloak to protect.* The choice of the threads of testimony, their infinite variety and combinations of type, substance, and presentation will reflect the skill and artistry of the weaver—the advocate.

Thus, for example, the testimony of a witness who relates what he saw in response to the question, Q. *What, if anything, did you see?* attains greater persuasiveness if, before he states what he saw, he testifies as to what he did to put himself into position where he could observe without any obstructions to his view; his state of mind, his reason or motive to observe, etc. His testimony will be further enhanced if he describes what he saw in detail and describes other things which he saw at the same time and place. Furthermore, perception may occur simultaneously by means of sight, hearing, touch, taste, and smell and his testimony as to these various sensory perceptions would corroborate each other.

Should the witness be there to testify as an expert, he is not asked directly to state his opinion. The experienced trial attorney will first go into the details of the witness' qualifications (*Knowledge*), then as to what he did with respect to tests and examinations of the subject matter (*Actions*) and then the details of what he observed (*Perceptions*). Only then will he call for the opinion of the expert witness.

In [developing such testimony], the advocate does not limit himself to one of the six categories of testimony, but should include as many as possible. The inferences arising from the answer to any one *Generic Question* can be strengthened by the inferences flowing from others. There is, for example, harmony between a man's thoughts and deeds. When, therefore, it appears from the testimony of a witness that his sensory perceptions, his actions, and his mental conceptions were all consistent with each other, there are a great number of inferences flowing from all his testimony, pointing in the same direction, *i. e.,* towards truth and credibility.

NOTES

1. *The Consistency Criterion in Direct Examination*

Many effective lawyers (with whom we agree) would take Schwartz quite literally: that is, they would attempt to link *every* item of information that might come out in the course of the examination into a consistent theory of what occurred and how it supports their claims. This essentially involves asking oneself: (i) What purpose do I have? (ii) What belief, proposition, or attitude do I want the hearer to adopt? (iii) What questions will lead to these results? (iv) What answers do I expect? (v) Why do I expect those answers to produce the desired beliefs? (vi) What weaknesses exist in the links of inference I am trying to establish? In this process one weaves together the elements of the dialogue between counsel and witness, in a pattern designed to have a particular effect on one's audience.

The difficulty is deciding what questions and answers are likely to maximize impact and minimize flaws in the testimony. Clearly the elements of the applicable legal standard must be satisfied, but this basic requirement provides little specific guidance in making the choices involved. Consider, for example, the following questions:

How Much of the Witness' Background Should be Introduced?

The witness should generally be introduced to the hearer of the case and his or her testimony should be placed in context. Since this makes the witness more real and human for the hearer and gives the witness an opportunity to dispel any initial nervousness by answering questions which are familiar, background becomes an important examination topic. But there is always a question as to how many background facts should be elicited. Bailey and Rothblatt, for example, suggest bringing out the defendant's present employment, employment history, marital status, residence, age, and parentage in a criminal case because such facts help to "personalize and humanize" the defendant.[45] There are, however, many instances in which you might not want to introduce such facts with respect to

----

45. F. L. Bailey & H. Rothblatt, FUN-
DAMENTALS OF CRIMINAL ADVO-
CACY 367 (1974).

every witness. Where witnesses are cumulative or where a lengthy introduction might open up unfavorable material, for example, a shorter introduction would be more appropriate.

Should Unfavorable Matter be Introduced?

Many lawyers do not elicit any unfavorable facts on direct. Their argument is that the negative matter is harmful and may never come out at all. Others take the view that introducing such unfavorable matter on direct can substantially undercut the effectiveness of cross-examination and enhance the impression of fairness and candor that the witness conveys. Perhaps Spellman's approach is closest to our own:

> One of the main functions of introducing a witness to the jury is, where the occasion arises, to deprive the opposition of the opportunity to bring out unfavorable facts on cross-examination. For example, if the witness is a relative or close friend of the party calling him, he should so testify. Similarly, if the witness has been convicted of crime, he should disclose this fact during the introduction.

> * * *

> The underlying strategic consideration is that it is better to have an unfavorable matter exposed through one's own witness than to let it appear either that an attempt was made to conceal that matter or that it was unknown to trial counsel because the witness was hiding it from him. A similar approach can be employed with regard to weaknesses in the case, itself.

> During preparation, counsel very often is compelled to conclude that there are certain unfavorable factors, which, in all probability, will come to light during the trial and the existence of which cannot be successfully denied. These facts cannot be swept under the rug. They must be faced realistically and careful plans should be laid how best to mitigate their effectiveness.

> Some unfavorable matters may be so unimportant when viewed against the entire background of the cause that emphasis placed upon them can only serve to enlarge their stature. It is wise either to treat these matters with skillful neglect, trusting to summation properly to belittle them, or not to mention them at all.

> * * *

> Where counsel is faced by an *important* unfavorable factor, resulting from facts that cannot be denied or minimized but will be harmful if unexplained, it is nevertheless often desirable to bring out these facts through his own witnesses. Here, the strategic concept is *anticipation*. If the trier of the facts has already heard testimony about an unfavorable factor, he will be impatient if it is rehashed later in the case. Counsel to whose client the unfavorable facts will be damaging should try to bring them out in a somewhat casual way on direct examination, preferably interjected in the course of testimony helpful to his client.

> * * *

It must not be assumed from the foregoing that in every case counsel should bring out unfavorable facts during the direct examination of his own witnesses. In a great many instances, the damning facts are so important that, no matter when they come out, they will be vitally harmful. It makes no sense to help one's opponent by admitting these facts in advance. Indeed, the admission may create an atmosphere so unfavorable that the case may be lost during direct examination. If unfavorable facts can be met by explanatory favorable testimony, it is often wiser to reserve the explanation so that it will come as late as possible in the case. "Final impression" is a tactical advantage not to be easily surrendered. . . .[46]

Whether in any particular case one can separate the important from the unimportant and the favorable from the unfavorable—as the jury or judge would see it—remains problematic. But the reasons Spellman urges for anticipating unfavorable matter on direct seem generally sound. Against them should be weighed (i) the possibility that the matter will not be brought out on cross (opposing counsel for example, may simply fail to recognize its value); (ii) the extent to which introducing such material detracts from the effect of the direct; (iii) whether the matter can readily be explained on redirect; (iv) the likelihood that anticipating cross-examination will serve to emphasize its legitimacy. There are many good reasons for not referring to any unfavorable testimony at all.

Should Favorable Matter be Reserved?

The considerations here are similar to those relating to unfavorable matter. Many lawyers recommend not introducing all the available favorable evidence, on the theory that it will have far more force if elicited on cross-examination. As Appleman writes:

. . . Occasionally it is well to refrain from bringing out all matters favorable upon a certain circumstance, particularly if opposing counsel is the ordinary type of tedious cross-examiner. He will plunge in and, upon cross-examination, bring out many additional matters seriously damaging to him and thus having a much more dramatic effect than if elicited upon direct testimony.[47]

The following, however, underscores the risks of pursuing such a course:

The temptation sometimes arises to have a witness tell only part of the story during direct examination, holding back the remainder of his knowledge of the facts for redirect examination or on rebuttal. This is an extremely dangerous course and should only be employed when the nature of the case requires it as a matter of law.

It is true that an element of surprise may be advantageously utilized through the holding back of some part of the story during the main examination of a witness on direct. But it is equally and

46. H. Spellman, DIRECT EXAMINA-
TION OF WITNESSES 85, 88, 90, 92
(1968).

47. J. Appleman, SUCCESSFUL JURY
TRIALS 181 (1952).

more generally true that, after a witness has been cross-examined, his redirect can look like an invention if there is no reasonable explanation for his failure to tell the whole story when he first had the opportunity to do so.

Furthermore, it is a general principle of law (subject, of course, to the exercise of discretion by the trial judge) that a witness will not be permitted to state anything during redirect examination which is not in direct rebuttal to matters brought out on cross. Thus, the failure of the witness to tell the whole story during direct examination may result in the irreparable loss of advantageous testimony.[48]

In light of the possibility that such favorable testimony will *not* be elicited in the course of cross-examination, ask yourself which of these views makes more sense to you. Can you think of cases where withholding certain pieces of testimony would be the better approach? For example, what about favorable testimony on matters on which the other party has the burden of proof?

How Much Detail on Any Issue Should be Brought Out?

This is a difficult question to address in general terms. Nevertheless, the following comments by Kenney Hegland underscore our own view of the importance of erring on the side of concreteness and specificity in determining what to cover in an examination:

> Compare the following:
>
> Q: Did you see the defendant get out of his car just after the accident?
>
> A: Yes, I did.
>
> Q: Were you able to form an opinion as to his sobriety?
>
> A: Yes, I was.
>
> Q: And what was that opinion?
>
> A: He was drunk.
>
>   *   *   *
>
> Q: Did you see the defendant get out of his car just after the accident?
>
> A: Yes, I did.
>
> Q: Where were you in relation to him?
>
> A: I was standing on the curb, about five feet from the driver's door. He got out of that door.
>
> Q: Was there anything interfering with your vision of him?
>
> A: No.
>
> Q: What were the lighting conditions?
>
> A: It was a clear day. Just after two in the afternoon.
>
> Q: How long did you observe the defendant?

---

48. H. Spellman, *supra* note 46 at 87.

A : Well, he looked at me when he got out of the car. He stood there facing me ten to fifteen seconds and then he staggered off.

Q : What was he wearing?

A : He had a T-shirt on with a picture of a tiger. Under the tiger, it said "I never met a man I didn't like."

Q : What was the defendant's condition?

A : His eyes were bloodshot, his clothes were messed up. I noticed a strong smell of alcohol and when he asked "is anyone hurt?" his voice was slurred. He could barely stand up.

Q : How do you know he could barely stand up?

A : Well, when he got out of the car, he leaned on the door. When he walked off, I saw him almost fall twice.

Q : Do you have an opinion as to his sobriety?

A : Yes, he was drunk.

The message of both is the same: the defendant was drunk. Legally, both are proper—a layman can form an opinion as to sobriety. Both versions seem equally *understandable*. But, when the time comes for the jury to sort out all of the bits of testimony it has heard, the longer version is much more likely to be *recalled*. First, more time was spent on developing it—no one can pay total attention and the shorter version may have been crowded out of consciousness by the jury's thoughts of dinner. The longer version is also more likely to be recalled because it was dramatic. The examiner did not go directly to the conclusion; he slowly built toward it. The longer version is much more *believable*. The witness has really testified to two conclusions: first, that he could adequately perceive the defendant, second, that what he saw and smelled led him to the conclusion that the defendant was drunk. And, what makes conclusions believable? *Details*.

People talk in conclusionary terms—"This is the man that robbed me," "I clearly overheard the plaintiff say it," "I knew from his behavior that the defendant was apologetic." What you must do is to break down these conclusions into the factual details upon which they rest. *Do this before trial.* Ask the witness: "How do you know he is the man that robbed you?" "That it was the plaintiff you overheard?" "What is there about the defendant's behavior that led you to the conclusion?" During this pretrial conference, the witness may not be able to articulate the factual basis on which his conclusion rests. If so, draw it out of him. The method is to ask yourself "If the witness' conclusion is true, what else would be true?" If it is true that the witness "got a good look at the robber," it is probably also true that the lighting was good, that the witness was close to the robber, that he had a sufficient time to observe him, that he can describe his clothing and so forth. Now, you simply ask the witness about these possible factual supports.

During the trial, develop the factual details upon which the conclusion rests.[49]

To establish a plausible basis for the witness' observations and recollections it seems clear that an examiner must go beyond the foundation the law requires. This is so obviously sensible that it is puzzling that this advice is so often ignored in practice.

Should Cumulative Testimony Be Offered?

This involves two separate issues: whether additional witnesses should be offered on the same subject, and whether cumulative matter in a single witness' testimony should be avoided. The standard advice on both these questions is to avoid repetition:

> (a) Economy of proof is universally recognized as the hallmark of a good trial lawyer. He tries to put in just enough to survive a motion to dismiss. He saves corroborative evidence for rebuttal if necessary. Or he makes use of it by making the standard offer:
>
> > I have a number of other witnesses who are prepared to testify to the same facts. I do not want to waste the time of the Court and jury unnecessarily. If my opponent will stipulate that they will in substance testify the same way, then it will not be necessary to put them on the witness stand.[50]
>
> (b) Direct examination should not be repetitious, should cover the testimony, and should give the witness an opportunity to tell what he knows and the examination should then be concluded.
>
> Echoing should be avoided. Frequently, lawyers will repeat the answer that the witness gives. This is not only annoying to the jury but unnecessarily lengthens the record, possibly to the detriment of your client later. Requesting the witness to repeat a particularly favorable answer is too shallow a tactic to indulge in. Usually the lawyer who does this is apparently unable to hear the unfavorable answers.[51]

Our own experience, however, often suggests otherwise. Despite the risks, meshing the testimony of different witnesses so that a basic pattern seems to emerge can be very persuasive. Moreover, there is always the possibility that adverse inferences will be drawn from the omission, whatever the instructions on this subject.

The same is true with respect to repetition within a single witness' testimony. To use Schwartz' metaphor, documentary and demonstrative evidence, though cumulative, weaves the "threads" of testimony more tightly together. And more than one description of the same events, if not obviously repetitive, may be necessary to gain the jury's comprehension and attention. This is the unstated rationale for the often-used approach of asking the witness to tell his or her

---

49. K. Hegland, TRIAL AND PRACTICE SKILLS IN A NUTSHELL 20–23 (1978).

50. H. Gair & A. S. Cutler, NEGLIGENCE CASES: WINNING STRATEGY 30 (1957).

51. J. Appleman, *supra* note 47 at 211.

"story," then going back over the narrative with specific questions to explore details. The net result is to reinforce the facts being presented, despite some repetition.

With Schwartz, we would emphasize congruence and corroboration in the presentation of evidence, fully realizing that such an approach offers, at most, an orientation. It only begins to inform the difficult task of deciding what witnesses to call and what to ask them.

---

2. *The Importance of Amplifying Material*

However the above issues are resolved, the metaphor Schwartz uses highlights the value of amplifying material in the development of a direct examination. This view is shared by a number of writers on the subject. Robert Keeton, for example, makes the following observations on the use of demonstrative evidence:

> The traditional way of proving a fact is by asking a witness who knows. Some trials conclude with no type of evidence having been offered other than what the witnesses say. Yet a moment's reflection will suggest to you that this type of evidence is in most respects the least convincing type of evidence you can offer. It is subject to all the frailties of human error in observation, memory, expression, and integrity. It is common knowledge that two witnesses standing side by side to observe the same event, if interrogated separately, will differ in their statements concerning what occurred. Jurors who are not already aware of these facts can usually be converted to belief in them with moderate attention to the question in the lawyer's argument. The lawyer who has more of real or demonstrative evidence than his adversary has a distinct advantage in the contest of convincing the jury. Some at least, though not all, of the chances for error are absent or reduced in the case of demonstrative evidence.
>
> Generally you should make use of all the favorable physical or demonstrative evidence that is available to you, and careful attention and some imagination in searching for such evidence will disclose that more is available than is customarily used in the trial of cases.[52]

This suggests that for each topic and subtopic in the examination counsel should consider whether there is any corroborative evidence available, including that which is demonstrative or documentary in character. This might involve:

—stipulations

—admissions obtained through interrogatories or other discovery devices

—judicial notice

—prior testimony of an unavailable witness

52. R. Keeton, TRIAL TACTICS AND METHODS 79–80 (2d ed. 1973).

—public records

—quasi-public records

—business records or memoranda

—correspondence

—photographs

—motion pictures

—diagrams and plans

—charts

—models

—views by the fact finder [53]

In addition, the way transitions and sequences are handled, as well as references to the testimony of other witnesses, can provide amplification. Hegland provides some examples:

> There is a tendency to be overly clever: to purposefully scatter evidence during the trial so as not to tip your hand until closing argument where, to the amazement and admiration of all, you "tie it all up," order emerges from chaos, and you victorious, trailing clouds of glory.

> There are two dangers. First, what you "tie up" at closing are the bits of evidence. However, unless the jury saw the importance of the evidence at the time it was presented, likely it is forgotten. There is nothing to tie up. Second, the jury may be asleep during your argument which may not, in fact, turn out as well as it did in front of the bathroom mirror. Thirdly, and most importantly, *most cases are decided before closing argument:* if you have important evidence, let the jury know its importance. How?

> Assume a case where a 15 year old girl has testified that her father sexually molested her on two separate occasions, September 17 and September 19. After her testimony, the state puts on two or three corroborative witnesses and then rests. The defense puts on the father who is to deny all charges. Once the preliminary questions are asked, the attorney might ask: "Directing your attention to the evening of September 17, what occurred when you arrived home?" This is a mistake as most of the jury will not recall that this is a key date. For

53. For the trial literature on the admissibility and tactical use of the above, *see, e. g.,* J. Appleman, PREPARATION AND TRIAL (1967); I. Goldstein & F. Lane, TRIAL TECHNIQUE Vol. 2 (2d ed. 1969); H. Hickam & T. Scanlon, PREPARATION FOR TRIAL (1963); S. Schweitzer, CYCLOPEDIA OF TRIAL PRACTICE, Vol. 1 (2d ed. 1970); J. Wigmore, EVIDENCE Vol. 3 (Chadbourn rev. ed. 1970); Belli, *An Introduction* to *Demonstrative Evidence,* 8 J. FORENSIC SCI. 355 (1963); Crocker, *Demonstrative Evidence Techniques,* 5 PRAC.LAW. 45 (Jan.1959); Gilbert, *Practical Problems in the Presentation of Evidence,* 28 F.R.D. 216 (1960); Hays, *Tactics in Direct Examination,* PLI, TRIAL TECHNIQUES LIBRARY (1966); Lay, *Mapping the Trial—Order of Proof,* 5 AM.JUR.TRIALS 505 (1966).

openers, refer to the day as well as the date—"Friday, September 17."
Better still:

Q: Did you hear your daughter testify in this matter?

A: Yes.

Q: Did you hear her say that when you returned home from work on Friday, September 17, you forced her into her bedroom and raped her?

A: Yes, I heard that.

Q: Did that happen?

A: No.

Q: What did happen when you returned home?

[Transitions can similarly be used to corroborate testimony.] . .
Assume you wish to develop several different points with a witness such as his relationship with the plaintiff, the plaintiff's physical abilities before the accident in question and his abilities after. Use transitions to make the testimony more clear:

"Mr. Witness, I would like to spend a few minutes with you discussing your relationship with Mr. Jones."

"Now, I would like to discuss Mr. Jone's physical condition prior to the accident."

Effective use of transitions, in addition to aiding the jury's understanding, can prune much irrelevant testimony. Suppose you have two pieces of evidence you wish to bring out with the witness:

1. That he saw the accident and also saw the Chevy run the red light;

2. That, when the ambulance arrived (20 minutes later), the witness heard the driver of the Chevy admit fault to the attendant.

After establishing the running of the red light and the ensuing crash, the beginning advocate, ever fearful of the dreaded leading question, will ask, "What, if anything, happened next?" With this question, it will take about ten minutes of irrelevant testimony to get to the point of the ambulance arriving. Instead, why not:

"Now, sometime after the crash, did an ambulance arrive?" Another approach to avoid the march through the irrelevancies is to advise the witness before trial that when you ask what happened after the crash he should relate the arrival of the ambulance.[54]

The references to other testimony, the connections created by transitions, and even the exclusion of irrelevancies are often neglected features of an effective examination.

---

54. K. Hegland, TRIAL AND PRACTICE SKILLS IN A NUTSHELL (unpublished draft, 1977). *See* pages 13–16 of the published version (West Publishing Company, 1978).

3. *Developing Examination Ideas*

All of this suggests that, given certain statements, documents, demonstrations and other evidence, one can begin to organize the case as a whole, dealing with difficult problems of what to include and exclude in an orderly way. But how can one be sure that all the available evidence is identified in the first instance? Is it enough to think in terms of whether the witnesses and topics corroborate each other or whether inconsistencies can be explained? How can one be sure that potential incongruities are even recognized? The following are some possible sources to which you might turn.

Sample Examinations

One possibility is to use transcripts of similar examinations and check-lists in thinking of examination ideas. These are readily available in the practice literature. Francis X. Busch, for example, offers sample examinations on the following topics:

> VERBATIM EXCERPTS FROM REPORTED DIRECT EXAMINATIONS
> OF WITNESSES .   .   .
>
> Specimen direct examination of witness to prove execution of a written contract.
>
> Specimen direct examination of witness testifying to an explosion.
>
> Specimen direct examination of a defendant indicted for murder.
>
> Specimen direct examination of a defendant in a murder case, where the plea was self-defense.
>
> Specimen direct examination to establish identity of defendant charged with knowingly passing a forged check.
>
> Specimen direct examination to refresh the memory of a witness.
>
> Specimen direct examination of identification and qualification of pieces of iron as real evidence.
>
> Specimen direct examination to identify and qualify photographs.
>
> Specimen direct examination of a witness who has unexpectedly proved hostile and given surprise testimony.[55]

Each of these examinations would be a source of ideas in structuring testimony in similar cases, and you will find such transcripts in numerous works on trial practice. Although no two cases are exactly alike, such models are very useful starting points for identifying and filling in possible gaps in testimony.

Narrative Sense

As we suggested earlier, the criteria generally applied to good fiction provide some preliminary standards for evaluating what needs to be done in preparing a direct examination. You have your own

55. F. X. Busch, LAW AND TACTICS
IN JURY TRIALS xvii (1949).

notions of what makes sense in a story line—what seems to be missing or incongruent. Take any piece of bad writing:

> Alfie raced up the stairs and burst in through the open door. "I've been accepted!" he cried. "I'll be going to law school in the fall!"
>
> "That's nice, dear," responded his mother, looking up.
>
> "Nice!" Alfie sputtered. "Nice! Is that all you can say?" He threw the letter onto the table where his mother was working and strode to the window, where he stood looking out. "Don't you realize how hard I've worked for this?"
>
> "You're not the only one!" His mother almost hissed the words. "You seem to forget that your father and I had something to do with it."
>
> Alfie turned on her. "Oh, sure," he snarled, brushing an invisible speck of dust off his sleeve, "It's all your doing. I didn't have anything to do with it."
>
> His mother stood up, pushing a strand of grey hair into place as she did. "I'm not going to stay here and take this abuse," she said. "I'll be in the kitchen when you're ready to apologize."
>
> Alfie felt a knot of pain in the pit of his stomach. He watched her walk across the room. "You're right, Mom," he said. "I'm sorry." She turned in the doorway, and the warmth of her smile made words of forgiveness unnecessary.

Think about what is wrong with this account. What makes it unconvincing? Our hunch is that similar criteria are applicable to any case. Or think about some occasion when you felt someone was lying, whether a witness encountered in your clinical work, a salesperson or someone else. What made you have doubts about that person's credibility? We all have ways of judging whether something we are told is true, and our own sense of what is "inherently" probable. If you apply these standards to the "story" you are putting together for trial, you will frequently find areas that need corroboration or further explanation.

Generative Questions

Finally, you might develop your own system of self-questioning. As you think through what all the witnesses have said to you and what all the documents, charts, and physical exhibits mean, you might ask some of the following questions:

—What theory of law do I want the decision-maker to accept?

—What theory of what occurred (or what was believed, felt, said, done) do I want to advance in support of this theory?

—What does this witness add to this factual picture?

—If what the witness says is true, what other details would be true?

—What aspects of the factual picture are inconsistent with what this witness says?

—What will opposing witnesses testify to? Can it be contradicted or explained by this witness?

To these would be added the sorts of "generic" questions suggested by Schwartz. The basic notion is that such inquiries trigger possibilities which help organize and give focus to an otherwise difficult task.

b. *Cross-Examination: Building Inconsistency*

GOLDSTEIN, THE CARDINAL PRINCIPLES OF CROSS–EXAMINATION

3 TRIAL LAWYERS GUIDE 331, 354–58, 380–83 (1959).

The cross-examination of every witness, at least the cross-examination of every important witness, should be planned in advance. The less experienced the trial lawyer, the more important becomes the preparation and the early planning of the cross-examination. The less the experience, the more detailed the planning of the cross-examination must be. The younger lawyer must realize that the more preliminary effort the less danger that he will forget some important subject matter during the stress and strain of the trial. He must be prepared to compensate for his lack of experience, his nervousness, and his inability to formulate the most effective forms of questions on the spur of the moment. He must realize that not only is the *form* of the question important, but the sequence also may be important. A full realization of these matters should convince him that it may be advisable to even write out the more important questions. He may want to do this to make certain that the questions and the answers will attain the results the lawyer hopes will come within the scope of the cardinal principles hereinafter set out. It must be understood that the form of the question frequently determines the results.

* * *

In planning cross-examination in advance, it is necessary to have several sheets of paper for use in apportioning your preparatory work within the framework of the purposes of cross-examination.

In blocking out a planned cross-examination, one of the blank sheets of paper should be headed *"Primary Purpose."* On this sheet should be listed all matters or subjects that the lawyer is certain the witness ordinarily must admit. These are the subjects and matters which tend to corroborate the trial lawyer's theory of the case. He may decide to complete each subject in sequence or he may decide to "jump around." Jumping around only can be done on the basis of a previously planned and prepared cross-examination. Thus the cross-examiner knows every moment just where he is going, what question and what subject he will cover next. There is no chance of forgetting or overlooking something vital and important. "Jumping around" for the inexperienced trial lawyer who has not planned and prepared his cross-examination in advance is fraught with danger. Generally, he should not attempt it.

Under "Primary Purpose" should be listed all admissions against interest and all documents to be used for this purpose. *All vital questions* should be written out in full. See that they do not violate the cardinal principle against "too broad a cross-examination" permitting possible harmful explanation.

Under the heading of *"Secondary Purpose"* on a separate blank sheet of paper list all items or information that tend to discredit the witness, such as

(1) Bias, prejudice, former convictions, bad reputation, interest in the outcome of the case, unusual compensation for testifying, relationship to party not disclosed on direct examination, etc.

(2) List all matters of impeachment by former oral contradictory statement, former written contradictory statement, former contradictory sworn testimony at coroner's inquests, and all court proceedings and hearings, former contradictory sworn statements in affidavits, applications, contradictory statements in sworn and unsworn pleadings, failure to talk or silence when the witness would be expected to speak out, etc.

It should be remembered that a foundation for impeachment must be laid on cross-examination for all witnesses not parties to the suit. The witnesses must be given an opportunity to admit, deny, or explain the apparent contradiction.

A third blank sheet of paper can be used to list the documents you require the witness to admit or to lay the foundation for their admission into evidence.

A well considered and well planned cross-examination prepared long in advance of the trial in the quiet of your office or your home will pay big dividends. The impromptu cross-examination by the inexperienced that is attempted under the stress and strain of the courtroom rarely produces results.

Illustration of a Planned Cross-Examination

Cornelius in "Cross-Examination of Witnesses," cites an instance of the method to be followed in planning cross-examination in advance in the following language:

"A careful study of the pleadings and a survey of the evidence which the adverse party will probably introduce in support of his contention almost invariably enables opposing counsel to forecast, with considerable accuracy, the trend which the testimony of the opposing witnesses will likely take. Thus in making a plan, counsel should prepare a statement of these probabilities which he may use advantageously as a foundation for the questioning of any number of adverse witnesses, provided they testify contrary to the probabilities thus worked out. For example, consider the following actual case:

"A. purchased an apartment house from an owner B. for $65,000 and paid $15,000 down, leaving a balance of $50,000 to be paid on the contract, at the rate of $600 per month.

"A. claimed that the owner B., from whom he purchased the property, misrepresented the facts in this transaction, in the following particulars:

"(a) That the rentals from this property of $700.00 per month had been reduced so that they were at absolute bed-rock at the time the transaction was closed and that all of the tenants were prompt in paying same, and that an expenditure of only about $300 *per annum* was required for heat.

"(b) That the owner represented that all of the apartments were in good repair as to decorations; that the buildings would easily carry the contract and pay for itself out of the rentals.

"A. purchased the property, entered into possession and discovered the following facts:

"1.   That it cost him $250 *per month* for heat.

"2.   That the tenants were not prompt in paying rent.

"3.   That heating plant required $500 repairs immediately.

"4.   That the property lacked approximately $300 *per month* of paying for itself from the rentals.

"A. brought suit for rescission against B. The defendant in his answer denied that he made any such representations as above set out.

"What, now, are the probabilities in this case? The lawyer for the plaintiff, in planning his cross-examination of the defendant and his witnesses, should reach the following conclusions respecting the same:

Statement of Probabilities
A. v. B.

"(1) A. as a purchaser would be vitally interested in knowing what income the apartment produced. B., the owner, had that information. A. did not. The probabilities, therefore, strongly support the contention of A. that he asked for this information. If B. had given him the actual facts he would have refused to purchase the property. So here again, the probabilities support A. that B. misrepresented the income.

"(2) Since heating costs of large apartment buildings vary widely, depending upon the efficiency of the heating plant as well as upon the construction of the building, the probabilities are strongly with A. when he stated that he asked B. what said cost would be and B. told him. If B. made any representations at all about the heating costs of the apartment, it would have to be a representation consistent with the purchase of the building by A. Had B. told the real facts, A. would not have purchased.

"(3) As to the condition of the interior decorations, the individual apartments being all rented, A. did not have access to them and he was compelled to depend on B. for information. Here again a true disclosure would, in all probability, have blocked the deal.

"(4) Since the tenants in the building were none of them prompt paying and since A. naturally would be interested in making inquiries as to their character, the probabilities are that A. did inquire and that B. concealed and misrepresented the real facts.

"Since one of the important objectives in cross-examination is to show that the witness is not testifying truthfully, one forceful method of doing this is to show the improbability of his story by emphasizing facts before the jury which render such story improbable. Counsel, therefore, cross-examined the defendant in this case as follows:

"Q. (Addressed to the defendant on the witness stand.) You, as the owner and operator of this property, knew the annual cost to heat this building?

"A. Yes, sir.

"Q. The heating costs of apartment buildings vary widely do they not, depending upon the condition and efficiency of the heating plant and the construction of the building?

"A. Yes, sir.

"Q. You had exact information as to what it cost to heat this building?

"A. Yes, sir.

"Q. Mr. A., your prospective purchaser, had no information as to what these costs were?

"A. No, sir.

"Q. And he, as a prospective purchaser of this building, would naturally be very much interested in knowing what these heating costs were?

"A. Yes, sir.

"Q. You were ready to answer his questions in this regard?

"A. Yes, sir.

"Q. And yet he asked you nothing about this important subject?

"A. No, sir.

"The same general line of questions were successfully applied to all the claimed misrepresentations in the foregoing statement of facts."

* * *

Cross-Examination as to Improbabilities

[What does this example suggest?]

In almost every case, in the eyes of the cross-examiner, at least one witness has testified to an unreasonable and improbable story. This is particularly true as to the opposing party—where it is a case of one man's word against the other. These situations emphasize the importance of the trial lawyer having a good working knowledge of cross-examinations as to improbabilities. He must know the various instances where it has been used and where it can be used. Pointing out the inherent improbabilities and the unreasonableness of the story told by the witness in his examination-in-chief is the basic aim of such a cross-examination. In the instances of testing the recollection of the witness—in showing that he should not be believed—that it is unreasonable to believe that he could have recalled all that he claims—a knowledge of cross-examination as to improbabilities is an absolute necessity. Proving false the testimony of the alibi witness and proving false representations and statements may be done by this type of cross-examination. Disproving claims that certain things or events took place or that certain happenings were seen or heard also may be shown or proved by cross-examination as to improbabilities.

The success of this type of cross-examination is usually founded on thorough prior investigation, study and analysis of the evidence— the frequently quoted "mastery of the facts."

—Planning the Cross-Examination as to Improbabilities

It is always advisable to plan this particular type of cross-examination in advance. For an illustration of this see the method referred to in the prior section . . . .

—Increasing the Improbabilities

One of the basic things that tends to help a cross-examiner in this type of cross-examination to prove that a witness' story is unreasonable and improbable is to increase the improbabilities. Preliminarily increasing the improbabilities will help to shake the belief of the court and jury in the testimony of the witness. In many instances there are a number of preliminary questions that a cross-examiner may use to accomplish this purpose:

(1) Have you talked to anyone about this case?

(2) With whom?

(3) When did you talk with him?

(4) Where did you talk with him?

(5) Who was present on that occasion?

(6) That was when you learned that you were to be a witness in the case?

(7) At the time of this occurrence you did not know that there would be a lawsuit concerning it, is that correct? (This question generally is used in contract cases.)

—Increasing the Improbabilities—"Have You Talked to Anyone About this Case?"

In a cross-examination as to improbabilities, this question is not used in the same light or with the same purpose as is the question referred to above, "To whom have you talked about the case?" Under increasing the improbabilities, this question is used to launch the series of questions listed in the preceding section. In utilizing this question for this purpose it is necessary to keep in mind that in most cases opposing counsel has warned the witness to answer this question truthfully and to admit that he has talked to the lawyer for the other side. If the witness does not admit it, advantage may be taken of the fact in the closing argument as illustrated in the section headed "To whom have you talked about the case?"

—Increasing the Improbabilities—"When Did You Talk with Him?"

This question should follow the answer of the witness that "I talked with Mr. Jones, the attorney." It is important to ascertain and fix the time for the record and as a basis for later argument to the jury. The improbabilities will be increased in proportion to the recentness of the talk. If, as assumed, many lawyers delay talking to their witnesses until just before the trial, particularly in contract cases, the answer of the witness that he talked to the lawyer "last week" or "two weeks ago" would have some psychological effect in those jurisdictions where the courts are three, four or more years behind in their trial calendars. There is far more chance that jurors will doubt the statements of witnesses who remember minute details of happenings, or conversations which took place a long time before trial. This is more true when the whole series of suggested questions are used. The more you can increase the improbabilities before attacking the main story of the witness the more you increase the possibilities of success in your cross-examination.

It is, therefore, important to fix the time of the "talk" between the witness and the opposing counsel as near to the time of trial as possible.

—Increasing the Improbabilities—"Where Did the Conversation Take Place?" "Who was Present?"

These two questions, when answered, may give you additional leads for further cross-examination and additional facts to argue to the jury as to why the witness should not be believed. If he admits that the conference included other witnesses at the same time it may be the "cue" for use of some of the other cardinal principles of cross-examination. It may be the basis for testing for identical stories told by the witnesses; it may indicate to the jury inordinate "coaching."

—Increasing the Improbabilities—"That Was When You Learned You Were to Be a Witness in the Case?"

If the answers to the prior questions, plus your preliminary investigation shows that opposing counsel had interviewed the particular witness only a week or two before the trial, the answer to the question "That was when you learned you were to be a witness in the case?" might indicate that the witness had not expected to be called. It also might indicate that this was the first time that he knew he was to be a witness in the case. This may lead the jurors to view his testimony with some degree of skepticism.

While in the average personal injury case a person witnessing the occurrence might expect to be called as a witness, this might not be true in many contract cases. If there has been laxity in early investigation in a personal injury case this may give rise also to a long delay in interviewing witnesses. This definitely would indicate the necessity of asking the witness "That is when you learned you were to be a witness in this case, is that right?"

—Increasing the Improbabilities—"At the Time of this Occurrence You Did Not Know There Would Be a Lawsuit Concerning It, Is that Correct?"

Basically, this question is used in contract cases. While as stated, it is natural to assume that those who witness accidents must realize the possibility of their being called to court to give testimony concerning what they witnessed, yet, in contract cases where the objective is to test the recollection of the witnesses, etc., it is possible to use this question to good effect.

HEGLAND, TRIAL AND PRACTICE SKILLS IN A NUTSHELL

(Unpublished draft, 1977).*

The essential question is not whether the witness has hurt you but whether you can do anything about it. Unless you have a theory of

* *See* pages 55–63 of the published version (West Publishing Company, 1978).

attack, your cross will simply result in the witness retelling the story and in the growing conviction of all that you cannot break it. Best to take your lumps sitting down.

The ideal attack is two prong: first, showing that the witness is wrong and second, showing why he is wrong—the jury should be shown not only why the story of the witness is incredible but also why it is that the witness apparently believes it. Of course, in many situations you will be able to develop only one line of attack. You may be unable, for example, to shake the alibi the witness has given the defendant—you would still be well advised to ask "Now, isn't it true that you are the defendant's mother?"

1.   Showing the Error: Attacking the Testimony

No work of this nature is worth its salt without a heuristic model showing, hopefully, an analytical schema. Hence:

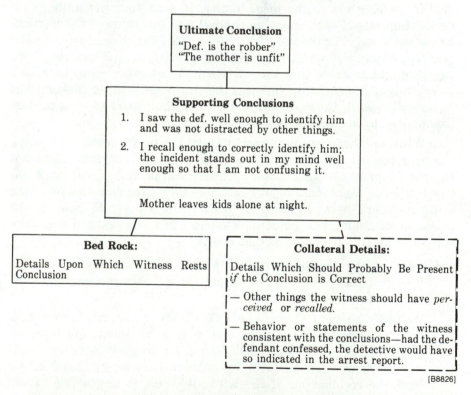

Ultimate Conclusion

"Def. is the robber"
"The mother is unfit"

Supporting Conclusions

1. I saw the def. well enough to identify him and was not distracted by other things.

2. I recall enough to correctly identify him; the incident stands out in my mind well enough so that I am not confusing it.

Mother leaves kids alone at night.

Bed Rock:

Details Upon Which Witness Rests Conclusion

Collateral Details:

Details Which Should Probably Be Present *if* the Conclusion is Correct

— Other things the witness should have *perceived* or *recalled*.

— Behavior or statements of the witness consistent with the conclusions—had the defendant confessed, the detective would have so indicated in the arrest report.

[B8826]

In cross examining a witness, forget frontal attacks on the conclusions—how many times, since your birth, have you admitted error? The attack must be on the supporting detail and the method will vary depending on whether you focus on "bedrock" or, for the lack of a better phrase, "collateral detail".

Collateral detail. "If the witness saw the accident well enough to testify as he did, what else would he have seen? "If the crime happened the way the witness claims, what would the witness likely have done immediately after it?" By using the hypothetical, you theorize the details which would be present if the witness' conclusion is correct. Your cross is now designed to show that the details do not exist —your argument will be that the conclusion is hence erroneous. Obviously, if the witness knows what you are about, the details will most likely line up to support the conclusion. Thus, your method must be somewhat devious: *close the doors* on the witness and try not to tip your hand. The witness should not know why you are asking the questions. Your tone should not be accusatory as this will simply alert the witness of the danger ahead.

Bedrock detail. Here the method is dogged persistence. It is a more frontal attack as it begins by asking the witness upon what he bases his conclusion. For example, a welfare worker testifies that the mother is "unfit": ask the reasons. The response will likely be another conclusion: "She doesn't take care of her child" which in turn, rests on another "She often leaves the child alone at night." Your job is to get to bedrock:

"Her neighbor told me she has left the child on two occasions during the last month." * It is only by getting to bedrock that you can hope to shake the superstructure. The argument will be, of course, that the witness improperly jumped to the conclusion, that there are simply not enough hard facts to support it. The danger, of course, is that your questioning may unearth granite. So be it.

In seeking bedrock, are you not asking the dreaded "why" question? Aren't you risking the murderous "unknown answer"? Yes. But, what then of the commandments? Scrapped. If the witness killed you—testified your client is unfit or that the fingerprints found on the gun are his—what further damage can be done? Additionally, assuming your opponent competent, you may not have too much to fear from the "why" question or from the unknown answer. A competent opponent, on direct, will have attempted to bolster the witness' conclusions as much as he can: if the welfare worker is partially basing the unfitness conclusion on the mother's long history of infanticides, probably this would have been brought out on direct. Unless, of course, your cagey opponent was laying a trap for you—in which case you should kill him.

Despite the obvious soundness of this analysis, experienced practitioners warn against "why" questions and questions you do not know the answer to. So, use them only if there appears no other way.

A related way to attack the professional "conclusion maker"— welfare worker, police chemist, experts in general—is to establish

* Before attacking one of the supports of the conclusion, be sure you have committed the witness to listing them all. Otherwise, the witness, realizing after the attack that the one support is insufficient, will likely fudge another— "She is also unfit because she drinks." The proper procedure is, at the offset, to ask "are there any other reasons?"

all the things they could have done to reach their conclusion but didn't do. What tests were not run, which neighbors were not talked to? Here, the argument is that the witness asks us to believe a certain conclusion—too bad more was not done so we could really be sure.

2. Explaining the Error: Attacking the Witness

The fact that someone has got up and sworn to a certain state of affairs is something to be reckoned with. Even though the story is incredible, it must be true because the witness believes it. Attempt to suggest the source of error.

It may be the witness is lying. If so, is there a sufficient motive? More probably, the witness is mistaken. There are several sources of error. As to the eyewitness, did the physical setting, such as shadows or movement, cause misperception? Did the witness' mental state—confusion, distraction, fear? Was the event distinct enough to be recalled uniquely or is there a probability that details of similar or routine events are spilling over? And, of course, people tend to see and recall what they wish. Hence, the relevance of bias, interest, prejudice. (Prosecutors to the contrary, police have an interest in the outcome of a trial—they made the arrest after all and their job is to arrest the guilty, not the innocent. Additionally, there is possible tort liability.) People may also fill in missing details, either because of a desire to present a total story or because of the suggestions of other witnesses with whom they have spoken. There are several excellent works on the sources of human error which you may wish to consult. But, be aware that the jury will ask, "If the witness is wrong, what explains the error?"

3. Asking Questions When You Know the Witness Will Answer "No"

Thus far, we have been viewing cross as a device to develop evidence—getting the witness to testify to facts favorable to your side or to admit facts which undercut the harm he did you on direct. Some students think that this is the only function of cross and hence, do not ask questions when they know the witness will answer "no". An example.

The victim of the crime has just finished direct. Your theory of defense is that the victim made the whole thing up because he hates your client. After you have attempted to show the inconsistencies in the story and after you have attempted to show the bias, should you ask on cross "Now isn't it a fact that you made this whole thing up because you hate my client?"

Some students will say "No—surely the witness won't admit it." But, the question has other justifications. First of all, it signals the jury that you do not accept the testimony and alerts it to your theory of the case. Second of all, it allows you to directly confront the witness with your theory. If you do not confront the witness but rather simply call your own witnesses to prove the accusation, then the jury may feel you have unfairly treated the witness. There is something about making accusations to one's face.

——————

NOTES

1. *Developing Cross-Examination Ideas: The Search for Inconsistency*

In thinking through what topics ought to be included in a cross-examination, you might begin by comparing these excerpts with Schwartz's comments on direct. Are the processes they discuss very different? Would it be meaningful to speak of cross-examination as weaving together threads of testimony?

Despite their different formulations, our own view is that the two perspectives are very similar. The cross-examiner who wants to elicit testimony which corroborates or credits aspects of his or her own case must think in terms of the same connections which are relevant on direct. Indeed, many lawyers consider the development of corroborative material on cross-examination its most important function: in so far as closing argument can be punctuated by references to what "counsel's own witness" or the adverse party said, it is bound to be more effective.

Even when counsel is seeking to discredit the witness, to contradict another witness' testimony, or to show how the witness' testimony supports contrary inferences, the process of pattern building is close to what Schwartz describes. The "threads" in these instances, however, are designed to lead the hearer to a belief or attitude *contrary* to the propositions being advanced by the witness. The witness implicitly asserts that he or she is sincere, careful, and accurate. The cross-examiner seeks to elicit testimony that the opposite is more probable. The witness asserts that X or Y is true and significant; the efforts of the cross-examiner are directed to establishing the falsity or insignificance of these propositions. In pursuing these goals, however, the same attention must be paid to such factors as unity, coherence, emphasis, plausibility and completeness. What the cross-examiner argues through questions and answers, even when cross-examination seeks only to raise doubts, must make sense. The examination must have a purpose: a set of attitudes and ideas that counsel wants the audience to accept.

Almost every commentator on this aspect of trial practice has emphasized the importance of planning around such objectives. The following is an example:

It might seem unnecessary, in a work designed for the use of law students and counsel, to discuss the objects of cross-examination. Those who undertake to cross-examine, it might be thought, will at any rate know what they are about. But experience shows that often they do not. Nor, indeed, are the efforts of those who stand up and question witnesses without any clear appreciation of their aims always unsuccessful. Luck plays a part in cross-examination, as in so many other human activities. But it is the mark of the competent cross-examiner that he creates the situations in which openings and advantages, which may appear to be fortuitous, are likely to come his way. And when they do, he makes skilful use of them. If he is to do these things, it is well that he should be clear about his aims.

* * *

The process is commonly thought of as one designed to expose the witness who is deliberately lying, and indeed it is that. But no less important is the achievement of counsel who demonstrates, by cross-examination, that a witness has been mistaken on one or more of the points in his evidence, or that he is biased, or otherwise unworthy of credence, or that material points have been omitted, or inadequately stressed, in the evidence in chief. And even when a cross-examination does not succeed in demonstrating matters of this kind, it is helpful if it reveals the probability (or sometimes even the possibility) that they exist. Courts work on probabilities of various degrees when certainty cannot be achieved; and although destruction of the evidence in chief constitutes success, a cross-examination may be equally valuable if it does no more than raise doubts about the reliability of the witness, or the accuracy of his evidence on a material point or points.[56]

In concrete terms, this objective requires that you know (and be able to articulate) the specific proposition (inference) you want the hearer to draw from the witness' testimony. It entails having a clear idea of what sort of answers are wanted, what contentions they would support (the witness lied, the witness was mistaken), and how they would be rebutted. What you are looking for is the "right question to weaken or destroy what the witness said." Generally it involves a "series of questions which lead up to the . . . question from which you seek a certain answer . . . . [I]n cross-examination all questions asked constitute a series . . . leading up to the one that does the damage."[57]

The problem, of course, is that it is extremely difficult to develop such ideas in the context of a specific case. How does one determine what lines of impeachment are available or whether they would be effective? Many of our students tell us that they just don't think of as many ways to challenge a witness' testimony as do more experienced lawyers. They find little solace in being told that knowing what to pursue on cross-examination is an art.

As with direct examination, there are a number of ways to approach this dilemma. To begin with, there are again the common sense ideas one has about what facts, motives, and themes fit in a

56. G. Colman, CROSS-EXAMINA-TION: A PRACTICAL HANDBOOK 3–5 (1970).

57. L. Lake, HOW TO CROSS-EX-AMINE WITNESSES SUCCESSFUL-LY 5 (2d ed. 1966).

given fact pattern. As you construct your own version of the facts, incongruities and inconsistencies in your opponent's case readily suggest themselves. What is important is to ask yourself how such incongruities can be explained. Which must be accepted as true? Which need to be challenged directly? Which can be turned in ways that are supportive of your own case? Consider, for example, the following analysis of potential lines of cross-examination of a doctor in a negligence action:

> Proper preparation will give you a critical approach to the expert's opinion. Are his conclusions in accord with recognized authority? Do they find support in the medical data at hand? In arriving at his diagnosis has he performed all the standard diagnostic tests?

> Let us list some opinions commonly given in court by defense doctors and point out the possible defect in such opinion.

The doctor says:	*The defect in his opinion:*
There is nothing wrong with the plaintiff because his symptoms are purely subjective.	But subjective symptoms are medically recognized as indicative of pathology and in many instances constitute the sole basis for the diagnosis.
That the general physical condition of the plaintiff, as shown by examination, prostatic smears, blood count, congenital anomalies and so on, could account for his present complaints.	But plaintiff had no such symptoms before the accident and it is fair to assume that the accident either caused them, exacerbated a quiescent condition, or aggravated a pre-existing condition.
That the neurological examination was negative.	But the doctor has failed to perform certain tests which are recognized as part of a standard neurological examination.
That since the X rays show perfect repair of the fracture, there are no permanent effects.	But the X rays do not show the condition of the nerves, ligaments, and surrounding soft tissue.
That, in a fracture case, since the bones have knit well and there is good union, the patient has been restored to status quo.	But that does not mean that the nerves, muscles, and ligaments are in status quo. There is frequently a permanent loss of power and function.
That there is no permanent injury to the plaintiff's brain.	But no brain wave study (electroencephalogram) was made, and if made, might have detected certain brain damage.[58]

58. E. Low, HOW TO PREPARE AND TRY A NEGLIGENCE CASE 172–73 (1957).

Each of these lines of inquiry represents possible defects in the anticipated testimony based on counsel's knowledge of the case and its details, and the sorts of weaknesses testimony of this nature typically entails. George Colman describes this process in more general terms:

The most useful type of planning for the cross-examination of a specific witness should follow upon an imaginative effort by counsel. He should visualize himself in the shoes of the witness (as the threadbare metaphor goes) and tread the witness's path through the events relevant to the case, as also through his contemplated cross-examination as it begins to take shape in counsel's mind. At every step counsel should ask himself:

'If his story is true, what would he have done at this stage'?

or

'Why did he do that (or say that)'?

Through this often painful exercise of the imagination counsel may well come upon improbabilities or inconsistencies in the known conduct of the witness, and he will note them as the basis for lines of cross-examination. Or, if no such openings reveal themselves to him, he may think of questions designed to test the conduct and motives of the witness against what could have been expected if his evidence were reliable. From the mental process described there will emerge the raw material of cross-examination in the form of such rough notes as these:

If you really thought he was dishonest, why leave him in charge during May?

Did you report it to the police?

Why didn't you scream?

If you knew all that, why was the item posted to a suspense account?

Had you ever been there before?

    (1) What was your financial position then?

    (2) Anyone you could have borrowed from?

    (3) Wife and how many children?

    (4) How could you take the risk?

Did you have a brief-case?

If that was what you thought, why no X-rays?

    (1) When first suspect?

    (2) What steps taken?

The search is for weaknesses in the version given by the witness, or in the character or reliability of the witness himself. If none are manifest, the search is for methods of exposing them, if they exist.[59]

Needless to say, projecting oneself into both the past (what really occurred) and the future (what the witness will probably say) is no

---

59. G. Colman, *supra* note 56 at 39–40.

mean feat.   Nevertheless, it is only out of this sort of analysis that the specific lines of examination can be generated.

A second and related approach to generating cross-examination ideas is to turn to the work of other lawyers.   Francis X. Busch, whose list of "specimen" direct examinations appears above, also discusses the handling of a variety of cross-examination situations:

> Cross-examination to show interest, motive or corrupt disposition of a witness ....
> Cross-examination to show relationship of witness to a party ....
> Cross-examination of witnesses who have a special relationship to the case ....
> Cross-examination of a witness to show friendship or hostility ....
> Impeachment; right of cross-examination as to previous contradictory statements ....
> Cross-examination as to previous contradictory statements; instruments of impeachment ....
> Cross-examination as to previous contradictory statements; laying foundation for impeachment ....
> Cross-examination as to previous contradictory statements; effect of admission or denial ....
> Cross-examination as to previous contradictory statements; where the witness is a party ....
> Cross-examination as to previous contradictory statements; where a witness testified to material facts omitted from his former testimony ....
> Cross-examination as to previous contradictory statements; practical observations as to the most effective use of such material ....
> Cross-examination of a witness called to impeach a previous witness ...
> Suiting the style of cross-examination to the particular witness ....
> Cross-examination of the stupid witness of poor perception ....
> Cross-examination of the timid and hesitant witness ....
> Cross-examination of the evasive witness ....
> Cross-examination of the flippant, "smart-aleck" witness ....
> Cross-examination to develop that a witness has been coached to recite a prepared story ....
> Cross-examination of the dishonest witness ....
> Cross-examination as to identity ....
> Cross-examination of the alibi witness ....
> Cross-examination of a witness who has testified to a previous witness' reputation .... [60]

Here, as elsewhere in lawyering, our experience is that such lists can be extremely useful.   For those who are inexperienced and have little knowledge of typical patterns, such formulations help to trigger ideas and identify areas that need further investigation.

Finally, additional cross-examination ideas can be developed by working through possible cross-examination objectives.   Schwartz

---

60.   F. X. Busch, *supra* note 55 at xi (1949).

offers one example of this approach. He identifies six "points of vulnerability" for cross-examination, similar to his "generic questions" on direct. These points are (i) knowledge, (ii) recollection, (iii) perceptions, (iv) actions, (v) state of mind, and (vi) opinions. In each of these areas he specifies particular cross-examination objectives:

(i) If the cross-examiner feels that the witness is qualified and *does* possess the knowledge he professes, it would be foolhardy to cross-examine him on this score. Instead, the cross-examiner may be able to make use of the witness' knowledge by inducing him to testify as to his knowledge of other facts which would be favorable to the cross-examiner's client.

* * *

(ii) The objectives, when cross-examining as to recollection, are to show:

- Circumstances negating recollection.
- Limitations on the witness' ability to recall.
- Lack of credibility as to the alleged recollection.
- Inability to recall collateral details.

* * *

(iii) The most telling testimony is usually that dealing with what the witness personally saw or heard, *i. e.,* his perceptions; and the outcome of the trial will often depend upon whether or not the witness can be successfully attacked on this score and the effect of his testimony weakened or destroyed. There are four main approaches to such a cross-examination: . . .

- Exposing limitations in the perceptive powers of the witness.
- The surrounding circumstances which adversely affect perception.
- Details of what was allegedly perceived.
- The insidious effects of bias and lack of credibility.

* * *

(iv) If the witness has testified that he did a certain act, it is hardly to be expected that he will admit that his testimony is false as a result of a direct, frontal attack by the cross-examiner. The best hope lies, not in questioning the act itself, but rather in probing into the details of how it was allegedly done and as to the circumstances surrounding its performance, both with the following objectives in mind:

- To elicit undisclosed details favoring the cross-examiner.
- To demonstrate that the witness lacked capacity, means, or opportunity to act as claimed.
- That the details testified to are improbable or impossible.
- Other acts, statements, reasons, or motives which contradict or indicate contrary actions.

* * *

(v) Cross-examination as to State of Mind is applicable to every witness irrespective of the nature of his testimony. The cross-examiner has a right to probe into any subjective feelings on the part of the witness which may affect his desire or ability to tell the truth, as this will affect the weight of every word he has uttered.

Because testimony as to State of Mind is subjective, the only hope of undermining it is by concentrating on matters which might cast doubt upon the witness' assertions. The objectives of the cross-examiner are:

- To have the witness acknowledge facts about his background and antecedents which reflect upon his credibility.
- To elicit prior statements or conduct which contradict his testimony.
- To reveal any interest, bias, or prejudice which might motivate the witness and vitiate his testimony.
- To demonstrate the inherent improbability or falsity of the testimony.

* * *

(vi) There is very little that can be done to demonstrate that the witness does not, in fact, hold the opinion he has expressed. What may be attempted is to expose any weaknesses in the foundation upon which the opinion rests. The objective in cross-examining is to demonstrate that the opinion is entitled to little weight because:

- The witness is limited as to his qualifications, knowledge and experience;
- The factual basis for the opinion is unsound;
- The hypothetical assumptions are incomplete and inadequate;
- Hidden motivations exist.[61]

Each of these "objectives" suggests lines which a cross-examiner can explore.

2. A Suggested Schema

Whichever of the above approaches (or any others) you use, you will have to begin with the witness' expected testimony on direct. Then, with as clear and detailed an idea as possible of what the witness will (probably) say, you ask the following questions:

1. Can I bring out any facts which the witness is likely to concede which contribute to or corroborate my theory of the case (or undermine the adversary's theory of the case)?

2. Can I bring out any facts which the witness is likely to concede which tend to discredit or contradict his or her testimony?

3. Can I bring out any facts which the witness is likely to deny or distort which, when contrasted with other facts in the case tend to discredit or contradict his or her testimony?

61. L. Schwartz, PROOF, PERSUA-
SION AND CROSS-EXAMINATION
1605–06, 1803, 1703, 1910, 2003, 2205,
2103 (1973).

4. Can I bring out any facts concerning the attitudes, capacities, and beliefs of the witness which tend to discredit or contradict his or her testimony?

Facts, as used here, include omissions and commissions, specifics (I did X) and characterizations (I was uncertain). In simplified form, this approach might be represented on the following matrix:

FEATURES OF WITNESS' TESTIMONY	LINES OF EXAMINATION			
	Likely Concessions Supportive of Examiner's Theory of the Case	Likely Concessions Unfavorable to Witness	Potential Contrasts	Potential Demonstrations at Trial
Conduct of the witness (things done and observed	Witness didn't call police/gave a description to police that didn't fit defendant	Witness tried to avoid testifying/many inconsistencies in subsequent versions of events	Witness will claim X was there/X can be shown to have been elsewhere	Witness can be shown to use a particular vocabulary which matches out-of-court statements he denies
Capacities of the witness (ability to perceive, know, communicate about)	Witness didn't have eyeglasses on at the time	Witness had no reason for remembering a particular date which he claims on an earlier occasion that he recalled	Witness will claim he was able to see X from window/can be shown that angle of vision and obstructions made this impossible	Witness can be shown to be very near-sighted
Character and motives of the witness (interest, bias, involvement)	Police said they had the man	Witness is a relative of the victim/has a criminal record	Witness will claim he has been made no promises to testify. He told Y he "had to burn the defendant to save his own skin"	Witness can be shown to be willing to lie if pressed with an inconsistency

[B8827]

The potential lines of examination involve the following inquiries.

Concessions Supportive of the Examiner's Theory of the Case

Inquiries in this area involve asking yourself what you might seek to establish through the witness if you called him or her in your own case. Because of the control which cross-examination offers, there is almost always an opportunity to bring out some corroborating or crediting material from the witnesses of one's adversary, and the source of such testimony makes it particularly credible (*e. g.*, "As you have heard from defendant's own expert, the specialist who examined the plaintiff and testified here is nationally recognized as the leader in his field . . ."). Often this involves simply translating basic contentions into question form (*e. g.*, "Even if what you say is true, _____ is just as likely, isn't it?"). Or it may simply require bringing out material the witness has omitted.

Concessions Likely to Weaken or Discredit the Witness' Testimony

This inquiry also centers on matters the witness is likely to admit. The emphasis, however, is on the accuracy and completeness of the testimony on direct rather than inferences directly supporting the examiner's case.   Thus an apparently disinterested witness can be shown to be a close friend or relative of the party for whom he or she appears, or to have a reason for testifying *against* the party represented by the examiner.   What counsel is working with here are facts from which unfavorable inferences may be drawn, which the witness either cannot deny, or could deny only with some embarrassment or the likelihood of being contradicted.   There are many examples of this type of examination; nearly all doctors will acknowledge the possibility of error in a diagnosis, and most bus drivers will concede that their driving records are an important concern.   Indeed, common weaknesses in testimony—*e. g.*, gaps filled in by inference or imagination, statements not made on the basis of personal knowledge, distortions produced by bias, or judgments made without full knowledge—will often be acknowledged by a truthful witness carefully brought to a realization of these problems.

Potential Contrasts

In this area of questioning it is expected that the witness will "stick to his or her story."   The strategy, then, is to encourage exaggerations, overstatement and even denials.   In rhetorical terms the examiner's argument is built not on inferences drawn directly from what the witness says, but on the contrasts between what the witness testifies to and some other evidence in the case.   This seems to us to be at the root of what Goldstein refers to as creating "improbabilities."   The improbabilities are inferred from comparisons of the witness' testimony with (i) physical facts; (ii) common understandings of how people behave or how events take place; (iii) standards agreed on by the witness or testified to by another qualified witness (*e. g.*, proper medical practice); (iv) other things done, said, or observed by the witness; and (v) things done, said, or observed by other witnesses.   There is, of course, an overlap here with other lines of inquiry: a prior inconsistent statement, for example, is an impeaching fact which the witness is likely to admit.   In this category, however, we are interested in the problem of preparing a cross-examination which sets up contrasts of which the witness is unaware, or which works with the refusal of the witness to concede the matter in issue.   One of the most famous examples of this sort of examination is drawn from a murder trial in which the accused was represented by Abraham Lincoln:

> "The mother of the accused, after failing to secure older counsel, finally engaged young Abraham Lincoln, as he was then called, and the trial came on to an early hearing.   No objection was made to the jury, and no cross-examination of witnesses, save the last and only important one, who swore that he knew the parties, saw the shot fired by Grayson, saw him run away, and picked up the deceased, who died instantly.

"The evidence of guilt and identity was morally certain. The attendence was large, the interest intense. Grayson's mother began to wonder why 'Abraham remained silent so long and why he didn't do something!' The people finally rested. The tall lawyer (Lincoln) stood up and eyed the strong witness in silence, without books or notes, and slowly began his defence by these questions:

"*Lincoln.* 'And you were with Lockwood just before and saw the shooting?'

"*Witness.* 'Yes.'

"*Lincoln.* 'And you stood very near to them?'

"*Witness.* 'No, about twenty feet away.'

"*Lincoln.* 'May it not have been *ten* feet?'

"*Witness.* 'No, it was twenty feet *or more*.'

"*Lincoln.* 'In the open field?'

"*Witness.* 'No, in the timber.'

"*Lincoln.* 'What kind of timber?'

"*Witness.* 'Beech timber.'

"*Lincoln.* 'Leaves on it are rather thick in August?'

"*Witness.* 'Rather.'

"*Lincoln.* 'And you think *this* pistol was the one used?'

"*Witness.* 'It looks like it.'

"*Lincoln.* 'You could see defendant shoot—see how the barrel hung, and all about it?'

"*Witness.* 'Yes.'

"*Lincoln.* 'How near was this to the meeting place?'

"*Witness.* 'Three-quarters of a mile away.'

"*Lincoln.* 'Where were the lights?'

"*Witness.* 'Up by the minister's stand.'

"*Lincoln.* 'Three-quarters of a mile away?'

"*Witness.* 'Yes,—I answered ye *twiste*.'

"*Lincoln.* 'Did you not see a candle there, with Lockwood or Grayson?'

"*Witness.* 'No! what would we want a candle for?'

"*Lincoln.* 'How then, did you see the shooting?'

"*Witness.* 'By moonlight!' (defiantly).

"*Lincoln.* 'You saw this shooting at ten at night—in beech timber, three-quarters of a mile from the light—saw the pistol barrel—saw the man fire—saw it twenty feet away—saw it all by moonlight? Saw it nearly a mile from the camp lights?'

"*Witness.* 'Yes, I told you so before.'

"The interest was now so intense that men leaned forward to catch the smallest syllable. Then the lawyer drew out a blue covered almanac from his side coat pocket—opened it slowly—offered it in evidence—

showed it to the jury and the court—read from a page with careful deliberation that the moon on that night was unseen and only arose at *one* the next morning.

"Following this climax Mr. Lincoln moved the arrest of the perjured witness as the real murderer, saying: 'Nothing but *a motive to clear himself* could have induced him to swear away so falsely the life of one who never did him harm!' With such determined emphasis did Lincoln present his showing that the court ordered Sovine arrested, and under the strain of excitement he broke down and confessed to being the one who fired the fatal shot himself, but denied it was intentional." [62]

In this category also fall those lines of inquiry in which counsel, by tone of voice or manner, invites a denial of facts which he or she can readily contradict. "You didn't talk to anyone about this case, did you?" or "Didn't you make a statement to the police?" are designed to generate an assertion which, when contrasted with other evidence, can be shown to be improbable or untrue.

Note that in Lincoln's cross-examination the impact would have been lost if the witness had been helpful, or more equivocal, or less positive about some of the details. The witness could have seen the incident whether or not there was a moon, just as a witness can truthfully describe an accident without being sure of every detail. The same is true of prior inconsistent statements or actions. If a witness says, "Yes, I did do that . . ." or, "Yes, I said that, but there was such and such a reason . . ." the effective inferences counsel can draw from such testimony are significantly limited. If you are to rely on contrasts and contradictions as the basis for challenging a witness' testimony (as distinguished from merely eliciting impeaching facts), you must also learn to foreclose opportunities for qualifying the helpful statement or explaining away the potential contradiction. The object is to elicit unequivocal statements from the witness which are apparently damaging to the examiner's case, but which can afterward be exposed as untrue or distorted. There is no aspect of the cross-examiner's task more difficult and more fraught with dangers.

Potential Demonstrations of Unreliability at Trial

Finally, the cross-examiner can focus on exposing characteristics or traits of the witness in the nature and manner of the testimony itself, which will bear on the credibility of all that witness' testimony. If a witness can be shown to be biased, prejudiced, emotionally involved, arrogant, or possessed of some other undesirable trait, his or her testimony is, of course, far less likely to be credited by the jury. It is this premise which underlies attempts to bait witnesses

62. F. Wellman, THE ART OF CROSS–EXAMINATION 74–75 (1903; Collier Books ed. 1962).

on cross-examination, to get them angry or to so exhaust them that they are no longer careful in the way they present themselves. Similarly, if the witness can be shown to be unable to do what he or she claims to have done on an earlier occasion, a strong case can be made against the truthfulness of the witness' testimony. Thus a witness who claims to have a clear memory of specific events occurring some months earlier can be shown to have no recollection at all of contemporaneous events. Or a witness who claims to have perceived fine distinctions in appearance, or to have stood a specific distance from events to which he or she testifies, can be shown to have faulty perceptions, or to be a poor judge of distance. In each instance the witness' performance on the witness stand is shown to be inconsistent with his or her claimed capacity or attitude. Although there are risks in such inquiries, they are certainly worth considering in the initial stages of preparation.

Will these suggestions generate cross-examination ideas in particular cases? We are not sure. Our own experience suggests that some combination of conscious self-questioning and the use of checklists makes some difference. But the feeling of not being able to see all the available paths will probably remain with you for some time.

———

3. *Lines of Inquiry at Trial*

An even more complex problem of assessing and shaping potential lines of examination relates to what has been described as "unarmed combat." In such circumstances:

> .   .   . [C]ounsel approaches his task unaided by any material. There are no documents which conflict with what the witness is deposing to; there are no tangible objects to contradict or throw doubt on his evidence in chief; and there are no other witnesses who will contradict him, or none whose evidence will necessarily be accepted in preference to his; counsel has nothing upon which to attack the character of the witness, and nothing which proves that he is biased. Yet it is necessary to destroy or weaken the testimony of the witness, if that is possible by legitimate means.   .   .   .
>
> Counsel's task, in the situation postulated, is to create his material out of the witness's own mouth; and in order to do that, he will have to be alert for weaknesses both in the substance of the testimony and in the manner in which it is given.[63]

What these circumstances require is an immediate assessment of potential discrepancies in the witness' testimony, as well as the likely effect of particular questions on both the witness and the judge or jury hearing the case. It is no wonder such judgments are considered a matter of art and not often discussed in terms of preparation.

---

63. G. Colman, *supra* note 56 at 61.

Nevertheless, in this situation as well there are possible patterns and clues to be looked for. That is, one can do some preparing, even for the unexpected. The following represent a few general approaches to this problem.

Building Consistencies

There is almost always some favorable testimony that can be elicited from any witness. Consider, for example, the following:

> *Q.* Following the accident a police radio car arrived at the scene, isn't that correct?
>
> *A.* Yes, sir.
>
> *Q.* Did you give your name and address to the police officer?
>
> *A.* Yes, sir, I did.
>
> *Q.* Wasn't there another man who had been standing near you on the same corner who likewise gave his name and address to the police officer?
>
> *A.* Yes, there was.
>
> *Q.* Do you recall his name?
>
> *A.* This was three years ago. I can't recall the name.
> (*Counsel turns to the back of the courtroom*) Mr. Portnoy, will you please stand up?
> (*Turns back to the witness*)
>
> *Q.* Mr. McCann, do you recognize this man?
>
> *A.* Yes, that is the man who was on the corner with me.

After requesting from Mr. Portnoy his full name and address for the record, counsel stopped his inquiry on this phase. The foregoing inquiry served to place Mr. Portnoy in the position where he would testify he was. This placement from a witness for the plaintiff serves to dispel any doubt that he was there and in a position to see.[64]

Even where a witness' testimony comes as a complete surprise there are almost always such possibilities.

Probing for Contradictions

Similarly, there are invariably possibilities that careful exploration will reveal bias or inaccuracy, or that something can be found to contradict other witnesses. The following is one example:

> When a witness has testified to an important, dramatic or interesting event in which others, who may also give evidence, took part, or which they saw or heard, it is often useful to question him about subsequent discussions with those others.
>
> *And when you got home, did you and your brother talk about the accident?*

64. D. Novok, THE DEFENSE OF PERSONAL INJURY ACTIONS 61–62 (1972).

A negative reply might cast doubt upon the candour of the witness, if the event was one which they would almost certainly have discussed. Moreover, the brother, if called, may give a different answer. If the witness answers affirmatively, the cross-examination may continue:

> *Was his recollection the same as yours?*
>
> Yes.
>
> *On every point?*
>
> Yes.
>
> *Had he noticed anything which you hadn't noticed?*
>
> Nothing.
>
> *Did you agree on every single detail which you have mentioned in your evidence?*
>
> Yes.

Three possibilities flow from this: The brother may not be called, and that may found a valid criticism of the litigant who could have been expected to call him. Or he may be called, and his testimony may differ from that of this witness, and a criticism may be based on that. If he is called, and his evidence does coincide completely with that of this witness, it may be argued that it is unlikely that two observers of a sudden and unforeseen event will notice and remember exactly the same things, and that it is more probable that some, at least, of the testimony is based not on direct observation, but upon what passed in conversation between the two brothers, so that what appears to be strong confirmation is nothing of the kind.

If the witness, in response to the questions, says that his brother's recollection did not coincide fully with his own, the matter can be probed further, and the impressiveness of one or both of the observers may well be weakened in consequence of what emerges.[65]

Such lines of inquiry are often fruitful, and negative answers would not seriously damage the examiner's case. Rarely can two witnesses give precisely the same version of a set of facts.

Exploring General Tendencies To Distort

This involves using more typical sources of distortions in testimony, including the witness' (i) perceptual capacities; (ii) memory of the event; (iii) relationship or interest in the case; (iv) opportunity and ability to have observed or known what was testified to; (v) withholding of details relating to the event; (vi) embellishment of aspects of the testimony; (vii) over- or underestimation of features of the case; (viii) certainty or uncertainty about particular matters; (ix) oversimplification of matters in question; and (x) emotional state at the time of the occurrence. Each of these topics can be tentatively opened up as a predicate for more searching questioning.

65.   G. Colman, *supra* note 56 at 10–11.

How effective you will be in such efforts will depend on your skill and your ability to pick up clues from the witness or the evidence in the course of the trial. For example, the witness may hesitate at a certain point in the examination, or may become evasive and unresponsive. A particularly useful clue is the very carefully-worded answer. Colman provides the following illustration:

> A witness who has been answering questions under cross-examination in a relaxed, informal manner, changes his tone when asked:
>
> > *Did you, during January, hear that the plaintiff was in financial difficulty?*
>
> He responds, slowly and carefully.
>
> > No. I did not hear that he was in financial difficulty.
>
> If counsel notices the change of tone, and the precise manner in which the answer is framed, his next question will be:
>
> > *What* did *you hear about him?*
>
> And the witness may, either at once, or after the point has been pressed, say:
>
> > Well, someone did tell me that he'd sold his wife's diamonds.[66]

Even where there are no such clues to suggest specific follow-up questions, you should be able to think of possible lines of further inquiry from the testimony itself. As Colman goes on to observe:

> Counsel cannot, of course, be confident that such opportunities as these will present themselves. His main search for a promising opening will be in the content of the evidence itself. He will bring the full force of his imagination to bear on the story which the witness tells, and he will be constantly asking himself such questions as these about the witness:
>
> > How did he come to be there?
> > What was he doing?
> > How much would he have seen, heard, noticed?
> > Why does she remember that?
> > What would she have done if that really happened?
> > Whom would she have told?
> > How did they find him?
> > Why should he lie?
> > How does she know that?
> > How will it affect him if I lose this case?—How if I win it? [67]

Here, as elsewhere, much depends on your imagination and your ability to construct alternative versions of a set of events.

Relying on "Trap" Questions

Finally, counsel can pose a number of questions which, because they build on knowledge of the way witnesses are usually prepared

66. *Id.* at 64.   67. *Id.* at 66.

for trial, can elicit helpful answers. Friedman suggests the following:

> *Q.* When did you last talk to the attorney calling you as a witness about the facts of this case?
>
> *Q.* How many times have you discussed this case with the attorney?
>
> *Q.* Have you discussed your testimony or the case with any of the parties involved?
>
> *Q.* Have you been allowed to read the deposition (*or prior testimony*) you gave in this case?
>
> *Q.* Have you any financial interest in the outcome of this case?
>
> *Q.* Did you appear here as a witness voluntarily or were you subpenaed?
>
> *Q.* Since this trial started, have you talked with the other witnesses about what their testimony was or is going to be?
>
> *Q.* At the time of this event or shortly thereafter, did you make any notes on what you saw or heard?
>
> *Q.* How many times before this trial started did you discuss this case with anyone who was to be called as a witness?
>
> *Q.* Did you discuss the facts with anyone who was to be a witness in order for each of you to refresh his memory about what he had seen or heard?
>
> *Q.* Was such a discussion entered into so that your testimonies would agree with one another? [68]

Ask yourself what other questions might be posed that develop the same sorts of possibilities. What constraints would you feel in using them?

---

4. *The Decision to Cross-Examine At All*

The foregoing discussion assumes that cross-examination is called for: that is, that there is something to be gained by asking questions of the witness after direct examination. There is hardly an article, speech or text on this subject that does not point out the significance of the prior judgment of whether to cross-examine at all. Sidney Schweitzer suggests some of the considerations involved:

> It is unwise to begin cross-examination of a witness knowing that the testimony given on direct examination is beyond contradiction, and that no possible avenue for impeachment exists. A cross-examination in such a situation usually results in no more than a repetition of the testimony already given, with even more devastating effect than if left alone.

68. L. Friedman, ESSENTIALS OF CROSS–EXAMINATION 97 (1968).

Where the witness has left no loophole in his direct examination, and you know of no weak points that could profitably be exploited on cross-examination, *do not attempt to cross-examine*. Dismiss the witness with a curt gesture that says: "too unimportant to bother about." It is often sounder strategy to waive a witness aside after he has completed his affirmative testimony, without any cross-examination, than to trust to providence that your interrogation will develop one or more weak points.

One of the most damaging of the hazards of cross-examination is that of causing the witness to give an unexpected, unfavorable answer. Such an answer carries more weight than it would have had it been elicited on direct examination because, generally, the jurors pay closer attention to testimony given on cross-examination, realizing that it is being given by an adversary. No cross-examination should be undertaken, therefore, unless the counsel knows, or is reasonably sure of, what the witness will say.

The direct examination of a witness may leave a clear hiatus, tempting the cross-examiner to develop the missing portion. This gap may be the result of an honest oversight on counsel's part, or it may be purposely designed to trap an unwary cross-examiner. In no event should the cross-examiner interrogate the witness about matters in this unexplored area unless he knows with reasonable certainty what the answers to his questions will be. He should not run the risk of receiving a damaging answer.

Counsel should make a quick decision at the trial as to whether there is a need for cross-examination in the first instance. The common impression among lawyers that it is a sign of weakness to allow a witness to step down from the stand without first cross-examining him, is basically wrong. Similarly it is an error to assume that juries will get the wrong impression from dismissal of a witness without cross-examination.[69]

A similar set of warnings (and accompanying illustrations) is directed to asking "one question too many." The following is an example of what this means:

Q. How far were you from the corner?

A. Sixteen feet. I was buying a paper at the news stand.

Q. You mean exactly 16 feet, and not 20 or 10 feet?

A. Yes, I mean exactly 16 feet.

Q. You mean you are so sure of yourself that you cannot even be a foot or two out of the way?

A. Yes.

Q. You do not expect the court or jury to believe that?

A. I surely do. I went back there this morning and measured it. I was sure that some technical lawyer like you would ask me just that question.[70]

69. S. Schweitzer, CYCLOPEDIA OF TRIAL PRACTICE, VOL. I, 614–15 (1970).

70. A. Cutler, SUCCESSFUL TRIAL TACTICS 119 (1949).

Beyond these familiar warnings, you will often hear from experienced trial lawyers that cross-examination should not be too long or too short, too aggressive or too acquiescent. And one frequently hears admonitions that one should not ask a question unless one "knows the answer." It should be obvious, however, that no one can ever be absolutely sure of what a witness will answer, even if the same question has been asked and answered before. One clearly takes large risks in asking questions which can elicit a harmful answer, particularly in situations where the witness has really caused no great harm, or where further questions would serve no useful purpose. Nevertheless, such risks seem to be what the examination process is made of. It is very difficult to ascertain when to ask or not ask a particular question, or whether its risks are outweighed by its potential benefits. It is probably better to analyze this issue as you would any other decision—with an emphasis on identifying alternatives and projecting of possible consequences—than to search for some ready rule of thumb. Inexact as they are, purpose and prediction seem to offer the only practical response to the uncertainties of trial practice.

2.　Framing the Questions

---

a.　*Direct Examination*

KEETON, TRIAL TACTICS AND METHODS

42–44 (2d ed. 1973).

Experienced trial lawyers invariably find it much easier to frame questions well than to tell a novice how to do it. They have developed habits of interrogation and a "feel" for what is and what is not appropriate; they find it easier to perform than to explain. This is not to say, however, that you must depend on inspiration of the moment, or what amounts almost to accidental construction of the form of your questions. Particularly as to direct examination, even if you do not have the benefit of extensive trial experience, you can anticipate accurately the subject matter that you will cover with each witness, and you can frame your questions in advance, at a time when you can consider and test each question in the light of rules such as those suggested here. In due course, that practice will help you develop good habits of framing questions, so that your phrasing of even your extemporaneous questions will tend to meet the requirements of proper interrogation. In short, the suggestions that follow admittedly can give you little help in phrasing a question during trial, because there is then insufficient time to think of a proposed question and subject it to tests such as these, modifying or abandoning it pursuant to the results of the tests. These suggestions are intended for advance preparation of specific questions and for use in developing good habits in the phrasing of questions.

(1) Ask only one question at a time, and not a question with several parts. Compound sentences are sometimes hard to understand. Answers to compound questions are worse; they are likely to be incomplete, ambiguous, or both.

(2) Avoid negatives in the question, if possible. Consider this exchange: Q—"You do not know whether Jones was there?" A—"Yes." Did the witness mean "Yes, I know," or did he mean "Yes, it is true that I do not know," or did he mean "Yes, Jones was there"? If you notice it, this doubt can be cleared by another question, and the loss is simply that of delay and a slight danger of confusion, but if you fail to call for clarification after an exchange such as this you may have lost a vital point by having the answer interpreted differently from what you yourself know that the witness meant.

(3) Make the question brief. Both the witness and the jurors must remember all of the question in order to understand it correctly.

(4) State the question in simple words—those used in everyday conversation. You want all of the jurors to understand both the questions and the answers, and this requires the use of words that the least educated among them will understand. This is not a recommendation for use of slang or bad grammar, however; that practice, unless it comes naturally with the lawyer, probably will be recognized and resented as talking down to the jury.

(5) In summary, make the question clear. It is not enough that you and the witness understand each other's questions and answers, though of course that is important. Understanding by the jury is also important. The jurors are the ones whose understanding is your primary interest. They are less familiar with the facts and circumstances than either you or the witness. It is no reflection on the intelligence of the jurors that simple questions are best.

NOTES

1. *Preparation and Question Formulation*

In literary terms, the problem of question framing is a problem of style—of choosing the right words for the particular circumstances. Although much will depend on the specifics of case and context, it is also possible to articulate some general criteria that can be used in reviewing question sequences. Keeton offers some helpful starting points. To these may be added the following:

—the question should conform to the applicable rules of evidence.

This is an obvious prerequisite; it is well to note here, however, that avoiding evidentiary objections is not the sole consideration in conforming to evidentiary rules. Leading questions, even if they would be permitted, can often be uninteresting to a jury and convey the impression that counsel lacks trust in the witness' memory, honesty or capacity. Similarly, compound questions—*e. g.*, "Did you get out of the car and call the police?"—can be confusing and unclear.

—*the question should be appropriately linked with prior questions.*

There are dangers here of repeating or excessively belaboring what the witness has said. On the other hand, as Spellman has pointed out:

> . . . [A] question, without being leading, can and should preserve the continuity of the witness' story. For example, if a witness has testified to a particular conversation and then has given some disconnected details in answer to a question by the trial judge, the first query propounded thereafter by examining counsel should steer the case back into its chronological course. After such an interruption, the first question by counsel could well be: "What did you do after you had spoken to Mr. Jones on June 9?" This is obviously better than the question: "What happened on the afternoon of June 9?" The former query relates back to the conversation previously testified to. The latter leaves the subject in a vacuum unless the trier of the facts happens to remember that the conversation with Jones took place on June 9.[71]

—*the question should not invite an answer which makes the witness unnecessarily vulnerable on cross-examination.*

A good example is the question "Exactly what was said?". If the witness tries to answer the question as worded, he or she is likely to give erroneous testimony or to give the impression this testimony was memorized. A better formulation would be: "Tell us, in substance, what, if anything, Mr. X said to you."

There are, of course, a number of other similar rules of thumb. The difficulty is applying them under the pressures of trial. In line with Keeton's suggestions, many lawyers write out most of their questions for the direct examination of their witnesses, going over them with the witness beforehand. They may or may not actually refer to these prepared questions at trial. (Some will read them, despite what seems to be a considerable loss of spontaneity and persuasiveness.) Others feel that it is better to reduce the witness' expected testimony to a detailed outline of the following type, framing the actual questions in the course of the examination:

Outline Of Proposed Testimony Of Individual Witness

WILLIAM SMITH, 22 Brook Avenue, Chicago, Illinois.

(a) Introduction of witness.

71. H. Spellman, DIRECT EXAMINA-
TION OF WITNESSES 82–83 (1968).

(b) Conversation of June 1, 1967:

    1. Who was present at conversation and where it was held.

    2. Contents of conversation.

(c) Meeting of June 19, 1967:

    1. Who was present and where held.

    2. What, in substance, was said by each participant.

    3. Signing of contract.

    4. Introduce contract (our #22).

    5. Read paragraphs 3, 21 and 22 of contract.

(d) Receipt of second installment of goods covered by contract on August 3, 1967:

    1. Examination of goods after receipt.

    2. Defects discovered in goods.

(e) Telephone conversation on morning of August 4, 1967.

(f) Letter of August 4, 1967:

    1. Establish mailing of letter.

    2. Request production of letter, pursuant to our notice to produce.

    3. If original not produced, introduce in evidence our notice to produce (our #7).

    4. Read original or copy of letter.

(g) Receipt of reply to letter of August 4, dated August 13, 1967:

    1. Establish receipt of letter.

    2. Read letter.

(h) Meeting of August 19, 1967:

    1. Who attended meeting, where was it held and in substance, what was said by each participant.[72]

Our own experience suggests that, at least in the initial stages of one's trial practice, you ought to write out your questions. Inexperienced lawyers tend to be more confident and effective at trial if they have reflected beforehand on the peculiar problems of mood, emphasis, clarity and meaning which arise when ideas have to be translated into specific questions. This does not mean that the questions should be read at trial; an outline may be all that accompanies counsel into the courtroom. Nor is it always necessary to write out *every* question in advance, especially those that are basic to direct examination. Most lawyers with a little experience can readily phrase the ordinary questions that induce a witness narrative—"Directing your attention to (date), what occurred? . . . What did you do then? . . . What was said after/before that? . . ." and so forth. The same is true of the typical foundation questions used in introducing documents or demonstrative evidence. Many lawyers

72. *Id.* at 93.

recommend memorizing these formulations, but this seems unnecessary if one is familiar with the elements that must be covered.

On the other hand, it does not seem to us enough to just "let the witness tell the story." Unity, congruence, emphasis and completeness do not arise automatically in ordinary discourse, particularly under the constraints imposed by the rules of evidence and the formal nature of the trial process. The lawyer is needed to aid in the process of translation "between cultures." As Louis Nizer has remarked:

> Put yourself in the position of the witness. He has never faced an audience before in his life. Suddenly he is placed on a platform, and to his right sits a Supreme Court justice with a black robe, which in itself is sufficient to put him in awe and in terror. To his left there are twelve jurors looking at him very skeptically and critically, and who examine every motion which he makes, as well as every word which he utters. In front of him are a sea of faces, and by this time he sees, out of the corner of his eyes, already dimmed, the leering faces of the defendant and his witnesses looking up at him. In front of those hostile faces he sees opposing counsel sitting anxiously on the edge of the seat. He imagines by this time that the cross-examiner is slowly sharpening a knife, waiting to spring at him and cut him to pieces.

> And while all these confusing surrounding circumstances are pressing in upon him and his blood is pounding in his head, you stand there presenting questions to him. It is surprising that he can even answer the first questions put to him by the court attendant: "What is your name and where do you live?" And if you expect him, in the light of these circumstances, to be descriptive, to be articulate, to be finely sensitive to a point that you wish him to develop—well, you are simply expecting too much from human nature. There is no use going to the restaurant during recess hour and complaining about your fool witness; how he made incredible answers against his own interest and in violation of the truth. The fault is yours and mine. If we put him on the stand without greater preparation and take that risk the fault is not his.

> The law permits you—it does more than permit you, it makes it your duty—to examine your witness carefully in advance to refresh his recollection as to dates and details by exhibiting documents to him which establish these matters; to acquaint him with the sequence of questions so that the truth may be established in orderly fashion and without confusion which may throw doubt upon it. It is the only way, in fact, in which you can present the truth. For the truth never walks into a court room. It never flies in through the window. It must be dragged in by you through evidence, so that the jury is subjected to the stimuli of the facts which you possess. And incidentally, if you examine your witness carefully in advance you will find out what kind of person he is. If he is timid, you must encourage him and lead him. If he is impulsive and talkative, you must restrain him.[73]

73. L. Nizer, *The Art of the Jury Trial*,
32 CORNELL L.J. 59, 65, 66 (1946).

Letting the witness hear what he or she is to be asked before trial seems to be an important part of this process.

---

2. *Staying Within the Evidentiary Rules*

In addition, of course, the questions and the answers you expect to receive to them must satisfy evidentiary standards of relevance, materiality and admissibility. This seems obvious, but is often ignored when questions are prepared. Counsel must anticipate the potential objections to questions on direct:

—question is leading
—question is compound
—question is ambiguous or unintelligible
—question has been asked and answered
—question is cumulative
—question calls for a narrative
—question assumes a fact not in evidence.

Although a fuller consideration of these rules is best handled in courses on evidence and trial practice, it is important to note here how important being able to phrase and rephrase questions to avoid these sorts of objections is to an effective direct examination. This takes a great deal of rehearsal and practice. It also requires that you be conversant with a number of evidence rules and their exceptions which are particularly important to the sort of examinations we have urged.

The Rule Against Crediting

Obviously an emphasis on corroboration and consistency may run afoul of evidentiary rules limiting the degree to which conforming material can be introduced. Background facts, prior consistent statements, post-incident conduct consistent with the witness' claims, and testimony revealing the type of person the witness is are all important corroborating elements which may be limited by the prevailing laws on relevance and disposition evidence. You should carefully study the local rules in this area.

The Opinion Rule

The same is true of the rule against conclusions and opinions. All fact statements are, to some extent, conclusory and the rule speaks essentially to matters of degree. To reinforce a presentation and give it more coherence and plausibility, you might well want to explore the witness' state of mind, intentions, beliefs, and motives for his or her actions. In many jurisdictions, testimony of this nature would be excluded as opinion. You will have to research your local law with some care if questions on such subjects are to be unobjectionable.

The Rule Against Leading

The problem of leading questions is often passed over in evidence courses, probably because such objections are virtually never the basis for reversal on appeal. Nevertheless, it is extremely important that you be able to avoid leading, and also to frame leading questions when it is necessary and permitted under existing rules. Except under unusual circumstances, some leading seems absolutely essential if any examination is to move smoothly through a narrative and a variety of topics. For example, consider the following questions:

Was X running or walking?

Were you on the corner when the accident happened?

Did you hear X say anything at that time?

What, if anything, did he say?

Are these leading? If so, how would you rephrase them to avoid the problem? Can you list the exceptions to the general prohibition against leading questions? [74]

The Rule on Foundation

A final reference needs to be made to an oft-neglected evidence problem: the need for foundation questions. The evidence rules and exceptions in cases and statutes must be translated into questions and answers if they are to be relied on as a basis for the questions counsel wishes to ask. If leading questions can be asked if the witness' memory is exhausted, it must be shown that the witness is having difficulty remembering (Can you recall _____?). The same is true if a foundation is needed to introduce certain documents or to introduce particular items of evidence. For example, in many jurisdictions a prior statement of one's own witness can be introduced to impeach only if counsel is surprised by the witness' testimony. Surprise itself must be shown by admissible evidence before the impeaching material can be properly introduced.

We mention these particular rules because our students seem to have the most difficulty with them. If you are systematic in preparing direct and trying to deal with problems you foresee, you will gradually develop your own set of memoranda on such evidence questions. It is important here, however, to at least test whether your general knowledge of evidence rules is adequate to guide your preparation. The rules generally inhibit our common sense ways of explaining and describing events. Whatever their wisdom, they present formidable obstacles to translating a witness' account into a persuasive presentation at trial.

---

74. *See, e. g.,* R. Keeton, TRIAL TACTICS AND METHODS 50 (2d ed. 1973).

3. *Some Typical Routines*

As a starting point in properly wording questions on direct it is helpful to refer to the established routines that are found in the practice literature. This helps to avoid the more common evidentiary problems and gives you language from which to begin revising the examination. The following are some examples:

Refreshing Recollection

1. Mr. Witness, directing your attention to [date], what [information desired]?

2. Do you recall making a statement to Mr. Doe or Mr. Roe?

3. Would that statement refresh your recollection?

4. At the time you made the statement, was it true and accurate?

5. And was it made shortly after the transaction?

[Mr. Clerk, will you mark this document as Defense Exhibit 2 for identification.]

6. I show you defense exhibit 2 for identification, and ask you whether that is the statement to which you referred?

7. How do you recognize it?

8. Will you read it to yourself?

9. Now having examined defense exhibit 2 for identification, do you have an independent recollection, without reference to the statement, of what occurred on [date]?

Introducing Business Records

1. Your Honor, I would like to have this instrument marked as defense exhibit #1 for identification.

2. State your name.

3. Where do you reside, Mr. [witness]?

4. And what is your occupation?

5. Where are you employed?

6. What is the nature of your employer's business?

7. And what is the nature of your work there?

8. Were you so employed there on [date in question]?

9. Now, as the [position title], do you have responsibility of keeping the records concerning [subject matter]?

10. What is the method utilized for keeping these records?

11. Is this followed with respect to every [entry] [patient, etc.]?

12. I show you defendant's exhibit #1 for identification, purporting to be [document title], and ask you whether these are the original records which you have kept in your position?

13. Were these records in your custody on [date]?

14. And were they in your custody prior to your bringing them to court this morning?

15. Where were they kept?

16. Were the entries made herein made shortly after the transaction they record?

17. Who provided the information contained therein?

18. Was it his duty to collect this data and pass it on to you?

19. And were these entries made in the usual and ordinary course of business?

20. To the best of your knowledge, are they true and correct?

* * *

Eliciting Testimony Regarding the Character Trait of Truth and Veracity

1. What is your name, please?

2. Where do you reside, Mr. [name]?

3. Where are you employed?

4. How long have you worked there?

5. In what capacity?

6. Do you know the defendant, [name]?

7. How long have you known him?

8. During that period, how often did you see him?

9. What was the nature of your association with him?

10. Did you know other people who knew him?

11. Did you discuss with these people, or hear discussed, the defendant's reputation for truth and veracity?

12. What generally is his reputation for truth and veracity among those people?

Establishing the Alibi Defense

1. Do you know Mr. [defendant]?

2. How long have you known him?

3. What was the nature of your relationship?

4. Did you have occasion to see him during the [month]?

5. How often?

6. Can you tell His Honor and the ladies and gentlemen of the jury generally how you happened to see him during that month?

7. Now, directing attention to the [day] of [month], did you happen to see him on that day?

8. Did anything unusual happen on that day?

9. Now, [number] days later, did you have occasion to see him again?

10. That was the [day] of [month]?

11. Do you remember what day of the week that was?

12. Did anything unusual happen that day?

13. Where did you see him?

14. About what time?

15. Can you tell the ladies and gentlemen of the jury what transpired at that time?

16. How long did you [talk, other activity]?

17. What occurred then?

18. Who else was with you?

19. Was [name] there? What was he doing?

20. At what time did you last see [defendant]?

21. Did you notice the exact time?

22. During the [length of time] you were with the defendant, was he wearing a [garment]?

23. Was he wearing a [another garment]?

24. At any time from [time] to [time] on that day, did the defendant leave from [place]?

25. At any time did you see him with [weapon used in crime, if any]?

26. At any time did you see him with [proceeds of crime, if other than money]?

27. At [time], [date], was he with you, Mr. [name]?

No further questions.[75]

Needless to say, excessive reliance on such aids is unnecessary and often self-defeating. The words one uses are a function of style in a variety of senses, for language must fit not only the situation but your own speech patterns and rhythms. On the other hand, it is often easier to find a comfortable formulation when one has "tried on" someone else's. Such models—which can be found in many trial practice books and drawn from transcripts of trials—are one of the available resources to which you might profitably turn.

—————

4. *Questions as Responses*

Finally, here, as elsewhere in trial work, there is the problem of anticipating the unexpected. Notwithstanding what can be accomplished by careful preparation, many decisions about what should be included and excluded, repeated or emphasized in an examination are made only upon hearing the witness' actual answer. Consider, for example, the following:

—what if the answer is dull and uninteresting and was probably not listened to by the hearer?

—what if the answer is incomplete?

—what if the answer is rambling and hard to follow?

75. G. Bellow & G. Shadoan, TRIAL MANUAL 2–1, 2–4 to 2–7, 2–10 to 2– 11 (Crim. Prac. Inst. of Md., D.C. & Va. 1964).

—what if the answer is untrue?

—what if the answer is at variance with what the witness previously told you?

—what if the answer is framed in a way which can be taken advantage of on cross-examination—*e. g.*, what if the answer is overly positive?

Ask yourself if you could readily frame questions which could get at these sorts of problems and which meet the criteria for "good" questions set out above. Our hunch is that without giving such problems some advance consideration, in most instances you could not. Neither could we. It is in developing a repertoire of back-up formulations, possible rephrasing, lead-in statements (*e. g.*, "Excuse me Mr. _____, you're going a little fast for me . . . let me go back a moment to . . ."), and reference points (*e. g.*, pinpointing the logical breaks in the narrative), that question planning seems particularly important.

Such planning, of course, is not a substitute for listening with your own and the "hearer's" ears throughout the examination. If the witness' narrative is incomplete or otherwise inadequate, it must be amplified or clarified. While the most persuasive story may be one told by the individual who testifies with no more than gentle guidance from counsel, witnesses can lose their way and become rambling, prolix, inaccurate, uninteresting or unconvincing (to name only a few of the potential problems). You must not only be able to recognize those moments, but must have considered ways to return the testimony to the course you intended.

b. Cross-Examination

———

LAKE, HOW TO CROSS–EXAMINE WITNESSES SUCCESSFULLY
328–29, 92, 102, 14, 16–18, 185–88, 195–98 (1966).*

There are two factors in cross-examination capable of considerable development:

1. The refinement of the English language, with so many words that are similar to each other yet which express many different subtle shades of meaning, requires that you use the words that express your precise thoughts. When you use a word that you are not satisfied with (I am speaking of the important, the key word, in a sentence) then look it up in a book of synonyms. You will be surprised how often you will find among the words listed one that is much more forceful, that gives your speech greater strength and grace.

2. Avoid abusing the English language. Remember that carelessly constructed sentences not only fail to express what you are

trying to say but can also convey meanings different from what you intend.

Cross-examiners should concentrate on (and even invent) methods of asking questions that can be answered in only one way—as they want them to be answered. They must also keep in mind that badly worded questions can yield answers that are adverse to their case.

When you read or hear cross-examinations, study how they could be improved by asking different questions or by refraining from asking certain ones. Do not be satisfied by seeing the mistakes of others but search for the reasons that cause them. Until you do this, you have not found the answer, nor are you fortified against making similar mistakes yourself. You know the problem. You know how it should be handled (you would not ask such a question under the same conditions), but that is not solving the problem. You must know why you would not ask the question. When you have that answer, you have created a principle that extends to many other conditions.

* * *

[You should therefore] . . . select the words you wish to use in phrasing specific questions . . . Make your questions logical and concise, reasonable and to the point, so that only the answer that you want the witness to give promotes reason. Thus, if the witness answers differently, it will raise a doubt in the minds of the jurors as to his bias or the honesty of his answers. . . . Do not ask a question the answer to which should have been obtained by your opponent. . . . Do not ask a question unless you have a reasonable right to believe that the answer will be what you expect it to be.

[All of this depends on propounding questions to hostile witnesses correctly and framing your questions artfully. The problem is one of language—of translating ideas into purposes and possibilities. Let me offer some examples.

First, take a case in which the witness has made contradictory statements . . .]

If there is a writing that you can confront the witness with after you have him firmly committed to his oral statement, you can make serious trouble for him. But a witness has to be carefully secured, or he will escape.

Example. A discharged real estate agent testified against a landlord for whom he had formerly collected rents and stated that a certain tenant, the defendant, had always paid his rent regularly on the first of the month. This fact had a strong bearing on the outcome of the case, but the agent had overlooked the fact that just before the plaintiff discharged him he had sent him, the landlord, a letter stating that he was enclosing a check that he had just succeeded in getting from the tenant for three months' rent in arrears.

Excerpts from the cross-examination follow:

    Q. During your direct examination you were asked by your counsel about the values of houses in the neighborhood from a rental standpoint and, without any provocation, at the end of one of your answers you volunteered the following statement, that the defendant "always paid his rent promptly." Was there any reason why you wished to volunteer that statement to the jurors?

    A. I thought that the answer was a responsive part of the question.

*   *   *

The first question was the lead question to the part of the cross-examination that follows. The answer to it switched the cross-examiner's plans, temporarily, to showing that the witness was evasive and biased. . . .

Cross-examination resumed:

    Q. You said that you thought that it would be helpful and that is what you said bias meant. Now let me ask—you knew the defendant?

    A. Yes.

    Q. He paid the rent to you?

    A. To my office.

    Q. Rents were collected under your supervision?

    A. Yes.

    Q. How did you know when they were paid?

    A. I told you they were collected under my supervision.

    Q. That was my phraseology. Do you wish to adopt it?

    A. Yes.

    Q. You followed the collections so closely that you knew when they were paid and when they were in arrears?

    A. I did.

    Q. You are sure of the truth of what you have said?

    A. Certainly I am.

    Q. And you swore that the defendant always paid his rent promptly. Didn't you?

    A. Yes.

    Q. And you would not have sworn to it unless you knew it was true, would you?

    A. No.

    Q. Won't you admit that when you made that oath that you knew it was not the truth?

A.   It was the truth.

Q.   You deny that that statement was a falsehood?

A.   You imply that I am a liar and I resent it.

Q.   That is your statement?

A.   Yes.

Q.   Is this your signature?   (*The letter was folded back so that only the signature was visible.*)

A.   It is.   Let me read the letter.

Q.   Don't worry.   You will hear what is in it sooner than you like.   Just answer my questions first.   The stationery the letter is written on is yours, is it not?

A.   It is.

Q.   What do these initials written at the bottom of the letter stand for?

A.   My stenographer's initials and my initial.

Counsel.   Letter is offered in evidence.   [*It was then read to the jurors.*]

It stated that three months' rent in arrears had just been collected and that the check for it was enclosed.

There was no escape for the witness under such conditions. He had placed himself in a very unfavorable light with the jurors by his evasiveness and his show of bias.

*   *   *

[Or consider the following cross-examination in a case] . . . for damages involving the driver of an automobile who ran over and killed a little . . . boy riding on a scooter.

The plaintiff kept his principal witness under cover. It turned out that she was a . . . woman who lived up the block from the place where the accident occurred. The plaintiff refused to give any information about her or what she would say until he put her on the witness stand. He had revealed only that he had an eyewitness as to what took place.

The scene of the accident. It occurred on a wide street having a 20 foot parkway in its center with two lanes 18 feet wide, one on each side of the parkway. The street had trees about 25 feet tall along the pavement curbing and in the parkway. The time was early fall and the trees were fully leaved. The accident took place at the intersection of a cross street. A man at the filling station at the corner where the accident happened said the place where the boy was killed was known to be a very dangerous place for children to play and that police constantly were chasing boys on scooters away from it.

Defendant's statement about the accident. The defendant said that he was traveling about 25 to 30 miles an hour when the boy shot out of the cross street right in front of him. The street had a down-grade and he claimed that the boy was coming fast coasting on his left side near the gutter, and that he, the defendant, was on his right side of the street. He said that the pavement at the intersection was about ten feet wide.

The corner house at the intersection prevented the defendant from seeing the boy as he coasted down the hill. The defendant applied his brakes. The boy screamed, ran right in front of his car and was killed. The defendant said that it happened so fast that there was nothing that he could do but jam on his brakes, which he said he did.

What the plaintiff's mystery witness said. The mystery witness said that she had been looking out of her second-story front window for about five minutes when she saw the defendant coming down the street very fast and also saw the boy on the scooter. She said that the defendant had plenty of time to stop after he saw the boy but that he kept right on and ran over him and killed him. She said that her house was about 100 feet from the scene of the accident and that she saw plainly all that took place. The number of her house she said was 1836.

The questioning had to be based on the impression the witness had made on the cross-examiner and the points in her direct testimony that he thought were contradictory and weak. His efforts were directed to magnifying the weak and contradictory spots in what the witness had said.

. . . As the cross-examiner listened to the witness testify, he felt that the witness had committed certain perjury on two points and was what is termed a willing witness or an affidavit witness. As counsel for the defendant had carefully studied the scene of the accident, he knew there were trees on the sidewalk and in the parkway; he knew that number 1836 was nineteen houses from the corner where the accident had occurred and that the distance was over a 100 yards to her house instead of a 100 feet as the witness insisted it was. The cross-examiner also knew that the trees made it impossible for her to have seen the accident in the detailed way she had described it.

* * *

With this knowledge the cross-examiner decided to try to uncover the complete falsity of the witness' whole testimony. This he undertook to do in what I have . . . called a chatty style of questioning, involving the witness' personal habits and surroundings, with no questions until the last about the accident.

Excerpts from the cross-examination follow:

Q. I believe that you said that your house, number 1836, is up the street from where the accident took place, did you not?

A. I did.

Q. How long have you lived there?

A. Over three years.

Q. You and your husband live there?

A. Yes.

Q. Do you have any children?

A. I have a son eight-years old.

Q. Do you occupy the whole house?

A. My husband, my child, and I live on the first floor. I have roomers on the second and third floors.

Q. Who occupies the second floor?

A. A man had the front room and a woman has the back room.

Q. Your husband works all day?

A. Yes.

Q. What do you do?

A. I am a housewife.

Q. You stay home and keep house for your family and keep the rooms clean and the beds made for your roomers?

A. Yes.

Q. And of course look after your little boy?

A. Yes indeed.

Q. That keeps you pretty busy. Does it not?

A. It certainly does.

Q. Do you ever loiter or rummage around your roomers' rooms?

A. I certainly do not. When I finish cleaning and straightening up I close the room and leave it.

Q. I did not mean to offend you.

A. Why should I stay in their rooms?

Q. Well, what were you doing in the second-floor front room the day of the accident?

A. I was cleaning up the room and making the bed.

Q. You were not just loitering around there then?

A. I was not.

Q. Just doing your housework?

A. Yes.

Q. And while you were doing that you heard the screeching of the automobile tires and the scream of the little boy who was killed?

A. Yes.

These answers were definite contradictions of statements she had made in her direct testimony. In it she said that she had been looking out of the window about five minutes when the accident happened and that she saw everything, even the little boy lying dead in the street. Contrast this with what she had just stated: She did not loiter around the rooms, but when she finished cleaning she shut them up and left. Secondly, when asked what she was doing in that room the day of the accident, she said that she was cleaning up and making the bed. How, then, did she see the accident?

* * *

[The cross-examiner then questioned the witness on her thoughts and actions at the time, as well as her relationship to the plaintiff, bringing out several damaging admissions and inconsistencies.]

The next section of the cross-examination referred to the two points the witness testified to on her direct examination. The cross-examiner felt there was no doubt that he could make her contradict them and utterly destroy her testimony. He actually had the witness under his control by this time and had no fear about any question he asked her. The defendant had a number of pictures taken in the neighborhood from the point of the accident. Though unintentional, one pointed directly at the witness' house.

Cross-examination continued:

Q. I want to ask you some additional questions about the distance of your house from the point of the accident. Are you still sure that the distance is only 100 feet?

A. I am.

Q. Your house is number 1836 which means it is the 19th house up the boulevard from the intersection of the cross street where the accident occurred. Is that right?

A. Yes.

Q. How wide do you think those houses are in feet?

A. I think about 14 feet.

Q. Will you multiply 14 feet by 19 houses and tell the jury what you get?

A. 266 feet.

Q. How wide is the street and how wide are the pavements on the cross street?

A. I think about 20 feet and 12 feet.

Q. How wide is the pavement and street and parkway in front of your house?

A. The pavement is about 12 feet, the street about 20 feet, and the parkway about 20 feet.

Q. Taking them diagonally to the place of the accident would be over 300 feet, would it not?

A. I think it would.

Q. Then instead of you being 100 feet away from the accident when you looked out of your second-story window, you were over a hundred yards away, were you not?

A. I must have been.

Q. I do not want any "must have been." Were you not over 100 yards away?

A. Yes.

Q. Didn't you know all the time that the distance was considerably over 100 feet?

A. I don't know.

Q. Now you swore on direct examination that you looked out of the window and saw not only the accident happen but saw the defendant coming down the boulevard and the boy on his scooter coming down the cross street and later the boy lying dead in the street. Is that correct?

A. Yes.

Q. On your side of the street—from your house down to the intersecting street where the accident took place—I want to ask you if there are any trees planted along the sidewalk?

A. There are.

Q. Try to count in your mind how many trees there are from your house down to the cross street?

A. I would say seven or eight.

Q. One to about every two houses?

A. Yes.

Q. Now, how about the trees in the parkway. Are there trees there?

A. Yes.

Q. Well, how many do you think there are from your home to the corner?

A. I can't say.

Q. Try.

A. I don't know.

Q. Are there as many as there are on the sidewalk?

A. I think so.

Q. Aren't there more than twice as many?

A. I believe there are.

Q. That would be more than 24 trees at least?

A. Yes.

Q. Will you look at this picture? Do you recognize any of the houses on the street your house is on?

A. Yes.

Q. The picture points toward your house does it not?

A. Yes.

Q. Do you see your front steps?

A. Yes.

Q. Will you point out to the jury the window you were looking out of in your house?

A. You cannot see it.

Q. Why can't you see it?

A. Because the trees are in front of it.

Q. If that is so, how could you have seen a little boy lying in the street and what took place, if the trees hide the window of your house that you were looking out of?

A. I don't know.

Q. Now, why don't you be honest and admit that you did not see the accident?

A. It looked to me like it was the accident.

Q. But you did not see the little boy lying there. Now, did you?

A. It must have been something else that I saw.

NOTES

1. *The Preparation of Questions for Cross-Examination*

As Lake suggests, the proper questions on cross-examination again involve the issue of finding the right words—words which in his terms "keep the witness in the dark," "condition" the answers, or "transform" the meaning of the witness' statements. It should be remembered, however, that the right questions in a cross-examination are always part of a sequence of inquiries. As Harris has remarked:

> . . . I would suggest it as a good and safe rule, that if you are desirous of getting an answer to a particular question, *do not put it*. The probability is that the witness will know your difficulty and avoid giving you exactly what you wish. If not altogether straightforward (and for such witnesses you should always be prepared) he will be on the alert, and unless you circumvent him will evade your question. It is in such a situation as this that the skill of the cross-examiner is shown. One advocate will sit down baffled, another will obtain all

that he requires. A series of questions, not one of them indicative of, but each leading up to the point, will accomplish the work. If the fact be there you can draw it out, or if you do not so far succeed, you can put the witness in such a position that from his very silence the inference will be obvious.[76]

As in direct examination, our own experience with students is that such sequences need to be prepared. Ordinary discourse does not lend itself to the sort of incremental, purposeful questioning that this perspective envisions. Can you formulate criteria which might be applied to such formulations? As you read the above material, does it point to generalizations that can be used in your own work?

Many of Lake's suggestions and examples are helpful here. Perhaps it would be useful to set them out in a more declaratory form and contrast them with other commentaries on the framing of cross-examination questions.

—The questions should have a specific objective in mind.

This is basic to the analysis Lake offers. You should know what you are trying to accomplish in cross-examining a certain witness, and you should be able to state such goals in terms of the propositions and attitudes you want the hearer to accept. The same is true of each question that is put to a witness.

For example, if you want the witness to characterize someone (he was a hot-head, vicious, etc.), you will have to plan your examination accordingly. Similarly, if you want to keep the answers in a particular frame of reference or have them phrased in particular terms, you will need to develop your examination towards those ends. Hegland offers the following illustration:

The more abstract the testimony, the more likely the jury will err in drawing conclusions from it. Some illustrations:

Testimony	Factual Conclusion You Want Jury to Reach	Ultimate Conclusion You Want Jury to Reach
"He was 40 feet away"	"He was a long way away"	"He couldn't see well enough"
"Mr. Smith told me . . ."	"Mr. Smith is the man who previously testified and he told the witness . . ."	"The man who previously testified told the witness . . ."

Where possible, have the witness testify in such a way as to minimize the danger that the Jury will make an incorrect factual determination. To some, "forty feet" may not seem "too far"—have the witness relate

76. R. Harris, K. C., HARRIS' HINTS ON ADVOCACY 57 (1881).

the distance in concrete terms—"about from here to that door over there." (To preserve your record, it is well to state, "Your Honor, let the record reflect that the witness is indicating a distance of about 40 feet." The clever lawyer has measured the courtroom.) Some members of the jury may not recall who "Mr. Smith" is—identify him as the previous witness who testified to thus and so.[77]

To say you need a concrete purpose is not the same as saying you should "ask no question to which you don't know the answer." Often the cross-examiner will have only a reasonable expectation that a particular answer will be forthcoming or, more frequently, will be pursuing multiple expectations of a very tentative nature.

—The question should restrict the witness' opportunity to give damaging testimony.

This venerable guidance is usually expressed in the form: "questions should call for yes or no answers" or questions should be "narrow, closed-ended and limited." Such advice, however, sometimes fails to make clear that restricting the opportunity of the witness to go into extensive explanation ("well, yes, that's true, but . . .") depends on much more than the form of the question. Your tone of voice, confidence, facial expression, facility in posing your next question, and the expectations you generate in the course of the examination—*i. e.*, what you "teach" the witness about how he or she is supposed to act—are far more important sources of control. Nevertheless, it is often advisable to frame questions in ways which sharply limit the possible answers. For example:

"The road was wet, was it not?"

"Isn't it true that the defendant applied his brakes before he entered the intersection?"

"After the accident, you heard the defendant and plaintiff talking?"

"Now, the plaintiff didn't say anything that you could hear concerning the color of the light?"

You should practice framing questions in this form until it feels entirely natural to do so (after which time you may never have a decent conversation again).

On the other hand, there are many instances when you will not want to restrict the form of the question. For example, a witness who in fact has no explanation of an inconsistency in his or her testimony is often more effectively impeached by being given a chance to explain it. Otherwise, the hearer is left to imagine that some explanation might have been forthcoming if it had been sought. Con-

---

77. K. Hegland, TRIAL AND PRACTICE SKILLS IN A NUTSHELL (unpublished draft, 1977).

versely, narrow questions improperly handled can be very damaging. Consider, for example, the following:

    Q. You say you saw the accident?

    Q. And you saw the plaintiff driving carefully down the street?

    Q. Keeping on the right-hand side?

    Q. And you say that the defendant was coming very fast?

    Q. On the wrong side of the street?

    Q. Could he see what was ahead of him?

    Q. Could he have stopped before hitting the plaintiff?[78]

Obviously, simple "yes" answers are not very effective here. How narrowly questions are framed is always a function of your purposes and the risks involved.

   —The questions should progressively narrow the opportunities for the witness to explain away impeaching or unfavorable material.

We will discuss this again when we deal with the sequence of questions. Here it is important to note that every question should build on the previous answers of the witness. Colman offers the following illustration:

> The accused, when arrested on a charge of housebreaking and theft, was wearing a leather belt. The victim has said that among the things stolen was a belt, and that he thinks that the one found on the accused is that belt. The accused, in evidence, says that he bought the belt at a shop months before the robbery. The accused is a slim man; the victim of the robbery is a good deal stouter, and prosecuting counsel notices, on the surface of the belt, not one, but two wear marks manifestly made by the edge of the buckle while the belt was in use. They are several inches apart, and with the buckle against one of them the belt would be far too large for the accused. Before drawing attention to this, counsel asks:

> *For what purpose did you buy the belt?*

> What do you think? To keep my trousers up.

> *Some men manage to keep their trousers up without belts, don't they?*

> Not I. My hips are narrow.

> *So you have always worn a belt?*

> Yes.

> *Every day?*

> Yes.

---

78. L. Lake, HOW TO WIN LAW-SUITS BEFORE JURIES 173–74 (1954).

Then I take it you already had a belt when you bought this one. Did you?

Yes, but it was getting very shabby.

What did you do with the old belt?

I gave it to my son.

Did you, then, wear this belt every day from the day you bought it till the day of your arrest?

Yes.

Every day, without exception?   Were you never ill in bed?

No.   My health is good.

Did you never lend the belt to anyone?

No.

And as your health was good, can I take it that you haven't gained or lost weight since you bought the belt?

(The witness now begins to see what is coming.)

May I see the belt, please?

Not at this stage.   Did you lose or gain weight?

Yes.   For the last six months before my arrest I was dieting.

Why did you want to see the belt before telling me that?

I thought I might be able to show you marks on the belt to prove that I'd been dieting.   I'm not sure they're there.   I haven't seen the belt since my arrest.   But they may be.

Here is the belt.   Are there such marks?

Yes, here, and here.

You have shown me a mark near the second hole in the belt, and another mark near the eighth hole.   Do they represent your waist before and after dieting?

It must be so.   Otherwise you wouldn't find the two marks.

There are no marks between those two.   Tell me please, what diet is it which shrunk your waistline about six inches so suddenly that at no stage did you buckle your belt on any hole between the second and the eighth? [79]

There are numerous such examples in the trial literature.   The object is to "close the escape route" before the witness feels the need to escape.   Counsel must imagine (i) all the possible non-damaging explanations that might be offered by the witness ("I loaned the belt to my brother for a few months. . . .   I was ill and had lost a lot of weight . . ."); (ii) construct questions which don't "tip the witness off"; (iii) ask them in a tone and sequence which gets

79. G. Colman, CROSS-EXAMINA-
TION: A PRACTICAL HANDBOOK
49–50 (1970).

the desired answers that provide the contrast the examiner is seeking. Kenny Hegland gives another example:

> You defend a woman accused of shoplifting. The store detective has just testified as to several incriminating statements made by her upon her arrest. In the arrest report, written by the detective, there is no mention of the statements. Your theory is that the statements were not made and your evidence is, if they had been, they would have been mentioned in the report. If you immediately confront the witness with this—"Now, you made no mention of these statements in your report"—the witness will recognize that this fact tends to conflict with his conclusion that the statements were made. Hence, the explanations: "Everything doesn't go into the report." "I was very busy that night," etc.
>
> . . . What you need is a way of eliminating these possible responses: *i. e.*, closing the door to them.
>
> Note that how you ask the questions is important: you are to close the doors, not *slam* them. If you ask in an accusing manner, "Now, it is true, is it not, that everything important is included in the arrest report" the answer will be a defensive "no," even though the witness is unaware of the important omission. Compare "Now, being a store detective is a very responsible position. In filling out arrest reports, I imagine you take all the care you can." Here the witness will likely describe the report as one prepared with the accuracy and care of an encyclopedia. Trickery? No. As to the inclusiveness of the report, there is no objective truth: the witness will maximize or minimize the degree of inclusiveness depending on his perceived interest. The testimony will be colored in any event—might as well color it with your colors.[80]

Trickery or not, this involves a very subtle form of questioning. Few tasks in trial practice pose a greater test of lawyer skill.

> —*The questions should be framed so as to conceal their purposes from the witness.*

This is a corollary of the prior proposition and one of Lake's major themes. He describes it as "legitimate deception." In his words, "if you do not deceive or hide from the witness what you are doing, but reveal your object to him, you will have a hard time getting any results . . . . To warn the witness what you are doing is to tell him what to expect and to give him opportunities to manufacture explanations for any false statements as he may have made."[81]

Although this is good advice, it should not be followed slavishly. In some instances, too much circumspection can make the witness more cautious rather than less so. In addition, such questioning can be boring or confusing to the jury. Generally it is important for the jury to know what you are doing as you are doing it. (Sometimes

---

80.   K. Hegland, TRIAL AND PRAC-
TICE SKILLS IN A NUTSHELL
67–68 (1978).

81.   L. Lake, HOW TO CROSS-EX-
AMINE WITNESSES SUCCESS-
FULLY 33 (1957).

you can use an opening statement for this purpose, if the witness is not present and there is no time to brief him.) Juries forget or misunderstand testimony which is not made salient for them, and often make up their minds as they go along. Your efforts to "tie it all up" at closing may come too late to be effective.

---

2. *Staying Within the Evidentiary Rules*

As in direct, the phrasing of the question on cross, and its sought-for answer, must not run afoul of the rules of evidence. You need to keep this potential constraint in mind as you consider the precise wording of the questions you plan to use.

The objections that are most commonly made against a cross examination are those addressed to form: that the question is (i) argumentative; (ii) ambiguous and unintelligible; (iii) compound; or (iv) too general; or that it (v) has been asked and answered; (vi) assumes a fact not in evidence; (vii) calls for a narrative; (viii) calls for opinion or speculation; or (ix) misquotes the witness. In addition, questions may be objected to as calling for matter which is (i) incompetent; (ii) privileged; (iii) hearsay; (iv) not supported by proper foundation; (v) not binding on the party; (vi) contrary to public policy; (vii) irrelevant; (viii) immaterial; or (ix) unduly prejudicial.[82]

Even when untenable, such objections often break the pace of the examination or otherwise insulate the witness from a question's effects. You will need to learn phrasings that can avoid such objections, and to develop some facility with rewording questions in response to objections without losing your timing or pace.

---

3. *Some Typical Routines*

As in preparing direct examination, your efforts to frame appropriate questions in an effective sequence can be aided by using some skeletal sequences for a starting point. These can be found in the trial literature, and were referred to in our earlier discussions concerning the problem of initially generating fruitful lines of inquiry at pages 275–86, *supra*. The following are sample sequences for use in cross-examining about prior inconsistent statements:

A. Written Report Signed by Witness (Contradiction)

1. Now, Mr. [name], you stated that [testimony] on direct examination, did you not?

---

82. Those of you interested in reviewing your knowledge of these evidentiary objections will find examples and a useful discussion in L. Schwartz, PROOF, PERSUASION AND CROSS-EXAMINATION 2304–14 (1973).

2.   Did you ever give a different version of that [incident, description, etc.]?

3.   You did talk to [name of person who recorded statement] after the incident, didn't you?

4.   That was on [date]?

5.   And [name] and [name] were present, were they not?

6.   And they recorded what you stated, didn't they?

7.   And you read what they wrote and then signed it, didn't you?

8.   Was that report accurate?

9.   And was it a reliable statement of what you observed or heard concerning the case?

10.   Would it be fair to say that it was made with the facts fresher in your mind than they are today?

Mr. Clerk, please mark this document as defense exhibit #1 for identification.

11.   I show you defense exhibit #1 for identification and ask you if this is your signature?

12.   And that is the document you read and signed on [date], is it not?

13.   Now, directing your attention to [line], [page], you stated at that time that [contradiction], did you not?

14.   That is contrary—directly contrary—to what you are saying now, is it not?

15.   You're not asserting that your recollection of those events is better now than it was [length of time] after?

16.   Then your testimony on direct examination was not entirely accurate, was it?

17.   You knew when you made this statement [or report] that it longer whether [fact which is the basis of contradiction]?

18.   Before I go further, Mr. [name], are there any other inaccuracies in the testimony you gave this morning?

B.   Written Report Signed by Witness [Additional Piece of Damaging Information in Trial Testimony]

13.   Now, Mr. [name], when you made that statement [or report] which you had in front of you, you were not trying to conceal any information, were you?

14.   You were attempting to be as accurate as you could, weren't you?

15.   You certainly attempted to include in the statement [or report] the facts you considered important in this case, didn't you?

16.   You knew the purpose of such a statement, didn't you?

17.   You knew when you made this statement [or report] that it would be utilized by people who did not have first-hand knowledge of the transaction?

18.   And that such people would gain their knowledge of this transaction from your description?

19.   You also knew that you would probably testify in this case?

20.   And that the trial would be a considerable period of time after this transaction?

21.   And you knew that you could utilize this statement [or report] to refresh your recollection before testifying today [if witness is police officer or professional]?

22.   In fact, you did read this statement [or report] prior to testifying today, didn't you?

23.   This would certainly be a good reason for including in the statement [or report] as much of what actually occurred that night as possible, wouldn't it?

24.   I show you, Mr. [name], defense exhibit #[no.] for identification and ask you, Sir, whether anywhere in that statement [or report] there is mentioned that [fact omitted]?

25.   Didn't you think if it happened, that it was important that [fact omitted]?

26.   When did you first decide to include this matter in your account of the transaction?

27.   You didn't mention it in any other statement [or report or testimony]?

28.   Today, for the first time, we hear about this matter, is that right?

29.   Your training includes report writing?

30.   You are taught to include the important facts of a transaction in such a report?

31.   If something of evidentiary significance actually occurs, do you usually fail to include it in your statement [or report]?

32.   Only in this case, is that right?

C.   Oral Inconsistent Statement by Witness

1.   Now, Mr. [name], you stated that [testimony] on direct examination, did you not?

2.   Did you give a different version [incident, description, etc.]?

3.   Did you have occasion to discuss this case with [name]?

4.   That was on the [day] of [month]?

5.   In [place]?

6.   And present at that conversation were [name] and [name]?

7.   You discussed the events to which you testified today, isn't that right?

8.   You didn't try to hide or falsify anything during that conversation, did you?

9.   You didn't lie to [name]?

10.   He wasn't discourteous to you, was he?

11.   He didn't in any way coerce or threaten you, did he?

12.   And you tried to be as accurate about what you said as you could, didn't you?

13.   Now, on that date, did you say to [name] that [the facts constituting contradiction]? [83]

You can find such models in any number of practice texts and manuals.   Compare each sequence with the general criteria for framing questions set out in the preceding notes.   How closely do these sequences follow those ideas?   In what ways do they depart from them?

Helpful as such exercises are, you should also recognize their limitations.   Particularly in cross-examination, where you may feel uncomfortable until you have gained experience, there is a real possibility of becoming too dependent on such sequences.   The result will often be a largely standardized and inflexible presentation at trial.

In addition, as we have said before, phrasing is peculiarly personal.   You may find the language of the above questions wooden, the transitions uncomfortable, the sentence structure too long or too short.   Try delivering these questions out loud and you will immediately get a feel for whether they fit you.   Even if an examination is written out (which we advise for planning purposes), it needs to be written out in your own words—with a sense of your own style and rhythm, as well as recognition of the fact that oral and written expression often exhibit very different characteristics and qualities.

3.   The Sequencing Problem

---

a.   *Direct Examination*

SCHWEITZER, TRIAL GUIDE

1275, 1277–81, 1298, 1305 (1945).

Direct examination can be dry, drab and dreary.   It can be akin to the reading of a piece from a book in a disconnected recital.   Or it can be a forcible, logically arranged presentation.   The art of direct examination is simply the technique of having a witness tell a story in an interesting narrative, natural, effective manner.

*   *   *

OBJECTIVES OF DIRECT EXAMINATION

In framing the direct examination of his witnesses, or in outlining the proof to be presented as part of his affirmative case, coun-

---

83.   G. Bellow and G. Shadoan, *supra* note 75 at 3–9 to 3–12.

sel should bear in mind the basic objectives of direct examination, and its principal purposes.

1.—The examination should tend to establish the elements of a prima facie case. Counsel should not rely upon the cumulative effect of testimony to spout forth a specific act of negligence, or other liability. He should bear in mind the specific elements of a prima facie case, or those factors that he *must* prove to establish a cause of action. . . .

2.—The examination should tend to portray a clear and dramatic picture of the main events. It is poor trial strategy to stick exclusively to the technical aspects of the case, being content with establishing a prima facie case, and proving the damages.

Counsel should evaluate the facts and circumstances of his particular case to determine how his proof can be presented in the most effective manner possible. In this respect, counsel is like a general before a battle, planning the disposition of his forces, deciding where to proceed first, at what times, and under what circumstances. The attack should be orderly, arranged for maximum effectiveness, and follow a logical pattern.

* * *

3.—The direct examination should place before the court and jury all documentary evidence that is relevant to the issues, and which will serve to clarify or establish a point in issue. . . .

* * *

Order of Witnesses

It is generally well to start the trial with a good witness, end with a witness of strength, and place the weakest testimony in the middle. The theory upon which this view is based is that first impressions generally tend to remain; a weak witness at the outset, who becomes confused and makes damaging admissions upon cross-examination, may create an unfavorable impression which will color all the testimony to follow.

Reserve a good witness for the last phase of your direct examination, upon the same general theory that the case should be opened in strength. The impression created by a bad witness closing the case may cause the jury to forget many of the important points raised by preceding witnesses, or possibly place less credence in the probability of their stories.

The best strategic position for a witness who must be called to the stand, because of his relationship to the parties or issues or the inference that would arise from failure to call him, is between other witnesses of greater strength and force. While there is obviously no assurance that this practice will make obscure or harmless the substance of his testimony, the tendency of juries is to remember less of the details of a witness' testimony which is placed in the middle of the plaintiff's case.

Counsel should be careful to exclude from his positive case any testimony that is properly in the nature of rebuttal. A witness whose testimony can only have the effect of rebutting affirmative matter which you assume will be offered by the defendant, should never be placed among your other witnesses in the presentation of your case.

Such witness should be called upon close of the defendant's case, when you will be in a better position to rebut specific points raised by the defense. To anticipate such points in advance is dangerous, because the defendant may shape his case in such manner as to neutralize the effect of your proof, or render it less damaging. Moreover, rebuttal testimony gives you the last word, which is inclined to create a more lasting impression in the minds of the jury.

ORDER OF DIRECT EXAMINATION

It is always advisable to arrange a direct examination in chronological order. The precise arrangement of a direct examination will, of course, depend upon the facts and circumstances of each case, but generally the prime objectives should continually be kept in mind in framing the questions.

Where, for example, the action is one to establish negligence, counsel for the plaintiff should be certain that his direct examination of the plaintiff establishes the necessary elements and proof of a prima facie case.

The following order of direct examination in a personal injury action is an illustration of an effective arrangement of questions:

1—*Preliminary identification of plaintiff*—Name, address, married, occupation, how long employed at work, nature of work, etc.

2—*Accident*—The manner in which the accident took place. Ask the witness to tell the story just how it happened. After he has told his story, complete his summary of the facts by your own questions.

3—*Injuries*—Ask the plaintiff simple questions designed to prove the nature and extent of injuries sustained. Fill in any gaps by your own questions. Be sure to cover all the injuries sustained.

4—*Treatment received*—At what hospital was the plaintiff confined, for how long? Specific treatment administered. Develop in full all treatments given to the plaintiff.

5—*Length of treatment*—Describe in full the duration of any treatment received by the plaintiff, as for example the wearing of a splint for a fractured leg, or the use of crutches.

6—*Nature and length of disability*—How long was plaintiff confined to bed? How long was he able to move around the house without going outside? For how long a period did he lose full motion of his leg or other injured part of his body?

7—*Loss of earnings*—Describe the nature of the plaintiff's work, his salary, and how long he was absent from work after the accident.

8—*Special damages*—Doctor's bill, nurse's bill, hospital expenses, special appliances, should all be fully developed.

9—*Future losses*—Where the plaintiff will in the future be deprived of the use of an injured part of his body, such fact should be fully established. Similarly, the need for future hospitalization, or medical treatment should be developed.

10—*Condition of plaintiff's health prior to accident*—Show that existing disability, or injury, was not existent in any form prior to accident.

* * *

REDIRECT EXAMINATION, GENERALLY

A well-conducted redirect examination can form an important part of a lawsuit. Too often attorneys fail to grasp the full significance of a redirect examination, or the wide opportunities it affords for development of decisive phases of the proof.

The cardinal purpose of a redirect examination is to restore unity to the examination of the witness, to straighten out inconsistencies developed upon cross-examination, and to aid in strengthening the credibility of a witness. The close of a well-planned and thorough cross-examination generally finds the theory of the case as developed on direct examination shaken and confused. A skillful cross-examiner will select one or two weak points in the affirmative proof, and magnify them to an importance where they threaten to weaken the entire structure of the direct examination, and thereby throw the whole case out of perspective.

It is the function of the redirect examination to avert such a situation, or stated differently, to gather up the loose and scattered bits of testimony and once more present some semblance of unity and consistency in the story related by the witness. . . .

REBUTTAL

It is well settled that a party has the right to offer testimony in rebuttal which has the effect of meeting or offsetting any affirmative proof offered by the other side. Rebuttal may also be used to support the credibility of a witness who has been attacked by proof as to his character.

Rebuttal should not be used unless the evidence to be offered meets affirmative matter presented by your opponent; furthermore it is inadvisable to use rebuttal testimony where there is no practical need thereof, as where the new matter offered by the other side is of no decisive value.　Evidence which is purely cumulative in character is not properly used in rebuttal.

* * *

Ordinarily it is improper to use rebuttal to offer evidence which should have been offered upon the principal examination but which through an oversight was not introduced.　Some courts, however, allow proof of this character to be offered in rebuttal, depending upon the facts and circumstances of the particular case.

NOTES

1.　*The Order of Examination: The Insights of Psychology*

The notion of using a chronological format, as Schweitzer suggests, has long been the dominant rule of thumb among trial lawyers. However, this general prescription leaves unanswered a number of difficult questions relating to the order of inquiry.　For example:

—how should favorable and unfavorable material be sequenced?

—at what point should exhibits, maps, charts, documents be introduced?

—what is the best order for introducing technical and nontechnical material?

—should familiar material precede unfamiliar material?

Consider whether the following analysis by Thomas Parker is helpful in addressing these issues:

.　.　.　We may have the best case in the world, but unless we can present it in such a manner that the jury will understand, and remember it when they reach the jury room, where, unfortunately, final deliberations depend almost exclusively on memory, we will have wasted our breath.

Obviously, nothing can be remembered which has not first been observed or perceived.　More important, to the lawyer, is the fact that nothing can be remembered which is not first learned.

It is therefore my purpose in this discussion to review with you some principles of learning and laws of memory which can be applied, and are applied, through good trial tactics, to assure that the average juror, when he is deliberating your case behind the locked doors of the jury room, will remember every facet of your case that you wish him to, and, consequently, be your advocate in the jury room.

In order to illustrate these points, a series of short learning exercises is employed.　The purpose of these exercises is to demonstrate to you that a lawyer can make it easier for a jury to learn the important facts pertaining to his case.　Also, you will discover some general principles that you, as a lawyer, may use to help your jurors learn.

Each exercise is a short test consisting of twelve words, syllables or digits.　Let us say that each exercise consists of twelve pieces of evidence, or twelve pieces of learning.　Look at each set of items for just twenty seconds. That is the time it will take you to read them through two times, reading at a normal speed. During that time, attempt to memorize the list. After you have read it through twice, cover the list and recall as many items as possible and write them down. It is not necessary that you list the twelve in order.

TEST 1

TIG
LEV
SAH
KIH
MEC
FEH
POH
CIX
YOD
ZEK
LDC
NOK

Wherever this test has been given, without exception, it has been shown that more people were able to recall the first two or three items and the last item than were able to recall those in the middle of the list.

Conclusion. Jurors tend to remember the evidence which is presented first and that which is presented last. They tend to forget the evidence which is presented in the middle of the trial.

Almost without exception, leading trial tacticians advise you to *start* your case with a strong witness and *end* with a strong witness. These are the most important parts of the trial insofar as the memory of the juror is concerned.

This illustrates certain laws of memory which we shall call the LAW OF PRIMACY and LAW OF RECENCY.

* * *

These "laws" can be illustrated further by the "learning curve" long familiar to educators and used in evaluating any memory or learning situation.

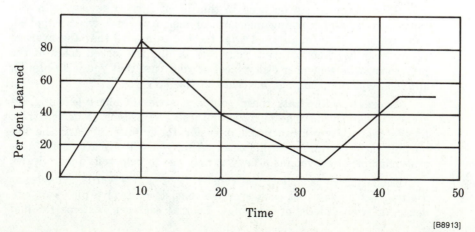

1.   This diagram represents the learning curve of an individual in a given situation.

2.   The general shape of the curve is independent of the ability of the lawyer or the intelligence of the jury.

3.   As the examination of a witness is lengthened or shortened the relative shape of the curve remains the same.

4.   The ability of the lawyer and the intelligence and the attitude of the jury will affect the position of the curve.

Thus it can be seen that, during the examination of a witness, you can expect to have the jury's maximum attention at the beginning of your examination, and at the end. The initial peak of the curve is primarily due to the inherent curiosity of men, curiosity as to the witness, as to what he has to tell, how the presentation is made, the subject matter you are bringing up, etc.

* * *

[The second test illustrates that jurors] tend to remember that which has meaning to them. They will remember very little of any evidence or demonstration which has no meaning for them. A lawyer who is aware of this fact will try to lead the jury to insight. He will try to avoid rote learning on such things as medical testimony, but will make sure that it is explained in a way that it will have meaning to the jury. . . .

This illustrates a principle of learning that we shall call PRINCIPLE OF MEANING.

* * *

[The third test shows that jurors] tend to remember new, unfamiliar or technical evidence if it is associated in some way with something they already know or can easily learn. This is called the LAW OF ASSOCIATION.

* * *

. . . Your presentation must be so well organized that the juror can associate each contribution of the witness with a theory of your case as a whole and with each part of it. For that reason, organize your case carefully and avoid taking a witness out of order, if possible.

Associate the new with the familiar. Insist that your doctor use such words as "bruise" instead of "contusion," "cut" instead of "incision," "black eye" instead of "ecchymosis," etc.

* * *

A case consisting of the testimony of several witnesses must be so organized that all relationships are clear and the testimony of each makes a well integrated whole.

. . . Jurors tend to remember individual items of testimony if they can fit it into an overall picture. This is called the PRINCIPLE OF THE WHOLE.

* * *

Choose your words with care in your opening and closing argument to make the portions of your case, which the jury must remember, vivid. Make sure that your witnesses do likewise, wherever possible, and if their command of the language is sufficient. And in all cases, bolster them with visual aids. This illustrates the LAW OF VIVIDNESS.

It is not necessary to demonstrate the law of frequency; instead you will readily grant that you could make a better score in each test in the above series if the whole procedure were repeated. Any one of you will be able to repeat numerous commercial slogans used on radio programs, slogans in which you had no interest but which are firmly fixed in your mind as a result of the sheer force of repetition. Important points of your testimony should be repeated five or six times during its presentation. For retention over a long period of time, key points of your testimony in a long case must be reviewed on as many successive days as time and the judge will permit. [This is the] LAW OF FREQUENCY.

* * *

A jury must be oriented. So, in the opening speech to the jury, tell them what you expect to prove to them. As we have demonstrated before, their interest is highest at that initial point. Then proceed to prove it to them, and in the concluding arguments, tell them what you have just proved to them—again, at a time when their interest is highest.

Stimulation of the mind is accomplished through the senses: sight, hearing, touch, taste and smell. Psychologists agree, generally, to the following percentages as representing the amount of learning accomplished by each of the five senses.

SIGHT	85%
HEARING	10%
TOUCH	2%
TASTE	1½%
SMELL	1½%

We must realize that this is a general average, applying to the average of all situations. In a particular situation, the percentages might not hold true.

We should, therefore, remember in preparing our files for possible presentation to juries:

1. The sense of sight should be used to the maximum in presenting material.

2. Since our juries are made up of individuals who are not segregated in accordance with their ability to learn, the more senses which are stimulated, the better chances for all of them to learn.

3. In certain situations, the sense of hearing, touch, taste or smell could be a major channel for stimulation. For instance, a liquor bottle, found in the wreck, might be exhibited to the jury and smelled by them.

4. The jury must know the reasons *why* an accident happened, in addition to knowing *how* it happened.

5. Previous experiences and knowledge of the jury should be utilized by forming associations between their knowledge and the evidence being presented.

6. Material must be presented in a logical, meaningful, striking and stimulating manner, using visual aids, demonstrative evidence and other interesting experiences to make intense impression on the jury.

If the five memory laws

THE LAW OF PRIMACY
THE LAW OF RECENCY
THE LAW OF ASSOCIATION
THE LAW OF VIVIDNESS
THE LAW OF FREQUENCY

are utilized by the attorney in presenting his case to the jury, together with the principles of learning

PRINCIPLE OF MEANING
PRINCIPLE OF THE WHOLE

with the full realization that he has the maximum attention of the jurors at the beginning and end of his case, and that 85% of what they learn will be through their eyes, he can be sure that the jury will learn, and thus remember, the facts of the accident as he wishes them remembered, and render their verdict accordingly.[84]

Parker's conception of the presentation of testimony as a teaching/learning process calls to mind our earlier comparison between trial testimony and good writing. The principles of "meaning" and "the whole" discussed by Parker embody the same idea of coherence. Both notions have the same practical implications for two specific choices in trial work: the order of topics within a particular examination, and the sequence of testimony within the overall structure of the case.[85]

How does one translate his insights into the specifics of a particular sequence of questions? In particular contexts, counsel must determine what witnesses to call, how to connect or relate their testimony, what matters of proof to leave to documentary evidence or stipulation, and how much of the opponent's proof to anticipate.

What guides such judgments? Consider, for example, the following general rules of advice:

(i) In a personal injury case it is generally more effective to prove damages before liability. This highlights the elements of damage which must be plaintiff's major concern. This means that plaintiff should start with medical witnesses and thereafter develop the underlying causal circumstances that led to the injury.

(ii) There is very little risk in covering minimally, or even failing to cover, some elements of the necessary proof in the case-in-chief if

---

84. Parker, *Applied Psychology in Trial Practice*, 7 DEF.LAW J. 33–36, 38–45 (1960).

85. A useful summary of some of the research that has been done on the ef-

fects of sequence choices is contained in THE ORDER OF PRESENTATION IN PERSUASION (C. Hovland ed. 1957).

the matter can be developed in cross-examination. The opposing party is left with the "Hobson's choice" of presenting no testimony on the issue or permitting the gaps to be filled in. The presentation of such evidence through cross-examination of hostile witnesses enormously increases its impact and credibility.

(iii) There is much to be gained by having the opposing party commit his or her case to a version of the facts that can thereafter be rebutted. For this reason, counsel should refrain from including too much in opening statement or presenting the entire case in the case-in-chief. It is important to save material for rebuttal. Similarly, counsel should consider raising issues which could be asserted in the answer as counterclaims in order to preserve the right to open and close.

(iv) Testimony is most effective when it moves from the general to the specific. If models or diagrams are to be used, they should be presented first and the events developed in relation to them. Similarly, since evidence is admissible subject to proper foundation and connection, the outlines of the story should be offered early and the underlying evidence developed thereafter.

(v) Since, despite the formal allocation of the burden of proof, it is human nature to be anxious about the fault of the parties, it is advisable to anticipate defenses in the case-in-chief. This takes the "wind out of the opponent's sails" and presents the case as a complete picture.

(vi) Testimony should not be so sequenced that it leaves opportunity for the hearer to fill in or develop doubts. For example, if a document is mentioned it should very shortly thereafter be introduced, or at least identified. If certain circumstances need explanation, there should be immediate testimony to that effect. For example, if it would be unusual for the witness to be doing X, he or she should be asked to explain that fact shortly after testifying to the activity. If doubt develops it filters all the rest of the testimony.

Do you agree with these suggestions? In what circumstances would such advice be inappropriate? In making such judgments, what predictions are you making about the probable responses of the hearer? Consider whether Parker's "laws" provide any guidance in evaluating these often-relied-on rules of thumb.

---

2. *Order of Proof in the Case as a Whole*

Although we cannot explore the full range of issues related to overall trial strategy, it is well to remember that any direct examination must inevitably be related to the function the witness is expected to play in the presentation of the case as a whole. Schweitzer's comments might be compared with the following observations on criminal cases by Charles Tessmer:

> The order in which witnesses are called and evidence is presented is within the control of the lawyer and can be used to advantage. A good strong beginning is half the battle. The beginning witness in a

criminal case should have a general knowledge and should be able to give evidence concerning the general background of the defendant and pertinent evidence as to his contentions and defense. It is often wise to open with a close relative or member of the defendant's family, particularly his mother, wife or father, who knows nothing of the actual facts of the case but who may testify to the background, education, employment, family, etc. while giving evidence as to the general reputation of the defendant or evidence of some unimportant fact which will permit the introduction of the background material. This type of evidence is often utilized to present the widow of the deceased in a murder case merely to testify that the deceased was her husband and is now dead. The obvious strategy of the prosecution in this type of procedure is to develop as much prejudice against the defense case by use of the dead man's widow as possible. By the same token, the defense may begin well with the presentation of the defendant's wife or family to create as much sympathy on his behalf as possible. It is true that character testimony from close members of the defendant's family may not have much weight, but the jury will become better acquainted with the accused by the development of his background by such a witness. The evidence put in by defense witnesses should be presented in an orderly manner and evidence relating to the same or similar points should generally be offered in a chronological sequence. Unimportant witnesses may be sandwiched in between the lengthy witnesses in order to avoid monotony and to hold attention. However, it is not wise to skip around with the witnesses and develop one phase of the case and then jump to some other completely different phase and then back to another witness along the same line of evidence. It is common sense that a weak beginning by a witness, who may be easily upset on cross-examination, creates an unfavorable atmosphere for the entire case which follows.

The ideal method of presentation would call for: (1) a strong witness (2) unimportant witnesses (3) technical proof of documents, attestation, etc., and (4) ending with the strongest witness. Of course, if the defendant is to testify in the case, it is generally considered to be sound strategy to call the defendant as the last witness because he may remain in the courtroom and listen to the testimony of all the other witnesses. It is also good strategy, where the prosecution will probably offer rebuttal evidence, to hold back a good, strong witness for rebuttal so that the defense may have the last word with the jury. It is unwise to anticipate the rebuttal testimony and to hold out such a witness unless you have reasonable grounds to believe that rebuttal testimony will be put on by the State. The Trial Judge may not exercise his discretion in permitting you to re-open your case and offer the withheld witness in the event rebuttal is not forthcoming from the prosecution.

If there are several witnesses to proof of the same fact, it is always wise to select one or two of the witnesses who make the best impression, both in appearance and in expressing themselves, to carry the load of the case. Of course, the other witnesses may be held for sur-rebuttal.[86]

86. C. Tessmer, CRIMINAL TRIAL
STRATEGY 76–78 (1968).

Note that Tessmer not only agrees with Schweitzer on risks involved in saving an important witness for rebuttal, but also urges taking advantage of "recency" and "primacy" effects in sequencing testimony. A number of lawyers would give different advice, emphasizing the importance of starting with a witness who can provide an overview of the case and developing a general chronological progression.

Tessmer goes on to develop suggested orders of proof in a variety of different types of cases. For example, in a case involving a charge of manslaughter arising out of driving while intoxicated he recommends the following:

> (1) Impeaching evidence of prosecution witnesses, (2) The background family witness—preferably the wife or mother of the accused, (3) Best witness who observed accused shortly before the arrest or who was present in the automobile with the defendant at the time of the accident, (4) Other witnesses who saw the defendant before arrest, (5) Police record relevant to show time of arrest and release (bearing on the short period of time accused was held in jail), (6) Any documents in possession of the police indicating a good steady signature of the defendant at the time he was supposed to have been intoxicated, including confessions or statements obtained from the defendant with his signature affixed thereto and any police photographs made at the jail at the time of arrest, (9) Witness defendant called from the jail to establish rationality and no drunk symptoms, (10) Witness who can testify to known samples of defendant's handwriting (compare with materials signed by defendant when allegedly drunk), (11) The defendant, (12) An expert witness who can testify concerning the validity of the tests and conditions that should be observed. Also hypothetical questions as to intoxication on two bottles of beer, etc., (13) Character witness as to law abidance and sobriety (14) Sur-rebuttal, a strong witness who observed defendant's actions shortly before arrest who can give opinion as to sobriety of the accused.[87]

Ask yourself if this makes sense to you. Would you try to develop similar sequences for various case types? What assumptions about human behavior and the trial context does Tessmer seem to be making? Here, as elsewhere, lawyers tend to disagree; your own intuition may again be the best (although hard to articulate) guide.

b. Cross-Examination

COLMAN, TIMING, CROSS–EXAMINATION: A PRACTICAL HANDBOOK

136–50 (1970).

A cross-examiner must decide not only what to do with his witness, but when to do it. In some situations the second question vir-

---

87. *Id.* at 80–81.

tually answers itself. In others the order in which topics are introduced or particular questions are put may be of little importance. But more frequently the question of timing deserves serious consideration.

One of the reasons is that the answer to a specific question is so often conditioned by what has gone before. What a witness has already said may coerce him to give a particular answer, or preclude him from saying what he might otherwise have said. An obvious illustration of that is the case where answers which might otherwise have been given are ruled out, from the point of view of the witness, because if he were to give them he would be contradicting himself. But even when that is not so, a witness may feel compelled to refrain from saying something which he is tempted to say because he sees that, in the light of what he has already told the court, the answer will not carry conviction.

Another possibility is that an answer may be influenced by the relationship which has been established between counsel and the witness. The witness may have come to like counsel, or to fear him. He may have been able to infer from what has already happened during his cross-examination, what the cross-examiner would like him to say, or how much information the cross-examiner has on a particular matter.

In what follows, an attempt will be made to show how considerations like these should influence counsel's decision about the stage at which he should turn to particular aspects of his inquiry, and about the order in which questions should be put. Reference will be made, also, to certain other factors to which weight should be given by counsel in selecting the most appropriate time sequence in which to put his questions.

An immediate problem which faces counsel when he has heard the evidence in chief (or learnt, at some earlier stage, what the witness would say) is how best to open the cross-examination. A well chosen opening question may take him a long way towards success.

It may be that counsel is lucky enough to have at his command a powerful piece of material, or a strong probability, with which he is able to strike a swift and damaging blow at the structure which the witness is seeking to build up. Even if the point is not a vital one, it is sometimes useful to deliver the blow at once. The impression thus to be made on the court will be helpful to counsel's case; and what is even more important is the effect on the witness. An initial reverse may make him much easier to handle than he would otherwise have been.

Thus, if the circumstances are appropriate, a cross-examination may usefully begin in some such manner as this:

> *You have told the court that at no stage did you see or handle the will. Can you explain how it comes about that your fingerprints appear on three of its pages?*

or:

> *You have convictions for fraud and perjury, have you not?*

or:

> *Why didn't you mention the revolver to the police?*

But counsel, before he takes so bold a line, should satisfy himself that the witness has no escape from the difficulty in which the question is designed to place him.

* * *

Whether counsel has useful material in hand, or whether he is merely hoping to create some as he goes along, he will be wise, often enough, to start off with questions whose main or sole purpose is to give him the measure of his witness. He may be uncertain whether the witness is shrewd or stupid, calm or nervous, candid or deceitful, partisan or unenthusiastic. He may not know whether the witness is educated or uneducated, experienced in some aspect of life or not, or whether he commands or lacks the ability to understand and use language clearly. He may not know whether the witness is a stranger to the litigant who has called him or not; and, if he is a stranger, how his testimony has been obtained. And counsel may wish to find out some of these things, or at any rate to gain impressions about them, before he decides how to go about the important parts of his cross-examination.

To that end, the cross-examiner may find it best to begin by asking questions about the witness himself, or about some matter which is no more than marginally relevant to the inquiry. He will be seeking replies which, even though they may have little bearing upon the case, will teach him something about the witness.

* * *

Patience   .   .   .   is an essential quality in a cross-examiner. If, for example, counsel's aim is to reveal the untruthfulness or unreliability of his opponent's witnesses by bringing out conflicts between them on points of detail, it may be his duty, at the risk of boring himself and the court, to spend a good deal of time inquiring into details which are of no great importance in themselves. And the process may have to be repeated with witness after witness. The easiest method of doing this is to take the events in chronological order. But, particularly when it is thought that the witnesses are being deliberately untruthful, another method is sometimes preferable. A fabricated story is usually invented and memorized in chronological order, and discrepancies are more likely to appear if that order is departed from in cross-examination. Counsel may dart back and forth, at random, among the details of the story, and that may help him to achieve his object. But it will be better still if he can build bridges across which to lead his witness from one part of the narrative to another. What is meant by that metaphor will appear from the following example:

In what counsel thinks may be a fabricated account, a mother has described how, on a winter's afternoon, she and her daughter walked together, for about a mile, to a doctor's house. Asked about the weather, she has said that it was raining quite heavily during the walk. Now the daughter is testifying. Counsel could ask her, as he did her mother, about the state of the weather during the walk, and then go on to deal with what happened at the doctor's house. He prefers to start with their arrival at the house, and build a bridge back to the question whether it had been raining:

Into what room were you shown at the doctor's house?

A waiting-room.

Was that a large, attractively-furnished room with a fire burning in it?

Yes.

What was the first thing that you and your mother did when you got into that room?

We sat down on a couch.

The couch is under the window, isn't it?

Yes, I think so.

You didn't, either of you, go and stand by the fire?

No, I wasn't cold. We'd had a brisk walk.

Physically, were you quite comfortable?

Yes, as far as I remember.

Did you keep your coats on in that room?

My mother did. I took mine off and held it on my lap.

Inside out?

No.

It didn't make your skirt wet?

No. The coat was quite dry.

If your shoes and stockings had been wet would you have gone to the fire?

I suppose so. But I don't think they were.

So it didn't rain during your walk?

No.

Another matter which governs the order in which counsel will put his questions is the one which has already been referred to as 'closing the escape routes'. This, too, relates to dishonest witnesses. When counsel has a question to put to a witness which ought to evoke a helpful answer, it is important to consider the likelihood that the witness will, if possible, lie his way out of giving that answer. Counsel, before he puts the important question, will consider the lies which the witness may resort to, and try to make it impossible for the witness to make use of them.

* * *

One of the difficulties about closing escape routes is this: An astute liar may see what counsel is about, and adjust his answers so as to leave one of the routes open. When there seems to be a danger of that, counsel will not set about closing the escape routes as soon as he sees his opening. He will, at that stage, start cross-examining about some other aspect of the case, and introduce the necessary questions later on, when the witness is less likely to remember the answer which suggested the line of inquiry to counsel. If possible, the blocking questions will not be asked one after the other, but will be scattered among other material. And each will be introduced in a context designed to mask its relevance.

* * *

When the witness has said something which is in conflict with what one of counsel's own witnesses will say later in the case, the conflicting version must be put to the witness. But it is not always advisable to put it as soon as the statement is made. If that is done, the witness may at once correct or modify his answer and suffer less damage to his credibility than he will suffer if counsel first attempts to pin down firmly the erroneous statement which he has made.

A business man, let us suppose, has said that a variation of a contract between his firm and a company in Italy was orally agreed upon when he had lunch with the chairman of the Italian company in London on a particular day. He gives a plausible explanation for the fact that the variation was never put into writing, and says that the Italian witness will be testifying untruthfully if he denies that the agreement was made, or that he lunched with the witness. It so happens that the restaurant at which the event is alleged to have taken place was not open on the day referred to by the witness, and counsel is able to prove that. He should not be precipitate in putting that fact to the witness. If, prematurely, he says:

> *I shall be calling evidence to prove that Bianchi's Restaurant was closed on the 11th of June. How, then, can you say that you and Signor Rosso lunched there?*

the witness may say:

Oh, did I say the 11th? I meant the 9th.

or

I beg your pardon. That was a slip of my tongue. I meant the other Italian Restaurant, Bardolini's.

Counsel might be more fortunate (though he might not) if he were to keep back his important piece of information until after something of this sort:

How, after all this time, can you be so sure of the date?

I have the lunch appointment noted in a pocket diary. Here it is, if you care to look at it.

Thank you. . . . The entry seems to have been squeezed in between two others. Why is that?

That is because I wasn't expecting to make a lunch appointment, and I didn't leave space for one. I fitted the note in when Signor Rosso telephoned me at about noon.

Who chose the restaurant?

I did. It's the place to which I always take visiting Italians. If you're interested, they give you a very good meal there.

Do they? What did you eat that day? Do you remember?

Yes. I had an excellent arrosto di vitello. And I can tell you what Signor Rosso had, too, if you like?

Yes, what was it?

Ossobuco.

Where, in the restaurant, did you sit?

In the alcove, underneath the picture of St. Peter's.

And, I take it, you shared a bottle of Italian wine. . . . What are you laughing at?

I'm laughing because Signor Rosso said his favorite wine was whisky and soda. And that is what we had.

Signor Rosso tells me that he did say that to you, but it was in Milan, a year or so earlier. And that he never lunched with you in London.

He is lying. I remember vividly his remarking that he'd never had a better ossobuco even in his own country.

So you are certain of the date, you are certain you lunched together at Bianchi's, you know exactly where you sat, and what you had to eat, and you remember clearly two things which were said on that day and in that place?

I've told you so.

You have no doubt on any of these points?

Not one iota of a doubt.

I shall prove that on the night of the 10th of June there was a fire at Bianchi's, as a result of which the restaurant was closed on the 11th and 12th of June. What do you say to that?

* * *

Among the many other things which a cross-examiner has to consider is the psychology of his tribunal. And not least important, under this heading, is the reluctance of human beings to change their minds. A court which has to resolve a dispute of fact will, however hard it tries to keep an open mind, be forming provisional views about the witnesses while the evidence is being given. And once a strong view of that kind has taken root, it may be difficult to displace. It is for that reason, mainly, that experienced counsel sometimes decide to ask questions . . . which do no more than summarize or emphasize what is already on the record. Another reason which sometimes operates is counsel's desire to jolt the witness into a realization of what he has said; in some situations and with some witnesses, the realization may have a salutary effect upon the manner in which the witness will respond to further questions.

These considerations may play a part, too, when the witness has given two conflicting answers, and counsel has to decide whether to face him with the conflict as soon as it arises, or to defer that process. His decision may depend upon the manner in which the answers to these problems present themselves to him.

Has the court probably noticed the conflict?

If not, is it desirable to point it out at once so that they will realize at this stage that the witness is not as reliable as they may think?

Is it likely to help me in my further cross-examination if the witness is made to see his blunder?

Or am I likely to do better with him if I don't put him on his guard by bringing the conflict to his notice at this stage?

The consideration raised in the last of these questions may be a decisive one. There is many a witness who, having made a bad impression throughout his evidence, leaves the courtroom feeling that he has done very well. Such a witness might do better if he had the benefit, during his cross-examination, of having his mistakes and deficiencies pointed out to him as they arose.

* * *

Lastly, on the subject of timing, a reference must be made to the effect which adjournments may have upon the success of a cross-examination. It is seldom that a case of any importance, which involves conflicts of fact, can be concluded during a single sitting of the court. Consequently, a witness who is under cross-examination often has the opportunity, overnight, over a week-end, or during some longer or shorter interval, of speaking to others, including people who have been or will be witnesses on the same side. If such a break comes at an inappropriate time, from counsel's point of view, a promising line of cross-examination may be frustrated.

* * *

If there is a question, or series of questions, which should be asked before the witness has time to speak to others, counsel should be careful to leave himself enough time to do this before the court adjourns. And to that end he may find it necessary to break off in the middle of some other topic. This sort of thing is quite common:

> *We'll come back to that part of the case tomorrow morning, Mr. White. Now, before the court adjourns, tell me about something else. Did you get any information about the dog from Miss Amber?*

I can't remember any.

> *I want you to think very hard please. If you have any recollection at all of any talk between yourself and Miss Amber about the dog, I want the court to hear about it now. Have you any?*

No, I haven't.

> *Can I take it that if she had told you anything about the dog, you would remember it?*

Yes, I think so.

> *Surely you can be more positive than that. Could you have forgotten such a conversation?*

No.

An alternative course which can effectively be followed by counsel who is sure that he is on strong ground, is to invite the witness to make full use of the coming adjournment:

> *I'm going to put a question to you, Mr. Green, which you need not answer now; think about it overnight, and tell the court tomorrow morning: If you were satisfied that you had a valid lease, how did you come to write the letter Exhibit 'J'?*

If, on the following morning, the witness can give no acceptable explanation, his failure to do so will perhaps seem more significant than if he had not had time for reflection.

———

NOTES

1. *Lawyers' Lore on Sequence in Cross-Examination*

You might compare Colman's observations with the following views of trial practitioners concerning the sequence of cross-examination:

(a) Most witnesses, whether coached or uncoached, recall events and conversations in chronological order and give their testimony in that sequence. They expect cross-examination to follow the same line. It is an extremely poor tactic to cross-examine in this order, allowing the witness to correlate each event or conversation with the one just before it and simply reiterate the facts testified to on direct examination. Even starting the cross-examination with the last matter covered on direct gives the witness this advantage of continuity and should be avoided.

Cross-examination usually produces the best results when it jumps from one subject to another in complete disregard of chronological order. Counsel may start the examination somewhere in the middle of the sequence of events, proceed to events and conversations occurring earlier, and then jump to later periods of time. This method may well throw the witness's line of thought out of kilter. He may become hesitant in his answers, thus casting doubt on his recollection. His answers may even be different from his testimony on direct examination. If he is confused, he may become annoyed and belligerent. Each of these results benefits the cross-examiner. Perhaps none of these responses will be elicited by jumping around, but it is fairly certain that they will not be brought forth by a chronological cross-examination. Thus, no harm and much good can come from jumbling the order.[88]

* * *

(b) While it is ordinarily impracticable to adopt a pattern for cross-examination, it is possible in the vast majority of cases to make a quick decision at the trial as to the logical arrangement of the questions to be asked in cross-examination. The following considerations are submitted in this connection:

1.—Where your cross-examination is directed to a specific objective, the bulls-eye of the case, it is rarely wise to strike this objective in your opening questions. It is well to start with a harmless line of questions, and to thereby place the witness at ease.

Handle the witness in a kindly, friendly fashion. Disarm him of suspicion as much as possible. Then abruptly switch your inquiries to the focal point, and in the same tone of voice, continue your cross-examination. As soon as you have made your point, sit down. Do not overplay your role.

2.—Where there are a number of inconsistencies that you would like to develop in your cross-examination, select the weakest to begin

88. L. Friedman, ESSENTIALS OF CROSS-EXAMINATION 90–91 (1968).

your interrogation. Start off with slight and apparently trivial inconsistencies, taking care not to overdevelop their importance. Place the strongest point at the end of the cross-examination.

3.—In those instances where counsel has the benefit of a signed statement by the witness, contradicting portions of his direct testimony, it is well to leave the strong punch for the end of the questioning.[89]

* * *

(c) 1. *Arrange your points* in the order that will be most convincing when you cross-examine the witness about them. This should be done by taking an over-all view of your case. You will have a number of points you will want explained to the jurors—points which, in a way, will appear to be separate but which in reality are facts that make up a whole case. For example: background, circumstances, your acts and those of the defendant, carelessness, the consequence of an act, and the omission of or by the defendant that caused the ultimate result. These and similar points should be carefully considered and worked into a pattern that will make the best possible impression on the jurors. Avoid having these factors jar each other, but instead let them fit together smoothly and logically, so that one point supports another.

* * *

2. *Arrange the questions you will ask* the witnesses and the sequence in which you will place them.

Do this much in the same way as you would your points. Your questions should be asked in such a sequence that you cannot be harmed by a reluctant witness' adverse answer.

3. *Select the words you wish to use* in phrasing specific questions.

* * *

4. *Never ask the witness a bold or blunt question* until you have tested him out with questions which, when standing alone, are harmless if answered adversely.[90]

Think about what these excerpts assume about the psychology of witnesses and the appropriate role of cross-examination. In some ways each envisions different circumstances, different available resources, and different needs for confrontation and direction. Each focuses on different aspects of the examination. Can they be reconciled? Can you begin to construct your own generalizations in regard to this dimension of cross-examination? For example, consider the questions we raised concerning order in direct examination at pages 772–77, *supra*. How might those discussions apply in this context? In what ways do arrangement problems in cross-examination differ from such problems in other contexts?

———

89. S. Schweitzer, TRIAL GUIDE 1310 (1946).

90. L. Lake, HOW TO CROSS EXAMINE WITNESSES SUCCESSFULLY 42–43 (1957).

2. *The Strategic Nature of Order Choices*

In some ways, a consideration of the order in which topics should be introduced in cross-examination involves an inquiry into all the issues we have discussed thus far. If you follow our suggestion that you begin preparation by writing out your examination, or at least outlining it in detail, you will find that there will be no clear line between the content, order and wording of the questions you decide to ask. Each will be an element of a larger plan or complex of purposes. In making sequence choices, you will inevitably be asking the following questions as well:

—*What is my purpose at this stage of the examination?*

Simply stated, what answers do I expect and how do I intend to use them, both in the examination and in the case as a whole? Has the order maximized my control over the examination?

Control is undoubtedly a key issue in any cross-examination. As the *ALI–ABA Civil Trial Manual* advises:

> No matter what technique of cross-examination is used, . . . the cross-examiner, not the witness, must control the situation. The use of a polite, quiet method of cross-examination is not inconsistent with maintaining control. The attorney who lets the witness win preliminary sparring matches in order to make the witness too confident is maintaining control, even though the success of the technique depends on his creating the impression that the witness has gained control. . . .[91]

Obviously, the order in which topics are introduced will affect the wariness and attitude of the witness and the flow of the examination. The *Civil Trial Manual* goes on to make the following suggestions:

> Repeated conferences with the direct examiner often condition the witness to expect the questioning to follow a particular order and sequence. The cross-examiner should not follow the same sequence as did counsel on direct. The witness will often give more candid answers when he is forced to abandon the comfortable prearranged format. Some effective cross-examiners appear to the uninitiated to have dumped all their questions into a grab-bag from which they casually select them at random. Not only do they not follow the direct examiner's format, they do not seem to the witness to be following any rational plan at all. What appears to the witness to be aimless wandering by the cross-examiner is actually a shrewd plan, which deliberately presents questions in seeming disarray so that the witness will not be able to calculate the importance of the question and gauge his answer accordingly. In closing argument, the cross-examiner weaves this seeming disarray into a structure never envisioned by the witness. The cross-examiner is cautioned, however, that the grab-bag technique

91. R. Figg, R. McCullough & J. Underwood, CIVIL TRIAL MANUAL 420 (ALI–ABA 1974).

of questioning should not always be followed because on some occasions cross-examination may be of value to the jury only if there is a discernible structure. But even then, the structure followed should usually not be the same as that of the direct examiner.

A closely related technique for denying the witness and the direct examiner controlling influence over the cross-examination is always to begin the questioning on a different phase of the issues than that on which the direct examination ended. Merely picking up where the direct examiner left off leaves the witness on familiar ground, on which he can begin to rehash his direct testimony. . . .[92]

In some ways, however, this does not get at the most important ways in which control is generated by sequence. The lawyer and the witness inevitably enter into a psychological as well as legal relationship. In a sense, it is not unlike a negotiation: the lawyer bargains with threats (I'll embarrass you) and promises (I'll let up on you) for the answers he or she wants. The witness similarly makes complex promises and threats (if you don't stop I'll hurt your case). How this relationship is initially shaped inevitably has a good deal to do with how and what answers are given later in the examination. Counsel may examine for hours just to establish the relationship he or she desires before the critical questions are asked.

Given this orientation, the first interchanges become critically important. The witness is interested in such questions as: Is the lawyer confident? Does he or she know a great deal about me? About the case? Does he or she have the skills to embarrass me? Thus, if an examiner begins the exploration of an area with such questions as: "You were at Wall Street and Vine? . . . That was on the northeast corner? . . . Where the grocery store is? . . . And you were directly across from the hydrant on the other side of the street? . . .," the examiner makes it clear to the witness that (i) the examiner has been there; (ii) he or she is well prepared; and (iii) he or she can challenge the witness if the witness is in error on details. This can also be done by referring to potential testimony from other witnesses who were there ("And John Jones was also there, wasn't he?"). Since most witnesses have trouble remembering under the strains of testifying, they will be less willing to go beyond the examiner's questions and into great detail when they are confronted with this sort of material early in the examination.

—*Has the order of questions created a motivation to give a different answer?*

If you want the witness to concede a fact, it is obviously not a good idea to create a situation where he or she would be contradicting prior testimony. If you want exaggeration, the witness ought not be confronted with the impeaching materials until the subject of the contradiction has been sufficiently emphasized and explored.

---

92. *Id.* at 422–23.

—Has the order maximized the witness' motivation to give the desired answer?

Since witnesses have a natural inclination to make their answers consistent, a series of earlier concessions will make the desired answer more probable. For example, suppose you want to show that credit harassment was not merely the work of unauthorized lower level employees. An examination which speaks supportively (and early) to a vice-president's responsibility, skill, and command over his or her employees is far more likely to get some exaggeration of the scope of executive control than an accusation of incompetence or irresponsibility. This effect will often be enhanced if you act as if you have material to contradict any other answer. As an old cross-examiner's adage suggests, "Act like you know what you don't know and like you don't know what you know."

—Has the order revealed the cross-examiner's purposes too soon?

Sometimes a helpful answer can and should remain unemphasized until closing. Colman gives the following illustration:

> . . . [W]ith some witnesses, and in some situations, the desire to deliver a *coup de grâce* would be better resisted. In an accident case, counsel for the defendant has had a measure of success in cross-examining a candid medical expert on the question whether the plaintiff's injury will produce traumatic arthritis in later years. He has reached this stage:
>
> > *So it will depend on a number of factors whether there will be arthritis or not?*
> >
> > Yes.
> >
> > *And many of these factors are unpredictable?*
> >
> > Some of them certainly are.
> >
> > *What is more, the X-ray plates are not clear enough to give you all the information you would have liked to have before making a prognosis?*
> >
> > No. That is one of my difficulties.
> >
> > *You cannot be certain that arthritis will ever appear?*
> >
> > No.
> >
> > *Or when it will appear if it does develop?*
> >
> > No.

That is substantial success. And (unless the point has already been made, adversely to his client) counsel might be acting unwisely if he seeks to round off his line of inquiry by putting this question:

> *In fact it is improbable that there will be arthritis?*

For the answer, unless there was a firm foundation for optimism, may well be:

> No. I can't say that. There are all these uncertainties, but even if I allow fully for them, I must say that I think it probable that he'll have arthritis within ten years.[93]

On the other hand, there will obviously be times when you will want to reveal what you are driving at. The question is whether, at the time you do so, any alternative answers to the one desired have been foreclosed or made considerably less credible. This is what Colman calls "closing escape routes," and is far and away the most important aspect of question sequence. In this connection, you might want to take another look at his example of the dieting defendant and the belt at pages 313–14, *supra*.

    —*Has the order provided an opportunity to fall back or retreat if a particular line of questioning does not prove fruitful?*

Although Colman doesn't dwell on this, it seems a fundamental aspect of sequencing. Since there are always risks of damaging answers in any examination, the questions should be planned so that less risky lines can be pursued in the face of difficulty.

    —*Does the order provide an opportunity to "build momentum" if a particular line of questioning is very successful?*

This is a corollary of the last inquiry. If some line is successful and can be emphasized, the order of questions should not foreclose this possibility. When an examiner has the opportunity to accumulate a large number of small contradictions, this is particularly important.

    —*Does the order offer a number of places to stop?*

This is again part of fall-back planning. You will want to stop at a "high point." However, you will also want to be free to stop before all the possible lines of inquiry are explored if the situation calls for it. The best way to plan for this seems to be to develop a number of possible stopping points.

    —*Does the Sequence Contain "Wrap-Up" Questions?*

As we mentioned earlier, despite the suggestion of many trial commentators to the contrary, our own view is that the jury or judge needs to be told what they have heard at various points in the testimony. Thus, it is important to prepare such questions as:

> —Then, you can't be sure that you saw Smith that night, can you?

> —Then your testimony is based on each of those elements, Doctor? If one of them was untrue, you might have to alter your testimony?

93. G. Colman, CROSS–EXAMINA-TION: A PRACTICAL HANDBOOK 89–90 (1970).

—Then you are saying flatly that the witness was incorrect, is that right?[94]

You may disagree with the way some of these reference questions are formulated, and you may want to add some of your own. Note, at least, how much these considerations overlap with the criteria governing what to ask and how to frame your questions. Each of these interwoven processes depends on the difficult judgments we discussed earlier concerning yourself, the witness, the fact-finder, and the material you have to work with. In the final analysis, it is your capacity to imagine your own performance—to project yourself into the future—that gives these decisions the specificity and concreteness they need.

----

4. Asking and Responding: The Examination Process Itself

Implicit in all of the foregoing is an image of the lawyer actually in court—examining, cross-examining, acting and reacting. Decisions made in preparation are only a predicate to the countless judgments that must be made in the course of the examination itself. The skills involved in this aspect of trial work are central, but difficult to define and to teach.

At the heart of the process are a series of relationships. First, there are your interchanges with the witnesses. In direct examination, you ask questions, hear responses, adjust new questions to your assessment of what has occurred and where it should be going. All the while attention must be paid to form, sequence, admissibility, topic and transition. But something more is happening as well: you are also in relationship—with the witness and with the observers of the scene. In a sense, you are making a dramatic presentation—following a prearranged script, yet improvising in the present—all in front of a skeptical, potentially judgmental audience. Similar interpersonal processes are involved in cross-examination. The central theme here is not partnership, however, but threat and control.

Second, there is your relationship with opposing counsel, whose job it is to protect, interrupt, and perhaps take advantage of your efforts and excesses. He or she is the person who is, in some ways, most like yourself in training, experience, and in relation to the situation—and is, most explicitly, your enemy.

----

94. Obviously such "wrap-up" questions can run afoul of the objection that they are argumentative, and this possibility should be taken into account in framing them.

Finally, there is the judge and/or jury, who are the focus of your efforts, but with whom you have the least interaction and about whom you know the least.

In each of these relationships, you are using words, actions, gestures, timing and other means to communicate who you are and what the case is about. Thus far, we have spoken primarily about how to get ready for this enterprise: how to plan, organize, and project possible approaches and actions. We might have gone on, but there is a limit to discussions of "what do you do when . . . .?" There are too many nuances in each situation to make a pre-selected technique precisely applicable, or to give the kind of guidance needed to fit advice to circumstances.

Is there, then, anything that can be said about actually "doing it"—about the qualities that are needed for this job and how they can be developed? Perhaps we might single out a few.

Command

First, you will need to develop the kind of command described in the literature on acting—command of self and command of situations. In direct examination, you will have to develop the ability to listen in public, to communicate warmth and support to the witness in a highly formalized situation, to rephrase questions in the face of objections, and to guide the witness and the testimony in the direction you desire. Witnesses may falter, testify differently than they were expected to, or forget important details. You can respond by (i) slowing witnesses down or reassuring them; (ii) shifting the focus to the past ("I want you to try to feel and see exactly what you felt and saw then . . .;" (iii) going back over material with more leading questions (leading is permitted to clarify testimony and recollection); (iv) bracketing ("Now, after _____, did anything happen?" or "what happened immediately before _____?"); (v) refreshing recollection with documents; or (vi) obtaining a recess. You will find such suggestions scattered throughout trial manuals and this chapter. But all of this will depend on concentration, a personal calm and a sense of the situation which is extremely hard to develop.

In cross-examination, the need for command is even greater. The witness is forewarned to distrust you and often ready to interject damaging testimony if pressed too hard. Here, too, techniques are available to help you perform this task. You can learn to (i) ask narrowly drawn questions; (ii) "clip" the witness' answer so he or she doesn't add to or digress from it; (iii) adopt a trial pace which draws the witness into a pattern of submission; (iv) "instruct" the witness to stay within the scope of the question (in ways that are persuasive); (v) change topics fluidly without losing your own train of thought; and (vi) mask your own reactions to damaging material.

What is required is a good deal of practice, experimentation, and feedback from others.

Conviction

In addition to maintaining control (and as a form of it), you will continually have to communicate conviction. If you examine a witness whom you have prepared, you must still hear the story as if for the first time—with what Stanislavski called "the memory of emotion." That is, it must be new, interesting and believable to *you*.

The same is true of your actions on cross-examination. If you are asserting implicitly that a witness is a liar, you must act as if you believe the witness is a liar. The hearer is often looking to you for "clues" to what is "really" the case, despite the restrictions on stating your personal opinion. There is no way you can avoid having inferences drawn from your conduct, and you will have to act accordingly.

The need to communicate conviction in the complex "public" circumstances of a trial is the source of a good deal of tension. Hegland has captured this problem very well:

> The beginning advocate faces two chief obstacles, the first, insecurity. How else can one explain:
>
>> "Ladies and Gentlemen of the Jury. The eyewitness, Mr. Jones, places the defendant at the scene of the robbery. Yet, Jones admits that he was 100 feet away from the robber and that the robber had a ski mask covering his entire face. Jones further admits that it was totally dark and that he, Jones, was asleep at the time. I would, therefore, suggest on the basis of this that you may decide that the identification may not be as good as it might be."
>
> And what accounts for the way an inexperienced lawyer deals with nervous witnesses? Although it is clear to everyone that the witness is about to pass out, the lawyer doggedly asks the next question. Why no reassuring words to the witness or a request for a recess? Because we know that we are on safe ground when we ask questions—television is quite clear about that. But, who ever heard of a lawyer stopping the testimony to tell the witness that everyone is nervous and that he should just answer the questions as best he can.
>
> Insecurity is perhaps the inevitable product of a law school education. Unlike other graduate schools, students come to law school with no idea of what to expect. They are quickly awed by their professors who obviously understand everything about a totally incomprehensible subject. Add to this general confusion the institutional commitment of instilling in its students the realization that "certainty is an illusion and repose is not the destiny of man" [a]—time and time again

a. O. W. Holmes, *The Path of the Law*, 10 Harv.L.Rev. 457 (1897).

they are argued out of what they once took as sure. And, sprinkle in a little of the benign contentiousness of the classroom encounter:

> The professor's method is to ask a student a series of questions, each becoming more difficult. One student answers five correctly but falters on the sixth and, after hemming and hawing, finally confesses ignorance.

> "That just proves," shouts the professor "that you didn't understand anything from the very beginning!"

No wonder beginning lawyers are afraid to state anything without qualifications, escape routes and other quibbles—the idea of boldly stating "Jones could not see the defendant" makes their mouths run dry—there must be a trap; there is always a trap. And no wonder beginning lawyers faced with an unexpected situation cling desperately to the certain—keep your head down and ask the next question.

How to cope with the insecurity? Make that shocking and ultimately disappointing realization that you are as competent as the next person—the student who missed the sixth question is now a distinguished law school professor. In closing argument, argue as if you believe in what you are saying, not as if you are walking across a land mine. In coping with unexpected situations at trial, do what comes naturally unless you know it is prohibited. Insecurity teaches that unless something is expressly allowed, it is prohibited; security that everything is allowed unless it is expressly prohibited. Loosen up.

Insecurity is one barrier to effective trial advocacy, laziness the other. For example, beginning lawyers often make arguments to the jury without really understanding why the argument is cogent. Consider an attack on the credibility of an eyewitness. The defendant is black. On cross-examination the eyewitness has expressed prejudice against blacks. Now, obviously, racial bias will have something to do with the believability of the eyewitness. Everyone knows that —even the judge. The key question is what is the precise relationship: is the prejudice such that it would cause the eyewitness to consciously lie about the identification? Or is it such to cause the eyewitness to be simply mistaken, prejudiced individuals tending to see all group members as "alike." Most beginning trial lawyers do not force themselves to ask this question—instead they simply argue that the jury should consider "the witness's racial bias in assessing his credibility" and, of course, the jury already knows that, assuming it knows the word "credibility."

What is required is the mental discipline to force yourself to ask precisely why are you making a given argument, asking a specific question, making a certain objection. But, don't lawyers do this naturally? Isn't this advice akin to telling tennis players that they should "watch the ball"? "But, of course, I watch the ball, you idiot. How else can I play tennis?" But, the fact of the matter is that most people do not watch the ball. Next time you play, force yourself to watch the ball as it hits your racket. You will find three things:

1. You currently do not watch the ball as it hits, but rather, you take your eye off the ball when it is 2–3 feet away;

2. If you watch the ball as it hits, you become a much better tennis player;

3. If you watch the ball, you will no longer enjoy playing, it has become mentally as well as physically exhausting.

With tennis, you may decide to simply play the game and refuse to expend the vast amount of mental energy required in playing and thinking about playing at the same time. Let Jimmy Connors pursue his own insane delusion.

Here, of course, we are dealing with yours.

There is a seeming paradox about the advice thus far. To overcome insecurity, you are told to loosen up. To overcome laziness, you are told to concentrate. Yet, there is no contradiction; not only can you concentrate and remain loose, the right kind of concentration helps you get loose. Insecurity stems from self-awareness—"How am I doing with this witness?" "Is the jury believing my argument?" "I'm probably going to screw this up." To cope with this, you must divert your attention from yourself to something outside yourself—to the witness you are examining, to the argument you are making. And, this is what you do when you concentrate on the trial rather than on your own performance. A recent book, *The Inner Game of Tennis*, asserts that most players defeat themselves by listening to the little voice which says such things as "Get ready for your backhand; remember, its your worst shot; you'll probably screw it up." The recommendation is to silence that voice by concentrating on something outside, the seams of the incoming ball. The inner game of advocacy suggests you do not concern yourself with how you are doing but rather focus on what you are doing.

* * *

[Take, for example, this problem confronted in cross-examination:] Obviously, you must have a good idea of where you are going with your cross. Generally, one will have a written outline which shows the general areas of inquiry followed by some specific areas of examination. However, during the cross, the witness will often give an unexpected answer which may open up another line of inquiry. Many beginners fail to pick it up because, after they ask a question, they begin thinking about their next question rather than listening to the answer. *Listen*. The next question will come naturally enough.

Listening has an additional advantage—it is a way to reduce nervousness. If you focus on your questions, you are really focusing on your performance and on yourself. Without getting personal, obviously, this is going to make you quite nervous. If, on the other hand, you focus on the answer, your attention is turned outward. Here our tennis analogy may help.

* * *

Most players beat themselves because of that little voice in their minds which keeps on telling them what to do—"Get ready for the backhand." . . . The solution recommended is to concentrate on something outside—the seams of the incoming ball. This quiets the internal voice and releases nervousness and tension. If tennis, why not cross? Tomorrow, ping pong.[95]

We concur: why not? But Hegland's advice, though it seems sound, it is far easier to state than to follow. Our hunch is that you will struggle with this problem for some time.

Judgment

Finally, there is the need to develop increasing sophistication in your trial judgment. Every one of the suggestions we have made requires drawing lines on the basis of assessments of complex situations. Such line drawing again requires not rules of thumb, but practice, feedback and the accumulation of examples.

Consider, for instance, the oft-quoted statement that "witness control is the essence of effective cross-examination" in relation to your own experience, if any, in examining witnesses. Did you exercise control? Did you find it necessary and/or possible to cut off non-responsive answers and to "keep the witness guessing"? Were you able to do so? As we have stressed, no piece of advice, no matter how valid it may be as a general proposition, can simply be accepted and applied. A cross-examination, like a direct, must have its own unity and coherence, and "controlling" it is not enough. Even if details are left to be tied in on closing argument, a judge or jury must have some idea of what you are getting at, and must understand how the weaknesses you have revealed in a particular witness' testimony are related to your client's theory of the case. And what if the jury understands the significance of the testimony you elicit, but is also aware of how tightly you controlled the questioning? At what point do such tactics give rise to doubts about your *own* honesty and fairness? How often do they invite intervention by opposing counsel or by the judge? Here, as elsewhere, we are often controlled by the social circumstances we create.

SECTION THREE. THE ETHICAL DIMENSION

———

Close to the surface of the cynicism and shrewdness you have just worked through are the moral issues of trial practice. In one sense the ethical questions here involve each of the relationships we have thus far discussed—relations with clients, witnesses, adversaries. To these must be added the lawyer's obligation to the court and to the law. All of these are summed up in the conflicting duties embodied in the idea of zealous advocacy.

The following transcript explores these themes in the context of events at and before a preliminary hearing in the case of People

95. K. Hegland, TRIAL AND PRACTICE SKILLS IN A NUTSHELL 1–6 (1978) (the concluding paragraphs of this excerpt were revised to some extent before publication).

v. Roger Link. The initial conversation is between Clyde Rollins, counsel for the government, and Polly Tate, the complaining witness. Counsel for the defendant, who overhears the conversation, is Al Wirtz. The defendant is charged with robbery and attempted rape, both felonies.

PEOPLE v. ROGER LINK

SCENE: *Prosecutor is talking to a victim of a robbery and attempted rape in a hallway outside of the courtroom.*

Rollins: I understand, Miss Tate.

Miss Tate: I'm just telling you that I can't be sure, that's all.

Rollins: All crime victims feel that way, Miss Tate. But look at it this way, there's a man in there who is guilty of robbery and attempted rape, and we won't be able to do a thing about it if you don't help us this afternoon in this preliminary hearing. We're never gonna be able to turn this problem of crime around if people like that continue to get off.

(Wirtz appears, undetected by Rollins and Tate. He overhears the following:)

Miss Tate: I don't know. It was so dark and I was scared, really scared. It all happened so fast, you know, it makes me wonder. You know, I saw something just like this on TV last night, and the girl picks this guy out of the line-up and then it turns out that she was wrong. That's what I wonder about. And besides, I had a couple of drinks before I left the bar. I mean, what if I made a mistake?

Rollins: Let me put your mind to rest about that. The man you identified is definitely the right person. We have a statement from his co-defendant that incriminates him. They got it right after he was arrested. We know he has a prior record for armed robbery.

(Wirtz withdraws, still undetected)

Miss Tate: Oh, well . . .

Rollins: Can we go in now? Can we?

Miss Tate: I still . . .

Rollins: Can we?

Miss Tate: Will I be first?

Rollins: Yes, but just relax. All you have to do is tell the truth and you'll be fine. Now when the, ah, defense attorney gets a chance to ask you questions, just answer what he asks. Don't volunteer anything that they might be able to use to get this guy off the hook. Oh, and you don't have to mention anything about these last-minute self-doubts that you have. You don't want to see a guy like this, with this kind of record, get off, do you?

Miss Tate: (*Shakes her head no*). I'm ready.

SCENE: *The courtroom.　The preliminary hearing is in progress.*

Judge: You may proceed, Mr. Rollins.

Rollins: State your name and address, please.

Miss Tate: My name is Polly Tate.　I live in the Royal Apartments in Arlington.

Rollins: And what is your occupation?

Miss Tate: I'm a student part-time, and I also work nights as a waitress, at Frank's Place.　It's a bar.

Rollins: Directing your attention to the evening of July 10th at or about 12:30 a. m.　Did anything unusual happen that evening?

Miss Tate: Yes, that was the night I was attacked.

Rollins: Would you please tell the court what happened in your own words?

(*Flashbacks of the attack appear intermittently as Miss Tate describes the event.*)

Miss Tate: I got off work a little late as usual.　My car was in the parking lot next door where I usually keep it and so I was walking, and you know, I've walked through that lot a hundred times, but there was something different about it that night.　I thought I heard something but I wasn't sure.　.　.　.　I never thought it could be so dark out there.　Anyway I started to hurry, and by the time I got to the car my hands were shaking, and I had trouble with the keys and that's when this guy came at me out of the dark.　I guess he was hiding behind one of the cars.　He, um, grabbed at me, and, um, he pulled on my purse, and I pulled back .　.　.　.　I don't know why .　.　.　. I guess I should have given it to him, maybe then he would have left me alone, but I didn't, and um, he had hold of me and the purse, and I could tell that he was angry.　You know what I mean?　And then he dropped the purse and that's when I broke and ran away .　.　.　.　.　. I was scared.　I was really scared.　I tried to run, you know, but the, uh, the ground was real uneven and I started to stumble and that's when he caught up with me .　.　.　.　I didn't see that he had a knife then, but he shov　.　.　.　shoved me to the ground, and I thought this is really it.　I can still see it.　The blade seemed to give off flashes of light.　The he said　.　.　.　"Shut up and hold still or I'll cut your face."　And then he was on top of me and he was tearing at my clothes and then, uh, I felt this smashing pain and my whole head was spinning　.　.　.　.　I guess that I decided that I was never going to get out of it alive.　And then this other guy, he came up and he started, uh, shaking the guy who was on top of me and he said something like, um, "Hey, this wasn't in the plan," and, uh, he said, uh, something like "Let's split, we've already got the pocketbook," and, uh, they must have run off then, but I didn't actually see them go. I must have passed out because the next thing I knew the policemen were there.

Rollins: Miss Tate, Miss Tate. Ah, I'd like to go back over your testimony to clarify some points. Did you say that you were shoved to the ground?

Miss Tate: Yes.

Rollins: And you were pushed into a sexual position?

Miss Tate: Yes.

Rollins: And the man that got on top of you, he said something else, didn't he?

Wirtz: Objection, your honor! This is leading, repetitious and aimed at prejudicing the court.

Judge: Overruled. You may answer the question.

Miss Tate: I guess I forgot to include this earlier. He said, uh, "Now you're gonna get what you want."

Rollins: Did you get a good look at the man who robbed and assaulted you that night?

Miss Tate: Yes.

Rollins: Do you see that person in this courtroom?

Miss Tate: I do. That's him.

Rollins: Let the record indicate that the witness has identified the defendant, John Link. Are you certain that this is the same man?

Miss Tate: Yes. I'm positive.

Rollins: When the defendant struggled with you, were you injured?

Wirtz: I object!

Rollins: I'm only trying to show the extent of the assault, your honor.

Judge: Overruled.

Rollins: What were your injuries?

Miss Tate: He broke my nose when he hit me.

Rollins: Were you taken to a hospital?

Wirtz: Objection, your honor!

Rollins: Tell us about the treatment, Miss Tate.

Miss Tate: I had to have surgery, twice.

Rollins: Were you hospitalized for some time after the assault?

Miss Tate: Yes.

Wirtz: I object to this entire line of questioning, your honor.

Judge: Cross-examine, Mr. Wirtz?

Wirtz: Thank you, your honor . . . . Have you discussed your testimony in this case with the prosecutor, Miss Tate?

Miss Tate: Yes, I have.

Wirtz: Did the prosecutor ever say anything to you about any of the other evidence in this case?

Miss Tate: No, not that I recall.

Rollins: Objection. I object to counsel's insinuation.

Wirtz: Are you prepared to take the stand and say that you haven't raised these issues with this witness?

Rollins: Your honor, I'm not the witness in this case.

Judge: Proceed, counsel. Let's get on with this.

Wirtz: All right, your honor. It is your testimony, then, that it was very dark when you were attacked and that you were very frightened? Is that correct?

Miss Tate: Yes, that's what I said.

Wirtz: And nevertheless you say that you're positive that you could identify John Link, that there's no question in your mind about that?

Miss Tate: No, none at all.

Wirtz: This man whose features you remember so clearly, had you ever seen him before the events you described?

Miss Tate: No.

Wirtz: The place you work, this Frank's Place. Can you describe the typical clientele, Miss Tate?

Miss Tate: Sure. They're almost always men, older guys, working types. They start coming in about cocktail hour, and it's pretty busy from then until closing time.

Wirtz: Did you ever leave the bar at closing time with one of the customers?

Miss Tate: Not very often.

Wirtz: Isn't it a fact, Miss Tate, that you regularly left the bar with customers?

Miss Tate: It was safer that way. That was the only reason. I wouldn't say it was regular, either.

Wirtz: Isn't it a fact that it was you who picked these men up? That you agreed to have sexual relations with them?

Rollins: Objection, your honor. Counsel is making wild allegations that he has no intention of substantiating. He is simply harassing the witness.

Wirtz: I can prove my allegations, your honor.

Judge: Are you prepared to produce witnesses in this matter, counsel?

Wirtz: I am, your honor. I'm calling two "customers" and I'm simply laying the foundation for that now. I will also establish that Miss Tate had been drinking immediately before she was allegedly assaulted.

Rollins: Whether counsel has witnesses or not, I don't see the relevance of this part of the cross-examination. The prior sexual conduct and drinking habits of this witness have no bearing on her veracity.

Wirtz: I'm showing that this witness made a regular practice of picking up men from the bar, just as she did on the night of July 10th, and that's highly relevant, your honor.

Judge: I'll overrule the objection.

Wirtz: Thank you, your honor.

Associate Counsel (whispering to Wirtz): Al, the judge is wrong on that. Prior bad conduct is not admissible to show credibility. There's a new case directly against us, and we don't have anything on her conduct for the night in question.

Wirtz (whispering): Let's not make the other side's arguments for them, okay? I've got enough problems already.

Wirtz: Miss Tate, I'm going to rephrase that last question. Is it your testimony that you did not leave Frank's Place with one of the customers that night?

Miss Tate: No, I didn't.

Wirtz: And you deny that you had a fight with one of them and then called the police with this story?

NOTES

1. *Relations with Courts and Other Decision-Makers: The Code*

The provisions in the Code governing zealous advocacy comprise over one-quarter of its content. Given that most lawyers spend only a small percentage of their time in the courtroom, the reason for this emphasis is somewhat unclear; perhaps it reflects a recognition that the same rhetorical and dramatic skills which make an advocate effective can also be the tools of a scoundrel. Certainly the paradox posed by the advocacy obligation seems highlighted in this area. What are we to make of an ethic which demands zealous advocacy, no matter how harsh the consequences, in the name of some greater, long-range good?

The most famous expression of the creed of partisanship is found in Lord Brougham's statement to the House of Lords on behalf of Queen Carolene:

"I once before," he said, "took leave to remind Your Lordships—which was unnecessary, but there are many whom it may be needful to remind—that an advocate by the sacred duty which he owes his client knows, in the discharge of that office, but one person in the world, *that client and none other*. To save that client by all expedient means, to protect that client at all hazards and costs to all others, and among others to himself, is the highest and most unquestioned of his duties. And he must not regard the alarm, the suffering, the torment, the destruction which he may bring upon any other. Nay, separating the duties of a patriot from those of an advocate, and casting them if need be to the wind, he must go on reckless of the consequences, if his part it should unhappily be to involve his country in confusion for his client's protection." [96]

The statement was a veiled threat that Lord Brougham intended, if necessary, to seek to impeach the title of the King of England to the Crown on the ground that, in marrying a Catholic, he had forfeited it under the Act of Settlement. Later commentary on the reality of the good Lord's intentions and even his conception of his professional obligations have found both somewhat extreme.[97] Nevertheless his statement provides an interesting benchmark from which to evaluate the actions of both Wirtz and Rollins and the contrasting visions of proper conduct by which the profession judges them.

The Decision to Proceed or Defend

As we have suggested before, Rollins' decision to go forward with the prosecution does not rest on the same ethical ground as the defendant's plea of guilty or the initiation of a civil action or defense. Even if the defendant has admitted his guilt to his lawyer, he is entitled in a criminal case to put the government to its proof. In a civil case, counsel must refrain from initiating an action or asserting a position only if such action "would serve merely to harass or maliciously injure another" or is "unwarranted" under existing law, and if a "good faith argument" cannot be made for change or modification.[98] In contrast, a prosecutor may not initiate a criminal prosecution if he or she knows or it is obvious that the charges are not supported by probable cause.[99] This standard, however, contains a number of ambiguities. It is not clear, for example, whether the prosecutor must determine whether (i) he or she would personally find probable cause on the evidence; (ii) a reasonable judge would find probable cause; or (iii) the particular judge who is likely to hear the case would find probable cause. Similarly, it is unclear what the prosecution should/must do if the probable cause standard is satisfied but he or she believes that (i) the defendant is innocent; (ii) the evidence is insufficient to find the defendant guilty; (iii) the evidence is insufficient to find the defendant guilty but a jury is likely to convict; or (iv) the evidence is sufficient to find the defendant guilty, but the jury, for some reason, is likely to acquit. The ABA Standards on Criminal Justice offer the following guidance on these problems:

> (a) In addressing himself to the decision whether to charge, the prosecutor should first determine whether there is evidence which would support a conviction.

---

96. W. Forsythe, HORTENSIUS 389 (1879).

97. *Id.*

98. DR 7–102(A)(1), (2). Further applications of this rule are discussed in Chapter One, *supra*, at pages 145–146.

99. DR 7–103(A). Note that this provision is limited to criminal cases. *Cf.* EC 7–14.

(b) The prosecutor is not obliged to present all charges which the evidence might support. The prosecutor may in some circumstances and for good cause consistent with the public interest decline to prosecute, notwithstanding that evidence exists which would support a conviction. Illustrative of the factors which the prosecutor may properly consider in exercising his discretion are:

(i) the prosecutor's reasonable doubt that the accused is in fact guilty;

(ii) the extent of the harm caused by the offense;

(iii) the disproportion of the authorized punishment in relation to the particular offense or the offender;

(iv) possible improper motives of a complainant;

(v) prolonged non-enforcement of a statute, with community acquiescence;

(vi) reluctance of the victim to testify;

(vii) cooperation of the accused in the apprehension or conviction of others;

(viii) availability and likelihood of prosecution by another jurisdiction.

(c) In making the decision to prosecute, the prosecutor should give no weight to the personal or political advantages or disadvantages which might be involved or to a desire to enhance his record of convictions.

(d) In cases which involve a serious threat to the community, the prosecutor should not be deterred from prosecution by the fact that in his jurisdiction juries have tended to acquit persons accused of the particular kind of criminal act in question.

(e) The prosecutor should not bring or seek charges greater in number or degree than he can reasonably support with evidence at trial.[1]

Does this resolve these ambiguities? To what effect? In the above transcript, Ms. Tate's doubts, even if admitted at the hearing, might not preclude the court from finding probable cause but would make a conviction beyond a reasonable doubt very unlikely. What is your understanding of the precise obligation of the prosecution under these circumstances?

This problem is further complicated by the prevalence of plea bargaining in the criminal process. Suppose Rollins believes the defendant to be innocent, but also believes that most judges, as a matter of course, will bind him over for trial—with the result that the defendant is likely to plead guilty without a trial. Consider what Rollins' obligation would be under the Code and the foregoing standards. Would your evaluation be different if Rollins thought the defendant was guilty? What policies and interests are served by these sorts of distinctions?

1. ABA Standards, THE PROSECU-
TION FUNCTION § 3.9 (1971).

"Preparing" the Witness

The prosecutor's obligations also differ from the defense lawyer's in the area of "coaching" the witness. In general, although a lawyer cannot participate in the creation of false evidence, he or she is entitled to help place the witness' testimony in a light favorable to the client. An illustration of the sort of instructions for witnesses suggested by experienced lawyers can be found on pages 231–35, *supra*. The leeway given counsel in this area would probably justify mentioning corrobative evidence to a witness or advising the witness to answer only what is specifically asked. If Ms. Tate were a defense witness, then, only the advice concerning not mentioning "doubts" would be ethically questionable, assuming it was interpreted as suggesting to her that she could lie about this aspect of her testimony.

The prosecutor's obligations in this area look rather different. There is a constitutional as well as an ethical requirement that he disclose "favorable evidence." And the injunction to see that "justice is done" would seem to require Rollins to disclose Ms. Tate's last minute doubts to defense counsel, and to prohibit his advising the witness not to mention her misgivings.[2] The same obligations would also seem to preclude Rollins from bolstering his witness by making (i) disclosures of damaging evidence against the accused, or (ii) statements about his own belief in the guilt of the accused.[3]

Most prosecutors with whom we have discussed this problem, however, disagree. They argue that all witnesses are entitled to be advised against exaggerating or talking too much in response to cross-exam questions and, furthermore, that all witnesses have doubts. Extending the disclosure obligation to minor inconsistencies or transitory "changes of mind," they feel, would make prosecution impossible and distort relations with victims and witnesses. At some point, they admit, such statements would properly be subject to disclosure—as in this case if Ms. Tate had said, at the end of the discussion, that she didn't believe they had the right man. They also concede that the information would have to be disclosed if it was directly requested. But short of these circumstances, they would argue, the prosecution is entitled to function in this situation very much as would a privately retained advocate.

---

2. *See generally* Brady v. Maryland, 373 U.S. 83 (1963); Giles v. Maryland, 386 U.S 66 (1967); DR 7–109(A); DR 7–102(A)(3); DR 1–102(A)(4), (5), (6); Note, *The Duty of The Prosecutor to Disclose Exculpatory Evidence*, 60 CAL.L.REV. 858 (1960). The prosecutor may, however, advise witnesses that they do not have to speak to defense counsel. Commonwealth v. McLaughlin, 352 Mass. 218, 369 F.2d 185 (D.C.Cir. 1966).

3. *But see* People v. McQuirk, 106 Ill. App.2d 266, 245 N.E.2d 917 (1969) ("a state's attorney may go over [a witness'] story with her, ease her embarrassment, familiarize himself with sexual terms she uses and perhaps suggest others. There is nothing wrong with this if the witness' essential testimony is neither altered nor colored by emphasis or suggestion").

Consider what your own judgment on these contentions would be, and whether it is consistent with the general provisions of the Code on prosecutorial conduct.[4] Give some thought as well to the propriety of Wirtz' listening in on Rollins' conversation with Ms. Tate. While the prosecutor is clearly not in a confidential relationship with the victim, there may be expectations of privacy in such relationships that warrant some protection.[5]

Trial Conduct

Similar contrasts can be drawn between the prosecutor's and defense attorney's conduct at trial. Rollins would clearly be acting improperly if he intentionally (i) asked another question in order to "get it in" before a ruling on the preceding one; or (ii) used leading questions without an evidentiary basis for doing so.[6] Much more difficult are the issues of (i) his failure to elicit testimony about Ms. Tate's drinking or her last minute doubts (presumably he would argue that she did not testify "falsely" as to this matter); [7] and (ii)

---

4. *See* DR 7–103(A), (B); EC 7–13, 7–14; Berger v. United States, 295 U.S. 78 (1935); ABA Standards, THE PROSECUTION FUNCTION § 3.11 (1971).

5. Although it was probably improper for Wirtz to continue to listen to the conversation, he would not seem to be prohibited from using the information so obtained. *Cf.* Canon 9 (requiring a lawyer to avoid "even the appearance" of professional impropriety). On the other hand, if he had inadvertently heard a confidential communication between a lawyer and his or her "client," he would have to withdraw. *See* ABA Opinions 47 (1931), 150 (1936).

6. *See, e. g.*, DR 7–106(C)(5), (6), (7). It is not clear whether the rules of evidence set the appropriate standard of conduct here and, if so, whether the prosecution is entitled to "see what the judge would do." *See, e. g.*, ABA Opinion 150 (1936) (even if evidence turned over to the prosecutor by the police would be admissible, it should not be used if it was obtained "by the setting of traps or by persuasion or duress").

7. The cases and opinions concerned with how tightly an attorney may question to elicit truthful but misleading evidence are collected at pages 143–145 in Chapter One. Whether the prosecutor has special obligations in

this regard is unclear. An interesting illustration is described in F. Frankfurter, THE CASE OF SACCO AND VANZETTI 76 (1927). Following the trial, the head of the state police, Captain Proctor, submitted an affidavit stating the following:

"At no time was I able to find any evidence whatever which tended to convince me that the particular model bullet found in Berardelli's body, which came from a Colt automatic pistol, which I think was numbered 3 and had some other exhibit number, came from Sacco's pistol, and I so informed the District Attorney and his assistant before the trial. This bullet was what is commonly called a full metalpatch bullet and although I repeatedly talked over with Captain Van Amburgh the scratch or scratches which he claimed tended to identify this bullet as one that must have gone through Sacco's pistol, his statements concerning the identifying marks seemed to me entirely unconvincing.

"At the trial, the District Attorney did not ask me whether I had found any evidence that the so-called mortal bullet which I have referred to as number 3 passed through Sacco's pistol, nor was I asked that question on cross-examination. The District Attorney desired to ask me that question, but I had *repeatedly* told him that if he did I should be obliged to answer in the negative; consequently, he put to me this question: Q. Have you an opinion as to whether bullet his pursuit of the line of questioning concerning her hospitalization. Suppose he personally believes the material has limited relevance and might prejudice the judge; indeed suppose that, were he ruling on the matter as a judge, he would not let it in. Should he, nevertheless, pursue this line of questioning? Even assuming that the judge is willing to allow this matter in evidence, the question remains whether it is proper for a prosecutor to elicit testimony which he or she believes ought to have been ruled inadmissible.[8] Though the distinction is not made explicitly in the Code, a defense lawyer would undoubtedly have more latitude on these issues.

On the other hand, much of Wirtz' conduct in the courtroom may violate even a private lawyer's obligations. Wirtz clearly may not allude to any matter which he has no "reasonable basis" to believe is relevant to the case.[9] It makes no difference that he can corroborate Ms. Tate's liaisons with "customers" generally, for he has no basis for asserting that one of these customers broke her nose on the night in question, as his conversation with co-counsel indicates. Would Wirtz' last question be considered such an assertion? Under the facts of this case the question cannot be justified as a challenge

number 3 was fired from the Colt automatic which is in evidence? To which I answered, 'I have.' He then proceeded. Q. And what is your opinion? A. My opinion is that it is consistent with being fired by that pistol." (Brief for Defendants on first appeal before Supreme Judicial Court, 161.) [Italics ours.]

He proceeded to state that he is still of the same opinion, "but I do not intend by that answer to imply that I had found any evidence that the so-called mortal bullet had passed through this particular Colt automatic pistol and the District Attorney well knew that I did not so intend and framed his question accordingly. Had I been asked the direct question: whether I had found any affirmative evidence whatever that this so-called mortal bullet had passed through this particular Sacco's pistol, I should have answered then, as I do now without hesitation, in the negative." (Brief for Defendants on first appeal before Supreme Judicial Court, 161.)

This example is reprinted in V. Countryman, T. Finman & T. Schneyer, THE LAWYER IN MODERN SOCIETY 295 (1976).

8. The contrary argument is a variant of Dr. Johnson's famous statement: I do not know it is inadmissible until a court determines that it is inadmissible. *See* Uviller, *The Virtuous Prosecutor in Quest of An Ethical Standard: Guidance from the ABA,* 71 MICH.L.REV. 1145 (1973). Monroe Freedman has pointed out the problems this view raises when the prosecutor knows or believes his or her adversary is inadequately prepared or incompetent. *See,* Freedman, *The Professional Responsibility of the Prosecuting Attorney,* 55 GEO.L.J. 1030, 1039–40 (1967). *cf.* Brown, *Ethics in Criminal Cases: A Response,* 55 GEO. L.J. 1048, 1060 (1967).

9. DR 7–106(C)(1). Note, however, that DR 7–106(C)(2), which deals with questions, prohibits asking a question which counsel "has no reasonable basis to believe is relevant to the case *and* that is intended to degrade a witness or other person." Certainly this permits him to explore areas on cross-examination where he does not know whether he will produce relevant answers; whether it permits him to suggest a version of the facts he knows is not true is doubtful. *See, e. g.,* Love v. Wolf, 226 Cal.App.2d 378, 38 Cal.Rptr. 183 (1964) ("did you know" question held improper when there was no factual basis for the implied assertion).

to her credibility, because the prevailing law has apparently excluded prior bad acts as a basis for impeachment. Indeed, he is obligated to inform the court of the adverse decision to this effect.[10] What then justifies his pursuit of this entire line of questions? Although a good many defense lawyers would disagree, our reading of the Code would prevent Wirtz from seeking to "create" such a defense on the basis of this kind of inference and innuendo. Again, in reviewing this material, you should think hard about whether you would reach a different judgment.

The Lawyers as Witnesses

There may also be differences in the propriety of either Wirtz or Rollins (i) testifying at the hearing, or (ii) calling each other to testify. Under the facts here, can you imagine circumstances in which either would want to testify or would consider calling the other? Would such a tactic be proper?

The general rule is that an attorney is competent to testify in a case he or she is handling and, when necessary, may do so without impropriety.[11] This is true whether a prosecutor or defense counsel is involved.[12] In practice, however, the necessity requirement is very rigidly construed and many courts routinely deny such requests.[13] Does this make sense? Should either Rollins or Wirtz be precluded from continuing in the case? Should a different rule be applicable to either of them? A recent comment on this issue sets out some of the reasons which have traditionally been given for this prohibition:

> The expressed reasons why an attorney should not participate in a trial in which he will testify are several. . . . [The] choice is compelled by the inconsistency of these roles and the resulting prejudice to a client's case. Because the attorney, as counsel, will be identi-

10. *See* DR 7–106(B)(1); *but see* ABA Opinions 146 (1935), 280 (1949). Note that the Code narrows the former rule to authority in the "controlling jurisdiction." *Cf.*, In re Greenberg, 15 N.J. 132, 104 A.2d 46 (1954). Whether this obligation is satisfied by an unobtrusive citation labelled "*cf*" or "*contra*," tucked away in a brief citing other authority, has not been clearly answered.

11. *See* DR 5–101(B); DR 5–102(A); EC 5–9, 5–10; see also DR 5–105(D). We briefly discussed these rules in connection with the transcript included in the ethics section of Chapter One, pages 141–42. You should consider how the situation of King there differs from that of the two attorneys in the instant case.

12. *See, e. g.*, People v. Stokley, 266 Cal. App. 1009, 72 Cal.Rptr. 513 (1968) (the

prosecutor was in the position of either doing nothing and thereby letting the jury think that he could not be trusted, or testifying in order to rehabilitate his position); Schwartz v. Wenger, 267 Minn. 40, 124 N.W.2d 489 (1963) ("certainly plaintiff's attorney could not have predicted before trial this unusual train of events. His failure to take the stand might well have been construed by the jury as a tacit admission.").

13. *See* Comment, *The Attorney as Both Advocate and Witness*, 4 CREIGHTON L.REV. 128 (1970). We assume, perhaps erroneously, that the rule is applied even more stringently against the prosecution. *But see* Robinson v. United States, 32 F.2d 505 (8th Cir. 1929).

fied with the cause of his client, his testimony as a witness will be susceptible to impeachment for interest and therefore ineffective.

* * *

A second reason advanced for disqualifying an attorney-witness—that public confidence in the legal profession would be shaken by the unseemly practice of lawyers testifying for their clients, derives from concern that the public would think that the lawyer tailored his testimony to the needs of his client. Support for this argument is found in Canon 9 of the Code, which provides that "(a) lawyer should avoid even the appearance of professional impropriety."

* * *

As a third reason for prohibiting testimony by a client's counsel, both the courts and the Code declare that the dual role is incompatible with the traditional judicial structure and disruptive of the orderly proceedings at trial. More specifically, courts have asserted that it is inconsistent for an attorney to drop the robes of a partisan advocate and to don those of an objective reporter of facts. The attorney thereby places himself in the awkward position of arguing his own credibility to the jury and places the opposing counsel in the embarrassing predicament of attacking the credibility of a professional colleague.[14]

Are these arguments persuasive? What counter arguments and alternative rules might be suggested?

The converse of this situation would arise if either attorney sought to call the other as a witness. Again, the practice is strongly "discouraged" and a number of courts have reversed criminal convictions where criminal prosecutors had been permitted to call defense counsel as a witness.[15] Are the policy issues different or similar here? Should a distinction again be drawn between defense counsel and the prosecutor?[16]

Disclosure of Perjury

There are also contrasts in the obligations of government and private attorneys in revealing "frauds" to the court. It is clear that Ms. Tate committed perjury when she denied that the prosecution said anything about "other evidence" in the case. Rollins has an unequivocal obligation under the Code to disclose this immediately. Instead, he compounds his failure to do so by his objections and denials.[17]

---

14. Comment, *The Rule Prohibiting an Attorney from Testifying at a Client's Trial: An Ethical Paradox,* 45 U. CINN.L.REV. 268, 269–71 (1976); see also Levy, *Time to Review the Code,* 62 A.B.A.J. 225 (1976).

15. *See, e. g.,* Rude v. Algiers, 11 Wis. 2d 471, 105 N.W.2d 825 (1960); Meeker v. Walraven, 72 N.M. 107, 380 P.2d 845 (1963); People v. Lathrom, 192 Cal. App. 216, 13 Cal.Rptr. 325 (1961).

16. With respect to defense counsel calling the prosecutor as a witness *compare* People v. Nelson, 89 Ill.App.2d 84, 233 N.E.2d 64 (1967) (not reversible error to refuse to hear witness), *with* State v. Lee, 203 S.C. 536, 28 S.E.2d 402 (1943) (court's refusal to permit prosecutor to be called denied defendant a fair trial).

17. *See* DR 7–102(B)(2); see also footnote 6, *supra.*

On the other hand, Wirtz' obligations in this interchange are more elusive. If Ms. Tate were his client, and he had not been advised beforehand that she would testify as she did, he would have no obligation to reveal the fraud.[18] If he learns of his client's intention to commit perjury before trial, his obligation is to withdraw.[19] If he learns of it during trial but before his client testifies, the ABA Standards suggest the following:

(a) If the defendant has admitted to his lawyer facts which establish guilt and the lawyer's independent investigation establishes that the admissions are true but the defendant insists on his right to trial, the lawyer must advise his client against taking the witness stand to testify falsely.

(b) If, before trial, the defendant insists that he will take the stand to testify falsely, the lawyer must withdraw from the case, if that is feasible, seeking leave of the court if necessary.

(c) If withdrawal from the case is not feasible or is not permitted by the court, or if the situation arises during the trial and the defendant insists upon testifying falsely in his own behalf, the lawyer may not lend his aid to the perjury. Before the defendant takes the stand

---

18. *See* DR 7–102(B)(1); DR 4–101(A), (B), (C); ABA Opinion 341 (1975). If you are unsure about the interaction of the several Code provisions and ethics opinions involved here, you should review pages 254–60 in THE LAWYERING PROCESS (1978). Bear in mind that a number of states have adopted DR 7–102(B)(1) without the clause relating to "privileged communications."

19. DR 7–102(A)(4)–(7); DR 2–110(B)(2); EC 7–26; *but see* M. Freedman, LAWYERS' ETHICS IN AN ADVERSARY SYSTEM 31–32 (1975):

In my opinion, the attorney's obligation in such a situation would be to advise the client that the proposed testimony is unlawful, but to proceed in the normal fashion in presenting the testimony and arguing the case to the jury if the client makes the decision to go forward. Any other course would be a betrayal of the assurances of confidentiality given by the attorney in order to induce the client to reveal everything, however damaging it might appear.

A frequent objection to the position that the attorney must go along with the client's decision to commit perjury is that the lawyer would be guilty of subornation of perjury. Subornation, however, consists of willfully procuring perjury, which is not the case when

the attorney indicates to the client that the client's proposed course of conduct would be unlawful, but then accepts the client's decision. Beyond that, there is a point of view, which has been expressed to me by a number of experienced attorneys, that the criminal defendant has a "right to tell his story". What that suggests is that it is simply too much to expect of a human being, caught up in the criminal process and facing loss of liberty and the horrors of imprisonment, not to attempt to lie to avoid that penalty. For that reason, criminal defendants in most European countries do not testify under oath, but simply "tell their stories". It is also noteworthy that subsequent perjury prosecutions against criminal defendants in this country are extremely rare. However, the judge may well take into account at sentencing the fact that the defendant has apparently committed perjury in the course of the defense. That is certainly a factor that the attorney is obligated to advise the client about whenever there is any indication that the client is contemplating perjury.

Is this a fair reading of these provisions? Do you agree with it as an interpretation of an attorney's moral obligation? Compare Meagher, *A Critique of Lawyers' Ethics in an Adversary System*, 4 FORDHAM URB.L.J. 289, 290–95 (1976).

in these circumstances, the lawyer should make a record of the fact that the defendant is taking the stand against the advice of counsel in some appropriate manner without revealing the fact to the court. The lawyer must confine his examination to identifying the witness as the defendant and permitting him to make his statement to the trier or the triers of the facts; the lawyer may not engage in direct examination of the defendant as a witness in the conventional manner and may not later argue the defendant's known false version of facts to the jury as worthy of belief and he may not recite or rely upon the false testimony in his closing argument.[20]

Does this resolve this issue satisfactorily? Why does the ABA not insist on withdrawal "if the situation arises at trial"? What alternatives to this approach would you propose?

With respect to Ms. Tate, Wirtz is dealing with a person "other than a client," and the disclosure obligation of DR 7–102(B)(2) seems to apply to him just as it does to the prosecution. Under these circumstances he could call the prosecutor to testify, despite his protestations, and could probably take the stand himself. But may he wait to disclose this perjury until trial? This might be the best course of action for tactical reasons—*e. g.*, to prevent the prosecution from preparing the witness to "explain" the answer at trial—but it is not clear whether it is consistent with the Code's requirements of prompt disclosure. If Wirtz' knowledge could be considered a "secret" within Canon 4, however, it could not be disclosed without his client's consent.

The Allocation of Decisional Authority

Finally, it is worth noting the differences between the prosecutor and defense counsel with respect to their authority to resolve these questions. The prosecutor owes a victim concern and cooperation, but the victim has no legal control over the government attorney's conduct.[21]

20. ABA Standards, THE DEFENSE FUNCTION § 7.7 (1971); see also Gold, *Split Loyalty: An Ethical Problem for the Criminal Defense Lawyer*, 14 CLEV.MAR.L.REV. 65, 69–70 (1965); *cf.*, McKissick v. United States, 379 F.2d 754 (5th Cir. 1967) ("If appellant told his attorney that he had committed perjury, that offense was in effect a continuing one so long as allowed to stay in the record to influence the jury's verdict. . . . The statement was good cause for the attorney to withdraw from the case, and he would have been subject to discipline had he continued in the defense without making a report. The attorney not only could, but was obligated to, make such disclosure to the court as necessary to withdraw the perjured testimony from the consideration of the jury").

A number of courts have indicated that in a civil case it is flatly unethical for the attorney to remain in the case after perjury has been committed. In re Carroll, 244 S.W.2d 474 (Ky.1951); In re Hardenbrook, 135 App.Div. 634, 121 N.Y.S. 250 (1909). At least one ethics committee has indicated that the attorney was required to "disclose the facts within his knowledge to those adversely affected." Disbarment Committee of the Supreme Court of Louisiana, Advisory Opinion # 4 (1930). Compare these holdings with the provisions cited in footnote, 18, *supra*.

21. There is, of course, some authority for a court, at the behest of a private

A defense counsel, on the other hand, must follow his or her client's wishes (within the bounds of law) on all matters which are not "merely technical." Ethical consideration 7–7 explicitly states:

> In certain areas of legal representation not affecting the merits of the cause or substantially prejudicing the rights of a client, a lawyer is entitled to make decisions on his own. But otherwise the authority to make decisions is exclusively that of the client and . . . binding on his lawyer.

In practice, it should be noted, the scope of authority exercised by lawyers at trial is much broader. Some hint of its scope is found in the ABA standards and accompanying commentary:

> (a) Certain decisions relating to the conduct of the case are ultimately for the accused and others are ultimately for defense counsel. The decisions which are to be made by the accused after full consultation with counsel are: (i) what plea to enter; (ii) whether to waive jury trial; (iii) whether to testify in his own behalf.

> (b) The decisions on what witnesses to call, whether and how to conduct cross-examination, what jurors to accept or strike, what trial motions should be made, and all other strategic and tactical decisions are the exclusive province of the lawyer after consultation with his client.

> (c) If a disagreement on significant matters of tactics or strategy arises between the lawyer and his client, the lawyer should make a record of the circumstances, his advice and reasons, and the conclusion reached. The record should be made in a manner which protects the confidentiality of the lawyer-client relation.

* * *

> In general, . . . it may be said that the power of decision in matters of trial strategy and tactics rests with the lawyer. . . . The lawyer must be allowed to determine which witness should be called on behalf of the defendant. . . . Similarly, the lawyer must be allowed to decide whether to object to the admission of evidence . . . whether and how a witness should be cross-examined . . . or whether to stipulate to certain facts. . . .

> Many of the rights of an accused, including constitutional rights, are such that only trained experts can comprehend their full significance and an explanation to any but the most sophisticated client would be futile. Numerous strategic and tactical decisions must be made in the course of a criminal trial, many of which will be made in circumstances which will not allow extended, if any, consultation. . . .

> Some decisions, especially as to which witnesses to call and in what sequence and what should be said in argument to the jury, can be anticipated sufficiently so that counsel can ordinarily consult with

citizen, to require that the prosecutor initiate a particular action. In general, however, a decision to charge is a matter of unreviewed and—sometimes—unreviewable discretion. *See* Breitel, *Controls in Criminal Law Enforcement*, 27 U.CHI.L.REV. 427 (1960).

his client concerning them. Because these decisions require the skill, training and experience of the advocate, the power of decision on them must rest with the lawyer, but that does not mean that he should completely ignore his client in making them. The lawyer should seek to maintain a cooperative relationship at all stages, while maintaining also the ultimate choice and responsibility for the strategic and tactical decisions in the case.[22]

The apparent conflict between this statement and Ethical Consideration 7–8 is hard to explain, and both are difficult to apply. For example, consider which of the decisions Wirtz has made or may have to make would properly be subject to the defendant's wishes. Even if Wirtz wished his client to participate in making such judgments, how could such a goal be realized?

At this point, you might look back at our discussions of the lawyer-client relationship in other contexts. To what extent is the issue of control different in interviewing, investigation and negotiation? In civil or criminal cases? Would it be possible and/or desirable to have a different standard to govern a lawyer's obligations to clients in carrying out the "technical" aspects of these tasks?

---

2. *The Larger Puzzle: The Lawyer's Responsibility for the Truth*

Admittedly there are many unanswered questions here. As you review the provisions of the Code, however, you might ask yourself whether your own notions of morality in advocacy are satisfied by the lines that are drawn between: (i) fact and law; (ii) advocacy and counseling; (iii) crimes and other wrongs; (iv) future crimes and past crimes; (v) non-disclosure and misrepresentation; (vi) acquiescence and participation; and (vii) public and private. Do these limits allow for the kind of relationship you would like to have with judge or jury? To what extent do they express judgments based on moral as well as institutional-policy (what works best) grounds? Not all forms of advocacy are governed by these standards. For example, compare the concept of zealous advocacy embedded in the Code with the following statements concerning ethics in debate and argument:

> (a) Persuasion .   .   . must promote deliberation and thought by the audience . . . Suggestion, deliberate omission or minimization of materials contrary to the speaker's case, and the deliberate use of non-rational motive appeals are inherently unethical because they shortcircuit the listener's critical thinking processes and, by so doing, deprive him of freedom of choice . . . The speaker must acquire the facts, present all the facts and must not go beyond the facts save where correct inferences lead. He must eschew suggestions as well as efforts to arouse interests or biases . . . An ethical

---

22. ABA Standards, THE DEFENSE FUNCTION § 5.2.

advocate is obliged to respect propositions which, when tested by his best thinking, prove to have a low truth probability.[23]

* * *

(b) *There is general agreement that some means of persuasion are unethical.* Let us list them:

(1) It is unethical to falsify or fabricate.

(2) It is unethical to distort so that a piece of evidence does not convey its true intent.

(3) It is unethical to make conscious use of specious reasoning.

(4) It is unethical to deceive the audience about the speaker's intent.

A person who wishes to be ethical must avoid these practices.
. . .

Second, some means of persuasion appear to be intrinsically sound. Advocacy which springs from reflective thought and systematic investigation leads most often to the wisest choices and the greatest probability of truth. . . .

* * *

. . . Although the advocate cannot experimentally test the conclusions he argues for, he can, by using reflective thinking and careful investigation, discover the probable degree of truth that his conclusions merit. *An ethical advocate is obliged to reject propositions which, when tested by his best thinking, prove to have a low truth-probability.* . . .

Finally, it should also be evident that some means of persuasion may be good or bad, depending upon the circumstances of their use. They appear, from an ethical viewpoint, to be intrinsically neutral. Rousing the emotions, for instance, may be a good tactic or it may be bad. The goodness or badness of it appears contingent upon the way in which it is done. . . . [The advocate,] having assured himself as well as he can of the soundness of his position, . . . may use such ethically neutral methods as suggestion, emotional excitation, and the like in ways which are consistent with and can be defended by reliable evidence and sound reasoning.[24]

(c) . . . in any area of activity, a man who seeks ethical behavior patterns . . . will probably guide his actions to conform with the values of truth, human welfare, and rationality . . . Argumentation is a part of the endeavor of the search for and communication of truth.

The argument that truth cannot always be ascertained is no excuse for superficial presentation . . . The standard requires that he engage in analysis and research for the purpose of discovering the available arguments and evidence which best reflect objective reality . . . Conversely . . . arguments framed for the

---

23. Haiman, *A Re-examination of the Ethics of Persuasion,* 3 CENTRAL STATES J. 4 (1952) (abridged).

24. W. Minnick, *The Ethics of Persuasion,* in THE ART OF PERSUASION 285–86 (1964).

sole purpose of winning   .   .   .   must be considered unethical.   The
primary responsibility   .   .   .   is to be rational   .   .   .   That is,
that sound evidence be marshalled to logical inferences.[25]

To what degree do these statements depart from your own aspirations?   From the norms that govern persuasion by lawyers?
Are the differences justified?   By this time the rationale for prevailing conceptions of the advocate's role must have a familiar ring.   Nevertheless, it is worth focusing more explicitly on the relationship of
this conception to the ideal of truth.   David Mellinkoff provides a
thoughtful discussion:

> Our system of justice   .   .   .   (although it insists that men
> cannot be permitted to perjure themselves)   .   .   .   searches not
> for truth but justice   .   .   .   .   It is a compound of honest testi-
> mony, rules of law and a not inflexible application of both to a particu-
> lar controversy between human beings.   .   .   .
>
> The great function of the lawyer in our society is not to establish
> or disprove guilt, but to see to it that an orderly process of justice is
> indeed continuous.   .   .   .
>
> The questions for the lawyer are not "Shall I defend a guilty
> man?", not "How can I argue for acquittal if I 'know' he is guilty?"
> The lawyer asks himself, "What is this man entitled to under the law?",
> "Under the established system of justice is there the required proof
> that this man is to be punished?"   Neither judge nor jury, legislator
> nor moralist, the lawyer is required to insist that his client be given
> what he is entitled to under the law, and that he not be punished
> unless there is the proof that our system of justice requires.   That
> is the lawyer's part of the system of justice in his prime role as the
> representative at law of another, less informed human being who
> places his life, liberty, or property in the lawyer's care.   On other
> occasions, when he has not assumed that representative role, the
> lawyer as legislator or citizen joins with others in attempting to im-
> prove the laws.   And at whatever level, if the system of justice as we
> know it and practice it ultimately does not achieve justice as we come
> to believe it, the system of justice will be in for change.
>
> In the meantime, the lawyer must be there to present a case for
> decision by others, advising according to the law, advising the witness,
> "Answer what you are asked!"   The law and the evidence.   Those are
> the lawyer's truths.   Certainly not "truth" in an absolute sense.   But
> close enough to "truth" to permit an orderly system of continuous
> justice to operate.   The language of "determination of truth" as the
> purpose of a trial confuses the public into believing that it is the
> will-o'-the-wisp we are after, God's truth, some sort of pure reason,
> as distinct from the truths that men live by.
>
> Whatever the torments of his private morality, the lawyer has got
> to know what the law of the land requires.   When Edward Coke fought
> his historic battle with King James over whether the law or the King
> ruled England, the King—so Coke later reported,

25. Rives, *Ethical Argumentation*, J.
AM.FORENSIC A. 79–85 (1914).

said that he thought the law was founded upon reason, and that he and others had reason, as well as the Judges: to which it was answered by me, that true it was, that God had endowed His Majesty with excellent science [i. e. knowledge], and great endowments of nature; but His Majesty was not learned in the laws of his realm of England, and causes which concern the life, or inheritance, or goods, or fortunes of his subjects, are not to be decided by natural reason but by the artificial reason and judgment of law, which law is an act which requires long study and experience, before that a man can attain to the cognizance of it: that the law was the golden met-wand and measure to try the causes of the subjects; and which protected His Majesty in safety and peace; with which the King was greatly offended, and said, that then he should be under the law, which was treason to affirm, as he said; to which I said, that Bracton saith, *quod Rex non debet esse sub homine, sed sub Deo et lege*. [that the King should not be under any man, but under God and the law.]

The lawyer's conscience like his law is a learned thing, not intuitive, untutored, abstract; it is not everyman's conscience. Applied to a specific case, the lawyer's conscience is a reflection of an educated sense of justice under law and of a thorough awareness of a lawyer's role in the system of continuing justice. The lawyer has got to know deep inside that even a guilty man is entitled to justice. To paraphrase what a California judge once said of the right of a drunken man to a safe street, a guilty man is as much entitled to a fair trial as an innocent one, and much more in need of it. In insisting that if even a guilty man is condemned it must be according to the regular forms that we have established, the lawyer serves his client today and the innocent tomorrow, and adds his passing encouragement to the old hope for a just society.[26]

Mellinkoff goes on to articulate distinctions between "personal and professional ethics," and a notion of a lawyer's "special moral requirements" as a rationale for the rules governing the lawyer's conduct as an advocate. Others have added the following to the justifications he offers:

—the need to encourage litigants and their counsel to ferret out all the possible facts and inferences relevant to the case;

—the desirability of having a counterweight to the tendency of judges and juries to reach their decisions too quickly and unreflectively;

—The sense of satisfaction a client may get from being able to turn his or her case over to a zealous advocate;

—the capacity of adversarial representation to narrow issues and to generate general agreement on basic facts;

26. D. Mellinkoff, THE CONSCIENCE OF A LAWYER 7, 157–59 (1973).

—the need to encourage disclosure by clients to lawyers (pre- sumably they would be less open if they knew the facts they provided could be revealed or would affect the zealousness of the representation);

—the priority given to human dignity by reconciling the inevi- table conflict between confidentiality and full disclosure in fa- vor of the former.

Ask yourself if this cluster of reasons warrants the pattern of obligations we have discussed. Are its assumptions realistic and valid? To what extent do they, necessarily, sacrifice truth, and what is the nature of this so often debated value?[27]

These inquiries set in sharper focus the question of alternatives. How many of these values could be preserved if the rules regulating counsel's obligations were modified? To what extent does the sys- tem in practice achieve the benefits thought to underlie the adver- sarial norms? Consider the following arguments for a very dif- ferent orientation advanced by Judge Marvin Frankel:

> Without opposing altogether the drive toward "clinical" training and certification, I am moved to deep skepticism. If, as I increasingly believe, the "art of advocacy" exhibits too much that is artful and not enough devotion to justice, how far should our law schools go in teaching it? Note in the list of subjects offered illustratively by the Chief Justice that the "arts" leading all the rest are those of "asking questions" and of "cross-examination, including the high art of when not to cross-examine." Consider to what a degree these arts consist in tailoring direct questions that will produce not the whole of the sprawling and unmanageable truth, but the portrayal that is most convenient and useful. All of us as advocates have sat in vital strategy sessions figuring out whether to ask a particular question or how to ask it so that the answer would be a properly controlled flow or trickle rather than a destructive geyser.
>
> * * *
>
> . . . [T]he need, I submit, is to reconsider our principles, not their teaching or application. In a system that so values winning and deplores losing, where lawyers are trained to fight for, not to judge, their clients, where we learn as advocates not to "know" in- convenient things, moral elegance is not to be expected. The morals of the arena and the morals of the marketplace . . . tend power- fully to shape our conduct.
>
> As for advocates specifically, the rule is essentially that they must not "knowingly" use "fraudulent, false, or perjured testimony" or "[k]nowingly engage in other illegal conduct . . . ." These are not sufficient rules for charting a high road to justice. The lawyer's capacity for ignorance is large. The proscriptions defining

---

27. The philosophical debate over the nature, meaning, possibility and desir- ability of this ideal is a very complex one. *See generally* THE LAWYER- ING PROCESS 84, footnote 32 (1978). *See also* Symposium, *On Liars and Ly- ing,* 29 SALMAGUNDI (Spring, 1975); M. Eck, LIES AND TRUTH (1970).

the "illegal" are narrow. The prohibitions, ethical or disciplinary, are under a canon telling the lawyer to *"represent a client zealously within the bounds of the law."* And the proscription of fraud and illegality is under an italicized heading proclaiming the *"Duty of the Lawyer to the Adversary System of Justice,"* not to the Truth or to Justice *simpliciter*.

Let us by all means stress ethics and seek to uplift ourselves. But let us not build our hopes for the system on a breed of lawyers and judges much better or worse than mere human beings. If we limit our fantasies in this respect, we will not expect that better rules of warfare are apt to produce peace and cooperative crusades for justice.

IV. Some Proposals

Having argued that we are too much committed to contentiousness as a good in itself and too little devoted to truth, I proceed to some prescriptions of a general nature for remedying these flaws. Simply stated, these prescriptions are that we should:

    (1) modify (not abandon) the adversary ideal,

    (2) make truth a paramount objective, and

    (3) impose upon the contestants a duty to pursue that objective.

A. *Modifying the Adversary Ideal*

We should begin, as a concerted professional task, to question the premise that adversariness is ultimately and invariably good. For most of us trained in American law, the superiority of the adversary process over any other is too plain to doubt or examine. The certainty is shared by people who are in other respects widely separated on the ideological spectrum. The August *Code of Professional Responsibility*, as has been mentioned, proclaims, in order, the *"Duty of the Lawyer to a Client,"* then the *"Duty of the Lawyer to the Adversary System of Justice."* There is no announced "Duty to the Truth" or "Duty to the Community." . . .

Our commitment to the adversary or "accusatorial" mode is buttressed by a corollary certainty that other, alien systems are inferior. We contrast our form of criminal procedure with the "inquisitorial" system, conjuring up visions of torture, secrecy, and dictatorial government. Confident of our superiority, we do not bother to find out how others work. It is not common knowledge among us that purely inquisitorial systems exist scarcely anywhere; that elements of our adversary approach exist probably everywhere; and that the evolving procedures of criminal justice, in Europe and elsewhere, are better described as "mixed" than as strictly accusatorial or strictly inquisitorial.

In considering the possibility of change, we must open our minds to the variants and alternatives employed by other communities that also aspire to civilization. Without voting firmly, I raise the question whether the virginally ignorant judge is always to be preferred to one with an investigative file. We should be prepared to inquire whether our arts of examining and cross-examining, often geared to preventing excessive outpourings of facts, are inescapably preferable to safeguarded interrogation by an informed judicial officer. It is permissible to keep asking, because nobody has satisfactorily answered, why our present system of confessions in the police station versus no confessions at all is better than an open and orderly procedure of having a judicial official question suspects.

If the mention of such a question has not exhausted your tolerance, consider whether our study of foreign alternatives might suggest means for easing the unending tension surrounding the privilege against self-incrimination as it frequently operates in criminal trials. It would be prudent at least to study closely whether our criminal defendant, privileged to stay suspiciously absent from the stand or to testify subject to a perjury prosecution or "impeachment" by prior crimes, is surely better off than the European defendant who cannot escape questioning both before and at trial, though he may refuse to answer, but is free to tell his story without either the oath or the impeachment pretext for using his criminal record against him. Whether or not the defendant is better off, the question remains open whether the balance we have struck is the best possible.

To propose only one other topic for illustration, we need to study whether our elaborate struggles over discovery, especially in criminal cases, may be incurable symptoms of pathology inherent in our rigid insistence that the parties control the evidence until it is all "prepared" and packaged for competitive manipulation at the eventual continuous trial. Central in the debates on discovery is the concern of the ungenerous that the evidence may be tainted or alchemized between the time it is discovered and the time it is produced or countered at the trial. The concern, though the debaters report it in differing degrees, is well founded. It is significant enough to warrant our exploring alternative arrangements abroad where investigation "freezes" the evidence (that is, preserves usable depositions and other forms of relatively contemporaneous evidence) for use at trial, thus serving both to inhibit spoilage and to avoid pitfalls and surprises that may defeat justice.

* * *

B. *Making Truth the Paramount Objective*

We should consider whether the paramount commitment of counsel concerning matters of fact should be to the discovery of truth rather than to the advancement of the client's interest. This topic heading contains for me the most debatable and the least thoroughly considered of the thoughts offered here. It is a brief suggestion for a revolution, but with no apparatus of doctrine or program.

We should face the fact that the quality of "hired gun" is close to the heart and substance of the litigating lawyer's role. As is true always of the mercenary warrior, the litigator has not won the highest esteem for his scars and his service. Apart from our image, we have had to reckon for ourselves in the dark hours with the knowledge that "selling" our stories rather than striving for the truth cannot always seem, because it is not, such noble work as befits the practitioner of a learned profession. The struggle to win, with its powerful pressures to subordinate the love of truth, is often only incidentally, or coincidentally, if at all, a service to the public interest.

We have been bemused through the ages by the hardy (and somewhat appealing) notion that we are to serve rather than judge the client. Among the implications of this theme is the idea that lawyers are not to place themselves above others and that the client must be equipped to decide for himself whether or not he will follow the path of truth and justice. This means quite specifically, whether in *Anatomy of a Murder* or in Dean Freedman's altruistic sense of commitment, that the client must be armed for effective perjury as well as he would be if he were himself legally trained. To offer anything less is arrogant, elitist, and undemocratic.

It is impossible to guess closely how prevalent this view may be as a practical matter. Nor am I clear to what degree, if any, received canons of legal ethics give it sanction. My submission is in any case that it is a crass and pernicious idea, unworthy of a public profession. It is true that legal training is a source of power, for evil as well as good, and that a wicked lawyer is capable of specially skilled wrongdoing. It is likewise true that a physician or pharmacist knows homicidal devices hidden from the rest of us. Our goals must include means for limiting the numbers of crooked and malevolent people trained in the vital professions. We may be certain, notwithstanding our best efforts, that some lawyers and judges will abuse their trust. But this is no reason to encourage or facilitate wrongdoing by everyone.

Professional standards that placed truth above the client's interests would raise more perplexing questions. The privilege for client's confidences might come in for reexamination and possible modification. We have all been trained to know without question that the privilege is indispensable for effective representation. The client must know his confidences are safe so that he can tell all and thus have fully knowledgeable advice. We may want to ask, nevertheless, whether it would be an excessive price for the client to be stuck with the truth rather than having counsel allied with him for concealment and distortion. The full development of this thought is beyond my studies to date. Its implications may be unacceptable. I urge only that it is among the premises in need of examination.

If the lawyer is to be more truth-seeker than combatant, troublesome questions of economics and professional organization may demand early confrontation. How and why should the client pay for loyalties divided between himself and the truth? Will we not stultify the energies and resources of the advocate by demanding that he judge the honesty of his cause along the way? Can we preserve the heroic lawyer shielding his client against all the world—and not least against the State—while demanding that he honor a paramount commitment to the elusive and ambiguous truth? It is strongly arguable, in short, that a simplistic preference for the truth may not comport with more fundamental ideals—including notably the ideal that generally values individual freedom and dignity above order and efficiency in government. Having stated such issues too broadly, I leave them in the hope that their refinement and study may seem worthy endeavors for the future.

C. *A Duty to Pursue the Truth*

The rules of professional responsibility should compel disclosures of material facts and forbid material omissions rather than merely proscribe positive frauds. This final suggestion is meant to implement the broad and general proposition that precedes it. In an effort to be still more specific, I submit a draft of a new disciplinary rule that would supplement or in large measure displace existing disciplinary rule 7–102 of the *Code of Professional Responsibility*. The draft says:

(1) In his representation of a client, unless prevented from doing so by a privilege reasonably believed to apply, a lawyer shall:

(a) Report to the court and opposing counsel the existence of relevant evidence or witnesses where the lawyer does not intend to offer such evidence or witnesses.

(b) Prevent, or when prevention has proved unsuccessful, report to the court and opposing counsel the making of any untrue statement by client or witness or any omission to state a material fact necessary in order to make statements made, in the light of the circumstances under which they were made, not misleading.

(c) Question witnesses with a purpose and design to elicit the whole truth, including particularly supplementary and qualifying matters that render evidence already given more accurate, intelligible, or fair than it otherwise would be.

(2) In the construction and application of the rules in subdivision (1), a lawyer will be held to possess knowledge he actually has or, in the exercise of reasonable diligence, should have.

* * *

. . . The draft provision for wholesale disclosure of evidence in litigation may be visionary or outrageous, or both. It certainly stretches out of existing shape our conception of the advocate retained to be partisan. As against the yielding up of everything, we are accustomed to strenuous debates about giving a supposedly laggard or less energetic party a share in his adversary's litigation property safeguarded as "work product." A lawyer must now surmount partisan loyalty and disclose "information clearly establishing" frauds by his client or others. But that is a far remove from any duty to turn over all the fruits of factual investigation, as the draft proffered here would direct. It has lately come to be required that some approach to helpful disclosures be made by prosecutors in criminal cases; "the suppression by the prosecution of evidence favorable to an accused upon request violates due process where the evidence is material either to guilt or to punishment, irrespective of the good faith or bad faith of the prosecution." One may be permitted as a respectful subordinate to note the awkward placement in the quoted passage of the words "upon request," and to imagine their careful insertion to keep the duty of disclosure within narrow bounds. But even that restricted rule is for the *public* lawyer.   Can we, should we, adopt a far broader rule as a command to the bar generally? [28]

Do you find merit in Judge Frankel's suggestions?   Is the system he envisions really very different from the present one, which, in his terms, "so values winning and deplores losing"?   In what ways and with what consequences?

In confronting these questions be careful that you are clear about precisely what lawyers do and do not do when they press claims adversarially.   Is it enough to say that lawyers don't "really lie," or to be content, with Mellinkoff, with "a lawyer's truth."   A legal proceeding certainly allows more omission, false inference and uncorrected error than one would find consistent with an undiluted passion for accuracy.   Take the demands of closing argument.   It is common for counsel to ask the judge or jury to draw inferences about a client's innocence, a witness' credibility, the "cause" or consequence of a given event, on the basis of evidence he or she knows is incomplete or distorted.   Even where such statements can be preceded by "the evidence shows," they are hardly what we mean when we give common sense content to the notion of "truth-statements."   Nor does one usually label as truthful the common assertions that "there is no evidence   .   .   .   that [X, Y, or Z] is the case" when such evidence has been withheld or excluded.   And it is surely a rigid formalism which fails to recognize that inferences drawn by counsel also convey some personal warrant of their correspondence to reality.

What is offered to justify these departures from "truth" are the claims of policy, tradition and practicality.   No one, it is urged, ever tells the whole truth.   And there are many conflicts in social experience in which deception may be the lesser of two evils.   There are occasions, for example, when it may be more "cruel" to tell the truth than to lie, and surely kindness has its place in any scheme of ends (if one's ends don't justify one's means, what does?).   The question for law and the lawyer is whether the sorts of distortions, omissions, silences and permissable inferences in which lawyers engage— in each of the contexts in which they work—are warranted.   As John Smith has commented in his discussion of Ibsen's deeply troubling treatment of truth-telling in the *Wild Duck:*

> There is always a creative element in human decision and action and this element expresses the moral quality of the moral self.   Nevertheless, there must be in all moral action a pole representative of stable

28.   M. Frankel, *The Search for Truth: An Umpireal View,* 123 U.PA.L.REV. 1031, 1047–48, 1051–59 (1975).   Judge Frankel's views have touched off a spirited debate.   *See* Freedman, *Judge Frankel's Search for Truth,* 123 U.PA. L.REV. 1060 (1975); Uviller, *The Advocate, the Truth and Judicial Hackles: A Reaction to Judge Frankel's Idea,* 123 U.PA.L.REV. 1067 (1975); *cf.,* Damaska, *Presentation of Evidence and Factfinding Precision,* 123 U.PA. L.REV. 1083 (1975).

principle, a standard by reference to which action is to be judged. Even if we refuse to accept casuistical justification of lying, some clear principle is necessary if we are to make any pronouncement about the situation at all.

Deliberate deception, we may say, could be a course of action for us, *if and only if*, we are reasonably sure that the situation satisfies two conditions. First, the end in view, must be such that it clearly outweighs in importance the denial of the validity of truth implicit in such deception. Secondly, the act of deception must be one which may reasonably be expected to achieve, or in some material way contribute to, the desired objective. There are situations in human life where telling the truth and especially what must pass in ordinary situations as the whole truth would result in a state of affairs worse than before. This much must be admitted. Violation, however, of so basic a principle as the universality of truth can be countenanced only with a deep awareness that disloyalty to truth in any instance is an action which ultimately strikes at the heart of the distinction between truth and falsity itself. As soon as we enter into a weighing of the evidence for or against telling the truth in a given case, we are essentially bartering truth and attempting to translate it into a value in exchange. We are attempting to give it a price and when we do that we are implying that truth is a piece of our property which we may keep or withhold at will, depending upon our belief that another person does or does not have the right to the truth we possess. In cases where we think we can see that telling less than the truth will achieve a result which is good, we are inclined to think that talk about the universality of truth and our unqualified commitment to it is rather high flown and that only a hopeless "absolutist" would continue to argue that the lie should not be told. Consider, however, whether there is any logical difference between the case where we deny truth to a man on the ground that he would misuse it if he possessed it, and the case where a government in propaganda denies truth to others on the ground that they would misuse it if they possessed it. In both cases there is a clear identity, namely, the judgment that truth is to be communicated only upon conditions which the one who possesses it can determine. What troubles me in all this, is that the will to truth in our Western tradition, empirical science being one of the most striking expressions of that will, has taught us to regard truth as no man's private property disposable at will upon any conditions a man wants to propose. It may be objected, of course, that the two cases cited are different in character, and I would certainly admit that they are, but, on the other hand, there is the underlying identity in both cases, the principle that truth can be withheld or communicated upon conditions specified by the one who "owns" the truth.

* * *

It will not do simply to say that man must distort the truth in order to live, for whatever need he may have for deception, the fact remains that man is still the being who can attain to truth and he continues to remain under its judgment. To whom much is given, much will be required; man continues to be the foremost exemplification of this truth. The dignity of man and at the same time the depth of his frailty and willfulness is made manifest by his being held accountable in terms of an ideal which he can never literally realize.[29]

It may be that, notwithstanding the problems described by Frankel and many others, Smith's conditions are met in the special circumstances of lawyer work. At the very least, however, we ought to be honest with ourselves. Where else could any discussion of deception begin?

29. Smith, paper delivered at the Jewish Theological Seminary of America, New York City (1956).

Chapter Three

ARGUMENT: THE CASE PRESENTED

SECTION ONE. PRELIMINARY PERSPECTIVES

A. IMAGES AND FRAGMENTS

KAPLAN AND WALTZ, THE TRIAL OF JACK RUBY

325–31 (1965).

Now came the real start of Belli's argument. It was a set speech, but in Melvin Belli's magnificent voice it hushed the room.

But let us see now in the beginning small hours of the morning, when great discoveries in the history of the world have been made in garrets and attics and basements, if here in a temple of justice we can't rediscover something that was never lost in your great city of Dallas, that we may rediscover justice.

It was a fine beginning, setting a mood that involved the true splendor of the law. But the mood was promptly shattered by the ego of its creator. The jurors sat stony-faced as Belli confided to them that

my life has been dedicated to the law. Perhaps except for the months that Howard Naffziger wanted me to leave the law and go into his specialty of brain surgery—other than for those perhaps few months I think I have dedicated my whole academic life to my discipline, the discipline of the law.

Leaving autobiography for the moment, Belli launched into what was to be his central contention: that Jack Ruby must be acquitted outright. "I can't find it in my heart that you want the blood of this man on your hands, this sick man, or that you want one year of his time." Even a suspended sentence would be too much: "[H]e's already had four months and you know what one week, two weeks, three weeks is in partial confinement."

Then he began laying out his medical defense before the glassy-eyed jurors.

We've only gone to the cortex or outer surface of it trying to determine whether this man was sick. . . . maybe they'll laugh at us . . . as we laughed at those not so many years ago who tried to transfuse sheep blood [The stenographic transcript, at this point, says "cheek bone" but we may assume that

377

the court reporter was tired too]. That wasn't very long ago. They knew nothing of the Rh factor, which now would be malpractice not to consider. They didn't even know the classifications of the blood at the beginning of the century.

Now, Belli hoped, an American jury would find itself capable of wedding law with science. He discussed the testimony of the defense's medical experts, beginning with psychologist Roy Schafer, who, "with his Rorschach and the rest of these things," had ruled out schizophrenia and paranoia and ruled in organic brain damage. Thereafter Dr. Towler, "your own Texan," had conducted electroencephalographic tests and found in Ruby "a psychomotor variant type of epilepsy, given to rage states." Schafer had been corroborated. And then "Dr. Gibbs himself came down here." Now Belli embarked upon a series of allusions to past medical greats—Semmelweis, Pasteur—that provoked an objection, technically correct perhaps but by no means magnanimous, that he was traveling beyond the trial record. Judge Brown curtly instructed him to "stay in the record" and Belli returned to the living. Dr. Frederic A. Gibbs, "one of the great scientists of this country," had seen psychomotor epilepsy in Jack Ruby's EEG tracings. Countering one of Bill Alexander's points in his cross-examination of Gibbs, Belli reverently remarked, "I know other healers who weren't licensed to practice either."

Ruby's chief counsel stressed the diagnostic importance of the EEG, pointing out that "there is now an electroencephalographic machine in every major hospital." Here Alexander interrupted again to object that the San Franciscan was going outside the evidence. But Judge Brown silenced the assistant district attorney. "I think it's in there. I remember the remark, Counsel."

The leader of the defense team altered the course of his argument and, for a moment, it seemed that he was requesting mercy for his client. "I don't advocate lynch law," he began. "But our legislature of the great Lone Star State has said that where there is great stress, such as a husband and a wife and an adulterer, that there should be an excuse. And if there is an excuse in the shooting of someone with a wife, how about someone shooting the assassin of the President?" However, Belli was not suggesting that Ruby's had been a crime of passion. He had turned his back on the defensive approach suggested months before by attorney Tom Howard. He advised the jury, "That isn't the case we have here."

There was a second category, said Belli, into which some might feel Ruby fit: "the man who has the unstable personality." Summoning up a story recounted by one of the prospective jurors on *voir dire*, Belli referred to "the man that runs out onto the football field to tackle the man on the opposing team." Someone, he added, with the sort of mind that Dr. Holbrook, "the jailhouse psychiatrist, said

Ruby had." As the defendant listened without expression, his chief defense attorney sketched a word-picture of his personality.

Ah, great sport to have a character in the community. In the old days we used to call them—what? The village clown, the village idiot? There's the chained wolf, there's the hunchback of Notre Dame, there's our own Emperor Norton out in San Francisco, the old humpty-dumpty who would bend over and allow people to hit him on the backside with a board. Ah, fine, until there's trouble and then the cry goes out, "Who do you suspect the most; who would do a thing like this?" The village character. You substitute the village idiot, the village clown, or who?

Nor did Ruby's expression change while Belli discussed the prosecution charge that Ruby had committed the crime to gain publicity:

Ah, Ladies and Gentlemen, I suppose before that handful of dust settles down on the plain to be scratched up by the dancing tumbleweed, that we'd all like to engrave our initials in some oak tree, that we'd like to be maybe in Bob Considine's or Inez Robb's or Dorothy Kilgallen's column [all three were in the audience at the time]. There are some of us even that are engraved on Mt. Rushmore. There are some of us who do the immortal Shakespeare, Gray's *Elegy in the Churchyard*. There are others of us who have other forms of immortality. I think it's a part of our craving to seek after some bit of immortality.

Now Belli turned to the State's evidence. "Archer!" he spat out in a voice tinged with contempt. It was Archer, Belli reminded the jurors, who had related Ruby's purported statement that, "I intended to shoot him three times," and "Do you think I was going to let the so-and-so get by with it?" "Mr. Archer," Belli asserted, "is the keystone." Belli, it seemed, had two strings in his bow. First, Ruby had not made the remarks which Archer attributed to him, and second, even though he had done so, the statements were mere confabulation. The jury could take its choice. Belli reminded the jurors that in Archer's written report "there is not one word of anything that Jack is reported to have said by this officer when he was on the stand," and then told them that "[E]ven if all those things were said, are you not satisfied on the mental process of what's called confabulation? . . . You know what confabulation is."

Belli next described a third category to which Jack Ruby might be assigned. This category, he explained, involved the person who not only has an unstable personality but "comes of bad stock" and has psychomotor epilepsy. "[W]ould you apply the law of Texas of the suspended sentence" to such a man? asked Belli. His answer was No. Any man in this third category, Belli argued, "should be not guilty by reason of insanity at the time of the act." The defense, in short, was still arguing that the accused had killed while unconscious. "Here we have an honest-to-God blackout, temporary fugue," he said—and his evidence was still the tangible evidence needed to convince the concrete-thinking Texans.

These tracings and these hold a man's, not life, not life, but his years, his years, his freedom in your hands.

Then he returned to the village clown theme:

And when you put your head on your pillow tonight, you search your own experience in what you were thinking and what you were saying about this man who shot the President. And then ask yourself, "Who would be the most logical candidate to do it [i. e., murder the alleged assassin]?" The village clown, the character, the man who knows the police, who's tolerated in the police department, who runs down and gets the sandwiches, and gets all the rest of it. And is with the big shots and can say hello to the officials. His little touch of recognition. His little touch of, if you will, immortality.

Now Belli etched a picture of the very event. He spoke of how circumstances had inexorably conspired to enmesh Jack Ruby. "The conspiracy—time, place, event." Down the basement ramp walked Jack Ruby. He was in turmoil. "The lid was on but it was bubbling." There were lights, people, noise. "The leering face comes out that he had seen before." A flashbulb explodes. "The man comes out, he goes up, and the shooting. . . ." Having shot Lee Oswald, Jack Ruby—the man who loved cops—kept his finger on the trigger of his revolver, a revolver that now was aimed at a policeman. And Ruby's finger—was it the middle one?—was "contracting, convulsing" on the trigger. "There you have it," said Belli, "the continuance of the state."

Melvin Belli turned to the Texas test of insanity, the unembellished *M'Naughten* rule. "It's a law that there has been a lot of criticism of, and I've been on a lot of programs pro and con." He told the jurors that he could not rely on a theory of irresistible impulse "because we don't have it in your state. . . . The law in the State of Texas," he continued, "is that this man cannot know what he was doing at the time." Again, Belli urged the jurors to conclude that Ruby had been "in a state of unconsciousness" when he shot and killed Oswald. He insisted that Gibbs had established that when one suffers from psychomotor epilepsy "it follows, as the sun follows the moon, that you get the rage states, you get the unconsciousness, you get the islands of memory." . . .

* * *

Belli's entire argument made it clear that he felt there was only one proper disposition of Jack Ruby's case: he must be acquitted outright, on grounds of insanity. Over and again Belli informed the jurors that there was no middle ground, no room for compromise. "I'll stand before you as long as you'll tolerate me to argue against putting a man in bedlam who has a personality disorder and who has epilepsy!" he boomed. If it were true, as suggested by the prosecution, that Texas made no provision for the treatment of the criminally insane, then "Acquit him, not guilty by reason of insanity."

> You cannot find this sick man guilty of anything. It would be an incongruity to compromise and say one year, two years, five years.

Then, in what turned out to be one of the prize ironies of the trial, Belli continued.

> Where do you have the right to take a man's liberty—not his life, we're not even talking about that—his liberty, when he is one of the afflicted? . . . You can't arrogate unto yourselves, you good jurors of this good town, the right to put a sick man in jail for six months, or to put a stigma on him by a suspended sentence. . . .

Again and again: "[T]his man should be not guilty by reason of insanity at the time of the act." "This poor sick fellow—and sick he is, and you know he's sick in your hearts, every one of the twelve of you." Belli repeatedly insisted that the jury could not consider even a suspended sentence.

> You can't give him a suspended sentence, you couldn't, he's already had four months.

A suspended sentence might be appropriate for a man who has killed the seducer of his wife, said Belli, but this case was different. "[S]o there will be no question about it—this man should be turned out. . . . You can't free him completely, he's already had four months. And you know what three weeks are there." In apparent seriousness, Belli added, "If you put a felony of any kind on him, he won't be eligible for Veteran's Administration. He is now, being an ex-serviceman. . . . They can give treatment for a case like this, and he'll get treatment."

Now Belli was beginning to ramble. It was late at night and the fatigue of the trial and of the late hour was having its effect. More and more he focused his argument on himself rather than on Ruby. The pronoun "I," already at least as prominent in Belli's argument as was the name of the defendant, became steadily more so. He advised the jury that "I have tried cases in any number of courts and jurisdictions in this country and abroad," and that "I once did a lecture on this." After having referred to Rabbi Silverman as "Father Silverman" Belli informed the Protestant jury, "I have a son who is a priest." He referred to Dr. Gibbs as "the man, the year before I was graduated from law school—and I graduated from Boalt Hall at the University of California, in 1933—the year before I got out of law school, was just inventing the encephalogram." "[A]gainst the criticism of my brothers at the bar, I marched this boy, or this man, before laboratory work." "I got the best I could." "I have my own views of penology." "I'd go before the governor of my own state, as I've done many times . . . I'd go before my own governor and say there must be a doubt." "I'm an avowed foe of capital punishment." "I brought Dr. Gibbs here." "I say, collectively, as the thirteenth juror . . ." "I told you the category that this man is in." Wittingly or unwittingly, Melvin Belli was inviting his Dallas jury to try Melvin Belli.

With a noticeable effort of will Belli drew his argument to a sudden close. He told the jurors, "You're an intelligent jury and I don't butter you up." He directed them to "use your God-given intelligence in this case" and to "be true unto yourselves." Belli was certain that "with the personality disorder and the psychomotor epilepsy, you'd send him where he belongs." "And, as I stated, thank you. Thank all of you for your attention."

It was 12:40 on Saturday morning, March 14, 1964, and Melvin Belli was very tired as he resumed his seat. Behind him at the defense table Joe Tonahill was weeping unabashedly, the tears coursing unchecked down his large face. Tonahill's reaction was not the only favorable one Belli evoked. Although the great majority of American reporters present in Dallas were less than impressed, the foreign contingent found Belli's summation much to their liking. Belli himself wrote, "I did my best, but the hour was too late; the jury had been assailed by too much noise and emotion."

It is all too easy to summon hindsight in the assessment of a trial lawyer's approach to a serious and intricate case. Those who do not bear the responsibility for drawing up a theory of the case and for making split-second tactical decisions can be too quick to criticize the man on the firing line. Nonetheless, of all of the tactical mysteries of a mysterious trial, probably the two greatest occurred in Melvin Belli's closing argument. First, he failed to suggest to the jury a conviction for murder without malice. Only Phil Burleson of the three defense attorneys had adverted to this, and then without the expenditure of much time or effort. The second, and probably the greatest, mystery of the case was why Belli did not even try to talk the jury out of imposing the death penalty on his client. In certain cases an all-or-nothing defense has some merit since, by preventing a compromise verdict, it makes the jury more likely to return an outright acquittal. But to do this in a capital case is a dangerous thing indeed, unless one is very sure of one's case for acquittal. And to do it when the case for acquittal on the ground of insanity has collapsed completely is almost inexplicable. . . .

LEONARD BOUDIN, ORAL ARGUMENT TO THE SUPREME COURT IN KENT v. DULLES

Supreme Court of the United States, 1958.
357 U.S. 116, 78 S.Ct. 1113, 2 L.Ed.2d 1204.

[Editors' Note: Early in 1956, Secretary of State John Foster Dulles refused to issue passports to Rockwell Kent, an artist, and Walter Briehl, a psychiatrist, because they would not file affidavits relating to Communist or alleged Communist activities, as required by regulations promulgated by the Secretary.

Kent and Briehl brought suit in the District of Columbia claiming:

(1) that the Secretary had no authority or inherent power to condition the issuance of passports on standards such as Communist affiliations or activities;

(2) that the regulations were not authorized by Congress and were in conflict with the controlling statutes;

(3) that the Secretary's refusal to issue passports to Briehl and Kent abridged their first amendment rights of free speech and association and their fifth amendment rights of travel and due process.

At this time, travel had not been held to be a constitutionally protected liberty and the "chilling effect" doctrine in the free speech area was not developed. Dombrowski v. Pfister was decided in 1965.

Although the government had claimed throughout the proceedings that there was no constitutionally protected right to travel, and that the Secretary had inherent power to promulgate the disputed regulations, it conceded these two points shortly before the Supreme Court argument. Thus the government's primary contentions at the argument were (i) that the Secretary's regulations and actions were authorized by the McCarran-Walter Act of 1952 and the Security Act of 1950; and (2) that there were no denials of first or fifth amendment rights.

Boudin and others had been litigating the passport issue in the District for five years. On analogous issues, the Supreme Court had split 5–4 with Justices Warren, Black, Douglas and Brennan in the minority and clearly in the civil libertarian camp; Justices Burton, Clark, Harlan and Whittaker were clearly in the government's camp and Justice Frankfurter with the majority but not firmly. In other words, one way of conceiving Boudin's task was that he had to persuade Frankfurter to shift sides and join Warren, Black, Douglas and Brennan. The argument was made on April 10, 1958.]

Mr. Chief Justice and your Honors. These cases, which are suits for passports by American citizens against the Secretary of State, arose in the District of Columbia and involve the following issue: whether the Secretary of State has the right to deny passports to American citizens on the basis of political standards devised by the Secretary of State. The issues involved are both statutory and constitutional. We shall, of course, address ourselves to the alleged lack of authority on the part of the Secretary of State under any statutes of the United States.

The facts, which I shall advert to very briefly, are these: Dr. Walter Briehl is an American psychiatrist of approximately 27 years. He served as a lieutenant colonel in the United States Army in charge of army hospitals, that is, the psychiatric parts of the hospitals. He is a practicing psychiatrist in Los Angeles and is connected with many medical societies, psychoanalytic, psychiatric and otherwise, which are specified in the record. As a member of these societies, as a delegate of these medical societies, he has had occasion to travel abroad—most recently in 1953—with an American passport for the purpose of attending international conventions on mental health and on psychoanalysis, and reporting back to his medical society. He did that in 1953 and when he attempted to renew his passport in 1955 for the same purpose, acting as a delegate of his medical society, he received instead a typical letter from the director of the passport office in which it said that certain allegations have been made against Dr. Briehl by persons who were not specified—the allegations were of course not sworn as far as we know—that he had at one time, unspecified, been a member of the Communist Party and that he had been a member of a number of organizations on the Attorney General's list—three or four or five, or associated with them—and that he had once petitioned the President of the United States not to prosecute communists under the Smith Act. And so the Department, having made these charges against Dr. Briehl, said to him in this letter, "we ask you now for an affidavit as to whether you have ever been a member of the Communist Party"—ever—"whether you are now, and we ask you also to explain under oath your connections with a communist front organization which we have described in our letter and any other communist front organization." Dr. Briehl demanded a hearing—a quasi-judicial hearing, in view of the recent decision of the Court of Appeals, Dulles against Nathan—and instead he received an informal hearing in the passport office in 1955 at which he was the only witness. No witnesses were offered by the government in support of any of the allegations, and instead the passport office sought to examine Dr. Briehl with respect to the subject matter of his letter. He declined to answer the question with respect to Communist Party membership, communist front organizations so-called, or his associations, and the department refused to issue a passport to him—indeed, refused to act upon his passport application at all.

The case of Mr. Rockwell Kent is essentially the same. Mr. Kent, a well-known explorer, writer, and artist—internationally known, of course—known, I assume, to the members of this court. He has travelled abroad very widely for more than 50 years, using passports when passports were required as they have more recently, and I assume travelling without passports in earlier years when they were not required. And the great creative works manifested in his writings and in his art have been the product of this international travel. Mr. Kent applied in 1955 for a passport to travel abroad for—as he said under oath—pleasure and profession. I assume that the two are intermingled with him. And he received a similar letter from the director of the passport office stating: "You, Mr. Kent, are alleged to have been a member of the Communist Party"—time, place unspecified; "You, Mr. Kent have been connected with many organizations on the Attorney General's list and you have done many other things, some of which we will now specify." And your Honors will see and I think be outraged at the kinds of things alleged on page 8 of my brief—alleged against an American citizen as a reason for denying him liberty of movement. For example, "It has been alleged that you sought the repeal of the Walter-McCarran law. It has been alleged that you urged clemency for Rosenberg. You urged a release on bail of Steve Nelson who was convicted of sedition in Pennsylvania. You were a sponsor of a petition addressed to Attorney General Brownell criticizing the use of paid informants." I surely do not have to rely upon the decisions of this court upholding the positions taken by Mr. Kent on many of these issues. The fact is that Mr. Kent had a constitutional right to take all of these positions and at the same time to have the liberty of movement which he has demanded. Mr. Kent also, I may say, was given the same kind of informal hearing. Oh, there were two variations: his autobiography, called *"It's Me Oh Lord*—in which he tells his entire philosophy of life as candidly as anyone could—was introduced into evidence by the passport office. This book was put in there for the purpose of showing that Mr. Kent had admitted that he had been connected with organizations on the Attorney General's list. And also the passport office introduced testimony given by Mr. Kent before the McCarthy Committee in 1953 because the department considered it significant that he had asserted his constitutional privilege against self-incrimination.

Both plaintiffs started these lawsuits, which were dismissed in the District Court under the Secretary's regulations, and the dismissal was affirmed in the Court of Appeals.

Now, I should of course give your Honors first the regulations, because they are .   .. Before I give your Honors the regulations, may I state two concessions made by the government which have never been made in the course of these two years of litigation, or indeed in the five years in which we have been litigating many other passport cases in the District? For the first time we learn in this court—and it's to the credit of the government—that there is a constitutional liberty of movement; they make that concession. They seek to undercut it, but we will discuss that later. Secondly, they for the first time disavowed the claim of inherent power on the part of the Secretary of State to control the movement of citizens abroad—a claim of inherent power that was made up to this Court's level. Therefore we come down to the preliminary question, where is the statute that authorizes the Secretary of State to prevent American citizens from going abroad for profession, pleasure, vagrancy or any other reason?

Now we turn to the regulations again. The regulations whose vagueness—whose, I must say, outrageous character is apparent from their reading [interruption by the Court] . . . very well, I shall withhold the term, your Honor. I shall let your Honors' judgments determine that after reading the regulations. The regulations provide in Section 51.135, on page 66, the following: that there are three categories of citizens who are not to be permitted the right to travel— three categories. The first, Category A, are members of the Communist Party or those who have recently terminated such membership under circumstances indicating that, in the view of the Secretary of State, they are still controlled by the Communist Party. Category B are persons—regardless of the formal state of their affiliation—who engage in activities which support the communist movement under circumstances indicating, in the view of the department, [they are subject to control]. And in Category C, on page 67, are persons— regardless of the formal state of their affiliation—as to whom there is reason to believe on the balance of all the evidence that they are going abroad to engage in activities which would advance the communist movement. We are not concerned in this case with 51.136, which talks about people who are going abroad to violate the laws of the United States, or people who would do things prejudicial to the orderly conduct of foreign relations, or even prejudicial to the interests of the United States. We are concerned with 51.135.

Now, the question is, where is the authority for 51.135? The regulations themselves, as your Honors will see on Page 66, cite a single statute: 22 U.S.Code 211 (a). And that statute, which is on Page 59 of my brief, is also disavowed in this court for the first time, although it's the only statute referred to in the regulations as a source of the Secretary's authority. Because of time I won't go into that statute because the Government has conceded that it does not give it the power to control travelling, but merely to issue passports, a somewhat different problem which I think I need not go into. The Government now, however, for the first time relies exclusively upon the McCarran-Walter Act of 1952, 8 U.S.Code, Section 1185, which is on Page 60 of my brief and which makes it a crime during a period of national emergency proclaimed by the President for American citizens to travel abroad, depart from the United States, or to enter the United States without a valid passport. Your Honors will note that this statute is not cited in the preamble to the Secretary's regulations. Your Honors will, as a matter of fact, note that this statute was not in effect at the time of the regulations of August 28, 1952, and finally that the statute says nothing about an authority to the Secretary of State to control travel. And if it has said anything about such authority, I would of course call your Honors' attention to the fact that there are no standards in the statute, and if this statute is to be given any meaning whatsoever, it would have to be read in conjunction with, as a complement to, the Internal Security Act of 1950, Section 6. That was a statute in which Congress decided what character of persons should not have passports, and that statute appears on Pages 59 and 60 of my brief. The standards set forth in that statute—the standard set forth in that statute—is a single one: Persons who are presently members of an organization found by a final order of the Subversive Activities Control Board to be a communist action organization—present membership in an organization found by that Board to be communist action. Your Honors can compare that particular statute with the standard set forth in the Secretary's regulations and the differences are quite obvious.

ARGUMENT OF WILLIAM KUNSTLER, SENTENCING IN STATE OF SOUTH DAKOTA v. SARAH BAD HEART BULL*

(1974).

[Editors' Note: Sarah Bad Heart Bull was an Oglala Sioux, and the mother of seven children. On February 4, 1973, her son Wesley was shot and killed by a white storeowner in Custer, South Dakota. Believing that the police were purposely not investigating the shooting, Sarah Bad Heart Bull charged publicly that there was a coverup and that the coverup was one more aspect of the dual system of justice in South Dakota, one for whites and one for Indians. She also announced that she would come to Custer to demand action from the district attorney.

On the morning of February 6, 1973, Sarah Bad Heart Bull appeared at the steps of the Custer Courthouse in which the district attorney's office was located. She was accompanied by between 30 and 40 members of the American Indian Movement (A.I.M.), which had previously announced support for her cause. On the day before and again on the morning of February 6, representatives of A.I.M. attempted to arrange a private meeting between the district attorney or his representatives and a committee of Indians. These attempts failed. Instead, on the morning of February 6, the Indians were met by armed police, who stood in front of the courthouse door behind a ringed barrier of police cars parked bumper to bumper. Sarah Bad Heart Bull sought entrance to the building and was forcibly rebuffed by the police. When she attempted to push her way in, several officers grabbed hold of her and placed her under arrest. Spontaneously, several members of A.I.M. and friends rushed the police, and a general melee ensued. The violence lasted approximately an hour and a half until tear gas dispersed the Indians who had not been arrested. A score of Indians and police were injured, some very seriously. During the conflict, several

---

* This example was suggested by Professor David Rosenberg of the Harvard Law School.

police cars, a gas station and the courthouse were set on fire. For the entire period of the fighting, Sarah Bad Heart Bull was in police custody.

Sarah Bad Heart Bull and two others were subsequently charged with engaging in a riot during which arson was committed. Under South Dakota statutes, any person who is found to have participated in a riot is vicariously responsible and punishable for arson committed at any time during the riot, regardless of the fact that the person has no knowledge that arson has been committed, has no intent to commit arson and, indeed, has no prior relationship of any kind with the arsonist.

There was a three-month trial, commencing in May, 1973. The three defendants were found guilty as charged.

On July 29, 1974, Sarah Bad Heart Bull appeared for sentencing. The lead counsel for the defendant was William Kunstler, assisted by Mark Lane. Arson is punishable under South Dakota law by a term of imprisonment not exceeding 10 years. Defense counsel presented testimony concerning the defendant's background, the plight of American Indians, and a similar incident in South Dakota occurring several weeks before the violent confrontation in Custer, where a local district attorney and a committee of Indians peacefully negotiated a procedure for settling their differences. Based on this showing, the defendant moved the court to impose a suspended sentence.]

STATE OF SOUTH DAKOTA ⎫
County of Minnehaha ⎬ ss.
For the County of Custer ⎭

IN CIRCUIT COURT
SEVENTH JUDICIAL CIRCUIT

STATE OF SOUTH DAKOTA, ⎫
              Plaintiff, ⎪
    vs. ⎬ Hearing in Mitigation
SARAH BAD HEART BULL, ⎪ and Sentencing
KENNETH DAHL, and ⎪
ROBERT HIGH EAGLE, ⎪
          Defendants. ⎭

DATE TAKEN: July 29, 1974

TIME TAKEN: 9:30 A.M.

PLACE TAKEN: Civil Defense Building,
              Minnehaha County, Sioux Falls, South Dakota

TAKEN BEFORE: Honorable J. H. Bottum

* * *

MR. KUNSTLER: Judge, if I could have just a few minutes in view of the time—

THE COURT: Yes.

* * *

MR. KUNSTLER: You have the pre-sentence reports before you which gives you a background.

I am asking, Your Honor, I guess, as I did in the beginning when we talked about the lawyers coming in here that perhaps we have reached the time, maybe long since reached it, for the only people in this country that seem to have any effect on what is happening are the Judges of the country, whether they be State Judges like yourself or Federal Judges, and that the only bulwark it seems any longer are the Judges.

* * *

Reverend Vine DeLoria who is the father of the Indian historian says, who is the criminal, those who harass or the ones who are finally forced to show anchor because of a harassment, and I think, Your Honor must understand. . . .

* * *

. . . that we have a special community in this country, a wronged community of native Americans, and there isn't a person in the United States or the world who doesn't recognize the centuries of wrong doing and deprivation and murder and pillage committed against the Indian people of the United States. That is well documented everywhere, and no reasonable person disputes that.

Now, the question is you come to a specific instance here of a sentencing, and what is Your Honor going to do about the sentencing of these three people who were, and I think all the evidence shows, who were in Custer for a specific purpose. I don't know what happened in Custer. I know violence erupted. I wasn't there, and I make no appraisal of it except that it is a continuum of many situations that have occurred in this country when people come to protest. It was a violence inflicted upon the aborigines attempting to end slavery in the United States, a violence inflicted upon the early labor unions organized in the United States which resulted in many of them being killed such as Samuel Dowell and Eugene Debs, of violence inflicted upon those who sought the end of the discrimination against women in the electoral polls in this country, a violence against civil rights workers in the south, violence against people who were opposing the war in Viet Nam, incalculable violence from the beginning of this country to the period we reach now.

* * *

You sit up there as a Judge, and probably what is going through your head at this moment is what do I do in a case like this, I have to reckon with the community, with my conscience, with the political life. I have to reckon with my own views and feelings inside, and I admit it is a difficult role to play. It is one I have never played, and will never play, but it is one I have to reckon with. . . .

* * *

What we are asking is that Your Honor consider all of this because I know words can change minds and I know words have an influence, and a sentencing procedure is supposed to be something that does come up against a foredoomed result, . . . because while what you do here, if you exercise common sense, compassion and mercy not to these individuals but to the spirit of what we are all professing to live under, while that might not change the world overnight, of course, but it will be one more little drop in a return to decency in this country that its citizens are struggling to attain. They have been hopelessly betrayed by people they trusted, and Your Honor has had a spectacle of person after person going into Court after Court in this land confessing to crimes of subverting the republic of violating their oaths of office, of stealing money—$2,000 a week contributed to the Vice President of the United States—and walking out of those Courtrooms with nothing more than a hundred dollar fine and himself suspended as in the case of the highest, former highest law enforcement officer in the land, Mr. Kleindeinst. I don't have to go over all of these with Your Honor, but Your Honor understands that there are a whole series of sentences coming down in [cases where defendants] . . . betrayed this republic which amount to nothing more than virtually a condemnation of that betrayal.

* * *

These people did not admit their guilt. They contested their guilt in return for nothing. These people did not admit their guilt. They contested their guilt, and they fought their cases through this Court, and now they are before you for sentencing. Are they more guilty than Kleindeinst or Agnew, or are they just people who thought when other means failed a way to reach an ear somewhere so that what they considered disparaged justice, what Your Honor figures is not material, what they consider and could be protested—when they did it in Gordon, Nebraska, it was handled with sanity. There was no violence, no trials, and a human rights commission emerged. When they did it in Custer, South Dakota, there was violence. Nothing came out of it except an increased continuum [of] tragedy and despair to not only the citizens of South Dakota, Indian and non Indian, but to the country as a whole. So I am asking Your Honor to suspend any sentence you impose in this case. You have the power.

* * *

. . . [The] tendency is to bring justice in line with the reality of the United States and its histories, and that is I guess what we are asking, to make justice. . . .

* * *

I would think that if the Judge would in every instance look beyond the case and do what Judges are supposed to do, judge their fellow men and women and do it with compassion and in light of the historical reality. . . . here; not justice for some criminal case unconnected with reality, unconnected with American Indians, unconnected with ideas of disparaged justice. . . . Otherwise if just one Judge after another, and one failure after another, then we reach the stage where a great many of the citizens of this country regard the system under which they live as hypocritical and false and then who knows where that leads in the future. So I would suggest to Your Honor that you give what sentences you wish, but that you suspend them, or sentence people as has been done in some cases in very similar situations. I am talking about demonstration cases in New York City where people were accused of assaulting policemen in the anti-war demonstrations and the Judge sentenced them to five minutes in the jury box, and that was the end of the matter. In this case, I suggest that under the law—we have argued it before—I think it is clear from reading the statute that you have the power to impose a sentence and then suspend it. What good is going to come to the people of South Dakota or of America that three people go to jail? Is that going to end the Indian problem? Is that going to make the reservation places where people can earn a decent living or end the problem of alcoholism or end the problem of teenage suicide—which is highest among Indian teenagers of this country, four times the national rate—or increase the longevity which is now less than 45 years of the lives of native Americans? It will do nothing of that sort. It may make a few people in Custer feel a little better for a moment, people who don't see what is happening before their eyes, but it will do nothing whatsoever to solve any of the problems which will remain no matter what Your Honor does, and remain to haunt us in the future.

Your Honor has a chance to send three human beings out of this Courtroom with maybe a beginning of an understanding that there is enough flexibility in our system to make an attempt here of a peaceable nature worthwhile. If they can understand that, and other people can learn through it, perhaps we will come to a better day.

Thank you, Judge.

THE COURT: If Mrs. Bad Heart Bull will remain, I will excuse the other two Defendants. I want to make each sentencing separate.

Thank you, gentlemen.

Mrs. Bad Heart Bull, will you please rise.

As you know, you were charged with and convicted by a jury of the crime of a riot where arson in the second degree was committed.

This Indictment, of course, or this Indictment charged you with a felony.

* * *

THE COURT: All right. Do you have anything which you care to say, Mrs. Bad Heart Bull?

MRS. BAD HEART BULL: No.

THE COURT: Very well.

May I say to all of you whatever I may do, regardless of what people say afterwards, I can't help, that this is not done with any degree of vindictiveness whatsoever. It is done with a very, very sad heart as far as I am concerned because for any one man to even have the right to interfere with the liberties of another is indeed an awesome terrible thing.

By the same token, I can agree, Mr. Kunstler, with many of the things that you have said as far as the right to protest, the right of people to get together and talk about their wrongs. Those things certainly must exist if this country is to endure but I cannot agree with you that people can get together and protest and engage in the violation of our laws. Maybe sometime in the future that thing will be changed and anything that will bring about the kind of a getting together where Indians are treated just as other people is one of the things that I desire I am sure as much as anyone else, and I believe that what I do today is a matter to me of duty and a matter of conscience, so it will be the judgment of this Court that you, Sarah Bad Heart Bull, upon your conviction of the crime of riot where arson was engaged in the second degree as set forth in the Indictment here, you are sentenced to confinement in the State Penitentiary, Sioux Falls, South Dakota, for a period of not less than one year and not to exceed five years, the term of such sentence to be determined by the Board of Pardons and Paroles of the State of South Dakota, in accordance with the provisions of the statutes of this State. It is ordered that this sentence shall be deemed to commence as of this date, the 29th day of July, 1974, the date of its pronouncement, for all purposes, including the computation of good time on said sentence. It is further ordered that you are remanded to the custody of the Sheriff of Minnehaha County to be delivered to the Warden of the State Penitentiary at Sioux Falls, South Dakota, and it is further ordered that the bond posted by the Defendant is hereby discharged.

* * *

[The court then denied defendant's motion for bail pending appeal. The other two defendants were each sentenced to prison terms of from five to seven years. Bail pending appeal was also denied these defendants.]

* * *

MR. LANE: Your Honor, I would like to make this one comment. You make me ashamed to be a member of the same profession you are a member of.

THE COURT: All right.

MR. KUNSTLER: Judge, I might say I join in that. I think that what you have done is a savage, vindictive act which can bring no credit upon you as a Judge in this country or this State.

THE COURT: Gentlemen, I am not looking for any credit.

MR. LANE: No, you are looking for reelection.

(End of these proceedings.)

NOTES

In every case, efforts at compromise are accompanied by a search for a different sort of consensus—agreement that one's views of the facts and law, as well as the conclusions that follow from them, are correct. One argues one's cause to adversaries, and sometimes to clients and colleagues. But most often argument is before some authority—be it judge, tribunal, administrative officer or jury—capable of deciding the issue in dispute.

Chronologically, argument in litigation might be made as early as an appearance on the first motion in the case or as late as the last appeal to the highest appellate court. As the examples you have just read illustrate, it is most often preceded by the presentation of evidence. We take up the subject of argument, then, at the chronological point where it frequently occurs. This does not mean, however, that it is the last thing to which you should give your attention. Our own experience is that the argument in any given case needs to be prepared *before* evidence is presented. Indeed, it is the framework around which to organize even the initial investigation of a case.

At one level, the task is a straightforward one. If one can cause the tribunal or jury to "see" the case in a particular way, the desired result will follow. What is sought for is an identity between advocate and decider. This purpose, however, must be realized in conformity with a variety of formalities and rituals. The lawyer must adapt to the tone, conventions, and civilities of the "occasion" and marshal these constraints to his or her purpose. Every advocate— because he or she must affect the decisions of specific individuals— must make judgments about the degree of confidence, deference, or even servility that must be projected.[1] Compare Belli's confident position before the jury, Kunstler's assertive arguments to the court, and Boudin's characterization of the facts and issues before the Supreme Court. Are any of these responses inappropriate for the advocate's purposes? How can such judgments be made? At either level, one is faced with the mystery of how anyone is persuaded at all. Can one ever ascribe the results in any of these cases to the advocate's efforts?

The jury rejected Melvin Belli's argument on behalf of Jack Ruby and brought in the death penalty; the court rejected Kunstler's rec-

---

1. For a very provocative discussion of the nuances and political symbolism involved in this process, *see* J. Cud- dihy, THE ORDEAL OF CIVILITY (1974); *cf.*, L. Friedman & N. Dorsen, DISORDER IN THE COURT (1974).

ommendations on sentencing; the Supreme Court "agreed" with Leonard Boudin. Is there any way to compare, evaluate, or even describe these very different situations? For example, we see all three advocates appealing to rules and principles—that is, to an internal logic which would bind any hearer who accepted the underlying norms. Can you identify the values, attitudes, fears, hopes and convictions to which each of these arguments appeals? Think about which of them might have influenced the audience—either negatively or positively—in each instance. What aspects of this process could actually be controlled by the advocates? How else might Belli, for example, have worded his arguments, and what other arguments might he have made? Would it have made a difference?

We think so; perhaps not in any of these cases, but generally, argument *can* make a difference. Suppose Boudin, instead of stating the issue as he did, had framed the question before the court as follows:

> The issue, your Honors, is whether John Foster Dulles, as Secretary of State, has the authority to limit the travel abroad of my clients—Rockwell Kent and Walter Briehl—on the basis of regulations under the McCarran-Walter act dealing with membership in the Communist Party.

Try to sort through in your own mind what makes this choice of wording, style and structure less effective than the one he chose. Look carefully also at his statement of facts. What judgments and appeals can be found there?

Because it can make a difference, argument always carries with it a complex of responsibilities. One question Kunstler, Boudin and Belli must ask themselves is whether they did enough—whether they did all they could to touch the fears, hopes, and beliefs that would provide a common ground with their audience. But the advocate also faces the question of going too far—of violating his or her own sense of justice and fairness, and perhaps of loyalty to the law itself. There are few places where the "public" responsibilities of the lawyer are as clear as when he or she stands, alone, before a tribunal or jury. What does this mean when one knows that what one argues is based so much on what one has made of the case itself—on the reality that has been created by the investigations, interviews, negotiations and presentations that preceded it?

Each of these processes potentially distorts and alters facts and relationships in the case. The advocate must come to terms not only with the past that gave rise to the litigation, but with the past of the case itself and the role he or she has played in it.

B. AN ORIENTING MODEL: ARGUMENT AS RHETORIC

WINTEROWD, RHETORIC: A SYNTHESIS

14–16 (1968).

Along with Aristotle, we define rhetoric as *the art or faculty of discovering the best possible means of persuasion in regard to any subject whatever*. Rhetoric impinges on all areas of human concern, for human beings do and must talk about everything within their ken. . . . It includes the tools of argumentation which lawyers, diplomats, and politicians employ to carry their points. But it also includes a theoretical treatment of the ways in which man can most effectively persuade. Men being what they are, other means must supplement bare dialectic. For human beings act not only on the basis of reason, but also in passion. Rhetoric must gain emotional assent as well as logical assent. Its study must extend to the ways in which we use discourse to ingratiate ourselves, to arouse sympathy, to evoke indignation, and so forth. And, to the elicitation of the sympathetic agreement of the reader or auditor, in precisely the way that a lyric poem arouses sympathetic agreement.

THE "DEPARTMENTS" OF RHETORIC

Rhetoric has five traditional divisions, generally called "departments." They are (1) invention, (2) arrangement, (3) style, (4) memory, and (5) delivery.

Invention is the process whereby subject matter for a discourse is discovered. . . .

* * *

Arrangement is the department of rhetoric that embraces all theories concerning the ways in which material can be effectively organized in discourse. Rhetorical pronouncements on arrangement run the whole spectrum, from a dogmatic listing of four—and only four—parts for an oration to the oversimplified and basically destructive (but extremely widespread) "law" that the writer or speaker should arrange his points in an ascending order of importance. Cicero, for instance, codified the theory of arrangement when he said that the oration must include these parts: (1) exordium, or introduction; (2) narratio, the statement of the case; (3) confirmatio, proof of the case, and reprehensio, refutation of the opponent's case; (4) peroratio, the summing up. . . . This rigid outline of organization was so influential that it dictated form in many instances well into the nineteenth century. . . .

Style is the department of rhetoric that embraces all theories about the *manner* of discourse that is effective. Roughly speaking, the history of rhetoric produced two "schools" of thought on style.

The first, by various and complicated ways, emerged from Aristotle; this Aristotelian school advocated a plain style, unadorned with "rhetorical flowers." . . . The second school derives from Cicero; the Ciceronians advocated a richer style than did the Aristotelians. In fact, at its extremes, the stylistic doctrine deriving from Cicero advocates ornateness to the point of eccentricity. . . .

Memory and delivery [involve] techniques for committing speeches to mind [and presenting them.]

CLARK, THE PRECEPTS OF RHETORIC
RHETORIC IN GRECO-ROMAN EDUCATION

71–72, 74–75, 118–19, 124, 75–76, 78–80, 83–92, 100–102 (1957).

Inventio [Invention]

Of the five parts into which the speaker's resources were anciently divided, *inventio*, or the art of finding out what the speaker or writer should say, is not only the first in time but the first in importance. . . . It refers to both . . . the investigation of facts . . . [and] . . . the art of discovering arguments. The student was taught how to determine the . . . main issues of the case he was preparing to argue . . . .

* * *

[He then had to discover] all possible means to persuade his audience. Aristotle in the *Rhetoric* points out that the means of effecting persuasion are three: "Of the modes of persuasion furnished by the spoken word there are three kinds. The first kind depends on the personal character (*ethos*) of the speaker; the second on putting the audience in a certain frame of mind; the third on the proof, or apparent proof, provided by the words of the speech itself. Persuasion is achieved by the speaker's personal character (*ethos*) when the speech is so spoken as to make us think him credible. . . . Secondly, persuasion may come through the hearers, when the speech stirs their emotions (*pathos*). Our judgments when we are pleased and friendly are not the same as when we are pained and hostile. . . . Thirdly, persuasion is effected through the speech itself when we have proved a truth or an apparent truth by means of the persuasive arguments suitable to the case in question"

In his *Rhetoric* Aristotle develops this analysis with great fullness, devoting the second book to *ethos* and *pathos* and pointing out in detail how to go about creating a favorable impression on the hearers and rousing or allaying their emotions. "There are three things which inspire confidence in the orator's own character—the three, namely, that induce us to believe a thing apart from any proof of it: good sense, good moral character, and good will. . . . It follows that any one who is thought to have all three of these good qualities will inspire trust in his audience. . . .

"The emotions are all those feelings that so change men as to affect their judgments, and that are also attended by pain or pleasure. Such are anger, pity, fear and the like, with their opposites. We must arrange what we have to say about each of them under three heads. Take, for instance, the emotion of anger: here we must discover (1) what the state of mind of angry people is, (2) who the people are with whom they usually get angry, and (3) on what grounds they get angry with them. It is not enough to know one or even two of these points; unless we know all three, we shall be unable to arouse anger in any one. The same is true of the other emotions".

* * *

[To persuade the audience the student also learns the use of particular proofs. Some of these] lie outside the art of rhetoric, such as laws, witnesses, contracts, torture, and oaths, and those rhetorical arguments which are provided by the words of the speech itself.

. . .

The kinds of proof or persuasive arguments which do belong to the art of rhetoric are two: the enthymeme, including the maxim, and the example.

The enthymeme is a rhetorical adaptation of deductive logic. "I call the enthymeme," says Aristotle in the *Rhetoric*, "a rhetorical syllogism. . . . When it is shown that, certain propositions being true, a further and quite distinct proposition must also be true in consequence, whether invariably or usually, this is called a syllogism in dialectic and an enthymeme in rhetoric". . . .

* * *

We are all familiar with the syllogism which demonstrates the mortality of Socrates. *Major premise:* All men are mortal. *Minor premise:* Socrates is a man. *Conclusion:* Therefore Socrates is mortal. An enthymeme on Socrates might be, "Socrates as a man is bound to die"; or, "Socrates must share the inevitable fate of all men." In this instance the enthymemes may be said to be incomplete syllogisms which omit the statement of the major or minor premise. On the other hand an enthymeme may differ from a logical syllogism in drawing its conclusion, not from a major premise of universal application, but from one based on opinions generally, or frequently, accepted, or on premises of dubious validity. Thus as an example of an indication from which no necessary conclusion can be drawn, Quintilian quotes Hermagoras, "Atalanta is not a virgin, because she strolls through the woods with young men". But Atalanta undoubtedly got herself talked about because there are always some people who would accept the unexpressed major premise that girls who wander in the woods with young men are less likely to be virgins than girls who stay at home. The argument of the enthymeme is based, not on a universal, but on a probability.

* * *

The second kind of proof belonging to the art of rhetoric is the example. In the same passage where he defined enthymeme as a rhetorical syllogism Aristotle defined an example as a rhetorical induction. But the rhetorical example does not move from particular to general as does a logical induction. Nor does it move from universal to particular as does a deduction. It moves instead from particular to particular in the same class or order. "When two statements are of the same order, but one is more familiar than the other, the former is an example".

[Finally] the student of oratory is . . . instructed in detail how to go about discovering or inventing arguments which will win over his audience, prove his case and move to action. On the school level, at least, the art was based on what were called the places of argument. . . . These "places" are also called "topics" from the Greek word "*topos*" meaning "place."

Clearly the doctrine of the "places" or "topics" of argument is based on a metaphor. One goes looking for arguments in some "places" of the mind as one looks for a book on a shelf or a letter in a pigeonhole. In practice the student was taught to ask certain questions. As Quintilian puts it: "In regard to everything that is done the question arises, Why? or Where? or When? or How? or By what means?". And the ancient student of rhetoric in seeking answers to these questions was guided, as is the modern student of newspaper reporting, to those "places" where information and arguments may be found. The places pointed to by Quintilian's questions were cause, place, time, manner, means.

Let me give a few other simple examples. One of the most important of the places or topics of argument is that of cause and effect. The teacher trains the student to ask, "What might have caused the effect we are investigating? What effects might result from this situation?" Other important places or topics of argument are similarity and dissimilarity. "What is it like? What is it different from?" Two very important places are definition and division. "What is it? What are its parts?"

* * *

For the student of rhetoric in antiquity, as today, the value of the places of argument is that in endeavoring to find answers to the questions posed, the student begins to see relationships amongst the data of his knowledge and experience. In a word, he begins to think. Or in terms of public speaking, he begins to discover means to logical persuasion. . . .

* * *

Dispositio [Arrangement]

. . . Cicero in *De oratore* stated that after finding out what he should say, the speaker should next "dispose and arrange what he has found, not only in an orderly way, but with a certain weight and judgment. . . . The methods of doing this are two, the one arising from the nature of cases, the other contributed by the judgment and prudence of the speaker". . . .

The first of these methods, arising from the nature of all cases, is the familiar division of any speech into *exordium*, statement of facts, proof and refutation, and peroration. . . .

There remain many problems of sequence: problems not basic for all speeches but growing out of the strategy involved in marshaling arguments to win over a given audience at a given time in a given case. The speaker needs all his prudence and judgment to decide rightly many problems of sequence. Should a given argument be introduced in his *exordium*, presented in the midst of his speech, or reserved for his peroration? Should he rebut his opponent's argument before or after presenting his own? Would it be more expedient to present his proposition first and then support it, or to present his evidence in such a way as to prepare the way for the acceptance of his proposition?

* * *

Elocutio [Style]

Crassus, in *De oratore*, states that the third task of a speaker is "to clothe and adorn his matter with language." This art of putting proper words in proper places is with us called "style." No other aspect of rhetoric or poetry in antiquity received so much attention in surviving treatises. . . . Aristotle in the *Rhetoric* felt that all the virtues of style could be included under clearness or under appropriateness. But most of his followers made four virtues of style: correctness, clearness, embellishment, and appropriateness. . . .

* * *

Correctness. What is correct? Standards of correctness in the use of language were to a degree uncertain in antiquity, as they are today. Quintilian lists four criteria: (1) reason derived from study of analogy and etymology; (2) antiquity; (3) the authority of the best authors; and (4) custom—not what the majority say, but the "consensus of the educated." To Quintilian, as to Horace, good current usage was the best criterion for establishing correctness in language. . . .

Clearness. "Style to be good must be clear," says Aristotle, "as is proved by the fact that speech which fails to convey a plain meaning will fail to do just what speech has to do" (*Rhetoric* III.2). He suggests that clearness is attained by using words which are current and ordinary, by introducing metaphors drawn from kindred and similar things, and by avoiding redundancy. In his discussion of correctness or purity of language he includes several caveats which subsequent writers have included amongst the aids to clearness: using specific rather than general words, avoiding ambiguous terms unless you want to deceive, avoiding overlong suspensions of thought through misuse of parentheses. . . .

* * *

Embellishment. Aristotle also insists that the use of embellishment must be controlled by appropriateness to the speaker, the audience, and the circumstances. Moreover, "A writer must disguise his art and give the impression of speaking naturally, not artificially. Naturalness is persuasive, artificiality is the contrary". And following the lead of Isocrates, he condemns all excess and recommends "a falling short rather than an overdoing of the effects aimed at." . . .

Naturally enough, countless writers and speakers in antiquity, intoxicated by the sound of their own voices, failed to observe these restraints. They enjoyed and practiced the devices of artistic prose for their own sake. . . .

In his distinguished treatise on the art prose of antiquity, Eduard Norden points out three postulates which remained constant from the sixth century B.C. to the Renaissance: that embellished prose should be figurative, similar to poetry, and rhythmical. . . .

The figures which were taught in the schools, analyzed by the critics, and employed by the orators and men of letters were in antiquity classified as tropes, figures of thought, and figures of language. Of these the tropes (*tropi, tropoi* in Greek) are the most familiar to us because they include metaphors and other figures of similarity. . . .

* * *

. . . [T]he figures of thought deal with the conception of ideas, and the figures of language deal with their expression. All of the figures of thought depart somewhat from direct and ordinary patterns of thinking and meaning. They do not mean quite what they say. Thus a simple question asking for information is not a figure. But the rhetorical question, which does not ask for information but is designed to emphasize a point, is a figure of thought. "How long, Catiline, will you abuse our patience?"

Quintilian's list, which I prefer to the elaborate discussion of Cicero because of its relative simplicity, is as follows: (1) The rhetorical question (*interrogatio*), which I have just used as an illustration, with the following variations: the reply which sidesteps or evades a question asked; dissimulation, or replying in such a way as to seem not to understand the speaker, asking a question and answering it oneself. (2) Anticipation (*prolepsis*), which forestalls objections. (3) Hesitation (*dubitatio*), when the speaker pretends to be at a loss where to begin, or end, or what to say. (4)

Consultation (*communicatio*), when the speaker asks the advice of the judge or pretends to take his opponent into his confidence, or otherwise endeavors to seem stupider than he is. (5) Simulation of any passion, as fear, sorrow, anger, and the like, in order to arouse the emotions of the audience. (6) Impersonation of characters (*prosopopoeia*). Here the speaker will compose lines as though spoken by his client, his opponent, the gods, his fatherland. A form of dramatic monolog or dialog adapted to pleading. (7) Apostrophe, which aims to divert the mind of the judge from the issue by turning away to address some other person or thing, real or imagined. (8) Illustration (*evidentia*), where the speaker gives a vivid word picture of an imagined scene as if it were before his eyes. (9) Irony, a rather full development of something contrary to what the speaker wishes to be understood. (Irony as a trope is shorter and simpler.) (10) Simulated reticence (*aposiopesis*), when the speaker breaks off in the middle of a sentence, but only after the audience has discovered what he means. (11) Mimicry (*ethopoeia*), an imitation of some person's manners in word or deed. (12) Pretended repentance for something said, or a transition managed by a pretended, "That reminds me." (13) Intimation (*emphasis*) of something latent, not expressed, when it would be unsafe or unbecoming to speak plainly.

In summing up his treatment of the figures of thought, all of which are devious devices for implying or suggesting what is not stated or proved, Quintilian points out that they should be used sparingly, for they betray themselves by their multiplicity. Their overuse may make the judge believe that the speaker mistrusts his own cause since he does not give it clear and vigorous support. For straightforward eloquence requires strength to win an audience, while doublings and turnings are the resources of weakness. If sparingly used, however, the figures of thought help to win audiences, for "The auditor delights to understand what is insinuated, applauds his own penetration, and plumes himself on another's eloquence".

The figures of language (*figurae verborum*, in Greek *schemata lexeos*), are verbal patterns which depart in some ingenious way from the patterns of everyday speech. The most familiar examples today are parallelism, antithesis, and climax. . . .

* * *

Appropriateness. That the style of prose should be appropriate as well as pure, clear, and embellished was the consensus of antiquity. Like the thoughts which it clothes, language should be appropriate to the speaker, to the audience, and to the subject. The following analysis offered in the *Rhetoric* by Aristotle was accepted with but slight modification and shift of emphasis by subsequent writers, including Cicero and Quintilian: "Your language will be appropriate if it expresses emotion (*pathos*), and character (*ethos*), and if it corresponds to its subject. 'Correspondence to subject' means that we must neither speak casually about weighty matters, nor solemnly about trivial ones; nor must we add ornamental epithets to commonplace nouns, or the effect will be comic. . . .   To express emotion, you will employ the language of anger in speaking of outrage, the language of disgust and discreet reluctance to utter a word when speaking of impiety or foulness; the language of exultation for a tale of glory, and that of humiliation for a tale of pity. . . .   This aptness of language is one thing that makes people believe in the truth of your story. . . .

"Furthermore, this way of proving your story by displaying these signs of its genuineness expresses your personal character. Each type of man, each type of disposition, will have its own appropriate way of letting the truth appear. Under 'class' I include differences of age . . . sex . . . or nationality. By 'disposition' I here mean those dispositions only which determine the character of a man's life."

Appropriateness to the character (*ethos*) of the audience Aristotle considers under the heads of the three kinds of rhetoric. Thus the style of a speech will be adapted to the different audiences of forensic and judicial speeches and, as Aristotle suggests, the readers of epideictic speeches, which he classifies as written rather than spoken: "It should be observed that each kind of rhetoric has its appropriate style. The style of written prose is not that of spoken oratory, nor are those of political and forensic speaking the same. . . . The written style is more finished: the spoken better admits of dramatic delivery. . . .   Thus strings of unconnected words, and constant repetitions of words and phrases, are very properly condemned in written speeches: but not in spoken speeches. . . .

"Now the style of oratory addressed to public assemblies (deliberative) is really just like scene-painting. The bigger the throng, the more distant is the point of view: so that, in the one and the other, high finish in detail is superfluous and seems better away. The forensic style is more highly finished; still more so is the style of language addressed to a single judge, with whom there is very little room for rhetorical artifices. . . .   It is ceremonial (epideictic) oratory that is most literary, for it is meant to be read; and next to it forensic oratory".

NOTES

The preceding excerpts give you only a general notion of the rich literature (and sometimes baffling vocabulary) that emerged from classical rhetoric.[2] Nevertheless, even this abbreviated discussion contains much that is useful in beginning to analyze argument in the context of law practice. Despite their modern association with public speaking and lecture-circuit presentations, rhetorical principles were developed in the context of legal proceedings. Happily or unhappily, the task of persuading judges and juries has been much the same for over two thousand years.

Try to imagine yourself engaged in preparing for an argument before a particular judge or jury. What concerns ought to be paramount in your mind? How would you select, organize and present the material available to you? If you were to follow the rhetorical tradition, the following questions would be central to your efforts:

First, *who is my audience and what do I want of them?*

Rhetoric's concern for the "best possible means of persuasion" assumes (i) an occasion, bounded by time, circumstance and role; (ii) an audience, subject to such influences as age, sex, knowledge, experience, personality, expectations and socio-economic status; and (iii) a sought-for response. Like the rhetorician, the lawyer is interested in a result—in convincing the audience to believe specific prepositions and/or take definite actions. These objects are the "reasons" for his or her advocacy. Much of what an advocate does is designed to confirm, justify, support and amplify such a rhetorical purpose.

Second, *what arguments are available to me and which of them should be used?*

This is the traditional concern of "rhetorical invention." Analytically, it involves the problems of generating, classifying, and choosing among the possible arguments which are available to support the advocate's purpose. As Winterowd points out, such contentions vary in tone, content and character and are often implicit in the structure of the argument as a whole. Nevertheless, they can be classified as follows:

—*Ethical concerns*—those arguments that concern the credibility or persuasiveness of the speaker. These would involve the lawyer in making statements, using gestures and other non-verbal conduct, and adopting approaches which would enhance the audience's belief that he or she (i) is not the sort of person who would distort or conceal (character); (ii) has no interest or bias towards the subject, or, if such an interest or potential bias exists, it is not influencing his or her sincerity (intentions); (iii) has knowledge and competence with respect to the matters in dispute (expertness). While some of these

2. *See,* Aristotle's *Rhetoric* in BASIC WORKS OF ARISTOTLE (McKeon, ed., 1941); *see generally* D. Bailey, ESSAYS ON RHETORIC (1965); A Baird, RHETORIC: A PHILOSOPHIC INQUIRY (1965); G. Campbell, THE PHILOSOPHY OF RHETORIC (F. Bitzer, ed., 1963); W. Fisher, RHETORIC: A TRADITION IN TRANSITION (1976); STUDIES IN RHETORIC AND PUBLIC SPEAKING (A. Drummond, ed., 1962).

qualities would be referred to directly, more often they would be conveyed indirectly by the lawyer's knowledge, analysis, organization, and style of delivery in the argument itself. (The traditional statement to juries by counsel in closing argument thanking them for their time and patience, and asking them to remember that what counsel says is not evidence, involves such an appeal to the ethos of the speaker).

—*Pathetic concerns*—those arguments that respond to qualities (needs, interests, attitudes, objectives, role conceptions, values and loyalties) of the audience. Such contentions would take account of the audience's (i) background characteristics; i. e., age, education, intelligence, socio-economic status; (ii) familiarity with the issue and the participants; (iii) interest and involvement in the outcome of the decision; (iv) responsiveness to the constraints and opportunities in the situation; and (v) initial attitudes toward any aspect of the case.

—*Logical concerns*—those arguments that seek to enlist traditional canons of logic and reasonable inference in support of the advocate's position. These would include (i) all the lines of inference which support each contention; (ii) any potential counterarguments that the evidence supports; (iii) the possible explanations, characterizations or further claims available to meet these counterarguments.

In each of these categories counsel would initially develop the available lines of argument as fully as possible and, thereafter, refine, support, amplify and choose among them in the context of the specifics of the particular case. For example, an argument designed to reinforce existing beliefs and dispositions will involve very different emphases than an argument which must persuade an audience to change an attitude or adopt a position different from one it already holds. All arguments, however, involve some combination of ethical, pathetic and logical elements.

Third, *how should these elements be organized, sequenced and formulated?*

In the language of rhetorical theory this question relates to both arrangement and style. Counsel as rhetorician would have to make some judgment about the structure of the presentation, the order in which specific arguments will be made, and the particular words, images, figures of speech and phrases which will be used to convey the message. Every argument presents the ethical, pathetic and logical contentions that are available in a particular order and with a particular quality and orientation. In this is much of the fascination and complexity of the rhetorical enterprise.

Finally, how should my presentation be given?

This is the traditional concern of "delivery" in rhetorical writing. It includes consideration of (i) the mechanics of elocution: e. g., voice, inflection, posture, facial expression, gesture; (ii) the qualities of one's actions: e. g., spontaneity, directness, conviction, clarity; and (iii) the possible relationships with the audience: e. g., formal, informal, conversational, authoritative, etc. In the terms of traditional argument, counsel would attempt "to control and adapt the available resources"—language, material, events and his or her own personal qualities—to the supposed perceptions and reactions of the audience.

Consider these inquiries in light of your own experience with arguing (not quarreling) with others. Are these the sorts of questions you ask yourself? Do you usually think consciously of "talking the language" of the audience? Of the logic, order or style of your presentation? When you think of the arguments you will make as a lawyer, are your answers any different? Look again at the three arguments set out in the prior section. Try to analyze or evaluate these presentations in terms of the questions we have asked in this note. Does it add to your insights to evaluate them in terms of the logic and appeal of particular assertions, the way in which they are organized, or the appropriateness of the style employed?

Our hunch is that you will, over time, give affirmative answers to these questions. It is true that rhetorical principles do not provide specific answers in particular circumstances. To be aware of the importance of presenting oneself as a competent or responsible person, or of gaining the attention and acceptance of an audience, does not tell you how one accomplishes these goals. Nor is it obvious how one identifies the best possible means of persuasion in a given argument. These are, of course, ubiquitous problems in relating thought to action in any area. Nevertheless, the rhetorical perspective offers some criteria for differentiating and judging a lawyer's competence in this elusive art. It also brings a rich body of literature to bear on the problems you will face as you prepare and present arguments in your own practice—one which is well worth the attempt to master its unfamiliar categories.

SECTION TWO. THE SKILL DIMENSION

A. ASSESSMENT: DIFFERENT AUDIENCES, DIFFERENT DISPOSITIONS

---

1. The Appellate Court as Audience

BROWNE, UNDERSTANDING APPELLATE ADVOCACY

90–101, 43–50, 53–55, 85–88 (1977)*.

An advocate should seek means to acquire a knowledge of each of the judges on the court to assist not only on some precise matters of arrangement or delivery of his argument, but, most importantly, in order to give him an understanding of the general orientation from which to present his argument and the general parameter of legal method within which to frame the argument in order for that argument to achieve a high level of compatibility with the perceived preferences of the judges.

All of the writers on advocacy, since the earliest times, have stressed the desirability of a knowledge of the court. For example, nearly two thousand years ago, Quintilian wrote:

> "I should also wish if possible to be acquainted with the character of the judges. For it will be desirable to enlist their temperaments, in the service of our cause where they are likely to be useful, or to mollify them if they are likely to prove adverse, just as accordingly they are harsh, gentle, cheerful, grave, stern, or easy going   .   .   ." [a]

But the important questions are: why is a knowledge of the judges desired, or, in other words, of what relevance or use will such knowledge be to an appellate advocate? What knowledge about the judges is desired? And, how can an advocate acquire such knowledge?

One purpose for considering information about the members of the court is to aid in attempting to forecast or predict the outcome of an appeal. Accuracy in such forecasts is important initially in deciding whether to proceed with the appeal at all. This decision may

---

* From an unpublished paper on file at the library of the Harvard Law School. The paper analyzes arguments of counsel before the International Court of Justice, the Supreme Court of the United States, and the High Court of Australia.

a. Quintilian iv.I.17 as quoted by Stryker, *The Art of Advocacy*, in SELECTED WRITINGS ON THE LAW OF EVIDENCE AND TRIAL (W. Fryer, ed. 1957).

be related to the question of costs to a client, but it may also be related to whether the particular case involves a particular pattern of facts and law which are the most likely to lead to the particular judges laying down a precedent that will be of the greatest value in the future settlement of situations involving the same considerations.

A second purpose for knowledge of the court is to assist in the framing of the argument. As Karl Llewellyn has shown, when any court approaches the authorities it approaches a "malleable, a manipulable mass of material." The question is: which view, among the possibilities, is the court going to accept? Therefore, upon which authorities and combination of facts should the argument be based for presentation to the particular court? This can only be forecast by an informed guess as to which choice among the various "doctrinally correct possibilities" the particular court, consistent with satisfying its notion of "duty to the law" and to "justice", will view as "right and decent for the community in regard to the outcome of the case." [b] The advocate, therefore, needs to know something of the judges in the areas of the factors that are likely to contribute to their decision as to what is "right and decent for the community."

* * *

It is not, however, some abstract notion of justice that the advocate needs to perceive in framing his argument. This will not be a complete guide. Nor will the advocate's guess as to how persons of the particular judges' background and supposed social philosophy would view the "justice" of the case be sufficient. Most decided cases confirm that members of an appellate court will frequently arrive at the same result even though they are drawn from diverse backgrounds and are of varied training. If possible, the better guide would be the views of the particular judges, expressed as judges, as best they can be deduced from previous decisions involving the same or similar considerations.

A further, but more menial purpose for a knowledge of the members of the court, is simply to be able to interpret and respond to a judge's questions in the most amenable fashion and, on the negative side, to avoid offense, irritation or estrangement. To take a simple example, if it happened to be fact that the fathers of some of the judges on the court had been policemen and if this were known to the advocate, he would obviously be less likely to make the mistake of engaging in unnecessary and subjective criticism of policemen as a class.

* * *

[Consider how this knowledge would be used. Take, for example, one of the arguments in the] *"South Carolina Case"* (*Briggs et al v. Elliott et al*) [c] .   .   .   one of the five "School Segregation Cases"

---

b. Llewellyn, *A Lecture on Appellate Advocacy*, 29 U.CHI.L.REV. 627, 224– 27 (1962).

c. 347 U.S. 483 (1954).

that, were argued before the Supreme Court . . . . Broadly, these cases all involved the same question: whether the segregation of white and black children in the public schools of a state solely on the basis of race, pursuant to state laws permitting or requiring such segregation, denies the black children the equal protection of the laws guaranteed by the Fourteenth Amendment of the Constitution—even though the physical facilities and other "tangible" factors of white and black schools may be equal.

* * *

The leading advocate for the plaintiffs was Mr. Thurgood Marshall. He was the grandson of a slave and he was later to become a Federal Judge, Solicitor-General and, in 1967, an Associate Justice of the Supreme Court.

Mr. John W. Davis appeared for the defense. He was the senior partner of a large and well-established Wall Street law firm. He had been Governor of West Virginia, Democratic presidential nominee in 1924, a member of Congress, Solicitor-General, Ambassador to England and adviser to President Wilson at Versailles.

* * *

Mr. Marshall began his argument by presenting as the central contention of his case that separation in and of itself is a denial of equality. . . . sought, as a first step in his argument, to destroy the factual basis or the confusion that opponents of his case could latch onto to say that equal facilities provided could be said to comply with the "equal protection" requirements of the Fourteenth Amendment.

[He] then moved on to set up step by step, by reference to the expert evidence in the record, the factual propositions that would later form the basis of his affirmative legal propositions. . . . The type of language he used was as follows:

> " . . . Witnesses testified that segregation deterred the development of the personalities of these children. Two witnesses testified that it deprives them of equal status in the school community, that it destroys their self-respect. Two other witnesses testified that it denies them full opportunity for democratic social development. Another witness said that it stamps him with a badge of inferiority.
>
> "The summation of that testimony is that the Negro children have road blocks put up in their minds as a result of this segregation . . ."

The language was measured, not bitter. The emphasis was on the effects on individual persons. The issue was not presented as a clash of interests or as a competition between the blacks and the whites as groups in the community. He stressed the failure to provide for the proper development of some individuals who were members of the total polity, even though they might be classified as a distinct group under the laws being challenged.

. . . In other words . . . he was obliquely reminding the judges that the legal and factual basis of his case was such that if they were to decide against it they would be adopting a shameful position of, in effect, deciding that there were differences relevant to the education process here between individuals because of their colour.

In a sense this was obvious and there may have been no need to remind the court of it. But its rhetorical value here would have been the presentation of it at the outset of the case to the judges approaching this issue for the first time in their roles as judges. It could have served to remind the judges that irrespective of their prior personal preferences on this issue as members of the general polity, the issue was now before them as judges of the highest court, to be decided by them under the Constitution on the basis of what Mr. Marshall claimed was uncontroverted factual and scientific evidence. . . .

Mr. Marshall [then] moved to [the] question [of whether segregation was a "legislative" or "legal" issue]. He tackled the issue before any question was put by a judge suggesting that it may have been regarded as a problem.

The argument put was as follows:

". . . this Court is being asked to uphold those statutes, the statute and the constitutional provision because of two reasons. One is that these matters are legislative matters, as to whether or not we are going to have segregation . . .

"So here we have the unique situation of an asserted Federal right which has been declared several times by this Court to be personal and present, being set aside on the theory that it is a matter for the state legislature to decide, and it is not for this Court. And that is directly contrary to every opinion of this Court.

"In each instance where these matters come up in what, if I say 'sensitive' field, or whatever I am talking about, civil rights, freedom of speech, et cetera—at all times they have this position. The majority of the people wanted the statute; that is how it was passed.

"There are always respectable people who can be quoted as in support of a statute. But in each case, this Court has made its own independent determination as to whether that statute is valid. Yet in this case, the Court is urged to give blanket approval that this field of segregation, is purely to be left to the states, the direct opposite of what the Fourteenth Amendment was passed for, the direct opposite of the intent of the Fourteenth Amendment and the framers of it. . . ."

This formulation .   .   .   did not plead with the Court to take the dangerous path of doing something novel. It did not argue the "political" case for the Court doing something that others had failed to do. It rather presented the issue as being capable of solution by the application of well-established legal principles. More importantly, however, it appealed to the sense of responsibility and importance of the judges. It made a good case for it being an avoidance of its responsibilities under the Constitution for the court to avoid deciding the case on the grounds that it was a "political" matter.

* * *

[Mr. Marshall then turned to the problem of precedent. Although there had been some recent civil rights decisions in favor of blacks, the Supreme Court had] not yet   .   .   .   overruled the Plessy v. Ferguson doctrine of "separate but equal".

Mr. Marshall sought to attack the validity of this doctrine but not by proposing that it was necessarily essential for the Court to overrule Plessy v. Ferguson, but, rather, he adopted what has been described as a "pincers strategy"—attacking both flanks simultaneously. He argued that in the earliest relevant cases, *Slaughter-House* (1873) and *Strauder* (1880) the Fourteenth Amendment was interpreted broadly to include all types of racial discrimination: in the middle period beginning with Plessy v. Ferguson (1896) the interpretation was narrowed to "separate but equal"; but in the latest cases, *e. g.*, *Sweatt* (1950) and *McLaurin* (1950), the Court returned to the broad interpretation. Then he closed the pincers: "The 'separate but equal' doctrine is just out of step with the earlier decisions .   .   .   and the recent cases in this Court."

This strategy obviously took account of the natural reluctance of judges, even those on the highest appeal courts, to directly overrule the court's previous decisions. The strategy was probably additionally prudent in this case because certain judges might well have been reinforced in such a reluctance because of the likelihood that an overruling of the "separate but equal" doctrine would be widely publicized and likely also to be the subject of intense controversy and the target of some criticism.

* * *

[Only on the problem of enforcement was his strategy unclear.] Mr. Marshall had almost reached the end of his allotted time   .   .   . when Justice Frankfurter indicated by a question that this problem had not been dealt with. He was concerned about how school district lines might be drawn in a case of desegregation in South Carolina, whether there might be gerrymandering and the development of Negro ghettos. He asked:

"JUSTICE FRANKFURTER: I think that nothing would be worse than for this Court—I am expressing my own opinion— nothing would be worse, from my point of view, than for this

Court to make an abstract declaration that segregation is bad and then have it evaded by tricks. . . ."

When Justice Frankfurter asked for a "spelling out" of what might happen, Mr. Marshall said:

". . . I think, sir, that the decree would be entered which would enjoin the school officials from, one, enforcing the statute; two, from segregating on the basis of race or color. Then I think whatever district lines they drew, if it can be shown that those lines are drawn on the basis of race or color, then I think they would violate the injunction. If the lines are drawn on a natural basis, without regard to race or color, then I think that nobody would have any complaint. . . ."

Perhaps it could be said that by ignoring this problem of enforcement in his argument Mr. Marshall may have sought to convey the impression that it was not, in fact, a problem that the Court need be concerned about at all. [Or perhaps this judgment, also, was based on what the judges wanted to hear].

* * *

Given these purposes for acquiring a knowledge of the members of the court, [how can such knowledge be acquired?] . . .

An advocate is unlikely to be able to relate meaningfully to his task any notion of a judge's "character" or "motivation" in the absence of the opportunity for a long and close personal relationship with that judge. In most instances this is not possible.

For the advocate's purposes the most worthwhile categories of knowledge are likely to be: first, the outcome and reasons for that outcome in past cases involving a similar issue or considerations that have been decided by the judges who comprise the court in the case being prepared; and, secondly, any indications given in cases decided previously by the judges as to their perception of their role and duty and their preferences as to the manner or method of performing their role.

The best means for gaining this information is, of course, by reading the written judgments of the relevant judges in appropriate earlier cases, particularly the most recent cases involving similar considerations. Much valuable information as to the judges' approaches and methods can be got by reading such judgments as published in the law reports. Karl Llewellyn, for instance, believed that this was of such importance that an advocate should study the "last half-dozen volumes of reports," and not only what a judge has written, but what he has concurred in as well.

It is not always possible, however—particularly, if a judge's method of judgment-writing is excessively legalistic or formal—to obtain a full understanding of a judge's underlying approach from his written judgments. Where this is not possible, an advocate may increase his understanding by discussion with other advocates who have appeared before the particular judges in similar cases. Such advocates may be able to guess the underlying approach of the judge on the relevant question because, through their detailed knowledge of the background of the cases they appeared in, they will know what the underlying issues were as they emerged in the argument and thus how the written decision of the judge relates to these issues. Such guesses at the relationship between the decision and the issues in previous similar cases should indicate the judge's preferences amongst the considerations involved in the particular issues. They should also indicate the view the judge adopts as to the scope or extent of his judicial role in relation to a particular issue and, thereby, what facts and considerations he regards as relevant for presentation to him in deciding the issue. The advocate's recollection of the comments and questions of the judge during the argument of an earlier case should also help him answer questions on the above matters in order to supplement the understanding being sought from the judge's earlier written decisions.

One American counsel has suggested, for example, that after a reading of the recent cases decided by the court it is important to ask other members of the bar who are better acquainted with the court about the accuracy of any conclusions you may have formed on such matters as whether the court is sensitive to what might be described as human problems rather than abstract rules of law or whether the court is reluctant or unwilling to make new law.[d]

Another method of acquiring knowledge about an unfamiliar tribunal is to attend the court when it is in session a day or two before the argument is due to be presented. By listening to the proceedings it is possible to get, so to speak, the feel of the court—for instance, how the judges react to particular propositions and approaches, to what extent they are willing to let counsel proceed in his own way, and to what extent and when they interrupt with questions. It has also been suggested that it is important to sit in on a particular court before arguing before it even to "see for yourself what the practice is and how the judges react" and that advantage may be gained from knowing how the court feels about even the speed of presentation.

A further suggested source of information about the judges is to consult the appropriate Who's Who. Lord Macmillan has commented that he often used to consult Who's Who before addressing a Parliamentary Committee. "It is unwise to attack too violently the practices of landowners when that invaluable manual has informed you that a member of the Committee owns 30,000 acres." [e]

d. Gates, *Hot Bench or Cold Bench*, in COUNSEL ON APPEAL 125 (A. Charpentier, ed. 1968).

e. Lord Macmillan, *Some Observations on the Art of Advocacy*, an address delivered at the Annual Dinner of the Birmingham Law Student's Society on December 1, 1933.

Many individual counsel and many law firms also keep "book" on all the judges before whom they appear. The idea is that this book should include much more than a biographical sketch such as that listed in Who's Who. It is regarded by some as helpful to be able to consult such a book for information such as: Does a particular judge treat the government as just another litigant, or does the government have a preferred or, sometimes, a prejudiced position? Does he seem impressed by the reputation or prestige of the lawyer making the argument? These and many other impressions are recorded for future reference.

* * *

The advocate-judge relationship in an appellate court is clearly more complex than suggested by many writers. For example, C. G. Walter has described a central aspect of appellate advocacy as follows:

". . . Where the argument is addressed to a question of law it consists of two things: reasoning and authorities. The proportion of the blend differs. Sometimes one predominates, sometimes the other, but there almost invariably is a blend of some sort. We analyze cases and state their holdings and quote from their opinions and endeavor to show their applicability to and controlling effect upon our controversies. We call attention to rules and principles and endeavor to show that our case comes within or falls outside of them. We generalize from and beyond the points decided in other cases and endeavor to show that they lead logically and justly to a certain rule or principle, not yet formulated or announced, which will cover our case. We compare our case with others and point out distinguishing features between them. We appeal, of course, to justice, to sound policy, to the rule which will work; but the courts administer justice under the law, and the field in which they are at liberty to consider policy is rather narrow. They legislate, but only interstitially. In the vast majority of cases, therefore, the true and only function of the brief-writer's argument is to refer the court to the law as it has been laid down by statute or prior decisions and point *what* statutes and *what* prior decisions apply to the facts of his case . . ." [f]

This may describe the basic structure of many arguments as they are in fact presented. But . . . the advocate's task is not just a matter, as Walter says, of pointing out "what prior decisions apply to the facts of his case." Most often there is also the aspect of selecting amongst the different lines of prior decisions that could be emphasized. There are also, of course, questions as to which aspect of the facts should be emphasized and whether or not possible choices

---

f. C. G. Walter, BRIEF WRITING AND ADVOCACY 137–38 (1931).

as to the policy preferences should be articulated at all and, if so, to which preferences the judges are most likely to be receptive.

* * *

The development by an advocate of a relationship with the judges of the court that is based on an acquired knowledge of the judges and, in particular, a knowledge of their perception of their role and duty, [thus seems to me to] coincide with the basic relations of the theories of art.

James Branch Cabell has explained that:

". . . The serious artist will not attempt to present the facts about his contemporaries as these facts really are. . . . for the simple reason that in living no fact or happening reveals itself directly to man's intelligence; but is apprehended as an emotion, which the sustainer's prejudices color with some freedom . . . All the important happenings of life, indeed, present themselves as emotions that are prodigally conformed by what our desires are willing to admit . . . We, in fine, thus fritter through existence without ever encountering any facts as they actually are: for in life no fact is received as truth until the percipient has conformed and colored it to suit his preferences . . ." g

Or, to put it another way, facts do not exist "out of relation to the rest of life."

A more encompassing theory of art is that found in Proust's "Remembrance of Things Past". This theory rests on the belief that each human being lives in his own universe and that no two universes are the same. The function of art is to communicate between them. What is important is to be able to crawl into another man's universe. In the case of appellate litigation we must learn to crawl into the universes of the judges of the court before which one argues. One must see the world from inside of each judge's universe, a universe which is frequently quite different from one's own.

NOTES

1. *Assessment of Appellate Tribunals*

Browne's analysis provides a useful starting point for the practical task of predicting how law courts will respond to particular arguments, and draws heavily on the insights of Karl Llewellyn in this area.[3] Many lawyers have made similar observations about the need to link argument to an understanding of the tribunal:

g. J. B. Cabell, BEYOND LIFE 268–70 (1921).

3. *See generally* K. Llewellyn, THE COMMON LAW TRADITION: DE-

CIDING APPEALS (1960). Llewellyn's notion that an advocate develops a "situation sense"—a feel for how the court will see the circumstances of the case and possibly resolve the com-

(a) ". . . The twin purposes of an appeal are to arouse the emotions of the members of the court so that they will be moved to act on behalf of your client; and to satisfy their intellect so that they will think it proper to take favorable action. Both of these objectives must be attained. If you can convince the appellate judges that the court below is wrong as an intellectual matter, but leave them with the impression that no worthwhile damage was done, the prior result will be affirmed. If, on the other hand, you convince them on the emotional level that your client had a raw deal, but fail to convince them on the intellectual level that there is anything they can properly do about it, the same result will follow. . . ."[4]

(b) ". . . If I were to select the rule which in my estimation above all others should govern the presentation of an argument in Court it is this—always keep steadily in mind that what the judge is seeking is material for the judgment or opinion which all through the case he knows he will inevitably have to frame and deliver at the end. He is not really interested in the advocate's pyrotechnic displays: he is searching all the time for the determining facts and the principles of law which he will ultimately embody in his decision . . .

". . . Counsel's task is to help the Court—to help the Court to reach a decision in his client's favour . . . He wants the clear phrase, the moderately-stated principle, the dispassionate array of facts which may appropriately find a place in his judicial findings. It is a good exercise to think out how, if you were the judge and not the advocate of your client's cause, you would yourself frame a judgment in your client's favour . . .

". . . After all, the problems of pleading are all problems of psychology. One mind is working on another mind at every point and all the time. The judicial mind is subject to the laws of psychology like any other mind . . ."[5]

(c) ". . . Courts of appeal are not filled by demigods . . . that (the judges) are honest, impartial, ready and eager to reach a correct conclusion must always be taken for granted . . . They are simply being called upon for action in this appointed sphere. They are anxiously waiting to be supplied with what Mr. Justice Holmes called the "implements of decision." These by your presence you profess your-

peting values it involves—is worth more discussion than we've given it here.

4. Lampron, *Observations on Appellate Advocacy*, Vol. 14, No. 3 NEW HAMP-SHIRE B.J. 106 (Winter, 1973).

5. Rt. Hon. Lord Macmillan, Some Observations on the Art of Advocacy, Address delivered at the Annual Dinner of the Birmingham Law Students' Society, December 1, 1933.

self ready to furnish. If the places were reversed and you sat where they do, think what it is you would want first to know about the case . . .

"... What would make easier your approach to the true solution? These are questions the advocate must unsparingly put to himself. This is what I mean by changing places with the court.

"If you happen to know the mental habits of any particular judge, so much the better. To adapt yourself to his methods of reasoning is not artful, it is simply elementary psychology . . ." [6]

The underlying thesis of each of these comments is that although rule formulations are not determinative of a court's decision, there is, nevertheless, considerable predictability in the judicial process. If a lawyer is skilled in the use of precedent and sensitive to the court's "sense" of the situation, he or she can often suggest an outcome which serves the court's commitments to both precedent and fairness.

What complicates the situation, of course, is that such commitments mean very different things to different people. A judge's idea of what is right and decent for the community will be a product of his or her background, experience, and orientations, and a court's collective judgment on these matters will be affected by a variety of interpersonal processes. Obtaining knowledge of a particular judge's "character or motivation" is an elusive goal at best.

What, then, is the value of the preparation efforts Browne suggests? Think of an appellate court whose opinions you have read. Consider what you would want to know about the judges sitting on a particular appellate court, how you would go about discovering these things, and how you would adapt your presentation accordingly. Is it possible to decide *what* predispositions and concerns are relevant to an individual judge's approach to a specific case, and how those attitudes, traits, needs and preferences can be turned to your client's advantage? If it is as simple as finding out what the judge had for breakfast, or a host of other "background factors" often mentioned in discussions of this nature, presumably that information could be obtained: but what would it tell you about the way the judge might rule in a specific case? No one has ever satisfactorily explained whether bacon and eggs are propitious for plaintiffs or defendants, or whether they foster activism or judicial restraint. Would the knowledge that the judge is Protestant, or Republican, or a graduate of Harvard tell you more? How would knowledge of these facts be used?

6. Davis, *The Argument of An Appeal*, 26 A.B.A.J. 896 (1940).

The psychological literature on "audience assessment" suggests that the following inquiries would be relevant:

—Who are the members of the audience? What is their age, education, intelligence, experience, economic, political and social background?

—What are their dominant interests, concerns, attitudes, objectives, role conceptions, values and loyalties?

—What is their interest and stake in the issue to be decided? How will they be affected by the decision?

—How familiar are they with the issue or the participants in the dispute? What is the nature of these past relationships?

—What are the immediate pressures, constraints, and influences in the situation?

—What is their prior relationship with and likely attitude toward counsel?

—What institutional process will guide the decision? Does it involve an individual judgment or group discussion? What information will be considered? [7]

But again, even if this information could be obtained, the question of how to connect it to specific judgments remains surprisingly difficult. For example, you may be relatively certain that the members of a particular appellate tribunal have read prejudicial news articles concerning your client, but how can you tell what effect this will have on their deliberations? Will it cause them to stretch the rules against your client, or result in their bending over backwards to prove to themselves (and to you) that they can still be fair and impartial? And if you reach a tentative conclusion on this question, how do you determine the effect it should have on your argument? Will you refer to the possibility of prejudice or not when you address the court? As useful as Browne's remarks are as a starting point, "seeing the world from inside the judge's universe" is no simple undertaking.

----

7. *See, e. g.*, W. Minnick, THE ART OF PERSUASION (1957).

2. *Research on Predicting Judicial Decisions: The State of the Art*

Perhaps it would be useful to visualize what seems to be implicit in an "audience assessment" analysis. The following is one such picture:

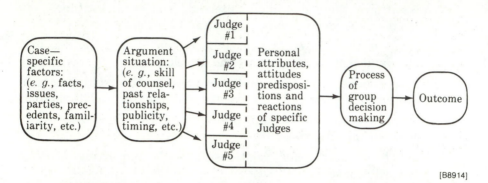

[B8914]

These categories and lines of influence represent what many practitioners mean when they speak of "changing places with the court."

Social science research on this subject uses a similar model.[8] But the lists of variables have been so enormous, and the task of finding meaningful relationships among them so complex, that very few directly usable generalizations have been formulated. Nevertheless, despite these problems, political scientists have offered the following rationale for continuing these efforts:

> . . . [C]entral in the judicial policy-making process . . . [are] the values of the individual justices and the issues—their shared perceptions about the factual questions raised by cases before them for a decision. . . . [But] the means by which each justice acquires his values is a very individual matter. An individual's values are a product of socialization, and his socialization experience results from a combination of chance considerations operating within the political culture in which he has been reared. Supreme Court justices acquire their values in part as a consequence of having been born into a particular family at a particular place and time; nationality, race, family, and early as well as later education all have some influence in building the political character of each justice, as do marriage, law school training, and subsequent professional experience. . . . Of course, it is not to be assumed that a mature man can be completely described by a handful of labels designated as 'attribute' or 'attitudinal' variables. His values, like his attributes, have been moulded by a lifetime of experience. Nevertheless, it is quite possible that when we ask why he votes as he does in a particular case or series of cases (raising, for him, the same policy issue), a small number of variables may approximate *what is most relevant about him closely* enough to be useful in analyzing

8. For an excellent summary of the work done thus far and some of its dominant concerns, see T. Becker, COMPARATIVE JUDICIAL POLITICS: THE POLITICAL FUNCTIONING OF COURTS (1969).

decision-making. If such a focusing of attention, for analytical purposes, were not possible, then we could say nothing of scientific value about the causes of the behavior of judges (or of any other complex living organisms, for that matter).[9]

In the work from which this quotation is drawn, Glendon Schubert goes on to describe studies of Supreme Court decision-making and to document their somewhat inconclusive results. As difficult as it is to ascertain the personal factors which will influence the decisions of an individual justice, he points out that it is even harder to explain the process by which these individual values are integrated in group decisions. However, he concludes that as research techniques become more refined, "it may be possible to predict the outcomes and other aspects of the decision-making behavior of the Supreme Court (and other courts as well) on a systematic basis and with considerable accuracy." [10]

Other researchers have made even more extravagant claims about the predictive and explanatory power of these efforts.[11] For example, in a study of correlations between (i) various background variables—including political party affiliation, pressure group affiliation (e. g., association with business or professional organizations), ethnic and religious affiliation, pre-judicial occupation, education, age, and size of hometown; (ii) attitudes ("liberalism" as regards criminal cases or economic issues), and (iii) decisional outcomes, Stuart Nagel—who has been engaged in such studies since the early sixties—felt he could draw the following conclusions:

> [Predictive variables can be identified in particular cases. The study has] . . . indicated the importance of political party as a predictor of judicial propensities in criminal cases and, especially, in cases involving economic conflict. It has also indicated in the multiple correlation context that the religious orientation of judges is an important predictor of their decisional propensities in criminal cases and their pre-judicial associations with the business world is an important predictor in economic cases.[12]

9. G. Schubert, THE POLITICAL ROLE OF THE COURTS: JUDICIAL POLICY–MAKING 113–14 copyright © 1965 by Scott, Foresman & Company. Reprinted by permission.

10. *Id.* at 114.

11. Although we need not describe it fully here, these assertions have been the subject of vociferous debate. Critics charge that such studies oversimplify the decisional process, neglect important variables, and rest on questionable methods and assumptions. The tasks involved in research of this type—selecting the variables to be studied, defining them in ways which would permit a researcher to recognize them in concrete situations, and determining and weighing correlations and causal relationships among them—present enormous difficulties. Moreover, the very notion of attribute, attitude, value and behavior are themselves very difficult to use as research concepts. *See, e. g.,* Grossman, *Social Backgrounds and Judicial Decision-Making,* 79 HARV.L.REV. 1551 (1966); W. Murphy & J. Tanenhaus, THE STUDY OF PUBLIC LAW (1972).

12. Nagel, *Multiple Correlation of Judicial Backgrounds and Decisions,* 2 FLA.ST.L.REV. 258, 278 (1974). Nagel has also urged that such research has

Nagel had even translated his theory into a set of formulas for the practitioner interested in predicting a particular court's decision in a particular case. This method essentially involves (i) compiling a list of the court's previous decisions on the issue; (ii) identifying the variables that "probably" influenced these decisions; (iii) determining correlations between the presence of particular variables and particular outcomes; and (iv) mathematically computing a "point value" for the case being predicted which should indicate how it will come out.[13]

One is naturally attracted to any method which could simplify the complex predicting job of the appellate advocate. But the limits seem obvious. How are the variables to be identified or weighed? How does the prediction take into account the interplay of individual elements in the case? In what way is this approach more valid than the "inspired hunches" of the practicing bar?

Clearly assessing the reactions of courts is something you must do as an advocate, and some of you will do it very well. You may also benefit from the research work in this area, which will continue to provide confirmations and challenges to the conventional wisdom. But a "science" of such judgments has a very long way to go.

2. The Trial Judge as Audience

Look again at our discussion of lower trial courts in Chapter Two at pages 201–13, *supra*.[14] How does Blumberg's description of the value even when it cannot be made the basis of specific predictions:

In spite of the limitations on judicial background analysis for predictive purposes, such analysis does help improve the legal process. It is useful for providing a better understanding of the determinative factors in judicial decision-making. It also enables one to demonstrate better the need for making judges more representative of the people over whom they judge, since it enables one to show that certain background characteristics have a substantial relation to certain judicial propensities. Furthermore, if one finds a relatively high correlation between the background characteristics of some judges and their decisional propensities, then one can make statements about methods of decreasing these correlations by analyzing how low-correlation judges, or their courts, differ from high-correlation judges. Finally, an analysis of these relations can provide some data that might be helpful to voters in the selection of judges and to lawyers in the selection of jurors.

Id. at 279–80. Note that the judgment of whether a case is an "economic" case has its own complexities. The same is true of the other organizing categories Nagel uses.

13. Nagel, *Using Simple Calculations to Predict Judicial Decisions*, PRACTICAL LAWYER 68–74 (March, 1961). On reading the article, however, you may find that the term "simple" is not quite descriptive.

14. *See also* J. Hogarth, SENTENCING AS A HUMAN PROCESS 50–61 (1971); R. Smith & H. Ehrmann, CRIMINAL JUSTICE IN CLEVELAND 259–61, 268–72 (1922).

lower court bureaucracy affect your assessments of the trial judge as a "audience." How should the arguments typically made in such settings—*e. g.*, on motions or evidentiary objections—be adapted to the situation he describes? For example, consider the following guidelines, which have been gathered in conversations with a number of lower court practitioners:

(1) *Lower court advocacy should be oriented to "the way we do things here."* Typical patterns of judgment should be appealed to where they favor counsel's position (*e. g.*, "Bail is usually allowed in these kinds of cases, Your Honor"), and departures from the typical patterns should be treated as exceptions to what counsel acknowledges are valid general rules of thumb (*e. g.*, "I realize that bail is usually high in a case of this type, Your Honor, but the defendant just was not involved in the crime . . . .").

(2) *Arguments should appeal to the dominant "bureaucratic values" of the court* (*e. g.*, "This approach will permit us to resolve the case quickly. . . ." "This course of action will save the time of the police and all the witnesses, Your Honor. . . .").

(3) *Arguments should be couched in ways that relieve the court from responsibility* (*e. g.*, "I'm afraid the recent decisions require this, Your Honor. . ." "The family and employer will vouch for the defendant's return to trial. . . ." "There just isn't enough to go on here. . . .").

(4) *Arguments should never challenge the authority or intentions of the court or its agents or deny the main theme that the lawyer and judge are "just doing their jobs" in an impersonal, detached way.* (*e. g.*, The judge should be addressed by honorific title; disagreement with the court should be firm but generally unemotional; sarcasm should never be used; disparagement of the good faith of any of the court's personnel or opposing counsel should be avoided; criminal defendants should be advised to express repentance, etc.).[15]

Ask yourself if you agree with this advice, and whether you would modify or add to it. Our own experience is that such suggestions do speak directly to prevailing attitudes and practices among judges in lower trial courts. We don't often get the audience we would like.

---

15. There is a growing literature on the dynamics of deference in the judicial process. See readings collected in J. Robertson, ROUGH JUSTICE (1974). Especially useful are Mileski, *Courtroom Encounters: An Observa-* *tion Study of a Lower Criminal Court*, 5 LAW & SOC'Y REV. 473 (1971); Stumpf & Janowitz, *Judges and the Poor: Bench Responses to Federally Financed Legal Services*, 21 STAN.L. REV. 1058 (1969).

3. The Jury as Audience

Assessments of the jury involve the same considerations as were discussed in Chapter Two at pages 214–27. You are arguing to a group with the following general characteristics:

1. Registered voters (most potential jurors are selected from the registered voter lists).

2. Willing to serve (most often an excuse can be invoked to evade jury service).

3. Conditioned by pre-service instruction (jury manuals or a film will have instructed them on the importance of their service).

4. Survivors of the selective process of voir dire.

5. Under oath to "well and truly try the issues." [16]

In argument, however, the presentations are made directly by counsel and the jury's reaction to the lawyer as an individual becomes more central. Assessing how others will respond to the case (facts, witnesses, documents, etc.) is always somewhat different (and less emotion-laden) than judging how they will respond to you.

B. PRESENTATION: CONSTRUCTING THE ARGUMENT

----

1. Invention: Deciding What to Argue

LLEWELLYN, 'THE MODERN APPROACH TO . . . ADVOCACY . . .'

43 COL.L.REV. 167, 179–84 (1946).

. . . [A]dvocates have in the main done their learning by trial and error, by "feel" rather than by considered theory. They have not in the main become conscious of what it is which their methods of advocacy have been adjusting to: to wit, to a sharp change in the work and thought of our appellate courts which has been marked increasingly over now three decades.

Thus in presenting the better advocates' realistic, operational approach one does better (as in any operational approach) by describing first the situation which the advocate is up against. His task is to persuade the court to his view of the law and of the facts of his case. What he is up against is therefore the court and *its* way of doing *its*

----

16. J. Jeans, TRIAL ADVOCACY 369 (1975). Reprinted by permission of West Publishing Company.

work, *its* way of seeing the law and the facts of *any* case. The new development in this picture is not so much that the courts' ways have changed greatly in these war years as that the best advocates are beginning to realize more accurately (though often still dimly) what the courts' ways are. It is not, again, that the best advocates' best ways of work have changed greatly, but that those best ways are now becoming conscious techniques, and so available for more consistent use, available also to any man within the range of his own powers, no longer limited to the odd gifted few who are "born" artists in the craft and who then come to have "sufficient experience".

The realistic or operational approach to advocacy rests on facts like these (and they are carefully tested facts):

(1) While the courts have and know a duty to the Law, their office forces on them also, and they have and know and labor to live up to, a duty to Justice, to decency and fairness of result.

(2) Despite this felt duty to Justice, it is also their office to stay within the Law as they seek for Justice; and they do so stay within the Law. But the range of *leeway* which our case-law system offers both in *readjustment* of the Law and in its *application* is much greater than most lawyers let themselves realize. And the fact that a case-law court's duty to its case-law system is (and always has been) to take advantage of that leeway to further Justice and to improve the Law—that is a thing that the schooling of our lawyers has been slow to make adequately clear.

(3) Justice is a thing easier to feel than to think about. The conscious thought of courts runs rather in terms of "What is fair in the situation", or "What is good sense and decent in the situation"; and of course judgments on fairness or good sense or decency can and to some extent must differ, so that one needs to study the personnel of the court, and *their* ways of seeing sense.

(4) No court can feel happy with a decision unless the decision fits comfortably, under our accepted techniques of handling authorities, with the accepted body of the law. But the techniques which are accepted and in standard use are contradictory and alternative techniques. This holds equally in regard to prior cases, to statutes, and to administrative regulations.

I give typical instances of each, just to remind of how the accepted and correct techniques run in opposing pairs throughout each field.

(a) *Case-law:* (i) The prior decided case stands only for a point actually necessary to the judgment. Anything else in the opinion is dictum. Even if the rule carefully laid down would lead to the decision in the case and was unmistakably meant to, the case is still "distinguishable" if you can distinguish it on either the facts or the issue. You can, you even should, disregard any case which is thus "distinguishable". (Thus the court can and does avoid the misguesses or misphrasing or misjudgments of prior cases which they now see have gone off-line on the job of sense and justice.) *Per contra,* (ii) anything said by a prior court (whether dictum or not) can be picked up as: "The true rule was laid down" or "We said" or "We expressly held" in *Zilch v. Gahoozis.* . . . And any "distinguishable" case can be recognized as distinguishable, and yet be followed: "But we think the reason (or: the principle) of that decision equally applicable here." The court can even rest on "the tendency of our decisions" and cite cases none of which is in point, even in its language. (Thus they can and do capitalize the good judgments or phrasings of the past, where in their quest for sense and justice they find such phrasings or decisions helpful.)

(b) *Statutes*: (i) Statutes in derogation of the common law are to be strictly construed. Preambles and captions are no part of the statute. Nor can a statute go beyond its text. *Per contra* (ii) Remedial statutes (which are of course by necessity in derogation of the common law) call for liberal construction; preambles and captions show purpose; purpose is a necessary part of any text. More: a statute must at need be implemented to effect its purpose by going far beyond its text.

(c) *Administrative regulation*: (i) When interpretative regulations have been issued and the legislature later amends the statute, it thereby incorporates the regulations as being the meaning of all unaltered language. *Per contra* (ii) Administrative usurpation is of course not sanctioned by an amending statute, which is directed only to correction of the legislative text.

These instances are, as noted, only illustrative. Our whole body of authoritatively accepted ways of dealing with authorities, ways in actual use in the daily work of the courts, is a body which *allows* the court to select among anywhere from two to ten "correct" alternatives in something like eight or nine appealed cases out of ten. That is, *technically* our system could find any of these alternatives to be correct. *Judicially,* our system does not allow most of them. That is not because the authorities and our accepted techniques for handling the authorities do not allow huge leeway. It is because judges have a duty to use the available leeways to make for sense and to accomplish decency, and because upright judges, these days, also want to and try to do just that. Whether consciously (as sometimes) or less consciously (as more often), they therefore use their two-faced or multi-faced accepted techniques to make the authorities take on some one of the (doctrinally) possible aspects which does seem to make for sense and to accomplish decency—always with the upright judge's ultimate and underlying drive to see the thing as best he can in terms of Justice-for-All-of-Us.

From these facts about the courts' methods and objectives a number of practical rules or principles or guides for the advocate emerge at once.

First, and negatively: it is plainly not enough to bring in a technically perfect case on "the law" under the authorities and *some* of the accepted correct techniques for their use and interpretation or "development". If the case is really worth litigating (and perhaps half of today's appealed cases are), then there is an equally perfect technical case to be made on the other side, and if your opponent is any good he will make it. The struggle will then be for *acceptance* by the tribunal of the one technically perfect view of the law as against the other. Acceptance will turn on something beyond "legal correctness". It ought to.

Second, a "technically" perfect case is equally unreliable in regard to the interpretation or classification of the facts. For rarely indeed do the raw facts of even a commercial transaction fit cleanly into any legal pattern; still less so do the "trial facts" as they emerge from conflicting testimony. No matter what the state of the law may be, if the essential pattern of the facts is not seen by the court as fitting cleanly under the rule you contend for, your case is still in jeopardy. This is of course the reason for the commercial counsellor's concern with "fixing" the transaction by a well-drawn document which does fit cleanly into known and certain legal rules. But even documents can have their difficulties (especially in commercial finance). Thus despite any and every document and the parol evidence rule, the "form" of outright sale will regularly be disregarded if oral testimony and circumstances persuade the tribunal that the "true transaction" was one for security only. Despite any document and the parol evidence rule, the "form" of legitimacy may even become an adverse factor if the tribunal from oral testimony and circumstance is led to see in that form a "mask" for usury.

Per contra, and third: *Without a technically perfect case on the law*, under the relevant authorities and some one or more of the thoroughly correct procedures of their use and interpretation, you have no business to expect to win your case. Occasionally a court may under the utter need for getting a decent result go into deliberate creative effort; but few courts like to. Such effort interferes with the court's sense of duty to the law; such effort requires also skill and labor from a hard-pressed bench. Sound advocacy therefore calls for providing in the brief a job all done to hand; it calls as of course for not stirring up any conflict between the court's two major duties. If there is any difficulty with or about the authorities, the solving rule that takes care both of those authorities and of the sound solution calls thus for careful, clear, adequate phrasing in the brief: "The true rule is . . ." (with any needed qualifications taken care of). A court can *recognize* the good solution which gives satisfaction in regard to a tough problem rightly worked out.

All of this serves only to lead up to the crux:

Fourth: the real and vital central job is to satisfy the court that sense and decency and justice require (a) the rule which you contend for in this *type* of situation; and (b) the result that you contend for, as between these parties. Your whole case, on law and facts, must make *sense,* must appeal as being *obvious* sense, inescapable sense, sense in simple terms of life and justice. If that is done, a technically sound case on the law then gets rid of all further difficulty: it shows the court that its duty to the Law not only does not conflict with its duty to Justice but urges along the exact same line.

The great change during these last few years in the approach of the best advocates lies here. As little as twenty or even ten years ago, leading advocates were still apologizing in private for that necessity of their profession that they termed "atmosphere". They meant the introduction, as a technical need, of matter and manner not really "legal" and in some undescribed way felt to be somehow illegitimate, which would make a tribunal *want* to decide their way. Today, as the courts' own sense of their felt duty to decency and justice becomes unmistakable in the decisions and increasingly articulate in the opinions, leading advocates have ceased apology and simply set to work. It is no longer a question of "introducing atmosphere". It is now a question of making the facts talk. For of course it is the facts, not the advocate's expressed opinions, which must do the talking. The court is interested not in listening to a lawyer rant, but in seeing, or discovering, from and in the facts, where sense and justice lie.

This leads to interesting corollaries. It is trite that it is in the statement of the facts that the advocate has his first, best and most precious access to the court's attention. The court does not know the facts, and it wants to. It is trite, among good advocates, that the statement of the facts can, and should, in the very process of statement, frame the legal issue, and can, and should, simultaneously produce the conviction that there is only one sound result. It is as yet less generally perceived as a conscious matter that the *pattern* of the facts as stated must be a *simple* pattern, with its lines of simplicity never lost under detail; else attention wanders, or (which is as bad) the effect is submerged in the court's effort to follow the presentation or to organize the material for itself.

Neither is it yet adequately perceived that the lines of argument just discussed lead of necessity to maximum simplicity on the legal side of a brief. Those who, complaining that "You never can tell on what peg an appellate court will hang its hat", throw in point after point after unrelated point, they scatter their fire, their impact, their unity of drive: they do it because they have not become clear that the vital matter is to satisfy the court that decision their way is imperative as a matter of sense and justice; they are still arguing as if "the law"—*before* the decision—were single and clear and in itself enough.   Whereas in fact one, two or three good points in law (*i e.*, technically sound and correct points) are enough, once the court is satisfied which way the case *ought* to, *must* come out.   Indeed three points, or two, are commonly enough troublesome, as being scatterers of attention, unless a way can be found to make them sub-points under a single simple line which receives reinforcement and cumulative power from each sub-point as the latter is developed.

FITZPATRICK, CLOSING ARGUMENT FOR THE PLAINTIFF

In Successful Jury Trials 411–31 (Appleman, Ed., 1952).

In a closing argument the lawyer has four aims.   First, to win good will, that is, to gain the favor of the jurors for his case in order to cause them to listen attentively to what he is saying and to assent to the ideas he is presenting.   The second aim is to give the jury an adequate explanation of his case which will include both an exposition of the law giving the right to recover and a clear statement of the facts entitling the plaintiff to the relief which the law guarantees. When he is certain that the jury understands his case he then seeks his third objective, which is to secure their belief in what he has stated.   He does this by establishing and confirming his own proof or weakening and overthrowing that of his opponent.   The fourth aim is to arouse the jury so that it will feel moved to return a verdict for his client.

These four aims a lawyer should have in mind throughout the closing argument.   But some parts of the argument will be concerned more with accomplishing certain of these aims than others.   Therefore, the average closing argument will fall into divisions according to the progress that the lawyer is making in achieving these aims.   Sometimes it is said that a good argument will be divided into four parts. The first part, which we may call *The Introduction,* is concerned principally with obtaining from the jury a favorable hearing for plaintiff's side of the case.   The second part we may call the *Statement* or *Explanation of the Case.*   The third is the *Proof of the Case,* and the fourth is the *Conclusion* or *Appeal to the Jury.*

* * *

The good will of the jury may be obtained by the behavior of the lawyer himself throughout the trial.   From the beginning of the case he should create the impression of being fair minded, generous, and considerate of others.   A display of these qualities will dispose a jury to give a lawyer's case a hearing for his sake alone.   Often there are certain things about the case itself which create a favorable impression.   .   .   .

* * *

The statement of the case is a most important part of any argument. This is particularly true when you argue on behalf of the plaintiff. If you make a good statement of your case, you might not have to argue it. If you have not stated your case so clearly that the jury understands what it is about and why you are entitled to recover, ordinarily your argument will be wasted. . . .

*　*　*

You have made a good explanation of your case if the person to whom you are talking immediately reacts by saying, "You certainly have a good case and you can't lose that one." But if the person frowns or shows that he wants to ask you questions when you finish or if he is non-committal, then you have not made a good explanation of the case. Some lawyers follow the practice, when they have an important case to try, of stating their case to many neutral parties before the trial to be sure that their explanation is full and complete and can give a person without foundation in legal matters or knowledge of the case a full and clear understanding. Lawyers are sometimes prone to forget that, although the jurors have been present in court during the trial of the case, at the commencement of the closing argument they still do not have the full understanding and feel of the case that the lawyer has who may have had the case under consideration for months.

In short, you must anticipate and answer all questions which may be in the mind of any of the jurors at the close of all the evidence, either about the law or about the occurrence itself. . . .

*　*　*

To avoid a pointless narration of all that has occurred, decide beforehand what is the greatest need of your case. For example, if it be to show that the driver of defendant's vehicle was negligent, emphasize all details tending to show that fact, including evidential items which some jurors may not have understood. In another case defendant's negligence may be clear, but plaintiff's exercise of care is strongly controverted. The same principle applies to any kind of trial. Knowing the need of your case will supply you with a standard determining what to include in your statement of facts, what to emphasize and what to omit or pass over quickly. Nothing is more discouraging than to be an unwilling listener to a detailed recounting of past events, replete with digressions and explanations without any point being made. In their private lives the jurors have had this experience and a lawyer must not identify himself with past unpleasant experiences of jurors. Narration should be purposeful. The purpose should be apparent.

*　*　*

Now, while the statement is made through the eyes of the plaintiff, the narration of what occurred must appear to be based upon the evidence and must appear to be in agreement with the judgment of mankind and the conduct of men generally. It must indicate honesty,

integrity, memory and truth. In that manner the lawyer builds up
confidence so that later the jury will accept his conclusions without
question. Throughout the statement of the case the lawyer is laying
the foundation for establishing belief in his case. Thus what he says
must appear to be true and all contention and controversy must be
avoided.

* * *

Two things make up the proof of a case: Confirmation of your
own case and refutation of the other side. A lawyer proves his case
and convinces the mind of the jury (1) by reference to direct testimony, (2) by inferences drawn from circumstantial evidence, and (3)
by indicating probabilities. Probabilities are indicated either by
pointing out those that are evident or by discovering probabilities
through the comparison of actions, ideas and persons in his case with
others both similar and opposite outside the case.

This part of the closing argument is truly argument. Perhaps
this portion of the speech should be introduced by a sentence which
will reawaken alertness in all the jurors. It might be a question,
"What proof has the plaintiff to support his case?" Or an invitation
to the jury such as, "Having stated the plaintiff's position, let's stop
for a moment and look at the proof—look at the evidence which supports the plaintiff."   .   .   .

* * *

Of course, the best of arguments is to be able to refer to the testimony of unimpeached witnesses who made a good impression while
they were on the stand and whose testimony corroborates the plaintiff's claim.   .   .   .   Generally it is best to refer to the witnesses by
name, perhaps allude to some act or characteristic or remark of the
witness that will almost recall his physical presence to the court room.
Then briefly show the vantage point from which the witness observed,
if it was a good one, and mark the different items on which the witness
corroborates and reinforces the position taken by the plaintiff.

* * *

.   .   .   Then proceed to argue inferences from circumstances.
They are the second source of proofs or arguments.

* * *

There is no case which a plaintiff may try, whether it be a will
contest, a negligence case or a dram shop case, where great advantage
will not come from a careful study of the case so as to pick out all the
strong points of circumstantial evidence which corroborate the plaintiff's contention.   .   .   .

It [is counsel's] duty all through the trial to lay a foundation for
a strong argument of the circumstances which silently but eloquently
corroborate the plaintiff. Occasionally this pointing up of corroboration from circumstances can be done unobtrusively. As a result, an
opponent does not comprehend the purpose in asking particular ques-

tions until the closing argument. Then the point is driven home that
it all fits into a pattern which spells out clearly and boldly a verdict for
the plaintiff.   That pattern will exist only in the mind of the plaintiff's lawyer before he commences the trial. Small details of it are
drawn or highlighted one at a time throughout the testimony.   The
whole clear picture for the first time is to be brought into focus in the
closing argument, so that it can be plainly read by the jury. One of
the principal aims during cross-examination of the defendant and his
witnesses should be to get each witness, if possible, to admit a point
or two which will fit into this pattern of circumstances which can
only be explained as corroborating the plaintiff's case. .   .   .

In the trial of the ordinary lawsuit, the questions in dispute regarding facts will generally be of two kinds, (1) did or did not an act
take place, and (2) what is the quality of an act whose happening is
not disputed? Does it indicate ordinary care or negligence? Does it
indicate mental capacity? Undue influence? Fraud? Argument
from probability may be used in both kinds of dispute. This form of
argument rests on the proposition that persons are more likely to believe something happened if they accept it as probable. In this connection it is hardly necessary to point out that everyone regards that as
most probable which he knows, or will accept, as actually having happened in the past. .   .   .

When you wish to use this method of securing belief, to what
sources do you go for material? Without being exhaustive, several
are mentioned. Historical event, folk tale or fable, proverb or short
saying, current witticism and anecdote. Illustrations of these sources
of argument from probability often may be found in the advertising
copy of the current issue of almost any magazine. There the writer,
of course is attempting to gain acceptance for a product or an idea.
Use only those which will be recognized at once and accepted by all
the jurors. Another source is a hypothetical happening which closely
parallels the occurrence under consideration and which is so true to
everyday life that the jurors will accept it as having happened.

*   *   *

Argument of this sort from probabilities is equally useful in interpreting acts about which there is no dispute. .   .   .

.   .   .   [I]f you are trying a case against a municipality, where
the plaintiff is injured by falling in a hole in the sidewalk, of which
the plaintiff has knowledge and over which the plaintiff has walked
many times in a period of years, you have to argue the probability
that a person in the exercise of care may still be injured by a defect
of which he has full knowledge. Referring to the ladies on the jury,
you might ask them to suppose that a corner of the linoleum in the
kitchen is turned up and you've called the attention of the head of the
house to the defect and warned him that he had better fix it before
someone trips on it. But he prefers to lie on the davenport and read

the paper.   Now after this turned up corner of the linoleum is in that condition for a month, one of the children trips on it and falls with a great clatter of dishes which he has been carrying from the dining room.   If the man of the house came out roaring from the living room and screamed at the child, "Didn't I tell you about that floor?   Why don't you watch yourself?"   You'd tell him to calm himself and explain to him that it wasn't the child's fault, but his.   He had better get busy and fix it.

This example may bring home to the jury that it is common experience that people give their attention to the task at hand, such as the child carrying the dishes.   It is hardly reasonable to require them at all times to concentrate on pitfalls, the result of another's neglect. The value of this arguing from a plausible illustration which the jury accept as a fair parallel is that if the opposing counsel later tries to argue the failure of the plaintiff to avoid the hole, it can be hoped that the jury may think not of the actual occurrence in the case before them, but rather of the parallel occurrence which they will accept as valid.   Although the above example deals with contributory negligence, it actually illustrates a method of discussing quality or meaning of any act done by the plaintiff or defendant.   It is a method of getting the jury to accept the interpretation which the plaintiff gives to his own actions and those of the defendant.   And the same method holds whether the interpretation contended for be negligence, fraud, undue influence, intoxication or other ultimate conclusion.

* * *

All of the ways in which probability may be argued in favor of our contention cannot be stated.   Many will occur to the lawyer trying a case.   For example, one can argue it is unlikely that a man would be negligent with his wife and children riding in the car with him. Would a woman who has worked hard and regularly at the same employment for many years make a dishonest claim?   Another would argue that youth is more reckless than age.   Where the defendant is a young driver the statement is heard, "Youth was at the wheel." This statement, while not the best example, may illustrate an unobtrusive method of enlisting the sympathy of the jury on the side of the plaintiff, where an open appeal or reference properly would be considered objectionable or otherwise ineffective.   Such statements invite recall of past experiences and grievances of the jurors themselves, instances wherein young people acted recklessly.   Look for opportunities to awaken a nostalgia, as it were, in the individual jurors through which they see the plaintiff in their own past, suffering wrongs identical with their own.

* * *

A useful method of refuting a contention of the defendant is to suggest a choice of one out of two or three possibilities, one of which is necessarily true and any of which will damage the opponent.   For example, suppose the defendant contends the reason his automobile went up on the safety island and injured the plaintiff is that he blacked out and he has no recollection from the time he was approaching the safety island until the accident was all over. Now you may say that the only answer that this argument needs is to tell to the jury that the defendant's story is unbelievable and unworthy of an answer. That suggestion may be followed, but there might be some of the jury that would be contrary-minded enough to say, "Why shouldn't you answer it? It's your job. Do you expect us to figure it out?" Others on the jury might feel the defense is believable and that you cannot answer it. Something can be said for the idea that if you don't intend to answer a point, it is better to ignore it. To state contempt of an opponent's point without arousing that contempt within in the jury may not work.

But to get back to the illustration, the defendant's contention that he blacked out, consider with the jury some of the reasons why a person would black out. Ask them if it is likely that a man in prior good health would suddenly lose consciousness. Inform them that they are entitled to use their experience as men and women in the affairs of life in deciding the case. Ask them if, in their experience, blacking out has ever happened to them or to anyone they knew and whether such happening, where it did occur in their experience, was not preceded or followed by some illness requiring medical attention. Remind them that in this case the defendant has brought in no doctor and he has not seen fit himself to take them into his confidence and tell them what, if anything, he was troubled with either before or after the accident that might explain his blacking out. "Are we then to believe the statement that he blacked out is a bare attempt to escape from responsibility for his act, which he cannot justify? Or does his statement demonstrate that because of his condition he is physically incapable of maintaining control over an automobile or driving carefully." This treatment usually will force the defendant to attempt an answer and care must be taken not to pose a dilemma to him that he can answer.

A similar procedure is to put a number of questions directly to the opponent. Again, care must be taken that no one of the series of questions is easy to answer. For if he answers one in an offhand fashion, it may create the impression that he could have answered the others in the same fashion if time permitted. Of course, having posed a dilemma or questions in other form to the opponent in the opening of the argument, remember to follow up with appropriate comments in the reply to defendant's argument, pointing up his failure to answer.

The above illustrations are meant only to suggest some possible sources of argument. Of course, each type of argument is not suitable in every case, nor is it desirable in trying a case that a lawyer in his mind run through a list of possible arguments so that by elimination he will assemble the most effective. With experience, industry in preparing a case will lead the lawyer almost automatically to the arguments needed in presenting his case.

NOTES

1. *Law Arguments: The Problem of Choice*

There is no legal argument that does not involve some interplay between law and fact; any distinction between them is necessarily an arbitrary one. Nonetheless, the differences in emphasis between jury summation and the sort of arguments discussed by Llewellyn offer a useful contrast in determining ways in which arguments may be formulated, selected and arranged. We will use the term "law argument" to refer to presentations whose primary focus is on the choice or applicability of a given rule or statute; "fact arguments" to designate those where the primary focus is on credibility and potential inferences from the evidence. Both types of arguments can be further categorized and analyzed.

The legal literature on this subject suggests that most lawyers have an ample understanding of how to choose among existing authorities and of the sorts of contentions that can be built on this foundation. As Wiener writes, "the initial arguments are generated out of research into the cases . . . new legal arguments are bound to suggest themselves to you once the statement of facts has been properly done."[17]

Our own experience, however, is that despite extensive case analysis in law school, you may have considerable difficulty with this aspect of the task. That is, many students cannot think of "what to argue," or of ways to "amplify" the basic arguments they do recognize. Nor can they readily discern which arguments are strong or weak, persuasive or unpersuasive, easily answered or difficult to answer. The reason, of course, is that this is a surprisingly difficult task. Although the approaches we suggest are limited, the problem warrants discussion, if only to stimulate you to do some thinking about it on your own.

The Need for Argument Ideas

If the primary problem for the advocate is not understanding the case materials but recognizing the possible arguments they suggest, it might be useful to turn briefly to the ways rhetoricians approach this task. Traditional writing on rhetoric assumes that argumentation is subject to systematic classification and that specific lines of argument can be identified by reference to a list of common "places" or types of arguments. Classifications of this sort not only

17. F. Wiener, BRIEFING AND AR-
GUING FEDERAL APPEALS (1967).

aid in identifying potential arguments, but offer insight into the nature of the justifications available to the speaker.

Is such an approach adaptable to legal work? Perhaps it is. Consider how such a typology might work. Suppose that you represent a tenant in a dispute with a landlord. For present purposes, the sole issue is whether the landlord, by leasing the premises (there is no written lease), should be held to have impliedly warranted to the tenant that the premises would be maintained in conformity with the local housing code. You can obviously list any number of arguments which might persuade the court to adopt such a rule. After you have set them down, ask yourself whether you have any way to identify *further* contentions. Would the following catalogue of argument "types" be helpful?

Type of Argument	**Specific Contention**
Definition (Arguments from the nature of the subject)	Defining property interests always requires some allocation of a "bundle of entitlements and obligations". There is no coherent limit on a landlord's responsibilities.
Analogy (Arguments from comparison)	There has long been case law in this jurisdiction holding that health and safety codes are implied as a condition of any contracts entered into after promulgation of the regulations. For example, contractors are held, whether or not they explicitly agree to do so, to comply with all building, plumbing and electrical codes when they build a house.
Authority (Arguments from expert opinion)	As the court of appeals and the leading treatise writer in this field has stated . . .
Consequences (Arguments from cause and effect)	In the absence of such a rule, tenants will continue to live in seriously deficient housing and be disadvantaged in any attempts to get their landlords to comply with even minimum standards of fitness. There will be no enforcement mechanism available to them, and they will have to rely on the efforts of overworked, understaffed local code enforcement officials.
Sympathy (Arguments to personal concerns)	In this case, the tenants themselves sought to make repairs wherever they could. The record shows that here, as

in many other cases, this landlord had a very profitable and successful rental business. Yet he delayed and procrastinated for over ten months on making repairs that were finally completed in three weeks, and cost less than six hundred dollars.

Policy (Appeal to additional value premises of the audience)

Unless there is an effective private right of action, the health and safety codes cannot be enforced in our community. The expenditure of public funds and resources would be prohibitive. (One health official estimated that the code enforcement staff would have to be increased five fold.) Not only does the warranty of habitability doctrine fairly allocate rights and responsibilities between landlords and tenants, it will enlist private energy and resources in support of an important public purpose.

This particular typology has been drawn (and somewhat modified) from writing on debate and public speaking.[18] You might compare it with the classifications mentioned in the Llewellyn excerpt.

Give some thought to a brief you have written, or an argument you have made, in which judicial precedent played a significant role (the law school practice of setting moot court arguments in some non-existent jurisdiction may limit your personal experience here). Outline the arguments that you made and consider whether each of the above categories is represented. Would these categories have suggested additional arguments? Does having such a checklist add to your ability to think of contentions? Is it detrimental?

The Need for Criteria

Your difficulties in deciding what to argue, of course, do not stop here. Whatever the uses of checklists as scanning devices for *identifying* possible lines of argument, they do not, in themselves, tell the lawyer how to select among them. Does Llewellyn's discussion offer standards for making such choices? What makes a point "weak" or

18. *E. g.*, J. McBurney & G. Mills, ARGUMENTATION AND DEBATE (1964); A. Mills, REASON IN CONTROVERSY (2d ed. 1968); J. Wilson & C. Arnold, PUBLIC SPEAKING AS A LIBERAL ART (1964). Obviously, in working in this way, it would be necessary to identify how these arguments might be refuted, as well as to anticipate contentions available to opposing counsel. In many cases one or more of these categories would fail to generate argument ideas, and some arguments might suggest themselves which would be difficult to classify.

"strong"? Can we do more than provide examples and begin to de-velop a "feel" for this distinction?

Again, consider some case you are handling or an issue on which you disagree with one of your classmates. List *all* the arguments both for and against your position that you can think of. Is there any way to rank them in some order of effectiveness or importance? A number of experienced practitioners have made the following suggestions:

(a) *Arguments and factual conclusions should be evaluated in terms of the probable attitudes and concerns of the audience.* The most important positions to assert are those that the court or jury would consider determinative of the case. For example, if there is a basis in the record for suggesting fraud or improper conduct of the opposing party it should be included even if it is not the most logically sound or direct argument in the case. No judge or jury wants to give a favorable decision to someone who "doesn't deserve it."

(b) *The most important subjects to include in an argument are those that respond to the likely arguments of opposing coun-sel.* These are the propositions upon which issue will be drawn, and they deserve the most attention. Focusing on the opponent's arguments provides a guide as to what is superfluous and sug-gests where the holes in your own presentation may lie. Indeed, the best way to choose arguments to assert in a case is to place yourself in the shoes of someone arguing against you. Your own argument should include restatements of the positions against you and their refutation.

(c) *The best way to select the material to present to a court is by a process of elimination.* Remove all the arguments that are so complex you can't make them intelligible to a non-lawyer friend, all the positions that can't be asserted without lengthy explanation and qualification, and all those you can't make with personal conviction (this doesn't mean you actually have to be-lieve in them but some arguments just don't "sit right"). Then remove any matter that does not lend itself to an easy oral rhythm (these should go in the brief) or fit into the most important theories of the case you are presenting.

You ought to be able to add other suggestions to this sampling of lawyer's lore on this subject, but you will probably not be entirely satisfied. Whatever guidance it may have given to Aristotle, the "most effective means of persuasion" is not exactly a rigorous cri-terion.

---

2. *Fact Arguments: Further Aspects of the Choice Problem*

The same problems attend efforts to identify and choose among factual contentions. Compare Fitzpatrick's comments on closing argument with what you know of appellate argument and brief-writing. In what ways do the different settings require different treatment of the statement of the case, the formulation of issues, the argument or proof, and the closing? Are the problems of persuasion involved essentially the same?

As you begin to construct arguments for a trial judge or a jury, you might give some thought to how you actually decide what arguments you are going to make. Do you focus, as Fitzpatrick suggests, on the "greatest need" of your case? Are there classification schemes that can be developed here as well?

In listing "sources of argument from probability," Fitzpatrick mentions historical events, fables, proverbs, "current witticism." and analogues. Our own experience suggests that working with a rough typology is again useful, even given the enormous variation in arguments from the facts in particular cases. Indeed, the argument types suggested by the debate literature have been surprisingly helpful to a number of students. Let us look once more at how this approach might work.

Assume this time that you are counsel for a client who has brought an action on the grounds that he was negligently struck by a truck while crossing a deserted country road. Using our earlier classifications, possible arguments might include the following:

Type of Argument	Illustration
Definition (Arguments from the nature of the subject)	The defendant was negligent in not slowing his speed after the heavy rain, or checking his brakes after going through that large amount of water. The plaintiff is entitled to ordinary care —that is, to conduct which reflects doing what can be done to avoid (i) possible mechanical failures or (ii) possibly unsafe conditions.
Analogy (Arguments from comparison)	Imagine that the defendant had just been told that his brakes were probably wet and might not hold on pavement at the speed he was going. You wouldn't have any trouble finding him liable in that situation. Well, how different are the circumstances here? What truck driver wouldn't know of the danger after going through water above his bumper level?
Authority (Arguments from expert opinion)	Now, two experts, including a police-officer, have testified that there is a high probability of brake failure or les-

Type of Argument   **Illustration**

	sened braking capacity in such circumstances on the basis of tests on trucks identical to the one driven by defendant. The defendant has driven these trucks for a number of years and certainly should have been aware, if he was not actually aware, of this probability.
Consequences (Causal instance to causal generalization)	He can't now claim that he couldn't have seen the plaintiff anyway. The fact is he skidded and he hit the plaintiff. If he had been going slower, or able to stop, the plaintiff would have been across the road. It was the defendant who caused the injury here.
Sympathy (Arguments from pity)	Of course, we don't have anything personal against the defendant. His employer is also a party here. But the dispute as to who should bear the loss here should be between them. That loss should not fall on a sixty-year-old man going for an evening walk.
Policy (Appeals to generally held values)	Now, there's been a lot of talk about how the plaintiff shouldn't have been crossing the road at that spot. Well, maybe so, if this were a large city or the road was a highway. But out here in the country a man ought to be able to rely on other people's common sense —and on their not being in such a hurry to get where they're going. If he doesn't do something foolish (like jump out in front of a truck) he ought not to have to walk a quarter mile to a crossing. It's a question of the kind of community you want to have here.

You might again apply this schema to an argument you have made or plan to make which relies heavily on factual inferences. Other arguments can, of course, be made on the basis of this list. And undoubtedly there are other categories which might also produce contentions. Judgments would still have to be made about how far to go in elaborating contentions, and what criteria to use in choosing among them. But, as a place to begin, there is much to be said for some such heuristic.

3. *Refutation and Amplification*

A complete analysis of invention in argument would require a treatment of supporting and counterarguments as well. An advocate must not only determine the basic assertions that can be made, but whether they can be "amplified"—that is, whether more content, explanation or repetition would make the presentation more persuasive. Just as there are categories of argument types that may be a source of ideas in specific cases, there are also ways of elaborating arguments which add accuracy, completeness, acceptability and interest to such presentations. The following potential amplifications appear throughout the debate literature and are well worth reviewing in the course of preparing any summation or argument: (i) anecdotes; (ii) comparison; (iii) contrasts; (iv) explanations of the way a condition or thing ordinarily functions (a predicate to comparison or contrast); (v) presentations of images of the whole; (vi) presentations of details; (vii) examples; (viii) restatements; (ix) visual aids; (x) statistical supports. Such reinforcement is sometimes the difference between covering what needs to be said and making what is said clear and credible. For example, consider the following list of "amplifying" ideas:

Universalizing Your Cause

Make the claim or defense bigger than the litigants. Transcend from a broken leg to speeding through school zones. Almost every case presents such an opportunity. The good advocate will find it.

Stressing Importance of Decision

A necessary corollary to the universalism pitch: Tell the jury that their decision is a pronouncement to the community as to how that community regards drunken drivers, shoddy products, sharp dealing store owners, etc.

Subliminal Suggestions

Few persons like to be hit over the heads with persuasive facts. Leave some at least to the jury to "discover" by themselves. Give a hint but hold off the complete revelation.

Presenting a Key

Most of us have a Rosetta stone complex. We like to believe that at the head of every complicated problem there is a simple truism that holds the secret to understanding. Tennyson put it much more prettily:

"Little flower if I could but understand

What you are root and all, all in all

I should know what God and Man is."

Provide an understanding of that key.

Appearing to be Fair

It sounds a bit cynical to be expressed in that fashion but fairness alone in a trial setting is ineffectual unless that fairness is apparent to the jury. The application of this rule is to be found in the illustrative argument, "If what I say isn't so, I shouldn't win—but if it is so, I should win." It is difficult to argue with that approach.

Holding the Offensive

Again a military analogy seems appropriate. We have all heard that "The best defense is a good offense." Well the best offense is a good offense too and, synthesizing the two, we reach the conclusion that good offenses are pretty important. Prior mention has been made that the establishment of the base of your argument is important and this is merely an extension of that concept. Establish *and hold* the base. You may achieve such a goal in a number of ways. The most effective of which is to advance arguments of such persuasive force that your opponent will be forced to respond thus, obligating himself to fight on your field. If deemed advisable confront your opponent with a direct challenge. "I have indicated my analysis of the damages in this case and I'll be waiting to hear how Mr. Stevens has analyzed the testimony." Two or three challenges like this and the opponent will have the major portion of his allotted argument time usurped by responses to issues chosen by you. That is what is meant by "holding the offense."

Concluding Appeal

Each oral presentation of a persuasive nature should conclude with a specific request for action. The story is told of a football coach who gave a stirring half time speech in the visitors locker room and concluded by exhorting his players to "go out that door and bring glory to ole Siwash!" The players unfamiliar with the surroundings ran through the door and fell into the swimming pool. The advocate on occasion is guilty of the same inadequate exhortation. The jury is duly aroused but they are sometimes led through the wrong door and into the swimming pool.

So rule number one is, be specific. For the defense lawyer this is a rather simple admonition. He will usually be requesting that the status remain quo. For the plaintiff it means not only a verdict be rendered but that guidance be afforded as to the amount. Few experiences are more frustrating than to have a juror approach the plaintiff's lawyer after verdict and anxiously inquire, "Did we give you what you expected?" Here is an obviously pro-plaintiff juror wishing to please but with an inadequate instruction as to what would be pleasing. Does that mean that in every case the plaintiff's lawyer should ask for a specific amount? Not necessarily so. There are some cases that just don't develop in the manner expected and by the end of the trial the plaintiff's lawyer might be happy to salvage any kind of verdict at all. Under those less than promising circumstances it might be ill advised to ask for a sizeable recovery. That just might be the final blow. Un-

der those circumstances your specificity will be satisfied if you ask for
"an amount that will fairly compensate my injured client." [19]

Can you think of others?

In addition, preparation of an argument requires anticipating
your opponent's arguments and how he or she will attempt to refute
what you will say. Nicholas Capaldi offers the following typology of
such planning:

> . . . all of your opponent's arguments can be shown to be de-
> fective. It is simply a question of your ingenuity and persistence. I
> shall begin by diagramming the form of attack, then exemplify some
> of the diagram's general principles, and then launch into a detailed
> analysis of specific refutation procedures.

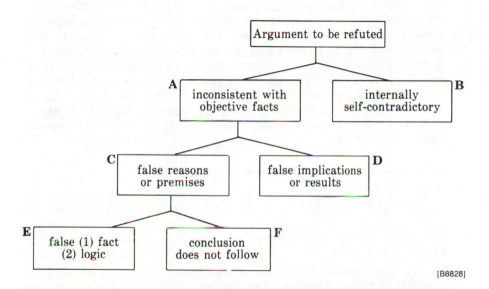

[B8828]

Every argument consists of a major point or conclusion supported
by premises or reasons which allegedly provide evidence for that conclusion. When attacking an argument we are claiming one of two things,
or perhaps both: an argument is defective (1) when the evidence contradicts the conclusion, or (2) when the evidence is simply false or inadequate. Since A above will be subdivided, let us examine B above
first.

B: An argument is internally self-contradictory either when one
of the premises contradicts the conclusion or the premises contradict
each other. For example, if I claim that Fidel cigars are better than
all others because they are so high priced that only a few men can buy
them, and, at the same time, that they are the largest selling cigar, then
I have made contradictory claims. You cannot claim that something

19. J. Jeans, TRIAL ADVOCACY 377–
79 (1975).

is good because it is exclusive and claim that something is good because it is popular at the same time.

A: An argument may be inconsistent with objective fact when either C the premises or reasons appealed to are simply false, or D the implications or results of the conclusion would be considered false. An example of the latter would be an argument which began with information about pollution and ecology and then concluded with a condemnation of all technology as being harmful to life. The false implications of this position are apparent in that a great deal of modern medicine which preserves and serves life is the result of technology. Surely we would not want to reject that.

C: Reasons or premises are false or unacceptable either when F the conclusion does not follow, or E we can simply show the premises to be false. In the case of F we say the argument is a nonsequitur. This differs from the case of B because in B we have a contradiction, whereas in the case of F there is no connection at all. For example, one may argue to the conclusion that Americans as a whole have greater innate intelligence now than they did forty years ago because there are more Americans attending college now than ever before. This is to offer a reason which is true but totally irrelevant to the conclusion. There is no direct connection between innate intelligence and attendance at a college. The colleges may have lowered their standards or expanded facilities for reasons having nothing to do with the intelligence of applicants.

E: A reason or premise can be seen to be false in either a direct or indirect way. In a direct way, if someone claims that it is raining we might show that he is wrong directly by looking outside, etc. A reason or premise may be shown to be false indirectly in a number of ways.

[This analysis may be used no matter what sort of appeal your opponent has made.]

If your opponent has appealed to pity, then you should act as if his example of pity is a general premise. Then add some premise of your own which you think would be accepted by the audience and derive a conclusion inconsistent with your opponent's. For example, . . . imagine a lawyer defending a juvenile client by claiming that *because* his client is a child, *therefore* we ought to make allowances. The appeal to pity has the following structure: because of x, therefore y.

We turn the tables by deriving a different conclusion from the same premise: because of x, therefore not y. Because he is a child, we ought not to make allowances, otherwise we shall be establishing or encouraging a bad habit.

* * *

There are two ways of undermining your opponent's use of authority, either by an *ad hominem* attack on his specific authorities, or by providing counter authorities. . . .

* * *

[If your opponent had made an *ad populum* appeal (to widely-shared values), the] major ploy . . . is to invoke another *ad populum* which supports you case and/or goes against the case of your opponent, one which you think might have an even greater appeal. For example, in redistricting or in choosing candidates it is frequently suggested that minority groups be placed into a stronghold or given a candidate with the same cultural background in order to guarantee them some kind of representation. This seems to be consistent with a democratic attempt to do justice to all legitimate interest groups within the society and is thus an *ad populum* appeal. To counter it you might point out that such a system gives the minority a voice but little power, since any one representative may be ignored. In the tenth Federalist paper, James Madison argued for another ideal which is also part of the American political system of ideals, namely the notion that a political representative should be encouraged by redistricting and other means to represent a wide variety of interests. In fact, by having a representative for a specific interest group we are encouraging factionalism which is just the evil we want to avoid. . . .

* * *

[If your opponent has made an appeal to precedent] the obvious refutation . . . is to invoke a counterprecedent . . . [or] to show that the precedent does not apply to the case at hand because of extenuating circumstances or significant differences. . . . [or] to show what happens when a precedent is extended to its extreme. For example, democratic procedure is a fine precedent but inappropriate in some cases. Imagine if we had elections to determine who should purify the city water supply or how it should be purified. This should be a matter of expertise and chemistry, not democracy. As a final example, to justify the use of violence on the grounds that there is a precedent for it is to base a case on shaky grounds. Anyone can invoke that precedent, including a lynch mob. . . .

* * *

[Finally, if all else fails you can directly attack your opponent's conclusions. This involves a number of specific steps. First] . . . summarize what you take to be the case of your opponent, but in order to clarify the case for the audience you should engage in a little translation so as to put that case in as bad a light as possible. Take the words used by your opponent and try to substitute those which will have a negative connotation in the mind of the audience. Below are a few examples of such translation.

discriminate = prejudice
alteration = radical innovation
existing order = antiquated prejudice
protective custody = thrown into a dungeon
religious zeal = fanaticism
law and order = political repression

In addition, you should be as picayune as possible by picking on his actual words rather than his meaning. This task will be made especially easy for you if your opponent takes the trouble of trying to make his presentation a little stylized or literary. For example, if he talks about the economy and mentions the mysteries of the stock market, you should pick him up on the word "mystery" and declare that you are not interested in mysteries or detective stories, thereby implying that he does not know what he is talking about.

Finally, in offering a general characterization of someone else's argument, you should dismiss it or categorize it emotively in terms of some generally known position that is rejected by your audience. Thus with some audiences an entire position might be dismissed as Marxist malarky, outmoded idealism, old-fashioned liberalism, racist, or irrelevant.

After a general characterization of the argument, you should attack the route taken by your opponent to his conclusion. . . . [by] criticizing the means he used to go from the evidence to the conclusion . . . [Y]ou can accuse him of certain traditional formal fallacies. . . . [These include (1) the fallacy of hasty generalization; and (2) the fallacy of composition (arguing from an instance to a whole, i. e., some X's are difficult to get along with; therefore all X's are difficult to get along with.] [20]

Concededly, Capaldi is "arguing" tongue in cheek. Nevertheless, this approach may offer some useful guidelines for anticipating arguments (fair and unfair) against you.

———

4. Invention and the Argument as a Whole

Implicit in all of this is some sense that counsel knows where he or she is going. Each of the examples we have used assumes that there is an underlying connection between proof and assertion which makes the argument sound. What sort of reasoning is involved here? Is it helpful to examine its structure more explicitly?

In rhetorical terms, every argument that is selected must be judged by its capacity to lead the reasoning of the audience to the advocate's desired conclusion. Arthur Hastings has attempted to describe the "implicit structure" of this process.[21]

To analyze an argument it should be broken down into elements more specific than the gross parts of premises and conclusion. The most practical structural analysis . . . identifies six elements in an argument:

1. Conclusion (C).

2. Data (D). The evidence or premises.

3. Warrant (W). This is a statement which asserts that the conclusion follows from the data. It is the reasoning process which leads to the conclusion. In some arguments it may not be stated explicitly, but only implied.

20. N. Capaldi, THE ART OF DECEP-   21. Hastings, *Reasoning Processes*,
TION, 76–80, 84–87, 100–101 (1971).   Chapter 7 in A. Mills, REASON IN
                                        CONTROVERSY (1964).

4. Backing (B). Evidence or reasoning which explains why the warrant is true.

5. Qualifier (Q). This states how probable or certain is the conclusion. In rhetoric, most conclusions are probable, not certain.

6. Rebuttal (R). This element covers reservations or possible refutations of the conclusion.

This is a diagram of the relations among these six elements:

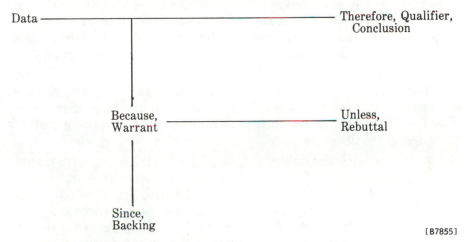

Data ——————————————————— Therefore, Qualifier, Conclusion

Because, Warrant —————————— Unless, Rebuttal

Since, Backing

[B7855]

To illustrate these elements in the context of an argument, consider this proof that the inhabitants of Grubnia do not like their government.

It is reliably reported that large numbers of Grubnian citizens are crossing the border daily and asking for asylum. We know from past experience that this is a good indication of domestic trouble in the political life of the country, so we can conclude that the Grubnian citizens are displeased and fearful of their government, unless, of course, those leaving are members of some minority faction.

CONCLUSION: Grubnian citizens are displeased with and fearful of their government.

DATA: Large numbers of Grubnian citizens are crossing the border daily and asking political asylum.

WARRANT: When citizens leave the country and ask for asylum there is usually dissatisfaction with the government and fear of the government.

BACKING: This has been the case when such situations occurred in the past.

QUALIFIER: "Probably." The qualification of the strength of the conclusion is implied, and the argument is clearly one of probability because a reservation is stated.

REBUTTAL: Those leaving may be a minority faction, which is not representative of the entire populace.[22]

22. *Id.* at 126–27. Hastings attributes this structural framework to Stephen E. Toulmin (THE USES OF ARGU- MENT, Cambridge University Press, 1964).

Look back on the examples we have been considering in this section. Such a structure, or a modification of it, is the framework for each of the examples that we have discussed and those suggested by Llewellyn and Fitzpatrick.

Fitting your arguments into this type of organization may suggest ways to increase, amplify or strengthen the claims you are making. It may also clarify whether there is really a "fit" between the arguments you have chosen and the conclusions you wish the hearer to reach. A number of lawyers suggest that you explicitly write out your desired conclusions and warrants before you write or deliver any argument. In addition, it may provide a basis for critiquing your own contentions.

Consider the following argument "on the facts." Suppose you are counsel for the defense attempting to argue to the jury that Jones shot Smith because he was in fear of his life. The governing statute provides in pertinent part:

> Murder is the unlawful killing of a human being with malice aforethought. . . .   A killing is perpetrated with malice aforethought if it is done . . .   (2) with intent to kill or inflict grievous bodily harm. . . .   One who perpetrates murder out of fear, however unreasonable, for his or her own life . . .   shall be guilty of murder in the second degree.

It is accepted by both parties that (i) Jones shot Smith; (ii) Smith was unarmed; (iii) Smith was walking toward Jones but made no threatening gestures; (iv) Smith was larger and stronger than Jones and had previously beaten him.

On the issue of Jones' *state of mind* you might argue some combination of the following warrants or backing for the claim that Jones was in fear of his life: (i) the victims of beatings often believe

---

Rhetoricians have refined these types of arguments even further and have developed some useful subcategories. One classification, for example, distinguishes different types of relationships between data, warrant and claim, depending on the nature of the premises and sort of reasoning involved. This scheme included arguments from (1) cause to effect (consequences); (2) effect to cause (cause); (3) attribute to class (sign); (4) class to attribute (classification); (5) instance to instance (parallel case); (6) relationship to relationship (analogy); (7) sample to generalization. Some of these will be explored more fully in the following sections. Aristotle's identification of two basic forms of argument—argument from example or instance and argument from enthy-meme—embodies a more general classification of these types. The enthymeme, it deserves repeating, is a syllogism in which one or more of the elements has been eliminated—*e. g.*, "Socrates, as a man, is bound to die."

Similarly, distinctions have been drawn concerning the types of claims that might be made. There is an obvious difference in the arguments used to establish (1) whether something exists; (2) what it is; (3) of what value it is; (4) how one ought to act in relation to it. In recent writings on argument these would be classified as designative, definitional, value, evaluative, and advocative claims. Each would be susceptible to different types of "proof." (Asserted relations between data and warrant.)

they will be beaten again when approached by their assailant; (ii) the circumstances of the prior beating exhibited the same characteristics, i. e., no initial threatening gestures as in the case in question; (iii) people who act the way Jones did before and after the incident meet the legal description of "in fear of their lives."

With respect to each argument, you would have to pay attention to the following canons of inference. When generalizations are employed (i) a reasonable number of instances must be cited; (ii) the instances must be typical; (iii) negative instances must be accounted for; and (iv) the relationship must exist in enough cases to support the degree of continuity embodied in the generalization. When analogies are used (i) the instances being compared must be alike in all essential respects; (ii) differences in the cases compared must be accounted for; and (iii) there must be a sufficient number of instances.[23] Most "factual" arguments involve precisely these sorts of contentions and claims.

Arguments "on the law" are both similar and different. Although there are many complications, from a general perspective the same combination of data-warrant-conclusion seems to underlie this sort of argument as well. In some instances the rule is accepted and forms one of the warrants in the reasoning process. It is the "reason" why Jones cannot be found guilty of first degree murder if the jury accepts the "data" that he acted in fear of his life. If the rule is in dispute, however, like other aspects of the argument it becomes one of the conclusions to be proved. This might result from a dispute as to the meaning of the rule, or the applicability of a subrule, or the applicability of the rule itself to the case in question. Suppose, for example, the prosecution contends that "the defendant cannot assert such a defense in circumstances where he had an opportunity to retreat," using as authority case law which adds such a requirement to claims of self-defense in manslaughter cases. Counsel for the defendant might argue that the statute contains no such exception (data) and that none should be implied (claim) on the basis of one or more of the following warrants: (i) criminal statutes should be strictly construed; (ii) the cases interpreting the statute have applied the rule only in manslaughter cases where the issue was the reasonableness of the conduct and not the subjective state of mind of the actor; (iii) the purpose of the first degree-second degree murder distinction is to distinguish cases where there is a less culpable state of mind; (iv) imposing a retreat rule in such circumstances would have no deterrent effect on future conduct involving such mental states. Using this same rhetorical scheme, you should be able to anticipate rebuttals to each of these claims.

23. *See, e. g.*, K. Anderson, PERSUASION: THEORY AND PRACTICE (1971); W. Minnick, THE ART OF PERSUASION (1957).

Perhaps this is an excessively complex way of making two general observations. First, arguments must be generated not only from argument types, but by working backward from the propositions you want accepted. Second, any argument, no matter how elegant, is sound only in so far as it supports such a conclusion. Asking yourself, "Why am I saying that" may be the most useful suggestion we can offer for choosing among contentions.

—————

5. *The Importance of Context*

Finally, all of the foregoing needs to be qualified to make allowance for the effects of different contexts and settings. Fashioning arguments depends on particular circumstances. Beyond such obvious differences as whether the argument is to a judge or jury, the following are some of the distinctions to which this statement refers.

Oral-Written

Very different demands are made on an advocate depending on whether he or she is making an argument orally or in writing. Not only are there differences in the way the opening statement to the court must be made: length and level of complexity, as well as the handling of case authority, often depart considerably from the brief. The following is a standard list of the ways in which any effective oral presentation differs from a written discussion of the same subject:

—more personal pronouns

—more variety in kinds of sentences

—more variety in sentence length

—more simple sentences

—more sentence fragments

—more rhetorical questions

—more repetition of words, phrases and sentences

—more monosyllabic than polysyllabic words

—more contractions

—more interjections

—more indigenous language

—more direct quotation

—more connotative than denotative words

—more figures of speech

Obviously the fact that an argument will be *heard* rather than read has an effect on one's planning. For example, many people have difficulty restating and remembering propositions heard for the first and only time. An oral presentation should thus involve more repetition, personal identification and simplification than its written counterpart. Even in appellate situations many lawyers recommend "starting fresh" in preparing oral argument, without referring to the brief at all. If you are going to write your arguments out before you make them, you might keep this straightforward advice in mind.

Trial-Appeal

What and how one argues similarly turns sharply on the composition and level of the court to which the argument is addressed. An argument to a trial judge involves very different strategies than essentially the same argument to a multi-membered appellate tribunal. In one of the few discussions in the literature on this subject, Myron Gordon offers the following suggestions:

> [In arguing to a trial judge, counsel] should stress those legal authorities that support his view. If contrary authorities cannot be distinguished or otherwise explained, and counsel cannot ignore them, he should acknowledge them rather than attempt a feeble explanation.

> The following suggestions are offered for stating authorities:

> 1. *Never assume that the court is familiar with a point of law or a specific case.* This applies even if the judge was personally involved in the case being cited; memories are surprisingly short.

> 2. *Never refer to a case without giving its citation to the court and your opponent.* It is sufficient, however, if the citation is contained in the written brief.

> 3. *If a citation is to a cardinal case, there should follow a clear and brief statement of its pertinent facts and how it was decided.* If the report includes a pithy quotation going to the very heart of the issue, it may be read.

> 4. *Avoid reading the authorities to the court in extenso.* Unless counsel is an extremely expressive reader (and the great majority are not), such a rendition usually results in a wandering of the judicial mind.

> 5. *Some reading to the court is beneficial, particularly when the material is short and directly on point.* Always be fair, however. Taking a quotation out of context will rarely benefit counsel and can be the source of criticism.

> 6. *Ascertain whether the authorities cited to the court have been overruled or modified.* Failure to heed this elementary suggestion can result in disaster. Lawyers frequently refer to this task as "Shepardizing."

Having asserted his views as to the applicable law, counsel is then ready to blend the facts of his case with those legal authorities. If counsel can show that public policy would be served by a holding in his client's favor, he should unhesitatingly urge this in his summation, thereby demonstrating that fairness and logic support his contentions.[24]

Appellate lawyers generally advise against reading quotations to an appellate tribunal, or belaboring the facts of particular precedents. You might ask yourself why Gordon apparently gives such different advice. Are his views very different from those of Llewellyn and Fitzpatrick, if the latter were adapted to an argument before a trial judge?

Criminal-Civil

Many writers also feel that the sort of arguments that can be made in a criminal case differ considerably from those appropriate to civil cases, at both the trial and appellate level. With respect to appeals, for example, Whitman Knapp observes:

> In the civil appeal, your basic objective as an appellate advocate should be to convince the court that, as between the parties, the substantive result below was fundamentally wrong and that the error was not attributable to your client or to your predecessor. And, if at all possible, you should convince the court that the legal position you are asking it to take will permit it either to provide for or to set the stage for a final disposition of the controversy.

> . . . [Y]our basic objective in a civil case is to convince the court that there is a fundamental wrongness (I don't like to use the word "injustice," because that gets me into all kinds of arguments over what it means) in the result below and that the court can, by adopting your argument, see some end to the litigation and not be opening a Pandora's box of interminable proceedings between the parties.

> . . . [W]ith respect to the criminal appeal . . . the considerations are exactly the opposite. It is my submission that, as an appellant in a criminal case, you should avoid like the plague any attempt to get the court involved in the question of whether substantial justice was done between your client and the government.

> Whatever individual judges may think of their attitude on this subject, and I have had some arguments about the point . . . I am convinced that to a man they have a fundamental reluctance to get involved in that question and will resent and resist you all the way if you attempt to involve them in it.

> Your objective then, I submit to you, should be to avoid any concern for ultimate justice as between the parties and, so far as possible, such matters as the sufficiency of the evidence, and to convince the court that there was some basic procedural irregularity in the process that resulted in the conviction. It doesn't make much difference whether that irregularity was in the prearrest process, in the grand jury proceedings, or at any point up to and including the verdict.

24. M. Gordon, *Non Jury Summations,*
6 AM.JUR.TRIALS 792 (1967).

It doesn't make a bit of difference whether some form of stupidity on the part of your client or your own produced the irregularity that you are complaining about. It is, however, of the utmost importance that the proposition you are urging will not bring an end to the case, will not forever foreclose the prosecution from another chance at conviction. All you want to do is to let your client live to fight another day.

The basic distinction, then, that I suggest between the civil and the criminal appeal is this: in the one, the court wants to get to the final issue and achieve a final result; in the other, the court shies from involvement in the substantive result and wants anything but finality.

Why the difference? Well, to understand the criminal appeal or at least my theories about it, you must first understand my theories about the entire criminal process; so let's take a look at them.

Criminal law is a nasty and archaic business: taking a man from his home, locking him up, or even killing him. It's an uncivilized business, and whether we admit it or not, we are all basically ashamed of it. . . .

We have gotten more civilized or more squeamish in the recent centuries, and no one wants to take responsibility for killing a man or for locking him up. . . .

So what have we done to protect law-enforcement officials—and they include the police, the prosecutor, the jurors, and the trial and appellate judges—from getting so mixed up in the mess that, being civilized human beings, they are unable to function? We have devised a complicated system, operating under well-defined rules, whereby no individual human being is required to take total responsibility for anything but whereby every individual can concentrate on his or her small task and leave ultimate responsibility up in the air. The police investigate. The prosecutor prepares and presents his case. The judge lays down the rules. The jurors, each sharing his responsibility with eleven others, make the finding of fact. The trial judge, with a complicated and formal statutory system and a detailed probation report to fall back on, imposes sentence. Finally the appellate court, from its Olympian heights, reviews the situation and makes sure that everyone has played the game according to the rules.

The essential lubricating agent that makes this process possible is the ability of each person in the chain to have confidence in the essential competence and integrity of every other such person. If the district attorney had no confidence in the police, he couldn't long run his office. If the trial court and the jurors had no confidence in the prosecutor, there would be no conviction. If the appellate judges didn't have essential confidence in the integrity and competence (basically, the integrity) of the prosecutor and of the entire judicial system over which they preside and felt that they had to examine the justice of every case before them, they would soon find themselves so overwhelmed that they could not carry out their functions.

The point is this: the appellate judges know that they must function and that the system must survive. They, therefore, have a strong vested interest in their belief in the integrity of the system, the belief that affords them the necessary isolation from individual responsibility.

It follows that if you come to them with a contention that the system has totally failed, that the jury's finding is so wrong as to require them to assume responsibility for reappraising it, the appellate judges are going to resent your argument and set their minds against agreeing with anything you have to say. In short, it is my oversimplified suggestion that no appellant's brief should ever have a point that "guilt was not established beyond a reasonable doubt." [25]

Ask yourself whether Knapp's distinction is a valid one. Would it lead you to make different types of arguments in other cases too— *i. e.*, tax, or civil rights, or antitrust cases? Or at different levels (trial, appeal)? Does it make sense to try to make such careful distinctions?

2. Arrangement: The Order of Presentation

———

To some extent—in oral arguments to courts and juries as well as in appellate briefs—sequence in legal argument is governed by the formalities of the occasion. Every first-year law student learns that a brief includes (i) statement of issues; (ii) statement of facts; (iii) summary of argument; (iv) argument; and (v) a conclusion, in essentially that order. Fitzpatrick and many other commentators on trial outline a similar set sequence for jury summation. Obviously, an advocate cannot entirely ignore these well-established conventions and the expectations that accompany them.

But there are still many choices to be made in this area, particularly with respect to the order of arguments *within* these general categories—*e. g.*, whether and when to anticipate counterarguments, or whether departing from a purely chronological statement of facts will best serve your client's purposes. The established ways of doing things still permit a great deal of latitude for persuasive "arrangement". It is with these subchoices—of sequences within sequences— that we are concerned in this section.

DAVIS, THE ARGUMENT OF AN APPEAL

26 A.B.A.J. 895, 896–99 (1940).*

(1) Change places (in your imagination of course) with the Court. . . .

---

25. W. Knapp, *The Civil and Criminal Appeal Compared,* in COUNSEL ON APPEAL, 66–69 (1968).

* *Editors' note:* The article from which these excerpts are taken has been widely quoted as a statement of the principles of appellate advocacy. We have included only those portions concerned with order and sequence.

[T]hose who sit in solemn array before you, whatever their merit, know nothing whatever of the controversy that brings you to them, and are not stimulated to interest in it by any feeling of friendship or dislike to anyone concerned. They are not moved as perhaps an advocate may be by any hope of reward or fear of punishment. They are simply being called upon for action in their appointed sphere. They are anxiously waiting to be supplied with what Mr. Justice Holmes called the "implements of decision." These by your presence you profess yourself ready to furnish. If the places were reversed and you sat where they do, think what it is you would want first to know about the case. How and in what order would you want the story told? How would you want the skein unravelled? What would make easier your approach to the true solution? These are questions the advocate must unsparingly put to himself. This is what I mean by changing places with the Court.

(2) State first the nature of the case and briefly its prior history.

Every Appellate Court has passing before it a long procession of cases that come from manifold and diverse fields of the law and human experience. Why not tell the Court at the outset to which of these fields its attention is about to be called? If the case involves the construction of a will, the settlement of a partnership, a constitutional question or whatever it may be, the judge is able as soon as the general topic is mentioned to call to his aid, consciously or unconsciously, his general knowledge and experience with that particular subject. It brings what is to follow into immediate focus. And then for the greater ease of the court in listening it is well to give at once the history of the case in so far as it bears on the court's jurisdiction. . . .

(3) State the facts.

[I]t cannot be too often emphasized that in an appellate court the statement of the facts is not merely a part of the argument, it is more often than not the argument itself. A case well stated is a case far more than half argued. Yet how many advocates fail to realize that the ignorance of the court concerning the facts in the case is complete, even where its knowledge of the law may adequately satisfy the proverbial presumption. The court wants above all things to learn what are the facts which give rise to the call upon its energies; for in many, probably in most, cases when the facts are clear there is no great trouble about the law. *Ex facto oritur jus*, and no court ever forgets it. . . .

Of course there are statements and statements. No two men probably would adopt an identical method of approach. Uniformity is impossible, probably undesirable. Safe guides, however, are to be found in the three C's—chronology, candor and clarity: Chronology, because that is the natural way of telling any story, stringing the events on the chain of time just as all human life itself proceeds; candor, the telling of the worst as well as the best, since the court has the right to expect it, and since any lack of candor, real or apparent, will wholly destroy the most careful argument; and clarity, because that is the supreme virtue in any effort to communicate thought from man to man. It admits of no substitute. . . .

(4) State next the applicable rules of law on which you rely.

If the statement of facts has been properly done the mind of the court will already have sensed the legal questions at issue, indeed they may have been hinted at as you proceed. These may be so elementary and well established that a mere allusion to them is sufficient. On the other hand, they may lie in the field of divided opinion where it is necessary to expound them at greater length and to dwell on the underlying reasons that support one or the other view. It may be that in these days of what is apparently waning health on the part of our old friend *Stare Decisis*, one can rely less than heretofore upon the assertion that the case at bar is governed by such-and-such a case, volume and page. Even the shadow of a long succession of governing cases may not be adequate shelter. In any event the advocate must be prepared to meet any challenge to the doctrine of the cases on which he relies and to support it by original reasoning. . . .

* * *

(6) [Invite] . . . questions.

. . . If the question does nothing more it gives you assurance that the court is not comatose and that you have awakened at least a vestigial interest. Moreover a question affords you your only chance to penetrate the mind of the court, unless you are an expert in face reading, and to dispel a doubt as soon as it arises. This you should be able to do if you know your case and have a sound position. If the question warrants a negative answer, do not fence with it but respond with a bold *thwertutnay*—which for the benefit of the illiterate I may explain as a term used in ancient pleading to signify a downright No. While if the answer is in the affirmative or calls for a concession the Court will be equally gratified to have the matter promptly disposed of. If you value your argumentative life do not evade or shuffle or postpone, no matter how embarrassing the question may be or how much it interrupts the thread of your argument. Nothing I should think would be more irritating to an inquiring court than to have refuge taken in the familiar evasion "I am coming to that" and then to have the argument end with the promise unfulfilled. If you are really coming to it indicate what your answer will be when it is reached and never, never sit down until it is made.

* * *

(10) Sit down.

This is the tenth and last commandment. In preparing for argument you will no doubt have made an outline carefully measured by the time at your command. The notes of it which you should have jotted down lie before you on the reading desk. When you have run through this outline and are satisfied that the court has fully grasped your contentions, what else is there left for you to do?

HEGLAND, TRIAL AND PRACTICE SKILLS IN A NUTSHELL

40–43 (1978).

Being explicit in closing argument requires that it is structured rather than simply a series of "good points". It is not enough to be explicit as to lower level conclusions—racial bias of the eyewitness *means* that he sees all minority group members as the same *means*, when coupled with other factors concerning the identification, that his identification of the defendant cannot be believed. One should explicitly tie these conclusions to the ultimate theory of your case: "the fact that you cannot believe the eyewitness *means* you cannot convict the defendant."

The easiest and perhaps clearest organization is "their side—our side". Hence, the Roman numerals:

I. Why our side is believable.

II. Why their side is unbelievable.

Next come the capital letters and some fillers:

II. Why their side is unbelievable—they must prove the defendant guilty and they have only three pieces of evidence.

    A. The eyewitness

    B. The money found on the defendant

    C. The gun

Then, of course, come the arabic numerals:

A. The eyewitness: he cannot be believed because:

    1. He is racially biased—his wife testified to that.

    2. He was 40 feet away from the robber—he admitted that himself.

    3. The lighting was dim—the clerk of the store testified to that.

Note that you *marshal* evidence, not simply recite it. That is, do not simply review what the first witness said and then what the second said, etc. Rather, state your conclusion—"Ladies and Gentlemen, the evidence will show that the eyewitness cannot be believed" —and, then combine all of the evidence supporting that conclusion— part of the wife's testimony, part of the eyewitness', part of the clerk's.

There are many possible organizing principles. Once you have chosen one, fit each of your "good points" into its rightful place.

By intuition, you know what is a "good point" but you should force yourself to ask "Just why does this point help my case?" Again, the need to be explicit.

And, once you have spent the time and effort organizing your argument, do not hide the structure from the jury or judge. Give an overview:

> Ladies and Gentlemen, we will first look at the State's case and then that of the defendant, Mr. Hall. The State's case rests on three pieces of evidence: the eyewitness identification, the money found on Mr. Hall and the gun. I will examine each piece of evidence and, upon inspection, each will prove untrustworthy. The testimony of the eyewitness does not prove Mr. Hall guilty nor does the money or gun. The State has not proved Mr. Hall guilty. The reason the State has failed is because he is innocent. We will look at Mr. Hall's case. It rests on the following evidence . . .

During the argument, continue to tie up the specifics to your general theory:

> "Hence, the eyewitness cannot be believed. He is racially biased, he was 40 feet away from the robber and the lighting was dim. The State cannot prove Mr. Hall's guilt by this witness. The State has only two other pieces of evidence linking him to the crime. Let's look at them."

Finally, you should generally summarize your argument. This will again review for the factfinder how all the various bits of evidence fit into your grand structure.

NOTES

1. *Order Effects in Argument: The Rhetorical-Psychological Literature*

The problem of sequence in argument has received considerable attention in traditional writing on rhetoric, and has been the subject of a good deal of modern research on persuasion. Undoubtedly there is a strong psychological need for structure in communication— for some pattern which organizes, focuses and limits the material which we hear, see and experience. What does this insight add to the advocate's task? Needless to say, an argument must have a beginning, a middle, an end and some appropriate transitions between them. Beyond this, however, the possibilities for arranging the ideas and topics of a presentation appear inexhaustible. For example, arguments might be sequenced in the following ways: (i) chronological; (ii) topical; (iii) by a process of elimination (presenting each contrary argument until only supportive arguments remain); (iv) problem-remedy; (v) climax (conclusion is reserved until the end); (vi) anti-climax (conclusion is stated at the beginning); and (vii) problem-inquiry (leaving conclusion to audience), to name only a few. Similarly, within each of these general arrangements any number of possibilities exist. James Jeans, for example, makes the following observations about "how to begin":

> The organization of the closing argument is critical. Your appeal will be either rational, emotional (or most likely a combination of both) and regardless of the selection or the mix, the argument must be structured to have an impact. The rational argument must unfold in logical order and the emotional argument must peak with a concluding appeal. Whether your target is the head or the heart, the key to hitting the bullseye is organization.
>
> The form of organization will not always be the same but regardless of the form which is employed, you will arrange your summation so that you will create a mood, establish a base for your argument, develop that argument and conclude with an appeal. Let us analyze each of those elements and consider the variations that are possible.

Creating the Mood

This appears to be that part of the summation most neglected by the advocate. The reason for the neglect is that too many consider this phase of the argument as simple salutation and the salutation employed is as perfunctory as a "How do you do? Haven't we had lovely weather?" For the lawyer there is a slight variation. "Good afternoon ladies and gentlemen of the jury. We have now reached that part of the case called the closing argument in which each of the lawyers have an opportunity to tell you what the case is about. First I want to thank you for your attentiveness. You have paid close attention to the witnesses and me and my client appreciate that . . . ." How many times have you heard that opening shot? Is it profound? sincere? eloquent? effective? No, but, they argue, it has some advantages.

First, it is traditional. We lawyers are always impressed by what has gone before. We take the path most traveled and heaven knows, this one has been stamped smooth.

Second, it is comfortable. Most of our social introductions are nothing less than ritual. Confrontation with a stranger provides a bit of concern so we put the mind and emotions into neutral while we mouth an automatic "How do you do?" We buy a little time while we shake hands and exchange smiles and by then, hopefully the minor trauma of meeting a stranger has been overcome and we are ready to ease into communications of heavier import. Sometimes lawyers feel this same need to "buy time" in order to warm up and the acceptable way to do this is to recite an innocuous salutation followed by a ritualistic "thank you."

Third, it is flattering to the jury and consequently will make them more receptive to your presentation. It would appear that to the seasoned advocate none of the aforegoing reasons would suffice to justify such a trite beginning to the dramatic highlight of the trial. Certainly it is traditional in the sense that it has often been done in the past, but the best definition of tradition is "that which we have done before and we wish to do again." Why should anyone wish to make such an introduction again? . . .

. . . [N]o doubt such a beginning provides comfort to those that feel the need to overcome the shock of a new confrontation. But why should you feel the discomfort of a confrontation and a new one at that? You have addressed the jury before, on voir dire, opening statement and certainly a few glances have been exchanged during trial. If your attitude has been right during trial, by now the jurors should at least be comfortable acquaintances if not old friends. Nor does the third reason, flattering them for their attentiveness, justify such an unimaginative beginning. Chances are your opponent will commence his summation in the same fashion so the generation of good will should be canceled out.

If we analyze this "thank you for listening" approach carefully we may conclude that it is in reality an offensive remark to these "officers of the court." All the participants in a trial are called together to perform the awesome task of dispensing justice. Everyone who is caught up in the procedure is there under compulsion—the judge and the coterie of courtroom attendants are elected or appointed public officials, the lawyers have contracted for the services, the witnesses and jurors are subpoenaed (too often we forget the Latin derivation, "under penalty") to appear and receive compensation for that appearance. Who are we to thank them? When they do their job well, it is because of their obligation to the state or to the concept of justice—not as a personal favor to the litigants. Perhaps it is time we abandon our traditional, comfortable flattering introduction to our summation.

Considering what not to do hardly solves our problem. How do we commence our closing argument? First of all don't think of an "introduction." If you do, you will fall right back into the ritualistic mouthings. Think in terms of the mood you wish to create in order that the jury will be ready to accept the body of your argument. It is surprising how often during a trial there will be certain incidents that have occurred or certain lines of inquiry developed which are foreign to the general theme of your presentation. Your initial task in opening argument is to neutralize these occurrences and create a proper climate for the jury's receptiveness.[26]

Ask yourself, with different purposes in mind, how else you might begin.

Rather than explore each of these possibilities in detail, it seems enough here to discuss the kinds of choices arrangement involves. Note that Davis, for example, like the classical rhetoricians, seems to assume that a chronological order is the best way to organize the facts, and that favorable arguments should precede those that refute

---

26. J. Jeans, TRIAL ADVOCACY 372–
   74 (1975).

the opponent's case. Is this supported by your own experience? Do you feel it makes any difference how the material is arranged?

John Cosier adds the following to Davis's suggestions:

> The late Mr. Justice Jackson once observed that although important to comprehension, good organization is not always controllable in argument before the Supreme Court. This observation is undoubtedly true. However, to the extent that interludes in questioning from the bench allow counsel to proceed with his preplanned organization, he is well advised to order his presentation so as to promote attention and acceptance as well as comprehension.

> I have already suggested that both sides of the argument should be discussed during the course of the presentation. But which side should be presented first? This question has been the subject of a surprising amount of research. Some studies have supported a primacy hypothesis (first presented "side" has greater persuasive impact) but others have supported a recency hypothesis (last presented "side" has greater appeal). The only thing which can be asserted with confidence is that arguments in the middle of a communication will have the least impact, other factors remaining constant. . . . In particular, theories of primacy-recency do not at present appear solid enough to support the use of rebuttal argument simply to have the last say.

> Another factor influencing the order of presentation is the perception of the argument by the receiver. McGuire has shown that the audience should be first presented with material of a desirable and acceptable nature before they are presented with material which might be unacceptable. Apparently the "momentum" created at the beginning of the communication helps carry the persuader through the more difficult sections of his argument.

> Utilizing the above theories regarding organization, a suggestion for the organization of appellate arguments might be tendered. If possible, the advocate should begin to develop such arguments favoring *his* view of the issues as he is fairly confident the court will accept. This is based somewhat on the common sense notion that the court initially wants to hear petitioner's (respondent's) view of the case from the counsel representing petitioner (respondent). Thus, counsel might lead with his strongest or second strongest argument—strength being evaluated in terms of the likelihood that the argument will carry his cause *with the particular court*. Next, he should develop further arguments in the order of estimated decreasing acceptance by the court. He should then state and refute opposing counsel's arguments beginning with the one which is easiest to refute. Finally, prior to his concluding remarks he should present the court with another very strong argument favoring his client, making use of the principle of recency. In some cases an especially good argument might be reserved for final presentation; in other cases this final appeal might be a summary of arguments offered during the initial portion of his presentation.[27]

27. J. Cosier, *A Theory of Appellate Oral Advocacy: A Psychological Perspective*, unpublished paper, Harvard Law School, 1972 (footnotes omitted).

Think about whether you agree with these observations. In what other order could the facts and law be combined? What order is more likely to generate questions?

Not all the research on persuasion would support Cosier's comments. For example, in reviewing the studies on this subject, Lawson concludes:

> In situations where a two-sided argument can be expected to have an advantage over a one-sided one [*i. e.,* where the opposing side will be presented subsequently] an arrangement of [two-sided] arguments in a refutational-supportive sequence should be more effective in persuasion than an arrangement of the same argument on a supportive-refutational sequence.[28]

Lawson bases this conclusion on two theories. First, persuasion depends on the communicator establishing his credibility. The reason that one-sided communications are generally not as effective as two-sided communications (except with favorably inclined audiences and without exposure to counterargument) is that the audience perceives the communicator as less credible because he is not evenhandedly presenting the issue. They will, therefore, not pay close attention to the rest of what he has to say or "read into" what he is saying a "biased" intent. Thus, it is necessary for the advocate to immediately establish his balance and truthfulness by beginning with opposing arguments. Secondly, Lawson suggests that a refutational-supportive order is necessary to counteract the natural tendency of an audience, particularly if it is not initially favorably inclined, to "rehearse" unfavorable arguments as they listen to the speaker. Presenting opposing arguments early in the presentation has "the effect of indicating to the opposed members of the audience from the very beginning that their point of view and supporting arguments would not be neglected."[29] Does this reasoning, at least as applied to arguments to a court, seem sound to you? Compare these conclusions with those of Cosier. Can you account for the differences?

A similar sort of analysis is necessary when one addresses the question of whether the strongest arguments should be placed first or last in the presentation. A number of trial lawyers have argued that the ideas should be arranged in a climax order:

> A speech must progress in order to move. It must press on from point to point. It must with each paragraph rise a little higher until

---

28. Lawson, *Experimental Research on the Organization of Persuasive Arguments: An Application to Courtroom Communications,* 1970 LAW AND THE SOCIAL ORDER 579, 602 (1970). A refutational communication mentions or challenges unfavorable arguments; a supportive communication presents only favorable arguments.

29. *Id.* at 600, quoting from C. Hovland, A. Lumsdaine and F. Sheffield EXPERIMENTS ON MASS COMMUNICATION 203–04 (1949).

at last, through an ever-ascending series of words and clauses it mounts finally to the bright pinnacle of a climax.[30]

If one assumes a "law of primacy" in persuasion, an anti-climax order (strongest arguments first) would seem to be preferable, and this position, too, has its supporters among trial lawyers.[31] Such an assumption is warranted by most research on learning and recall. When presented with a series of statements under experimental conditions people seem to remember the statements placed at the beginning of the sequence,[32] and at least one experiment purports to demonstrate larger shifts of opinion in an audience presented arguments in an "anti-climax rather than a climax order."[33] On the other hand, there is some evidence that weak arguments have less effect when they are preceded by a strong argument.[34] Does this suggest that a climax order is preferable, or simply reinforce the view that the "best" arguments should be placed first, where they will have the greatest effect? Without going into the validity of these studies, or of the methodologies employed (assume they are within an acceptable range), can you think of a hypothesis of argument arrangement which would reconcile these results? Can you think of any experiments or data which might help you resolve these sorts of issues?

-----

2. *The Idea of Coherence in Ordering Arguments*

In considering the foregoing, one should not stray too far from a more general rhetorical insight—effective advocacy depends on the audience feeling that what is presented expresses some overall coherence. The following sets out what this would mean to a writer or critic:

> "To achieve its purpose, to confirm its position, a work must have unity, coherence and emphasis . . . How can we determine unity? The determination must be done in terms of the relation of its parts to the whole. A student calling upon his science instructor may come upon him in a laboratory that looks like the last word in disarray. The

30. L. Stryker, THE ART OF ADVOCACY 148 (1954). *See also* M. Belli, MODERN TRIALS 1265 (1954).

31. *E. g.*, B. Palmer, COURTROOM STRATEGIES 177 (1959); J. Appleman, SUCCESSFUL APPELLATE TECHNIQUES 1032 (1953); H. Goodrich, R. Carson & J. Davis, A CASE ON APPEAL 60–61 (1967); E. Low, HOW TO PREPARE AND TRY A NEGLIGENCE CASE 132 (1957); R. Stern & E. Grossman, SUPREME COURT PRACTICE 502 (4th ed. 1969); F. Wiener, EFFECTIVE APPELLATE ADVOCACY 182 (1950).

32. Jersild, *Modes of Emphasis in Public Speaking*, 12 J.APPL.PSYCH. 611 (1928).

33. Sponberg, *A Study of the Relative Effectiveness of Climax and Anti-Climax Order in an Argumentative Speech*, 13 SPEECH MONOGRAPHS 35 (1946).

34. *See* Cramwell, *The Relative Effect on Audience Attitude of the First Versus the Second Argumentative Speech of the Series*, 17 SPEECH MONOGRAPHS 105 (1960).

student can see no sense in the clutter of meters, tubing, and glass. If the instructor can explain to the student the purpose of the experiments he is conducting and how various parts of the equipment make their contribution toward the completion of the experiment, the student may see some kind of sense, some unity, in the midst of what first seemed to be mere clutter. If the student can be made to see the purpose and the relationship of the various parts to that purpose, he may leave the laboratory feeling, as does his instructor, that there was not clutter, but purpose, in the arrangement of laboratory materials.

* * *

The goal .   .   . can be thought of as a final cause that motivates or holds together the entire work. It can also be thought of as an underlying principle from which the entire work grows or develops. Whether thought of as a final cause or an organic principle, the purpose is the factor that integrates a work and gives it vitality and impact.

* * *

The writer who wants to achieve unity in his work can best begin by developing an ability to recognize how an integrating principle functions in effective writing. He must constantly ask himself: What is it that this selection intends to accomplish? Is it trying to explain something? To prove something? To make me want to do something? Can it be formulated into a specific proposition?

This formulation of the unifying principle should then be treated as would a hypothesis in science: that is, it should be tested. If the student is correct in his formulation of the principle, he should be able to show how every part of the essay helps develop the principle. The hypothesized basis of unity ought to explain why the writer used a given illustration, why he used certain references, why he organized his material one way instead of another.

Secondly, the writing must have coherence. A work is considered coherent if the sequence of its parts—ideas, imagery, paragraphs, sentences—is intelligible to the reader. The sequence will be intelligible if it is based upon a principle of organization that is meaningful to its intended audience.

Though both unity and coherence are based upon principles, they are different qualities, and the principles upon which they are based are different. The principle of unity is the *purpose* the work tends to fulfill; the principle of coherence is the basis of *organization* that controls the sequence of the parts in the work. Unity is the quality attributed to any writing that has all its necessary parts. Coherence is a quality attributed to any writing wherein these parts are arranged according to a sequence meaningful to a careful reader. A work may be unified without being coherent, for it can contain all that is necessary to its purpose without having these parts arranged in a sequence its intended audience can follow. Conversely, work may be coherent without being unified, for it can progress logically without including all the necessary information.

Logical coherence [is based] on the sequence of parts being controlled by objective, impersonal, and analytic relations among the various ideas in the work. When the progression of ideas is determined by logic, the order of those ideas is usually based on relationships such as that of the part to the whole, the effect to the cause, the antecedent to its consequence, or the conclusion to its premises. For example, paragraph *B* may follow paragraph *A* because *B* describes the effect of the operation of a cause described in *A*; paragraph *C* may follow paragraph *B* because it states a generalization that follows from the evidence presented in paragraphs *A* and *B*.

. . . The tenth *Federalist Paper*, written by Madison to prove the proposition that the new Constitution would control internal factions, is an example of an essay whose coherence is based upon the logical progression of ideas. The excerpt here shows Madison moving from a definition of faction to a consideration of the means of controlling it. These means must fall into one of two possible categories: cause or effect. There are two possible ways of controlling the causes, neither of which is desirable or feasible.

By faction, I understand a number of citizens, whether amounting to a majority or a minority of the whole, who are united and actuated by some common impulse or passion, or of interest, adverse to the rights of other citizens, or to the permanent and aggregate interests of the community. There are two methods of curing the mischiefs of faction: the one, by removing its causes; the other, by controlling its effects.

There are again two methods of removing the causes of faction: the one by destroying the liberty which is essential to its existence; the other, by giving to every citizen the same opinions, the same passions, and the same interests.

It could never be more truly said than of the first remedy, that it was worse than the disease. Liberty is to faction what air is to fire, an aliment without which it instantly expires. But it could not be less folly to abolish liberty, which is essential to political life, because it nourishes faction, than it would be to wish the annihilation of air, which is essential to animal life, because it imparts to fire its destructive energy.

The second expedient is as impracticable as the first would be unwise.

The logical coherence in this passage is so clear that it may be diagrammed:

Faction which is an impulse contrary to the public good, is a mischief.
 Mischief may be cured through its causes or effects.
  Causes may be cured in two ways: destruction of its principle of existence and the universalizing of this minority impulse.
   The first cure would destroy freedom.
   The second cure is impractical.
    (Madison's next step, logically and obviously, will treat of the cure through effects.)

Associational coherence . . . As logical coherence is based on objective and verifiable relations among ideas, associational coherence is based upon subjective and personal relations among ideas, images, details—anything. The sequence in informal essays is frequently based upon the associations called up by experiences, and these associations follow one another in a sequence that is based upon accidental interrelationships. Detail *B* may follow detail *A* because that is the way they came together in the writer's life; there may be no other connection between them. . . . At its best, writing that is coherent associationally dramatizes the writer's mind in action, moving from one idea to another, showing the reader not only what the writer has on his mind but how he came to think the way he does . . .

. . . The writer [using associations] must try to avoid two real dangers: employing associational leaps so private no one can follow them, or associations which leave out too many intermediary steps. . . .

Spatial coherence . . . advances the sequence of details according to their arrangement in space. The coherence of descriptive passages is commonly based upon a spatial sequence, the writer presenting the details of the object he is describing in an order that reflects the order they occupy in space. A writer who wants to describe a scene can begin by asking his readers to imagine themselves occupying a particular position in relation to the scene he wants to describe, and then presenting his details in relation to that point. Thus a historian about to describe the Battle of Gettysburg might "place" his readers on a hill overlooking the field. He would locate the Northern Army to his right, the Southern to his left, and all important landmarks in relation to these original lines of orientation.

The clarity of a passage organized according to spatial coherence is . . . ensured by an imposed frame of reference. The writer can use some common figure—a square, a triangle, the letter "A"—as a frame or pattern to which he can refer all the details of the scene he is describing. . . .

Once a writer has introduced a frame of reference, whether it be the scene itself or an imposed fundamental image, he can further ensure the coherence of his writing by presenting his details according to an ordered pattern of progression, for example, in a sequence from left to right, top to bottom, clockwise or counterclockwise.

Chronological coherence involves, of course, the passage of time. Details in chronological ordered writing such as news stories, biographies, histories, personal reminiscences—are presented in a succession that parallels the succession in which they originally occurred. Detail *B* follows detail *A* because that is the way it originally happened. The possibilities of confusion in following or writing a passage organized according to chronology are less than in passages organized according to other patterns, for reader and writer can always refer the details to the time sequence itself.

[Even here, however, the work must have the third essential quality,] emphasis.

It is important to recall that no matter how well organized and well argued any piece of writing may be, if it lacks emphasis it will not be effective. Mark Antony's speech in *Julius Caesar* beginning "Friends, Romans, countrymen, lend me your ears," is one of the most familiar landmarks in literature. Few people recall, unless they are prodded, that Mark Antony's speech was immediately preceded by one from Brutus. Brutus' speech is a model of clear argumentation—brief and pithy argumentation. It is the speech of a man who believed that all that was required for effective expression was clear organization and logical argumentation. . . . The same crowd listened to Mark Antony with attention, hung on his every word and when he had finished, did exactly what he had intended—rioted.[35]

Your own arguments must reflect these qualities. That is, you must be able to relate each of the parts to a central proposition or image you wish to convey. Similarly, whatever mode of organization you select—topical, chronological, associational, or spatial—you must, even when reading your argument, be able to trace its primary emphasis. All of the foregoing assumes this simple injunction.

3. Style: Wording and Phrasing

COSIER, A THEORY OF ORAL APPELLATE ADVOCACY: A PSYCHOLOGICAL PERSPECTIVE

(1972).*

Argument is inevitably a mix of feelings, organization and language—a search for the "proper words in the proper places." At each stage of the presentation the advocate is faced, not only with what to say, but when and in what form to say it. The following is a cursory review of some of the choices and possibilities this involves.

THE OPENING AND THE CHARACTERIZATION OF THE CASE

Psychologists divide human responsiveness to verbal messages into three "aspects": attention, comprehension, and acceptance. The opening minutes of the argument positively must gain the first and should lay the foundation for the other two. . . .

* * *

From a strictly psychological perspective counsel for both sides should be aware that "(t)he most important natural factor of attention seems to be that of change or variety."[a] This realization im-

---

35. R. Hughes and P. Duhamel, RHE-
TORIC: PRINCIPLES AND USAGE,
2nd edition, © 1967, pp. 15–23. Reprinted by permission of Prentice-Hall,
Inc., Englewood Cliffs, New Jersey.

* From an unpublished paper on file at
the library of the Harvard Law
School.

a. K. Andersen, PERSUASION: THE-
ORY AND PRACTICE 100 (1971).

mediately suggests two techniques for presenting effective openings. First, since judges hear arguments practically every day, they no doubt become weary listening to the routine argument. If the *manner* of presentation is significantly different from the routine case, the advocate stands a better chance of eliciting the court's attention. Second, judges no doubt listen to many frivolous and boring appeals. Their attention is quite naturally drawn to one in which the issues are unusual and interesting. Thus, during the opening the advocate should lead the court to believe that the issues presented will challenge their intellect and stimulate their imaginations. This should be the approach even though the issues may indeed be routine; the advocate simply must involve the court at the outset.

Perhaps the ultimate in attention-getting techniques is one which might be appropriately called the "shock effect." Wiener offers an opening he once used in a denaturalization case before the Supreme Court which fits this characterization: "The question in this case is whether a good Nazi can be a good American." [b] The "shock effect" is probably most appropriate when the advocate feels the court is generally predisposed one way or the other, making the oral argument somewhat of a formality. It is perhaps crucial when the predisposition runs counter to the position being advocated—the court may be "shocked" into listening to an argument they would otherwise not attend.

[The most fundamental aspect of the opening, however] is the "characterization" of the substantive issues, i. e., the psychologically favorable language used to describe the legal questions to be decided by the court. Viewed from the acceptance perspective the problem is how to phrase the question such that it admits of but one answer— in other words, how to set in the court's mind the manner in which the advocate wishes the case to be perceived. For example, characterizing the issues of Griswold v. Connecticut, 381 U.S. 479 (1965), as presenting "the question of whether a state can invade the sanctity of the marital bedroom" is clearly more effective than simply saying the case presents for decision "the constitutionality of a law forbidding the use of contraceptives." It is obvious that tactful use of covert emotional appeals is a key ingredient to effective characterization. . . .

MAXIMIZING PERSUASIVE IMPACT: POLISHING THE MESSAGE

The intent of this section is to offer general guidelines for maximizing the effectiveness of an already structured appellate argument. It focuses primarily on the use of language *per se* in promoting persuasiveness and increasing communion between the advocate and the

b. F. Wiener, BRIEFING AND AR-
     GUING FEDERAL APPEALS 289
     (1961).

court. . . . No attempt is made to canvass the entire field of rhetoric as applied to argumentation. Indeed, as with the emotional appeal, caution is mandated in the use of rhetoric in an appellate argument; the appellate court is not a jury and does not wish to be treated as one. But the appellate advocate should nonetheless be [cognizant of] Andersen's observation:

> (P)eople who have good language choice and style are generally more effective persuaders than those who do not. Even if the perfecting of style is only the perfecting of thought, the persuasive impact should still be heightened.[c]

The use of linguistic techniques in oral advocacy should be functional—mere eloquence is not tantamount to persuasiveness. The focus should once again be on the mediational processes of attention, comprehension, and acceptance.

* * *

While the focus of language use vis-a-vis attention is on novelty, its focus vis-a-vis comprehension is on meaning—*meaning to the receiver*. In this regard it may be worthwhile to recall the distinction between denotative and connotative meanings: "Denotative meanings deal with the relationships between the sign (word) and the object or the thing referenced . . .. Connotations have to do with the *feeling* or sense that a *person* has toward the object and sign . . .." [d] Of course, the distinction is not a clear-cut one, but the important fact is that a grouping of words persuasive to one individual may totally alienate another due to the associations those words carry for *him*.

Thus, though it may be difficult, word choice should be geared to the particular judges who will hear the appeal. . . .

* * *

Just what effect appropriate choice of words has beyond promoting attention and comprehension is not at all clear. Whereas one can focus on novelty and change to gain attention and on meaning to gain comprehension, it is difficult to perceive a "focus" for gaining acceptance of the argument through the use of rhetoric *per se*. Intuitively it seems as if some linguistic forms are "persuasive" in and of themselves, although this intuition is as yet unsupported by psychological research. Perhaps the best that can be done is to offer some of the specific techniques which are used in argumentation together with some plausible explanations for their presumed effectiveness. . . . Many of these techniques seem to leave a definite impression on the mind and to that extent seem to promote *retention* apart from any force they may bring to bear on the receivers adoption, *i. e.*, acceptance, of the argument.

---

c.　Andersen, *supra* note a, at 126.　　　　d.　*Id.* at 178 (emphasis added).

The first of these techniques which can be isolated is that falling into the general category of redundance—repetition, restatement, and parallel structure. Redundancy has the effect of "presence"—making the "object of discourse present to the mind." Obviously, the more times a judge hears a phrase the more likely he is to remember it. Furthermore, to the extent that the phrase which is repeated is linked to a major argument, each repetition of it in a new context presents the judges with yet another opportunity to accept the argument subtly posed in a new light. A prime example of repetition and restatement is presented in [Arthur Kinoy's argument for the petitioner in Powell v. McCormack, 395 U.S. 486 (1969).]. One of the central themes of petitioner's argument was that aside from the qualifications for membership in the House of Representatives *specifically* enumerated in the Constitution, the House had no basis for excluding a duly elected Representative. Kinoy chose to frame this argument in terms of the interference by the House with the *free choice* of the constituents of the congressional district. . . . The phrase "free choice" or "freely select," etc., is thus linked to a major argument. By the time Kinoy sat down he had used that phrase or variations on it a total of six times in a variety of contexts. And not surprisingly, the opinion of Chief Justice Warren states:

> Had the intent of the Framers (of the Constitution) emerged from these (historical) materials with less clarity, we would nevertheless have been compelled to resolve any ambiguity in favor of a narrow construction of the scope of Congress' power to exclude members-elect. A fundamental principle of our representative democracy is, in Hamilton's words, "that the people should *choose whom they please* to govern them." [e]

Parallel structure magnifies the "presence" of repetition with rapid-fire rhythmic emphasis which exerts a compelling psychological impact. Perhaps the best example of this technique is the portion of Kinoy's argument in which he demonstrates the futility of respondent's attempts to deal with petitioner's constitutional analysis. . . . The phrase "they have difficulty" is used five times to introduce very brief but persuasive dismissals of respondent's points. If the passage is read aloud, the monotonous message comes through— "they have difficulty" with X, "they have difficulty" with Y, "they have difficulty" with Z, "they have difficulty" with everything. [The net effect is that] respondents cannot find a single flaw in petitioner's analysis.

· Another technique which should be mentioned is the use of imagery or a striking phrase. By definition these devices leave an impression on the mind and hence promote retention. But more than

---

e.   Powell v. McCormack, 395 U.S. 486, 547 (1969).

that, an image may be so appealing and "catchy" that it is adopted by the receivers. We all occasionally find ourselves unconsciously whistling the tune accompanying an advertisement we have heard or repeating an advertising lyric or "jingle." The image offers the receiver a shorthand for remembering and adopting a complex argument. It promotes an economy of effort. Perhaps the most familiar example of such an image is the "chilling effect" used to describe the repressive impact of certain governmental action on civil rights and liberties.

Finally, through his knowledge of the individual judges, their styles, and linguistic preferences, the advocate is in an especially good position to choose words and phrases that identify him with the thinking of the judges. "The phrase 'he talks my language' is a common indication of praise and identification. As a man uses words that unite him with my ideas, my values, my reference groups, I may accept him, his proposition, and his attitudes." [f] [This is rooted in a psychological] model of attitude change [which suggests] that accepting the source of a statement may exert psychological pressure in the receiver to accept the statement itself. Undoubtedly, however, the advocate must use care in overtly regurgitating the judge's own ideas and language as the judge may take such an approach as blatant flattery and nothing more. Nevertheless, an argument couched in language with which the judge can readily identify is simply an intelligent refinement of the communication-persuasion process—a process necessarily receiver-oriented.

HEGLAND, TRIAL AND PRACTICE SKILLS IN A NUTSHELL

37–40 (1978).

Arguments often appear tentative because the advocate has not really focused on them so as to understand their true cogency. The argument which "sounds good" before the bathroom mirror suddenly weakens as it is given to the factfinder, holes appear and general relevancy fades. The advocate begins to meander and backtrack.

What you must do is to force yourself to think through the arguments. The racial prejudice of an eyewitness has "something" to do with the worth of this identification. But, precisely what? Does it mean that the identification is mistaken or that it is perjured? And, how does the fact of racial prejudice fit with other facts surrounding the identification? And, how does the issue of the identification fit into your overall theory of the case? What is suggested is that you become quite *explicit* both with yourself and with the factfinder: ask yourself exactly why an argument is cogent and then, tell the factfinder why it is so.[*]

f. *See, e. g.*, Andersen, *supra* note a at 168.

* The need for explicitness is an insight taken from Binder, et al., *Materials on Trial Advocacy.*

Turning now to the specific advice.

1. *Be Explicit, Not Implicit*

"Ladies and gentlemen of the jury, in assessing Jones' credibility, recall that he testified that the lion laid down with the lamb.   Recall also that Jones is President of Free the Lions Committee."

Why is it that we are generally implicit in our argument?   Partly because we do not wish to state the obvious, and partly because we lack the mental discipline to ask "What is it that is so obvious, anyhow?" Recalling that what is obvious to you may not be to the next person and that upon analysis, the "obvious" often isn't, you should generally be explicit:

Ladies and Gentlemen of the Jury, part of your job is to determine whether or not to believe Jones' story.	
One way we test a story to see if it is believable is to see if it makes sense from what we know of the world; if it conforms to how the world operates.	Explicit as to reasoning process
For example, if someone tells you in July that they had just returned from Tucson and that it was snowing there, you would naturally tend not to believe that story.	Example
In this case, Jones testified that the lion laid down with the lamb. [Counsel could stop here or make the tie-ups explicit, to wit]	Facts of case explicitly stated
In this world, it is our experience that lions eat lambs, not lie with them.	Explicit as to factual conclusion
Therefore, Ladies and Gentlemen of the Jury, you should not believe Jones' story	Explicit as to ultimate conclusion
———	
And, in addition, Ladies and Gentlemen, we tend to judge the truth of a story not only by that story but by who tells it to us. Does the person have a motive to lie to us? If he does, then we tend to lose faith in what he tells us.	Explicit as to reasoning process

For example, we tend not to believe the used car salesman when he tells us that the car was owned by an old maid school teacher.

Example: myth?

Now, in this case, Jones testified he is the President of Free the Lions Committee and as such wants lions to walk free.

Facts of case, explicitly stated

Jones has an interest in us believing that he actually saw a lion lie down with a lamb.

Explicit as to factual conclusion

Therefore, Ladies and Gentlemen, you should not believe Jones. Jones should be eaten!

Explicit as to ultimate conclusion, plus poetic license

PROBERT, SEMANTICS IN THE COURT ROOM

5 AM.JUR.TRIALS 723–25, 735–38, 743–51, 754–55, 762–63 (1966).

[All argument in the courtroom must deal with "word magic"— the association of words with particular things in ways which cause us to believe that a single interpretation is the only one feasible. . . . We forget that words are clues to meaning rather than things with meanings. . . .] A witness, by his own pattern of word association, may oversimplify and thereby tell only part of his story. . . . A jury in judging and interpreting may not recognize the role the word association plays in the witness's testimony. . . . The attorney who wants to manage the interpretive capacity of the jury will try to establish these channels of inquiry. . . . In argument [he] can lead the jurors beyond or beneath the signal words (*i. e.*, probable cause, breach of duty, duty) by taking the words off their pedestal and pointing [to their source and the conditions to which they refer. . . .]

* * *

There is a wide variation in the possible degrees of generality and abstraction involved in the descriptions of events, persons, places, or things. The first and lowest order is contained in the observation of the thing itself, as with so-called real evidence, or certain forms of demonstrative evidence. On the other hand, a statement such as "I saw defendant hit plaintiff," which seems about as general as one can get, is psycho-logically of a rather high order of abstraction.

A high order of generality or abstraction fails to call attention to the uniqueness of the matter being described, and therefore details are apt to be omitted, ignored, or de-emphasized. Confusions arise from the fact that in our language there is simply not a unique word for every unique event. If your client is a nineteen-year-old driver and he is referred to as a teenager, you may have difficulty overcoming the image produced. The witness and jury may ignore what he is actually like as an individual, and resort to their own personal images of teenagers. Similarly, in speaking of an automobile, a Cadillac is not the same as a Volkswagen and the difference may be important in an accident case. In this instance the adjectives serve to differentiate. In notes or trial briefs where adjectives are not so readily available, subscripts noting the differences may be used, such as car /1 is not car /2. Counsel must be mindful of the uniqueness of every thing and every event, and of the potentiality of treating it that way at trial.

* * *

To create maximum effectiveness in communication there should be a skillful mixture of generality and detail. Therefore, there can be no hard and fast rule about using concrete references in preference to high order abstractions. For example, general statements do not tell much about the details, but they better indicate the way a thing or event fits into the bigger picture. If you show that the defendant drives a car in his work, you give information that is missing in describing him as a common carrier, and vice versa. Therefore, your courtroom arguments and examinations should move your listeners back and forth between detail and generality. If the witness is dealing in high order abstractions, counsel can clarify the testimony by eliciting more explicit information. The term "great pain and suffering," for instance, can be better understood by the jury if the witness describes in detail the specific ailments that constituted his pain and suffering. When the testimony concerns concrete references, there may be a need to put them in more general terms to enable the jury to have a picture of the situation as a whole. When counsel handles testimony in this way he overcomes the natural tendency to assume that words used have the same meaning to both the witness and the jurors.

There are times, however, when strategy calls for leaving out the details. If plaintiff is claiming injury from a bullet in a hunting accident, counsel will spend little or no time in calling attention to its ricochet characteristics if the bullet had to take a right angle bounce to hit its mark. Rather, his attorney will stress the risk involved, that someone was likely to have been hit, and that plaintiff was in fact hit.

From the defense view, however, it would be advantageous to stress every twist and turn of the bullet, and every branch it hit, in order to stress the uniqueness of the particular event. The term "foreseeable" could be applied to the accident by both sides, its meaning dependent on how it is used. If the word is taken literally, nothing that happens is foreseeable in every detail and aspect of its happening. On the other hand, almost any accident is foreseeable if described in general terms.

Note that the position of both attorneys is "true" in that both sides give the jury the opportunity to make a decision on the facts as most favorably presented. We see, however, that the questions may be arguments, and the seemingly objective descriptions may be loaded. The level of generality or abstraction becomes the focus of presentation of proof and argument. . . .

* * *

Words and expressions come to have "meaning mostly" through our usage of them. Since we all learn words under different circumstances, there is a great deal more latitude to usage than we recognize. We do have some control, however, because we can narrow down an interpretation to a particular area of meaning. Because the process of interpretation works so very subtly, often unconsciously, and because we do have latitude in usage, there follows a technique of persuasion and manipulation that we call definitional technique.

* * *

It is easy in many situations to persuade another person to accept one's own definition. This is especially so since it does not seem to cost the listener any effort, and he comes to accept the speaker's definition without realizing it. He may be gullible, dependent on the speaker's approval, or he may wish to be accommodating. Prestidigitation can be at its height in such circumstances. Fortunately, there is another attorney to point out that magic is being worked, although he can do this only if he himself is aware of it.

* * *

In some instances you may use certain attitude words as the focus of your definitional complex, fitting your facts into a more or less common usage. Take, for example, the word "science" used in an argument against the testimony of an expert witness:

> "His evidence was hardly scientific. Science does not involve just guessing. He had not seen the patient more than once, and then only for fifteen minutes. Instead, he relied on rumor."

"Science" here is an information word but, in the context used it calls on the jury's attitude toward science. Certainly, doctors are scientific, and if this doctor was not scientific then his evidence is hardly credible.

* * *

Loaded words, associations, and definitions do not work by themselves. You cannot argue that a feather is a dangerous weapon, except perhaps in metaphor. You cannot argue that a ten-year-old boy should exercise the skill of a surgeon. You must work within the psycho-logical framework that is presented to you. Also, your own definitions and associations must be attractive as well as reasonable and appropriate. If you develop an imaginative flexibility with your definitions, in addition to good communication sensitivity, you will more readily acquire effective rebuttal techniques.

Where simple words or phrases or definitional devices are involved, the simplest rebuttal technique would be to attempt a different definition or word association. In this regard, it helps to have an appreciation of the attitudinal connotation of words. Consider, for instance, such words as "boy," "kid," "brat," "child," "minor," "offspring," "youngster," "teenager," and "infant." In a given situation several or all of these words might be available variations. If a witness or opponent uses an unfavorable one, you may wish to dispute that usage or simply to use the word more favorable to you. . . .

The word loading may be more complex. Your opponent may argue that there were automobiles on all sides of your client, thus putting him in a special situation of due care. You may wish to counter that the highway was no more crowded than usual. If an opponent's witness says that your client could have taken a certain "simple precaution," you may wish to point out that while it might have been possible to take such an "extreme measure," it was not called for on the facts.

* * *

We should analyze the jury's interpretation of the evidence in terms of inference. When a witness makes a report to a jury, we should analyze the jurors' acceptance of the report, and the number of inferences involved in the acceptance. The jurors take an inferential leap, and assume that the witness is credible, remembers accurately, is not lying, has average powers of observation, uses words in customary ways, and has the capacity to articulate his observations in normal fashion. The instantaneous move from "the witness *said* X was so," to "X *is* so" may not be justified under logical analysis of the testimony. The testimony should be analyzed in detail to reveal its strengths and weaknesses. Eventually such analysis should become second nature.

NOTES

1. *Phrasing and Characterization in Argument*

Cosier's concern for "characterization" and imagery finds its counterpart in the literature on rhetoric in discussions of "style." The ideas and chains of inference that comprise an argument must inevitably be turned into *words* that will produce the desired effect on judge or jury. Although logically this seems to involve merely giving the themes which are to be argued more specificity and content, one need not be a rhetorician to recognize the possibilities involved in such a process. The statements, (i) "the facts show defendant to be innocent," (ii) "the defendant's innocence cries out from the facts," and (iii) "are we to say of such facts that they shall imprison and degrade?" may all mean the same thing at one level of understanding, but convey very different nuances and images.

The nature of the difference between such formulations has fascinated students of language and argument for centuries. While some have seen this concern as a shallow interest in decoration and cleverness, others have considered the problem or style—and its way of relating thought to language—as the fundamental element of communication.[36] All of the foregoing excerpts, in one way or another, reflect this view. Probert, for example, points out that a single phrase or characterization can sum up and favorably influence the outcome of an entire case, just as it can provide the opening an adversary needs to attack and undermine an entire line of argument. Our own observation of lawyer argument leads us to share this concern. "Polishing the message" is a separable and significant stage in the process of preparation—and one which we have only begun to understand.

As the readings suggest, the problem of phrasing and formulation is a problem of assessing the impact of language. Words have many meanings and effects. A particular combination of words, phrases, ideas and expressions, when taken as a whole, may be heard as dry, plain, elegant, florid, simple, balanced, concise, diffuse or irregular. How is one to choose among them?

Modern rhetoricians have focused on the following criteria:

Accuracy—This refers to the degree of precision the message conveys, *i. e.*, whether the words and phrases used delimit the experience, object, or relationship with which the speaker is concerned in ways which guide attention to the particular feelings and ideas he or she wishes to communicate.

Clarity—This calls attention to the completeness and comprehensibility of the message—its capacity to communicate what is meant. Note that a message may be precise but unclear (beyond the level of comprehension) of a given audience. Conversely, misinformation can be communicated quite clearly.

Force and Vitality—This notion concerns an argument's urgency and excitement—its energy and movement. It focuses, not only on emotional intensity, but on the animation, proximity or sense of reality which a presentation generates.

Propriety—This idea speaks to the appropriateness of the language used to the subject matter, the nature of the occasion, or the particular audience. There are many examples in the legal literature: "Any judge who would buy that is a damn fool". But, perhaps a classic example of inappropriateness—"the sunset

---

36. *See, e. g.*, J. Wilson & C. Arnold, PUBLIC SPEAKING AS A LIBERAL ART (1964).

was red, like a radish or a tomato"—conveys a better sense of what this concern encompasses.

This list, of course, is not exhaustive, nor does it answer many questions concerning the communicative quality of words. What interests us is the significance of these criteria for understanding lawyer advocacy. Look again at Cosier's analysis of appellate argument. Is he using this rhetorical frame of reference? In what ways should/could he go further? Take, for instance, the notion of propriety. How do we begin to sort out what formulations and phrases are appropriate in a given situation? How can arguments remain within this frame of reference and nonetheless convey force, vitality, and a persuasive message? Wiener offers a number of interesting illustrations from appellate practice.

(a) Here are some examples of oral openings, drawn from my own practice and observation . . .

(i) [For petitioner.]

Respondents were convicted by a jury of conspiring to defraud the United States of the disinterested services of one of its officers. Their judgments of conviction were reserved by the Second Circuit on four separate grounds, and the case is now here on certiorari.

Two of the questions, involving alleged errors on the part of the trial court, concern only the Bayers. Two concern only Radovich—whether a confession of his was admissible, and whether his plea of double jeopardy was a valid one. I shall deal with each of those questions separately in the course of the argument.

The basic facts can be briefly stated. Etc., etc., etc.

* * *

(ii) [For petitioner.]

This case, which is here on certiorari to the Ninth Circuit, involves the protection to be accorded the Government-soldier relationship.

* * *

(iii) [For petitioner.]

(b) This case comes here on certiorari to review a judgment of the Circuit Court of Appeals for the Eleventh Circuit which reversed an order of the District Court for the Western Caroline Islands that dismissed a bill of complaint for lack of federal jurisdiction.

The facts involve an action for damages brought by a native chieftain of those islands against a medical officer in the Navy. Etc., etc., etc.

* * *

Here are two examples of how a case can be stated in court; the question is whether post-mortem declarations are admissible in evidence.

(i) Post-mortem declarations have been held to be utterly inadmissible for any purpose, ever since Chief Justice Marshall's justly celebrated opinion in Schmaltz against the Chosen Freeholders in the 13th of Wheaton. Their inadmissibility has never been questioned since the time of that decision, which has stood as a landmark of the law of evidence, and which has been followed and affirmed and reaffirmed in a whole stack of cases, all of which are collected and discussed in our brief. Indeed, but for the decision below, we should have thought that the proposition was not subject to successful question.

(ii) The question of the admissibility of post-mortem declarations was first passed upon in the case of Schmaltz against the Chosen Freeholders of East Overshoe, reported at 13 Wheaton 743. That is a leading case, hence it may be helpful to state the facts out of which it arose:

One Oscar Schmaltz claimed a tract of 120 acres in the Township of East Overshoe, as devisee under the will of his uncle, Joseph Schmaltz. New Jersey had a statute at that time—this was in the year 1799—to the effect that the estates of Revolutionary War veterans should be exempt from taxation. If the elder Schmaltz were such a veteran, then the land in question passed to his nephew Oscar, the plaintiff-in-error. But if Joseph Schmaltz were not a veteran, then his estate escheated for nonpayment of taxes to the township, represented by the Chosen Freeholders. Now, Joseph Schmaltz's status as veteran or nonveteran turned on a declaration made, etc., etc., etc.

* * *

(c) —In order to present your contentions in simplified form, it is frequently useful to employ a striking phrase—a dignified slogan, if you please, but a slogan nonetheless. Perhaps this point will become clearer after a discussion of examples.

(i) . . . "Petitioner is not being denied due process; on the contrary, this statute affords him undue process."

(ii) . . . The question in this case is whether a woman, who all her life has been a civilian, may be tried by an Air Force court-martial in time of peace, here in the District of Columbia and literally within the shadow of the Capitol dome.

(iii) . . . "The question is whether a correction of a military record 'for all purposes' means something less than 'all', so that it is to be interpreted as 'for all purposes except pay and allowances.'"

(iv) . . . "The issue is whether a good Nazi can be a good American."

(v) . . . [The issue is whether], after a fair trial and painstaking review of the record by the agencies provided by law for that purpose, the convicted person will be set free because of alleged errors occurring in the hinterland of the proceedings, long prior to the actual commencement of the trial."

If the slogan you have devised is good—really good—it will make an indelible impression, one that will persist in the minds of the judges long after the rest of the argument has evaporated and been forgotten.[37]

---

37. F. Wiener, BRIEFING AND ARGUING FEDERAL APPEALS 287– 89, 320–23, 328–29 (1961) (citations omitted).

Think about which of these formulations are "better," and whether standards like clarity, force, and vitality are helpful in making such judgments. How would one use this knowledge in actually planning a presentation?

Bear in mind that each of these judgments must be made with one's adversary in mind. As Probert's analysis suggests, the phrases and characterizations we "select" must always compete with the labels attached by opposing counsel, as well as withstand direct attack. This is especially true in the context of jury summation, where an argument's effectiveness may be substantially undermined if the words in which it is framed can be "picked apart" by the opponent.

Look, for example, at a number of typical arguments suggested by the trial literature. If you were an adversary faced with these statements, how would you meet them?

(a) Here you have heard that the defendant has been indicted.

What is an indictment? An indictment is a complaint; it's a piece of paper that brings the defendant into court. It's like a summons in a civil case. The summons in the civil case brings the defendant into court for his trial; the indictment in a criminal case brings the accused into court.

Just because a man is sued does not make him liable. By the same token, just because a man is indicted does not make him guilty. The civil lawyer must prove that his client, the plaintiff, is right. Also, the plaintiff, the prosecutor in this case, must prove that he has a case. When you are in a civil court suing for money, there is no presumption favoring the plaintiff's being right, nor is there a presumption favoring the defendant's being right.

In a criminal case, however, it is a different matter. The law in the criminal case says every defendant is presumed to be innocent. That is a presumption of fact. But realize that the State with all of its power, resources and moral persuasion is the plaintiff and is fighting against one lonely defendant!

For example, take an ordinary baseball game. Both teams start from scratch—that would be like a civil case. No runs, no hits, everything is equal before the pitchers start. In a criminal case, however, the law gives the team—the defendant—one run to start off with. That one run I would call the presumption of innocence. It is the job of the other side, the prosecution, to overcome that one run lead and bat in an extra run to win the game or case.[38]

* * *

(b) "During the four days in which we were presenting the facts of this occurrence and the consequent results of that occurrence on the life of Dan Trotter there have been a few times when certain events occurred which provoked a laugh—from all of us. There is certainly

---

38. D. Cohen, HOW TO WIN CASES BY ESTABLISHING A REASONABLE DOUBT (1970).

nothing improper about a laughter in a court room. For the law deals with life, and laughter, thank goodness, is a substantial part of life. And perhaps in a case such as this laughter can be further justified for it has provided some periods of momentary relief from the catastrophe which most often has occupied our minds. But now the time for laughter has passed and we are confronted with another aspect of life which is the concern of the law, the suffering of Dan Trotter".[39]

* * *

(c) "There is one situation in which a person has an opportunity to evaluate pain in terms of dollars and cents. When the dentist advises that a tooth must be pulled or a cavity filled and questions whether novacaine is desired, the intended victim must answer the question: Is it worth five dollars to avoid the pain? The response is obvious. When confronted with a choice like this we have no problem. The five dollars is little enough to pay in order to avoid the pain. But the pain with which the plaintiff is cursed is not the transitory pain that's experienced in the dentist's chair but the continuous nagging discomfort that haunts him at work and at his home, night and day."

* * *

"Suppose there appeared in the want ad section of our local paper an opportunity for a job opening such as this: the pay will be ten dollars a day. There will be no responsibilities. You'll not have to report to work. No forms to fill and no calls to make. In fact, you will not have to do anything. The day will be free to spend in whatever way you choose. There's really only one feature to the job—you're going to have to endure pain, a continuing unrelenting pain. And, once the job is taken, it will be a permanent commitment. No weekends off, no chance of retirement. The pay and the pain will continue until you die.

"Do you think the ad would be answered? Would anyone voluntarily accept a position such as that? Well, plaintiff has just such a future for him. The acceptance of the job was not his choice, but the job is his. The pain, the constant pain, will follow him to the end of his days. The job obligations are established, it is up to you to determine the fair wages that should be his." [40]

All lawyers quite properly rely on stock arguments in specific situations; you will find there are stock counterarguments as well. They suggest ways immediacy and clarity can be introduced into a presentation. But they also illustrate the danger of basing an important argument on a single image. For example, ask yourself how difficult it would be to turn the baseball game analogy against counsel's position, or modify the "definition" of an indictment? Are there similar answers to the personal injury arguments as well?

The same examples also suggest important differences between arguments made to a jury and those made to a trial judge or appellate court. Generally there is far more play for rhetorical "turns" in jury

---

39.　J. Jeans, TRIAL ADVOCACY 374　　40.　*Id.* at 387–88.
(1975). Reprinted by permission of
West Publishing Company.

arguments. The arguments set out at the beginning of this chapter are worth reviewing in this connection.

It might also be interesting to compare these examples with arguments made over a hundred years ago.[41] Even in jury arguments the use of figures of speech and other forms of rhetorical embellishment has diminished as the world-view and exposure to mass communication of audiences has changed. It is generally agreed that, in modern trials, (i) the advocate must demonstrate sincerity and fairness, as well as commitment to his or her cause; and (ii) the argument should be presented in a way which avoids excessive length, emotionality or oratorical flourish. This does not mean that the choice of specific words and phrases is any less important. It is merely adapted to a different milieu.

---

2. *The Literature of Style*

There is a surprisingly large literature offering details on literary forms, figures and modes of expression. Many of you will not find these materials helpful, but others will draw heavily on them. For this reason, we have included a number of illustrations on the following topics:

Sentence Length and Structure

The good speaker pays attention to sentence length and structure because certain types of sentences are more effective than others to ful-

---

41. The closing argument of Daniel Webster, appearing as a special prosecutor in the murder trial of John Francis Knapp, makes an interesting comparison. Webster closed his summation with the following:

Gentlemen, your whole concern should be to do your duty, and leave consequences to take care of themselves. You will receive the law from the court. Your verdict, it is true, may endanger the prisoner's life, but then it is to save other lives. If the prisoner's guilt has been shown and proved beyond all reasonable doubt, you will convict him. If such reasonable doubts of guilt still remain, you will acquit him. You are the judges of the whole case. You owe a duty to the public, as well as to the prisoner at the bar. You cannot presume to be wiser than the law. Your duty is a plain, straightforward one. Doubtless we would all judge him in mercy. Towards him, as an individual, the law inculcates no hostility; but towards him, if proved to be a murderer, the law, and the oaths you have taken, and public justice demand that you do your duty. With consciences satisfied with the discharge of duty, no consequences can harm you. There is no evil that we cannot either face or fly from but the consciousness of duty disregarded. A sense of duty pursues us ever. It is omnipresent, like the Deity. If we take to ourselves the wings of the morning, and dwell in the uttermost parts of the sea, duty performed or duty violated is still with us, for our happiness or our misery. If we say the darkness shall cover us, in the darkness, as in the light, our obligations are yet with us. We cannot escape their power, nor fly from their presence. They are with us in this life, will be with us at its close; and in that scene of inconceivable solemnity, which lies yet farther onward, we shall still find ourselves surrounded by the consciousness of duty, to pain us wherever it has been violated, and to console us so far as God may have given us grace to perform it. THE WORLD OF LAW, VOL. II: THE LAW AS LITERATURE 439 (E. London, ed. 1960).

fill the purpose of the speaker. In the first place, generally speaking, the shorter simple sentences are to be preferred over the complex. Since it is the obligation of the speaker to make his meaning instantaneously clear, the long complex sentence may be difficult to follow. Thus, it is to be avoided. Various studies have revealed that the great speakers of the past with simpler styles have tended to use shorter sentences. On the other hand, the continuous use of the very short sentence could be monotonous. Thus, the variation between the short and the medium-length sentence is the preferred style by most.

Second, one should be alert to the use of periodic sentences rather than loose sentences particularly when driving toward a climax. A periodic sentence is one in which the meaning is incomplete until the very end. On the other hand, the loose sentence is one in which the meaning would be complete were it to have been ended before it was. In other words, in those sentences the period could have been placed earlier without any particular loss of meaning. The following are examples: Loose: He was an invalid until he was ten. Periodic: Until he was ten, he was an invalid. The first sentence is a loose one because a period could appear after the word invalid; in the second, the period could not be placed earlier. In many cases the periodic sentence is to be preferred, as is true in the foregoing example. If our hearers can be prevented from completing the picture too soon, we will be easier to follow as speakers. . . . In the periodic sentence, on the other hand, the clause "until he was ten" will cause the hearer to withhold the creation of any image because he knows that more is coming. We are not advocating that one always make use of periodic sentences instead of loose ones, but it frequently "economizes the mental effort" of the hearer. Periodic sentences, on the other hand, tend to have power of persuasion superior to the loose and thus are frequently utilized in building climactic portions of the speech.

Third, a speaker should be aware of the rhythmic possibilities of balanced sentence structure. A balanced sentence is one in which words, phrases, or even clauses of one part correspond both in form and in position to words, phrases, or clauses of another part. Here are some examples:

When reason is against man, he will be against reason.

The modern generation is more concerned with the achievement of joy than in the joy of achievement.

The good speaker will be very aware of the value of parallel structure, which is particularly valuable in the well-worded main headings. Parallel structures are formed when two or more phrases, clauses, or even sentences, have identical or similar structure. Often this type of structure is used to word an evil of the present system and to show how a new proposal will remove that evil. . . .

A special form of parallel structure is the "grouping of three." Often, speakers wishing to emphasize some idea and at the same time achieve the rhythmic flow of language will resort to this technique. Three words, three phrases, three clauses, or three sentences will be grouped together for this emphasis. Here are some examples: The

Franks, the Janes, the Sallys of the world are of great concern to all of us. You will become a Washington, a Lincoln, a Jefferson. "A government of the people, by the people and for the people shall not perish from the earth."

The following examples of groupings of three utilize sentences: "I would call him Napoleon, but Napoleon made his way to empire over broken oaths and through a sea of blood. This man never broke his word. . . . I would call him Cromwell, but Cromwell was only a soldier and the state he founded went down with him into his grave. I would call him Washington, but the great Virginian held slaves. This man risked his empire rather than permit the slave trade in the humblest villages of his dominion." Making use of a variety of these devices for more effective sentence structure will bring greater persuasion. Beauty of language through sentence structure has the power to stir audiences.[42]

Language Choice

The English language is rich in synonyms, most of which do not have identical meanings, much less the same association. A wise advocate chooses carefully among synonymous expressions to find those which persuade.

Language also must have color. It is sometimes difficult to identify and far more difficult to define. Apparently it embraces at least these factors:

Vividness

[We have previously] . . . considered the associative and pointing qualities of words. Some associative words we call "vivid" or "emotive." They constitute the language which calls us to look, to hear, to be awake. Many words, of all sorts, have this power to arouse intense feelings in those who hear them. Adjectives like "greedy," "kindly," "stingy," "rumpled," and "villainous" fit the category. Each carries a load of connotations and a built-in appraisal of the things it modifies. "Castigated," "reviled," "sneaked," "badgered," "temporized," and "haggled" are verbs charged with emotion.

* * *

Figures of Speech

Color is also injected into language by the use of figures of speech. Metaphors, similes, and other figures constitute a study in themselves. Briefly, we will note the two mentioned.

Similes, like the analogies discussed in an earlier chapter, call attention to an alleged similarity between what is being considered, and something else which is more familiar to the audience. "There he stands, like a stone wall," was the famous simile that gave Stonewall Jackson his name. "Communism, like cancer, consumes all that it infects," is a modern example.

42. R. Huber, INFLUENCE THROUGH ARGUMENT 341–43 (1963).

Metaphors are more powerful, assuming identity rather than mere similarity. From the cross Jesus said to John regarding Mary, "Behold your Mother," and to Mary, regarding John, "Behold your Son." . . .

Figures of speech do not, *per se*, get or hold attention. The only attention which "hard as a rock," "cold as ice," and "black as tar" would be apt to attract would be a tired yawn. Dozens of figures have been used so much that they have lost whatever freshness they once had.

* * *

Imagery

Phrases whose major appeal is to the senses—which cause us almost literally to see, feel, touch, taste, smell, or otherwise sense—we call *imagery*. They hold attention and create impressions as plain language cannot. Some words, like the following adjectives, are especially loaded with sensory values:

visual—blue-black, sparkling, dingy, golden, speckled, curlicued

auditory—raucous, harsh, strident, tinkly, shrill

gustatory—sweet, sour, salty, bitter

olfactory—smoky, acrid, rotten, putrid, sweet

tactual—rough, slick, velvet, hot, cold, greasy, smooth

Variety

The best English dictionaries have over a half million words; other thousands in the language are not yet included. With such an array at hand, it is depressing indeed to hear the same phrases used over and again. Debate judges hear "colleague," "case," "plan," "opponents," "the opposition," "we see," and "we have proved" to the point of nausea. . . . Listeners to political campaigners hear the same words and phrases a seemingly endless number of times.

This dependence upon the same word to carry all vaguely related meanings is not necessary. The English language is rich and full. Roget's *Thesaurus*, for example, gives the following synonyms for the common word "pretty":

beautiful	ornamental	goodly	harmonious
beauteous	immaculate	bonny	bright-eyed
handsome	delicate	good-looking	rosy-cheeked
lovely	dainty	well-favored	rosy
graceful	becoming	well-proportioned	blooming
elegant	comely	shapely	trim
exquisite	fair	symmetrical	tidy
neat	spruce	smart	shining
sparkling	radiant	splendid	resplendent
dazzling	glowing	sleek	gorgeous
superb	grand	magnificent	fine
aesthetic	enchanting	attractive	

This list does not include such other meanings of "pretty" as its use as an intensifier in expressions like "pretty fast." Of course some of the above words do not have meanings identical to the original word, but it is also true that we do not always refer to identical things when we use "pretty" One or another of these synonyms will undoubtedly be better in certain contexts.[43]

Figures of Thought

Over the course of time all the various methods used by a speaker to carry the audience along with him have been classified under the title of figures of thought. Each figure has been given a specific name.

It is helpful to be familiar with them, for once knowing them you will find more opportunities for their use. The original work of classification was performed thousands of years ago by the great Greek and Roman students of the speaking arts.

We all use these figures without giving them special attention and analysis. But analysis improves understanding.

Here is a list of some of the most interesting figures with an illustration or two.

1. *Interrogation*

The speaker states a fact in question form:

Is the world round? Is life cruel?

2. *Prolepsis*

The speaker anticipates an objection in advance in order to refute or weaken it by depriving it of novelty:

The defense will tell you my client has a criminal record. Yes, he has. We admit it. But he served his sentence. He paid his debt to society. Is he now to be sentenced again?

3. *Dissimulation*

The speaker pretends that he is no match for his opponent because of his opponent's great skill:

If I could use words like my opponent does, I could tell you what it means to suffer like my client has. But I cannot and so my client's cause must suffer.

4. *Dubitation*

The speaker expresses doubt concerning the matter or the manner of his own speech, or the mode in which the interests he advocates should be promoted or defended:

Should I scream that an injustice is being done or should I calmly tell you to beware of the temptation being held out to you.

43. E. Abernathy, THE ADVOCATE: A MANUAL OF PERSUASION 245–49 (1964).

5. *Simulation*

The speaker acts out an emotion such as anger, grief or despair.

6. *Communication*

The speaker appeals to his opponent for advice or aid:

We do not know how the fire started because we were not there. If anyone does my opponent does and I ask for him to tell you, here and now, how the fire did start.

7. *Submission*

The speaker, for the purpose of showing his confidence in the justice of his claims, offers to submit them to the decision of his opponent:

There can be only one result—even my opponent must decide for us. Let him be the judge in these facts.

8. *Imprecation*

The speaker invokes vengeance on the head of another for some past action or omission:

He is trying to escape in a cloud of generalities and confusion. Well—you will not escape, you will pay for the harm you have caused.

9. *Optation*

The speaker promises under a vow to do or to refrain from doing:

I made a bond with you to present the case honestly and you vowed to bring in a verdict based on the evidence.

10. *Exclamation*

The speaker expresses some vivid thought which has suddenly seized his mind—a figure usually introduced by interjections:

But no, oh no, this cannot be the end of this young man's life.

11. *Hypotyposis*

The speaker depicts a person or an object to the imagination of the hearer, in all the details of its exterior or interior characteristics, its actions, places, times and positions.

12. *Hyperbole*

The speaker magnifies the details of the subject he is discussing:

The witness's voice trembled with the emotion of truth, the whole truth and nothing but the truth.

13. *Diminution*

The speaker underplays:

He had a broken leg and a broken arm. He probably was in pain.

14. *Signification*

The speaker describes some things and leaves others to be inferred:

He raised his hand and brought it down and a man was lying dead.

15. *Suspension*

The speaker, having excited the hearer's curiosity, holds him in suspense, intending to exhibit to him at a later period an object very different from that which he expects:

All these things I have described bore fruit, bitter fruit. But now is not the time to tell that part of the story. That will come later.

16. *Preterition*

The speaker affirms that he will not disclose what he then describes:

I will not tell you his secret. Let him tell you that he was a conspirator.

17. *Reticence*

The speaker in the midst of his discourse interrupts himself, and passes to another subject, as if he feared to explain further, or has more to tell than he is able to relate.

18. *Correction*

The speaker reproves himself for not having spoken better than he has done.

19. *Postponement*

The speaker, after he commences discussing a subject, puts off its further discussion to a later time:

We shall prove who was negligent; who was driving 40 miles over the speed limit—but this will come later.

20. *Periphrase*

The speaker uses a roundabout method of description where more brief expression would be harsh or vulgar:

Old soldiers never die, they fade away.

21. *Antithesis*

The speaker places ideas in opposition to each other in order more clearly to illustrate their elements and differences:

He can bribe, but he cannot seduce. He can buy but cannot gain. He can lie but he cannot deceive.

22. *Paradox*

The speaker affirms two contrary attributes of the same subject:

Like all things human he is good and bad.

23. *Epiphonema*

The speaker closes a thought or an argument with a short and striking sentence, in which he sums up the substance or conclusion of what has previously been said:

All I offer is blood, sweat, toil and tears.

24. *Assumption of Agreement*

The speaker assumes that the audience is already in agreement with him:

Erskine in his speech for Stockdale, thus expressed himself:

"Gentlemen of the jury, I observe plainly, and with infinite satisfaction, that you are shocked and offended at my even supposing it possible you should pronounce such a detestable judgment."

25. *Permission*

The speaker throws himself or his cause upon the jury for guidance and protection:

Now you see why we asked for a jury trial. To protect us from these charges.

26. *Concession*

The speaker concedes something not injurious though perhaps unfavorable and not of serious consequence to his adversary:

We admit the defendant was there—yes he was there but he left long before the crime was committed.

27. *Exaggeration*

The speaker exaggerates the difficulties of his own position, in order to increase the importance of the arguments or facts by which he overcomes them:

It has been a difficult job to find the witnesses to prove our case. It was expensive; it was time-consuming, but now they are here and you have heard them.

28. *Irony*

The speaker intends that the opposite of what his words naturally signify shall be understood—a common form, in which blame, contempt or hatred are expressed under the guise of praise, respect, and love:

The government has accused, merely accused the defendant, so he is, of course, guilty without any opportunity to prove his innocence.

29. *Apostrophe*

The speaker addresses his remarks to some absent person or thing:

John Doe, this jury will not throw your possessions into the hands of those who ignored you during your lifetime.

30. *Prosopopoeia*

Persons present or absent are supposed to speak:

If John Doe were to come back into this courtroom, he would say —"Will contest—what will contest—I never made a will."

31. *Dialogism*

The speaker imitates a dialogue carried on between two or more persons.

32. *Obsecration*

The speaker commands another to speak or act:

The real killer has not been prosecuted but he is present here in this courtroom and I demand him to speak out and stop this miscarriage of justice![44]

44. J. Stein, THE ART OF CLOSING ARGUMENT 122–27 (1969). There are also lists of figures of speech which are obviously usable in any argument—*e. g.*, simile, metaphor, etc.

Obviously, one can overdo stylistic concern. Note, however, how many of the examples in this chapter have used variations of these suggestions. After you have prepared an argument, you might usefully review it with this material in mind. You might find that, like writing prose, you have been "speaking rhetoric" all your life.

4. Delivery: Presentation and Presence

————

WIENER, ORAL ADVOCACY

62 HARV.L.REV. 56, 60–63, 69–75 (1948).

An effective appellate advocate must have an appreciation of and ability to apply the fundamentals of good public speaking—and that does not mean oratory, because oratory is not necessary. . . . The play on an appellate court's emotions must be subtle and restrained if it is to be effective. Nonetheless, any argument differs from a dinner-table conversation; and while of course this article does not and cannot purport to be a text on public speaking, there are certain fundamentals which can be briefly stated.

(a) *You Must Be Heard.*—If you are arguing to a bench of five, seven, or nine judges, all of them must be able to hear what you are saying. Once you are up on your feet, talk is the only medium by which you can communicate your thought to the court; and unless you can make yourself heard you are wasting your time and the court's time and endangering your client's cause.

It is all very noble to assert that the advocate should not stoop to the artificial. But consider actors who, in portraying quiet dinner conversation, must talk in a considerably louder tone of voice so that the people in the back of the theater may hear them. Artificial? Yes, but without that kind of artifice the audience cannot obtain an impression of realism. The lawyer in a courtroom must use the same technique. He must speak loudly enough so that he can be heard and understood.

(b) *You Must Use Proper Emphasis.*—Here again, emphasis is a kind of artifice; but the spoken word without emphasis would be as ineffective—and often as unintelligible—as the written word without punctuation or capitalization. A lawyer worthy of the name cannot afford to use the same tone for "This case comes here on appeal from a decree of the District Court for the Eastern District" as for "This is the gross and shocking fraud which was perpetrated by these respondents."

The matter of proper emphasis can be broken down into four basic admonitions:

(I) Avoid a monotone. Perhaps the best way to attempt to reproduce a monotone in print is to omit punctuation:

At this point the shipper called on the railroad to deliver livestock directly to its siding but the railroad refused to do so contending that by reason of its contract with the stockyards it was bound not to deliver such competitive traffic over the track in question without the payment of yardage charges which yardage charges it was no longer willing to absorb and thereupon the shipper instituted its complaint against the railroad before the Commission.

That statement is just as difficult to follow by ear as by eye.

(II) Avoid the ministerial cadence. Here the voice goes up and down but without emphasis on the proper words:

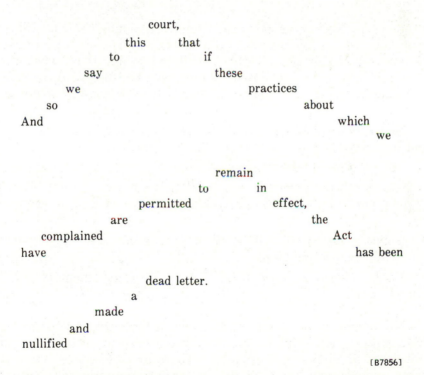

[B7856]

(III) Avoid mumbling. This-ah-case, turns on the-ah-validity of the-ah-Gadget Restriction Act of-ah-1948. We—that is, the petitioners—ah-contend-ah-that the measure-ah-clearly transcends-ah-the powers vested in the-ah-Congress.

(IV) Use the pause. The only way that an oral statement can be punctuated is by a pause—a short one for the commas (which, after all, are simply signals for a breath), a longer one at the end of sentences, and a still longer one when you reach the end of a paragraph.

If more emphasis is desired, as to mark the taking up of an entirely new point, underscore the pause and make it longer by taking a sip of water.

The pause is also helpful as a device to regain the court's attention. Sometimes the court's lack of interest is the fault of the case; more often it is the fault of the lawyer; and sometimes for no good reason the justices just aren't paying attention. They are whispering, and passing notes, and reading the record. Your main proposition is coming up. How to make certain that it will have their full attention? Very simple; just use the public speaker's oldest trick—pause. The sudden silence makes everyone look up; every member of the court eyes the speaker expectantly. It's an ancient dodge, but still one of the most effective.

. . . High on the list of essentials is the use of a good opening sentence or paragraph to catch the court's interest and attention. . . .*

* * *

. . . No lawyer, no matter how able he may be, can afford to argue any case in ignorance of the record . . . . I have seen lawyers of reputation utterly demolished when they went free-wheeling away from a record they obviously had not read, and were then caught up short by opposing counsel, who knew it inside out. . . .

There are a number of aids to learning a record. First of all, read it. Don't rely on abstracts. Read it yourself . . . .

Second, reread the critical portions . . . .

Third, tab the record . . . so that you can readily find any material portion without thumbing through it or looking in the index . . . .

Fourth, the record will stick in your mind more firmly when you write the brief yourself . . . .

Fifth, a good memory helps . . . [and] memory can be trained . . . .

* * *

No lawyer would dream of filing with the clerk the rough first draft of his brief. But too many lawyers present to the court the first draft of their oral argument. There are, of course, some virtuosos—people who have a flair for the extemporaneous. But, unless you are one of those fortunate few, a carefully rehearsed, prepared, and revised presentation will always be better than one that is off the cuff.

I feel it worthwhile to go over what I am to say if only for one reason: to time the remarks. When a firm chief justice leans over

---

* Excerpts from this portion of Wiener's discussion have been reproduced at pages 476–77, *supra*.

and says, "Your time has expired"—well, you sit down. Consequently you should know before you start just how much or how little time the direct presentation will take. If you have three points to make, and find you can only cover two in the allotted 45 or 60 minutes, revision is imperative. And the discovery that a change is necessary had better be made before you address the court.

But apart from timing, I feel that going over what I want to say is helpful in many other respects. In going over the case orally, I generally think of other points to make. Questions arise in my mind which must be checked, questions both of fact and of law. I progress gradually to a smoother presentation, and feel a sense of what to stress and what to eliminate, where to expand and where to compress. Preparation and rehearsal avoid unprofitable or even untenable digressions, and substantially assist in eliminating unhappy turns of phrase. After going over the argument three times, the infelicities are largely smoothed out, I know just precisely how many minutes I am using, and the emphases have become settled. Consequently, by the time I get up in the courtroom, the court hears, not the first draft, but the fourth. Frequently the fourth draft still leaves considerable to be desired, but at least it is a much more finished performance than the first one was.

* * *

.   .   .   Essential to an effective argument is a proper mental attitude on the part of the advocate.

.   .   .   [If] the lawyer approaches a court with an appreciation so great that it amounts to awe, perhaps verging on fear, he will not be able effectively to stand up to the court's questioning.   .   .   .

I have witnessed the loss of case after case—cases which could have been won—because counsel was so terrified of the tribunal, and so in awe of its individual members, that their questions threw him completely off balance. The mere fact of being asked quite disabled him from answering. If you set out to argue an appeal, you must be able to engage in give-and-take with the court, for the judges will point out errors only as errors are pointed out to them.

.   .   .   It is just as important, however, not to talk down to a court, no matter how much the individual advocate may be more generously endowed with quick perception than some of the judges whom he addresses. Sometimes the lawyer's attitude of superiority rests simply on his own keen sense of self-appreciation. On other occasions its basis may be a view widely prevalent at the bar that a certain judge just isn't very bright. Or the lawyer may feel that he is such an outstanding expert in the particular field of law involved that he is the professor and the judges simply students listening to an expository lecture. Whatever the cause, such an attitude of superiority is wrong as a matter of protocol, for it flies in the face of the theory that the judiciary is superior to the bar. And it is particularly wrong as a matter of advocacy, because advocacy is the art of persuasion, and you do not, by talking down to him, ever persuade a man who has the power to decide against you.

. . . The only proper attitude is that of a respectful intellectual equality. The "respectful" part approximates the quantum and type of respect that a younger man should show when speaking to an older one, or a junior officer in the military service when engaged in official discussion with a superior much senior to him, or a parishioner talking to a priest, or the law clerk taking up a point of law with the senior partner. It is not inconsistent with this element of respect, however, for the advocate to argue an appeal on the basis that it is a discussion among equals, whether the argument is made directly or whether it is made in response to questions from the bench. . . .

* * *

. . . An appellate argument is not a set piece. In most courts, it is far from being a monologue; and it must be adjusted and trimmed according to the reaction which it evokes.

. . . Naturally, counsel must make allowance for questions [and, as petitioner or appellant, for rebuttal] when he plans his argument. If the rules of court permit only 45 minutes to each party, and judges are prone to ask questions, counsel will simply not be able to cover all of his points, unless the direct presentation is kept to 30 minutes.

. . . [T]he lawyer must have the essentials of his case so firmly in mind that, whenever his time is in fact cut down, he will know where and what to cut, so that, by the close of the argument, he will still have covered all of the vital points. Only rarely is the argument split, permitting counsel to reframe his remarks overnight, or during the recess; he must be prepared to make his revisions on a substantially extemporaneous basis. Condensation is never an easy process, particularly when the argument as finally prepared is already drastically pruned. And, absent preliminary trimming, cutting, and planning, condensation is well-nigh hopeless. . . . Counsel must also be sufficiently flexible to vary his argument on the basis of the reception it receives. If he has planned to spend ten minutes on Proposition A, and finds that his initial statement thereof gets nods of approval from the bench, he need not—indeed, he should not—proceed to elaborate that proposition further. If his statement of the second principle evokes a similar attitude of assent, he should once more move on. But if the court does not react favorably, he should elaborate upon the bare statement. And if he encounters doubts or active opposition, he may have to expand and detail his argument on a particular proposition far beyond what he had originally planned.

* * *

Good oral advocacy requires constant effort, but no twelve tasks of Hercules are necessary to attain the skill. Any competent lawyer can do it if he keeps in mind the precepts discussed above: Don't read your argument, apply the fundamentals of good public speaking, make an indelible impression in the first few minutes, state the facts clearly, know your record, prepare thoroughly for the argument, maintain an attitude of respectful intellectual equality toward the court, and keep your argument flexible. True, these things are easier said than done; but doing them is the lawyer's job.

FIGG, McCULLOUGH & UNDERWOOD, CIVIL TRIAL MANUAL
447–49 (ALI–ABA 1974).

Perhaps the single most important factor in presenting an effective summation is the impression the lawyer makes on the jury. If the jury is turned off by his manner of delivery, he will have an uphill fight, even in cases where all of the evidence is in his favor. Though there are many factors that will determine the impression the lawyer makes on the jury, the most important is an appearance of sincerity on his part. Above all, he must convince the jury that he believes that what he is saying is fair, right, and honest, and that he is convinced of the justice of his client's position.

One of the quickest ways for the lawyer to convince the jury of his insincerity is to employ an artificial manner of speech. Not many lawyers are naturally gifted orators, and any attempt to employ an unnatural manner of speaking will be spotted at once by even the most unsophisticated juror. Counsel's final argument should be opened in a restrained and impartial manner to leave the jury with the impression of an extemporaneous presentation. As was pointed out by Alan E. Morrill, extemporary argument is not to be confused with an impromptu argument. While the impromptu argument is given on the spur of the moment without any preparation, the extemporary argument can be well prepared and outlined, and even practiced orally before its delivery. A clear, direct, and logical discussion of the case, delivered in a friendly conversational tone, has been found to be highly effective by many advocates. This is not to say the address to the jury need be a dull and emotionless discourse. When the facts under discussion appeal to the emotions of men, it is only natural that counsel will tend to appeal to emotion; but this is a natural reaction and the spontaneity of an occasional emotional outpouring can be highly effective in making a lasting impression on the jurors.

While addressing the jury, it is absolutely essential that counsel has their undivided attention. Although it is inadvisable to give the appearance of talking to any one juror or any particular group of jurors, an effective means of holding their attention is to establish eye contact with them. As counsel talks, he should look at the jury, not at the floor or some spot above their heads. Similarly, though it will undoubtedly be necessary to glance at his notes from time to time, he should avoid giving the appearance of reading a prepared statement. Such conduct not only detracts from the feeling of sincerity that he is trying to convey but also tends to distract the jury from what he is saying.

One highly distracting factor that can readily be controlled is personal appearance. Any lack of neatness or eccentricity in dress or appearance, while it may well draw the jurors' attention to counsel personally, will distract them from what he is saying. Likewise, counsel's file of papers should be neat and orderly, for it is distracting to the jury to have them constantly shuffled during argument. It is also important that counsel avoids mannerisms of speech or gesture, such as hemming and hawing or monotonous repetition of gesture, which may tend to annoy or distract jurors.

Another questionable factor that is controllable by counsel is the use of a ten-dollar word where a nickel word would do. In addition to causing a juror's attention to shift from what he is saying to what the ten-dollar word means, such verbosity could impart to the jury an impression that counsel is "putting on airs." However, the other extreme of needless repetition or explaining the obvious can be just as disastrous, as the jurors may get the feeling that counsel is "talking down" to them. The middle ground, which one should try to reach here, is to speak to the jury in their own language. This is not to say, however, that technical words must be avoided. Where a technical word is called for by the nature of the case, it should be used and explained, if necessary, but the use of "legalese" should be avoided. This last point is best illustrated by the following story told by Welcome D. Pierson of the Oklahoma Bar:

There is a story told of the trial of a lawsuit in Oklahoma which may be only legendary. A case being tried in one of the rural communities of the state involved the proverbial story of a train striking a cow. The evidence had been concluded. The attorney for the railroad was one of the distinguished and great scholars of the state. After the attorney for the plaintiff made a few remarks, the railroad attorney rose to his feet and said to the jury, "This case is a simple case. It is just a plain case of *damnum absque injuria*." After he had resumed his seat, the young lawyer commenced his closing argument. He said to the jury, "I am not skilled in the classics. I understand that the distinguished railroad attorney knows a great many languages. He can translate Latin into English and English into Latin. He has a conversational knowledge of many languages. I do not know very much Latin. As a school boy I attended Wapanucka High School, where I studied Latin I. I will translate the phrase *"damnum absque injuria."* *"Damnum absque injuria"* translated from Latin into English means that it is a damn poor railroad which will kill a cow and won't pay for it." He needed to say nothing further—he won his case.[a]

NOTES

1. *Delivery as a Subject of Study*

Although these excerpts represent some of the best of the genre, they are typical of the "rules of thumb" approach which characterizes discussions of delivery in argument. While such rules are often helpful, they are only starting points in what may be the most difficult and complex aspect of argument. An individual lawyer might obey all the precepts set out in these selections, yet still fail to engage the attention of the audience or persuade them to his or her point of view. Moreover, it is difficult to particularize this kind of advice except by adding to the list of what the advocate must control and combine in an effective presentation. In contrast to the other tasks we have discussed, argument lends itself to detailed preparation. An argument can be written out ahead of time, rewritten, and rehearsed.[45] In some ways this makes the delivery of an argument more manageable than other tasks, but it also creates a number of problems in learning and improving performance in this area.

First, even without special difficulties with voice or coordination, most of us behave quite woodenly in formal settings. Second, familiarity and repetition seem to habituate performance in a way which, while enabling us to reach some tolerable level of competence, also tends to limit self-awareness. Third, attempts to be conscious of our own behavior, or to respond to feedback from others, often disturb these basic adjustments and are experienced as discomforting. Thus our original patterns of argument style and delivery are very difficult to change even if they are recognized as inadequate. As with any learned performance, the problem is to develop approaches to delivery which escape the confines of rule and habit and encourage originality and flexibility, without losing structure and command of what, in legal arguments, is often complex material.

Although rhetoricians have been concerned with learning and teaching the delivery aspect of argument for centuries, this "department" of rhetoric has received comparatively little attention in the literature. Nevertheless, through the years there have been a number of attempts to reduce the problem of delivery to a descriptive system

---

a. Pierson, *Instructions and Argument to the Jury: the Defense Point of View*, 39 A.B.A.J. 877, 943 (1953).

45. In appellate argument, of course, there is often some interaction with the court, a subject we deal with at pages 504–07, *infra*. The performance of counsel still admits of a higher degree of structure and control than is possible in other situations, however, as Wiener's analysis indicates.

and a set of prescriptive generalizations.[46] What emerges from these discussions is a further specification of factors playing a significant part in persuasive communication, along with some rhetorical "rules of thumb" which—like those offered by Wiener and writers on trial practice—are distilled from a considerable body of experience and analysis. Some of these may be helpful to you. In *The Working Principles of Argument*,[47] for example, O'Neill and McBurney list (i) external appearances (including physical traits such as size and coloration as well as clothing, grooming, etc.); (ii) visible action (which includes facial expression, posture, movement and gesture); (iii) vocalization (referring to voice characteristics such as force, pitch, time and quality); and (iv) rhythm and melody, as central concerns in delivery. These elements of delivery are linked to the need of the speaker to control his or her emotions.[48] They also offer a number of detailed suggestions for preparing for extemporaneous delivery, which they feel is the type "undoubtedly best suited to the

---

46. *See, e. g.*, S. Curry, THE PROVINCE OF EXPRESSION (1927); R. Whately, THE ELEMENTS OF RHETORIC (1841).

47. J. O'Neill and J. McBurney, THE WORKING PRINCIPLES OF ARGUMENT 274–88 (1932).

48. O'Neill and McBurney discuss the "uses" of emotion in argument in the following passage:

> Realizing the power of the emotions in conditioning and regulating these delivery factors, it follows that emotional control is highly desirable in the speaker if he hopes to be most effective in delivery. The individual who is apparently unable to feel very intensely regarding anything and constantly displays a cold, indifferent, unruffled front is not in our estimation exercising effective emotional control. Neither is the person who is unable to inhibit emotional excesses in his delivery exercising proper control. . . .

> There is no type of speaking in which emotional repression is more disastrous than in argumentative speaking. Here the speaker has a cause to defend; he is trying to win the beliefs of people and direct their actions. Unless his voice and movement indicate enthusiasm, sincerity, and emotional earnestness for the cause he is arguing, it certainly cannot be hoped that his speech will arouse any very intense feeling for

his cause among the members of his audience.

> On the other hand there are those speakers who permit themselves to be completely carried away by their emotional reaction. . . .

> . . . [T]hree types of emotional behavior [are especially] helpful to the speaker, confidence, sympathy, and differentiation. . . .

> We may say that *confidence* is that air of assurance and self-reliance about an individual which is bred by adequate preparation and properly controlled and regulated emotional activity. "Unless a speaker can somehow give those to whom he speaks an impression that he knows what he is about, that he is reasonably sure of his powers, and that he is comfortable, he has little chance of influencing the audience to do what he wants them to do."

> *Sympathy* is a readiness to notice, understand, and interpret the emotional responses of other people. It is the ability to adjust one's own behavior to the emotional disposition of others. Not only must the speaker be confident then, but he must be sensitive to the emotional attitude of his audience and capable of adjusting his own reactions to them.

> A third quality to be sought in emotional behavior is *differentiation*. Monotony is just as deadly in emotional behavior as it is everywhere else. . . .

Id. at 285–87.

presentation of argument." [49]   Finally, they describe the personal qualities that are most desirable:

Sincerity.—There is probably no single personal quality more persuasive in argument than sincerity or earnestness. If everything a speaker does or says indicates that he "means it," that he himself is interested and enthusiastic about the cause for which he is arguing, this interest and enthusiasm will almost invariably carry over to the audience.

* * *

Fairness.—Next to sincerity the personal quality most to be desired in an argumentative speaker is fairness. Every persuader should be enthusiastic for his own proposition, but that enthusiasm should never lead him to say or do anything which will appear to be unfair either to an opponent or to an opposing position. Always state your opponent's position fairly; recognize the strong points in his argument; quote him correctly, and answer what he really said. If an advocate of the other side is not present, be equally careful to recognize the strength of opposing positions, and be entirely fair in every reference to them.

Sarcasm and ridicule (unless very, very tactfully employed) are usually non-persuasive in argument, because they appeal to the average person as being unfair. All too frequently they are used to screen an inability to meet an argument by other methods. Many debaters, for example, resort to sarcasm when they are otherwise unable to refute the argument of an opponent. Nothing is more demoralizing to an arguer and his cause than to have his sarcastic remarks met by a carefully reasoned rejoinder, fairly and forcefully presented, restating and reaffirming the argument under discussion, thereby exposing the weakness of the attack and at the same time bringing into contrast one man's sarcastic attitude and the fair, reasonable attitude of his opponent.

Modesty.—Modesty is a third personal quality desirable in argument. People dislike conceit in any one, and most audiences are not only intelligent enough to recognize any evidence of it almost at once, but they are just illogical enough to close their minds to the conceited speaker. I say they are just illogical enough, because the attitude of the speaker has nothing whatever to do with the probative force of the argument, but it has everything to do with its persuasive power. The conceited speaker simply is not effective in argument. Delivery must display modesty and reserve if it is to be persuasive.

Akin to conceit is affectation. While it is not good advice to all persons to be *natural* in delivering a speech, it is a rather helpful suggestion to most people. Evidence of affectation whether in manner or voice is usually non-persuasive in argument.

Friendliness.—Friendliness is a fourth personal quality which is helpful in argument. A speaker should not attempt to fight his audience or his opponent. An argument should not be a fight; it should not even

---

49. *Id.* at 293.

be a battle of words, unless it is possible to have such a thing as a friendly battle. Ill-temper not only stirs up a reaction against the speaker among his listeners, but it seriously impairs his own effectiveness. It should not be thought that we are condemning the arguer who "warms up" to his cause. It is one thing to be sincere, earnest, and enthusiastic; and it is quite another thing to be ill-tempered and pugnacious. The casual, indifferent speaker is just as weak as is the ill-tempered, antagonistic speaker, but it is possible to achieve the greatest sincerity in argument and still remain even-tempered and friendly.

As in the case of meeting sarcasm by a show of utter fairness, there is no better attitude to assume in the face of a hostile or bitter opponent than one of friendliness. It carries the audience and disconcerts an opponent more than would any show of anger on the speaker's part.

* * *

Aside from the four personal qualities which we have just commended to the arguer, there is one additional quality which should characterize good delivery. That quality is directness, or communicativeness. Directness means talking straight to the audience, but it means much more than that, too. By directness or communicativeness we have reference to that contact between speaker and audience such as exists in everyday conversation. There should be a mutual interchange of reactions in public address just as there is in good conversation. To be sure, the audience will not respond in so many words, but a trained speaker will be sensitive to every detectable reaction in his audience and constantly alert to adjust his presentation to these reactions. It is just as nonsensical and just as fatal to ignore the reactions of the audience in public speaking as it would be to ignore the replies of a friend in conversation. In delivering an argument the speaker should be able to lead his audience along with him; he should be able to realize when he has done enough with one point and when another argument needs additional support; he should be able to note signs of restlessness and fatigue and inattention in his audience, and be competent to meet the situation; he should be able to tell when arguments are hitting the mark and when they are not. In conversation the listener can ask for more, question, and contribute as the argument progresses; but in public speech the speaker can be sure that the audience is following the argument only as he develops the ability to converse without these definite and compelling responses which exist in conversation. . . .

It is good advice for the student of argument to urge that he make every effort simply to talk with his audience. To be sure, this conversing style of delivery should be animated and forceful, nor does the conversational basis of public speech imply anything else. Far be it from us to discourage force and power in delivery; there are many situations which demand it. The chief implication of the concept we are discussing is the importance for public speech of a lively sense of communication, and the natural inflections and intonations resulting, all of which are characteristic of good conversation.[50]

50. *Id.*, 298–302.

You might ask yourself whether these observations (which are typical) are more or less helpful than what lawyers have written on this subject.

In our experience, the characteristics that this writing identifies —directness, voice, gesture, sincerity—*can* be controlled and adapted in ways that are neither forced nor unnatural. Like the ways an actor learns to read, grasp and finally internalize the lines of a drama, a lawyer can "learn" to convincingly make a particular argument. This requires:

—carefully reading the "script"
—searching for its meaning and central ideas
—blocking out its rhythms and pauses
—finding its points of emphasis and significance
—rehearsing and rehearsing and rehearsing.

In this process a logically well-developed argument takes on force and coherence.

---

2. *Delivery and Adaptation: The Role of Role in Argument*

In some ways, however, the very idea of "delivery" is misleading. Argument is never solely a presentation, and the audience is never passive, even when it is silent. Counsel must continually read the reactions to what he or she has said and respond accordingly.

Examining this process affords some interesting perspectives on the limits and opportunities in this phase of advocacy. Take, for example, the familiar interaction between judge and advocate. If we schematized the exchange of "clues" as a social scientist might, the encounter could be visualized as follows:[51]

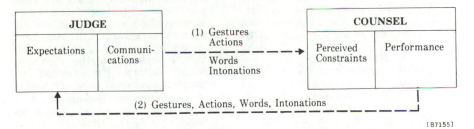

[B7155]

---

51. This analysis is drawn from the extensive literature on "role". You might find the following definitions helpful:

Role Position

This refers to a location in a social structure, a "place" (albeit social rather than physical in nature) which can be described in contrast and comparison with other such places in the social system. The designations lawyer, legislator, opposing counsel and judge all refer to role positions. A role occupant is a particular person in a role at a given time. The obligations and privileges that normally attend that position, however, are independent of whoever the particular occupant happens to be.

Role Expectations

This refers to those beliefs which embody the demands, entitlements and reality definitions associated with occupying the role involved. For example, a lawyer is *expected* to remain sufficiently "detached" from a case to permit judgments

The broken lines represent, in simplified form, the primary sequences of communication in the interaction. In this context expectations are conceived, sent, perceived, and acted upon. These actions, in turn, affect the nature and intensity of the expectations that are thereafter communicated. For example, a judge in the course of an argument might feel that counsel is (i) taking too much time; (ii) arguing improperly; (iii) otherwise violating some norm or value associated with oral advocacy. The judge might then, by a raised eyebrow or less ambiguous signal, communicate the demand that counsel limit the presentation, alter his or her manner, change the subject, etc. (line 1). Counsel will interpret and respond to this message in a variety of ways, which in turn will affect how and what is further done or communicated by the judge. (line 2). At the same time, although supported by considerably less enforcement power, counsel is communicating his or her conceptions of proper role behavior to the judge (lines 1 and 2 in reverse direction). Since these two processes overlap, the entire interchange involves a continuing pattern of adjustments and readjustments.

In addition, both participants are influenced by (i) personality, (ii) the history of the interaction, and (iii) the cultural and institutional setting. Simplifying our analysis so that we are again looking only at the influences on counsel, these additional factors require the following changes in the diagram:

which are not distorted by emotion or bias. Role expectations can differ in specificity, formality, clarity, intensity, legitimacy, applicability and potential sanction, to name only some of the dimensions involved. Moreover, expectations always involve images of both required and typical behavior and, potentially, multiple points of view. I expect (and will feel "betrayed" if my expectation is not met) that opposing counsel will not intentionally deceive me. I also expect (and will be "surprised" if my anticipation is not met) that he or she will be courteous to me. Opposing counsel has similar expectations concerning my conduct. I have further anticipations (based on "taking the role of the other") concerning his or her beliefs in this regard, and so forth.

Role Adjustment

This refers to responses to role expectations and demands in a given situation. Such obligations are communicated by some "other" (a role sender), or embedded in one's own conceptions of self and appropriate role behavior. In the discussion which follows, for example, the judge is portrayed as a role sender. Although our analysis is based on these concepts, we have eliminated most of this technical language in this discussion. For an excellent treatment of these ideas, see J. Turner, THE STRUCTURE OF SOCIOLOGICAL THEORY (1974).

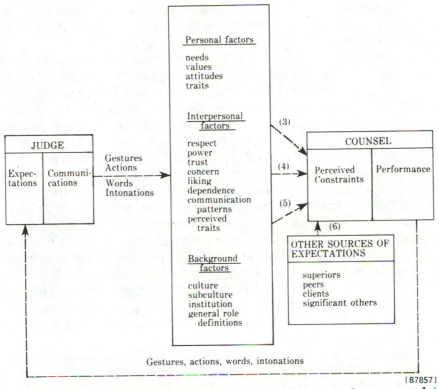

Filter of other
factors influencing
perception and
performance

Personal factors

needs
values
attitudes
traits

Interpersonal
factors

respect
power
trust
concern
liking
dependence
communication
   patterns
perceived
   traits

Background
factors

culture
subculture
institution
general role
   definitions

JUDGE

Expec-
tations | Communi-
cations

Gestures
Actions

Words
Intonations

COUNSEL

Perceived
Constraints | Performance

(3)
(4)
(5)
(6)

OTHER SOURCES OF
EXPECTATIONS

superiors
peers
clients
significant others

Gestures, actions, words, intonations

[B7857]

Note that, to be complete, the diagram would have to be reversed to show the same influences affecting the judge.

Counsel's interpretations of the judge's behavior and the conduct such interpretations evoked would initially be influenced by counsel's own needs, attitudes, and personal characteristics (line 3). The same is true of the judge's interpretations and responses to counsel's actions.

Similarly counsel's responses will be influenced by his or her perceptions of the judge's intentions, capacities and sincerity, themselves a product of the prior interactions between them (line 4). The same contacts, as perceived and interpreted by the judge, will in like manner affect the judge's conduct. That is, the history of any relationship (even when relatively short in duration) generates stable patterns and expectations.[52]

Finally, counsel's interpretations and responses are affected by the institutional and cultural background of the transaction (line 5)

52. Indeed, over time these attributes of the relationship and, less certainly, the personality characteristics of the participants are affected by the actions that are taken. In a very real sense, our needs, attitudes and more enduring personality dispositions are shaped by the tasks we are asked to perform and the roles we are required to play. *See* Turner, *supra* note 51 at 160–69.

and by the demands and anticipations of other role senders (line **6**).
The general outlines of the role of counsel, the assumption that the
court must "decide" the case (rather than functioning as a mediator
or therapist), the conventions of dress, speech and gesture (imagine
refusing to approach the bench) are among the background factors
which influence any particular interchange.

What does such a schema tell you about the problems of delivery
in argument? What possibilities does it suggest? First, it may give
some of you a clearer understanding of the sources of strain in argument.[53] Throughout your argument, whether before a judge or jury,
you will be faced with (i) the ambiguities in the messages you receive; (ii) multiple and conflicting demands; and (iii) the limited
resources (time, skills, knowledge) you have to cope with them. Since
you are being judged by yourself and others for your failure to resolve
these conflicts, they may be the source of considerable strain.

In the foregoing interaction, for example, the judge's demand
that counsel limit the argument can produce a number of conflicts.
Counsel might believe that the client wants him or her to continue
arguing. Or counsel might feel unwilling to be backed down in front
of other lawyers in the courtroom. Counsel might also believe that
it violates his or her own conception of proper conduct to "give in,"
or, more typically, might not feel *able* to adjust to the judge's demands
without surrendering the argument. Indeed, the judge might be communicating inconsistent messages.

Whatever their precise source, the existence of such conflicts can
produce considerable tension. You will want to reduce these anxieties
without acting inconsistently or ignoring those demands considered
most legitimate. The available options include: (i) selection of a
course of action which is rationalized as reconciling the conflict; (ii)
sequential compliance (first one, then the other); (iii) the preference of one demand over another; (iv) delay and inaction; (v) deception; (vi) withdrawal; and (vii) persuasion of one or more role

---

53. This analysis, of course, could be
applied to any facet of lawyer work
and to much more general ideas about
motivation and social experience. For
example, McCall and Simmons write
of role as follows:

> This imaginative view of oneself
> in a position is usually rather ideal-
> ized, incorporating standards of con-
> duct and achievement that are un-
> likely to be consistently attained
> . . . in the individual's actual
> day-to-day performances relevant to
> the role. . . . [Nevertheless]
> they exert important influences on
> daily life. . . . They serve as
> the primary source of one's plans of
> action. . . . [They] give mean-
> ing to our daily routine, for they
> determine our interpretations of the
> situations, and other people we en-
> counter . . . And because

. . . the realities of life are
constantly jarring them . . .
they necessitate continually seeking
perspectives that allow us to maintain them . . . despite contradictory occurrences. As a crea-
ture of ideals, man's main concern
is to maintain a tentative hold on
these idealized conceptions of himself, to legitimate his role-identities
. . . He has not only to persuade
himself that his views of himself
are true enough, but he also has
to act in ways that the identities
he has claimed before other people
are not disconfirmed in their eyes
. . . that is, he *needs* role-
support.

G. McCall & J. Simmons, IDENTI-
TIES AND INTERACTIONS 67–76
(1966).

senders to drop or modify the demand. The form these "avoidance strategies" take, of course, depends on the possibilities and evaluations that attend a particular situation. There are many lawyers who would sit down in the situation described above and tell the client that "the case couldn't have been won anyway" without an awareness of the forces that shaped this decision. If you would avoid this sort of temptation, you will need some means of analysis which will permit you to talk systematically about them.

Second, understanding the need to "take the role" of another in making an argument may make you more sensitive to the situation from the judge's point of view. True, such an understanding does not suggest particular ways to shift the content or tone of the argument to counter the judge's expressed impatience. But it does offer a starting point for rehearsing in your mind what the consequences of choosing a particular alternative might be. A judge's impatience, for instance, may be a function of an array of factors that look something like this:

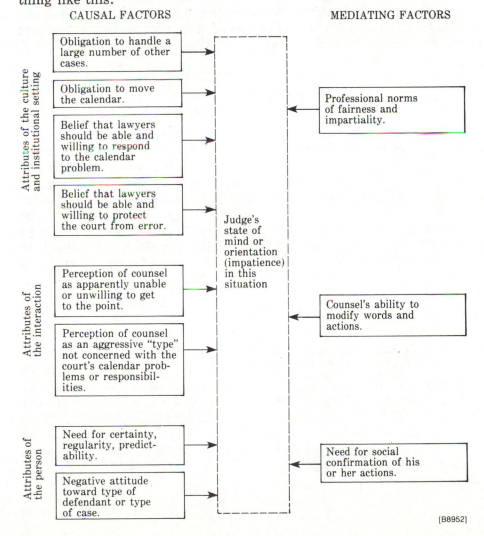

CAUSAL FACTORS   MEDIATING FACTORS

Attributes of the culture and institutional setting

- Obligation to handle a large number of other cases.
- Obligation to move the calendar.
- Belief that lawyers should be able and willing to respond to the calendar problem.
- Belief that lawyers should be able and willing to protect the court from error.

Professional norms of fairness and impartiality.

Judge's state of mind or orientation (impatience) in this situation

Attributes of the interaction

- Perception of counsel as apparently unable or unwilling to get to the point.
- Perception of counsel as an aggressive "type" not concerned with the court's calendar problems or responsibilities.

Counsel's ability to modify words and actions.

Attributes of the person

- Need for certainty, regularity, predictability.
- Negative attitude toward type of defendant or type of case.

Need for social confirmation of his or her actions.

[B8952]

Your ability to alter the judge's perceptions and behavior in this situation will depend on accurately assessing these circumstances (the area within the dotted lines) as they appear to the judge, and acting appropriately to control them.

For example, faced with the court's impatience you might immediately state that you have "two major points that can be briefly summarized" to assure the court of (i) your concern for the court's interest in dispatch; (ii) the importance of what is going to be said; (iii) the likelihood that it will not consume an unreasonable amount of the court's time. Or you might refer to the judge's role responsibilities to abide by the mandates of the upper courts: "I don't see how we can avoid going into this, your Honor, in light of the recent decisions on this subject." Or you might "break role" in order to emphasize the importance or exceptional nature of the matter, or your desire that the judge adhere to different role imperatives: "I don't usually ask for so much time, your Honor, but there is great danger in this case that an injustice could be done if we don't sort through these details." In each instance you are appealing to influences, values and norms of which both of you can be only dimly aware.

---

3. *The Question of Questions*

When the cues to which counsel must respond take the form of questions, counsel's ability to respond appropriately becomes even more crucial. For the court (in some jurisdictions, juries are also permitted to ask questions) such inquiries are a basis for testing and clarifying the issue it must resolve. For counsel, questions are a source of information about what is troubling the court and how far from the mark counsel's initial judgments about its likely response may have been. If a contention obviously has support, it might be given less emphasis than had been planned. If the court is bothered by a particular point, it can be further amplified. As John W. Davis has stated, "rejoice" when a court begins to ask questions.[54]

Desirable as a colloquy with the court may be, the question of questions generally raises some difficult choices. First, there are times when counsel does *not* want questions. For example, in a complex case where the arguments need to be fully developed to be effectively presented, it is often desirable to defer questions—at least for some period of time. The difficulty is to signal a desire not to be challenged without raising the ire of the court. On the other hand, it is often difficult to invite questions when counsel desires them. Jeffrey Browne makes the following comments on this problem, with particular reference to the argument of John W. Davis in the school segregation case discussed earlier:

54. Davis, *The Argument of an Appeal*,
26 A.B.A.J. 895, 897 (1940).

Rhythm and tempo in an advocate's delivery may also be important particularly in determining whether questions are asked and at what stage. Too much rhythm or continuous flow in an arument may discourage interaction with the judges. If such a delivery leads to less questions it might have an advantage in maintaining greater coherence in the argument, but by discouraging questions an advocate may lose opportunities to detect the directions of thought or the unanswered problems and concerns of the judges. By encouraging questions also the advocate is more likely to draw out any counter arguments in the minds of judges unsympathetic to his case. By drawing out such arguments he has an opportunity to provide an answer and thereby to protect himself against that judge using that argument unanswered in the judge's conference room.

In the School Segregation Case, for example, Mr. Davis' overbearing style of advocacy led to twelve times fewer questions than were addressed to Mr. Marshall. This may be accounted for partly by the clarity and coherence of Mr. Davis' argument. His language usage was masterful and accounted greatly for the clarity of his arguments. But it also made him more difficult to interrupt.[55]

A number of experienced lawyers have suggested the following ways to encourage colloquy with the court: (i) word some positions so that they need clarification; (ii) plan for long pauses in the course of the argument; (iii) directly ask the court if there are any questions; (iv) characterize parts of the argument as being important, or conversely, insignificant. But none of these offers any assurance of getting the response you might want.

Finally, preparing for questioning is very difficult, though it has been suggested that questions can be anticipated within fairly patterned categories. Consider the following typology:

(a) *Questions seeking information as to the facts of the case:* If the statement of facts has been adequate and the court has some idea of which facts were crucial, many time-consuming questions may be avoided. However, if factual items are central, a judge will often want to read them directly from the record. Consequently, counsel should be prepared to answer such questions with a reference to the page in the record where the fact is to be found. And it is important to know the possible relevance of facts which are absent from the record.

Questions as to the facts may also come from the judge who feels that counsel has wandered too far from the facts of the case into an abstract discourse on the law. Consequently, when such questions are asked, counsel may well want to "react" to the questions by sticking a little more closely in the argument to the factual setting of the case. This involves also the wording of arguments to bring out the facts of the case. For instance, in making an argument concerning a plaintiff's

---

55. Browne, Understanding Appellate Advocacy 122–23 (1977) (unpublished paper on file in the library of the Harvard Law School) *See also* Dickens & Schwartz, *Oral Argument Before the Supreme Court: Marshall v. Davis in the School Segregation Cases,* 57 Q.J. OF SPEECH 32 (1971).

reliance on a statement by the defendant, counsel might say, "Mr. Jones relied on William's flat statement that there was a ton of coal in the load" rather than dryly saying, "Reliance by the plaintiff is indicated in this case."

(b) *Questions about "policy considerations:"* Quite often, questions of this nature are phrased in terms of "Counsel, would you comment upon . . .." Here the court desires to hear a fuller exposition of the factors which counsel deems relevant to a decision, and possibly a countering of opposite policy considerations. The question will usually point up something that is troubling the judge. Counsel's problem is finding ways to recast and supplement points covered in the briefs, as well as emphasizing to the court the relative weight to be given to the factors advanced by both sides.

Sometimes, questions of this sort are phrased in argumentative form, such as, "But, counsel, isn't it clear that . . .." The form of the question does not mean that the judge has necessarily decided against the position advanced. It may well be that his thinking is presently adverse to that position, yet the proper answer is not to give up but rather to put the point in a new light and use utmost persuasion to change his mind. Of course, if it has become clear that the judge is simply stating good law, counsel may well want to admit the validity of the judge's comment and direct the discussion to new ground.

(c) *Questions directed at the authorities cited:* When a judge asks about a cited case, he wants something more than the dry recitation of the facts and the holding. He wants to know how it relates to this case. Does it constitute binding precedent on the point (not likely in a mythical jurisdiction where every issue is one of first impression) or does it show the existing framework of law into which the desired result must be fitted? Above all, the judge wants to know why the earlier court decided as it did. What considerations did it think controlling? Has the weight to be given these factors changed since the court decided the earlier case? The advice of Justice Shaefer is relevant:

> "Do not argue your case . . . in terms of rules. The law does not live in the statements of rule, including past statements of the rule by the court, any more than it lives in the black letter of the hornbook. The law lives and cases are decided . . . in that area of policy and in the considerations out of which the black-letter rules evolve . . .. Keep your . . . argument pitched to take account of these considerations—not ostentatiously, I am sure I do not have to tell you that—but do not put your argument solely in terms of a bare absolute rule which the court may have announced in a particular case." [a]

(d) *Questions directed at particular legal arguments:* Questions of this type test the logic of an argument. Loose statements of holdings, overbroad analogies, and imprecise wording in general can unleash a veritable barrage of questions.

However, there remain questions directed at legal arguments, which legitimately spring from the complexity or the implications of them.

[a]. Schaefer, *The Appellate Court*, 3 U. CHI.L.SCH.REC. 1, 13, No. 2 (March, 1954).

Mastery of the case and the depth of understanding of the whole realm of the law surrounding it will be tested. The judges often desire to know how far an argument will take the court down an uncharted path of the law. "Where will it end?" The question requires line drawing, yet this is precisely where the court needs guidance. If the judge is persuaded that a distinction can be drawn between the case at bar and a future case where the doctrine espoused seems applicable but where the result is untenable, then he is well on the way to adopting a favorable result. Thought concerning the implications of the doctrines advocated will help counsel to make responsive answers and will help the court decide the case.

A judge is not an adversary. Inexperienced counsel have more than once refused the argument set out on a silver platter by a judge who restated counsel's argument in a new way or supported his position with a new argument. Counsel can accept the help of a judge without losing face. If the question or its implications are unclear, counsel should talk with the judge, attempting to clarify the problem which is troubling the court so that he can give the right answer the first time.[56]

Is this helpful? What further guidance is needed?

No matter how much one prepares, there is always reason to expect the unexpected in this phase of argument. One's plans have to include (i) alternative closings and transitions (in the event counsel *is* interrupted by questions or has to elaborate on an argument in response to cues from the court); (ii) additional arguments and support on each of the points being made, should time and contingency call for them; and (iii) routes for bringing answers to anticipated questions back in line with the main themes of the argument. The skilled execution of such plans can make a presentation much more forceful. Conversely, the unanswered or poorly answered question may say far more to the court than the advocate intends.

SECTION THREE. THE ETHICAL DIMENSION

In argument, as in other lawyering activities, there is inevitably an ethical dimension to the task. The advocate has obligations to his or her art, to self and to the audience to which the argument is addressed. As Lord Chief Justice Cockburn expansively remarked, the tools of the advocate are the "arms of the warrior and not the assassin. It is his duty . . . to seek to reconcile [his clients'] interests which he is bound to maintain . . . with the eternal and immutable interests of truth and justice." [57]

56. Board of Student Advisors, Harvard Law School, INTRODUCTION TO ADVOCACY 93–95 (1976).

57. Costigan, *The Full Remarks on Advocacy of Lord Brougham and Lord Chief Justice Cockburn . . . November 8, 1864,* CAL.L.REV.INC. (1931), cited in S. Thurman, E. Phillips & E. Cheatham, CASES AND MATERIALS ON THE LEGAL PROFESSIONS 281 (1970).

The way these interests are to be reconciled, however, seems largely to be left to the individual lawyer and the general provisions of the Code. The professional and moral strictures governing argument are substantially similar to those imposed on a lawyer presenting evidence. That is, in argument a lawyer may not:

—express his or her personal opinion about the facts or justice of the case;

—appeal improperly to the sympathy or prejudice of the hearer;

—make a false statement of law or fact;

—refer to a matter not properly presented in evidence or not relevant to the dispute in issue;

—conceal legal authority adverse to his client's interests;

—be disrespectful to the court or refuse to comply with a legitimate judicial order;

—go beyond fair comment or improperly characterize the conduct of any of the parties, witnesses or opposing counsel;

—single out and address a particular juror.[58]

ARGUMENT IN PEOPLE v. ROGER LINK

With these rules in mind, you might consider the following argument in the case of State v. Link: (The testimony in this preliminary hearing is set out in the preceding chapter, *supra* at pages 350–54. You might want to review the evidence briefly before considering the propriety of the argument that Wirtz, counsel for the defendant, makes on the basis of it.)

JUDGE: If there are no more witnesses, I'll hear from the defense counsel.

WIRTZ: Thank you, your honor. I'm sorry that I had to be so aggressive in the cross-examination of the complaining witness, but I'm afraid that I've seen a great many cases just like

---

58. *See* cases collected in F. X. Busch, TRIAL PROCEDURE MATERIALS 523–31 (1961). Most of these standards are stated in the context of an appellate court's reversal or affirmance. *See also* Singer, *Forensic Misconduct by Federal Prosecutors and How It Grew*, 20 ALA.L.REV. 227 (1968). Vess, *Walking a Tightrope: A Survey of Limitations on the Prosecutor's Closing Argument*, 64 J.CRIM. L. & CRIMINOLOGY 22 (1973). The most relevant Code provision is DR 7–106. *See also* DR 7–101, 7–102; EC 7–23, 7–24. The number of disciplinary actions taken against lawyers for breach of these rules is rela-tively small, and usually involve egregious and repeated misconduct.

In addition, a number of rules have developed which directly relate to particular types of arguments. A lawyer may not: (i) ask the jurors to put themselves in the party's place (e. g., "What would you sell your own leg for?"); (ii) comment on the respective financial status of the parties; (iii) refer to the insured status of a party if evidence of insurance is inadmissible; (iv) make reference to other recoveries or trials. *See* Busch, *supra; see also* M. Belli, MODERN TRIALS 1656 *et seq.* (1966).

this. The girl picks someone up, something happens, she gets beaten up and then she wants to blame someone. This time it happens to be the defendant. I've been in front of your honor in a great many preliminary hearings, and I know that the required standard of proof is not high. But I've never seen a weaker preliminary showing than this. If your honor will think back for just a moment, I believe you will agree with me. I frankly don't know why the prosecutor would present such a case relying on this kind of testimony.

I've been able to do some investigation on this case and I think I should call your honor's attention to the fact that Miss Tate may have made accusations like this before. In fact, several times like this before. I don't see how anyone can believe her. No jury would believe her, and I ask you not to believe her as well, your honor.

A man's reputation, his liberty and his property ought not to be put in jeopardy on evidence as weak as that which we've heard today. This charge should be found to be without probable cause and should be dismissed.

NOTE

In this brief excerpt Wirtz may have violated a number of provisions of the Code.[59] Can you identify them? Even so limited an exercise demonstrates that the precise line between proper and improper conduct in this area is not always clear. Suppose, for example, that Wirtz offered the following defenses of his choice of words:

> (a) "I'm sorry I had to be so aggressive" was merely designed to eliminate any prejudice against my client that might result from the judge being upset with me.[60] Starting with an apology or a personal remark to "create a mood" is standard advice in most trial tactics books.

---

59. In a criminal case there is, of course, no recourse other than discipline or contempt proceedings against the attorney. The double jeopardy clause would prevent an acquittal from being set aside because of the defense attorney's misconduct. Whether a mistrial could be granted the prosecution without running afoul of double jeopardy is still somewhat unsettled. *See* F. Inbau, J. Thompson & C. Sowle, CASES AND COMMENTS ON CRIMINAL JUSTICE: CRIMINAL LAW ADMINISTRATION (3d ed. 1968).

60. The courts have evolved a doctrine of "fair reply" as grounds for upholding some otherwise improper statements. *See, e. g.,* People v. Ruppuhn, 25 Mich.App. 62, 180 N.W.2d 900 (1970), *rev'd on other grounds* 390 Mich. 266, 212 N.W.2d 205 (1973) (defense argument on credibility justified prosecution comments on defendant's character); Mobile Cab & Baggage Co. v. Busby, 277 Ala. 292, 162 So.2d 314 (1964) (comment on defendant's insurance coverage proper in light of defendant's inference that there was no insurance).

(b) Mentioning "other cases" was merely a reference to matters of common knowledge; false accusations do get made in precisely the way I described.[61]

(c) My claim that she was beaten up by a customer is a "fair and reasonable inference" from her admission on cross-examination that she regularly did go home with customers.[62] Even if my client has told me otherwise, if I can suggest an alternative theory of what happened from the facts, I am entitled—indeed, obligated—to do so.[63]

(d) At no time did I express any improper personal opinion. I referred to (i) the practice in the court (the standard actually used by the judge rather than the formal one); (ii) the weakness of their showing (which I believe I am permitted to argue); [64] (iii) the fact that no jury or anyone else would believe her. "I don't see" and "I've never seen" are not expressions of a personal opinion; they express nothing different than the "evidence does or doesn't show." [65]

(e) It was perfectly proper for me to refer to the impropriety of the prosecutor in bringing the case. The question is whether this was a fair comment about the weakness of the case.[66]

(f) I did not go outside the record; my reference to my investigation was just a request that the court take judicial notice of the court records.[67]

61. Arguments may be based on matters of common knowledge. *See, e. g.,* Kuehl v. Hamilton, 136 Or. 240, 297 P. 1043 (1931). Common knowledge usually refers to historical facts, public personalities, Biblical references, or common sense interpretations of evidence. United States ex rel. Coleman v. Mancusi, 423 F.2d 985 (2d Cir. 1970) (even in absence of expert testimony, prosecutor could argue gun had to be cocked); *see also* Hotel Riviera, Inc. v. Short, 80 Nev. 505, 396 P.2d 855 (1964).

62. This is the usual standard applied by the courts. *See* United States v. Alexander, 415 F.2d 1352 (7th Cir. 1969) (testimony that there was no way of knowing who punched time card; prosecutor could properly argue that defendant did not punch it); McAllister v. State, 44 Ala.App. 511, 214 So.2d 862 (1968) (reference to defendant's financial status as a possible motive for crime is not fair inference).

63. *Cf.*, EC 7–24 (". . . a lawyer may argue, on his analysis of the evi-

dence, for *any* position or conclusion with respect to [credibility, guilt or innocence, and the like]. . . .").

64. *See, e. g.*, People v. Acuff, 94 Cal. App.2d 551, 211 P.2d 17 (1949) (prosecutor's comment that he was satisfied that the defendant was guilty held proper inference from the evidence).

65. *See* Collins v. State, 87 Nev. 436, 488 P.2d 544 (1971); (not error for prosecutor to use phrases "I think" and "I feel" in argument); *but see* United States v. Barber, 303 F.Supp. 807 (D.Del.1969).

66. *Cf.*; EC 7–37; People v. Speck, 41 Ill.2d 177, 242 N.E.2d 208 (1968), *rev'd on other grounds* 403 U.S. 946 (1971) (prosecutor's statement that cross-examination of a government witness was an "exhibition" designed to confuse jury was proper).

67. We probably shouldn't even try to help him here. For typical rules on judicial notice see the Federal Rules of Evidence, Rule 201, 803(18).

(g) The idea that my reference to my personal experience before the Court was an appeal to personal sympathy is just specious. You should see the sort of appeals to emotion and prejudice that are regularly permitted in argument, even to juries.[68]

Look carefully at the relevant provisions of the Code and ask yourself if these arguments are sound. How would you answer them? How would you rewrite Wirtz's argument so that, in your view, it does not violate the Code? How different is it? What policies justify the line between proper and improper conduct in this area?

Note that none of these rules seem to prevent Wirtz from conveying implicitly, by tone and emphasis (rather than explicitly), his personal disbelief of the witness or his belief in his client's innocence.[69] Robert Keeton makes the following comments on the dilemma this poses for the trial lawyer:

> Probably you will be at your best as an advocate when you cause the judge and jury to believe that the decision you are urging them to reach is a decision you would reach yourself. Yet the Code of Professional Responsibility, in one of its Disciplinary Rules, prohibits any direct statement of belief in your cause. Should this rule be construed as prohibiting not only direct assertions of belief in your cause but also the kind of conduct through which, without making any direct assertion, you convey to the jury the impression that you believe in the cause you are presenting? Perhaps the general proposition that rules of conduct should not be subject to evasion by indirection points toward an affirmative answer. But quite clearly that interpretation of the Disciplinary Rule would be contrary to the prevailing practice in the courts, before and after adoption of the Code of Professional Responsibility as well as before and after adoption of earlier canons that expressed essentially the same idea. It seems more consistent with the apparent objectives of the rule, as well as the prevailing practice, to treat it as a regulation of the form and manner of your conduct as an advocate rather than a regulation requiring that you not display, even indirectly, any appearance of commitment to your cause. Indeed, if interpreted as precluding even an indirect display of commitment to your cause, the rule could hardly be reconciled with your acknowledged duty as an advocate to bring "zeal" to your representation of your cause.[70]

---

68. *See generally* Levine, *Summation—Inflammatory or Proper Argument*, 7 PLF.ADV. 28 (1963); Griffin, *Prejudicial Elements in Plaintiff's Argument for Damages*, 11 DEF.L.J. 1 (1962).

69. For an extreme example recognizing the distinction between words and acts, *see* Ferguson v. Moore, 98 Tenn. 342, 39 S.W. 341 (1897): "Tears have always been considered legitimate argument before a jury . . . . Indeed, if counsel has them at his command, it may be seriously questioned whether it is not his professional duty to shed them whenever the proper occasion arises."

70. R. Keeton, TRIAL TACTICS AND METHODS 2–3 (2d ed. 1973).

Do you agree with him? Does a distinction between form and substance square with the rationale of the Code's provisions?

———

2. *The Larger Puzzle: The Lawyer's Responsibility for the Process*

In the background of this discussion of proper "means", is the question of the lawyer's responsibility for the integrity of the judicial process itself. To what extent is the lawyer obligated to insure that whoever decides the case is informed, deliberate, and unmoved by "irrelevant" considerations?

The rule against expressing personal opinion might suggest that there is no such responsibility: that beyond avoiding violating specific rules in argument, there is no general obligation "to the system," or for the results it produces. David Mellinkoff describes the history of this rule as follows:

> In his popular Cambridge lectures, published as *The Principles of Moral and Political Philosophy* (1785), William Paley said that the evil of lying lay in the breaking of a tacit promise to speak the truth, and in the possibility that someone might suffer from a lie. But, he continued, "There are falsehoods which are not lies . . . ," because " . . . no one is deceived." This was the case not only with jokes and fairy tales, but with "a prisoner's pleading not guilty, an advocate asserting the . . . [rightness of his client's claim." Most American writers, however, have not adopted such a position.]
>
> * * *
>
> . . . [T]he influential Judge Sharswood [in] 1854, . . . [for example,] . . . told his law students and the American bar generally:
>
>> Moreover, no counsel can with propriety and a good conscience express to court or jury his belief in the justice of his client's cause, contrary to the fact. Indeed, the occasions are very rare in which he ought to throw the weight of his own private opinion into the scales in favor of the side he has espoused. If that opinion has been formed on a statement of facts not in evidence, it ought not to be heard,—it would be illegal and improper in the tribunal to allow any force whatever to it; if on the evidence only, it is enough to show from that the legal and moral grounds on which such opinion rests.
>
> After quoting [others], Judge Sharswood then pictures the unfair position of the young lawyer faced by a veteran's expression of his personal opinion:
>
>> In proportion, then, to the age, experience, maturity of judgment, and professional character of the man, who falsely endeavors to impress the court and jury with the opinion of his confidence in the justice of his case, in that proportion is there danger that injury will be done and wrong inflicted—in that proportion is there moral delinquency in him who resorts to it.

[For Sharswood, it would have been wrong for a lawyer] " . . . even to stand up and falsely pretend a confidence in the truth and justice of his cause, which he did not feel." [And approving Baron Park's advice to use all fair arguments arising on the evidence, Sharswood added his own carefully constructed comment:] "Beyond that, he is not bound to go in any case; in a case in which he is satisfied in his own mind of the guilt of the accused, he is not justified in going." George Warvelle agreed.

In all of this, there is the suggestion by Judge Sharswood . . . that in a good cause the lawyer is justified in greater efforts, in laying everything on the line, including himself, involving himself as personally as Erskine ever did, giving his personal, honest belief in the cause he advocates. This is a legacy of the religious, the moralist background of the profession of law, though it is to be observed that Sharswood says the occasions for expressions of personal belief are "very rare." . . . Others have ever further restricted such expressions.

Despite the fact that the first American code of ethics leaned heavily on the teachings of Judge Sharswood, that Code (Alabama State Bar Association, 1887) did not follow Sharswood . . . in distinguishing between permissible and impermissible expressions of counsel's belief in his client's cause. All expressions of belief were disapproved. This followed from the Code's preliminary advice to lawyers not to testify for a client except as to "formal matters" or in exceptional cases "when essential to the ends of justice . . ." a rule still of general application today. The Code continued:

> The same reasons which make it improper in general for an attorney to testify for his client, apply with greater force to assertions, sometimes made by counsel in argument, of personal belief of the client's innocence or the justice of his cause. If such assertions are habitually made they lose all force and subject the attorney to falsehoods; while the failure to make them in particular cases will often be esteemed a tacit admission of belief of the client's guilt, or the weakness of his cause.

Even that fleeting nod to Judge Sharswood's distinction, in the reference to "falsehoods," was omitted in the American Bar Association's version of the rule adopted as a part of Canon 15 in 1908. Like the current rule in England the prohibition is unequivocal:

> It is improper for a lawyer to assert in argument his personal belief in his client's innocence or in the justice of his cause.

American judges have repeatedly reaffirmed the principle of Canon 15: no-personal-belief, whether that belief be dishonest or honest, in a "bad" cause or a "good" cause. . . . [71]

Consider the alternatives that are set out here. Are any of these views (Sharswood's, Paley's?) more or less desirable? Does the "American rule" answer the question of the lawyer's responsibility? In what way? Is it fair to describe the rule as an effort by the pro-

---

71. D. Mellinkoff, THE CONSCIENCE OF A LAWYER 249, 258–60 (1973).

fession to insulate lawyers from responsibility for the consequences of their advocacy?

Some would argue that—whatever the lawyer's obligations to be silent about personal views—*as a public official,* he or she has special responsibilities to be sure that the institutions of the law work properly. Indeed, similar arguments have been made about the responsibilities of all persons who influence others. Insofar as an advocate obfuscates or manipulates outcomes, he or she no longer contributes to the "rational" settlement of disputes.

This traditional view of the advocate's role was articulated in a classic statement by Fuller and Randall.[72] It should be compared with the following comments on the ethics of persuasion:

. . . The method of subliminal cues is but a farther step along the . . . road that . . . hidden persuaders have been traveling for centuries—the road which circumvents man's mind and reason in order to elicit non-reflective, semi-conscious or unconscious responses. Those who have at last been shocked, by the discovery of the subliminal cue technique, . . . into facing the problem of the ethics of persuasion may now join hands with those who since the time of Plato's argument with the Sophists have been seeking to find a satisfactory answer to this dilemma.

* * *

The hidden persuader, whether he is aware of it or not, is engaging in a non-democratic practice. He takes advantage of the fact that although men may have the latent capacity for making rational, conscious choices, they are also part animal and as such can be exploited. They can, within limits, be made to respond reflexively. They can be moved to action by suggestions and pressure in the fringes of their consciousness. But because they can be so moved does not mean they should be so moved. . . .

* * *

[Does this not also mean that a speaker must dress] in a manner that will be accepted by his audience, that he avoid using language which will offend them, and that if his views are diametrically opposed to theirs he make some adaptation in order to avoid incurring their hostility? Are these not attempts to influence the listener in the fringes of his consciousness?

It must be admitted that such factors do influence an audience and that they are responded to in a semi-conscious way. The speaker, however, by observing these amenities, is not necessarily attempting to gain

---

72. Report of the Joint Conference on Professional Responsibility, 44 A.B. A.J. 1159–62 (1958) (Fuller and Randall, co-chairmen); for example:

. . . The advocate plays his role well when zeal for his client's cause promotes a wise and informed decision of the case. He plays his role badly, and trespasses against the obligations of professional responsibility, when his desire to win leads him to muddy the headwaters of decision, when, instead of lending a needed perspective to the controversy, he distorts and obscures its true nature.

* * *

Id. at 1161.

Id. at 1161. A lengthy excerpt from this report is set out in THE LAWYERING PROCESS 58–60 (1978).

uncritical acceptance of his ideas. He may simply be trying to avoid uncritical rejection. It must be recognized that people can respond reflexively *against* something as well as for something. If a speaker comes before them who sharply violates their norms in dress, language, or viewpoint, they might automatically close their minds to him and absorb nothing of what he says. There is no real chance for his cause to gain a fair, objective hearing. If, therefore, in the interests of rationality, he seeks to avoid being blocked by their prejudices, he is in no wise attempting to circumscribe the listeners' freedom of choice. He is, in fact, attempting to broaden it. If, however, he goes so far in his adaptation to the audience that he never reveals in any way his differences with them, and attempts to use his prestige and fluency, if he has them, to gain acceptance of an idea or product they would not accept if they examined it carefully, he has then misused this particular method of persuasion.[73]

Imagine yourself delivering an argument before a judge or jury. Would you follow these suggestions in measuring your own work as an advocate? Is it meaningful to say that in this context an advocate is *obligated* to refrain from seeking "uncritical acceptance" of his or her ideas?

There is, of course, a paradox here. The advocate under the Code *is asked to assist the decision-maker by maximizing his or her control* over the decision-maker's judgment. The more biased and uncritical the decision-maker is toward counsel's position, the less responsibility counsel has for changing the decision-maker's mind. The more "spontaneous" the lawyer becomes in communicating conviction and sincerity, the less the profession has to say about the ethics of this conduct. Is it fair to say that this projects a paradigm of the totally "natural," totally controlling persuader as an "ideal"?[74] How

---

73. Haiman, *Democratic Ethics and the Hidden Persuaders*, 44 Q.J. SPEECH 385, 387–89 (1958). *See also* the statements by other writers concerned with the ethics of advocacy in Chapter Two, *supra* at pages 365–67.

74. Haiman makes the following interesting comments about "intentionality" in his analysis:

Does all this apply, it may be asked, to individuals who manipulate others unconsciously—men who believe so devoutly or fanatically in the causes they advocate that they engage in hidden persuasion without knowing it? Here, of course, we have the problem of determining whether . . . the attempts at manipulation were truly unconscious. Was Mark Antony simply thinking out loud and communicating his own true feelings about Caesar's assassination to the friends,

Romans, and countrymen who lent him their ears, or did he deliberately plan the masterful hidden persuasion which roused them to riot? Did Adolf Hitler really believe that the Jews were a menace to the "Aryan race," or did he coldly calculate and promote this scapegoat mechanism as a device to unify the German people behind him? These questions may be impossible to answer. But for the sake of argument, let us assume that these men were completely sincere and entirely unaware of the techniques they were employing. Are they then any less guilty of unethical practices?

Id. at 391. For a view that unethical conduct *requires* intentionality, *see* Flynn, *The Aristotelian Basis for the Ethics of Speaking*, 6 THE SPEECH TEACHER 179 (1957).

can even an approximation of this view be considered desirable? Are there counterpressures enough in the legal system to mitigate it? Perhaps a war between advocates is ultimately necessary to an informed, deliberate legal process. But some of you will surely wonder if this is the only way to run the railroad.

†